Music in

ARDEN SHAKESPEARE DICTIONARY SERIES

Series Editor
Sandra Clark (Birkbeck College, University of London)

Class and Society in Shakespeare	Paul Innes
Music in Shakespeare	Christopher R. Wilson & Michela Calore
Shakespeare and the Language of Food	Joan Fitzpatrick
Shakespeare's Books	Stuart Gillespie
Shakespeare's Demonology	Marion Gibson and Jo Ann Esra
Shakespeare's Legal Language	B. J. Sokol & Mary Sokol
Shakespeare's Medical Language	Sujata Iyengar
Shakespeare's Military Language	Charles Edelman
Shakespeare's Non-Standard English	N. F. Blake
Shakespeare's Plants and Gardens: A Dictionary	Vivian Thomas and Nicki Faircloth
Shakespeare's Political and Economic Language	Vivian Thomas
Shakespeare's Religious Language	R. Chris Hassel, Jr
Shakespeare's Theatre	Hugh Macrae Richmond

Forthcoming titles:

Shakespeare and National Identity	Christopher Ivic
Shakespeare's Insults	Nathalie Vienne-Guerrin

ARDEN SHAKESPEARE DICTIONARY SERIES

Music in Shakespeare

A Dictionary

CHRISTOPHER R. WILSON & MICHELA CALORE

BLOOMSBURY
LONDON • NEW DELHI • NEW YORK • SYDNEY

Bloomsbury Arden Shakespeare
An imprint of Bloomsbury Publishing Plc

50 Bedford Square	1385 Broadway
London	New York
WC1B 3DP	NY 10018
UK	USA

www.bloomsbury.com

Bloomsbury is a registered trade mark of Bloomsbury Publishing Plc

This edition of *Music in Shakespeare* by Christopher R. Wilson and Michela Calore, first published 2005 by Thoemmes Continuum

© Christopher R. Wilson and Michela Calore, 2005
This paperback edition © Christopher R Wilson and Michela Calore, 2014

Christopher R. Wilson and Michela Calore have asserted their right under the Copyright, Designs and Patents Act, 1988, to be identified as Author of this work.

All rights reserved. No part of this publication may be reproduced or transmitted in any form or by any means, electronic or mechanical, including photocopying, recording, or any information storage or retrieval system, without prior permission in writing from the publishers.

No responsibility for loss caused to any individual or organization acting on or refraining from action as a result of the material in this publication can be accepted by Bloomsbury or the author.

British Library Cataloguing-in-Publication Data
A catalogue record for this book is available from the British Library.

ISBN: PB: 978-1-4725-2031-9

Library of Congress Cataloging-in-Publication Data
A catalog record for this book is available from the Library of Congress.

Typeset by Integra Software Services Pvt. Ltd.
Printed and bound in Great Britain

Contents

Series Editor's Preface   vii

Preface (including acknowledgements)   viii

Abbreviations   xi

Introduction   1

A–Z   9

Bibliography   477

Index   505

Series Editor's Preface

The Arden Shakespeare Dictionaries aim to provide the student of Shakespeare with a series of authoritative guides to the principal subject areas covered by the plays and poems. They are produced by scholars who are experts both on Shakespeare and on the topic of the individual dictionary, based on the most recent scholarship, succinctly written and accessibly presented. They offer readers a self-contained body of information on the topic under discussion, its occurrence and significance in Shakespeare's works, and its contemporary meanings.

The topics are all vital ones for understanding the plays and poems; they have been selected for their importance in illuminating aspects of Shakespeare's writings where an informed understanding of the range of Shakespeare's usage, and of the contemporary literary, historical and cultural issues involved, will add to the reader's appreciation of his work. Because of the diversity of the topics covered in the series, individual dictionaries may vary in emphasis and approach, but the aim and basic format of the entries remain the same from volume to volume.

Sandra Clark
Birkbeck College
University of London

Preface

The Elizabethans seem as reluctant to commit themselves to a definition of music as modern-day commentators are. It was only in the most recent edition of the *New Grove Dictionary of Music and Musicians* (2001) that 'music' appeared as a dictionary term. Previous editions, like many specialist music dictionaries, had not thought it necessary to include it 'on the assumption that no definition is needed, or perhaps because none would be totally satisfactory' (vol. 17, p. 431). *New Grove* distinguished between language dictionary definitions of 'music' and the place the term has in musicology. Language dictionaries concentrate on either a broad-ranging definition, attempting 'to specify all salient traits of music' using 'Western music in the fine art tradition' as the basic model, 'seeing music principally as a series of sounds and . . . compositions' (vol. 17, p. 426). Musical activity was seen primarily as composition whose art lay in 'combining sounds'. Musicology has sought to locate music in composition, performance and cultural contexts. Its meaning has changed, developed, varied from age to age and from country to country. Musicologists have provided 'a bewildering set of definitions' (vol. 17, p. 431).

For the Elizabethans, music was either a performing art, or composition, or a philosophical concept, or all three. In his laudatory verse, 'In Musicam Thomae Tallisii, et Guiliemi Birdi' in *Cantiones . . . Sacrae* (1575), Richard Mulcaster, for example, alludes to all three elements whilst defending the pedagogical qualities of music. He refers to the power of music and its basis in mathematical science in his opening words: 'Quanti sit precii res Musica, quamque regendis / Insanis animi motibus apta, docent . . .' ('How precious a thing is Music, and how appropriate for governing the mad passions of the mind, is revealed by those who teach that numbers are the foundation of everything having form, and that music is formed from these', *The Byrd Edition*, 1977, vol. 1, p. xxvi, ed. Craig Monson). He reminds his reader that for a healthy and sound human 'exercise should maintain the body and sober music govern the mind'. The Queen herself, he continues, not only

Preface

takes pleasure in hearing music, she also delights in practising music – 'she sings and plays excellently'. He rejoices in the fact the English composers, namely Tallis and Byrd, may now rival the distinguished composers of 'other nations' and that their reputation will spread abroad.

Shakespeare's use of music depends on the contemporary signification of music, the Elizabethan understanding of trumpet signals, different meanings of bells ringing, knowledge of the Orpheus myth, the opposition between stringed instruments and pipes, 'haut' versus 'bas' and many other symbolic musics. Where appropriate, discussion of the Elizabethan usage of a musical term is dealt with under that term. For wider ranging accounts of music in Elizabethan England, see David Wulstan's *Tudor Music* (1985), Iain Fenlon (ed.), *The Renaissance* (1989), David Price's *Patrons and Musicians of the English Renaissance* (1981), Bruce Pattison's *Music and Poetry of the English Renaissance* (2nd edn, 1970), Peter Holman's *Four and Twenty Fiddlers* (1993) and Walter Woodfill's *Musicians in English Society* (1953, reprint 1969).

Music in Shakespeare: A Dictionary includes terms which an Elizabethan and Jacobean commentator would quickly recognize. Many are unique to the Elizabethan age and are no longer in use as musical terms. Others, such as 'ordnance', 'noise', 'thunder', might puzzle some because they do not appear to be connected with music. But the dictionary aims to include any term which could have a musical meaning or relevance in the broadest sense of the word, either created sound or 'the combination of sounds' relating to the human world, which includes, for example, the songs of birds. It is not restricted to terms of Western art music. If it were, 'trumpet', 'horn', 'drum' and many other musical instruments which were not art-music instruments until the seventeenth century would be excluded. On the other hand, this is not a dictionary of vocal songs, ballads, instrumental music or other music that is intended to be performed in the plays. Where the name of a ballad (e.g. 'Greensleeves') is found as a term, it is there because it occurs in the body of the text of a play and has symbolic reference.

Each entry is divided into three sections. The first (A) explains the meaning of the term in music; the second (B) discusses its signification in specific Shakespeare locations; the third (C) offers selected bibliographical references. The entries are not intended to be comprehensive. Some terms occur only once in the Shakespeare canon in a musical sense (e.g. 'degree', 'pavan'); others are numerous ('music' is found in

Preface

143 instances) and for reasons of space every occurrence could not be cited. Cross references are in bold and are identified only the first time they occur in an entry.

The music definitions are concise. For fuller, more detailed and wider-ranging musical analyses of terms the reader is advised to consult the *New Grove Dictionary of Music* (2001). Other, very useful, smaller compendiums are Anthony Baines, *The Oxford Companion to Musical Instruments* (1992), Alison Latham (ed.), *The Oxford Companion to Music* (2002).

Quotations from Shakespeare's plays are from *The Riverside Shakespeare* (2nd edn, 1997). When specific editions have been consulted on Early English Books Online (for instance when editions of the same play contain different sound and music stage directions), quotations are in the original spelling.

This dictionary, which started life as an Athlone Press commission, has been a long time in the making. A large number of people have been involved at various stages. We would like to acknowledge a debt to the late F. W. Sternfeld, the late Graham Midgley, Melvin Bird, Cedric Brown, John Caldwell, Christopher Cipkin, Ross Duffin, Lesley Dunn, Bryan Gooch, Christopher Hardman, Ian Harwood, Elizabeth Heale, Oliver Hemming, Peter Holman, Ralph Houlbrooke, Ron Knowles, John Morehen, Richard Rastall, Paul Rhys, Jamie Savan, Susan Weiss and Julia Wood. The generous input by our consultants, Andrew Gurr and David Lindley, has been especially significant and appreciated. The help, encouragement and expert advice given by our general editor, Sandra Clark, has been invaluable. A generous research project grant by the Leverhulme Trust, commencing in 2001, enabled us to bring the work on music in Shakespeare to its conclusion. We should also like to thank the University of Reading for a small start-up grant from the Research Endowment Trust Fund.

Abbreviations

Shakespeare's Works
Ado   Much Ado About Nothing
Ant   Antony and Cleopatra
AWW   All's Well That Ends Well
AYLI   As You Like It
Cor   Coriolanus
Cym   Cymbeline
Err   The Comedy of Errors
Ham   Hamlet
1H4   The First Part of Henry IV
2H4   The Second Part of Henry IV
H5   Henry V
1H6   The First Part of Henry VI
2H6   The Second Part of Henry VI
3H6   The Third Part of Henry VI
H8   Henry VIII
JC   Julius Caesar
Jn   King John
LC   A Lover's Complaint
LLL   Love's Labour's Lost
Lr   King Lear
Luc   The Rape of Lucrece
Mac   Macbeth
MM   Measure for Measure
MND   A Midsummer Night's Dream
MV   The Merchant of Venice
Oth   Othello
Per   Pericles
PhT   The Phoenix and Turtle
PP   The Passionate Pilgrim
R2   Richard II
R3   Richard III

Abbreviations

Rom	*Romeo and Juliet*
Shr	*The Taming of the Shrew*
Son	*The Sonnets*
TGV	*The Two Gentlemen of Verona*
Tim	*Timon of Athens*
Tit	*Titus Andronicus*
Tmp	*The Tempest*
TN	*Twelfth Night*
TNK	*The Two Noble Kinsmen*
Tro	*Troilus and Cressida*
Ven	*Venus and Adonis*
Wiv	*The Merry Wives of Windsor*
WT	*The Winter's Tale*

Periodicals

EM	*Early Music*
GSJ	*Galpin Society Journal*
JAMS	*Journal of the American Musicological Society*
JEGP	*Journal of English and Germanic Philology*
LSJ	*Lute Society Journal*
MaRDiE	*Medieval and Renaissance Drama in England*
ML	*Music and Letters*
MQ	*Musical Quarterly*
MP	*Modern Philology*
N&Q	*Notes and Queries*
RD	*Renaissance Drama*
RES	*Review of English Studies*
ShQ	*Shakespeare Quarterly*
ShS	*Shakespeare Survey*

Frequently Cited Works

FWVB	Fitzwilliam Virginal Book
Grove	*The New Grove Dictionary of Music*, 2nd edn (2001)
Grove Online	The Grove Dictionary of Music Online
Introduction	Thomas Morley, *A Plaine and Easie Introduction to Practicall Musicke* (1597)
MB	Musica Britannica
MLNB	My Lady Nevells Booke
OED	*The Oxford English Dictionary*

Abbreviations

Miscellaneous
Ed.   editor, or edited by
Edn   edition
Folio   First Folio of Shakespeare's plays (1623)
OSD   opening stage direction
Q   quarto
Q1 (2, 3 . . .) first (second, third . . .) Quarto
SD   stage direction
Tr.   translator, or translated by

Books of Ayres and Madrigal Collections Cited
The abbreviations to books of madrigals and ayres in the main text of the Dictionary (e.g. Attey, 1622; Weelkes, 1598) refer to texts (without music) taken from, for the sake of convenience, the collected modern-spelling edition, *English Madrigal Verse*, eds F. W. Sternfeld and David Greer, 3rd edn, Oxford: Clarendon Press, 1967. The short full titles are listed below.

Alison, Richard, *An Howres Recreation in Musicke, apt for Instrumentes and Voyces*, 1606.
Attey, John, *The First Booke Of Ayres*, 1622.
Bartlet, John, *A Booke Of Ayres*, 1606.
Bateson, Thomas, *The first set of English Madrigales*, 1604.
———, *The Second Set Of Madrigales*, 1618.
Bennet, John, *Madrigalls To Foure Voyces*, 1599.
Byrd, William, *Psalmes, Sonets, & songs of sadnes and pietie*, 1588.
———, *Songs of sundrie natures*, 1589.
———, *Psalmes, Songs, and Sonnets*, 1611.
Campion, Thomas, *A Booke of Ayres*, 1601 (cf. Rosseter).
———, *Two Bookes Of Ayres (The First; The Second)*, c.1613.
———, *The Third and Fourth Booke Of Ayres*, c.1617.
Carlton, Richard, *Madrigals to Five Voyces*, 1601.
Corkine, William, *Ayres To Sing and Play To the Lute and Basse Viol*, 1610.
———, *The Second Booke of Ayres*, 1612.
Daniel, John, *Songs For The Lute[,] Viol and Voice*, 1606.
Dowland, John, *The First Booke of Songes or Ayres*, 1597.
———, *The Second Booke of Songs or Ayres*, 1600.
———, *The Third And Last Booke Of Songs Or Aires*, 1603.
———, *A Pilgrimes Solace*, 1612.
Dowland, Robert, *A Musicall Banquet*, 1610.

Abbreviations

East, Michael, *Madrigales . . . apt for Viols and voices*, 1604.
——, *The Second set of Madrigales*, 1606.
——, *The Third Set Of Bookes*, 1610.
——, *The Fourth Set of Bookes*, 1618.
Ferrabosco, Alfonso, *Ayres*, 1609.
Ford, Thomas, *Musicke Of Sundrie Kindes*, 1607.
Gibbons, Orlando, *The First Set Of Madrigals*, 1612.
Greaves, Thomas, *Songes of sundrie kindes*, 1604.
Handford, George, *Ayres To be sunge to Ye Lute, and Base Vyole*, 1609.
Hume, Tobias, *The First part of Ayres*, 1605.
Jones, Robert, *The First Booke Of Songes & Ayres*, 1600.
——, *The Second Booke of Songs and Ayres*, 1601.
——, *The First Set Of Madrigals*, 1607.
Kirbye, George, *The first set Of English Madrigalls*, 1597.
Morley, Thomas, *Canzonets. Or Little Short Songs To Three Voyces*, 1593.
——, *The First Book Of Ayres*, 1600.
Morley, Thomas (ed.), *Madrigales The Triumphes of Oriana*, 1601.
Mundy, John, *Songs And Psalmes*, 1594.
Peerson, Martin, *Private Musicke. Or The First Booke of Ayres and Dialogues*, 1620.
Pilkington, Francis, *The First Booke Of Songs or Ayres*, 1605.
——, *The First Set Of Madrigals And Pastorals*, 1613.
——, *The Second Set Of Madrigals, and Pastorals*, 1624.
Ravenscroft, Thomas, *Pammelia*, 1609.
——, *Deuteromelia*, 1609.
——, *Melismata*, 1609.
Rosseter, Philip, *A Booke of Ayres*, 1601. See Campion, 1601.
Tomkins, Thomas, *Songs*, 1622.
Ward, John, *The First Set of English Madrigals*, 1613.
Watson, Thomas, *The first sett, Of Italian Madrigalls Englished*, 1590.
Weelkes, Thomas, *Madrigals*, 1597.
——, *Balletts And Madrigals*, 1598.
——, *Madrigals Of 5. and 6. parts*, 1600.
——, *Ayeres Or Phantasticke Spirites*, 1608.
Wilbye, John, *The First Set Of English Madrigals*, 1598.
——, *The Second Set Of Madrigales*, 1609.
Youll, Henry, *Canzonets To Three Voyces*, 1608.

Introduction

Music pervades Shakespeare's plays and poems. In addition to numerous stage directions for music and sound effects and the many vocal songs in the plays, Shakespeare's dramatic and poetic work is permeated by references to music, involving over 300 terms. The traditional associations of music, its divine and degrading powers, often play their part in providing the drama and poetry with a wider network of allusions than modern readers can usually comprehend. The practical and metaphorical functions of music and sound often serve important structural and thematic purposes, and are an integral part of Shakespeare's dramatic technique and poetic language.

The existing major studies of the role of music and the use of song in the drama of Shakespeare's day have limited their focus to aspects such as imagery drawn from Renaissance musical iconography and theories of symbolic music. As the bibliography of this book shows, the most comprehensive works concentrating on these aspects were published between the 1950s and the late 1970s (among these are books and essays by John Long, J. S. Manifold, Peter Seng, F. W. Sternfeld and John Stevens). More recent publications on music in Shakespeare – which in the current dictionary appear both in the general bibliography and in the discrete bibliography at the end of each entry – have shifted their focus to some important issues including gender, performance and the role of acoustics and soundscapes not only in Shakespeare but also in early modern literature and society at large. The settings for Shakespearean songs and ballads have also received the attention they deserve in Ross Duffin's *Shakespeare's Songbook*.

The magisterial five-volume *Shakespeare Music Catalogue* (eds Gooch and Thatcher, 1991) lists all the musical works from the seventeenth century to c.1989 which are based on a Shakespeare text or theme. However, it does not discuss musical terms as discrete entities. Rather, it documents over 20,000 entries alphabetically under the headings: 'Incidental Music', 'Operas and Related Music', 'Non-Theatrical Vocal Music' and 'Obliquely Related Works'. Musical stage directions for

Introduction

each play are included but there is no attempt to contextualize them or explain their significance.

Graham Strahle's *An Early Music Dictionary* (1995) is a compilation of musical terms and their definitions in English from the sixteenth century to the early eighteenth century. Quoting from sources from the Renaissance to the Baroque, Strahle reveals 'how terms and definitions were understood by musicians of the time'. He gives cross-references to related headwords but does not discuss the meaning and significance of a term outside its musical citation nor does he mention occurrences in the literature of Shakespeare and his contemporaries.

Although the function of the aural dimension in Shakespeare and his contemporaries has been analysed from various perspectives, to date the only study which has dealt with the topic in a systematized form is an unpublished doctoral dissertation of 1968: M. L. Robbins's 'Shakespeare's Sweet Music'. However, this thesis includes significantly fewer terms than the present dictionary and omits the discussion of quite a few important words. Robbins does not provide detailed musical background of terms and references, whereas such explication is one of the main concerns of the present dictionary.

In the numerous modern editions of Shakespeare's works (with some exceptions such as David Lindley's New Cambridge edition of *The Tempest*), glosses to musical terms are usually minimal. When these are compared to the more detailed discussions of other recurrent themes in the Shakespeare canon, it becomes clear that this topic has been considered of secondary importance. Few editors of Shakespeare have much expertise in the historical place of musical terminology. Hence, comprehensive analysis of the musical lexis in the dramatic and poetic works of Shakespeare is at the centre of this dictionary, which tries to overcome the inevitable limitations deriving from the selective choices made in previous studies of this topic. The main objective of the dictionary is to provide a comprehensive survey of Shakespeare's musical vocabulary – his knowledge of technical terms, his allusion to instruments, musical genres and performance techniques. Analysing each musical term as a self-contained entity is an effective way of understanding the manifold nuances of meaning which it can acquire.

Unlike a number of its predecessors, *Music in Shakespeare: A Dictionary* draws on some vital discoveries about the layout and use of acting spaces in the early modern professional theatre. These have been prompted by the partial unearthing in 1989 of the foundations of the Rose theatre in

Introduction

Southwark, and by the productions at the new Globe on Bankside since its opening in 1997. The excellent acoustics of the reconstructed Globe and the employment of early music practitioners in some of its productions have challenged many post-Restoration assumptions about music and acoustics in the Elizabethan theatre. They have also revealed the unique power of music symbolically to evoke settings and atmospheres.

The importance of music, song and sound effects used by Shakespeare and his contemporaries can only partly be grasped by today's playgoers. Our enjoyment of a theatrical event is based on the predominantly visual experiences we have when we sit in a darkened auditorium with an acting space often defined by a proscenium arch. On the other hand, in the playhouses of the late sixteenth and early seventeenth centuries, the aural dimension carried out a more significant function, which reveals a different approach to sound in Elizabethan and Jacobean society at large.

Bruce Smith has recently argued that 'the multiple cultures of early modern England may have shared with us the biological materiality of hearing, but their protocols of listening could be remarkably different from ours' (*The Acoustic World of Early Modern England*, p. 8). Wes Folkerth expands on this idea:

> This perceptual domain held many related associations for the early modern imagination, among which are notions of vulnerability, community, the idea of 'cognitive nourishment', access to the deeply subjective or pre-articulated self, grotesque forms of continuity and transformation, radical provisionality, free-flowing expenditure, and related ethical dispositions such as obedience, receptivity, assent, and belief.
>
> (*The Sound of Shakespeare*, p. 9)

Among the acoustic communities, Folkerth includes the public theatre itself, 'the sounds of which regularly carried from the loose acoustical confines of the theatre out to the wider culture' (ibid., p. 17).

That the London theatres relied on music is apparent from the evidence found in a unique set of documents, the so-called *Henslowe's Diary*. This is a day-to-day record of the activities that took place at the Rose theatre in Southwark, kept by its impresario Philip Henslowe between 1592 and 1603. In 1598 he drew up inventories of the stage props, costumes and play books belonging to the Admiral's Men, who

Introduction

occupied this venue on an exclusive basis between May 1594 and July 1600. Henslowe listed as many as three trumpets, a drum, a treble viol, a bass viol, a bandore, a cittern and a sackbut.[1] Furthermore, in their wills some actors bequeathed musical instruments to their apprentices or fellow actors: clearly, playing music was an expertise in which a number of actors were skilled.[2]

Instrumental music during a performance usually framed supernatural atmospheres and metatheatrical devices such as dumb shows, visions and dreams. Songs, either accompanied or unaccompanied by instruments, also served the purpose of underlining the mood of a character or situation. In a similar way, sound effects were employed to evoke specific events, most notably storms (often working as a sign of ill-omen or of the presence of supernatural forces), battles (which required, for instance, the sounding of alarums, parleys, charges and retreats) and ceremonial entries/exits (these are sometimes preceded by cues such as 'flourish', 'sennet' and 'tucket'). The subtle nuances of meaning implied by many of these sounds are unfamiliar to modern readers and playgoers, but they were highly significant five centuries ago. A quick glance at Alan Dessen and Leslie Thomson's *A Dictionary of Stage Directions* confirms that these sound effects were part of a highly specialized theatrical code.

This theatrical code can be better understood in connection with the conditions of early modern performance: we must not forget that play scripts belonging to the repertoires of Renaissance professional companies were meant to satisfy ever-changing acting circumstances.[3] Actors could not rely on performing exclusively at purpose-built venues through the Elizabethan and Jacobean ages; they had to resort to travelling around the country on several occasions, for instance when a plague outbreak made it necessary for the authorities to close the London playhouses temporarily. Theatrical productions had to be as flexible as possible. In J. L. Styan's words: 'a prerequisite of a playwright's technique in Elizabethan times was his ability to write a play that could be put on anywhere'.[4] In the specific case of the integration of music and sound in performance, a lot depended on how many people were able to play instruments and on how many musical instruments were available at a specific moment. This preoccupation is nicely exemplified by a permissive stage direction in an allegorical play of the Queen's Men's repertoire written c.1590 by the dramatist Robert Wilson (also actor and shareholder in that company): '*Here Simplicity sings first, and Wit after,*

Introduction

dialoguewise, both to musicke if ye will.[5] This instruction reveals the awareness that instrumental music to accompany the song was not always practicable. But these limiting circumstances would not have had a major impact on vocal music and on the creation of basic sound effects, which could have been achieved even when an acting company's resources were limited.

The purpose-built London amphitheatres (commonly referred to as 'public' playhouses) were the best-equipped acting venues of the late sixteenth and early seventeenth centuries in England. Unfortunately, not much is known about their structure. What the recent archaeological discovery of the Rose theatre foundations in Southwark has revealed is that it is unwise to suppose that all public playhouses shared the same dimensions, basic structure and features.[6] This has a number of implications for our understanding of which areas were used to achieve sound effects and to play music during a performance.

It is thought that consorts of professional musicians would have often occupied a portion of the stage gallery (referred to as 'above' in Elizabethan stage directions) where they would play their instruments. However, both the stage directions and dialogue of some plays reveal that instruments would have been played on the main stage on several occasions. This is the case, for instance, when Ariel plays his tabor and pipe in *The Tempest*, or when the entry of an army in historical plays – often symbolized by 'three or four soldiers' – is accompanied by the sounding of martial instruments by some of the people belonging to the military procession. Other stage directions tell us that the 'within' area (behind the tiring-house wall or *frons scenae*) was required in several cases. Dessen and Thomson give the following definition of 'within':

> Widely used [. . .] to indicate the location of a sound or the presence of a figure within the tiring house and therefore offstage out of sight of the playgoer; most of the examples (1) anticipate an entrance so that a voice, knocking, or other offstage sound is followed by the appearance of a figure/figures or (2) suggest by means of sound an unseen action/event.
>
> (*A Dictionary of Stage Directions*, p. 253)

More than any other area, the 'within' is associated with the creation of aural signals. It is possible that this term was used to refer to an offstage

Introduction

space in a more generic way in the event that purpose-built theatres could not be used.

Resorting to aural metonymy, either off or onstage, was a very effective and economical device to evoke situations such as battles, or scenes involving rioting mobs. This type of metonymy was also suitable for venues where complex staging was not achievable. As the often-quoted prologue of Shakespeare's *Henry V* tells us, the audience was expected to make their 'imaginary forces work' (Prologue 18) in order to compensate for the limitations imposed by the 'unworthy scaffold' (10) of the playhouse (in this case the Globe in Southwark) when historical events were staged on it. The playgoers are exhorted to: 'Piece out our imperfections with your thoughts; / Into a thousand parts divide one man [. . .] / Think, when we talk of horses, that you see them' (23–4; 26). Shakespeare could not have chosen better words to express the symbolic and synecdochic quality of his and his fellow playwrights' stagecraft. The warning about the impossibility of displaying historical subjects at a purpose-built theatre in a proper manner is even more relevant when considered in the context of touring and of changeable theatrical resources. The unspecific nature of cues for music and sound in the plays of Shakespeare and his contemporaries may be frustratingly evasive to us, but their vagueness reveals that they were meant to be adapted to venues ranging from the London custom-built theatres to the guildhalls and market squares in the provinces.

The full significance of the musical code adopted in the theatre of Shakespeare's day can be grasped when attention is devoted to extant early printed editions of Elizabethan and Jacobean plays. In these texts, cues for sound effects and music often occupy a prominent position on the page, a characteristic which is mirrored in the linguistic features of this category of stage directions. Indications for music and sounds tend to be concise clauses (e.g. 'music plays', 'music ceases'), clauses in the imperative mood (e.g. 'sound alarums'), or noun phrases (e.g. 'music', 'alarums still'). These linguistic features make sound and music cues easily recognizable when compared to other aspects of stage business.

Ultimately, the way in which the main components of dramatic discourse – speech prefixes, stage directions including those for aural signals and dialogue – are distinguished on the page of early printed and manuscript play texts is linked to the performative needs that had to be addressed in the early modern professional theatre. As Linda McJannet has explained, 'the conventions governing speech attribution in Elizabethan printed editions suggest how page design may enhance readability and still emphasize the play as theatrical event'.[7] While freestanding speech prefixes are normally placed in a left-hand position, directions for stage action which interrupt the flow of the dialogue (for instance those for battles and dumb shows) are signalled through breaks in the text column. McJannet goes on to say:

> The left-hand speech prefix and the usually right-of-center exit direction represent the entry of the character into the reader's ken and his or her subsequent departure from our imaginative field of vision. The mature Elizabethan page design thus has a mimetic dimension; keyed to the way we read a page (top to bottom, left to right), it suggests aspects of an audience's aural and visual experience in the theater.
> (*The Voice of Elizabethan Stage Directions*, p. 69)

Her observations can be applied to the aural dimension, whose framing function in performance is reflected in the special prominence it is given linguistically and visually on the page.

The emphasis on the mimetic function of page design placed in early printed and manuscript theatrical play texts is lost in modern editions of Elizabethan and Jacobean plays, where the position of stage directions (not only for sound, music and songs but also for other aspects of stage business) tends to be standardized. A similar principle applies to the language of stage directions, which are often amended and implemented when they are deemed not to be clear enough. This practice is meant to satisfy a modern reader's expectations about consistency and linearity in the written text, but ultimately runs the risk of making us lose sight of the function of aural symbols in the theatre of Shakespeare's day. Hence, throughout the present dictionary, particular attention has been devoted to early printed editions, a task facilitated by the use of Early English Books Online, which gives quick access to most quarto and Folio editions of Shakespeare's (and his contemporaries') works.

Notes
1 Detailed studies of *Henslowe's Diary* are: Neil Carson, *A Companion to Henslowe's Diary* (Cambridge: Cambridge University Press, 1988); R. Foakes (ed.), *Henslowe's Diary*, 2nd edn (Cambridge: Cambridge University Press, 2002); and Carole Chillington Rutter (ed.), *Documents of the Rose Playhouse*, rev. edn (Manchester: Manchester University Press, 1999).

Introduction

2 E. A. J. Honigmann and Susan Brock scrutinize these documents in *Playhouse Wills, 1558–1642: An Edition of Wills by Shakespeare and his Contemporaries in the London Theatre*, The Revels Plays Companion Library (Manchester: Manchester University Press, 1993).
3 This topic has been analysed, among others, by Andrew Gurr, *The Shakespearian Playing Companies* (Oxford: Clarendon Press, 1996); and Siobhan Keenan, *Travelling Players in Shakespeare's England* (Basingstoke: Palgrave Macmillan, 2002).
4 J. L. Styan, *Shakespeare's Stagecraft* (Cambridge: Cambridge University Press, 1967), p. 8.
5 *The Three Lords and Three Ladies of London*, C1r.
6 For a discussion of the pictorial, documentary and archaeological evidence of Elizabethan and Jacobean theatres see Andrew Gurr, *The Shakespearean Stage, 1574–1642*, 3rd edn (Cambridge: Cambridge University Press, 1992). Another interesting essay is Glynne Wickham, ' "Heavens", Machinery, and Pillars in the Theatre and Other Early Playhouses' in *The First Public Playhouse: The Theatre in Shoreditch, 1576–1598*, ed. Herbert Berry (Montreal: McGill-Queen's University Press, 1979), pp. 1–15. Wickham's intuitive remarks about the dangers implicit in trying to gain a definitive insight into the architectural features of early-modern public venues have found confirmation after the unearthing of the Rose foundations in 1989. For a description of the discovery of the Rose foundations, see Julian Bowsher, *The Rose Theatre: An Archaeological Discovery* (London: Museum of London, 1998).
7 Linda McJannet, *The Voice of Elizabethan Stage Directions: The Evolution of a Theatrical Code*, (London: Associated University Presses, 1999), p. 69. McJannet applies the adjective 'Elizabethan' also to the Jacobean and Caroline periods; she is mainly concerned with historical plays written for adult professional companies.

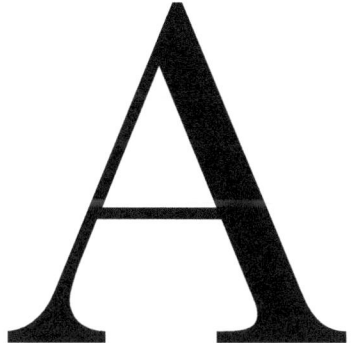

accent (A) In speaking as in **sing**ing, 'accent' can refer to either vocal quality or to verbal emphasis. The former is often associated with geographical region, human condition (age, emotion, state of being) or some other external circumstance. The latter is more a prosodic matter and concerns syllabic stress.

Definitions and concepts of accent in early modern poetry treatises and **music** manuals frequently overlapped to such an extent that poetry borrowed language from music in an effort to explain the complexities, and vice versa. It was thought that pitch variables determined accent. Thus:

> An *accent* is that, whereby the word is as it were **tune**d: and there is but one *accent* in a word, although there be many syllables: & it is ***sharp**e*, or ***flat***. By the *sharpe accent* a syllable is lifted up. The *flat accent* is either *grave* or *bended*: by the *grave accent* the syllable is depressed: by the *bended* it is both lifted up and also depressed.
> (*The Latine Grammar*, p. 11)

The rising and falling accents here are akin to the pitch inflections of the **voice**. (The Elizabethans found it extraordinarily difficult to say what governed accent in theory.) In music:

> *Accent* . . . is a certaine law, or rule, for the raysing, or low carrying of sillables of each word. . . . The *Graue* [accent] is that, by which a

accent

sillable is carried low: but to speake musically, it is the regular falling with finall words, according to the custome of the Church.... An *acute Accent* grammatically, is that, by which the syllable is raised. But musically, it is the regular eleuation of the finall words or syllables according to the custome of the Church.... The *Circumflex* is that, by which a sillable first raised is carried low. For it is, ... contrary to the *acute*, for it begins with the *acute*, and ends with the *graue*, vnknowne to Church-men.

(Dowland, *Micrologus*, 1609, pp. 69–70)

When accent has to do with tone or context its definition comes as it were halfway between music and poetry, as Dowland puts it: 'And it is called accent, because it is *ad Cantum*, that is, close by the **song** ... for as an adverbe doth determine a Verbe, so doth *accent* determine *Concent*' (ibid., p. 69).

(B) Many occurrences of 'accent' in Shakespeare imply simply verbal emphasis or syllabic stress. Other examples, however, do relate to 'word tuning', some more musical than others. Pitch, emphasis, vocal quality all combine in Sir Toby's advice to Sir Andrew after the latter has resolved to challenge Viola (disguised as Cesario) to a duel. It is important that Sir Andrew curses since 'it comes to pass oft that a terrible oath, / with a swaggering accent sharply **twang**'d off' (*TN* 3.4.179–80) gives the challenger a higher reputation for valour.

A musical image is present when Nestor talks about the 'thing of courage' (i.e. the courageous creature) which, in stormy conditions,

> As rous'd with rage, with rage doth sympathize,
> And with an accent tun'd in self-same **key**
> Retires to chiding fortune.
>
> (*Tro* 1.3.52–4)

Nestor's desire for harmony is, however, frustrated by the present condition of the Greek army, in which lack of discipline prevails.

Pitch inflection and vocal quality are involved in Mercutio's disparaging comments on the behaviour of men in love: 'The pox of such antic, lisping, affecting phantasimes, / These new tuners of accent!' (*Rom* 2.4.28–9).

accent

In his attempt to justify Coriolanus' abrupt manners and disdainful attitude, Menenius makes the following plea to the plebeians:

> Consider further:
> That when he speaks not like a citizen,
> You find him like a soldier; do not take
> His rougher accents for malicious **sound**s,
> But as I say, such as become a soldier
> Rather than envy you.
> (*Cor* 3.3.52–7)

The emphasis of line 55 is on pitch and vocal quality in relation to sound, which seems to confirm the reading 'accents' in preference to 'actions' (the latter is found in Folio, the first extant edition of this play).

(C) Attridge, *Well-weighed Syllables* (1974); and *The Rhythms of English Poetry* (1982).
   The Latine Grammar of P. Ramus Translated into English (1585).

accord (A) In his Italian–English dictionary, Florio (1598) defined *Accordare* as 'to **tune** an **instrument**'. In his French–English dictionary, Cotgrave (1611) stated that '*Accordance*' was 'a **concord**, or concordance in **musi**cke'. A century later, Chamber's (1728) definition summarizes the meaning as it would have applied in Elizabethan times: '*Accord*, in Musick, is more usually call'd *Concord*. The Word *Accord* is *French*, form'd according to some, from the Latin *ad cor*; but others, with more probability, derive it from the French *Corde*, a **String**, or Cord; on account of the agreeable Union between the **Sound**s of two Strings struck at the same time'.

(B) The only musical usage of this word in Shakespeare occurs when Hortensio, disguised as a **lute** teacher, clumsily tries to reveal his real identity to Bianca. He asks her to read his **gamut**:

> '*Gamouth*' I am, the **ground** of all accord:
> A *re*, to plead Hortensio's passion;
> B *mi*, Bianca, take him for thy lord,

accord

> C *fa ut*, that loves with all affection.
> D *sol re*, one **cliff**, two **note**s have I,
> E *la mi*, show pity, or I die.
> (*Shr* 3.1.73–8)

'Accord' here seems to be synonymous with 'concord', a concept which entails agreement of notes and pleasantness of sound (see also 'gamut' for a detailed analysis). It obliquely hints at Hortensio's hope that Bianca will accept his courtship, a hope which is dashed by her curt reply: 'Call you this gamouth? **Tut**, I like it not' (79).

See also **concent, harmony**.

air see **ayre**.

alarum (A) This term literally means 'to arms' (from the Italian 'all'armi'). The **sound**ing of alarums by various **instrument**s, especially **trumpet**s, **drum**s or **bell**s is connected with military atmospheres, and is most frequently called for in historical plays and tragedies. Unfamiliar as it might be to modern readers and audiences alike, this sound effect was extremely significant in a theatre which strongly relied on symbolic rather than realistic renditions of battles, and in which aural signals were often as important as visual ones. In *Apology for Actors* (1612), Heywood gives an account of a performance in a Cornish town in 1595, during which '. . . the players . . . presenting a battle on the stage with their drum and trumpets strook up a lowd alarme' (G2r).

(B) Folio *Richard III* has three explicit indications for alarums during the scenes showing the unfolding of the Battle of Bosworth Field. The last stage direction follows Richard's famous invocation 'A horse! A horse! My kingdom for a horse!' (5.4.13) and reads: '*Alarum. Enter Richard and Richmond. They fight. Richard is slain*' (3.5.OSD). Other outstanding instances of the importance of this sound effect in battle scenes with symbolic stage action are: '*Alarums. They fight. Edmund falls*' (*Lr* 5.3.152.SD); and '*An alarum. Excursions. Bedford brought in sick in a chair*' (*1H6* 3.2.41.SD).

Some stage directions prescribe that the alarum must be **play**ed 'within' the tiring-house rather than onstage, as in: '*Alarum within. Enter*

King, Malcolm, Donalbain, Lennox, with attendants, meeting a bleeding Captain' (*Mac* 1.2.OSD). Similarly, the use of the locution 'alarum afar off' appears to imply that the sound effect was expected to be achieved offstage (see Introduction for a discussion of the areas where aural effects were normally achieved in Elizabethan playhouses).

The references to alarum(s) in the dialogue also often occur in military contexts, and sometimes differentiate between trumpet and drum signals, as in: 'Now when the angry trumpet sounds alarum' (*2H6* 5.2.3); and: '**Strike** alarum, drums!' (*R3* 4.4.149). However, far more frequent is the generic indication 'alarum(s)', for example in: 'And with **loud** 'larums welcome them to Rome' (*Tit* 1.1.147); or: 'Patroclus, arming to answer in a night alarm' (*Tro* 1.3.171). It has been argued that in some instances of offstage battles, a cannon would be used to achieve this sound effect, as in: '*Alarum afar off, as at a sea fight*' (*Ant* 4.12.3.SD).

Shakespeare uses 'alarum' in a number of martial metaphors. When Gertrude expresses her concern about Hamlet's mental state, she compares his hair to that of 'sleeping soldiers in th' alarm' (*Ham* 3.4.120). Macbeth's qualms about committing regicide are well expressed in his soliloquy when he likens murder to a ghost 'alarum'd by his sentinel, the wolf' (*Mac* 2.1.53). In a more light-hearted context, we have Hortensio describe Katherina's spiteful attitude in the following terms: 'Tush, Gremio; though it pass your patience and mine to endure her loud alarums . . .' (*Shr* 1.1.127).

Adonis resorts to military language when trying to dissuade Venus from her intent: 'Remove your siege from my unyielding heart, / To love's alarms it will not ope the gate' (*Ven* 423–4). The tension immediately preceding Tarquin's rape of Lucrece is expressed with yet another powerful war metaphor: 'Anon his beating heart, alarum striking, / Gives the hot charge' (*Luc* 433–4).

The use of an alarum-bell occurs twice in the Shakespeare canon (there is also a reference to an alarum-bell in *2 Henry IV*, but this does not imply the actual use of the stage property). In *Macbeth*, it signals danger which may or may not have military consequences. After the murder of Duncan, Macduff exhorts everybody to awake: '**Ring** the alarum-bell! Murther and treason!' (2.3.74). Later in the play, Macbeth gives the same order, this time before the battle in which he will be slain: 'Ring the alarum-bell! **Blow wind**, come wrack!' (5.5.50). 'Bell' is used as a shorthand form for 'alarum-bell' in *1 Henry VI* (4.2.39), *Romeo and Juliet* (5.3.206) and *Othello* (1.1.90, 2.3.161 and 2.3.175).

alarum

(C) Dessen and Thomson, *A Dictionary of Stage Directions* (1999), pp. 3–4, is a ground-breaking study drawing upon a large database of stage directions (over 22,000) taken from 500 plays written for adult professional companies between 1580 and 1642.

de Somogyi, *Shakespeare's Theatre of War* (1998).
Edelman, *Brawl Ridiculous* (1992), esp. pp. 52–3, 121, 152.
Jorgensen, *Shakespeare's Military World* (1956), pp. 1–34.
Manifold, *The Music in English Drama* (1956), pp. 24ff., 76.

alarum-bell see **alarum, bell**.

allemande see **almain**.

almain (A) That French and Netherlands printers felt compelled to append the title 'allemande' in mid-sixteenth-century published collections of **chanson**s and **dance**s for the German variant of the *basse danse* indicates that the 'allemande' was a relatively new **dance**. In art **music**, it is characterized by its moderately slow duple (4/2) rhythm and three-**strain** sectionalized form. The middle strain is often contrasted with the first and third strains both in its tonality and inner structure. As for the dance itself, Arbeau described it as a 'simple, rather sedate dance ... familiar to the Germans' (*Orchesography*, 1589, p. 125). The dance comprises three walking steps and a *grève* or lifted step. The 'almayne leaps' sometimes alluded to in contemporary literature, occur in the third, more lively section of the dance.

English keyboard composers of the late sixteenth and early seventeenth centuries wrote a significant number of almains, second only in popularity to **pavan**s and **galliard**s. The largest number appear in the FWVB manuscript collection. Half of those adhere to the continental type described above. The others develop the form along individual lines. But as with the continental form, it is the tonal contrast of sections and the ponderous tempo rather than the melodic and rhythmic element which distinguish the almain.

(B) To set his trap for Othello in motion, Iago gets Cassio drunk while they are on watch duty. Iago sings a **song** praising drunkenness and *almain*

says that he learned it in England, a country famous for its people's drinking habits. He goes on to explain that an Englishman:

> . . . drinks you, with facility, your Dane
> dead drunk; he sweats not to overthrow your Almain;
> he gives your Hollander a vomit ere the next pottle
> can be fill'd.
>
> (*Oth* 2.3.82–5)

'Almain' allows Shakespeare to make an oblique allusion to the German dance and its ponderous slow tempo along with a more obvious reference to the German people. Moreover, 'Hollander' could also mean 'German' here; a similar usage is found for instance in Sidney's *A Defence of Poesy* (1595), where 'Dutch' or 'Hollander' is synonymous with 'German'. The musical nuance of Shakespeare's line is often overlooked, but it makes sense in the wider context of a scene where singing and an apparently merry atmosphere prevail. The German cultural frame is established earlier in the scene by Iago's first song (69–73), whose opening two lines contain the word 'canakin' (small drinking can): the suffix *-kin* is similar to the German *-chen*, normally employed in that language to form diminutives (Honigmann, p. 187).

(C) Dolmetsch, *Dances of England and France* (1949).
   Grove, 'Allemande'.
   Honigmann, *Othello* (1996).
   Payne, *The Almain in Britain, c. 1549-c. 1675* (2003).
   Sachs, *World History of the Dance* (1937).

alman see **almain**.

aloud (A) In nearly every case 'aloud' refers to reading audibly or speaking in a **loud voice**. But sometimes musical inferences are present, suggesting volume or intensity, generally in a public context.

(B) The use of this term in York's claim to the throne before the Battle of St Albans is interesting for its theatrical implications:

aloud

> From Ireland thus comes York to claim his right,
> And pluck the crown from feeble Henry's head.
> **Ring bell**s, aloud, burn bonfires clear and bright
> To entertain great England's lawful king!
> (*2H6* 5.1.1–4)

During a production of this history play in Shakespeare's time, these lines possibly worked as a cue to **sound** bells from an offstage position. Explicit stage directions for sound effects and **music** were sparingly used by Elizabethan and Jacobean playwrights and annotators, hence the dialogue often contained implicit stage directions similar to that at line 3.

In another military context, victory is celebrated after the French have defeated Talbot and his followers in Orléans, thanks to Joan of Arc's help. The Reignier orders:

> Why ring not out the bells aloud throughout the town?
> Dolphin, command the citizens make bonfires,
> And feast and banquet in the open streets,
> To celebrate the joy that God hath given us.
> (*1H6* 1.6.11–14)

'Aloud' suggests vocal intensity when Cordelia describes the deteriorated mental state of her father:

> ... He was met even now
> As mad as the vex'd sea; **sing**ing aloud,
> Crown'd with rank femiter and furrow-weeds,
> With hardocks, hemlock, nettles, cuckoo-flow'rs,
> Darnel, and all the idle weeds that grow
> In our sustaining corn ...
> (*Lr* 4.4.1–6)

It is possible that Shakespeare had a line from Chaucer's *Troilus and Criseyde* in mind: 'The kinges foole is wont to crie aloud' (2.401, quoted in *OED*). Having the King singing in the same manner as his fool (whose songs earlier in the play remind Lear of his mistakes) is an effective way of developing the theme of reversal of values running throughout this tragedy. Although Lear's singing is reported and not *aloud*

rendered on the stage, the image conjured up by Cordelia strikingly resembles that of the distracted Ophelia singing and distributing flowers and herbs on the stage in *Hamlet*, 4.5.

Isabella's hypermetrical use of 'aloud' in her exchange with Angelo 'Or with an outstretch'd **throat** I'll tell the world aloud / What man thou art' (*MM* 2.4.153–4), possibly adds quasi-musical passion to her disgust at Angelo's proposal that she should lose her virginity to him if she wants to save her brother from death.

See also **noise**.

(C) Cressy, *Bonfires and Bells* (1989), alludes to the collocation of bonfires and bells in popular celebration.

alter (A) Morley defines 'alter' as 'the doubling of the value of any **note** for the obsarvation of the odde **number**, . . . the note which is to be altered is commonly marked with a pricke of *alteration*' (*Introduction*, 1597, p. 24). In other words, a note is increased in **time**-value by half as much again by the addition of a dot (e.g. a **minim** which has two **beat**s lasts three beats when subject to alteration). If the dot is not written, then the time-value will depend on the rhythmical interpretation or '**mode**' of the **piece**. Dowland qualifies alteration as:

> The doubling of a lesser note in respect of a greater, or (as *Tinctor* saith) it is the doubling of the proper value. Or it is the repetition of one, and the selfe-same Note. And it is called *Alteration, Quasi altera actio*, it is another action, to wit: A secundary **sing**ing of a Note, for the perfecting of the number three.
>
> (*Micrologus*, 1609, p. 57)

Again, this is the elongation of a note by a half. 'Secundary singing' is equivalent to tying two notes in today's notation.

(B) In Shakespeare's *Sonnet* 116, which praises constancy in love, the poet plays on the polysemic quality of this term. He claims that 'Love is not love / Which alters when it alteration finds' (2–3), and that 'Love alters not with his [Time's] **brief** hours and weeks, / But bears it out even to the edge of doom' (11–12). The biblical tone of line 12 implies that 'the love defined here appears not merely life-long, but world-long' *alter*

(Duncan-Jones, p. 342). But the musical implications evoked by 'brief' (**breve**) and **bear** (**a part**) should not be missed: love (the singing or 'bearing a part') will always be constant, even when the breve (or note-value) changes.

(C) Duncan-Jones, *Shakespeare's Sonnets* (1997).

alteration see **alter**.

angel (A) The tradition of angels **sing**ing or **play**ing **instrument**s is a comparatively short one in the history of Christian and Jewish iconography. It is hardly older than the Middle Ages. In neither the New Testament nor the Old do the many angels who appear sing. Moore (pp. 89–99) argues that a more likely origin for musical angels is to be found in Eastern liturgies, in the Cherubic **Hymn** at the Great Entrance, where the angels, personated by singers, are perceived as joining invisibly with the congregation to glorify Christ. In the prayer of the **priest**, he describes the scene about the throne, where angels

> Cry one to the other with incessant **voice**s and perpetual **praise**, singing, vociferating, glorifying, crying, and saying to the Majesty of thy glory, the triumphal Trisagion: Holy, Holy, Holy, Lord of Sabaoth; Heaven and earth are full of Thy glory.
>
> (ibid., p. 90)

There seems, however, to have been a compounding of angelic singing with the singing of the elders in the Apocalypse, as in the prayer above, which aided the development of the tradition of angelic singing. This in turn was also incorporated into the notion that **music** was a 'heavenly thing'. In the Middle Ages, angels singing and playing were a common emblem in Miracle Plays and early religious dramas, symbolizing heaven, a heavenly presence or an intense religious moment.

Of the various instruments actually employed in church or religious contexts (e.g. weddings), **wind** instruments are preferred. Representations of angels playing instruments usually involve wind instruments.

The association of angels singing and heaven is commonly found in English Renaissance literature. An elegy to Henry Noel, for example,

angel

connects the heavenly music of the angels with the translation of the soul of the faithful departed:

> Hark! Alleluia cheerly
> With angels now he singeth,
> That here loved music dearly,
> Whose **echo** heaven **ring**eth,
> Where thousand cherubs hover,
> About th' eternal Mover.
> (Morley, 1601, no. 21)

Angels singing at special occasions, notably at Christmastide, is exploited in varying contexts. Christmas **carol**s, for example, often include angels, as in:

> This day Christ was born.
> This day our Saviour did appear.
> This day the Angels sing in earth,
> The Archangels are glad.
> (Byrd, 1611, no. 27)

(B) Shakespeare's musical angels are related to the heavenly or 'celestial music', the music of the spheres, as in Lorenzo's description to Jessica of the starry night sky:

> There's not the smallest orb which thou behold'st
> But in his **motion** like an angel sings,
> Still quiring to the young-ey'd cherubins.
> (*MV* 5.1.60–2)

The **harmony** evoked by these words perfectly suits the context of the final scene, in which love and forgiveness triumph. The notion of angels singing on the spheres is one which developed during the Middle Ages – a Christianizing of classical notions – but which fairly rapidly translated to angels singing in the *primum mobile*, rather than on each planetary sphere (Meyer-Baer).

In a more serious context, when Horatio bids farewell to the dead Hamlet, he calls upon the angels: 'Now cracks a noble heart. Good night, sweet prince, / And flights of angels sing thee to thy **rest**! (*Ham*

19

angel

5.2.359–60). That a **chorus** of angels should be present to receive the soul of the dead was a traditional image, dating back to the antiphon of the old Latin burial service (Jenkins, p. 416).

Before committing regicide, an anguished Macbeth foresees that Duncan's virtues 'will plead like angels, **trumpet-tongu'd**, against / The deep damnation of his taking-off' (*Mac* 1.7.19–20). Here, angels are described as neither singing nor playing instruments, but rather as divulging to the world the horror of Macbeth's dark secret with the power and intensity of a trumpet's **sound**.

A musical connotation in the use of 'angel' can also be discerned in Edgar's speech while disguised as Tom o'Bedlam. This time, however, it is the 'black angel', i.e. the devil, who is singing:

> The foul fiend haunts poor Tom in the voice
> of a **nightingale** ... Croak not, black angel, I have
> no food for thee.
> (*Lr* 3.6.29–30; 31–2)

Since these lines are preceded by the Fool's song 'Come o'er the bourn, Bessy, to me', it is possible that Edgar's reference to the nocturnal **chorister**, the nightingale, is an allusion to the Fool singing (Weis, p. 197).

(C) Jenkins, *Hamlet* (1982).
   Meyer-Baer, *Music of the Spheres* (1970), traces the way the classical notion of the daemons or spirits attaching to the spheres was in the Middle Ages translated to angels.
   Moore, 'The Tradition of Angelic Singing in English Drama' (1923).
   Rastall, *The Heaven Singing* (1996).
   Weis, *King Lear* (1993).

anthem (A) At its outset in the sixteenth century, the anthem was a peculiarly English choral **piece** using words from the Bible or sacred texts and usually **perform**ed as a separate item at the beginning or end of a church service. In cathedrals and chapels it had a special devotional function and was sung by the **choir** alone in order to intensify the act of worship of the people or congregation.

In the years following the Henrician Reformation, the English vernacular replaced Latin as the language of the English Church according to the edicts of the First Act of Uniformity (January 1549). The new English services were published in *The Booke of Common Prayer* (1549) and were based on pre-Reformation liturgies. The new rubrics did not state the part **music play**ed in these services, but evidence from the earliest surviving source of Anglican choral music (the Wanley Partbooks, Oxford: Bodleian Mus. Sch. E. 420–2, c.1546–8) indicated what sort of music was used. Among the contents are settings of biblical and prayer-book texts many of which are labelled 'antem'. The specific context in which these anthems were sung is uncertain, but they were primarily intended, like their Roman predecessor (the antiphon), to be inserted as preludes and postludes to parts of the liturgy, in the English context at the beginning and end of Morning and Evening Prayer (also called Matins and Evensong) and certain Festal services.

It is clear from the Elizabethan Injunctions (1559) that the anthem or '**hymn**' had a special place in the prayer-book services where **sing**ing was the norm:

> In the beginning, or in the end of common prayers, either at morning or evening, there may be sung an Hymn, or such-like song, to the **praise** of Almighty God, in the best sort of **melody** and music that may be conveniently devised, having respect that the sentence of the Hymn may be understood and perceived.
>
> (Le Huray, 1978, p. 33)

The first printed collection of English church music, John Day's *Certaine Notes* (1565), employs the terms 'anthem' and 'prayer' synonymously. By the beginning of the seventeenth century, 'anthem' was used widely in printed and manuscript sources to denote a choral piece employing an English text derived from the Bible, prayer book or even a moralizing verse. Whilst the anthem had primarily a sacred purpose, it was not necessarily confined to the church as it had been in the previous century. Consequently, many anthems or 'divine songs' appeared in early seventeenth-century printed books together with **madrigal**s, **ayre**s and part-songs. Like Amner's collection of anthems, his *Sacred Hymnes* (1615), they were intended for domestic consumption.

The types of anthems composed up to c.1565 were mainly unpretentious four-**voice** pieces suitable for small choirs. The simple style of the

anthem

early anthems found in the Wanley and Lumley part-books accord with the Protestant ideal of clarity of diction and solemnity in presentation, although such simplicity was not necessarily extended to other parts of the liturgy. Elaborate settings of the Canticles and of the Ordinary of the Communion survive from this time.

During the Elizabethan period and through into the seventeenth century the anthem became more elaborate and expressive. The most significant development was the creation of the 'verse' anthem technique in which passages for solo voice or voices accompanied by **viol**s or **organ** alternated with sections for full choir. Such anthems were particularly favoured by the choir of the Chapel Royal, especially during Richard Farrant's time as Master of the Choristers, 1569–80 (in this post, Farrant was also in charge of a company of choirboy actors and was required to present a play before the Queen each year). The most impressive verse anthems were written by composers associated with the Chapel Royal, namely Byrd, Morley, Tomkins and Gibbons; and the early seventeenth century saw a great flowering of anthem writing.

(B) Intense expression, often involving melancholic rhetoric, is characteristic of many late Elizabethan anthems. Valentine refers to this mournful mood after being banished from Milan. The banishment will prevent him from seeing Silvia, with whom he is in love. He apostrophizes Proteus who is hypocritically comforting him:

> No more; unless the next word that thou speak'st
> Have some malignant power upon my life;
> If so – I pray thee breathe it in mine **ear**,
> As ending anthem of my endless dolor.
> (*TGV* 3.1.239–42)

Here Shakespeare also alludes to the ending the anthem customarily brought to the church service in which it was sung. The musical metaphor is sustained by Proteus' subsequent comment that 'hope is a lover's staff' (248).

An **extempore** solo song or **ditty** is contrasted with the solemn anthem in *Venus and Adonis*: 'Her heavy anthem still concludes in woe' (839). Again the sense of ending is present. Likewise, mournful solemnity surrounds the following passage in *The Phoenix and Turtle*:

anthem

> 'Mongst our mourners shalt thou go.
> Here the anthem doth commence:
> Love and Constancy is dead.
>   (20–2)

With Falstaff it is **loud** singing in the choir that is appropriate to the anthem: 'For my voice, I have lost it with / hallowing and singing of anthems' (*2H4* 1.2.188–9).
See also **psalm**.

(C) Fellowes, *English Cathedral Music* (1969).
Le Huray, *Music and the Reformation in England* (1978).
Morehen, 'The English Consort and Verse Anthems' (1978).
Temperley, *The Music of the English Parish Church* (1979).
Wulstan, *Tudor Music* (1985).

Apollo (A) In Greek mythology, Apollo is represented variously as the god of medicine, **music**, poetry and eloquence and the fine arts of which he was the inventor. Among other attributes, he is reputed to have received from Jupiter the power of prophecy; his oracle at Delphi was famous throughout the world. His amorous encounter with Daphne is best known among several liaisons. He is also sometimes identified with the Sun, confounding together Apollo, Sun, Phoebus and Hyperion in Elizabethan sources although in classical mythology these deities are all different.

As the 'poetical god of music', Apollo appears frequently and diversely in early modern literature, poetry and drama. He is credited with having invented the lyre (in fact it was given to him by Mercury) and is either metaphorically connected with or depicted holding **string**ed **instrument**s, namely **lute, harp** or **viol**. For instance, in the 1616 title page of the Folio edition of Ben Jonson's *Workes*, Apollo is portrayed with his lyre in a small niche to the left of Tragicomedy (Dionysos is on the right). This image signifies that 'either the shepherd [Apollo] or the Wild Man [Dionysos] was considered to be a proper character in the mixed genre of tragicomedy. Both may also appear together in the same play with propriety . . .' (Simonds, p. 33).

The symbolic meaning of the ill-matched contest with Pan (or

Apollo

Marsyas), championed by Midas, is essential to Elizabethan mythography, representing, in the quiet string music of Apollo, order, sobriety and control in contrast to the less refined **wind** music of Pan which symbolizes disorder, lust and strife. The Elizabethan source of the story of the contest between Pan and Apollo is Ovid, *Metamorphoses* XI.146–93. It is transmitted by various writers. Wythorne, for example, summarizes it as follows:

> *Midas* aforesaid was a covetous king of *Phrygia*. *Pan*, the poeticall god of the sheppards contending in music with *Apollo*, the poeticall god of music. They chose one named *Tmolus* to be their judge in that controversy, who gave sentence on *Apollos* part. But *Midas* preferred *Pan* with his screaking **pipe**s before the music of *Apollo*. Wherfor, *Apollo* gave unto *Midas* a pair of asses **ear**s.
>
> (Osborne, p. 184)

Campion versifies the myth in his fourth book of **ayre**s:

> To his **sweet** Lute *Apollo* sung the motions of the Spheares,
> The wondrous order of the Stars, whose course divides the yeares,
> And all the Mysteries above:
> But none of this could *Midas* move,
> Which purchast him his Asses eares.
> Then *Pan* with his rude Pipe began the Country-wealth t'advance,
> To boast of Cattle, flockes of Sheepe, and Goates on hils that **dance**,
> With much more of this churlish kinde:
> That quite transported *Midas* minde,
> And held him rapt as in a trance.
> This wrong the *God of Musicke* scorn'd from such a sottish Judge,
> And bent his angry bow at *Pan*, which made the Piper trudge:
> Then *Midas* head he so did trim
> That ev'ry age yet talkes of him
> And *Phoebus* right revenged grudge.
>
> (c.1617, no. 8)

(B) The oracle of Apollo and the deity's association with Daphne are both found in Shakespeare's *The Winter's Tale*, *The Taming of the Shrew* and *A Midsummer Night's Dream*. Apollo's musical **skill**s are also well represented in *The Taming of the Shrew*, when the lord asks Sly:

Apollo

>   Wilt thou have music? Hark, Apollo **play**s,   *Music*
>   And twenty caged **nightingale**s do **sing**.
>   (Ind. 2.35–6)

It is fitting that the quiet domestic stringed-instrument music of Apollo should attend the lord. The stage direction for music in the margin shows that the lord's lines were intended as a cue for **musician**s. The actors were expected to occupy an 'aloft' position (see Ind. 2.OSD). At a purpose-built public playhouse, the stage gallery would have been used and it is possible that the musicians occupied part of that area. Alternatively, music could have been played within the tiring-house, as a number of musical cues in Shakespearean and non-Shakespearean plays indicate (see Introduction for a detailed analysis of the areas of Elizabethan theatres used for sound effects and music).

Sometimes, disparate aspects of Apollo are drawn together in one image, as when Berowne finally admits the importance of love to himself and his companions:

>   For valor, is not Love . . .
>   . . . as sweet and musical
>   As bright Apollo's lute, **strung** with his hair.
>   (*LLL* 4.3.337; 339–40)

Whilst Apollo was often represented wearing long hair, it is uncertain from where Shakespeare derived the image of Apollo stringing his lute with his hair. The closest image to that developed by Shakespeare is found in a passage from *How a Man May Choose a Good Wife from a Bad* (1602): 'Hath he not torn those gold **wire**s from your head, / Wherewith Apollo would have strung his harp, / And kept them to play music to the gods?' (David, p. 114).

The succeeding two lines of *Love's Labour's Lost* develop the metaphor of love and music intertwining: 'And when Love speaks, the **voice** of all the gods / Make heaven drowsy with the **harmony**' (4.3.341–2). The play concludes with a song, at the end of which Armado comments: 'The words of Mercury are **harsh** after the songs of Apollo' (5.2.930): the constant connection of Apollo with music, harmonious and lyrical, is contrasted with prose, a regular and less harmonious medium. Cohen (p. 836) explains that 'the words of Mercury' are a reference to Mercade's announcement that the Princess of France's

Apollo

father has died (the messenger enters at 5.2.716). It seems that Armado's concluding statement brings into question the very essence of a play which, as has often been noted, is among the most linguistically elaborate and verbally witty – starting from the title – in the Shakespeare canon.

Apollo's instrument, be it lute, harp or viol, is properly associated with either domestic or courtly environments. So, when the scurrilous Thersites refers to 'the **fiddler** Apollo' (*Tro* 3.3.304), his remark is especially disparaging.

(C) Cohen, *Love's Labour's Lost*, The Norton Shakespeare (1997).
David, *Love's Labour's Lost* (1951).
Osborne, *The Autobiography of Thomas Whythorne* (1961).
Simonds, *Myth, Emblem, and Music in Shakespeare's 'Cymbeline'* (1992).
Wells, *Elizabethan Mythologies* (1994).

ayre (A) In his *Introduction* (1597, p. 180), Thomas Morley described as 'ayres' all kinds of English **song**s which were not the more 'serious' Italianate **madrigal**s of, say, Weelkes and Kirbye. By 'ayre', Morley mainly intends **canzonet**s, 'villanelle', **ballet**ts. These are varieties of light madrigals and should not be confused with **lute** ayres.

The ayre or English lute song was essentially a simple **melody**-dominant song with lute or **viol** accompaniment, although more than a third of the 600 songs published between 1597 and 1622 offered an alternative part-song version to the solo song, printed on the same and adjacent page. The ayre was one of the major vocal genres of the English Renaissance. Unlike its counterpart, the madrigal, the musical substance of the ayre was contained in its solo melodic **voice** and largely harmonic accompaniment. The madrigal, in contrast, was distinguished by its equal-voice polyphonic texture and contrapuntal imitation between the voices. It did not require an **instrument**al accompaniment. The words of the ayre were more clearly audible than in the madrigal; and because musical mannerisms such as word-painting and repetition did not alter poetic form, **metre** and content as much as they did in the madrigal, the ayre was able to represent the poem it set more closely and directly. This made it more suitable for insertion in dramatic dialogue and it is the ayre that is invariably found in plays and **masque**s, not the madrigal, which hardly ever occurs.

In 1597, Peter Short published John Dowland's *The First Booke of Songes or Ayres of Fowre Parts with Tablature for the Lute*. Although ayres had existed in manuscript sources since the 1560s, this book started a vogue for the published lute song or ayre which continued until Attey's *First Book of Ayres* of 1622. Among the composers represented, in addition to Dowland, were Thomas Campion, Robert Jones, Thomas Ford, Philip Rosseter, Thomas Morley, Francis Pilkington, Alfonso Ferrabosco the younger and others most of whom had connections with London theatres or courtly entertainment. They were described by twentieth-century editors and musicologists as the English School of Lutenist songwriters, not only because their approach to the ayre had common artistic principles, but also because their published songs followed the same format established by Short in 1597.

The characterizing melodic element of the ayre resulted in the word 'ayre' also being used to denote the melody or **tune** itself. Campion, for example, refers to the melodic line as 'ayre' when, in explaining the genesis of his alternative part-song versions, he says, 'if wee consider well, the **Treble** tunes, which are with us commonly called Ayres, are but Tenors mounted eight **Note**s higher' (*Two Bookes of Ayres*, c.1613 'To the Reader'). Interestingly, in the same preface, he goes on to state what he regards as the best quality in songs or ayres, which is that they are 'light', cleverly made and concise: 'Short Ayres, if they be skilfully **frame**d, and naturally exprest, are like quicke and good Epigrammes in Poesie, many of them shewing as much artifice, and breeding as great difficultie, as a larger Poeme'. He claims that ayres can show as much artistry and invention as the **solemn** motet or intricate madrigal.

(B) Shakespeare employs 'air' either to signify the song type, or simply to mean a tune. The description **'sweet'** is commonly used to imply a **pleasant** pretty air. It also has special English connotations going back to the fifteenth century, when English **music** was described as 'sweet', notably by French writers, because of the **concord**ant **sound** of its thirds and sixths in contrast to the more open harsher fourths and fifths of continental polyphony. This is implied, for instance, when Armado exclaims 'Sweet air!' (*LLL* 3.1.4) after Moth has sung 'Concolinel'. Similarly, Helena's description of Hermia's beauty resorts to a musical metaphor: 'Your eyes are lodestars, and your **tongue**'s sweet air / More tuneable than **lark** to shepherd's **ear**' (*MND* 1.1.183–4).

In *Cymbeline*, Cloten decides to employ **musician**s to court Imogen

ayre

with the song 'Hark, hark, the lark' (2.3.20–6). The 'wonderful sweet air, with admirable rich words to it' (18) was accompanied by instruments which were **play**ed by **fingering** – possibly the lute or the **recorder** (Nosworthy, p. 53). Cloten's instruction to the musicians 'If you can penetrate her with your / fingering, so; we'll try with tongue too' (14–15) gives Shakespeare the opportunity to create a sexually suggestive word-play (see also 'fingering').

For a play like *The Tempest*, dominated by magic and music, it is not surprising the musical term 'air' is used on more than one occasion. After **hear**ing Ariel's song 'Come unto these yellow sands', and still believing that his father has drowned, Ferdinand comments:

> Where should this music be? I' th' air, or th' earth?
> It sounds no more; and sure it waits upon
> Some god o' th' island. Sitting on a bank,
> Weeping again the King my father's wrack,
> This music crept by me upon the waters,
> Allaying both their fury and my passion
> With its sweet air . . .
>
> (1.2.388–94)

The air that Ferdinand breathes blends seamlessly with the air sung by the invisible Ariel and is an integral part of the magic atmosphere pervading the island. The same idea is reinforced about 100 lines later when the young man, seeing Miranda, believes that she is 'the goddess on whom these airs attend' (1.2.424). Lines 392–4 manifest 'the belief that earthly music, by its imitation of celestial **harmony**, could order both nature and the human passions' (Lindley, p. 122). The same concept is expressed by Lorenzo when he explains that herds of wild colts can be tamed when they hear 'any air of music **touch** their ears' (*MV* 5.1.76).

The healing power of song is touched upon by Leonato when he still believes his daughter Hero to be dead. He rejects his brother's attempt to console him by saying that he will not listen to anyone who tries to '**charm** ache with air, and agony with words' (*Ado* 5.1.26).

Once again in *The Tempest*, a drunken Caliban inveigles Stephano to murder Prospero. The invisible Ariel intervenes and creates confusion among the conspirators by playing music while Stephano and Trinculo sing. The two friends get scared, and Caliban tries to reassure them:

'Be not afeard, the isle is full of **noise**s, / Sounds, and sweet airs, that give delight and hurt not' (3.2.135–6). The reference to 'sweet airs' has an ominous slant in this context of political scheming.

Shakespeare seldom eschews the opportunity for a play on the word, with its musical and simple atmospheric meanings. Apart from the scene in *The Tempest* analysed above (1.2.388–94), usages of this kind occur, for instance, when Lorenzo orders that music be brought 'forth into the air' (*MV* 5.1.53): here 'air' primarily means the open air, but the close proximity of 'air' and 'music' may also suggest musical allusion. Similarly, in the scene in *Macbeth* where Hecate and the witches conjure up the apparitions for Macbeth, 'air' indicates not only the atmosphere but also implies a musical meaning when one of the witches exclaims: 'I'll charm the air to give a sound' (4.1.129). Another such example is found in *All's Well That Ends Well* when Helen, fearing for Bertram's life (Bertram is at war), describes how bullets, or 'leaden messengers', are shot:

> . . . O you leaden messengers,
> That ride upon the violent speed of fire,
> Fly with false aim, move the still-peering air
> That sings with piercing, do not **touch** my lord.
> (3.2.108–11)

Shakespeare's awareness of the different kinds of Elizabethan airs, from serious to light, is manifest in Prospero's line while he is restoring harmony in the concluding scene of *The Tempest*: 'A solemn air, and the best comforter / To an unsettled **fancy**' (5.1.58–9), where he juxtaposes the homophonic rhythmically straightforward air with the contrapuntal rhythmically more complex fancy, as well as building on the image of the disturbed imagination. The opposite type of air is mentioned in Orsino's remark that a song he had heard the previous night relieved his passion 'More than light airs and recollected terms' (*TN* 2.4.5).

In a musically rich context, before the song '**Sigh** no more, ladies, sigh no more' (*Ado* 2.3.63–74), Benedick observes in an aside: 'Now, divine air! Now is his soul **ravish**'d! / Is it not strange that sheep's guts should hale souls / out of men's bodies?' (2.3.58–60). His scornful remark is directed at the music of **string**ed instruments and is dramatically ironic, since Benedick will soon fall in love with Beatrice.

(C) Caldwell, *The Oxford History of English Music*, vol. 1 (1991).

Doughtie, 'Words for Music: Simplicity and Complexity in the Elizabethan Air' (1965), contains considerations of music to poetry; *English Renaissance Song* (1986) discusses both musical and poetical angles.

Fellowes (ed.), *The English Lute Songs* (1959–).

Greer, 'The Part-Songs of the English Lutenists' (1967–8).

Lindley, *The Tempest* (2002).

Maynard, *Elizabethan Lyric Poetry and Its Music* (1986), includes a substantial section on Shakespeare.

Nosworthy, *Cymbeline* (1955).

Pattison, *Music and Poetry of the English Renaissance* (1948), has chapters on madrigals, airs and aspects of setting poetry to music.

Poulton, *John Dowland* (1982), is an extensive study of Dowland including detailed commentary on the songs.

Spink, *English Song: Dowland to Purcell* (1974), offers a good historical survey.

Toft, *Tune thy Musicke to thy Hart. The Art of Eloquent Singing in England 1597–1622* (1993), considers affect and rhetoric in the lute ayre.

Warlock, *The English Ayre* (1926), is a concise and interesting, if somewhat dated, account by a song composer (alias Philip Heseltine) who also edited a number of Elizabethan airs.

Wilson, *Words and Notes Coupled Lovingly Together* (1989), is a full-length study of Campion's poetry, songs, masques and theoretical works.

B

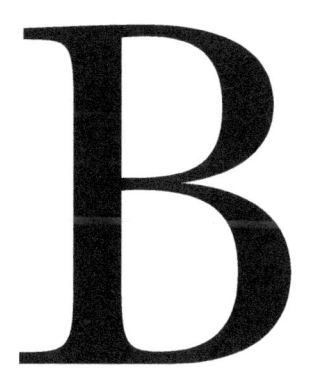

Babylon (A) The occurrence of 'Babylon' alludes to the **ballad** titled 'of the godly constant wife Susanna' (registered 1562–3) whose first line is 'There dwelt a man in Babylon'. It uses the **tune** *King Solomon* which survives as a **cittern** piece in the Mulliner Book (c.1560) and in the Dublin Virginal Manuscript which forms part of the so-called Dallis **Lute** Book (c.1570). Both 'Solomon' and 'Babylon' contain the 'lady, lady' refrain.

(B) In *Twelfth Night*, Sir Toby replies to Maria when she rebukes him, Feste and Sir Andrew for being too **loud** (Feste has just sung 'O mistress mine') by **sing**ing the ballad of *Constant Susanna*, whose story is derived from the Book of Susanna of the Apocrypha and whose opening lines are: 'There dwelt a man in Babylon'. These lines are followed by the refrain 'lady, lady' (2.3.79). The ballad touches upon one of the main themes of the play, that of women's constancy, which is discussed at length by Orsino and Viola (disguised as Cesario) in 2.4. 'Babylon' is also mentioned in *The Merry Wives of Windsor*, 3.1.24 (see '**madrigal**' for a discussion of the relevant passage).

See also **psalm**.

(C) Duffin, *Shakespeare's Songbook* (2004), discusses the ballads 'King Solomon' and 'There Dwelt a Man in Babylon'.

Sternfeld and Wilson (arr.), 'An Old English Carol', Oxford Carols (1978).

Ward (ed.), *The Dublin Virginal Manuscript* (1983).

bagpipe

bagpipe (A) A **wind instrument** with its distinctive air bag, originating in Ancient Greece and Arabia. In the Middle Ages it had become a popular and common instrument of many different kinds and sizes. After the shawm, it was the most frequently depicted wind instrument in paintings and carvings. Despite their differences, all bagpipes had three basic parts: the bag, the blowpipe and the chanter. The bag was usually made of leather or animal skin and sometimes covered by a cloth, as is suggested in Shylock's reference to the 'woollen' bagpipe (*MV* 4.1.56). The blowpipe allows the air to enter the bag, most often **blow**n by the player but sometimes by bellows. The chanter, connected to the bag, is a **pipe** (shawm) with finger holes and an enclosed reed which makes the (musical) noise. Many bagpipes, at least from the second half of the thirteenth century, had an additional pipe which provided a **drone** or **burden**.

(B) Throughout the Middle Ages and Renaissance, the bagpipe was generally an outdoor folk instrument, used to accompany dancing and eating at social occasions. This allusion is clear in the servant's comment preceding Autolycus' entry:

> O master! If you did but **hear** the pedlar at
> the door, you would never **dance** again after a **tabor** and
> pipe; no, the bagpipe could not move you.
> (*WT* 4.4.181–3)

The wailing sound of the bagpipe and its continuous drone has led writers to allude to its melancholic character. Such melancholy appears to be the subject of the reference in *The Merchant of Venice*: 'And laugh like **parrot**s at a bagpiper' (1.1.53). Like the foolish parrots, the bagpiper, having discarded the lute and harp finds solace in his sad instrument (see also '**bird**').

Falstaff is as melancholy as 'the drone of a Lincolnshire bagpipe' (*1H4* 1.2.76). The symbolic association of the bagpipe with gluttony and lechery, and by extension with the tavern, was well known from the Middle Ages and was a common theme in sixteenth-century symbolist painting (e.g. Bosch and Bruegel). That 'the bibulous Falstaff should be compared, among other "unsavory similes", to a "Lincolnshire bagpipe" is not inappropriate' (Wells, pp. 51–2). Exactly what a 'Lincolnshire' bagpipe is, is not known. In the late eighteenth century,

Steevens (*Works* VIII, 1793, p. 377) asserted that it referred not to the wind instrument but to the 'dull croak of a frog, one of the native **musician**s of that waterish county' (taken from Marder, p. 384). This seems unlikely. Other references indicating the instrument are found, for instance, in *Nest of Ninnies* (1608), where Robert Armin attests that at 'Christmas time, when . . . a noyse of **Minstrell**s and a Lincolnshire bagpipe was prepared: the minstrels for the great chamber, the bagpipe for the hall . . . for common dancing' (cited by Boswell and Malone, Third Varorium Edition, 1821, XVI, p. 197). In *Poly-Olbion* (1622), Michael Drayton notes: 'And **Bell**s and *Bag-pipes* next belong to *Lincolneshire*' (no. 22, 266). Writing about John Hunsley, the 'Lincolnshire bagpiper', Binnal (1941–2, p. 72) says that his bagpipe was 'little more than the Oaten Pipe improved with a bag'. Little or no iconographical evidence exists for a Lincolnshire bagpipe, unlike for example the comparatively large number of carvings of bagpipes in the glorious English Gothic minster at Beverley, East Yorkshire. Here, no two representations of the instrument are the same. But, with one exception, they all 'have a bag with a prominent seam' which might be called the 'Beverley bag' (Montague, p. 59). Because bagpipes were so variable it may have been that the Lincolnshire bagpipe was identifiable by a similar unique feature.

The classical opposition between **string**ed and wind instruments is invoked in the reference to the wind instruments which 'speak i' th' nose' in *Othello* (3.1.4). That these are bagpipes is confirmed by a similar description in *The Merchant of Venice* (4.1.49). The symbolic contrast is between the ethereal 'Musicks that may not be heard', the **music** of the spheres, the heavenly **harmony** (see *MV* 5.1.57) of stringed instruments and the base nasally sonorous bagpipes, associated in *Othello* with venereal disease and flatulence or 'breaking wind'. According to Ross, 'the opposition of two musics, one symbolising and conducing to virtue or order, the other error, is a common late medieval and Renaissance theme, and very frequently involves string music in contrast to wind instruments' (1966, p. 119). The bagpipe with its crude noise and unsophisticated **play**ing technique could not be a more apposite contrast to the refined **viol** or lute.

See also **pipe**.

(C) Baines, *Bagpipes* (1960).
   Binnall, 'A Man of Might' (1941–2), p. 72.

bagpipe

Block, 'Chaucer's Millers and their Bagpipes' (1954).
Carolan, 'Shakepeare's Uilleann pipes' (1981), p. 4.
Jones, 'Wittenwiler's *Becki* and the Medieval Bagpipe' (1949).
Marder, 'Shakespeare's "Lincolnshire Bagpipe"' (1950).
Montague, *Minstrels and Angels* (1998).
Oakley, 'Shylock's "Woollen Bagpipe"' (1960), p. 65.
Ross, 'Shakespeare's "Dull Clown" and Symbolic Music' (1966).
Sternfeld, *Music in Shakespearean Tragedy* (1967), pp. 226–35.
Wells, *Elizabethan Mythologies* (1994), pp. 50–2; p. 247 fn. 29.

ballad (A) There are two broad categories of ballads, namely folk – also known as traditional or popular – and street or broadside. Folk ballads owed their continued existence, at least until the late nineteenth century, to oral transmission. Street ballads, from the mid sixteenth century, were a printed genre. Communication conditions, therefore, distinguish the category into which a ballad falls. Folk ballads were recited or sung from memory. Street ballads were sung or read out **aloud** from a printed broadside at point of sale.

There is no single definition of 'ballad', nor any strict rule governing its form, unlike the French *'balade'* of the fourteenth and fifteenth centuries and its counterpart in Chaucer. The origins of the English ballad are not certain, but A. B. Friedman argues strongly that it derived from the French verse type, the *'balade'* referred to above, and not the Italian **dance** *'ballata'*.

The English street ballad was printed on a single sheet (usually folio) in 'black letter' typescript on one side of the page and usually contained pictorial woodcuts at the top of the page and/or side margins. Very rarely a melody was notated; nearly always, the instruction 'To the **tune** of . . .' was given, in other words to a simple familiar tune. About 1,000 tunes are mentioned (400 of which survive). They come from a variety of sources, including popular **song**, folk song, working songs, as well as art **music** from the early Tudor court and contemporary publications. There was no significance attached to the choice of tune, with one or two exceptions (e.g. 'Fortune my foe'); often the same tunes were used for different ballads. The familiar tune would help sell a new ballad. The tunes employed, give or take minor adjustments, would fit the **metre** and stanzaic form of the ballad text. The 'author' of the ballad, the 'ballad maker', would have control over its creation and dissemination at point of deliverance.

Twentieth-century commentators on the street ballad frequently denigrated the form as 'essentially an urban variety of subliterary expression' (Simpson, p. x). To compare the street ballad to art literature is to misrepresent its essential genre characteristics. The most important aspect of establishing its identity, according to Würzbach (p. 11) is the examination of the relationship between the text and the socio-cultural environment in which a ballad was manufactured and distributed, so that the link between 'textual construction and non-textual determining factors' (ibid.) may be established.

The street ballad was the target of Puritan reformers in their attempt, as Boyd points out (pp. 53–4), to supplant 'vague and trifling ballads' with uplifting and moralizing metrical **psalm** singing. Their aspirations must have been daunting. According to Tessa Watt, more than 3,000 ballads were printed between 1550 and 1650, and their circulation must have been well in excess of 1,000,000 copies. The centre for the street ballad was London but it was distributed throughout the country by itinerant balladmongers. Ballads reported a diverse range of topics from sensational national events, political propaganda, public executions of notorious criminals (generally to the tune of 'Fortune my foe') and so on to more mundane everyday occurrences. Whilst the 'story' was regarded by many modern literary critics as the main feature of the street ballad, it was by no means always the case.

The ballad crossed social boundaries but the status of the balladmaker varied from professional writers held in high esteem such as Thomas Deloney (d.1600) and Samuel Rowlands (d.c.1630) to rogues and vagabonds frequenting places of ill repute in order to sell their scurrilous ballads, ostensibly as Watt suggests to draw a crowd together so that their associates may indulge in petty crime. The pickpocketing of Autolycus, as Lindley contends, 'dramatises the association of balladseller and petty criminal'.

(B) In Shakespeare's plays, ballads 'might be not only commented upon and quoted, but **perform**ed and *meta*performed' (Smith, p. 168). For instance, characters sometimes remark on the quality of ballads; ballads were also performed on the stage, most notably Desdemona's

ballad

'Willow song'; the **jig**s can also be considered to be ballads narrated through singing and dancing.

In *The Winter's Tale*, ballads are mentioned in a scene dominated by disguise, with four characters concealing their real identities (Florizel, Polixenes, Camillo and Autolycus). Among his pack of trinkets, the cheat Autolycus has (street) ballads on various topics, as the following exchanges reveal:

> AUTOLYCUS: . . . for I have about me many parcels of charge.
> CLOWN: What hast here? Ballads?
> MOPSA: Pray now buy some. I love a **ballet** in print, a-life, for then we are sure they are true.
> AUTOLYCUS: Here's one to a very **doleful** tune, how a usurer's wife was brought to bed of twenty money-bags at a **burthen** . . .
> Here's another ballad, of a fish that appear'd upon the coast
> . . . and sung this ballad
> against the hard hearts of maids . . .
>
> (4.4.258–64; 275–8)

He is urged to sell a merry ballad, to which he replies: 'Why, this is a passing merry one and goes to / the tune of "Two maids wooing a man"' (4.4.288–9). The shepherdess Mopsa explains that this is in three **part**s, and proceeds to sing it with Autolycus and Dorcas. That ballads were considered to be goods for trading is clear from Autolycus' soliloquy in which he talks disparagingly of his customers and boasts that he has been able to sell all his 'trompery' (4.4.597), which includes ribbons, knives, shoe-ties, counterfeit stones and table-books, along with ballads.

The function of ballads as satires and purveyors of news is hinted at when Cleopatra fears that her reputation and that of Iras will be torn to pieces if they surrender to the enemy and are paraded through the streets of Rome. She tells Iras that 'Saucy lictors / Will catch at us like strumpets, and scald rhymers / Ballad's out a' tune' (*Ant* 5.2.214–6), and argues in favour of committing suicide rather than accepting this humiliation. Falstaff expresses his frustration and contempt when he discovers that his friends have hidden his horse by threatening them to

ballad

have 'ballads made on you all and sung to filthy tunes' (*1H4* 2.2.45). In his famous speech on the seven ages of man, Jaques tells us that the lovesick youth sighs 'like a furnace, with a **woeful** ballad / Made to his mistress' eyebrow' (*AYLI* 2.7.148–9). The quality of such a ballad can only be amateurish.

Sometimes the emphasis is on the role of the ballad as a means to divulge news and to celebrate an event. Helen tries to persuade the King of France, who is seriously ill, to take her father's remedy. She is convinced about the efficacy of this remedy to the point that she is prepared to have her shame 'traduc'd by odious ballads' (*AWW* 2.1.172) should it not work. Falstaff mentions a 'particular ballad' (*2H4* 4.3.48), clearly a street or broadside in which he alludes to the embellishing of ballad sheets, in this case depicting his capture of the 'furious knight', Sir John Colevile: 'with mine own picture on / the top on't (Colevile kissing my foot)' (4.3.48–9).

'Ballet' is used as a synonym for 'ballad' in some cases. Trying to find inspiration to write poetry for Jaquenetta, Armado enquires whether there is 'a ballet . . . of the King and the Beggar' (*LLL* 1.2.109–10). This was a popular ballad which told the story of King Cophetua and the beggar maid with whom he fell in love. Armado's self-conceited nature transpires from his choice of ballad: he implicitly likens himself to King Cophetua, and his beloved to the humble maid. In *A Midsummer Night's Dream*, after all the spells are revoked and Titania leaves him, Bottom awakes thinking that what has happened between him and the Queen of the Fairies has been 'a most rare vision' (4.1.205). He intends to ask Quince 'to write a ballet of this dream' (215) and to entitle it 'Bottom's Dream' because 'it hath no bottom' (216); the ballad will be sung during the wedding celebrations.

Whilst Shakespeare usually refers to subject matter, he occasionally intends form when talking of ballads. The very simple metrical form of the ballad is contrasted with art poetry when Henry V is wooing Princess Katherine and tells her that 'a **rhyme** is but a ballad' (*H5* 5.2.157–8). 'Rhyme' here is used synonymously for rhyming poetry, a usage common in Elizabethan times. Hotspur makes disparaging remarks about repetitive ballad metres when he asserts: 'I had rather be a kitten and cry mew / Than one of these same metre ballet-mongers' (*1H4* 3.1.127–8).

There are three references to balladmakers in Shakespeare. In *Much Ado About Nothing*, Benedick declares that he would rather have Don

ballad

Pedro 'pick out mine eyes with a ballad-maker's pen' (1.1.252) than fall in love – an exaggerated remark given that his aversion to love is short-lived and that he composes poetry and sings for Beatrice later in the play. In *The Winter's Tale* 5.2, some gentlemen narrate how Perdita's true identity is revealed. One of them comments that this was an exceptionally moving event and that even 'ballad-makers cannot be able to express it' (5.2.25). In a different context, Aufidius' servants reveal their diffidence of Coriolanus' alliance with their master: 'This peace is nothing but to rust iron, increase / tailors, and breed ballad-makers' (*Cor* 4.5.219–20).

See also **make**.

(C) Boyd, *Elizabethan Music and Musical Criticism* (1940).
Bronson, *The Traditional Tunes of the Child Ballads* (1959–72).
Chappell, *Popular Music of the Olden Time* (1855–9).
Chappell and Ebsworth, *The Roxburghe Ballads* (1869–99).
Child, *The English and Scottish Popular Ballads* (1882–98).
Duffin, *Shakespeare's Songbook* (2004), focuses on the lyrics and tunes of the ballads in Shakespeare's plays.
Friedman, *The Ballad Revival* (1961).
Gerould, *The Ballad of Tradition* (1932).
Rollins, 'The Black-letter Broadside Ballad' (1919), analyses the early history of the street ballad; *Old English Ballads* (1920); *Handefull of Pleasant Delites* (1924); and *Pepys Ballads* (1929–32).
Simpson, *The British Broadside Ballad and its Music* (1966).
Smith, *The Acoustic World of Early Modern England* (1999), pp. 168–205.
Watt, *Cheap Print and Popular Piety* (1991).
Würzbach, *The Rise of the English Street Ballad* (1990).

balladmaker see **ballad**.

ballet see **ballad**.

balletmonger see **ballad**.

base see **bass**.

base-string see **bass; string**.

base-viol see **bass; viol**.

bass (A) In a general musical sense, 'bass' signifies a **low** frequency **sound** or the lowest part of several sounding above. It also has specific meanings as a noun, an adjective and even as a verb.

The bass is the lowest sound or pitch when other parts are sounding. Thus a **chord** has a bass **note**. Most compositions from the later fifteenth century onwards, written in several **part**s or **voice**s, have a consistently identifiable bass usually called the 'contratenor bassus'. Consequently, a voice known as the 'bass' became established in vocal **music**. It was the lowest male voice below the tenor, alto (**mean**) and **treble**. In **instrument**al **consort**s the lowest sounding instrument similarly became known as the bass (e.g. bass **recorder**, bass **viol**, etc.). The lowest **string** on a **lute** or viol was called the 'bass string'.

In differing musical contexts, 'bass' can have various meanings. The bass, for example, can be the same or something other than the bass voice. It could be the lowest part without being an actual bass voice. Or, it could simply be a low or deep voice, a **soft** barely audible sound – a meaning current in the late fifteenth and sixteenth centuries.

In the seventeenth century, the structural and harmonic importance of the bass in compositional technique and performance style hugely increased. The term 'basso continuo' emerged, affecting the English spelling which had previously been more commonly 'base'. Despite its orthography, 'base' in sixteenth-century music would not have implied a harmonic foundation or support, even when used as a verb. According to Renaissance music theory, the bass provided a sonorous foundation to the musical texture.

(B) A literal use of the word occurs in *The Winter's Tale*, where the Clown complains that the shearers – 'three-man **song**-men all' (4.3.42) – are 'most of them means and bases' (4.3.43), in other words middle and low voices. Some editors (e.g. Pafford, p. 84) take 'mean' to indicate

bass

a middle man's voice between **high** and low, that is a tenor. In keeping with what had been old-fashioned practice, the tune would be in the tenor. Because Elizabethan songs survive in many different versions and were **perform**ed in various arrangements, it is not possible to say that a song had a predetermined performative configuration. However, secular part-songs for three men's voices were common in the fifteenth and sixteenth centuries in England. Popular songs and courtly **ballad**s, dating from the time of Henry VIII, survive in this form (Henry VIII and Ritson MSS) and would be known in Elizabethan circles as 'three men's songs' (see also 'mean') suited to amateur and unrehearsed singing.

The metaphor of a '**ground** bass' is implied when Shakespeare, having prepared us for a musical word-play with **organ pipe**, uses the word as a verb:

> ... and the **thunder**,
> That deep and dreadful organ-pipe, pronounc'd
> The name of Prosper; it did base my trespass.
> (*Tmp* 3.3.97–9)

The music of the elements here enforces Alonso's consciousness of the **discord** of his wrongs. The thunder is like a deep pedal-bass to his guilt. The image was commonplace in Renaissance literature. It is the moral law of nature and not human stimulus that will cause guilt to bite in a man. 'Base my trespass' has strong religious connotations and reminds us of the Lord's Prayer (Lindley, p. 178).

The musical term is cognate with the adjective 'base', meaning 'morally low', 'menial', 'unrefined'. This provides Shakespeare with opportunities for further metaphor as in the lute **lesson** in *The Taming of the Shrew* (3.1), where the word is employed in both senses and also gives the opportunity for bawdy jokes. When Hortensio, disguised as the music teacher, tells Bianca 'my instrument's in **tune**' (38), Lucentio, disguised as Cambio the schoolmaster, admonishes him that 'all but the base' (47) is now in tune. Hortensio retorts angrily to his rival: 'The bass is right, 'tis the base knave that **jar**s' (48).

The principal strings on the lute were the Trebles, according to John Dowland (1610). So Prince Hal's intention is clear when he tells Poins that he has 'sounded the / very base-**string** of humility' (*1H4* 2.4.5–6) with his drinking partners Tom, Dick and Francis at the Boar's Head

Tavern. The bass string is softer, gentler than the treble and less prominent in music; but it provides vital support.

More complex musical word-play occurs in *Henry V* when the Dauphin extols the virtues of his horse. He claims that 'the basest **horn** of his hoof is more musical than the **pipe** of/Hermes' (3.7.17–18). Here the two senses of 'base' are combined with the two senses of 'horn', the instrument and the substance of a horse's hoof. The note of the lowest horn and the sound of the horse's trotting feet both exceed in beauty the pipe music of Hermes.

(C) Dowland 'Other Necessary Observations belonging to the Lute' in *Varietie of Lute-Lessons* (1610).
Lindley, *The Tempest* (2002).
Pafford, *The Winter's Tale* (1963).
Stevens, *Music and Poetry in the Early Tudor Court* (1979).

bear a diapason see **bear a part**, **diapason**.

bear a note see **bear a part**.

bear a part (A) In this context, a 'part' refers to the single line or **voice** of a part-**song** or, more generally, of vocal or **instrument**al polyphony. Thus the **perform**er singing or **play**ing a part would 'bear a part'. The sense of supporting or sustaining a line in a contrapuntal texture, in combination with other voices, is inherent in the phrase. To 'sing' or 'play' a part is more common in musical contexts and commentaries, but 'bear a part' occurs in several literary sources. For example, Edmund Spenser uses this expression: 'The trembling streames . . . were by them right tunefull taught to bear / A **Base**s part among their **consort**s oft' (*The Teares of the Muses*, 1591, 25–28). George Herbert more specifically applies it to three-part singing:

> Consort both heart and **lute**, and twist a song
> **Pleasant** and **long**:
> Or, since all **music**k is but three parts vied
> And multiplied,

41

bear a part

> O let thy blessed Spirit bear a part,
> And make up our defects with thy **sweet** art.
> *(Easter)*

(B) A 'singing in parts' metaphor is employed in Shakespeare's *Sonnet* 8. The poet chides the beloved youth for becoming melancholy when he hears music, like Jessica in *The Merchant of Venice*, who is 'never merry' when she hears 'sweet music' (5.1.69). In the sonnet, the **harmony** of music is then compared with the harmony of marriage which the youth dislikes and rejects. The beauty of music's union and **concord** gently rebukes him for choosing a single life and the impossibility of a son to continue his beauty. 'Thou single wilt prove none' (14). Thus:

> If the true concord of **well-tuned sound**s,
> By unions married do offend thine **ear**,
> They do but sweetly chide thee, who confounds
> In singleness the parts that thou shouldst bear.
> (5–8)

It has been argued that Shakespeare has in mind the (Tudor) three-part song (see '**mean**' for a detailed discussion), implied a few lines later by: 'Resembling sire, and child, and happy mother, / Who all in one, one pleasing **note** do sing' (11–12). However, the union the youth must forge (between himself and a wife to bear the longed-for son) is bipartite, suggested in the lines: 'Mark how one **string**, sweet husband to another, / **Strike**s each in each by mutual ordering' (9–10). The reference is presumably to the lute whose strings, except for the bass, are **strung** in pairs and when tuned sound a single note 'sweet husband to another'. Alternatively, these lines could be alluding to the sympathetic vibration of tuned strings, which was a commonplace image.

In *The Winter's Tale* Mopsa proposes that, if Autolycus can sing his part, then together with Dorcas they can perform a three-part **ballad**, which they have already learnt: 'We can both sing it: if thou'lt bear a part, / Thou shalt hear; 'tis in three parts' (4.4.292–3). Autolycus assures them that he can hold his part since, as a balladmonger, he was used to 'rendering' his wares: 'I can bear my part, you must know 'tis my occupation' (295).

In the Hecate scene in *Macbeth* (usually ascribed to Thomas Middleton), a musical meaning is possible. Hecate angrily rebukes the witches for having excluded her from their 'trading and trafficking' with Macbeth:

> And I, the mistress of your **charm**s, . . .
> Was never call'd to bear my part,
> Or show the glory of our art . . .
> (3.5.6; 8–9)

When the witches are casting their spells, they **chant** in a circle: 'chant' is in a sense musical, and this scene includes 'Come away, Death', a part-song in which Hecate joins. In her reproach to the witches, Hecate is stressing that she has both a practical and a musical part to play.

Not to be confused with 'bear a part' is 'bear a note', as when Maria, ridiculing the pompous tone of the love letters that she and her friends have received from their respective suitors, comments: 'Folly in fools bears not so strong a note / As fool'ry in the wise, when wit doth dote' (*LLL* 5.2.75–6). A musical interpretation can be suggested: 'the folly of fools doesn't play as loud a tune as the foolishness of wise men when wit grows old' (Robbins, p. 115). There is however another possible sense for 'note' in this context, i.e. 'notable', 'obvious'.

To 'bear a diapason' is not an uncommon phrase in sixteenth-century literature and has a distinct musical meaning. The term 'diapason' was current in Elizabethan theory and was the interval between one voice and another, being an 'eight' or octave. It was the most perfect of the concords. An interesting example of 'bear a diapason' in the Shakespeare canon is observed when Lucrece reacts to Tarquin's violence by contemplating suicide. In her distress she addresses **Philomela** (another victim of rape, who was transformed into a **nightingale**), and asks her to sing of ravishment:

> So I at each sad **strain** will strain a tear,
> And with deep groans the diapason bear . . .
> And whiles against a thorn thou bear'st thy part
> To keep thy **sharp** woes waking, wretched I,
> To **imitate** thee well, against my heart
> Will fix a sharp knife . . .
> (1131–2; 1135–8)

The musical terminology poignantly expresses Lucrece's need to vent

bear a part

her despair, and anticipates the way in which she will commit suicide; 'groaning' and 'sharp' also acquire sexual connotations.

(C) Robbins, 'Shakespeare's Sweet Music' (1968).
 Wilson, 'Thomas Campion's "Ayres filled with parts" reconsidered' (1983).

beat (A) Whilst 'beat' has several distinct musical meanings, only two apply in Shakespeare. One is straightforward, namely the striking of an **instrument** such as a **drum** to make a (rhythmical) **sound**. The other, less direct, has to do with the impact of sound as an acoustic property. Further meanings such as 'tactus' or pulse, and melodic ornament or **grace note** are not used. 'Beating **time**' is not found.

(B) Most references to beating drums are uncomplicated and occur in military contexts, such as in Agamemnon's order to his followers: 'Beat loud the **taborin**s, let the **trumpet**s **blow**' (*Tro* 4.5.275). Similarly, Timon exhorts Alcibiades to beat the drum (*Tim* 4.3.97). In *King John*, word-play on 'beat' (meaning both '**strike**' and 'defeat') and the drum's warlike connotations are evident in the Bastard's defiance to the Dauphin:

> Indeed your drums, being beaten, will cry out;
> And so shall you, being beaten. Do but start
> An **echo** with the **clamor** of thy drum.
>   (5.2.166–8)

An interesting image involving the beating of the drum appears in *King Lear*. Shocked at the sight of Kent (disguised as Caius) in the stocks, Lear demands to see Regan and Cornwall. He wants an explanation about their decision to punish his servant in such a humiliating manner:

> . . . Bid them come forth and **hear** me,
> Or at their chamber-door I'll beat the drum
> Till it cry sleep to death.
>   (2.4.117–19)

At a time when he is being deprived of his few remaining privileges, the drum is the only weapon that the old King can use against his ungrateful daughter.

The sense of notes sounding in the air by beating is present in Romeo's contention that it is no longer night but dawn and that he must leave Juliet. The girl argues: 'It was the **nightingale**, and not the **lark**, / That pierc'd that fearful hollow of thine **ear**' (*Rom* 3.5.2–3). Romeo however observes that the **bird** they have just **hear**d was the lark 'herald of the morn . . . whose notes do beat / The vaulty heaven' (6; 21–2). A similar notion of sound hitting the air is suggested in *2 Henry IV*: 'with what loud applause / Didst thou beat heaven with blessing Bullingbrook' (1.3.91–2).

Ariel's **skill** in beating the **tabor** has a magical effect on the drunken Caliban, Trinculo and Stephano, as he narrates to Prospero:

> . . . Then I beat my tabor,
> At which like unback'd colts they prick'd their ears,
> Advanc'd their eyelids, lifted up their noses
> As they smelt **music** . . .
>
> (*Tmp* 4.1.175–8)

The comparison of the three drunkards to animals is founded on the Renaissance belief that 'animals could be influenced by the **harmony** of music' (Lindley, p. 193). The emphasis on the characters' physical experience of music is on their sense of smell. The speech concludes with another reference to the sense of smell: 'the foul lake o'erstunk their feet' (4.1.183–4), thus reiterating the base carnal nature of Caliban, Stephano and Trinculo.

(C) Lindley, *The Tempest* (2002).

bell (A) Not so much a musical **instrument** as a metal object designed to make a sonorous **noise**, the bell in its most characteristic form is one of the largest and most public of contrivances. The most common (in England) and distinctive type is the church bell, whose history can be traced back to early monastic times and the building of towers to house large bells. The earliest records, relating to the casting of seven bells for the abbey of Croyland, date back to the tenth century. In 1251, Henry III gave Westminster Abbey two bells to add to the

bell

'great bell'. In succeeding centuries, bells were installed in church towers throughout the land to make **peal**s which were, in theory, to be 'concordant and agreeable in **music, tune, sound**, and **harmony**'. Very few ancient bells exist, due largely to their widespread destruction during the Henrician Reformation and partly to the introduction of change-ringing, originating in Elizabethan times and flourishing during the late seventeenth century, which caused the old pre-Elizabethan bells to be recast and retuned. The church bell also doubled as the **chime** and **toll** of the church clock, the public timekeeper for most Elizabethans. Large 'tower' bells were hung in secular buildings such as castles, town-halls and great houses.

The ringing of bells was far more common in Elizabethan England than it is today. Bells would announce the start and end of the working day; they would announce times of the day, special events and warn of dangers. They played important functions in both sacred and secular contexts. Today we tend to associate bells with churches and ecclesiastical foundations. In Elizabethan times, town halls and secular establishments equally relied on the ringing of bells for various public signals. The ringing of bells is contrasted, in certain circumstances with tolling. The passing bell, for example, is tolled whereas the death **knell** is rung. The clock bell is tolled but the passing knell is rung to signify the end of the day and beginning of the night curfew (when in force).

The symbolic powers of bells are various and well known. The funereal or 'passing' bell was tolled to announce the death of a person (as John Donne's famous 'Ask not for whom the bell tolls' signifies) and, depending on one's creed, to protect the soul of the dead and dying from evil spirits. Church bells were rung to avert disaster and pestilence. Or they may be rung to summon the faithful to worship. The fifteenth-century motto runs: 'I call . . . I lament . . . I fracture' (calls the living [to church], laments the dead, fractures the lightning). Another, 'festa decoro', signifies joyous occasions when bells are specially rung to mark notable events, as Chapman writes (1607), 'bells jangling together in untuned confusion' to celebrate 'high births of kings, deliverances and coronations' (*Bussy D'Ambois*, 1.1.9).

(B) Shakespeare's joyous bells ring out, sometimes in conjunction with lighting beacons after the Elizabethan practice associated with the Armada, to celebrate civil or military triumphs as when Richard, Duke of York, makes his claim to King Henry's crown: 'Ring bells, **aloud**,

46

bell

burn bonfires clear and bright, / To entertain great England's lawful king' (*2H6* 5.1.3–4). These lines may have worked as a musical cue: there are several stage directions in plays of the period 1580–1642 requring the imitation of tower bells (Dessen and Thomson, p. 28). The ringing of bells would have complemented the other numerous sound effects (e.g. **alarum**s and **flourish**es) characterising *2 Henry VI*.

Victorious bells herald an English triumph in France:

> Rejoice, you men of Angiers, ring your bells,
> King John, your king and England's, doth approach,
> Commander of this hot malicious day.
> (*Jn* 2.1.312–14)

The dying King Henry IV, thinking that his son is eagerly waiting to inherit the crown, reproaches him in the following terms:

> Then get thee gone, and dig my grave thyself,
> And bid the merry bells ring to thine **ear**
> That thou art crowned, not that I am dead.
> (*2H4* 4.5.110–12)

King Henry is superimposing the image of bells accompanying his own funeral ceremony on that of festive bells to be **play**ed at his son's imminent coronation: this may explain why there is no mention of a beacon in his speech (which is linked with joyous occasions).

The metaphoric 'passing' bell tolls for the father who has killed his son at the Battle of Towton, and:

> My heart, sweet boy, shall be thy sepulchre,
> For from my heart thine image ne'er shall go;
> My **sigh**ing **breast** shall be thy funeral bell . . .
> (*3H6* 2.5.115–17)

Whilst in *Sonnet* 71 Shakespeare exhorts his young friend to mourn for him no longer 'than you shall **hear** the surly sullen bell' (2), no funeral bell shall toll for Tamora Queen of the Goths, as Lucius brings the tragedy of Titus Andronicus to a close: 'No funeral rite, nor man in mourning weed / No **mournful** bell shall ring her burial' (*Tit* 5.3.196–7).

47

bell

In *Romeo and Juliet*, Capulet orders that melancholic bells be sounded after Juliet's (apparent) death:

> All things that we ordained festival,
> Turn from their office to black funeral:
> Our instruments to melancholy bells,
> Our wedding cheer to a sad burial feast.
> (4.5.84–7)

The funeral bell not only signifies melancholic events, it also denotes the passing of time, as in *Much Ado About Nothing*:

> ... If a man do
> not erect in this age his own tomb ere he dies, he
> shall live no longer in monument than the bell rings
> and the widow weeps.
> (5.2.77–80)

The metaphorical funeral bell warns Lady Capulet of approaching death in her old age when she realizes that she has outlived her daughter: 'This sight of death is as a bell / That warns my old age to a sepulchre (*Rom* 5.3.206–7).

Much has been said about the anachronistic sounding of a bell when the conspirators part in *Julius Caesar*:

> *Clock strikes.*
> BRUTUS: Peace, count the clock.
> CASSIUS: The clock hath stricken three.
> TREBONIUS: 'Tis time to part.
> (2.1.192–4)

This anachronism is justified in that 'the bell-**note**s signal a change from ethical debate to urgently deciding what to do, when' (Daniell, p. 209). In other words, the striking of the bell at this important moment would have worked very well in a performative context relying upon symbolic signals.

Antony's exhortation to Cleopatra to 'mock the midnight bell' (*Ant* 3.13.184) indicates that his nocturnal activities are unconventional.

This leads Enobarbus to the painful decision to desert him. The midnight bell also announces Falstaff's mockery: 'The Windsor bell hath strook twelve; the/minute draws on' (*Wiv* 5.5.1–2).

Lady Macbeth's 'parlour' or little domestic bell is rung at 2.1.61 to inform Macbeth that he can proceed with the murder of the King. In Macbeth's over-heated imagination, this sound is connected to that of the sinister 'passing' bell:

> *A bell rings.*
> I go, and it is done; the bell invites me.
> Hear it not, Duncan, for it is a knell,
> That summons thee to heaven, or to hell.
> (*Mac* 2.1.61–4)

Warning bells sound in *Othello*, symbolizing both a moment in actual time and a **mood** of impending doom. As Iago lays the seeds of his evil he stirs up a commotion in Brabantio:

> . . . An old black ram
> Is tupping your white ewe. Arise, arise!
> Awake the snorting citizens with the bell,
> Or else the devil will make a grandsire of you.
> (1.1.88–91)

That same symbol of evil happenings, the alarm bell, arouses the citizens and summons Othello as Iago plots Cassio's downfall: 'Who's that which rings the bell? – Diablo, ho! / The town will rise' (2.3.161–2). As Othello enters, he commands: 'Silence that dreadful bell, it frights the isle / From her propriety' (2.3.175–6). Earlier in the same play, the bell announces a more joyful occasion, signalling the time span for Othello's nuptial celebrations: 'All offices are open, / and there is full liberty of feasting from this present / hour of five till the bell hath told eleven' (2.2.8–10).

The midday meal was often the main meal of the day in Elizabethan times, announced by the bell as in: 'The clock hath strucken twelve upon the bell' (*Err* 1.2.45). In a comedy where mistiming is prominent, this reference acquires particular significance.

49

bell

The (church) bell conventionally summons the faithful, as Prince John of Lancaster makes clear to the Archbishop of York:

> My Lord of York, it better show'd with you
> When that your flock, assembled by the bell,
> Encircled you to hear with reverence
> Your exposition on the holy text.
>
> (*2H4* 4.2.4–7)

This speech is meant as an admonition to a man of the Church who has got himself dangerously involved in military affairs, and who is 'cheering a rout of rebels with [his] **drum**' (2.4.9): the bell and the drum metonymically stand for the spiritual sphere as opposed to the military arena.

Mention of having been '**knoll**'d to church' by the 'holy bell' (*AYLI* 2.7.114, 121) also involves a play on the concept of the passing of time, symbolized by the bell: 'True is it that we have seen better days, / And have with holy bell been knoll'd to church' (*AYLI* 2.7.120–1)

The 'sacring bell' in *Henry VIII* (3.2.295), properly referring to the consecrating bell rung at the elevation of the host in the Catholic rite, is used anachronistically here in the post-Henrician Reformation sense of a bell rung to announce Morning Prayer.

With advances in ringing techniques and the introduction of change-ringing in the late sixteenth century, it became increasingly important that bells should be in tune with one another both in relative pitch and tone. Thus, a peal of bells when rung rhythmically and sequentially correctly would be 'in tune'. Shakespeare alludes to rhythm in *Twelfth Night* when he has the Clown say: 'The triplex, sir, is a good tripping **measure**, or the bells of / Saint Bennet' (5.1.37–8). Peals of bells most commonly comprised six in a sequence 1 2 3; 4 5 6 and in various combinations of the two sets of three.

The concordant aspect is considered when Theseus compares the cry of a pack of hounds to **well-tuned** bells:

> My hounds . . .
> [are] match'd in mouth like bells,
> Each under each. A cry more tuneable
> Was never hollow'd to . . .
>
> (*MND* 4.1.119; 123–5)

On the other hand, when bells are not tuned, the result is dreadful cacophony. This vivid metaphor is employed in *Pericles*:

> ... I would have kept such a jangling of the bells, that he should never have left till he cast bells, steeple, church, and parish up again.
>
> (2.1.40–3)

Similarly, in *Hamlet* we have: 'Now see that noble and most sovereign reason / Like **sweet** bells **jangle**d out of tune and **harsh**' (3.1.157–8).

The bell that is well made has both clarity and acoustical strength, acknowledged in the proverbial phrase 'sound as a bell'. When Don Pedro asserts 'he hath a heart as sound as a bell', he enlarges the metaphor with 'and his **tongue** is the clapper' (*Ado* 3.2.11–13).

(C) Daniell, *Julius Caesar* (1998).
Dessen and Thomson, *A Dictionary of Stage Directions* (1999).
Morris, *Bells of All Nations* (1951), provides a wide-ranging survey.
Price, *Bells and Man* (1983), concentrates on more specific functions; and *The Carillon* (1933), discusses peals of bells.
Wilson, Wilfrid G., *Change Ringing* (1965), focuses on peals of bells.
Wulstan, *Tudor Music* (1985), pp. 49–58, scrutinizes the practical and magical properties of bells.

bergamasca see **bergomask**.

bergomask (A) A folk **dance** probably originating in Bergamo, northern Italy, and which spread through Europe in the later sixteenth century. It has a simple musical structure employing a recurring major-**key** harmonic **bass** pattern (I IV V I) or **ground** and short melodic phrases in a duple **metre**. Variations for keyboard and **lute** on the *bergamasca* were written by Italian, Flemish and English composers. One fine example for keyboard is Bull's 'Het nieu Bergomasco' (BL Add MS 23623, f. 68 published in MB 19 no. 124) which has the characteristic *bergamasca* Italian standard bass and melodic outline:

bergomask

(B) At the end of their performance of 'Pyramus and Thisbe', the mechanicals are keen to have either an epilogue or a dance to bring their play to a suitable conclusion. Bottom enthusiastically asks Theseus: 'Will it please you to / see the epilogue, or to **hear** a Bergomask dance between / two of our company?' (*MND* 5.1.352–4). Theseus declines the offer of an epilogue, probably because he is not impressed by the amateurish quality of the production. The very fact that the mechanicals intend to end their play with a bergomask rather than with a **jig** (the latter commonly adopted by professional companies) might further imply that their acting is unskilful.

(C) Foakes, *A Midsummer Night's Dream* (1984).
Howard, 'Hands, Feet, and Bottoms' (1993), pp. 325–42, expounds the meaning of dance in *A Midsummer Night's Dream*.
Spiessens, 'De Bergamasca' (1989), refers to Italian sources.

bird (A) Unlike other animals, birds have been associated with **music** since pre-history. The vocal **noise** they make is most frequently referred to as '**sing**ing'. Some birds, such as the lark, nightingale, robin and canary, are more musical than others. Different kinds of birds are identified by their **song**s.

Singing birds and their songs often feature in early modern literature. The full panoply of Elizabethan daylight songbirds feature in:

> The thrush did **pipe** full clear,
> And eke with merry cheer
> The linnet lifted up her **pleasant voice**.
> The goldfinch chirped and the pie did chatter,
> The blackbird **whistle**d and bade me rejoice,
> The stockdove murmured with a solemn flatter,
> The little daw, ka-ka he cried;
> The hic-quail he beside

Tickled his part in a parti-coloured coat.
The jay did **blow** his **hautboy** gallantly.

The wren did **treble** many a pretty **note**.
The woodpecker did hammer **melody**.
The kite, tiw-whiw, full oft
Cried, soaring up aloft,
And down again returned presently.
To whom the herald of cornutos all sung cuckoo
Ever, whilst poor Margery cried: Who
Did **ring** night's 'larum **bell**?
Withal all did do well.
O might I **hear** them ever.
Of **strain**s so **sweet**, sweet birds deprive us never.
            (Bartlet, 1606, nos 20 and 21)

In a song 'made for the King and Queen's entertainment at Highgate on May-day, 1604' several birds are invoked to sing the welcome of the royal party:

> Up, nightingale, and sing
> Jug, jug, jug, jug.
> Lark, raise thy note and wing,
> All birds their music bring.
> Robin, linnet, thrush,
> **Record** from every bush
> The welcome of the King and Queen.
>   (Peerson, 1620, no. 24)

In another poem, 'pretty' songbirds are contrasted with the imperious cuckoo:

> The nightingale, the **organ** of delight,
> The **nimble** lark, the blackbird, and the thrush,
> And all the pretty quiristers of flight,
> That **chant** their music notes in every bush,
> Let them no more contend who shall excel;
> The cuckoo is the bird that bears the bell.
>   (Weelkes, 1608, no. 25)

bird

The songs of certain birds can have especial significance. Migratory birds, such as the cuckoo, can signify the spring. Night birds, notably the nightingale, represent love. Morning birds, like the lark, herald the approaching day.

During the sixteenth century, composers were not averse to representing birdsongs in music. One of the most famous settings was Janequin's Parisian **chanson**, *Le chant des oiseaux* (1537).

(B) Imagery of birds is extensively exploited by Shakespeare in his poetry as well as his drama. There are many references to the generic term 'bird', and also to particular species. Ornithological metaphors allude to activities such as hunting, preying, nesting and bird-catching. On several occasions there are references to the birds' singing, an ability which has fascinated poets and writers for centuries.

The noise made by some birds of prey is associated with ominous events, as when Casca (one of the conspirators against Caesar) comments on the signs of impending doom he has witnessed recently. A number of animals have behaved in an unnatural way, among them the screech owl:

> And yesterday the bird of night did sit
> Even at noon-day upon the market-place,
> Howting and shrieking.
>
> (*JC* 1.3.26–8)

In contrast to the sinister voice of this nocturnal bird, the harmonious singing of the birds in springtime is praised in the **song** 'It was a lover and his lass':

> It was a lover and his lass,
> With a **hey**, and ho, and a hey nonino,
> That o'er the green corn-field did pass,
> In spring time, the only pretty ring time,
> When birds do sing, hey ding a ding, ding,
> Sweet lovers love the spring.
>
> (*AYLI* 5.3.16–21)

References to birds can sometimes have a paradoxical effect, as when Tamora tries to evoke an idyllic atmosphere before proposing to Aaron that he should become her lover. She observes that 'the birds **chaunt** melody on every bush' (*Tit* 2.3.12). These words acquire a disquieting nuance, spoken as they are by a lascivious woman who will soon instigate the rape and mutilation of Lavinia.

When specific birds are alluded to, they are often compared or contrasted with other birds. For instance, in *Romeo and Juliet* an important dichotomy is introduced: the lark's singing habit is opposed to that of the nightingale. Juliet wishes that it was night and that she could spend some more time with Romeo (who has been banished and must leave Verona at dawn). She addresses him as follows:

> Wilt thou be gone? it is not yet near day.
> It was the nightingale, and not the lark,
> That pierc'd the fearful **hollow** of thine **ear**;
> Nightly she sings on yond pomegranate tree.
> Believe me, love, it was the nightingale.
>   (3.5.1–5)

However, Romeo replies that 'it was the lark, the herald of the morn, / No nightingale' (6–7). The two lovers have no choice but to part now that the morning light is approaching. Even though the nightingale does sing in daytime as well as at night, it is its nocturnal habit which has struck poets' imaginations over the centuries. Similarly, the lark's song has been commonly associated with dawn in literature (Harting, pp. 128 and 131).

Another play in which the nightingale's nocturnal associations are stressed is *The Two Gentlemen of Verona*. Valentine expresses the intensity of his love for Silvia when he explains to the Duke: 'Except I be by Silvia in the night, / There is no music in the nightingale' (3.1.178–9). This bird's singing is mentioned in a gloomy context when Edgar, disguised as Tom o'Bedlam, fakes madness and claims that 'the foul fiend haunts poor Tom in the voice / of a nightingale' (*Lr* 3.5.29–30).

'Philomela' is sometimes used as a synonym for the nightingale since, according to Latin authors, this mythological figure was transformed into a nightingale after being raped by her brother-in-law Tereus and having her tongue cut out. Several references to this myth are found in *Titus Andronicus*, where an obvious parallel can be drawn between Lavinia and Philomela. For instance, before the rape takes place, Aaron

bird

comments that this will be the day of doom for Bassianus, since 'his Philomel [Lavinia] must lose her tongue to-day' (2.3.43). Another raped woman, Lucrece, expresses her affinity to Philomela in her despair: 'Come, Philomele, that sing'st of ravishment . . .' (*Luc* 1128). She then goes on to describe the nightingale as singing 'against a thorn' (1135). This passage supports the belief that the nightingale's leaning against a thorn caused its **mournful** singing.

The lark is almost invariably identified as the harbinger of morning. In *Venus and Adonis*, there is a reference to the 'gentle lark, weary of rest' which 'wakes the morning' (853 and 855). We find another musical description: 'the lark at break of day arising / From sullen earth, sings **hymns** at heaven's gate' in *Sonnet* 29 (11–12). A very similar metaphor is employed in a song in *Cymbeline*: 'Hark, hark, the lark at heaven's gate sings, / And Phoebus 'gins arise . . .' (2.3.20–1). In *King Lear*, Edgar mentions the pitch of the lark's voice ('the **shrill**-gorg'd lark', 4.6.58) to his blind father. The 'morning lark' is heard by Puck (*MND* 4.1.94), whereas in *Richard II* the King, deprived of his powers, comments on the unnaturalness of his current state: 'Down court! down king! / For night-owls shriek where mounting larks should sing' (3.3.182–3). The unpleasant quality of the nocturnal bird's voice ('shriek') is contrasted with the pleasantness of the lark's voice ('sing'). In *A Midsummer Night's Dream*, Puck observes that at night:

> . . . The screech owl, screeching **loud**,
> Puts the wretch that lies in woe
> In remembrance of a shroud.
> (5.1.376–8)

Just before Macbeth murders Duncan, his wife persuades him that this crime has to be committed: 'It was the owl that shriek'd, that fatal bellman, / Which gives the stern'st good-night' (*Mac* 2.2.3–4). The ominous connotations of the owl and other scavenging birds are highlighted also by King Henry when he prophesies Gloucester's downfall, just before the latter kills him:

> The owl shriek'd at thy birth, an evil sign;
> The night-crow cried, aboding luckless time;
> . . .

> The raven rook'd her on the chimney's top,
> And chatt'ring pies in dismal **discord**s sung . . .
> *(3H6 5.6.44–5; 47–8)*

'Pie' is a shortening for 'magpie', a bird which is customarily described in early English literature as 'chattering'. When two or more magpies chatter they make an unmusical cacophonous noise, as Henry explains.

Listening to music **play**ed at night-time, Portia remarks that it **sound**s 'much sweeter than by day' (*MV* 5.1.100). She goes on to explain how 'season' (occasion) influences our appreciation of music:

> The crow doth sing as sweetly as the lark
> When neither is attended; and I think
> The nightingale, if she should sing by day,
> When every goose is cackling, would be thought
> No better a **musician** than the wren.
> How many things by season season'd are
> To their right praise and true perfection!
> *(102–8)*

Portia's comment alludes to the commonplace belief that the nightingale does not sing in the daytime because she would not be heard above the cacophony of all the other birds.

The **sharp**, shrill quality of the wren's song is opposed to the negative associations evoked by the raven's raucous voice. The King directs his anger at Suffolk, who has just informed him of the death of Gloucester:

> What, doth my Lord of Suffolk comfort me?
> Came he right now to sing a raven's note,
> Whose dismal **tune** bereft my vital pow'rs;
> And thinks he that the chirping of a wren,
> By crying comfort from a hollow **breast**,
> Can chase away the first-conceived sound?
> *(2H6 3.2.39–44)*

Negative qualities are also evoked at the beginning of one of the most powerful soliloquies in the Shakespeare canon, delivered by Lady Macbeth after she resolves that Duncan must be killed to allow Macbeth to become king:

bird

> The raven himself is hoarse
> That croaks the fatal entrance of Duncan
> Under my battlements. Come, you spirits
> That tend on mortal thoughts, unsex me here . . .
> (*Mac* 1.5.38–41)

The hoarse voice of this bird of ill-omen introduces on a metaphorical level Lady Macbeth's renunciation of her feminine qualities, which will give her the courage to convince her husband to commit regicide.

The raven is invoked by Hamlet during the staging of the itinerant players' tragedy. Addressing the actor playing the murderer (and, obliquely, his uncle), he exclaims: 'Begin, murtherer, leave thy damnable faces and begin. / Come, the croaking raven doth bellow for revenge' (*Ham* 3.2.252–3).

Another bird, the swan, evokes conceits of death even if it is not a bird of prey. Since ancient times, the swan (associated with **Apollo**) was thought to sing immediately before its death. Pliny the Elder had questioned this unfounded belief as early as 77 A.D. in his *Natural History* (Book 10, ch. xxiii), which appeared in an English translation by Philemon Holland in 1601. Nonetheless, this legend persisted in poets' imagination for many centuries. For instance, in the famous **madrigal** lyric set by Orlando Gibbons (1612) there is a reference to 'The silver swan, who living had no note / As death approached, unlocked her silent **throat**'. In the Shakespeare canon, Lucrece is likened to the swan just before she commits suicide: 'And now this pale swan in her wat'ry nest / Begins the sad **dirge** of her certain ending' (*Luc* 1611–12). In *Othello*, Emilia compares herself to the swan before dying: 'I will play the swan / And die in music' (5.2.247–8). She then sings words from the 'Willow song', which was sung in a previous scene by Desdemona. In *King John*, Prince Henry laments his father's imminent death (King John has been poisoned and is in a state of delirium):

> . . . 'Tis strange that death should sing.
> I am the cygnet to this pale faint swan
> Who chaunts a **doleful** hymn to his own death,
> And from the **organ-pipe** of frailty sings
> His soul and body to their lasting **rest**.
> (5.7.20–4)

The musical metaphor is sustained by the use of terms such as 'organ-pipe', 'doleful', 'hymn' (22) and 'rest' (24), which add powerful religious overtones to the speech.

A song in *A Midsummer Night's Dream* is worth quoting in full for its references to birds. The ass-headed Bottom sings to overcome his fear of being alone after the other mechanicals have fled from him:

> The woosel cock so black of hue,
> With orange-tawny bill,
> The throstle with his note so **true**,
> The wren with little quill,
> . . .
> The finch, the sparrow, and the lark,
> The **plain-song** cuckoo grey,
> Whose note full many a man doth mark . . .
> (3.1.125–8; 130–2)

Whereas some birds are praised for their singing qualities (the throstle or song thrush, the wren for its piping voice and the cuckoo with its plain-song voice), the woosel cock or blackbird is mentioned in relation to its striking orange bill. In another song, this time in *The Winter's Tale*, the thrush is mentioned along with other birds: 'The lark, that **tirra-lyra** chaunts, / With heigh, with heigh, the thrush and the jay!' (4.3.9–10). The same bird is mentioned when Portia observes that Le Bon, like his French fellow countrymen, 'falls straight a-**caper**ing' (*MV* 1.2.61) 'if a throstle sing' (60).

Speed understands that Valentine is in love when he observes that the latter has learnt various skills, among which is 'to **relish** a love-song like a robin-redbreast' (*TGV* 2.1.20). This is the only mention of the robin in the whole Shakespearean canon.

In *1 Henry IV* we find a reference to the song of the cuckoo, harbinger of spring:

> So when he had occasion to be seen,
> He was but as the cuckoo is in June,
> Heard, not regarded.
> (3.2.74–6)

This passage means that 'in June the cuckoo has been in song for a

bird

month, and is therefore less noticed than on its first arrival in April, when listened to as the harbinger of Spring' (Harting, p. 155). The association between the cuckoo and the warm weather is also found in *The Merry Wives of Windsor*, 2.1.122. In *The Merchant of Venice*, Portia remarks to Nerissa that Lorenzo is able to recognize her even at night-time: 'He knows me as the blind man knows the cuckoo, / By the bad voice!' (5.1.111–12).

Another bird is mentioned in relation to sound rather than song. Rosalind explains to Orlando that women change when they get married, and warns him: 'I will be more jealous of thee than a Barbary cock-pigeon over his hen, / more **clamor**ous than a parrot against rain...' (*AYLI* 4.1.150–1). The vociferous quality of the parrot is also implied in Solanio's comment about different dispositions in human beings. Whilst 'some... laugh like parrots at a **bagpipe**r / other[s are] of such vinegar aspect' (*MV* 1.1.53–4) that they will never smile (see 'bagpipe'). The latter also refers to the proverbial foolishness of the parrot, which reacts to the melancholy sound of the bagpipe in the most inappropriate way, i.e. by laughing.

See also **ayre**.

(C) Harting, *The Ornithology of Shakespeare* (1871), gives a detailed – if based on some outdated assumptions – account of the references to birds in the Shakespeare canon, including those relating to the musical sphere. Chapter 5 is dedicated to the songbirds.

Hartshorne, 'The Relation of Bird Song to Music' (1958).
Head, 'Birdsong and the Origins of Music' (1997).
Jellis, *Bird Sounds and their Meaning* (1977).
Jensen, 'Birdsong and the Imitation of Birdsong in the Music of the Middle Ages and the Renaissance' (1985).

blow (A) All **wind instrument**s (as opposed to **string**ed instruments) such as **trumpet**s, **hoboy**s and **recorder**s are blown. The **play**er places the instrument's mouthpiece, unique to that instrument, to or between the lips and makes the instrument **sound** or '**speak**' by blowing air through it. The harder or faster the player blows, depending on the instrument's capabilities, the louder the instrument sounds. **Organ pipes** are made to 'speak' mechanically by blowing air through them.

blow

(B) As opposed to his use of **breath**, 'blow' is generally connected by Shakespeare with trumpets and the sound is **loud**, a blast, most often in military and battle contexts. Ajax's instructions to his trumpeter splendidly capture this violence and volume:

> Thou, trumpet, there's my purse.
> Now crack thy lungs, and split thy **brazen pipe**.
> Blow, villain, till thy sphered bias cheek
> Outswell the colic of puff'd Aquilon;
> Come, stretch thy chest, and let thy eyes spout blood;
> Thou blowest for Hector.
> (*Tro* 4.5.6–11)

Similar loudness is integral in Aeneas' command earlier in the same play: 'Trumpet, blow loud, / Send thy **brass voice** through all these lazy tents' (1.3.256–7). In both instances the quality of the brass instrument 'trumpet' is underlined.

Before attacking the Volscian city of Corioles, Caius Martius orders that a **parley** be sounded: 'Come, blow thy blast' (*Cor* 1.4.12). The use of 'blow' implies that he is referring to the trumpet rather than the **drum**.

During the Battle of St Albans, Young Clifford discovers the dead body of his father and evokes the biblical image of the Day of Judgement:

> O, let the vile world end,
> And the premised flames of the last day
> Knit earth and heaven together!
> Now let the general trumpet blow his blast . . .
> (*2H6* 5.2.40–3)

'Blow' sometimes occurs in non-military contexts, for example when Philip the Bastard comments on Lady Faulconbridge in the following terms:

> But who comes in such haste in riding-robes?
> What woman-post is this? Hath she no husband
> That will take pains to blow a **horn** before her?
> (*Jn* 1.1.217–19)

blow

The sexual connotation of 'horn' hints at her unfaithfulness with King Richard I, which resulted in her becoming pregnant with Philip.

A figurative use of this verb occurs in the Induction of *2 Henry IV*, when Rumor compares himself to 'a pipe / Blown by surmises, jealousies, conjectures' (Ind. 15–16). These words recall the image of 'Rumour's' (or 'Fame's') trumpet in Chaucer's *House of Fame* (3.1624–8). Presumably Shakespeare's pipe, here, is more likely to be the figurative loud trumpet than a **soft** recorder because of his use of 'blow'.

branle see **brawl**.

bransle see **brawl**.

brass see **brazen**.

brave see **breve**.

brawl (A) The 'brawl' was an English version of the French 'brawle', a moderately slow **dance** of uncertain Medieval origins, which existed in many differing forms in the late sixteenth century ranging from simple duple-time dances to more complicated triple-time mixed 'brawles'. It is a round dance sometimes including little hops and 'springs'. Arbeau describes more than 20 brawles in *Orchesography* (1589). The dance was characterized by sideways movement possibly involving a swaying (braulé) gesture. Morley refers to both the simple 'braule' and the quicker or 'bransle double' (*Introduction*, 1597, p. 181). The brawl, known in courtly circles in England throughout the sixteenth century, became especially popular in the second half of the century and is mentioned by several writers, including Sidney, John Davies and, in particular, Marston, who describes its steps in *The Malcontent* (1604), 4.1.65: "'Tis but two singles on the left, two on the right, three doubles forward, a traverse of six round . . .'. It was an elegant dance as described by the agent of Savoy at the Somerset **masque** (1613) 'when [the **coranto**] was over, the Earl again offered his hand to the queen, and they began a *brawl*

French brando [brawl], which was by far the most beautiful and praiseworthy thing in all of the festivity' (Orrell, p. 304).

(B) Most references in Shakespeare mean a noisy quarrel or *ad hoc* fight. But its appearance in 3.1 of *Love's Labour's Lost* is unmistakeably musical. This scene is dominated by vocabulary relating to **music, song** and dance. Moth asks Armado how he intends to conquer Jaquenetta: 'Master, will you win your love with a French brawl?' (3.1.7). Don Armado's misunderstanding builds on the pun: 'How meanest thou? Brawling in French?' (3.1.8). These exchanges may also hint at contemporary events: the London riots of May 1593 against Huguenot refugees, accused of usurping housing and employment in the capital, as part of the satire of 'foreigners', a significant element in the topicality of the play (Yates, pp. 65–7).

Lord Hastings puns on 'brawl' in its musical nuance when commenting on the tasks that the King's army must face:

> For his **division**s, as the times do brawl,
> Are in three heads: one power against the French,
> And one against Glendower . . .
>
> (*2H4* 1.3.70–2)

This state of affairs encourages Hastings and his allies to pursue their plan of rebelling against Henry IV. 'Division' has an obvious military and political connotation, but can also mean 'elaboration' on the pattern of a dance, as is clear from *Orchesography* (1589), where Capriol asks Arbeau: 'Do I **make** no divisions [elaborations] in dancing these braules?' (p. 131). Mention of 'divisions', the French and 'three heads' in the space of two lines could indicate that Shakespeare also had the dance in mind.

(C) Arbeau, *Orchesography* (1589), not only provides background information on 23 braules, it also gives details of their music with steps.
Orrell, 'The Agent of Savoy at the Somerset Masque' (1977).
Yates, *A Study of Love's Labour's Lost* (1936), examines the French theme in the play.

brazen (A) 'Brazen' literally means 'made of brass', but often refers (in a musical context) to the **sound** emitted by a brass **instrument**.

brazen

(B) The sound of the **trumpet** is described as 'brazen' by Bolingbroke during the siege of Flint Castle, when he orders that a **parley** be sounded: 'Through brazen trumpet send the **breath** of parley / Into his ruin'd **ear**s' (*R2* 3.3.33–4). Antony describes the military sound of the trumpet in a similar fashion when he exhorts his followers to revel following Caesar's defeat: 'Trumpeters, / With brazen **din** blast you the city's **ear**' (*Ant* 4.8.35–6).

In *Troilus and Cressida*, the trumpet's sound is referred to as a 'brass **voice**' (1.3.258). Later in the same play, an interesting metonymic transposition is observed when Ajax addresses a trumpeter: '. . . Trumpet . . . / . . . crack thy lungs, and split thy brazen **pipe**' (4.5.7–8). The 'brazen pipe' refers to the trumpeter's **throat** (*The Riverside Shakespeare*, p. 513).

Only once does the adjective apply to an instrument other than the trumpet. The midnight **bell** has an 'iron **tongue** and [a] brazen mouth' (*Jn* 3.3.38): in addition to the human analogy, there is a specific reference to the components of the bell.

break time see **time**.

breast (A) The poetic word for chest, 'breast' is often found in a musical context particularly in association with **bird**s **sing**ing:

> **Sweet Philomel** in groves and deserts haunting
> Oft glads my heart and **ear**s with her sweet **chant**ing.
> But then her **tune**s delight me best
> When perched with prick against her breast,
> She sings, 'fie, fie', as if she suffered wrong,
> Till seeming pleased, 'sweet, sweet' concludes her song.
> (Jones, 1600, no. 16)

In some sources when singing is mentioned, breast is used specifically in juxtaposition with **throat, tongue** or mouth, as in:

> The **nightingale**, so soon as April bringeth
> Unto her rested sense a perfect waking,
> While late bare earth, proud of new clothing, springeth,
> Sings out her woes, a thorn her song-book making.

breast

> And **mournfully** bewailing,
> Her throat in tunes expresseth
> What grief her breast oppresseth.
> (Sir Philip Sidney, *Certain Sonnets*, 4, 1–7;
>   set by Bateson, 1604, no. 3)

Elsewhere, 'breast' can mean the lungs which produce the **breath** to **make music**:

> Music, all thy sweetness lend
> While of His high power I speak,
> On whom all powers else depend.
> But my breast is now too weak;
> **Trumpet**s **shrill** the air should break.
> All in vain my sounds I raise;
> Boundless power asks boundless praise.
>   (Dowland, 1612, no. 12)

(B) Shakespeare uses this last nuance when Sir Andrew praises the Clown's singing ability: 'the fool has an excellent breast' (*TN* 2.3.19). He wishes he had 'so sweet a breath to sing, as the fool has' (21). The reference to the lungs as the organs producing breath and **voice** is unmistakable.

The image of a bird's breast is conjured up in *2 Henry VI*. Suffolk's comforting words for the death of Gloucester are judged by King Henry VI to be coming from the '**hollow** breast' of a **wren** (3.2.43). (See 'hollow' for a detailed analysis of this passage).

The cruelty of civil war characterising *3 Henry VI* is encapsulated in 2.5, where a son kills his father and a father kills his son during the Battle of Towton. The father vents his despair when he addresses his dead son as follows:

> These arms of mine shall be thy winding-sheet;
> My heart, sweet boy, shall be thy sepulchre . . .
> My **sigh**ing breast shall be thy funeral **bell**.
>   (114–15; 117)

The father's disconsolate sighing will **echo** in the cavity of his breast, making it sound like a sombre funeral bell.

breast

breath (A) **Sing**ing and **play**ing **soft wind instrument**s (e.g. **recorder**s) involves 'breath'. Indeed, not only is breath required to produce a **note**, breathing articulates the **music** made in singing and playing. The idea that breath is required both to **make** music and to live is alluded to in the word-play in: 'Call him again, let him not die, / But live in Music's **sweet**est breath' (Wilbye, 1609, no. 25).

(B) In the Shakespeare canon, 'breath' (rather than '**blow**') in connection with singing and breathing through a wind instrument, generally implies that a sweet, soft and gentle music is being produced. This is the case in Hamlet's directions to Guildenstern on playing the recorder, where a gentle breath is needed:

> . . . **Govern** these **ventage**s
> with your fingers and thumbs, give it breath with
> your mouth, and it will discourse most eloquent music.
> (*Ham* 3.2.357–9)

The soft, calming, even seductive nature of the mermaid's **song**, 'uttering such **dulcet** and harmonious breath' (*MND* 2.1.151) is alluded to by Oberon. Sir Andrew wishes he had as good a **voice** as the Clown when he tells Sir Toby: 'I had rather than forty shillings I had such / a leg and so sweet a breath to sing, as the fool has' (*TN* 2.3.20–1). Once again, sweetness is the quality highlighted with reference to 'breath' in a musical sense.

The one exception appears to be Bolingbroke's use of 'breath' in his directions to Northumberland, where 'blow' would be expected:

> Go to the rude ribs of that ancient castle;
> Through **brazen** trumpet send the breath of **parley**
> Into his ruin'd **ear**s . . .
> (*R2* 3.3.32–4)

It may be, however, that he calls for a softer parley call, as preface to his ensuing conciliatory words. Furthermore, 'breath' rather than 'blow' ties the word to the play's imagery of the four elements, where air is the medium for language.

breve (A) Not much used today except in church **music**, the breve was a standard **note**-value of the Medieval and Renaissance periods in music. It was one of the eight separately identifiable notes of white mensural notation used from the mid fifteenth century to the end of the sixteenth. In Common **Time** (C or 4/2) it is equal to two semibreves, four **minims**, eight semiminims, etc. It was written as a white square note without a tail, thus: ▢. Though, paradoxically, it had become a relatively long note-value by the end of the sixteenth century, it is called 'brevis' in contrast to the 'longa' which was twice its length and notated with a tail, and which in turn was half the value of the 'maxima'.

(B) Even though 'breve' is not found in the Shakespeare canon, and 'brief' is never used in its musical meaning, one pun on 'braves' acquires a musical nuance. While courting Bianca, Lucentio and Hortensio (disguised, respectively, as a tutor and as a music master) have a heated exchange:

> LUCENTIO: Preposterous ass, that never read so far
> To know the cause why music was ordain'd!
> . . .
> Then give me leave to read philosophy,
> And while I pause, serve in your **harmony**.
> HORTENSIO: Sirrah, I will not bear these braves of thine.
> BIANCA: Why, gentlemen, you do me double wrong
> To strive for that which resteth in my choice.
> (*Shr* 3.1.9–10; 13–17)

The phrase 'bear these braves' ('bravadoes', 'boasts') points to the musical expressions '**bear a part**' and 'bear a **burden**': Hortensio is expected to carry a **lute**, and the musical connection would have been created visually as well as verbally on the stage. In her reply, Bianca sustains the musical tone of the dialogue when she uses the adjective 'double': 'under the rules of **alteration**, a breve could be doubled in value. (Double might also mean lower pitch, as in "double octave", or "double bassoon")' (Robbins, p. 132).

(C) Apel, *The Notation of Polyphonic Music* (1953), pp. 87–195, offers an extensive discussion of White Mensural Notation.

breve

Robbins, 'Shakespeare's Sweet Music' (1968), analyses the homophonous pun on 'braves' in *The Taming of the Shrew*.

brief see **breve**.

broken see **consort, division**.

bugle see **horn**.

burden (A) The word 'burden' has two usages in musical contexts, one concerned with poetic form, the other with the musical shape or performance of a **song**. The first refers to the refrain which may recur at the end of stanzas, or as interjected lines within stanzas. In manuscript sources (viz. early English popular **carol**s of the fifteenth century) and subsequently in printed copies of Tudor miscellanies, the burden was often given at the head of the song rather than after each stanza. In musical performance, a solo singer might **perform** the stanzas whilst the burden could be taken up by several singers as **chorus** (see also Gerould, p. 121). The burden would often carry the gist or theme of the whole poem. Or, it could act as a counterpoint to the stanza, employing quasi-**instrument**al or nonsense words, e.g. 'fa-la-la', '**ding-dong**', **hey**, '**nonny-no**', 'downe a downe', etc. The relationship between the continually changing stanza and the constant refrain is both structural and semantically variable, and has endless possibilities.

The second meaning has a more specific musical nuance which dates back to the eleventh century, and is especially English. The thirteenth-century round, 'Somer is icumen in', has a 'burden' for two **voice**s, '**Sing cuckoo**'. This was equivalent to Chaucer's 'stift bourdoun', under-song or **drone** (**bass**), a practice common in Medieval English songs and well known in the sixteenth century. The burden, **holding** or foot (pes) is sung throughout the stanza rather than being a separate entity at its end. As a constant and repeating entity, however, it is clearly related to the refrain.

(B) In addition to the refrains printed with the songs in Shakespeare's plays, there are also several references simply to 'burden' as 'refrain'. In *The Winter's Tale*, the servant explains that Autolycus sells **ballad**s which meet different tastes. Among them are

> ... the prettiest love-songs for maids, so without
> bawdry, which is strange; with such delicate burthens
> of **dildos** and **fadings**, 'jump her and thump her' ...
>
> (*WT* 4.4.193–5)

The servant is alluding either to actual refrains or to nonsensical refrain words: 'dildo', 'fading' and 'jumping' refrains are common in seventeenth-century ballads, mostly of a bawdy nature (Pafford, p. 101). Autolycus's choice of 'delicate' (l. 194) to describe the burdens is contradicted by the musical terms he uses in the following line: hence, his speech acquires a sarcastic nuance.

Whether or not ballads are complete without a burden or refrain has been the subject of debate. Many traditional ballads survive in modern printed sources without refrains; certain commentators suggest this does not necessarily preclude the existence of a refrain in performance. That the burden would be an addition to a ballad accords with the pun made by Shakespeare in several places on 'burden' adding weight. The wild **music** that 'burthens every bough' (*Sonnet* 102.11) is not only sung by many poets as a sort of refrain but also weighs down the branch on which the **nightingale** sings. Also, this line implies that the burdens crowd the air (Duncan-Jones, p. 102).

Margaret puns on 'burden' when she tries to change Beatrice's sombre mood to one of joy: 'Clap's into "Light a' love"; that goes / without a burden. Do you sing it, and I'll **dance** it' (*Ado* 3.4.45–6). This pun is appropriate in a scene where the experienced Margaret has just referred to sexual intercourse in her conversation with the bride-to-be Hero. It is further confirmed in the choice of the popular song, 'Light o' love' referred to in similar circumstances in *The Two Gentlemen of Verona*:

> JULIA: Best sing it to the **tune** of 'Light o' love'.
> LUCETTA: It is too heavy for so light a **tune**.
> JULIA: Heavy? belike it hath some burden then?
> LUCETTA: Ay; and **melodious** were it, would you sing it.
> (1.2.80–3)

The quibble over the weightiness or seriousness of love is the subject of the debate between Julia and Lucetta. 'Light o' love' seems to have been a well-known ballad in Elizabethan times. The text written by Leonard Gibbons c.1570 'may have been a response to an earlier poem' (Duffin,

burden

p. 255). The same ballad is also mentioned in *The Two Noble Kinsmen*, when the Gaoler's daughter describes her beloved Palamon as follows: '[He] gallops to the tune of "Light a' love"' (5.2.54).

When Celia says to Rosalind: 'I would sing my song without a burthen; / thou bring'st me out of tune' (*AYLI* 3.2.247–8), she probably means that a refrain sung **sharp** or **flat** between her stanzas would distract her from her **true note**. But she could also be referring to the meaning of burden as a sort of drone or under-song which, if sung off-**key**, would adversely affect her singing. A few lines earlier, the following exchange takes place:

> CELIA: There lay he, stretch'd along, like a wounded knight.
> ROSALIND: Though it be pity to see such a sight, it well becomes the **ground**.
> (3.2.240–2)

Whilst 'ground' here clearly refers to the forest floor, it may also have a figurative meaning which could include music. And this would connect with the sense of the 'burden' as under-song or even ground.

The same idea occurs when Petruchio tells Hortensio that he is willing to marry a wealthy woman, no matter how ugly, old or bad tempered she is. He explains that 'wealth is burthen of my wooing dance' (*Shr* 1.2.68). In other words, wealth in a prospective wife is the principal attribute or recurring feature (a sort of 'ground') of his courtship. Here, as in *Much Ado About Nothing*, dancing is connected with the burden.

The term 'holding' may indicate a burden in the context of a round **dance** when Enobarbus, during a feast on board Pompey's galley, instructs his fellow revellers:

> All take hands.
> Make battery to our ears with the **loud** music;
> The while I'll place you, then the boy shall sing.
> The holding every man shall bear as loud
> As his strong sides can volley.
> (*Ant* 2.7.108–12)

Mention of holding, according to Elizabethan usage, would indicate an under-song or ground. The men could sing 'Cup us till the world go round' (2.7.117) as the boy sings 'Come, thou monarch of the vine'

(2.7.113). Contrast in timbre between **treble** and bass would ensure that the boy's **voice** is heard. But, if the men were to sing as loud as possible, the boy's song would be drowned. So, the men probably sang and danced a loud refrain.

Singing and dancing under-songs to accompany Ariel's songs, 'Come unto these yellow sands' (*Tmp* 1.2.375) and 'Full fathom five' (1.2.397) are probably indicated by Ariel's

> Foot it featly here and there,
> And, **sweet** sprites, the burthen bear.
> Hark, hark!
> *Burthen dispersedly.*   Bow-wow.
>   (1.2.379–82)

The burden 'bow-wow' may derive from James Rosier's account in *Purchas this Pilgrimages* (1613, p. 637), of a ceremonial Virginian dance (Kermode, xxxiii). Such burdens could hardly be confined to refrains. The dispersed burdens were probably sung continuously rather than only at the ends of the stanzas. Such an effect would indeed add magic to the airy music. However, the textual ambiguities derived from the punctuation and layout of the songs in Folio (the only authoritative source for this late play) make it very difficult to draw a definitive conclusion as to the way in which the songs would have been performed onstage. For instance, it has alternatively been argued that the burden was sung by offstage spirits:

> . . . though . . . what words they sing and when is not obvious . . . In this song, and in 'Full Fathom Five' which follows, at least two spirits probably echoed words from Ariel's song, either moving about the curtained music-room, or else positioned above, behind and possibly below the stage to give a stereophonic effect.
>   (Lindley, p. 121)

In other songs whose words are printed in the text of the play, burdens are often abbreviated or merely alluded to. In *King Lear* (3.6.25), only one line of the very popular song (refrain), 'Come o'er the bourn, Bessy', is printed. Manuscript and printed sources supply the missing lines:

burden

> Come o'er the bourn, Bessy, to me
> [My little pretty Bessy,
> Come o'er the bourn, Bessy] to me,

To which the Fool improvises a sung response:

> Her boat hath a leak,
> And she must not speak
> Why she dares not come over to thee.
> (3.6.26–8)

The effect of adapting an abbreviated verbal refrain to extant contemporary music is to expand the text. Thomas Morley's version of 'It was a lover and his lass' (*AYLI*, 5.3.16) in his *The First Booke of Ayres* (1600) repeats the refrain words, adding a line:

> It was a lover and his lass,
> With a hey, and a ho, and a hey **nonino**,
> That o'er the green corn-field did pass . . .
> (5.3.16–18)

Snatches of burdens from popular songs may be included in the texts of songs, as in Justice Silence's

> Be merry, be merry, my wife has all,
> For women are shrows, both short and tall;
> 'Tis merry in hall, when beards wags all,
> And welcome merry Shrove-tide.
> Be merry, be merry.
> (*2H4* 5.3.32–6)

This is probably part of a Shrovetide **wassail** song (Long, pp. 86–9). ' 'Tis merry in hall' has been identified as a proverbial refrain dating back to the fourteenth century (Tilley, H55).

(C) Bukofzer, *Studies in Medieval and Renaissance Music* (1950), focuses on the structural independence of the burden.
   Duffin, *Shakespeare's Songbook* (2004).
   Duncan-Jones, *Shakespeare's Sonnets* (1997).

Gerould, *The Ballad of Tradition* (1932).
Kermode, *The Tempest* (1954).
Lindley, *The Tempest* (2002).
Long, *Music in English Renaissance Drama* (1968).
Pafford, *The Winter's Tale* (1963).
Tilley, *A Dictionary of Proverbs in England* (1966).
Wulstan, *Tudor Music* (1985), discusses the 'use and misuse' of the term, arguing that 'burden' is not the equivalent of 'refrain'.

burthen see **burden**.

C

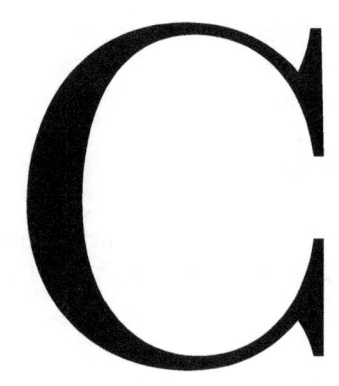

cadence (A) The association of 'cadence' with falling or a descent of **note**s in **music** at a pause or ending derives from Medieval and Renaissance practice. The cadence became a formal closure point either at various stages in the middle of a composition or at its end. Cadence therefore became synonymous with 'close' in music. Morley defined a cadence as: 'A *Cadence* wee call that, when coming to a close, two notes are bound togither, and the following note descendeth thus:

or in any other keye after the same manner' (*Introduction*, 1597, p. 73). In Renaissance music and earlier, a cadence was a melodic event and the main consideration was a linear descent to the 'final' of the predominant **mode**. In the late Renaissance, cadences became more concerned with bringing several **voice**s or **part**s to a close and were determined by harmonic procedure. Campion, for example, was more progressive than Morley and stated that cadences or closes helped define **key**. In *A New Way of Making Counterpoint* (c.1614) he endeavoured to show how the progression of the **bass** (voice) determined this and articulated cadences. For the Elizabethans, there were three main or 'formal' closes depending on function and key. Dowland notes that 'euery **Song** is graced with *formall* Closes, we will tell what a *Close* is. Wherfore a Close

cadence

is (as *Tinctor* writes) a little part of a Song, in whose end is found either **rest** or perfection' (*Micrologus*, 1609, p. 84).

The musical sense of falling and coming to an ending, either in the middle or conclusion, can be applied to poetry. Cadence is, of course, only applicable when the poetry is heard or spoken.

(B) There is only one occurrence of 'cadence' in the Shakespeare canon. In *Love's Labour's Lost*, Nathaniel is asked by the illiterate Jaquenetta to read the love letter that Armado has written to her. The letter contains a sonnet, and Holofernes criticizes Nathaniel's way of delivering it:

> You find not the apostraphas, and so miss
> the **accent**. Let me supervise the **canzonet**.
> Here are only **number**s ratified, but for
> the elegancy, facility, and golden cadence of poesy,
> caret.
>
> (4.2.119–23)

This rather complicated passage is meant to highlight Holofernes' pedantic nature. He is worried that Nathaniel has not respected the **metre** of the poem. The reference to cadence 'in the sense of rhythmical **measure**' (David, p. 89) is the most obvious meaning of the word. But the speech has other musical terms in it – 'accent', 'canzonet' and later '**fancy**' (125) – as does the sonnet quoted in the love letter: these seem to reveal Shakespeare's willingness to evoke different layers of meaning in this passage.

See also **harmony, melody, strain**.

(C) David, *Love's Labour's Lost* (1951).
Herrisone, *Music Theory in Seventeenth-Century England* (2000).
Wilson (ed.), *A New Way* (2003), includes discussion of cadences.

canary (A) A lively duple-**time dance** of possible sixteenth-century Spanish origin. Whilst Arbeau (*Orchesography*, 1589) gives an example in 'simple' (¢) time, seventeenth-century versions appear more often in 'compound' rhythms (*à la gigue*), for example Cesare Negri, *Le gratie d'amore* (1602), and Praetorius, *Terpischore* (1612), no. 31. The dance *canary*

begins on the first **beat** of the bar and is characterized by a dotted rhythm within a repeated two-bar phrase structure.

Arbeau relates the canary to the Spanish **pavan**. Whether the dance hails from the Canary Isles (the 'Fortunate Isles') is doubtful; but, as Arbeau suggests, its name connects it with the slightly wild and exotic: 'sections are gay but nonetheless strange and fantastic with a strong barbaric character' (*Orchesography*, p. 180). This makes its inclusion among English courtly dances (especially the revels of the courtly **masque**s) doubtful but not impossible. It also has licentious and Bacchanalian overtones which Middleton observes: 'Plain men dance the **measure**s, the sinque pace the gay . . . You / Drunkards the canaries; you whore and bawd, the **jig**' (*Women Beware Women* 3.3.218–19). Dekker seems to confirm this in *The Wonderfull Yeare* (1603): 'A drunkard, who no sooner smelt the winde, but he thought the ground under him danced the canaries' (F4v).

(B) Shakespeare mentions the canary three times out of a total of some fifty references to dances in his plays and poems. Another three references allude to 'canary wine', as in 'O knight, thou lack'st a cup of canary. / When did I see thee so put down?' (*TN* 1.3.80–1). A reference in *The Merry Wives of Windsor* involves a pun on both the dance and the alcoholic drink:

> HOST: Farewell, my hearts. I will to my honest knight Falstaff, and drink canary with him.
> FORD [*Aside*]: I think I shall drink in pipe-wine first with him; I'll make him dance.
>
> (3.2.87–90)

Word-play on 'canary', the dance or the drink, is found in Mistress Quickly's explanation of Mistress Ford's state of confusion and excitement. She tells the foolish Falstaff that he has managed to bring Mistress Ford 'into such a canaries as / 'tis wonderful' (2.2.60–1) and that not even the best courtier ever 'brought her to such a canary' (63). The bawdy context of the scene (which opens with a reference

canary

to Mistress Quickly's loss of virginity) gives a sexual nuance to the lines.

Allusion to the lively, wild and bawdy nature of the dance is unmistakable when Lafew informs the King:

> . . . I have seen a medicine
> That's able to breathe life into a stone,
> Quicken a rock, and make you dance canary
> With spritely fire and motion . . .
> (*AWW* 2.1.72–5)

Lafew's reference to 'breathing life' into inert things becomes more explicitly bawdy in the next few lines with the use of words such as 'pen' and 'arise'. That same liveliness and innuendo are found when Moth advises Armado not to '**brawl** in French', but 'jig off a **tune** at the **tongue**'s end, canary to it with your feet' (*LLL* 3.1.12–13).

(C) Brissenden, *Shakespeare and the Dance* (1981), p. 54.
   Dolmetsch, *Dances of Spain and Italy* (1954).
   Pulver, *A Dictionary of Old English Music* (1923), notes the dance (pp. 27ff.).

canton (A) A variant form of the Italian 'canto', meaning 'a **song**'. It may also recall the French term, '**chanson**', as well as being connected with the Italian 'canzone'. Another form, 'cantion', appears in sixteenth-century English sources, e.g. Thomas (1587), meaning a [**sweet**] song, **charm** or enchantment.

(B) Shakespeare uses the word in *Twelfth Night*, when Viola, disguised as Cesario, woos Olivia by proxy and claims that, if she loved her as much as Orsino does, she would: 'Write loyal cantons of contemned love, / And **sing** them **loud** even in the dead of night' (1.5.270–1). In this context, 'cantons' is clearly synonymous with 'songs'. Viola's mention of unrequited ('contemned') love is dramatically ironic given that Olivia, thinking that Viola is a young gentleman, is falling in love with her.

(C) Thomas, *Dictionarium Linguae Latinae et Anglicanae* (1587).

canzonet (A) This word derives from the diminutive form of the Italian for **'song'**, generally of a popular style. It comes next after the **madrigal** in order of musical sophistication, according to Morley (*Introduction*, 1597, p. 180). Like the madrigal, each line of the poem set receives a contrapuntal treatment, or, as Morley puts it, 'some **point** lightly **touch**ed'; and except for the middle section is repeated, thus A A' B C C'. Like the English madrigal, the canzonet sets vernacular lyric poetry of a 'light' kind. It tends to be more syllabic in its treatment of the poem than the madrigal. Canzonets were both imported into England from Italy, where they were also known as 'Canzoni alla Napoletana', and also 'Englished', that is given English words to the Italian original, e.g. Morley *Canzonets, Or Little Short Songs to Three Voyces* (1593). Whilst the musical form of Morley's canzonets is fairly consistent, the stanzaic form of the poems he sets is not. Stanzas vary between four and twenty lines.

(B) Holofernes requests that Nathaniel read 'a staff, a stanza, a verse' (*LLL* 4.2.103) of a canzonet. The musical nuance is established by 'staff', which could mean either 'stanza' or 'musical stave'. Although musical imagery, relating to celestial and mundane **music**s, is present in the last four lines of the canzonet:

> Thy eye Jove's lightning bears, thy **voice** his dreadful **thunder**,
> Which, not to anger bent, is music and **sweet** fire.
> Celestial as thou art, O, pardon love this wrong,
> That sings heaven's **praise** with such an earthly **tongue**.
> (4.2.114–17)

the pedantic schoolmaster's main concern is prosodical:

> You find not the apostrophas, and so miss the **accent**...
> Here are only **number**s ratified, but for the elegancy,
> facility, and golden **cadence** of poesy, *caret*.
> (4.2.119; 121–2)

At first, it seems that Holofernes wishes to 'supervise the canzonet' in a literary rather than musical sense. The sonnet is read not sung. Shakespeare seems to be employing 'canzonet' as a poetical adjunct, related to the Petrarchan 'canzone', rather than as a musical type. However, the use of words such as 'staff' and 'accent', as well as Holofernes' humming the **note**s of the **gamut** in the wrong order (100), undoubtedly adds to the musical flavour of the exchanges between the two men.

(C) All commentators on the Italian madrigal deal with 'canzone', and its diminutive form the 'canzonetta', as a verse form for the madrigal, e.g. Harrán, 'Verse Types in the Early Madrigal' (1969) and Kerman, *The Elizabethan Madrigal* (1962).

caper (A) A **dance** step which became very popular in Elizabethan England at the end of the sixteenth century. It took various forms but was essentially a vigorous step comprising a jump and movement of the feet whilst high in the air. Because of the skill ('tricks') and energy required, the caper was a young man's dance step, related in many ways to the fashionable **galliard**. In *A Friendlie Dialogue betweene Paule and Demas* (1580, fol. 38v) Samuel Byrd, as Baskervill notes, 'speaks of the turning on the toe, the capers, and other tricks of the young man who dances' (*The Elizabethan Jig*, p. 336). No separate **music** for a caper survives from Elizabethan sources, but given its association with the galliard and other leaping dances, similar lively music would be an appropriate accompaniment.

(B) The liveliness and vigorousness required by this dance are evoked when Sir Toby instructs Sir Andrew on how to 'cut a caper' (*TN* 1.3.121) with his legs and thighs: 'Let me see / thee caper. Ha, higher! Ha, ha, excellent!' (140–1). These lines were meant to work also as an implicit instruction to the actor playing Sir Andrew to jump high in order to achieve the best movement possible of the feet.

Elsewhere Fenton, in love with Anne Page, is described as somebody who 'capers, ... dances, ... has the eyes of youth' (*Wiv* 3.2.67). The association between love and dancing is also found in Richard's famous soliloquy at the beginning of *Richard III*. He cynically observes that peace brings about frivolousness:

>Grim-visag'd War hath smooth'd his wrinkled front;
>And now, in stead of mounting barbed steeds
>To fright the souls of fearful adversaries,

caper

>He capers nimbly in a lady's chamber
>To the lascivious pleasing of a **lute**.
>(1.1.9–13)

The energy which should be spent in war is now being wasted in wooing ladies with dances. The result can only be a 'weak piping time of peace' (24), and Richard is determined not to succumb to it.

See also **cinque pas, coranto**.

(C) Baskervill, *The Elizabethan Jig and Related Song Drama* (1929).

care-tun'd see **well-tuned**.

carman's whistle (A) A 'carman' was a cart driver (carter, carrier), who was 'wont to whistle to his beasts a comfortable **note**' (Henry Chettle, *Kind-Hart's Dreame*, 1592). The **tune**s carmen whistled were popular, often bawdy, **songs**. William Byrd **set** one as the theme of his variations for keyboard in MLNB (1591), no. 34 (cf. FWVB I, p. 214).

(B) Falstaff highlights Shallow's lustful nature when soliloquizing about the Justice's habit of visiting prostitutes. He

>. . . Sung those tunes to the
>overscutch'd huswives that he heard the carmen
>**whistle**, and sware they were his fancies or his
>good-nights.
>(*2H4* 3.2.316–19)

The bawdy tune of the carman's whistle perfectly fits this context. 'Fancies' and 'good-nights' also have a musical connotation and reinforce the notion that Shallow is a creature of the night given to lascivious activities.

See also **fancy**.

(C) Chappell, *Popular Music of the Olden Time* (1855–9), vol. 1, pp. 137–40. Neighbour, *The Consort and Keyboard Music of William Byrd* (1978), p. 146.

carmen whistle see **carman's whistle**.

carol (A) The carol was the most popular form of late Medieval, fifteenth-century English lyric verse. It was a **song** on any subject ranging from religious solemnity to amorous conceits and was distinguished by its stanzaic regularity and ever-present **burden**. The burden was often structurally independent of the stanzas. The carol, as both popular and ceremonial song, was associated with early pagan **dance**-songs **perform**ed at midwinter (solstice) festivities, hence the modern (Christian) adaptation of it as specifically a Christmas song.

(B) The popular type with accompanying ring dance occurs when Titania reproaches Oberon for having changed the season pattern as a result of his disagreements with her. She observes that he has 'disturb'd our sport' (*MND* 2.1.87) with his **brawl**s when the fairies wished to 'dance our ringlets to the whistling **wind**' (2.1.86). The winter gloom will not be relieved by celebrations: 'The human mortals want their winter cheer: / No night is now with **hymn** or carol blest' (2.1.101–2). A distinction is implied between the solemn, perhaps religious hymn and the more joyous, earthly carol.

A popular carol of the springtime is alluded to in the Page's song, 'It was a lover and his lass' (*AYLI* 5.3.16–33). The characteristic burden structure of the carol suits the song the pages sing, with its nonsense refrain:

> This carol they began that hour,
> With a **hey**, and a ho, and a hey **nonino**,
> How that a life was but a flower,
> In spring-time, the only pretty ring-time.
> (5.3.26–9)

carol

If 'ring-time' also refers to the ring dance, then the carol is particularly apposite since it is the song type associated with such a dance.

(C) Greene, *The Early English Carols* (1977), is the most important study of the English carol, with a definition on p. xxiii.

Routley, *The English Carol* (1958), provides a survey particularly of the nineteenth-century Christmas carol.

Stevens, *Music and Poetry in the Early Tudor Court* (1979), refers to the ceremonial and popular carol.

case (A) A case is the wooden box or leather or cloth bag to hold an **instrument** when it is not being **play**ed. Most cases were custom-made for the instrument they contained.

(B) Shakespeare emphasizes the notion that when an instrument is in its case it is unplayed and worthless. There is no sense that the case has a beauty as a piece of craftsmanship, although sometimes he refers to the latent quality of the instrument enclosed in its silent case.

During one of the many misunderstandings in *The Comedy of Errors*, Dromio resorts to musical metaphor which provides an interesting word-play. He describes the leather apparel worn by the sergeant who arrested Antipholus of Ephesus (who Dromio believes to be his master, Antipholus of Syracusa) as follows: ' 'Tis a plain case; he that went / like a **base-viol** in a case of leather' (4.3.23–4).

A play on the meaning is also present in Hero's remark to Don Pedro, who is wooing her on behalf of Claudio during a masked ball: 'When I like your favor, for God defend / the **lute** should be like the case!' (*Ado* 2.1.94–5). The girl is referring to the rustic or grotesque mask worn by Don Pedro (Mares, p. 70). The musical metaphor is appropriate in a festive scene which probably involved the playing of **music** in the background. It is also possible that there is an allusion to Don Pedro's belly, since the lute case would necessarily have the same distinctive bellied shape as the instrument.

In cutting Justice Shallow down to size, Falstaff says: 'The case of a **treble hoboy** was a mansion for him' (*2H4* 3.2.326). The treble hoboy was a small thin instrument, and is meant to evoke Shallow's slender build. There are several musical allusions in this passage, as there are in *case*

Richard II when Mowbray vents his sorrow and despair after being banished from England for life:

> My native English, now I must forgo,
> And now my **tongue**'s use is to me no more
> Than an unstrung viol or a **harp**,
> Or like a cunning instrument cas'd up,
> Or being open, put into his hands
> That knows no **touch** to **tune** the **harmony**.
> (1.3.160–5)

The emphasis is on the unfulfilled potential of the instrument enclosed in its case. The same allusion is more straightforward in *Timon of Athens* where Timon observes that friends 'would most resemble **sweet** / instruments hung up in cases, that keeps their **sound**s to / themselves' (1.2.98–100) if they were not prepared to give help when needed.

A pun on 'case' in its musical connotation is clearly intended after the apparently dead body of Juliet has been discovered. The **musician**s who had been employed to play at her wedding with Paris are sent away. One of them exclaims: 'Faith, we may put up our **pipe**s and be gone' (*Rom* 4.5.96). To which the Nurse replies: 'Honest good fellows, ah, put up, put up, / For well you know this is a pitiful case' (4.5.97–8). The 'pitiful case' of Juliet's death is arguably linked to the case where the musicians would put their instruments.

(C) Mares, *Much Ado About Nothing* (1988).

catch (A) A **song** or sometimes an **instrument**al piece in which three, four or more **part**s follow each other in the manner of a **round** or canon. It involved a simple quasi-improvisatory technique in that the **part**s **imitate** at the unison or octave, unlike the canon where parts can also enter at different pitches. In his *Introduction* (1597), Morley briefly described the construction of a catch, likening it to that of a canon: 'in this manner also be the catches made, making how many parts you list and setting them all after one' (p. 176). Catches were not meant to be sophisticated formal songs. They were about having fun as **perform**ers, not listeners, and could be just as effective if performed crudely. They were the preserve of male society of all social groups. A

catch

poem in Ravenscroft's miscellany, *Pammelia* (1609), summarizes the attributes of **perform**ing a catch:

> Come, follow me merrily, my mates,
> Let's all agree and make no faults:
> Take heed of **time, tune** and **ear**,
> And then, without all doubt,
> We need not fear
> To **sing** this catch throughout.

First applied to collections of songs in the late sixteenth century, the catch became very popular in Elizabethan England. Because of the way the words were sung and their subject matter, punning humour often tending to bawdiness and vulgarity became an essential feature, distinguishing the catch from the round.

It is not certain where the term 'catch' came from, but the earliest known collection from the Elizabethan period, Cambridge, King's College MS KC 1 (1580), equates catches with rounds: 'Here are wth in this rowle divers fine catches, otherwise called Roundes of 3, 4, and 5 parts in one' (title page). This manuscript contains a version of 'Hold thy peace' (*TN* 2.3.65). It is number 32 and is different from the one Ravenscroft printed in *Deuteromelia* (1609), no. 10. Jill Vlasto (p. 228) suggests this earlier version may well have been the one used in *Twelfth Night* and not the Ravenscroft which is invariably cited in modern editions of the play.

(B) The sexual content of catches is clear when Feste makes bawdy innuendos involving the title of one such song:

> SIR TOBY: Shall we rouse the night-**owl** in a catch that will draw three souls out of one **weaver**? Shall we do that?
> SIR ANDREW: And you love me, let's do't: I am dog at a catch.
> CLOWN: By'r lady, sir, and some dogs will catch well.
> SIR ANDREW: Most certain. Let our catch be 'Thou knave.'
> CLOWN: 'Hold thy peace, thou knave' . . .
>
> (*TN* 2.3.59–65)

catch

There seems to be a reference to the three-part catch in line 59 (Lothian and Craik, p. 46). The lines quoted above are followed by more bantering between the three men and further puns on 'peace/(cod)piece', for instance Feste's line 'I shall never begin if I hold my peace' (70): the codpiece is an obvious allusion to male genitalia (Partridge, p. 102), and Feste does not miss the opportunity to comment on his own and Sir Andrew's sexual desire.

The dialogue in this part of the scene is complemented by the stage direction '*Catch sung*' (2.3.71.SD), but unfortunately the text is not given: this may point to the improvisational nature of catches. It is possible that early modern actors would modify the words of the catch to suit the occasion. Malvolio's scandalized reaction after hearing the catch confirms that the content of the song and the manner of delivery are unsophisticated:

> My masters, are you mad? Or what are you?
> Have ye no wit, manners, nor honesty, but to gabble
> like tinkers at this time of night? Do ye make an
> alehouse of my lady's house, that ye squeak out your
> coziers' catches without any mitigation or remorse
> of **voice**? Is there no respect of place, persons, nor
> time in you?
>
> (2.3.86–92)

'Time' refers both to the inappropriate time of the night chosen for singing and to musical time (rhythm), as Sir Toby's reply reveals: 'We did **keep time**, sir, in our catches' (93).

In another 'drunken' situation a catch is sung. After plotting against Prospero's life, Caliban exhorts his fellow conspirators Stephano and Trinculo to be merry: 'Let us be jocund. Will you **troll** the catch / You taught me but while-ere?' (*Tmp* 3.2.117–18). However, their singing is made impossible by Ariel's intervention (the spirit is invisible to the drunken party). He '***plays** the tune on a **tabor** and **pipe***' (3.2.124.SD) and confounds them to the point that Trinculo comments: 'This is the tune of our catch, play'd by the / picture of Nobody' (3.2.126–7). This catch and the catch in *Twelfth Night* may in some ways be perceived as subversive, as the group solidarity that the sharing of a single musical tune implies.

85

catch

A final passage is worth quoting in relation to 'catch'. In *A Midsummer Night's Dream*, Helena praises Hermia's beauty in the following terms:

> Your eyes are lodestars; and your **tongue**'s **sweet air**
> More **tune**able than **lark** to shepherd's **ear**,
> When wheat is green, when hawthorn buds appear.
> Sickness is catching; O, were favor so,
> Yours would I catch, fair Hermia, ere I go;
> My ear should catch your voice, my eye your eye,
> My tongue should catch your tongue's sweet **melody**.
>
> (1.1.183–9)

The repetition of 'catch' is most appropriate in a speech dominated by musical references.

See also **snatch**.

(C) Lothian and Craik, *Twelfth Night* (1975).

Partridge, *Shakespeare's Bawdy* (1968).

Robbins, 'Shakespeare's Sweet Music' (1968), pp. 147–9, comments in detail on the passage in *Twelfth Night*.

Stevens, 'Rounds and Canons from an Early Tudor Song Book' (1951), includes an explanation of the differences between canons, catches and rounds.

Vlasto, 'An Elizabethan Anthology of Rounds' (1954), discusses Cambridge MS KC 1.

catling (A) The thin high-pitched **string**s on a **lute, viol** or violin made of catgut. 'Catling' is the diminutive of 'cat'.

(B) Whilst **Apollo** is typically depicted with a lute or stringed **instrument** of noble quality, in *Troilus and Cressida* the reference to Apollo 'the **fiddler**' (3.3.303) is disparaging. Thersites is cynical about Apollo's ability to restore '**harmony**' (i.e. sanity) in Ajax:

> ... What **music**
> will be in him [Ajax] when Hector has knock'd out his brains,
> I know not; but I am sure none, unless the fiddler
> Apollo get his sinews to make catlings on.
>
> (3.3.301–4)

Thersites reinforces the contemptuous nature of his comments by reminding us that the **fiddle**'s small strings come from gut. Analogies between stringed instruments and the human anatomy were Elizabethan commonplaces.

The three **musician**s in *Romeo and Juliet*, summoned for the wedding celebration between Paris and Juliet and dismissed after the discovery of the girl's (apparent) death, have names relating to stringed instruments: Hugh **Rebec**k, James **Soundpost** and Simon Catling. The tenet of this part of the scene, meant to provide comic relief, suggests that these are not high-brow musicians. This impression is reinforced by their exchanges with Peter, which reveal that they are more interested in the '**sweet sound**' (4.5.131) of **silver** [money] than in 'music with her silver sound' (4.5.129).

(C) Bonta, 'Further Thoughts on the History of Strings' (1976).

change (A) 'Change' can have either a specific or more general musical meaning. It is used specifically by Morley and Campion, for example, to mean moving erroneously from one **key** to another. Morley claims that to 'change' is a 'great fault, for every key hath a peculiar **ayre** proper unto it selfe, so that if you goe into another then that wherein you begun, you change the aire of the **song**, which is as much as to **wrest** a thing out of his nature' (*Introduction*, 1597, p. 147). Campion confirms that the tonality of a **melody** (the 'ayre') must remain constant and that to 'change' is 'not lawfull'. He suggests, ahead of his time, that the **bass** signifies the tonality: 'To make the key knowne is most necessary in the beginning of a song . . . Now if this be the right **Base** (as without doubt it is) what a strange unaireable change must the key then make' (*A New Way*, c.1614, D6v–D7r). Inability to change from one key to another in the same piece of music – to modulate, as it became known – was a mark of Renaissance music. The new music of the baroque was characterized by interrelated tonal modulations.

In a more general sense, a change in music implied a shift in **mood** or a move to another kind of **piece**, or melody (the proverbial 'change his **tune**'), or type of musical utterance. A shift in mood is expressed in:

>Free from love's bonds I lived long.
>But now to love I change my song

change

> With **discord**s **sweet** in every **strain**,
> And of my joy and pleasing pain.
> (Ward, 1613, no. 11)

Altering the tune is found, for example, in:

> Fain would I change that **note**
> To which fond love hath **charm**ed me
> **Long**, long to sing by **rote**,
> **Fancy**ing that that harmed me.
> (Hume, 1605, no. 112)

(B) This term acquires different connotations when used in a musical context by Shakespeare. A change in mood is intended by Capulet when he dismisses the **musician**s who had been employed to **play** at the wedding celebrations for Juliet and Paris:

> All things that we ordained festival,
> Turn from their office to black funeral:
> Our **instrument**s to melancholy **bell**s,
> Our wedding cheer to a sad burial feast;
> Our **solemn hymn**s to sullen **dirge**s change.
> (*Rom* 4.5.84–8)

Capulet has just discovered the apparent death of his daughter, and the resulting dramatic change in his disposition, from joyful to mournful, is reflected in the type of music he wants to **hear**. A 'change' is necessary since 'each **mode** had particular qualities, e.g. the **mournful** Lydian mode' (Robbins, p. 152).

Barely able to conceal her jealousy towards Silvia, Julia comments negatively on the song which has just been performed by a group of musicians in honour of her rival:

> JULIA: He plays **false**, father.
> HOST: How, out of tune on the **string**s?
> JULIA: Not so; but yet so false that he grieves my very heart-strings.
> . . .
> HOST: I perceive you delight not in music.

change

JULIA: Not a whit, when it **jar**s so.
HOST: Hark, what fine change is in the music.
JULIA: Ay; that change is the spite.
HOST: You would have them always play but one thing?
JULIA: I would always have one play but one thing.
(*TGV* 4.2.59–62; 66–71)

Julia wishes that Proteus could love her, hence her remark on the constancy of love at line 71. 'Playing false' discloses her fear of Proteus' unfaithfulness but has also a musical connotation as it means 'out of tune' and evokes the idea of discord. This conceit is expanded on with the use of 'change' relating to key **alteration**, which could potentially lead to mistakes and cause jarring **sound**s.

Disclosing her intention to disguise herself as a doctor of law, Portia explains that she will have to change the tone of her **voice**: 'And [I'll] speak between the change of man and boy / With a **reed** voice . . .' (*MV* 3.4.66–7). This remark has an interesting metatheatrical resonance: in Shakespeare's time, Portia would have been played by a young male actor whose voice would have possessed the very quality described in lines 66–7.

(C) Lester, *Between Modes and Keys* (1989), considers the transition from modal to tonal harmony.

Lewis, 'Incipient Tonal Thought in 17th-century English Theory' (1981), discusses tonality in English theory.

Robbins, 'Shakespeare's Sweet Music' (1968).

Wilson (ed.), *A New Way* (2003), pp. 61–3.

chanson (A) In the sixteenth century, *chanson* came to denote a **song** with a French text not confined to any specific poetic form as it had been particularly in the fourteenth and fifteenth centuries. Thus the term embraced many kinds of songs ranging from frivolous, bawdy, drinking songs to more serious, sombre, often quasi-religious types. For most of the sixteenth century, *chansons* were **compose**d for three and four **voice**s to sing in simple polyphony. Towards the end of the century, songs for solo voice and **lute** accompaniment (also known as *airs de cour*) began to be written in greater **number**s.

chanson

The *chanson* was one of the most widely disseminated genres in the sixteenth century; nearly 10,000 pieces appeared in printed or manuscript sources. Several collections were published in England from the 1570s, notably by Vautrollier.

(B) Hamlet's reference to 'the pious chanson' (*Ham* 2.2.419) is not altogether clear. A religious *chanson*, properly speaking, would imply a vernacular setting of a **psalm** or chorale text. Here, Shakespeare seems to denote a stanza of a serious or biblical song or **ballad** ('Jephthah Judge of Israel') which he cites in **part** a few lines earlier, borrowing the term simply to mean a song without necessarily a French text. Since Hamlet addresses his words to Polonius, and since the ballad is about the virgin daughter of Jephthah, it seems that the Prince is obliquely referring to Ophelia. The insertion of the ballad anticipates the fate of Ophelia who will die a virgin.

(C) Dobbins, *The Oxford Book of French Chansons* (1987), provides a well-chosen selection of *chansons* and useful introduction.

chant (A) As a verb, 'chant' means 'to **sing**' and is used in both a general and a specific ecclesiastical sense. What is sung is also called a chant (i.e. the noun). In general, 'chant' was employed synonymously with 'sing', as in Morley's **ballet**, 'Sing we and chant it / Till love doth grant it' (1595). In an ecclesiastical context, it refers to the singing (chanting) of **hymn**s, **psalm**s and canticles. The melodies used for Latin texts in the pre-Reformation liturgy were known generically as 'Gregorian chant' or 'plainchant'. Many of these were adapted and new ones made for the English Church in the later sixteenth century, notably John Merbecke's *Book of Common Praier noted* (1550). Psalm chants later came to be known as 'Anglican chants'.

(B) Shakespeare uses 'chant' in both its specific ecclesiastical context and in its more general usage. In *King John* for instance, Prince Henry meditates upon his father's imminent death:

> 'Tis strange that death should sing.
> I am the cygnet to this pale faint **swan**
> Who chaunts a **doleful** hymn to his own death,

> And from the **organ-pipe** of frailty sings
> His soul and body to their lasting **rest**.
> (5.7.19–23)

The passage is dominated by musical terminology ('sing', 'hymn', 'organ-pipe' and 'rest'). 'Chaunt' fits the solemnity of the passage with its swan emblem of death, singing the last and final **note**, an emblem widely used in Elizabethan times, as in Orlando Gibbons' famous **song**:

> The **silver** swan, who living had no note,
> When death approached unlocked her silent **throat**;
> Leaning her **breast** against the reedy shore,
> Thus sang her first and last, and sang no more.
> (*First Set Of Madrigals*, 1612, no. 1)

In another context of pain and distress, Gertrude recounts to Laertes, in one of the most lyrical speeches of the Shakespeare canon, how Ophelia drowned. After Ophelia fell into the brook:

> . . . Her clothes spread wide,
> And mermaid-like awhile they bore her up,
> Which time she chaunted **snatch**es of old **laud**s
> As one incapable of her own distress.
> (*Ham* 4.7.175–8)

It is interesting that 'lauds' (177) only appears in Q2 (1604/5), and that both Q1 (1603) and Folio have '**tune**s' instead. The use of the verb 'chaunt' does not help in clarifying which of the two words is the better option, since the verb can refer either to the act of singing in general or, more specifically, to singing religious songs.

Talk of religious matters, shady cloisters and nuns, appositely involves chanting as Theseus asks Hermia whether, rather than obey her father's order to marry Demetrius, she

> . . . Can endure the livery of a nun,
> For aye to be in shady cloister mew'd,
> To live a barren sister all your life,
> Chaunting **faint** hymns to the cold fruitless moon.
> (*MND* 1.1.70–3)

chant

In contrast, secular **bird**s 'chaunt **melody** on every bush' (*Tit* 2.3.12) and 'The **lark**, that **tirra-lyra** chaunts / With heigh' (*WT* 4.3.8–9) sings with the **thrush** and the **jay**. Interestingly, in these two examples Shakespeare prefers 'chaunt' to mean 'sing' when more than one person (or bird) is singing, perhaps recalling a church image of several monks or nuns chanting together a psalm or hymn.

In a non-specific way, the term is used when Autolycus sings **ballad**s 'so chaunts to the sleeve-hand' (*WT* 4.4.209); and 'free maids that weave their thread with bones, / Do use to chaunt it' (*TN* 2.4.45–6), 'it' being the Clown's song, 'Come away, death'. Venus '**hear**s no tidings of her love' from Adonis as she 'hearkens for his hounds and for his **horn**; / Anon she hears them chaunt it lustily' (*Ven* 868–9).

chantry (A) Chantries were established in cathedrals, monastic foundations and parish churches in Medieval times by royal, noble or notable persons for the purpose of **sing**ing plainchant, especially the requiem mass, for the repose of the souls of that person and his family.

(B) On the eve of the Battle of Agincourt Henry V addresses the 'God of battles'. He recalls having established chantries (at monastic houses) in penitence for his father's (Henry IV) deeds:

>   . . . I have built
> Two chauntries, where the sad and solemn **priest**s
> Sing still for Richard's soul.
>   (*H5* 4.1.300–2)

Henry is hoping that God will regard these pious acts with favour and help the English win the battle.

In a more light-hearted context, Olivia asks Sebastian (whom she mistakes for Cesario) to exchange vows of love:

>   . . . If you mean well,
> Now go with me, and with this holy man,
> Into the chantry by, there, before him,
> And underneath that consecrated roof,
> Plight me the full assurance of your faith,

chantry

    That my most jealous and too doubtful soul
    May live at peace.
                           (*TN* 4.3.22–8)

Olivia is referring to the betrothal ceremony: the wedding will take place later and will be celebrated in style 'according to [her] birth' (31).

charm (A) In his Latin–English *Thesaurus* (1565), Thomas Cooper equates 'charme' with '**song**e'. Other usages suggest charm is a song **tune** or **melody**, particularly associated with **bird**s: 'The small Birds **warbled** their harmonious Charmes' (Michael Drayton, *Owle*, 38). There is also evidence to suppose charm, as a song, could have magical connotations relating to the practice of **chant**ing or reciting verse with magic power, going back to the fourteenth century.

(B) The scene of the apparitions in *Macbeth* is dominated by the witches' **rhyme**s accompanying their spells. The apparitions are underlined by **sound** effects (for instance **thunder** and **hoboy**s). Of particular interest is the First Witch's exhortation before she, Hecate and the other witches disappear: 'I'll charm the **air** to give a sound / While you **perform** your antic **round**' (4.1.129–30). These lines are followed by the stage direction: '**Music**. *The Witches dance and vanish*' (4.1.132.SD). A musical connotation is evoked here, as the use of 'round' and 'air' (which was pronounced like the musical term '**ayre**') confirm (see also 'round' for a comment on this passage).
  Another play pervaded by magic, *The Tempest*, makes use of 'charm' both as a noun and as a verb on eleven occasions. For instance, Ariel explains how he managed to foil the plot to murder Prospero devised by Caliban, Stephano and Trinculo:

                . . . Then I **beat** my **tabor**,
    At which like unback'd colts they prick'd their **ear**s,
    Advanc'd their eyelids, lifted up their noses
    As they smelt music. So I charm'd their ears . . .
                             (4.1.175–8)

The music of Ariel's tabor charms the conspirators' ears. The three men follow their senses and behave like wild animals which can be

charm

tamed by music. However, in this case Ariel's aim is to humiliate them by leading them into the 'foul lake' (183) beyond Propsero's cell rather than make them enjoy the soothing effect of music.

The final scene combines magic and music in the reconciliation between Prospero and his enemies. Prospero renounces his magic:

> . . . But this rough magic
> I here abjure; and when I have requir'd
> Some heavenly music (which even now I do)
> To work mine end upon their senses that
> This airy charm is for, I'll bury my staff . . .
> (5.1.50–4)

In this speech the musical ayre is connected to 'charm' whilst conveying the idea that 'the music, sounding in the air, [. . .] works as a magic spell' (Lindley, 2002, p. 201). The ensuing stage direction ('**Solemn** *music*', 5.1.57.SD) confirms that practical music was deemed to be a vital element in the staging of this scene, where the supernatural plays a major role in the denouement.

A play on 'charm' in its musical sense is possible in Vincentio's observation that 'music oft hath such a charm / To make bad good, and good provoke to harm' (*MM* 4.1.14–15). This comment is in response to Mariana's stern dismissal of the boy who has just sung 'Take, O, take those lips away' (1–6), whose words painfully remind her of Angelo's rejection. It also betrays Angelo's ambiguous feelings about the concept of pleasure, a question which affects most characters in *Measure for Measure*.

(C) Cooper, 'Cantus' in *Thesaurus linguae romanae & britannicae* (1565).
Lindley, 'Shakespeare's Provoking Music' (1990); and *The Tempest* (2002).

chaunt see **chant**.

chime (A) 'Chime' denotes the **sound** of a **bell** most usually of a clock. The chimes or bells rung mechanically sometimes to make a **tune** were used to tell the hours of the day. A chime can also refer to a set of attuned bells, to a diatonic scale.

chime

(B) Falstaff uses this term when he tells Justice Silence of his and Shallow's nocturnal exploits: 'We have **heard** the chimes at midnight' (*2H4* 3.2.214). Elsewhere, the allusion to **time** is reinforced by the sound of the bell in Pericles' dangerous observations on Antiochius' daughter:

> You are a fair **viol**, and your sense the **string**s . . .
> But being **play**'d upon before your time,
> Hell only **dance**th at so **harsh** a chime.
> (*Per* 1.1.82; 84–5)

Ulysses draws on the second meaning, that a chime (of bells) should make a **concord**ant sound, when dismissing Achilles' disrespectful behaviour towards his superiors and peers in the Greek army: 'When he speaks, / 'Tis like a chime a-mending, with terms unsquar'd' (*Tro* 1.3.158–9). Bells wrongly chiming would indeed make a harsh **noise**.

choir (A) A choir is a group of **voice**s, male and/or female, most often but not exclusively associated with church **sing**ing, notably in post-Reformation England, of **anthem**s. In cathedrals and large chapels the choir was also a section of the building where the singers performed, hence the phrase at the end of Evensong in the Elizabethan *Book of Common Praier*, 'In Quires and Places where they sing, here followeth the anthem'. Cathedral choirs in Elizabethan England were exclusively male. Almost every cathedral supported its own choir, a tradition which continues to this day. Boys and men from certain choirs, notably St Paul's and the Chapel Royal, performed as both singers and actors at courtly **masque**s and entertainments and in the London theatres. Women would sing in **madrigal** and other 'domestic' ensembles as well as in masques but would rarely be designated as a 'choir'.

(B) Shakespeare alludes to the architectural choir, the enclosed part of a cathedral progressing eastwards from the nave (equivalent to the chancel in a parish church) in *Henry VIII*. In his description of the coronation of the new queen, Anne Boleyn, a gentleman records that a train of lords and ladies had withdrawn from Anne after she had been 'brought . . . / to a prepar'd place in the choir' (4.1.63–4). Then, during the ceremony 'the choir / With all the choicest **music** [i.e. musicians]

choir

of the kingdom / Together sung **Te Deum**' (90–2). Contemporary accounts relate that on state and other grand occasions the cathedral choir – in this case Westminster Abbey – would be augmented and other professional musicians employed by the Court would take **part**. That the staging of Anne Boleyn's coronation was spectacular is confirmed by the lengthy and detailed stage direction, which begins as follows:

> THE ORDER OF THE CORONATION:
> 1. A lively **flourish** of **trumpet**s
> 2. Then, two judges
> 3. Lord Chancellor, with purse and mace before him
> 4. Quiristers, singing.   Music.
> (4.1.36.SD)

Further stage instructions follow for another 22 lines. Clearly, the presence of choristers on the stage was deemed to be vital to enhance the sense of grandeur characterizing this scene.

When Venus improvises a **song** about unrequited love, reference to anthem in her '**woeful ditty**' (836) suggests that the church choir is meant: 'Her heavy anthem still concludes in woe, / And still the choir of **echo**es answer so' (*Ven* 839–40). Elsewhere, when referring to the fairies as the 'whole quire' (*MND* 2.1.55) who laugh at the tricks he performs on humans, Puck reinforces the simple meaning that they are a company, a group, of individuals. A group of singing **bird**s is described as a 'choir' in *2 Henry VI* when Suffolk reassures Queen Margaret that he is plotting against her enemy Eleanor, Duchess of Gloucester:

> Madam, myself have lim'd a bush for her,
> And plac'd a choir of such enticing birds
> That she will light to listen to the **lay**s,
> And never mount to trouble you again.
> (1.3.88–91)

As a vocal group, a choir must sing together in **harmony** or **concord**. When Coriolanus feels that he is losing this harmony after agreeing to fake respect for the plebeians, he asserts:

choir

> ... My throat of war be turn'd,
> Which quier'd with my **drum**, into a **pipe**
> Small as an **eunuch**, or the virgin voice
> That babies lull asleep! ...
> *(Cor 3.2.112–15)*

Emphasis is placed on the concept of agreement. By stooping to compromise, Coriolanus fears that his virile soldierly voice will turn into a weak voice more appropriate to a eunuch or a woman.

Heavenly choirs and celestial music colour Lorenzo's description of the music of the spheres as he tells Jessica:

> There's not the smallest orb which thou behold'st
> But in his **motion** like an **angel** sings,
> still quiring to the young-ey'd cherubins;
> Such harmony is in immortal souls.
> *(MV 5.1. 60–3)*

There are two references to the architectural choir besides that in *Henry VIII* 4.1.64 (see above). In *Sonnet* 73, Shakespeare meditates on the effects of growing old. He vividly captures the image of a ruined abbey church, which by the 1590s would be showing significant aspects of decay following the Henrician dissolution of the monasteries in the 1530s:

> That time of year thou mayst in me behold
> When yellow leaves, or none, or few, do hang
> Upon those boughs which shake against the cold,
> Bare ruined choirs, where late the **sweet** birds sang.
> *(1–4)*

The human choristers have become birds 'sweet singing in the choir', as the refrain of the **carol** of 'The Holly and the Ivy' has it.

That the choir as the place in which to sing is separate and enclosed is alluded to in the following passage:

> ... our cage
> We make a choir, as doth the prison'd bird,
> And sing our bondage freely.
> *(Cym 3.3.42–4)*

choir

Here, Arviragus is complaining to Belarius (whom he believes to be his father) that his life in a 'pinching cave' (38) is too limiting. Arviragus and Guiderius are in fact Cymbeline's sons: they were abducted by Belarius who wanted to 'bar [Cymbeline] of his succession' after Cymbeline had deprived him of his lands and banished him. The comparison between the two young men (who are unknowingly prisoners to Belarius) and a caged bird is particularly fitting.

(C) Fellowes, *English Cathedral Music* (1969), focuses on post-Reformation choirs.
Le Huray, *Music and the Reformation in England* (1978).
Wulstan, *Tudor Music* (1985).

chord (A) A chord is a **string** on an **instrument** such as a **harp** or **lute** or on a keyboard instrument (harpsichord, clavichord, **virginals**). On the harp or lute, the strings were made of gut and the name 'chord' may be derived from the Greek 'xopdai' meaning intestines. On the harpsichord the strings were **brass** or **wire**-wound.

In the sixteenth century, chord also meant the distance or interval between two **note**s either consecutively or vertically. During the seventeenth century it came to mean the simultaneous **sound**ing of three or more notes in a polyphonic texture.

(B) There is only one usage of 'chord' ('cord') in its musical connotation in Shakespeare's works. Observing Wolsey's displeasure at the news that Henry wants to marry Anne Boleyn, Surrey comments to other noblemen: 'I would 'twere something that would **fret** the string, / The master-cord on 's heart!' (*H8* 3.2.104–5). Given that instrument strings, like frets, were of animal origin, mentioning them in relation to the heart strings (a recurrent image in Elizabethan and Jacobean literature) gives this speech a special potency. To fret the string is to '**stop**' it and **change** its pitch or note. The alarming news of Henry's intention to marry would stop or break Wolsey's heart-string (Robbins, p. 229).
See also **catling; degree**.

(C) Robbins, 'Shakespeare's Sweet Music' (1968).

chorister see **choir**.

chorus (A) The term 'chorus' refers to a group of players (actors) or dancers who may also **sing** and **dance** together. More specifically it indicates a **choir** or ensemble of singers. It may be used to denote the **music**, usually vocal, inserted between or at the end of acts in a tragedy or comedy.

In the English Renaissance dramatic tradition, this term indicated a character 'who speaks the prologue, and explains or comments upon the course of events' (*OED* 1c). This type of device, developed from the chorus of Attic tragedy, was sometimes necessary to overcome the physical limitations imposed by Elizabethan and Jacobean playhouses, where important battles, changes of settings and the passing of **time** could only be represented symbolically.

(B) A chorus figure reports events throughout *Henry V*. He is the first character to enter the stage and to address the audience announcing his vital role. He apologizes for the impossibility of representing the imposing scale of the Battle of Agincourt on the bare stage of the Globe theatre, and concludes by pleading with the audience to 'admit me Chorus to this history' (Pro. 32) and 'gently to **hear**, kindly to judge, our play' (34). The summarizing task assigned to this figure is also what Ophelia has in mind when she tells Hamlet: 'You are as good as a chorus, my lord' (*Ham* 3.2.245). The whole court is assembled to watch the play put on by the travelling actors (a ploy used by Hamlet to put Claudius' innocence to the test), and Hamlet is explaining the plot details to Ophelia.

In *The Phoenix and Turtle* we find the only reference to 'chorus' in its classical meaning, with a probable musical nuance. This occurs in an **anthem** sung by **bird**s in honour of the dead phoenix and turtle. The anthem is followed by a threne, i.e. a **dirge**. To understand the full musical implication, it is important to quote the two previous stanzas:

> Reason, in itself confounded,
> Saw **division** grow together,
> To themselves yet either neither,
> Simple were so well compounded:
> That it cried, 'How **true** a twain
> Seemeth this **concord**ant one!
> Love hath reason, Reason none,
> If what **part**s, can so remain'.

chorus

> Whereupon it made this threne
> To the Phoenix and the Dove,
> Co-supremes and stars of love,
> As chorus to their tragic scene.
> (41–52)

The love between the two birds is alluded to in musical terms ('division', 'concordant', 'parts'), and the procession of mourning birds described at the beginning of the poem evokes the image of a singing chorus delivering the threne.

cinquepace see **cinque pas**.

cinque pas (A) The French '*cinque pas*' were the five **dance** steps which formed the basis of the **galliard** and tordion. According to Arbeau (*Orchesography*, 1589), they comprised four movements (hops and kicks on alternate feet) and the '***cadence***' (a leap '*sault majeur*' and **rest** '*posture*'). The steps were reasonably energetic and required some dexterity. Variations on the basic step pattern are described, for example, in sixteenth-century Italian dance manuals (e.g. Caroso, *Il ballarino*, 1581, and Negri, *Le gratie d'amore*, 1602), and Arbeau gives a number of different versions in his tabulations of the galliard. If the galliard was for those who wished to show off, then the cinque pas was better suited to more straightforward performing, or as Riche asserts: 'Our galliardes are so curious, that thei are not for my daunsyng, for thei are so full of trickes and tournes, that he whiche hath no more but the plaine sinquepace, is no better accoumpted of then a verie bongler' (Preface, *Farewell to Militarie profession*, 1581). Unlike the galliard, no compositions called 'cinque pas' were written for keyboard or **lute**.

(B) The cinque pas is mentioned by Sir Toby Belch in *Twelfth Night*, 1.3.130 (see 'galliard' for a discussion of this passage). In *Much Ado About Nothing*, Beatrice explains the differences between the cinque pas and other types of dance when warning Hero about the disadvantages of falling in love and marrying:

> ... Wooing, wedding, and repenting, is as a

> Scotch **jig**, a **measure**, and a cinquepace; the first
> suit is hot and hasty, like a Scotch jig, and full
> as fantastical; the wedding, mannerly-modest, as
> a measure, full of state and ancientry; and then
> comes repentance, and with his bad legs falls into
> the cinquepace faster and faster, till he sink into
> his grave.
>
> (2.1.73–80)

The excitement of wooing is likened to the liveliness of a Scottish jig. However this liveliness is soon replaced by the formality and moderation of the wedding celebration, which is compared to a measure (a more stately dance). Marriage, on the other hand, is dominated by repentance: like the cinque pas, it is less exciting than the jig, and no matter how hard one tries to 'escape back into jigtime' by dancing faster and faster (Berger, p. 302), this effort is doomed to fail. Marriage is described in this passage from a male perspective through the personification of repentance as a male bad-legged dancer, who cannot escape from a relationship which is restricting his freedom (ibid., p. 302).

(C) Baskervill, *The Elizabethan Jig* (1929), ch. 10, mentions the cinque pas in his summary of English dance forms.

Berger, 'Against the Sink-a-Pace'(1982), analyses the patriarchal values surfacing in the passage from *Much Ado About Nothing* quoted above.

cittern (A) A metal-**string**ed plucked **instrument**, originating in fifteenth-century Italy (called the *citole*) and very popular in England during the sixteenth and early seventeenth centuries. It was to be found as a solo recreational instrument or as a member of a **consort**. It had a pear-shaped body, shallow sides and a flat back. Generally **play**ed using a plectrum, the thin wire strings made a bright, clear **sound** in contrast to the more mellow, subdued tone of the **lute**. At the top of the **fret**ted neck, above the **peg**head, the instrument was distinguished by its carved ornamental figure or face.

The ancestry of the Renaissance cittern was thought by Italian humanists to lie in the classical Greek kithara. The stylized scrolls or 'buckles' of the Renaissance instrument, arguably represent the symbolic link with its classical forebear. Other physical features of the

cittern

cittern betray its classical provenance, notably its 'shell' body connecting it with the classical legend that the lyre Hermes presented to **Orpheus** had a (tortoise-) shell body (Wells, pp. 149–55). It is this feature which gives the cittern's noble offspring, the stately orpharion, its rich symbolism.

The cittern head, often grotesque, was more specifically a Renaissance feature emphasizing the instrument's erotic associations. Fletcher, for example, in *Love's Cure* (1622), refers to 'You cittern-head ... you nasty ... ill-countenanced cur' (2.2). In Dekker's *Honest Whore, Part 2*, the low-cast associations are invoked when Bellafront is accused of being 'a barber's cittern, for every serving man to play upon' (5.2.151). Elsewhere, the barbershop context is evident, for example in Dekker's *Match mee in London*, 'a citterne with a man's broken head at it, so that I think 'twas a barber surgeon' (1.4.137). It is thought that the cittern was commonly kept in the barbershop, to be taken down and played by waiting customers. The hook at the back of the peghead is an integral feature and would make the instrument easy to hang on a wall or other suitable place.

(B) Augustine Phillips, a sharer in the Chamberlain's Men, bequeathed a cittern to a boy in the company for whose teaching as a player he was responsible (Gurr, p. 79). Given the popularity of the cittern and the wealth of its associations, it is surprising that there is only one reference to the instrument in Shakespeare, namely when Holofernes' various facial guises are described:

> HOLOFERNES: I will not be put out of countenance.
> BEROWNE: Because thou hast no face.
> HOLOFERNES: What is this?
> BOYET: A cittern-head.
> DUMAINE: The head of a bodkin.
> BEROWNE: A death's face in a ring.
> LONGAVILLE: The face of an old Roman coin, scarce seen.
> (*LLL* 5.2.607–13)

Likening Holofernes' face to a cittern head is probably meant to evoke the grotesque features associated with this instrument.

(C) Abbott and Segermann, 'The Cittern in England before 1700' (1975).

Dart, 'The Cittern and its English Music' (1948).

Forrester, 'Citterns and their Fingerboard' (1983).

Gurr, *The Shakespeare Company* (2004).

Hadaway, 'The Cittern' (1973).

Holborne, *The Cittharn Schoole* (1597), is a source of English art music.

Robinson, *New Citharen Lessons* (1609), is another source of English art music.

Tyler, 'Checklist for Music for the Cittern' (1974).

Ward, 'Sprightly & Cheerful Musick' (1979–81).

Wells, *Elizabethan Mythologies* (1994), pp. 149–55, discusses 'shell' symbolism and the cittern's relationship with the orpharion.

Winternitz, *Musical Instruments and their Symbolism in Western Art* (1967), pp. 57–65, expounds the theory that the Renaissance cittern is a revival of the classical kithara; recalls a similar contemporary account by Galilei, *Dialogo della musica antica e della moderna* (1581).

cittern-head see **cittern**.

clamor (A) A non-specific term, in a musical context it suggests agitated **sound**. It is sometimes used to denote the **loud noise** of **bird**s and musical **instrument**s.

(B) Lennox (still unaware that Duncan has been murdered) expresses the sense of ill-omen pervading Macbeth's castle when he notes the **owl**'s behaviour:

> The night has been unruly . . .
> . . . The obscure bird
> clamor'd the livelong night.
> (*Mac* 2.3.54; 59–60)

The same bird is defined as 'clamorous' also in *A Midsummer Night's Dream* (2.2.6). In *As You Like It*, Rosalind uses this adjective to describe the **parrot**'s vociferous nature (4.1.151).

The sounding of **alarum**s is described as 'ungracious clamors' in

clamor

Troilus and Cressida (1.1.89). In *King John,* Blanche pleads with her newly wed husband that he refrain from moving war against her uncle:

> Upon thy wedding day?
> Against the blood that thou hast married?
> What, shall our feast be kept with slaughtered men?
> Shall braying **trumpet**s and loud churlish **drum**s,
> Clamors of hell, be **measure**s to our pomp?
> (3.1.300–4)

The instruments connected with battles are perceived to be 'clamors of hell' because of the death and destruction they bring. The musical nuance of this line is enhanced by the reference to measures, a term suggesting moderation and stateliness, in opposition to the confusion created by the clamour of martial instruments.

The connection between martial sounds and death is made explicit when Macduff incites his followers to the fight in Dunsinane: 'Make all our trumpets **speak**, give them all **breath**, / Those clamorous harbingers of blood and death' (*Mac* 5.6.9–10).

Richard tries to withstand the curses of Queen Margaret, the Duchess of York, and Queen Elizabeth by silencing them with the loud sounds of trumpets and drums:

> A **flourish**, trumpets! **strike** alarum, drums!
> . . .
> Either be patient and entreat me fair,
> Or with the clamorous report of war
> Thus will I drown your exclamations.
> (*R3* 4.4.149; 152–4)

But this display of military power is not enough to intimidate the three women.

See also **clang, din**.

clamour see **clamor**.

clang (A) Derived from the Latin 'clangere', it refers to the **loud**

resounding **noise** made by metallic **instrument**s such as **trumpet**s, **cymbal**s or objects such as swords. It is often used in a military context, but it can also allude to raucous **bird**s. 'Clangor' indicates a succession of clanging **sound**s.

(B) The final scene of *2 Henry IV* shows Henry V's formal procession through Westminster following his coronation, accompanied by the sounding of trumpets: '*Trumpets sound, and the King and his train pass over the stage*' (5.5.4.SD). The verb 'pass over' implies that the King and his followers would have left the stage after this wordless procession. Later in the scene, Pistol remarks: 'trumpet-clangor sounds' (40). This line is followed by the stage direction '*Enter the King and his train*' (5.5.40.SD), and was probably meant to work as an implicit cue for the **musician**s to **play** the trumpets once again to announce this second ceremonial entry.

Petruchio announces his intention to woo Katherina even though he has been warned about her spiteful nature. He will not be deterred from his intent:

> Think you a little **din** can daunt mine **ear**s?
> Have I not in my time heard lions roar?
> Have I not **hear**d the sea, puff'd up with winds,
> Rage like an angry boar chafed with sweat?
> Have I not heard great **ordnance** in the field,
> And heaven's artillery **thunder** in the skies?
> Have I not in a pitched battle heard
> Loud 'larums, neighing steeds, and trumpets' clang?
> And do you tell me of a woman's **tongue**,
> That gives not half so great a **blow** to **hear**
> As will a chestnut in a farmer's fire?
> (*Shr* 1.2.199–209)

This speech is built on aural metaphors, which culminate in the image of the loud sounds heard in battle. No wonder that the din caused by a woman is only 'little' in comparison to the frightening noises described by Petruchio.

During the Battle of Towton, Richard exhorts Warwick to take vengeance for his brother's death:

clang

> Thy brother's blood the thirsty earth hath drunk,
> Broach'd with the steely point of Clifford's lance;
> And in the very pangs of death he cried,
> Like to a dismal clangor heard from far,
> 'Warwick, revenge! brother, revenge my death!'
> (*3H6* 2.3.15–19)

Even though trumpets are not explicitly mentioned in this case, the allusion to these instruments is unmistakeable.
See also **clamor**.

clangor see **clang**.

clef (A) Morley says that 'A *Cliefe* is a charecter set on a rule [i.e. line] at the beginning of a verse [i.e. stave], shewing the heigth and lownes of euery **note** standing on the same verse' (*Introduction*, 1597, p. 3). The clef is the sign written at the beginning of the musical stave to indicate, in Elizabethan times, either where the '**ut**' (C), '**fa**' (F) or '**sol**' (G) lies. This depends on what kind of clef is used and on which line of the stave it is placed.

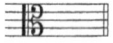

shows that 'ut' holds the middle line. The pitch of the notes above or below that line can then be determined. Today, we invariably employ only the **treble** 'G'

and **bass** 'F'

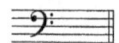

clefs, but in the Renaissance seven clefs were used (i.e. the G clef, two F clefs and four C clefs). In a piece for more than one **part** or **voice**, each part or voice could have a different clef depending on its *tessitura* or pitch. The clef and stave are fundamental to the notation of Western **music**.

(B) 'Cliff' is used in an interesting way when Bianca reads Hortensio's **gamut**:

> '*Gamouth* am I, the **ground** of all **accord**:
> *A **re***, to plead Hortensio's passion;
> *B **mi***, Bianca, take him for thy lord,
> *C fa ut*, that loves with all affection.
> *D sol re*, one cliff, two notes have I,
> *E **la** mi*, show pity, or I die.'
>
> (*Shr* 3.1.73–8)

Hortensio is disguised as the **music** teacher Litio in this scene, and the gamut provides him with the opportunity to reveal his love to Bianca. Exactly what 'one clef, two notes have I' means is uncertain, but for a musical explanation see discussion under 'ut' or 'gamut'. It has been suggested that his 'clef' is his love and the 'notes' his real and assumed personalities (Morris, p. 222) On a strictly musical level, what can be deduced from the passage quoted above is that Hortensio's gamut or music scale is in the bass F fa ut clef:

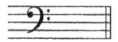

In the Renaissance system, the clef indicates the pitch of the note – in this case D. The name of the note is determined by the hexachord to which it relates – 'sol' to the hexachord starting on G and 're' to the hexachord starting on C. Shakespeare's usage here of Renaissance music notation is accurate in both theory and practice.

In *Troilus and Cressida*, a pun on female genitalia is probably intended in Thersites' comments on Cressida. He resorts to musical terms which point to the woman's sexual promiscuity: 'And any man may **sing** her, if he can take / her cliff; she's noted (5.2.10–11).

(C) Morris, *The Taming of the Shrew* (1981).
Partridge, *Shakespeare's Bawdy* (1968), p. 100.
Wulstan, *Tudor Music* (1985), pp. 203–10, discusses clef configurations.

clef

cliff see **clef**.

close see **cadence**.

coinage see **extempore**.

compass (A) The technical term 'compass' refers to the pitch range from the **low**est **note**s to the highest a particular **instrument** or **voice** is capable of sounding. On an instrument, the compass is determined by the physical properties of the instrument, mainly to do with size. Voices are less predetermined, although by the sixteenth century there was sufficient commonality for voices to have generic terms, e.g. **bass, treble**, etc. Morley (*Introduction*, 1597) writes that 'the Musicions do include their **song**s within a certaine compasse ... because that compasse was the reach of most voyces' (pp. 6–7).

(B) There are only two instances in the Shakespeare canon when this word appears in a musical context. Realising that Guildenstern and Rosencrantz are trying to assess his mental state and that they are going to report back to Claudius, Hamlet quizzes Guildenstern:

> Why, look you now, how unworthy a thing
> you make of me! You would **play** upon me, you would
> seem to know my **stop**s, you would pluck out the
> heart of my mystery, you would **sound** me from my
> lowest note to the top of my compass . . .
> (*Ham* 3.2.362–6)

He goes on to reproach his old friend for refusing to play a **recorder**. Hamlet is holding this instrument in his hands: the visual metaphor provided by the recorder effectively underlines the point which the Prince is making, i.e. that Guildenstern wishes to know the whole range of Hamlet's thoughts. However, Hamlet makes it clear to him that he will not accept being a tool in the courtiers' hands by concluding his speech in a defiant mode: 'Call me what instrument you will / . . . you cannot play upon me' (3.2.370–1).

In the concluding scene of *The Merry Wives of Windsor*, Falstaff watches the 'meadow-fairies' (who are in fact Anne Page, Mistress Quickly and boys in disguise) **sing** 'Like to the Garter's compass, in a *compass*

ring' (5.5.66). Although there is a reference here to singing, 'compass' denotes the fairies' circle and not the range of their voices.

complement (A) 'Complement' can have a specific musical meaning, namely a simple (as opposed to compound) interval equivalence inverted within the octave. In other words, a fifth inverted is a fourth; a third is a sixth.

(B) There is one occurrence of 'complement' in Shakespeare with a possible musical significance. In *Love's Labour's Lost*, Moth gives Armado advice on how he should woo Jaquenetta. Among other things, he recommends his master to 'keep not too long in one **tune**, but / a snip and away: these are complements, these are humo[u]rs' (3.1.21–2). Editors are inclined to think that the reference here is to 'compliments', i.e. 'gentlemanly accomplishments' (e.g. Hibbard, p. 133). However, it is possible that a musical meaning is being invoked: Moth is suggesting that even when he **change**s the **note**s the tune is too confined. Further evidence of a musical context is provided by the use of 'humours' which is found as the title of a short keyboard piece by Giles Farnaby in FWVB II, p. 262.

(C) Hibbard, *Love's Labour's Lost* (1990).
    Woudhuysen, *Love's Labour's Lost* (1998).

compose (A) The act of 'putting together' or inventing **music** in a transmittable form is one of the most significant identifying features of Western art music from the twelfth century onwards. Composing music invariably involves writing it down and is intrinsically bound up with the history of notation from the tenth century. It led to the emergence, in the twelfth century, of the named individual as the 'composer' of a musical work, a phenomenon which has dominated Western music ever since. 'Composition' has almost exclusively been the domain of the **musician** and is rarely applied to the act of creativity of poets, painters or sculptors.

Today the word 'compose' is used exclusively in art music to denote the act of creating music. But in the early seventeenth century, '**make**' and 'compose' were sometimes employed synonymously, as was occasionally the term 'invent'. In the 'Description of the *Somerset*

compose

Masque' (1613), for example, Campion says that some **song**s were 'made . . . by Mr. Nicholas Lanier', whilst others 'were composed by Mr. Coprario'. In his preface 'To the Reader' to *A Booke of Ayres* (1601), Campion refers to the 'well invented Motet'. Poets were also designated 'makers' or 'inventors' of (lyric) verse.

(B) Shakespeare applies 'compose' to the invention of both music and poetry, in particular of lyric poetry. For instance, although music is mentioned when the Widow explains how Bertram woos her daughter Diana, the words of the song is the likely interpretation:

> . . . Every night he comes
> With musics of all sorts, and songs compos'd
> To her unworthiness . . .
> (*AWW* 3.7.39–41)

On the eve of the Battle of Agincourt, the over-confident Dauphin boasts that he once wrote a sonnet to his horse beginning with the line 'Wonder of Nature . . .'. When one of his courtiers observes that he knows a sonnet beginning with the same line dedicated to a woman, the Dauphin replies: 'Then did they **imitate** that which I compos'd / to my courser, for my horse is my mistress' (*H5* 3.7.43–4). To him, war is clearly more important than love.

Thurio is exhorted by Proteus to woo Silvia with 'wailful sonnets, whose composed **rhymes** / Should be full-fraught with serviceable vows' (*TGV* 3.2.69–70). As *OED* explains 'composed' is synonymous with 'elaborately put together' in this context. Proteus describes the process of composition itself, which brings to the foreground the intimate connection between poetry and music:

> Write till your ink be dry, and with your tears
> Moist it again, and **frame** some feeling line
> That may discover such integrity:
> For **Orpheus' lute** was **strung** with poets' **sinews** . . .
> (3.2.74–7)

In view of this speech, it is possible that Proteus is referring to lyrical poetry in general at line 69 rather than to the sonnet form proper (this was a common usage until the mid seventeenth century).

concent (A) The application of the Elizabethan term 'concent' was concerned both with the harmonious relationship of **voice**s and, more specifically, with **sing**ing in **tune**. In his Latin–English dictionary, Thomas (1587) defines it as '*Concentio*: A consent of manie voices in one, an **accord**e in musike, **concord**e, agreement'. The pleasing **sound** of **part**s sung in concent is further emphasized by the addition of '**sweet**' in a number of poems and commentaries.

> Sing out, ye nymphs and Shepherds of Parnassus,
> With sweet delight your merry **note**s consenting,
> Sith time affords to banish love relenting,
> Fortune she smiles sweetly still to **grace** us.
> (Bennet, 1599, no. 7)

In a more sophisticated context, 'concent' invokes the philosophical relationship between practical and speculative **music**. As Robbins points out (p. 165), 'the ever-present relationship between the Human Music and the World Music was also mentioned by George Gascoigne, in his *Steele Glas*, 1567: "A sweet consent of music's sacred sounds/Doth raise our minds, as rapt, all up on high" (150–1)'.

Disagreement has arisen among commentators over the precise meaning of 'concent' in differing contexts, mainly in non-musical passages. In sum, in musical references it most often means simply the agreement of parts; however, literary critics should also be aware of the possibility that it also implies the concord between heaven and earth, the **harmony** of the spheres, the peace and unity of mankind in 'divine concent'.

(B) Of the hundred or so usages of 'concent'/'consent' in Shakespeare's works, two have a distinct musical flavour. The first example is observed when Capulet expresses his favourable view on a possible match between Paris and his daughter through musical imagery:

> But woo her, gentle Paris, get her heart,
> My will to her consent is but a part;
> And she agreed, within her scope of choice
> Lies my consent and fair **accord**ing voice.
> (*Rom* 1.2.16–19)

concent

The agreement on a political level that would ensue from a match between Paris and Juliet is like musical tuning ('accord'), which ultimately leads to harmony and concord.

The second usage of 'consent' occurs in a simile employed by Exeter, who believes that a good government,

> Put into parts, doth keep in one consent,
> Congreeing in a full and natural **close**,
> Like music.
>
> (*H5* 1.2.181–3)

'Congree' is synonymous with 'accord' (*OED*), and 'close' means **cadence**. As in the metaphor in *Romeo and Juliet*, emphasis is placed on the necessity for different vocal or instrumental parts (i.e. the subjects of a kingdom) to be in tune if concord is to be achieved.

(C) Robbins, 'Shakespeare's Sweet Music' (1968).
Thomas, *Dictionarium Linguae Latinae et Anglicanae* (1587).

concord (A) Concords are certain intervals between two or more **note**s which, when sounded together, make a pleasing **sound**. In Renaissance theoretical parlance they were also called consonances and were identified as intervals ('**chord**s') of the third, fifth, sixth and eighth and their compounds. Two sorts were recognized, namely 'perfect' and 'imperfect'. The 'perfect' concords were the fifth and eighth; the third and sixth constituted 'imperfect' concords. The latter were also divided into 'greater' and 'lesser', equivalent to our major and minor thirds and sixths. Morley defines concord as 'a mixt sound compact of divers voyces, entring with delight in the **ear**e, and is eyther perfect or unperfect' (*Introduction*, 1597, p. 70). The sense of agreement between disparate elements is noted by Dowland:

> Consonance (which otherwise we call *Concordance*) is the agreeing of two unlike Voyces placed together. Or is (as *Tinctor* writeth) the mixture of divers Sounds, **sweet**ly pleasing the eares. Or according to *Stapulensis lib*. 3. it is the mixture of an **high**, and **lowe** sound, coming to the eares sweetly, and uniformely.
>
> (*Micrologus*, 1609, p. 79)

(B) *Sonnet* 8 exposes these Renaissance theoretical principles with its rich musical imagery. The young man is saddened by **music** 'because its **harmony** and concord prompts him to confront his obligation to marry' (Duncan-Jones, p. 126). The poet tries to convince him of the importance of marriage:

> If the true concord of **well-tuned** sounds
> By unions married, do offend thine ear,
> They do but sweetly chide thee, who confounds
> In singleness the **part**s that thou shouldst **bear**.
> (5–8)

The young man, addressed as 'Music to **hear**' in the opening line, is reminded that he will not enjoy any harmony in his life if he does not **change** his mind.

In *Sonnet* 128, dedicated to the Dark Lady, the tone is much lighter. Shakespeare observes her while she is **play**ing the **virginal**s; her 'sweet fingers' (3) produce 'the wiry concord that mine ear confounds' (4) when she plucks the wires of the **instrument**. This has a pleasingly confusing effect on the poet (Duncan-Jones, p. 128).

In *The Two Gentlemen of Verona*, we are reminded that the harmony and pleasantness created by concord are easily disrupted. While Julia is trying to sing a song found in Proteus' love letter to her, her waiting-woman Lucetta tells her that she is marring 'the concord with too **harsh** a **descant**' (1.2.91) and suggests that only the **voice** of a tenor (Julia's suitor) can improve the quality of Julia's singing. 'Descant' here seems to be used in its meaning as the technique for improvising two-voice polyphony, of which the tenor was an essential part.

Lorenzo explains to Jessica the harmonious and soothing power of music, and goes on to warn her that:

> The man that hath no music in himself,
> Nor is not moved with concord of sweet sounds,
> Is fit for treasons, stratagems, and spoils...
> (*MV* 5.1.83–5)

If a man cannot be touched by the most pleasing music, the 'concord of sweet sounds', then he cannot be trusted.

The association between concord and harmony is evident when

concord

Malcolm pretends that he is not worthy to be king in order to test Macduff's loyalty. Malcolm claims that he does not have the qualities of a good king:

> ... The king-becoming **grace**s,
> ... I have no **relish** of them, but abound
> In the **division** of each several crime,
> Acting it many ways. Nay, had I pow'r, I should
> Pour the sweet milk of concord into hell.
> (*Mac* 4.3.91; 95–8)

Terms with a musical meaning, such as 'graces' and 'division', reinforce the musical pun. As already observed in relation to the passage in *The Merchant of Venice*, 'concord' is associated with sweet music: this association is evoked by the presence of the adjective 'sweet' in the same line as 'concord' in these lines from *Macbeth*. A similar effect is achieved in *Sonnet* 128, when 'sweet' is used to describe the Dark Lady's fingers producing concord while she plays the virginal.

See also **discord**.

(C) Duncan-Jones, *Shakespeare's Sonnets* (1997).

consent see **concent**.

consort (A) The noun 'consort' is used in a general sense to mean a 'company of **musician**s together' and more specifically as an ensemble of **instrument**s of the English Renaissance. According to *Grove*, the term is first found in its musical meaning in Gascoigne's description of the entertainment at Kenilworth in July 1575 (*The Princelye Pleasures*, 1576, lost; repr. in *The Whole Woorks*, 1587). Gascoigne mentions a 'Consort of **Music**ke' which, in Robert Laneham's account of the Queen's visit to Kenilworth, is described as an ensemble 'compoounded of six severall instruments' (*A Letter*, ?1575). These 'severall' or different-family instruments were **lute**, bandora, **bass viol**, **cittern**, **treble**-viol and **flute** (either transverse flute or **recorder**). This combination became the standard for the consort of the early seventeenth century as is attested by Morley in his *Consort Lessons* (1599) and

Rosseter, *Lessons for Consort* (1609). Today, we identify this as the 'mixed consort'. In the late sixteenth and early seventeenth centuries, 'consort' was generally but not exclusively associated with ensembles of different-family instruments.

During the late twentieth century many commentators erroneously used the term 'broken consort' to mean mixed consort. Neither 'broken' nor 'whole' nor 'full' are found in Elizabethan times used to designate types of consort. 'Broken musicke', however, does occur and refers to the manner of **play**ing **division**s or **extempore** embellishments (breaking **long note**s into several short ones), generally by the lutenist, whilst the other instruments of the consort accompanied. Because 'divisions' were a feature of mixed consorts, it is possible that 'broken musicke' became synonymous with 'consort', as defined for example by Francis Bacon in *Sylva sylvarum* (1627): 'In that Musicke, which we call Broken musicke, or Consort Musicke'.

Combinations of instruments varied according to function. In the professional theatre of the early seventeenth century, the Morley/Rosseter mixed consort was most common. Other consorts would be used as denoted by their symbolic associations. **String**ed instruments signified **harmony** and **concord**; **loud wind** instruments could allude to evil portents and **discord; soft** wind instruments, such as flutes, could signify death. There was also a distinction between instruments used by professionals (violins, **hoboy**s, **cornett**s, etc.) and amateurs. Invariably, music for consorts of viols was intended for amateur domestic consumption. This did not, however, preclude consorts of viols from appearing on the professional stage. **Song**s, accompanied by viol consort, were favoured by the children's companies and were possibly known as 'consort songs' as a unique reference in William Leighton's *Teares or Lamentacions* (1614) might suggest where the author distinguishes between accompanied songs ('consort songs') and unaccompanied '**part** songs'.

(B) In *Romeo and Juliet*, Tybalt tells his enemy Mercutio: 'thou consortest with Romeo' (3.1.45). 'Consort' may at first be interpreted as simply meaning 'keep company with'. However, Mercutio's defiant reply puns on the polysemic quality of the word:

> Consort? what, dost thou make us **minstrel**s?
> And thou make minstrels of us, look to **hear** nothing

consort

but discords. Here's my **fiddlestick**, here's that shall make you **dance**. 'Zounds, consort!

(3.1.46–9)

By describing himself as part of a consort of playing minstrels (rather than professional musicians) creating discord, Mercutio is using the word pejoratively. The comparison of his rapier to a fiddlestick, and the brandishing of this weapon implied by the wording of this speech, gives it a comical slant while emphasizing visually the musical metaphor.

On the other hand, Proteus is thinking of a consort of professional musicians when he advises Thurio on how to woo Silvia:

> Visit by night your lady's chamber-window
> With some **sweet** consort; to their instruments
> **Tune** a deploring **dump** . . .
>
> (*TGV* 3.2.82–4)

This consort's aim is to serenade the young woman with harmonious, if melancholy, music. Thurio is very keen to find capable musicians to make as good an impression as possible: 'Let us into the city presently / To sort some gentlemen well **skill**ed in music' (3.2.90–1). In the following scene, dominated by quite a different mood, an outlaw invites Valentine to join him and his partners in crime: 'What say'st thou? Wilt thou be of our consort?' (4.1.62). The choice of 'consort' to mean a company of criminals creates an ironic contrast with the use of the same word in the musical context of 3.2.

Cursing his enemies, Suffolk wishes that their music be as 'frightful as the serpent's hiss, / and boding **screech owl**s make the consort full' (*2H6* 3.2.326–7). In his mind, the unpleasant **sound**s associated with these animals of ill omen are the only music that his enemies deserve to hear.

(C) Beck, *The First Book of Consort Lessons: Collected by Thomas Morley* (1959).

Edwards, 'Consort', in Grove Online; and 'The Performance of Ensemble Music in Elizabethan England' (1970–1).

Holman, *Four and Twenty Fiddlers* (1993).

Wulstan, *Tudor Music* (1985).

coranto (A) Originating in Italy, and different from the early seventeenth-century French 'courant', the English **dance** was characterized by its speed and continuity. Morley notes that 'courantes' are danced 'travising [traversing] and running' and, interestingly, groups them with 'voltes' danced 'rising and leaping' (*Introduction*, 1597, p. 181), though the precise connection is unclear and is not amplified in other Elizabethan descriptions. It was never a popular dance and is invariably found in courtly or formal contexts. In Elizabethan **virginal music** it is the most common form after **pavan**s, **galliard**s and **allemande**s. There are 15 pieces in FWVB, for example, which demonstrate the fluidity of movement and both the simple Italianate triple-**time** kind and the more complex French type with its distinctive juxtaposition of triple and duple rhythm.

(B) After the King of France's unexpected recovery from a serious illness, Lafew comments that the King is now 'able to lead … a coranto' (*AWW* 2.3.43). This observation points to the liveliness of the dance, as opposed to the infirmity suffered by the King up to that point, and also reveals the coranto's courtly associations. The coranto and other dances are mentioned in a courtly context also in *Twelfth Night*, 1.3.129 (see 'galliard' for a commentary of this passage).

In *Henry V*, one of the King of France's courtiers complains that the victories obtained by the English are tainting their reputation. For instance, French noblewomen treat their men like cowards and bid them go 'to the English dancing-schools, / And teach lavoltas high and swift corantos' (3.5.32–3) since their '**grace** is only in [their] heels' (34). The French, incompetent as they are in battle, can only teach the English the art of dancing.

(C) Baskervill, *The Elizabethan Jig* (1929), pp. 344–5 refers to Arbeau's description of the dance steps.

cord see **chord**.

cornet see **cornett**.

cornett

cornett (A) The cornett (so spelt to distinguish it from the nineteenth-century valved **brass** cornet) was at the height of its popularity between c.1550 and 1650. Thereafter it went into decline becoming more-or-less obsolete in the eighteenth century, although recent research has shown that in parts of Germany and Scandinavia it was used into the early part of the nineteenth century. Furthermore, there has been something of a revival in cornett **play**ing over the past three decades. Three main sizes were known, namely **treble**, tenor and small treble (*cornettino*). The 'curved' treble cornetts were by far the most common, being made of wood, covered with thin black leather and played with a small **trumpet**-like cupped mouthpiece. The tone, said to approximate most closely to the human **sing**ing **voice**, is a cross between the smoothness of the clarinet and the brightness of a trumpet. It is not especially **loud** and can sustain both solo and accompanying roles.

In the Venetian poly-choral **music** of the late Renaissance, the cornetts together with trombones and **organ**s, were the preferred **instrument**s to support **choir**s. There is evidence that they were used at least on ceremonial occasions to accompany the choir in English cathedrals. In English ceremonial **music** collections, cornetts appear with music for violins and other **consort**s, as for example in the London Waits cornett player, John Adson's *Courtly Masquing Ayres* (1621), a collection of **masque dances** for violin band and other pieces for mixed ensembles of cornetts and **sackbut**s. The pieces for cornetts are idiomatically distinct from the pieces for violins, being much more linear and employing lower *tessitura* than the **string** pieces. As a solo instrument, the Renaissance cornett was famed above all other **wind** instruments for its capabilities in the hands of expert players of virtuoso display in its brilliant execution of **division**s or diminutions. The mute or straight cornett did not have the detachable cupped mouthpiece and had a **soft**er mellower tone more suited to indoor consort music. There was also a third type of cornett, a straight instrument with a detachable mouthpiece. This instrument was very popular in Germany in the early sixteenth century and can be seen alongside the curved and mute cornetts in the illustrations in Praetorius (Crookes, Plate VIII).

(B) It is generally agreed that cornetts were preferred to the louder trumpets in indoor theatres, a hypothesis corroborated by the larger number of directions for this instrument in the plays of the seventeenth century, when indoor venues such as the second Blackfriars were being used on a regular basis. Textual evidence derived from the Shakespeare canon points in the same direction. All stage directions for cornetts in his plays are found in Folio and in the only extant edition of *The Two Noble Kinsmen*, a quarto published as late as 1634. The only play mentioning cornetts for which we have editions other than Folio is *The Merchant of Venice*: interestingly, the earlier editions of this play (Q1, 1600 and Q2, 1619) have no indications either for the **sound**ing of cornetts or for other offstage sounds, suggesting strongly that they were not used in the play's original performance at the Globe. One of the directives for cornetts in Folio *The Merchant of Venice* occurs when the Prince of Morocco makes his first appearance on stage: '*Enter Morochus a tawnie Moore all in white, and three or foure followers accordingly, with Portia, Nerrissa, and their traine. Flo.[urish] Cornets*' (2.1.OSD). In Q1 and Q2 we have exactly the same wording except for the sound effect. Most critics agree that Folio represents a version of the play derived from a theatrical manuscript because of the larger number of musical cues indicated in this edition. Frances Shirley goes one step further and argues that the presence of cornetts 'suggests the infusion of stage directions from a later revival or from an indoor performance' (Shirley, p. 75). Cornetts accompany Morocco's exit at the end of this scene (2.1.45.SD) and are prescribed on two other occasions in Folio (2.8.OSD and 2.9.3.SD).

King Henry's first entry in *Henry VIII* is signalled by the sounding of cornetts, as are the entries of the King of France in *All's Well That Ends Well* (1.2.OSD and 2.1.OSD). As Shirley has noted (pp. 75–6), directions for cornetts to accompany royalty bring into question Manifold's theory (based on the directives in *Coriolanus* which require cornetts for the senators' entries) that these instruments 'serve to distinguish minor dignitaries [where]as the trumpets distinguish royalty and major dignitaries' (Manifold, p. 49). Trumpets were less likely to be used in an indoor context; 'the versatile cornett was apparently used more frequently than any other instrument in the children's theatres' (Austern, p. 63).

There is one single reference to this term in the Shakespearean dramatic dialogue, namely when York exclaims: 'O God, that Somerset, who in proud heart / Doth stop my cornets, were in Talbot's place!' (*1H6* 4.3.24–5). However, this is unlikely to be a reference to the instrument as such. Cornetts were depicted on the standard of companies of

cornett

cavalry (Rothery, p. 68), and York is accusing Somerset of failing to rescue Talbot by holding back York's squadrons of horse.

(C) Austern, *Music in the English Children's Drama of the Later Renaissance* (1992), pp. 63–7.

Baines, *Woodwind Instruments and their History* (1977), ch. 10 'The Sixteenth Century and the Consorts.

Basler Jahrbuch für historiche Musikpraxis, 5 (1981) (issue devoted to the cornett incl. E. H. Tarr, 'Ein Katalog erhaltener Zinken', 11–262).

Cairncross, *King Henry VI, Part I* (1962).

Collver and Dickey, *A Catalog of Music for the Cornett* (1996).

Crookes (ed. and tr.), *Michael Praetorius: Syntagma Musicum II* (1986).

Galpin, *Old English Instruments of Music* (1965).

Manifold, *The Music in English Drama* (1956).

Rothery, *The Heraldry of Shakespeare* (1930).

Shirley, *Shakespeare's Use of Off-Stage Sounds* (1963), analyses in detail the use and meaning of sound effects in Shakespeare's plays.

courant see **coranto**.

crack (A) Today we talk about a boy's **voice** 'breaking' when it deepens and becomes a man's. Thus a **treble** choirboy's voice is said to have broken when it changes into a tenor or **bass**. Alternatively, the change from a **low** to a **high** octave on a **wind instrument** such as the **recorder** or the **hoboy** is known as 'the break'.

(B) Shakespeare uses 'crack' twice in connection with voice to mean 'break'. Cressida expresses her despair to Pandarus after he tells her that she must be separated from Troilus:

> Tear my bright hair, and scratch my praised cheeks,
> Crack my clear voice with sobs, and break my heart,
> With **sound**ing Troilus. I will not go from Troy.
> (*Tro* 4.2.107–9)

This speech with its metatheatrical tone has an ironic slant. The boy actor playing Cressida draws attention to the very features which

crack

underline his ambivalent sexual status: the bright hair (symbolized by a wig), the cheeks (which would have probably shown the first signs of a growing beard) and the voice (which would have been on the verge of breaking).

The post-pubescent state reached by Arviragus and his brother Guiderius is noted by the former when he comments to his brother that their voices have 'got the mannish crack' (*Cym* 4.2.236).

(C) Smith, *The Acoustic World of Early Modern England* (1999), esp. pp. 226–32, discusses the importance of voice volume and pitch in early modern performance in relation to boys' voices.

Wulstan, *Tudor Music* (1985), ch. 8 'A High Clear Voice', deals with pitch, voice ranges and other factors including the breaking of boys' voices (223–5) although he does not refer to 'crack'.

crotchet (A) 'Crotchet' was and still is a peculiarly English term, not known in continental Europe and even today in the English-speaking world beyond the UK (in America for example) the **note**-value is called a quarter-note. Its value in Common **Time** is half of a **minim** and twice a quaver. It is equivalent to the white mensural semiminim (see '**breve**') which was a lozenge-shaped filled-in note (in black or red ink) with a tail. Dowland referred to the filled-in characteristic as 'colour', a Renaissance convention: 'A *Crotchet*, is a Figure like a *Minime* in colour varying' (*Micrologus*, 1609, p. 39). The origins of the note-value, either as a crotchet or semiminim are, according to Morley, not known: 'Who inuented the Crotchet, Quaver, and Semiquaver is uncertaine. Some attribute the invention of the crotchet to the aforenamed *Philip*' [i.e. Philippe de Vitry, c.1290–1361] (*Introduction*, 1597, The Annotations to the First Part); but by the end of the sixteenth century it had become widely used, especially in printed **music**.

(B) This word is used in its musical connotation twice, in both cases with a word-play on 'crotchet' as 'whimsical **fancy**': in *Romeo and Juliet*, 4.5.118 (see '**ut**' for a detailed discussion of this passage) and in *Much Ado About Nothing*, 2.3.56. Don Pedro exhorts Balthasar to **sing** (he, Leonato and Claudio are setting a trap for Benedick to make him declare his love for Beatrice) '**Sigh** no more, ladies', but the latter is *crotchet*

reluctant to deliver the **song**. The exchange that follows puns on the meaning of 'crotchet' and 'note':

> BALTHASAR: Note this before my notes:
> There's not a note of mine that's worth the noting.
> DON PEDRO: Why, these are very crotchets that he **speak**s –
> Note notes, forsooth, and nothing.
>
> (2.3.54–7)

'Crotchet' can be interpreted here as either a quarter-note or a whim. 'Note' evokes even more puns: as well as its musical connotation, it means 'take notice of', 'brief comment'. Furthermore, '"not" and "nothing" (with the "th" pronounced as "t" as it commonly was) are also involved' in this entertaining passage (Mares, p. 83). The verb 'speak' also had a musical meaning ('make to **sound**' or 'make musical notes') in early modern English.

(C) Mares, *Much Ado About Nothing* (1988).
   Rastall, *The Notation of Western Music* (1998).

cuckoo see **bird**.

cymbal (A) The reference to cymbal in Psalm 150 is one of the most famous of many found in the Bible: 'O Praise God in his holiness ... Praise him in the cymbals and **dance**s'. The reference is to the ancient Jewish metallic **instrument**s, 'mesiltayim' and 'selselim'. As is often noted, Asaph, King David's principal **musician**, was a cymbalist. Cymbals were used in ancient religious ritual to mark events, significant moments and methods of **chant**ing.

The cymbal was basically a flat plate of metal, usually **brass** or copper, and was made in differing sizes ranging from very small to reasonably large. Cymbals were **play**ed either in pairs, by being **beat**en or clashed together, or singularly, hit by a stick or hammer.

Small pairs of cymbals, generally played by **angel**s or females, are depicted frequently in Medieval iconography. These relate back to the pairs of cymbals in Graeco-Roman antiquity where they were intimately associated with various rites, especially the orgiastic religious rites

cymbal

of the goddess Cybele, and the wild ecstatic rites involved with the worship of Dionysus and Bacchus. Such 'ecstasy-inducing' **music** often included the use of the tympanum and aulos (**pipe**). In addition to religious contexts, cymbals were used by dancers, in instrumental bands and in battle. In certain situations, cymbals were thought to have special, even magical powers.

In the initial letter of Psalm 150 in a number of Medieval illustrated manuscripts, King David is depicted seated playing a row of small **bell**s with a hammer. These bells were known as 'cymbala'. There is no evidence elsewhere, however, to suggest that this was standard performance practice or that the Medieval cymbal and cymbala were interchangeable. Cymbala, mentioned in Greek and Roman sources, are in fact pairs of cymbals played together with **drum**s and **wind** instruments.

(B) The only reference to cymbals in Shakespeare is in *Coriolanus*, when a messenger reports to Menenius and Sicinius:

> The **trumpet**s, **sackbut**s, psalteries, and **fife**s,
> **Tabor**s and cymbals, and the shouting Romans,
> Make the sun dance. Hark you!
> (5.4.49–51)

The play here acquires a pageant-like quality to celebrate the triumphant entry of Volumnia into Rome (Brockbank, p. 61). That music was expected to be played in performance seems to be confirmed by the stage direction immediately preceding these lines: '*trumpets,* **hoboy**s*, drums . . . all together*' (5.4.48.SD).

(C) Brockbank, *Coriolanus* (1976).
La Rue, 'The Problem of the Cymbala' (1982).

D

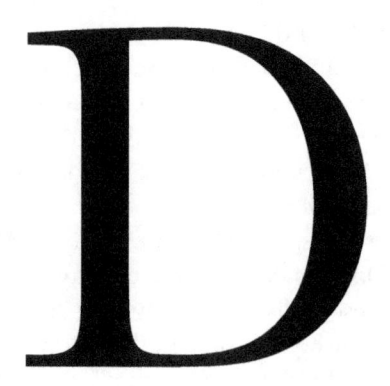

dance (A) Throughout history, **music** and dance have been intrinsically linked and frequently interdependent. It is very rare for a dance not to be accompanied by music even if that accompaniment is only a single percussive **sound**. Many dances have shaped musical forms and types to such an extent that the name of the dance has also become the designation of the music.

Dancing in Elizabethan times was especially popular in all levels of society: 'the English in general, and English courtiers in particular, were almost as famous in the sixteenth century for their love of dancing as for their gluttony' (Holman, p. 113). Queen Elizabeth took a special delight in both dancing herself and in watching other people dance. In a conversation with the Queen in January 1598, Monsieur de Maisse, King Henri IV's ambassador to the English court, recorded that, as Holman reports, the Queen:

> takes great pleasure in dancing and music. She told me that she entertained at least sixty **musician**s; in her youth she danced very well, and composed **measure**s and music, and had **play**ed them herself and danced them. She takes such pleasure at it that when her Maids dance she follows the **cadence** with her head, hand and foot.
> (p. 114)

The dancing-masters at court were often the musicians who composed and played the music for the dances, notably members of the violin **consort**, most of whom came from Italy. Dancing was not, of course, exclusive to the court. There is ample evidence that street musicians, Whythorne's 'pettifoggers of music', attempted to eke out a meagre living by playing **fiddle**s, **pipe**s and **drum**s for impromptu dances at taverns and other meeting places. Records of city waits show that they played at more organized occasions to accompany dancing.

Dance music for the court and other professional settings was invariably composed and written down, not least because it was mostly played by consorts. Street musicians, **minstrel**s and waits frequently improvised their music or played remembered music. Consequently, most of the dance music that survives from the sixteenth and early seventeenth centuries is notated stylized art music. Indeed, a large body of dance music from the period was composed as independent **instrument**al music and not as functional dance music intended to accompany dancing.

The combination of **sing**ing and dancing is pervasive in Elizabethan literature and dramatic sources. Dance **songs**, for example, are common in courtly **masque**s and entertainments. In his *Entertainment at Cawsome-House* (1613), Campion has a 'Song and Dance of sixe': 'Dance now and sing the joy and love we owe: / Let cheerfull **voice**s and glad gestures showe'.

In his *Discourse of English Poetrie* (1586) William Webbe observes that many songs for dances were set to popular **tune**s:

> Neither is there anie tune or stroke which may be sung or plaide on instruments, which hath not some poetical ditties **frame**d according to the numbers thereof, some to Rogero, some to Trenchmore, to downe right Squire, to **Galliarde**s, to **Pavin**es, to Iygges [**jig**s], to **Brawl**es, to all manner of tunes which everie Fidler knowes better then my selfe.
>
> (Smith (ed.), vol. 1, p. 272)

It is not surprising, then, that pastoral themes often invoked singing and dancing. Thomas Watson's 'Englished' version of Marenzio's **madrigal** 'Vezzosi augelli' is one such example:

> Every singing **bird**, that in the wood rejoices,
> Come and assist me with your **charm**ing voices;
> Zephyrus, come too, and make the leaves and the fountains

dance

> Gently to send a whispering sound unto the mountains;
> And from thence **pleasant Echo, sweet**ly replying,
> Stay here playing, where my Phyllis now is lying;
> And lovely **Grace**s, with wanton satyrs come and play,
> Dancing and singing, a **hornpipe** or a **roundelay**.
> (*Italian Madrigalls Englished*, 1590, no. 6)

That we know a considerable amount about sixteenth-century dances is largely due to Arbeau's dance manual, *Orchesography*. It was first published in 1589 at Langres. A second printing was issued in 1596 and except for the title page is identical to the first. It contains descriptions of the steps of stylized martial and recreational dances used at court and in organized social occasions. Each tabulation of a dance includes a musical **melody** suitable for accompanying the steps. The manual is in the form of a pedagogical document, not unlike Morley's *Introduction* (1597), in which the master (Arbeau) discusses a dance with his pupil (Capriol) at the same time reaffirming the importance of dancing in social etiquette.

(B) As can be expected, stage directions for dancing, sometimes followed by indications for music or singing, are omnipresent in Elizabethan and Jacobean drama (Dessen and Thomson, p. 64, calculate that there are about 350 stage directions for dancing in the plays of the period 1580–1642). Dance with its strong metadramatic quality was a stock feature of theatrical production in Shakespeare's day. Even when dance was not inserted in the narrative of the play, productions (not only of comedies but also of history plays and tragedies) would routinely end with the dancing of a jig. The Swiss doctor Thomas Platter recounts this custom when he comments on a production of *Julius Caesar* he saw at the Globe in 1599 while he was travelling in England: 'when the play was over, they [the actors] danced very marvellously and gracefully as is their wont, two dressed as men and two as women' (Williams, p. 166).

As far as the Shakespeare canon is concerned, dancing underlines different occasions and moods. Whilst it usually has positive connotations, for instance when it accompanies celebrations of various kinds, it can, like music, take on more ominous tones. To the first category belong stage instructions such as '*Music. Dance*' (*H8* 1.4.76.SD) during the court masque in which *Henry VIII* falls in love with Anne Boleyn; or:

'Here a dance of shepherds and shepherdesses' (*WT* 4.4.165.SD) to evoke the joyful atmosphere of the sheep-shearing feast; another example is *'Dance'* (*Ado* 2.1.154.SD) during the masked ball in Leonato's house. To the second category belong stage directions such as *'the Witches dance and vanish'* (*Mac* 4.1.132.SD) after they have conjured up the ominous apparitions for Macbeth; and *'Enter several strange shapes, bringing in a banket; and dance about it with gentle actions of salutations; and inviting the King [of Naples], etc., to eat, they depart'* (*Tmp* 3.3.18.SD). This dance, which accompanies an apparently celebratory banquet for the hungry Alonso and his retinue, soon shows its real sinister purpose when Ariel appears as a harpy, causes the banquet to vanish and accuses Alonso, Sebastian and Antonio in biblical tones of being 'three men of sin' (53).

The dialogue of Shakespeare's plays has several references to dances. Marina lists a number of respectable qualities she possesses when persuading Boult (one of the bawds) that she would not be suitable to work as one of his prostitutes. She explains to him: 'I can sing, weave, sew, and dance / With other virtues, which I'll keep from boast . . .' (*Per* 4.6.183–4). The ability to dance gracefully was a desirable attribute for a lady in early modern England.

Boyet points to the importance of dancing as part of the ritual of courtship when he explains to the Princess of France that the King of Navarre and his followers have devised to disguise themselves as Russians and provide musical entertainment for the Princess and her ladies:

> Their purpose is to **parley**, to court, and dance,
> And every one his love-feat will advance
> Unto his several mistress . . .
> (*LLL* 5.2.122–4)

However, when the dancing takes place later in the scene, things do not go according to plan: the Princess and her ladies exchange masks before the arrival of their suitors, who end up courting the wrong women.

Oberon and Titania will 'dance in the Duke Theseus' house triumphantly, / And bless it to all fair prosperity' (*MND* 4.1.88–9) to celebrate the couples whose love prevails at the end of the play. Benedick too proposes a dance (*Ado* 5.4.118) in a wedding scene.

One example which reveals the potential for subversion of the commonly accepted values attributed to dancing, is found when Queen

dance

Margaret sadistically humiliates York (the humiliation ends with her putting a paper crown on his head):

> ... Thou should'st be mad;
> And I, to make thee mad, do mock thee thus.
> Stamp, rave, and fret, that I may sing and dance.
> (*3H6* 1.4.89–91)

Instead of accompanying a harmonious and joyful celebration, Margaret's singing and dancing aim to cause as much suffering as possible to her helpless enemy.

Following Bolingbroke's banishment, his father tries to console him by telling him that he should use his imagination to make the pain of his exile less excruciating. First of all, Bolingbroke should 'suppose the singing birds musicians' (*R2* 1.3.288), and then he should consider his exile's steps 'no more / Than a delightful measure or a dance' (290–1). Even if motivated by the best of intentions, these references to the pleasures of courtly life inflict even more pain on Bolingbroke.

Like music, dance is sometimes associated with aspects of the natural world. **Orpheus**' music has a powerful soothing effect over the wildest animals and forces of nature, as it can 'make tigers tame, and huge leviathans / Forsake unsounded deeps, to dance on sands' (*TGV* 3.2.79–80). Titania and the fairies 'dance ... to the whistling **wind**' (*MND* 2.1.86), thus confirming their close link with the natural phenomena of the forest they inhabit. A messenger announces that 'the shouting Romans / Make the sun dance' (*Cor* 5.4.50–1) after Coriolanus has decided to spare their city from the ravages of war.

See also **bagpipe, bergomask, canary, hay, morris dance, tabor**.

(C) Baskervill: Brissenden, *Shakespeare and the Dance* (1981).

Cunningham, *Dancing at the Inns of Court* (1965), analyses the role of the dance in London society.

Dessen and Thomson, *A Dictionary of Stage Directions* (1999), pp. 64–5.

Holman, *Four and Twenty Fiddlers* (1993), discusses the importance of dances and dancing.

Sabol, *Four Hundred Songs and Dances from the Stuart Masque* (1978).

Smith (ed.), *Elizabethan Critical Essays* (1904).

dance

Sorrell, 'Shakespeare and the Dance' (1957), 367–84 is specifically on Shakespeare and less on music.

Walls, *Music in the English Courtly Masque* (1996), is an excellent account of music and dance of the English masque.

Williams (tr.), *Thomas Platter's Travels in England, 1599* (1937).

Wulstan, *Tudor Music* (1985), esp. ch. 5, surveys dances and dance music.

defunctive (A) An unusual musical usage of the adjective pertaining to death or dying is Shakespeare's application of 'defunctive'. (B) It describes the **music** of the symbolic **swan**, as is clear from a reference in *The Phoenix and Turtle* to the 'death-divining swan' (15) that sings 'defunctive music' (14). (See '**requiem**' for an analysis of this passage).

degree (A) Definitions for two sorts of 'degree' are given in Elizabethan musical treatises. One refers to adjacent **note** or stepwise linear movement in contrast to disjunct, leaping intervallic motion. Campion, for example, articulates this when he talks about 'Notes rising and falling . . . not so much by degree as by leaps . . . rising is said to be by degrees, because there is no Note betweene the two Notes' (*A New Way*, c.1614, B7r). This meaning is common in musical commentary throughout the seventeenth century.

The second has to do with rhythm and recalls late Medieval mensural notation theory. The anonymous *Pathway to Musicke* (1596) says that degree 'is a certaine rate, by the which the value of the principall notes is **measure**d and knowne by a certaine marke' (C iii). The 'certaine marke' is the predecessor to the modern **time**-signature. Morley is more expansive:

> Those who within these three hundreth yeares have written the Art of **Music**ke, have set downe the **Mood**es otherwise then they eyther have been or are taught now in England. . . . Those which we now call Moodes, they tearmid degrees of Musick: the definition they gave thus: a degree is a certayne meane whereby the value of the principall notes is perceaved by some signe set before them, degrees of musicke they made three, *Moode: Time* and *Prolation*.
>
> (*Introduction*, 1597, p. 12)

degree

Again, Morley refers to the 'signe' which was to become the time-signature. 'Moodes' are the Medieval rhythmic **mode**s which essentially divided music into either triple or duple rhythms. Both of these definitions, the one scalic the other rhythmic, could apply to Shakespeare's unique and remarkable use of degree with a musical meaning.

(B) Ulysses' first speech is Shakespeare's best known and most extensive exposition specifically on degree. The Greek commander's understanding of degree involves both hierarchy, in particular rank in the Greek army and in general law and order in the civil state with its levels of importance among those holding office and responsibility. When order is displaced by disorder, then strife and **discord** will ensue in both civilian and military societies:

> What plagues and what portents, what mutiny!
> What raging of the sea, shaking of earth!
> Commotion in the **wind**s! frights, changes, horrors,
> Divert and crack, rend and deracinate
> The unity and married calm of states
> Quite from their fixure! O, when degree is shak'd,
> Which is the ladder of all high designs,
> The enterprise is sick.
>
> (*Tro* 1.3.96–103)

The concept of degree and the political theory of order were vital to Elizabethan society and its well-being. This is reflected in many contemporary historical and political writings. The significance of Ulysses' speech is its 'general account of disorder in society' (Palmer, p. 45), propounding the Elizabethan ideal of control by law, justice and order and the terror of civil war – a common theme in Shakespeare. As in other plays involving conflicts between order and chaos, Shakespeare invokes a musical metaphor which builds on the imagery evoked in the passage quoted above: 'Take but degree away, un**tune** that **string /** And hark what discord follows' (1.3.109–10).

Tuning and discord are aspects of **harmony**. Strings that are in tune are harmonious and **concord**ant. Strings that are out of tune are discordant and lacking harmony. The application of degree is specific. Campion's scalic theory explains this concept clearly. A musical scale is determined, either rising or falling, by its tones and half tones, the *degree*

adjacent intervals which follow one another, its degrees: the relationship between its degrees brings order. Shakespeare's 'ladder' at line 102 plays on the meaning of 'scala', which in Italian refers both to 'musical scale' and 'ladder'. A stringed **instrument** such as a **lute** or **viol** when it is out of tune distorts the scale. If the rhythmic theory is applicable then we must understand that music is ordered by the temporal relationship of notes as indicated in the rhythmic mode, degree or time sign. In Medieval and Renaissance music, before the advent of the time signature and the organization of notes into metrical bars using bar lines, the interpretation and meaning of tempo and rhythm were implicit in the hierarchical relationship of the longest and shortest notes.

(C) Apel, *The Notation of Polyphonic Music* (1953), discusses the notation of Medieval rhythm.
Collins, *From Divine Cosmos to Sovereign* (1989).
McAlindon, *Shakespeare's Tragic Cosmos* (1991).
Palmer, *Troilus and Cressida* (1982).
Talbert, *The Problem of Order* (1962).
Wilson (ed.), *A New Way* (2003), p. 47.

descant (A) In the sixteenth century, the term had several interrelated meanings. It could either refer to a type of contrapuntal vocal piece, or to an improvisatory method of **sing**ing, or it could signify the top or **treble voice** or the high register of certain 'vocal' **instrument**s such as the **recorder** or **viol**, or it could mean to sing or **play** the top **part** in a multivoiced piece. Morley reports that

> The name of Descant is vsurped of the musitions in divers significations: some **time** they take it for the whole **harmony** of many voyces: others sometime for one of the voyces or partes: & that is, when the whole **song** is not passing three voyces. Last of all, they take it for singing a part **extempore** upon a playnesong, in which sence we commonly use it: so that when a man talketh of a Descanter, it must be understood of one that can extempore sing a part upon a playne song.
>
> (*Introduction*, 1597, p. 70)

Descant, improvised (extempore) on a slow-moving **plainsong** or

descant

cantus firmus used **note**s of shorter time-values than the plainsong but was not the more florid, faster **division**. Moreover, descant was more commonly associated with sacred **music** whereas divisions were most often found in secular song and instrumental music.

In its origin in the twelfth century, descant (known today by scholars as 'discant') was a method or technique for improvising two-voice polyphony, using a plainchant tenor and another voice in note-against-note manner. The word is derived from the Latin 'discantus' (adopted into Middle English; Old French is *deschant* or *descant*) implying not merely '**sound**ing apart' but more definitely 'singing apart' and is closely related in Medieval treatises with 'organum' and 'diaphonia', other terms for 'polyphony', though it is not commonly used with this general meaning. The idea of performing a descant in one voice against a **ground** (**bass**) in another is alluded to in: 'Yet one the ground must be, which you shall prove / Can **bear** all **part**s that descant on my love' (Corkine, 1612, no. 17).

The gradual widening of the vocal range in the later fifteenth century saw a new-found predilection for three-voice descant. The topmost voice was called the descant, hence to sing descant also meant to sing the top voice (see above). The contrapuntal rules observed in the late fifteenth and sixteenth century meant that the sound of English descant was **concord**ant or '**sweet**', avoiding **harsh** dissonance.

(B) The traditional concordant sound of descant was obviously known to Shakespeare and his audience when he has Lucetta remark to Julia that the latter is marring 'the concord with too harsh a descant' (*TGV* 1.2.91). The exchanges between the two women in this scene are full of references to music, including the popular song 'Light o' love'.

Knowledge of other characteristics, namely the skilful extemporization of one part against a plainsong or 'ground', as Shakespeare calls it, and of the sacred context are manifest in Buckingham's advice to Richard that he should look pious when he is offered the title of king:

> And look you get a prayer-book in your hand,
> And stand between two churchmen, good my lord –
> For on that ground I'll **make** a holy descant –
> And be not easily won to our requests.
>
> (*R3* 3.7.47–50)

descant

Earlier in the play, Richard describes his own deformity in musical terms. In his famous opening soliloquy, he claims that he has

> . . . no delight to pass away the time,
> Unless to see my shadow in the sun,
> And descant on mine own deformity.
> (1.1.25–7)

Hence, he intends to be a villain rather than a lover, and to disrupt the fragile political stability established by his brother Edward's accession to the throne. 'Descant' here also means 'remark', 'comment upon', but a musical pun is intended since other terms alluding to music and dance are used by Richard in this soliloquy – for instance **alarum**s (7), **measure**s (8), **caper**s (12), **lute** (13) and **piping** (24).

A passage rich in musical imagery in *The Rape of Lucrece* contains a reference to descant: 'While thou on Tereus descants better **skill**' (1134). Lucrece is invoking **Philomela**, who was transformed into a **nightingale** after being raped by Tereus. The choice of the nightingale with its high-pitched voice is appropriate since here 'descant' means to sing the upper part with extempore skill.

See also **diapason**.

(C) Kenney, '"English Discant" and Discant in England' (1959); and 'The Theory of Discant' in *Walter Frye and the 'Contenance Angloise'* (1964).

diapason (A) Originating in Ancient Greek theory and continuing its usage in Medieval and Renaissance **music** treatises, the term was generally used to mean the distance or interval of an eighth or an octave between two **note**s. Because the diatonic scale was not yet in use in Elizabethan times, theorists defined the 'eight' as comprising five whole tones and two half tones, that is seven notes with the eighth being the same as the first but an octave higher (or lower). The eight was a 'perfect' interval or **concord**. 'Diapason' also came to denote the range of a **voice** or **instrument**, normally of a low octave, so that when Campion observes that an 'inner voice' will fill up 'the whole distance of the *Diapason*' (*Two Bookes of Ayres*, c.1613, 'To The Reader'), he means the range between the lower and upper voices.

The extra **bass string**s on the **lute** were sometimes called the

diapason

diapasons. A bass course could be added to the principal six courses (pairs of strings, except for the single top string). These bass strings are 'open' in that they run at the side of the fingerboard and cannot be 'stopped' at the **fret**s in order to **play** different pitches. When played they **sound** as a sort of **ground**.

(B) Shakespeare uses this word only once: he refers to the range or **compass** of the voice when he characterizes his diapason. Lucrece compares herself to **Philomela**, who was transformed into a **nightingale** after being raped by Tereus. Lucrece exhorts her to:

> Make thy sad grove in my dishevelled hair;
> As the dank earth weeps at thy **languishment**,
> So I at each sad **strain** will strain a tear,
> And with deep groans the diapason bear;
> For **burthen**-wise I'll **hum** on Tarquin still,
> While thou on Tereus **descant**s better **skill**.
> (*Luc* 1129–34)

Not only does Shakespeare imply a low voice at line 1131, he also suggests the voice acts as a kind of 'ground' on which the high descant is **perform**ed, as lines 1132–3 confirm. 'Groans' (Partridge, p. 149) and 'burthen' are suggestive of sexual intercourse as well as evoking the musical sphere.

(C) Partridge, *Shakespeare's Bawdy* (1968).

dildo see **fading**.

din (A) 'Din' is associated generally with **noise** and more specifically with **loud** cacophony. It does not have a specific musical usage but usually refers to unpleasant **discord**ant **sound**s, made by several **instrument**s or **sing**ers.

(B) 'Din' is mentioned in connection with the noise of martial instruments when Antony urges his **trumpet**ers as follows: 'With **brazen** din blast the city's **ear**, / Make mingle with our rattling **taborine**s'

(*Ant* 4.8.36–7). The powerful sound of the **brass** instrument is opposed to the more subdued sound of the taborines in the celebration of the victory against Caesar. Another possible reference to the sounding of instruments in battle is found in *Coriolanus*, where Cominius talks about the 'din of war' (2.2.115) piercing Coriolanus' **hear**ing.

This term is employed to achieve a different effect in *Pericles*. Gower, who acts as a **Chorus** figure, describes the celebrations held at Mytilene in honour of Pericles. He asks the audience to use their imagination:

> . . . You aptly will suppose
> What pageantry, what feats, what shows,
> What **minstrel**sy, and pretty din,
> The regent made in Metelin,
> To greet the King . . .
>
> (5.2.5–9)

The oxymoronic expression 'pretty din' may refer to **music** sung or **play**ed by the minstrels to entertain the guests at the festivities.

See also **alarum, bird, clamour, clang, ding-dong, drum**.

ding-dong see **burden**.

dirge (A) A Medieval English term, first used in the thirteenth century, to denote the Roman office for the dead. It derived from the first word of the opening antiphon of the Latin funeral liturgy, 'Dirige, Domine Deus meus, in conspectu tuo viam meam'. The term also took on a more general meaning and was used for any **song** or lament in the vernacular sung at a funeral, particularly the funeral procession or burial itself. Consequently, many dirges have a **doleful, march**-like tread. Among the best known is the anonymous fifteenth-century north country Lyke-wake dirge, set a number of times to music, famously in the twentieth century by Stravinsky in his Cantata (1952) and Britten in his Serenade (1943). Shakespeare's dirge for Fidele in *Cymbeline* ('Fear no more the heat of the sun' 4.2.258–81) has been set to music a number of times over the years, notably by Thomas Arne (c.1759), William Boyce (c.1746), Gerald Finzi (1929), Constant Lambert (1942), Hubert Parry (1906), Roger Quilter (1921), Ralph Vaughan Williams (c.1895) and in a jazz version by John Dankworth (1964).

dirge

Instrumental dirges or 'dead marches' were a convention in Elizabethan tragedy and often concluded these plays, as in Marston's *Antonio's Revenge* (1602) or the mock funeral march which ends his *Antonio and Mellida* (1602). The burial scene at the close of Thomas Kyd's *Spanish Tragedy* (1594) is accompanied by an **instrument**al dirge. A dead march brings the *Tragedy of Hamlet* to a close. Funeral **strain**s are heard at the burial of Martius at the end of *Coriolanus*. Dead marches are not employed by Shakespeare or his contemporaries when a character is sullied by crime. There are no dirges in *Macbeth*, *Othello* or *Troilus* for example, just as they are lacking in Chapman's tragedies *Bussy D'Ambois* (c.1604) and the *Revenge of Bussy D'Ambois* (c.1610).

(B) Shakespeare uses 'dirge' in its general sense as a **mournful** song or lamentation sung at a burial, for instance after Capulet discovers Juliet's apparent death on the day of her wedding to Paris:

> All things that we ordained festival,
> Turn from their office to black funeral:
> Our instruments to melancholy **bell**s,
> Our wedding cheer to a sad burial feast;
> Our **solemn hymn**s to sullen dirges **change**.
> (*Rom* 4.5.84–8)

Before Lucrece starts the account of her rape to her husband, Shakespeare likens her to a dying **swan**: 'And now this pale swan in her wat'ry nest / Begins the sad dirge of her certain ending' (*Luc* 1611–12). These lines confirm to the reader that Lucrece will soon commit suicide, and evoke the image of her imminent funeral, reinforced by the use of 'laments' later in the same stanza (1616). The expression 'wat'ry nest' (1611) is interesting: it alludes to Lucrece's tears of despair while obliquely hinting at the tears that will be shed for her after her death.

A direct connection between a funeral ceremony and the singing of dirges is also established in *The Two Noble Kinsmen*. On her way to meet Palamon, whom she has freed from prison, the Gaoler's daughter is worried that her illegal action may be discovered and that she may be sentenced to death. If the worst should happen, she hopes that 'Some honest-hearted maids, will sing my dirge, / And tell to memory my death was noble' (2.6.15–16).

dirge

Claudius explains why he has married Gertrude notwithstanding the sadness caused by the death of his brother:

> Therefore our sometime sister, now our queen,
> Th'imperial jointress to this warlike state,
> Have we, as 'twere with a defeated joy,
> With an auspicious, and a dropping eye,
> With mirth in funeral, and with dirge in marriage,
> In equal scale weighing delight and dole,
> Taken to wife . . .
> *(Ham* 1.2.8–14)

He is trying to convince his courtiers that his decision was taken after careful thinking and for the greater good of the state. The use of the oxymoronic expressions 'mirth in funeral' and 'dirge in marriage' is an interesting example of Claudius's rhetorical skills, which enable him to involve several people in his machinations.

See also **drum**.

(C) Surprisingly little has been written on dirges in plays. In one of the few sections, Sternfeld mentions dead marches and funeral music in *Music in Shakespearean Tragedy* (1967), ch. 1.

discant see **descant**.

discord (A) Both technically and conceptually 'discord' is the opposite to '**concord**' and is created by the **sound**ing together of certain intervals between two **note**s which seem **harsh** and unpleasing. Morley defines a discord as 'a mixt sound compact of divers sounds naturallie, offending the **ear**e, & therefore commonlie excluded from **music**ke' (*Introduction*, 1597, p. 71). The intervals which constitute discords are a second, a fourth, a seventh and their compounds or octaves. Not only do discords 'offend the ear', they are said to be '**jar**ring' and 'out of **tune**' (Cotgrave, 1611, 'Discord'). Their only redeeming feature seems to have been when they were judiciously and sparingly mixed with concords, bringing extra delight to the concords and introducing some

137

discord

variety to the soundscape. According to the rules of Renaissance counterpoint, they were to be used in an ordered and strictly controlled fashion, otherwise chaos and disagreement would ensue:

> Rest now, Amphion, rest thy **charm**ing lyre,
> For Daphne's love, **sweet** love, makes **melody**.
> Her love's concord with mine doth well conspire,
> No discord jars in our love's sympathy.
> Our concords have some discords mixed among;
> Discording concord makes the sweetest **song**.
> (Bennet, 1599, no. 17)

(B) Shakespeare sometimes puns on the musical meaning of 'discord' to elaborate on the idea of political unrest, for instance when Exeter soliloquizes about the internal strife afflicting the English aristocracy. He **laments** that there is 'jarring discord of nobility' (*1H6* 4.1.188) and foresees that 'when envy breeds unkind **division** / There comes the ruin, there begins confusion' (193–4). The musical colour of these lines is reinforced by 'jarring' and division, both commonly used in Renaissance music theory.

Concern about civil unrest is also at the heart of Ulysses' speech, which resorts extensively to musical metaphors. After speaking at length about the importance of **degree** (i.e. hierarchy) in society, he observes: 'Take but degree away, untune that **string**, / And hark what discord follows' (*Tro* 1.3.109–10). This is an effective 'analogy with the disruptions of social order with its hierarchical scale or "ladder"' (Wilson, p. 11): when the stringed instrument (possibly a **viol** or a **lute**) is out of tune, it distorts the stepwise movement of the scale. There is a second musical meaning in these lines, since 'the interpretation of tempo and rhythm was implicit in the hierarchical relationship of the longest and shortest notes' (ibid.) in Renaissance music, which did not rely on the metrical bar-line and numerical **time** signature.

The harshness and unpleasantness associated with discord also emerges in a context of sexual violation, when Lucrece laments that her 'restless discord loves no **stop**s nor **rest**s' (*Luc* 1124), and then warns the **bird**s to '**relish** your **nimble** notes to pleasing ears / Distress likes **dump**s when time is kept with tears' (1126–7).

On some occasions, a paradoxical effect is achieved when 'discord' is coupled with an adjective suggesting **harmony**, as in Hippolyta's

discord

comment about the barking of the hounds during a hunt: 'I never heard / so musical a discord, such sweet **thunder**' (*MND* 4.1.117–18). Similarly, the contrast between concord and discord can result in an oxymoron: when Helen imagines Bertram's amorous adventures at the court of France she argues in the conventional paradoxical **mode** of Renaissance love poetry that 'His jarring [will have] concord, and his discord **dulcet**' (*AWW* 1.1.172).

In another amorous situation, Venus explains to Adonis why she is attracted to him. She wishes that she could feel otherwise, and explains that to her his **voice** is like a 'melodious discord, heavenly tune harsh sounding, / Ear's deep sweet music, and heart's deep sore wounding' (*Ven* 431–2). These oxymoronic lines betray the intensity of Venus' passion and her intuition that it will cause her bereavement – the 'deep sore wounding' anticipates Adonis' death resulting from the wound inflicted on him by a boar.

(C) Wilson, C. R., 'Shakespeare's "Fair Viols, Sweet Lutes, and Rude Pipes"' (1998), discusses the opposition between stringed and wind instruments in the imagery adopted by Shakespeare and contextualizes it within the theoretical landscape of English Renaissance music.

ditty (A) The term 'ditty', frequently used in Elizabethan **time**s, can simply mean the words of a **song** or **ayre**, or more specifically a song in which the rhyme or poem has been **composed** with a musical setting in mind, in some cases to fit a pre-existent **tune**. There are many examples of the latter so-called 'parody' or contrafactum technique, in the Elizabethan period, ranging from a number of poems in Sir Philip Sidney's *Certain Sonnets* (c.1577–82; print 1598) to a variety of popular songs. Indeed some of the songs in Shakespeare's plays may themselves have been written in this way to fit tunes that the actors would already know. The term is used to mean both a light-hearted song or poem and a sad one. When the latter, it is often coupled with 'doleful' as in:

> Lend your **ear**s to my sorrow . . .
> For no eyes will I borrow,
> Mine own shall **grace** my **doleful** ditty . . .
> **Chant** then, my **voice**.
> (Dowland, 1603, no.11)

ditty

'Ditty' may also be used as a verb. Morley (*Introduction*, 1597) discusses ways in which words and **music** may be coupled together in his 'Rules to be observed in dittying' (ibid., p. 177). Here he does not employ 'ditty' in its strict parodical sense but rather as a way of setting words to appropriate music: 'you shall have a perfect agreement, and as it were a harmonicall **consent** betwixt the matter and the musicke' (ibid., p. 178).

(B) In the Shakespeare canon, this term is only used as a noun. Ariel's song 'Full fathom five' convinces Ferdinand that his father died in the shipwreck. At the end of the song, he comments:

> The ditty does remember my drown'd father.
> This is no mortal business, nor no **sound**
> That the earth owes. I **hear** it now above me.
> (*Tmp* 1.2.406–8)

Here 'ditty' refers to the words of the song. This term contributes to the alliterative pattern of the line. The concluding sentence of this speech ('I hear it now above me') reveals that Ferdinand, to whom Ariel is invisible, thinks that the song has a supernatural quality comparable to that of the music of the spheres (*musica mundana*). On a metatheatrical level, it is possible that this line alludes to the gallery above the stage of Elizabethan and Jacobean playhouses, sometimes used by **musician**s while **perform**ing (Lindley, p. 123).

The same meaning of 'ditty' is observed in two other Shakespeare plays. The celebratory mood characterising the end of *A Midsummer's Night's Dream* is reinforced by Oberon's exhortation to Titania and the fairies: 'And this ditty, after me, / Sing, and **dance** it trippingly' (5.1.395–6). In *As You Like It*, there is a clear distinction between the musical setting and the words of a song when Touchstone criticizes 'It was a lover and his lass' by observing that 'there was no great matter in the ditty' and that 'the **note** was very untuneable' (5.3.35–6).

There are occasions when 'ditty' is synonymous with 'song'. For instance, the song 'Sigh no more ladies, sigh no more' exhorts women to 'Sing no more of ditties, sing no moe [sic], / Of **dump**s so **dull** and heavy' (*Ado* 2.3.70–1). In *Venus and Adonis*, the goddess is rejected by Adonis and sings about the grief accompanying love: 'She . . . begins a wailing note, / And sings **extemporally** a **woeful** ditty' (835–6).

ditty

'Ditty' can be used to describe songs of **bird**s (*OED*, 2). This nuance of meaning is found in *The Passionate Pilgrim*, where the poet observes that the atmosphere of happiness surrounding him is spoilt by the **nightingale**'s sorrowful singing:

> She, poor bird, as all forlorn,
> Lean'd her **breast** up-till a thorn,
> And there sung the dolefull'st ditty,
> That to **hear** it was great pity.
> (20.9–12)

In another poem belonging to the same collection, the nightingale's singing is described as follows:

> While **Philomela** sits and sings, I sit and mark,
> And wish her **lay**s were tuned like the **lark**.
> For she doth welcome daylight with her ditty,
> And drives away dark dreaming night.
> (14.17–20)

The allusion to the myth of Philomela, who was transformed into a nightingale after being raped and having her **tongue** cut out, gives the word 'ditty' a sad and melancholic nuance.

(C) Alexander, 'The Elizabethan Lyric as Contrafactum' (2003), focuses on the writing of new lyrics to existing tunes.
Lindley, *The Tempest* (2002).

division (A) In the sixteenth and well into the seventeenth century, division was the practice of breaking up a line of long **note**s (especially a *cantus firmus* or '**ground**') into much shorter florid movement. It was a particular kind of embellishment containing a significant element of improvisation or **extempore**. Its origins lay in the vocal polyphony and **music** treatises of sixteenth-century Italy.

No treatises on divisions of the Italian kind appear to have been compiled in sixteenth-century England, but references in scattered printed sources attest to the practice of making or 'adding' divisions. In 1591 it was recorded that the 'Dittie of *Come againe* was sung,

division

with excellent division, by two, that were cunning' (*The Honourable Entertainment given to the Queenes Maiestie in Progresse, at Elvetham in Hampshire, by the right Honorable the Earle of Hertford*, fol. E2v). Christopher Marlowe alludes to the rapidity of the notes in divisions in 'That kisse againe / she runs divisions of my lips' (*Jew of Malta*, c.1592, H2v). In a poem ascribed to Walter Raleigh, the jocular effect of the quick movement is alluded to: 'What is our life? A play of passion. / Our mirth the music of division' (Gibbons, 1612, no. 14). Tobias Hume included a **galliard** with divisions for **bass viol** in his *The First Part of Ayres* (1605). William Corkine provided examples of division for lyra viol in his *Second Books of Ayres* (1612). Thomas Campion noted that a '**Song** was sung by an excellent counter-tenor **voice**, with rare varietie of division' in his *Entertainment . . . at Cawsome-House neere Redding* (1613).

Within a few years, division **play**ing developed into an accomplished art of its own so that by 1650 a special **instrument**, the division viol, was made especially for the idiom. In 1659, Christopher Simpson codified the principles in his *The Division Violist: or An Introduction to the Playing upon a Ground*. He separated division-playing into three main categories: ornamenting the ground (bass); extemporising a **melody** (i.e. **descant**) above the ground in quick notes; and mixing the bass and descant techniques so that it 'presents unto our **Ear**es, the Sounds of Two, or more **Part**s moving together'. Simpson states in his preface that the first two techniques are applicable to any suitable instrument and not just the viol. Mixed division is more apt for the viol.

(B) The reference to division in *1 Henry IV* is reasonably straightforward. It occurs in a remark on the beauty of Glendower's daughter's Welsh speaking which adds ornament to the simple expression of her looks and gestures:

>   . . . thy **tongue**
> Makes Welsh as **sweet** as ditties highly penn'd,
> Sung by a fair queen in a summer's bow'r,
> With **ravish**ing division, to her **lute**.
>   (3.1.205–8)

It is possible that a lute would have accompanied the song sung later in the same scene by Glendower's daughter, as indicated by the stage direction '*Here the lady **sing**s a Welsh song*' (3.1.244.SD).

division

When Romeo (who has been sentenced to banishment) departs for Mantua, Juliet protests that:

> It is the **lark** that sings so out of **tune**,
> Straining **harsh discord**s and unpleasing **sharp**s.
> Some say the lark makes sweet division;
> This doth not so, for she divideth us.
> (*Rom* 3.5.27–30)

The concept of a **voice perform**ing division is strange until we remember that it is the lark which sings the quick notes. 'Division' is an appropriate polysemic choice in a context where separation is about to happen. The idea that Elizabethan **bird**s were accomplished in the art of division is suggested in Robert Nichol's description of the preparations made by the **Nightingale** for her singing contest with the **Cuckoo**:

> The little **Philomel** with curious care,
> Sitting alone her ditties did prepare,
> And many tunes . . .
> Dividing sweetly in division
> Now some sweet **strain**e to mind she doth restore.
> (*The Cuckow*, London, 1607, p. 12)

When Malcolm claims that he does not deserve to become king since his personality is tainted by serious weaknesses (in fact, he is just testing Macduff's loyalty), he says:

> The king-becoming **grace**s . . .
> I have no **relish** of them, but abound
> In the division of each several crime,
> Acting it many ways. Nay, had I pow'r, I should
> Pour the sweet milk of **concord** into hell.
> (*Mac* 4.3.91; 95–8)

This speech is built on a complex musical image: 'graces' is first used in the sense of moral qualities but suggests musical reference (meaning 'ornament') when 'division' is employed for the alleged horrid variations in Malcolm's crimes, which in turn suggests concord in the sense of political peace but with hinted musical overtones.

143

division

(C) Brown, H. M., *Embellishing Sixteenth-century Music* (1976).
Cyr, 'A 17th-century Source of Ornamentation for Voice and Viol: British Museum MS Egerton 2971' (1971).
Duckles, 'Florid Embellishment in English Song of the Late 16th and Early 17th Centuries' (1957).
Jones, E., *The Performance of English Song* (1989).
Poulton, 'Graces of Play in Renaissance Lute Music' (1975).
Simpson, C., *The Division-violist* (1659).
Till, 'Ornamentation in English Song manuscripts, 1620–1660' (1975).
Toft, *'Tune thy Musicke to thy Hart'* (1993), pp. 85–99.

doleful (A) Perhaps the best-known allusion to 'doleful' in an Elizabethan musical context is the application by Dowland to one of the **pavan**s in the second **part** of his *Lachrimae* (1604) with the title 'Semper Dowland semper dolens', attesting to the composer's assumed emotional persona of sadness and melancholy. This sorrowful disposition may have originated in his failure to secure a post at the English court in 1594 and for many years afterwards, despite being the most famous **lute**nist in Europe.

'Doleful' in **music** refers to slow-moving minor-**key piece**s whose melodies usually involve falling 'dying' movement (such as Dowland's famous 'Flow my teares') invoking melancholy.

(B) This adjective is sometimes used by Shakespeare to qualify musical terms with a generic meaning, i.e. without emotional bias. For instance, Autolycus claims that he sells **ballad**s for all tastes, including 'one to a very doleful **tune**' (*WT* 4.4.262). The dying King John is likened to a **swan** singing 'a doleful **hymn** to his own death' (*Jn* 5.7.22) when his end is approaching. '**Ditty**' can be used to describe **song**s of **bird**s (*OED*, 2). In *The Passionate Pilgrim* the poet argues that that the **nightingale**'s sorrowful song has a negative influence on the otherwise joyful atmosphere around him:

> She, poor bird, as all forlorn,
> Lean'd her breast up-till a thorn,
> And there sung the dolefull'st ditty,
> That to **hear** it was great pity.
> (20.9–12)

doleful

On other occasions, 'doleful' aims to emphasize musical words with a specific sad connotation. 'Doleful **dump**s the mind oppress' (*Rom* 4.5.127) according to Peter, who is quoting freely from a poem in *The Paradise of Dainty Devices* (1576) (Duffin, p. 443). Lucrece's sorrow after she has been raped is compared to a **bell** ringing a 'doleful **knell**' (*Luc* 1495).

See also **ayre**.

(C) Duffin, *Shakespeare's Songbook* (2004).
Holman (ed.), *Dowland: Lachrimae (1604)* (1999), pp. 36–60 and 63–5, analyses Dowland's melancholy.
Poulton, *John Dowland* (1982), p. 78, on the same topic as Holman.
Wells, *Elizabethan Mythologies* (1994).

drone (A) The continuous **sound** produced by the **bass pipe** or pipes of the **bagpipe**, as in:

> And when the bagpipes **play**
> For this the merry day,
> Then comes in little Joan
> And bids **strike** up the drone.
> (Peerson, 1620, no. 10)

When two or more **note**s form the drone they make an open sound usually based on intervals of fourths and fifths. A notated example of this can be found in 'The bagpipe and the drone' from Byrd's famous keyboard piece *The Battell* (MLNB, no. 4). As a recurring feature in a **piece**, the drone can also act as a **ground** or **burden**.

(B) This word is used in its musical meaning only once in the Shakespeare canon, when Falstaff says that he feels as melancholy as 'the drone of a Lincolnshire bagpipe' (*1H4* 1.2.76) (see 'bagpipe' for a commentary of this passage). The static ground and the simple repetitive sound would suggest boredom or frustration as well as sadness.

drum (A) The drum is one of the most widespread **instrument**s of world **music**s and also one of the most ancient. Drums vary

drum

immensely in shape and size but essentially contain two elements, a 'skin' stretched tightly over a body-shell of wood, metal, pot or bone. The body-shell acts as the resonator and the skin is the **sound** originator. In the West, drums are normally sounded by being **beat**en with the hands or with sticks. They are classified according to the shape and size of their body-shells. Kettledrums are so called because of the bowl shape of their body-shell. A second more varied category are the tubular drums.

During the fifteenth century, larger kettledrums (generally in pairs) began to appear in military contexts in western Europe, in particular with the cavalry and often associated with **trumpet**s. The idea was taken over from Turkish army practice. The use of smaller drums in military circles also came from the East, encountered during the thirteenth-century crusades. The military side-drum or large **tabor** was often associated with the **fife** and connected with the infantry. Unlike the tabor, the side-drum was **play**ed with two sticks. The side-drum was also known to the navy, being used for action calls, burials, on-board punishment and internal ship signals. Drake's drum of 1596 reportedly survives, preserved at Buckland Abbey, Devon. Very little military drum music of the sixteenth century was notated but rhythms for various **dance**s are given in Arbeau (*Orchesography*, 1589). Elizabethan drummers were known as 'drumsleds' or drum-beaters.

(B) In the plays of Shakespeare's day, drums were often played in conjunction with trumpets on ceremonial occasions and in military contexts. It is not surprising that the drum, the quintessential military instrument, is mentioned in numerous explicit and implicit stage directions for battles and **march**es. By extension, the drum is used in several martial metaphors. 'The drum, rather curiously in view of modern standards, was a more precise as well as a more connotative military instrument than the trumpet' (Jorgensen, p. 24).

This point is further supported by the instructions for drummers to enter accompanying an army, or for 'drum(s) and colour(s)' 'drum and ensign' (these two expressions clearly refer to the people carrying the props on stage): the build-up to a military clash and/or its outcome would be signified by this effective theatrical metonymy, which worked both on the aural and on the visual level. In *3 Henry VI*, Montgomery is instructed to enter before the city of York '*with Drum and Soldiers*' (4.7.39.SD) and later exhorts his followers thus: 'Drummer, **strike** up,

drum

and let us **march** away' (4.7.50). This is the only instance in the whole Shakespeare canon that the word 'drummer' is used.

One of the most effective uses of drums and colours is observed in Folio *King Lear*. The preparations for the battle between the French and the British armies are made clear to the audience when, at the beginning of 4.4, we have the direction '*Enter, with Drum and Colors, Cordelia, and soldiers*'. A messenger tells Cordelia that 'the British pow'rs are marching hitherward' (4.4.21); '*drum afar off*' (4.6.283) reminds the audience of the imminent battle. In the theatrical jargon, 'afar off' would have worked as an instruction to beat the drums from behind the tiring-house (see Introduction).

After the touching reconciliation between Lear and Cordelia, the two enemy armies are ready for the fight. Act 5, scene 1 begins with the entry of the British faction: '*Enter, with Drum and Colors, Edmund, Regan, Gentlemen, and Soldiers*' (5.1.OSD). Similarly, the French army enters '*with Drum and Colours*' (5.2.OSD). The battle itself is not displayed on stage – in a stroke of dramatic genius, Shakespeare makes his audience witness it from the perspective of the blind Gloucester: '***Alarum** and **retreat** within*' (5.2.4.SD). Edgar informs his father of the outcome, and then we have: '*Enter in conquest, with Drum and Colors, Edmund, Lear and Cordelia as prisoners, soldiers, captain*' (5.3.OSD). The drum plays a fundamental role in this sequence of brief eventful scenes.

As has been discussed, drums are mostly played in conjunction with trumpets in martial contexts. However, there are occasions when fifes are used, as in: '*Enter Alcibiades, with Drum and Fife, in warlike manner, and Phrynia and Timandra*' (*Tim* 4.3.48.SD). '*Drum within*' (which, as in 'afar off' would have implied the beating of the instrument offstage) in *Macbeth* 1.3.29, informs the witches of the imminent entry of Macbeth and Banquo, as is clear from the ensuing lines spoken by the Third Witch: 'A drum! A drum! / Macbeth doth come' (30–1).

Military and dead marches were usually accompanied by drums. The former often have an 'informative quality' (Shirley, p. 68), i.e. they would be associated with specific countries. A frequently quoted example is taken from *1 Henry VI*: '*Here sound an English march*' (3.3.30.SD), followed by a '*French march*' two lines later. Another important instance is the '*Danish March*' mentioned in Folio *Hamlet*, which accompanies the entry of Claudius, Gertrude and their followers before they watch the 'mousetrap' put on by itinerant actors. Folio is the only version to specify that a march be sounded; whereas Q1 (1603) simply indicates the

drum

entry of these characters, the direction in Q2 (1604/5) reads: '*Enter Trumpets and Kettle Drummes, King, Queene, Polonius, Ophelia*' (Q2, G4v). It is therefore possible that the stage direction in Folio for the Danish march would employ kettledrums.

Dead marches would be played on muffled drums, for instance when Salisbury's funeral is accompanied by '*Drums beating a dead march*' (*1H6* 2.2.OSD). Aufidius's speech at the end of *Coriolanus* contains precise instructions about how the drum should be played during a funeral. He exhorts the onstage drummer in the following terms: 'beat thou the drum, that it speak **mournful**ly' (5.6.149). The play concludes with a stage direction indicating '*A dead march sounded*' (5.6.153.SD).

Outside the display of martial events as such, the connection between different instruments and different **mood**s is clear, for instance when Benedick disparages Claudio's love for Hero in a soliloquy:

> ... I have known when
> there was no music with him but the drum and the
> fife, and now had he rather hear the tabor and the **pipe**.
> (*Ado* 2.3.12–14)

The drum and fife, used in the battlefield, are now less important to Claudio than the tabor and pipe which accompanied singing and dancing and, by implication, were associated with recreational or social activities.

When Armado confesses to Moth his love for Jaquenetta, he renounces martial values in favour of poetry:

> Adieu, valor, rust, rapier, be still,
> drum, for your manager is in love; yeah, he loveth.
> Assist me, some extemporal god of **rhyme**, for I am
> sure I shall turn sonnet.
> (*LLL* 1.2.181–4)

That love and war are considered to be mutually exclusive is clear also from a passage in *All's Well That Ends Well*, a play which makes ample use of drums both in metaphors and in stage business. Bertram, who has just been appointed general of the Duke of Florence's cavalry, exclaims:

> This very day,
> Great Mars, I put myself into thy file;
> Make me but like my thoughts, and I shall prove
> A lover of thy drum, hater of love.
> (3.3.8–11)

Military valour symbolized by the drum is inseparable from virility in the mind of some Shakespearean characters. For instance, when Coriolanus is convinced by his mother not to express his dislike of the plebeians in order to appease their anger, he reluctantly accepts:

> ... Well, I must do't.
> Away, my disposition, and possess me
> Some harlot's spirit! My **throat** of war be turn'd,
> Which **quier**'d with my drum, into a pipe
> Small as an **eunuch**, or the virgin **voice**
> That babies lull asleep! ...
> (*Cor* 3.2.110–15)

To the soldier Coriolanus, this compromise amounts to emasculation. In the following scene he cannot bring himself to accept it and, after speaking his mind, he is banished.

Hamlet is the only Shakespeare play to make reference to the kettledrum. This has led a number of scholars (for instance Jenkins) wrongly to infer that the kettledrum is a characteristically Danish instrument. Kettledrums and trumpets accompany the celebrations ordered by Claudius in honour of Hamlet (1.4.11). These are heard by Hamlet on the night when his father's ghost appears to him. This celebratory sound effect provides a stark contrast to the gloomy account given by King Hamlet's ghost about the circumstances surrounding his death. In Q2 (G4v) the staging of the 'mousetrap' is underlined by a stage direction for kettledrums: '*Enter Trumpets and Kettledrums and sound a* **flourish**'. Towards the end of the play, the signal to start the fencing bout between Hamlet and Laertes is given by Claudius when he orders: 'And let the kettle to the trumpet speak, / The trumpet to the cannoneer without' (5.2.275–6). Once again, the kettledrum introduces a seemingly festive occasion which turns into a tragedy.

(C) Jenkins, *Hamlet* (1982).

drum

Jorgensen, *Shakespeare's Military World* (1956).
Shirley, *Shakespeare's Use of Off-Stage Sounds* (1963).

drummer see **drum**.

dulcet (A) Derived from the French 'doucet', 'dulcet' describes the **sweet** and delicate **sound**s of **music**, which can have a pleasant soothing effect upon the senses.

(B) This effect is well described by Oberon who once

> ... sat upon a promontory,
> And heard a mermaid on a dolphin's back
> Uttering such dulcet and harmonious **breath**
> That the rude sea grew civil at her **song**.
> (*MND* 2.1.149–52)

The impact that the mermaid's vocal music has is so significant that it can control one of the wildest forces of nature. Its quality is supernatural. This attribute is also emphasized in the Induction to *The Taming of the Shrew*, when the lord explains to his followers how to treat Christopher Sly:

> Carry him gently to my fairest chamber ...
> Balm his foul head in warm distilled waters ...
> Procure me music ready when he wakes,
> To make a dulcet and a heavenly sound.
> (Ind.i.46; 48; 50–1)

The sounding of **pleasant** and heavenly music, while creating the illusion in Sly that he is the lord of the house, also works as a metatheatrical reminder to the audience that a trick (framed by music) is being played on the drunken Sly.

Portia orders that music be **play**ed while Bassanio is choosing between the three caskets. If he makes the right choice, then music will be to her:

> As are those dulcet sounds in break of day
> That creep into the dreaming bridegroom's **ear**,
> And summon him to marriage.
>
> (*MV* 3.2.51–3)

Portia's wish that Bassanio be successful prompts the conceit of an imminent wedding celebration with the music accompanying such a festive occasion.

Helen comments on Bertram's possible love encounters at the French court with a musical metaphor: 'His **jar**ring [will have] **concord**, and his **discord** dulcet' (*AWW* 1.1.172). These paradoxical combinations of terms are in line with Helen's feeling of anxiety about her future with Bertram.

See also **harmony**.

dull (A) Rarely used in a musical context, 'dull' evokes a sense of despair and sadness, as in:

> Out from the vale of deep despair
> With **mournful tune**s I fill the air,
> To satisfy my restless ghost,
> Which Daphne's cruelty hath lost.
> O'er hills and dales in her dull **ear**s
> I'll send my **note**s with bitter tears.
>
> (Ward, 1613, no. 21)

(B) In Balthasar's song 'Sigh no more ladies, sigh no more', which urges women not to indulge in the melancholic and sad feelings caused by men's inconstancy, **dump**s are described as 'dull and heavy' (*Ado* 2.3.71).

A sick King Henry IV orders that soothing **music** be **play**ed:

> Let there be no **noise** made, my gentle friends,
> Unless some dull and favourable hand
> Will whisper music to my weary spirit.
>
> (*2H4* 4.5.1–3)

The hands that **touch** the musical **instrument**s, probably **viol**s, make

dull

dull music: to accompany the King's death, they 'whisper' **soft** music rather than play loudly.

A connotation of absence of **sound** is implied when Lorenzo uses this adjective in a speech expounding the importance of music. He explains to Jessica that a man who is not touched by **harmony** is deceitful:

> The man that hath no music in himself,
> Nor is not moved with **concord** of **sweet** sounds,
> Is fit for treasons, stratagems, and spoils;
> The motions of his spirit are dull as night.
> (*MV* 5.1.83–6)

A lack of response to the sweetness of music can only result in a dull disharmonious spirit.

In *Troilus and Cressida*, Aeneas orders a **parley** to be sounded in order to summon the Greeks and then explains to the Greek general:

> We have, great Agamemnon, here in Troy
> A prince call'd Hector...
> Who in this dull and long-continued truce
> Is resty grown. He bade me take a **trumpet**,
> And to his purpose **speak**...
> (1.3.260–4)

The dull quality of the truce, characterized by the absence of martial sounds, has been interrupted by the '**brass voice**' (258) of the trumpet sounding the parley.

In *Sonnet* 102, the poet claims that he loves his friend even though he does not express his feelings openly. Whilst in the past he **compose**d **lay**s to praise his friend, he now prefers to 'hold my **tongue** / Because I would not dull you with my **song**' (13–14). The verb 'dull' here can mean either 'bore you' or 'represent you in a **tedious** manner in my verse' (Duncan-Jones, p. 102), but it also reinforces the musical theme of the sonnet (terms such as 'sing', '**stop**s', '**pipe**s', 'music' and '**burden**' appear in the previous lines). There is possibly an oblique reference to an understated musical performance.

(C) Duncan-Jones, *Shakespeare's Sonnets* (1997).

dump (A) It is uncertain exactly what a dump was in **music**. In early modern English literary contexts, it had sad melancholic connotations indicating a distressed mind or perplexed psyche. 'To be in the dumps' meant that one felt dejected. Musical dumps were variously referred to as **doleful, mournful, solemn** and **still**. Except for the earliest surviving example, 'My Lady Careys Dompe' (MB, 66, no. 37), dumps were not particularly melancholic. Some twentieth-century commentators have argued that the dump was either a **song** form, **dance** form or **instrument**al variation form. But there is no evidence to support this kind of categorisation. In his seminal article, John Ward (p. 120) contends that the English musical dump was the equivalent of the '*deploracion*' or '*tombeau*', that is commemorative music for a deceased person. In other words, the dump is a funeral song or musical lamentation without a specific musical form. In his Latin–English dictionary (1587), Thomas simply includes dump under '*Cantus*' to mean song, **melody** or **tune**.

Of the 20 dumps which survive in English manuscript sources c.1530 to 1620, the majority are for solo **lute** and the remainder for keyboard. Dumps for ensemble or **consort** are not found but references to consort dumps are found in plays, for example *Fedele and Fortunio* (c.1576–84), 3.2. '*The third Act being doone, the Consort* **sound**s *a sollemne Dump*' (cited in Ward, p. 119 fn. 29).

(B) Proteus advises Thurio to woo Silvia with music:

> Visit by night your lady's chamber-window
> With some **sweet** consort; to their instruments
> Tune a deploring dump – the night's dead silence
> Will well become such sweet-complaining grievance.
> (*TGV* 3.2.82–5)

Through this piece of music, the consort of skilled professional **musician**s (as is clear from line 91) will convey Thurio's melancholy, which is an essential element of his love for Silvia. The use of 'deploring' here suggests the hypothesis (put forward by Ward) that 'dump' is connected with the French '*déploration*'.

Balthasar's song 'Sigh no more ladies, sigh no more' exhorts women to give up their sadness at men's inconstancy: '**Sing** no more ditties, sing no moe [sic], / Of dumps so **dull** and **heavy**' (*Ado* 2.3.70–1).

dump

Once again, the melancholic and heavy-hearted quality of the dump is stressed, as it is in Lucrece's invective against the joyful **bird**s after she has been raped: '**Relish** your **nimble note**s to pleasing **ear**s, / Distress likes dumps when **time** is kept with tears' (*Luc* 1126–7).

While these lines evoke a sombre tone, the use of 'dump' in *Romeo and Juliet* achieves the opposite effect. The context is serious but the arrival of the musicians (who have just been dismissed after the apparent death of Juliet on her wedding day, betrothed to Paris) provides comic relief. Peter requests that the musicians **play** 'some merry dump' (4.5.108). Dumps are anything but 'merry', hence this 'sudden comic incongruity' (Evans, p. 174) encapsulates the spirit of the concluding part of the scene. It provides a perspective on death in opposition to that offered at the end of the play.

(C) Evans, *Romeo and Juliet* (2003).

Sternfeld, *Music in Shakespearean Tragedy* (1967), includes a short section on 'dump' (pp. 254–5) in which he emphasizes the mournful overtones of the form, and elsewhere (pp. 102–5) includes a discussion of the ironically 'merry dump' in *Romeo and Juliet*.

Thomas, *Dictionarium Linguae Latinae et Anglicanae* (1587), gives a definition under '*Cantus*'.

Ward, 'The "Dolfull Domps" ' (1951), lists (pp. 112–13) fifteen dumps from sources ranging from the early Tudor manuscript BL Royal App.58 to the early-seventeenth-century FWVB.

E

ear (A) In relation to **music** the ear is the vital physical attribute which enables a person to **hear** the **sound**s of music. It is the part of the body which allows other parts to be affected by music. As John Dowland put it: 'Lend ears and tears to me, most hapless man, / That **sing**s my sorrows like the dying **swan**' (1597, no. 14). The word may also be used metaphorically to signify that a person who has a 'good ear' is especially receptive to music or gifted in musical utterance.

In *The Anatomy of Melancholy* (1621), Robert Burton describes the sense of hearing in the following terms:

> *Hearing*, a most excellent outward sense, *by which we learn and get knowledge*. His object is sound, or that which is heard; the *medium*, air; the *organ* the ear. To the sound, which is a collision of the air, three things are required: a body to **strike**, as the hand of a **musician**; the body strucken, which must be solid and able to resist, as a **bell**, **lute-string**, not wool, or sponge; the *medium*, the air, which is *inward*, or *outward*.
> (Dell and Jordan-Smith, p. 138)

The importance of auditory reception and perception in comparison to visual was more significant in Shakespeare's theatre than many modern commentators have allowed. The soundscape of the early modern English theatre in its contemporary acoustical environment is vital to an understanding of the impact and meaning of a play. According to Bruce Smith, 'We need a cultural poetics of listening. We must take into

ear

account, finally, the subjective experience of sound. We need a phenomenology of listening' (Smith, p. 8). To this end, we need to be more aware of how Shakespeare used both the concept of hearing and actual sound, and how his audiences reacted to sound and hearing. As Wes Folkerth explains, we need to realize 'Shakespeare's close association of sound with the deeply subjective self [so-called "interiority"]' (p. 10) and the 'cultural contexts of the Shakespeare soundscape'. In particular, this would apply to music and the signification of the ear as both anatomical receiver and perceptual organ associated with 'notions of obedience, duty, receptivity, penetrability, transformation, and reproduction' (ibid.).

(B) Of the many occurrences of 'ear' in Shakespeare, a good handful – some 29 – use the word with reference to the ear receiving and being affected in various ways by the sound of music. Music of many kinds and force enter through the ear, for instance in a military context in *Antony and Cleopatra*. A metonymical transposition is implied by Antony when he orders the **trumpet**ers that they 'blast . . . the city's ear' (4.8.36) when sounding their instruments to celebrate his victory against Caesar.

Earlier in the same play, reference is made to music affecting the ears during the feast on board Pompey's galley. Enobarbus invites his revelling companions to join him in a **song** and **dance**:

> All take hands.
> Make battery to our ears with **loud** music;
> The while I'll place you, then the boy shall sing.
> The **holding** every man shall bear as loud
> As his strong sides can volley.
> (2.7.108–12)

The boy is expected to sing the main part of 'Come, thou monarch of the vine', while the men will sing the undersong as powerfully as they can.

The sounds of music 'creep in our ears' (*MV* 5.1.56) according to Lorenzo who is expounding the power of music to Jessica. Only a few lines after this comment, Lorenzo wishes that the musicians 'with **sweet**est **touch**es pierce [Portia's] ear / And draw her home with music' (5.1.67–8). In *The Two Gentlemen of Verona*, Proteus hopes that Silvia's feelings will be affected by hearing the song in her honour, when he and Thurio 'give some evening music to her ear' (4.2.17).

The pleasant effect that music has on the sense of hearing is emphasized by Timon when he exhorts his guests to 'feast your ears with the music' (*Tim* 3.6.33) accompanying the banquet. Marcus' horror at Lavinia's mutilation is articulated through a musical metaphor, in which her **tongue** is likened to 'a sweet **melodious bird** [which] sung / Sweet varied **note**s, **enchant**ing every ear' (*Tit* 3.1.85–6) but can no longer be heard. The melodious quality of a bird's singing is also noted by Helena, according to whom Hermia's voice is 'more **tune**able than **lark** to shepherd's ear' (*MND* 1.1.184).

The ear can also receive musically seductive and hostile messages, for instance when the mermaid entices the ear of those who listen to her song (*Luc* 1411). The same conceit is found when Antypholus of Syracuse vows that he will not give in to his attraction for Luciana: 'I'll stop mine ears against the mermaid's song' (*Err* 3.2.164). Laertes warns his sister Ophelia not to give in easily to Hamlet's advances, since it can be detrimental if she 'with too credent ear . . . list[s] his songs' (*Ham* 1.3.30).

'Ear' is infrequently used in the sense of a 'good ear', an ability to understand and appreciate music, but it does occur in *Cymbeline* when Imogen is advised to offer her services to Caius Lucius under the assumed identity of a page. Lucius will take her into his service 'if that his head have ear in music' (3.4.175), since Imogen has a musical voice. In one instance 'ear' is used comically when Bottom, who has no talent for music, tells Titania 'I have a reasonable good ear in music' (*MND* 4.1.28), and calls for the most unmusical of **instrument**s: 'Let's have the **tongs and bones**' (29). Bottom's high opinion of himself as a good musician and singer may be derived from Titania's exhortation to him in an earlier scene: 'I pray thee, gentle mortal, sing again. / Mine ear is much enamoured of thy note' (3.1.137–8). Titania's flattering comment occurs after Oberon's spell has led her to fall in love with Bottom, which reveals how deceived she is in her judgement – in the same speech she compliments the ass-headed Bottom on his good looks.

The sense of 'ability to understand music' also appears in a passage exposing the loutish character of Cloten in *Cymbeline*. Double entendres on 'penetrate' and '**fingering**' occur as he instructs the musicians to serenade Imogen, and dismisses them with 'If this penetrate I will / consider your music the better. If it do not, it is a / vice in her ears' (*Cym* 2.3.27–9).

ear

(C) Dell and Jordan-Smith (eds), *The Anatomy of Melancholy* (1938).

Folkerth, *The Sound of Shakespeare* (2002), is an absorbing study which deals with the effect sound and hearing had on Shakespeare's audiences and the ways in which Shakespeare's plays relate to the soundscape of Elizabethan England. The function of Bottom's 'grotesque ear' is discussed on pp. 91–102.

Smith, *The Acoustic World of Early Modern England* (1999).

echo (A) As a term, 'echo' has both a literal and a figurative meaning. It can refer to the audible reverberations made by an **instrument** or **voice**. Or, in the particular acoustic world of Elizabethan England, it implies more than mere sonic repetition. It conjures up a magical world, a specialness where nature itself, hills, woods and dales, are capable of reverberating man's thoughts and emotions. The fantastical world of fairies and spirits is invoked in:

> Come, let's begin to revel't out
> And tread the hills and dales about,
> That hills and dales and woods may **sound**
> An echo to this warbling **round**.
> (Weelkes, 1608, no. 1)

Birds and other animals create echoes, especially in deep woods:

> In the merry month of May
> The fields are decked with flowers gay. **Fa** la.
> The woods and groves, where birds do **sing**,
> Redoubling echoes, **sweet**ly **ring**. Fa la.
> (Youll, 1608, no. 19)

Voices and instruments combine in Campion's:

> **Sing** we then secure,
> Tuning well our **string**s,
> With voice as echo pure,
> Let us renown the King of kings.
> (c.1613, no. 15)

Campion's reference to the 'echo pure' is interesting, alluding to the quality of the repetition which is dependent on the context and acoustic source (voice or instrument), ranging, for example, from a deep wood, a cavernous church, a steep hillside and so on. Not surprisingly, the mythological figure, 'Echo', invariably inhabits a cave or dark grove.

Even the role of the preacher was seen in early modern England as that of an echo of the Word of God. As John Donne remarked in a sermon of 1625: 'The Scriptures are Gods Voyce; The Church is his Eccho; a redoubling, a repeating of some particular syllables, and **accent**s of the same voice' (quoted in Smith, p. 263).

The use of echo, both as a musical device and aural signification, was an important attribute in Renaissance theatrical production. Sixteenth-century French and Italian dramatic settings and early opera exploit echo as do English courtly **masque**s. Of its symbolic associations, Walls points out that 'as a supernatural response to human supplication [echo] is an idea that ... fits naturally into the Neo-platonic or Boethian view of music's position in the world order' (Walls, p. 44). An elegy for Henry Noel encapsulates that philosophy:

> Hark! Alleluia cheerly
> With **angel**s now he singeth,
> That here loved **music** dearly,
> Whose echo heaven ringeth,
> Where thousand cherubs hover,
> About th'eternal Mover.
>   (Morley, 1597, no. 21)

(B) 'Echo' is often mentioned in connection with the **noise**s of hunting in the Shakespeare canon. In the second scene of the Induction to *The Taming of the Shrew*, for instance, Sly is induced to believe that he is a lord and is offered various pastimes by 'his' servants. He is asked whether he would like to hunt, and is told that the 'hounds shall make the welkin answer them / And fetch **shrill** echoes from the **hollow** earth' (45–6). In *A Midsummer Night's Dream*, Theseus announces that he intends to 'mark the musical confusion / Of hounds and echo in conjunction' (4.1.110–11). According to Titus, the 'hunter's **peal**' (*Tit* 2.2.5) will make 'all the court ... echo with the noise' (6); during the hunt, Tamora observes that 'the babbling echo mocks the hounds / Replying shrilly to the **well-tun'd horn**s' (2.3.17–18). Venus anticipates the

echo

dangers that await Adonis in the boar-hunt and describes to him how confusing its sounds become when 'echo replies [to the hounds], / As if another chase were in the skies' (695–6).

After being rejected by Adonis, Venus vents her despair at her unrequited love:

> And now she **beat**s her heart, whereat it groans,
> That all the neighbor caves, as seeming troubled,
> Make verbal repetition of her moans;
> Passion on passion deeply is redoubled:
> 'Ay me!' she cries, and twenty times, 'Woe, woe!'
> And twenty echoes twenty times cry so.
>
> (*Ven* 829–34)

Her distressed sounds are reverberated by the caves, making them all the more pervasive and poignant. The connection between caves and echo is also established in *Romeo and Juliet*, in the mythological reference to the 'cave where Echo lies' (2.2.161).

Other usages of 'echo' achieve diverse effects. In a martial context, the '**clamor** of [the] **drum**' (*Jn* 5.2.168) beaten by the French 'start[s] an echo' as the English reply to it with their own drum. Palamon criticizes the tyrannical rule of his uncle Creon and remarks in a biblical tone that 'the echoes of his shames have deaf'd / The **ear**s of heavenly justice' (*TNK* 1.2.80–1). Gremio recalls that Petruchio kissed Katherina at the end of the wedding ceremony 'with such a clamorous smack / That at the parting all the church did echo' (*Shr* 3.2.178–9). Unlike the echoes of Creon's shame, this echoing sound in the church is very perceptible and has little to do with the spiritual sphere.

See also **report**.

(C) Smith, *The Acoustic World of Early Modern England* (1999).

Sternfeld, 'Écho et répétition dans la poésie et la musique' (1981), pp. 242–53; and *The Birth of Opera* (1993), ch. 7, both on echo in Italian settings and opera.

Walls, *Music in the English Courtly Masque* (1996), pp. 44–6, discusses the use of echo in masques.

e-la see **gamut**.

enchant (A) The power of **music** to move the emotions and affect the senses is denoted by this word. It can mean the pleasing effect **sweet melody** has upon the listener, but it can also suggest extra magical and special sensations. **Bird song** is often described as enchanting the **hear**er, as in:

> Happy streams, whose trembling fall
> With still murmur softly gliding,
> Happy birds, whose chirping call
> With sweet melody delighting
> Hath moved her flinty and relentless heart
> To listen to your **harmony**,
> And sit securely in those downs apart,
> Enchanted with your melody.
> (Wilbye, 1609, no. 10)

(B) In Shakespeare, 'enchanting' occurs with reference to both words and music – more often to words and discourse – expressing their power to affect and overcome the senses and the reason of the listener in an almost magical way. Marcus Andronicus bewails the **tongue**less mouth of his niece 'where like a sweet **melodious** bird it sung / Sweet varied **note**s, enchanting every **ear**' (*Tit* 3.1.85–6). After the horrible ordeal suffered by the young woman, the harmony that characterized her **voice** is lost forever.

In a more light-hearted situation, Don Armado is mocked for being under the spell of his own false eloquence, so different from the true power of music. According to the King of Navarre, the self-conceited Spaniard is 'one who the music of his own vain tongue / Doth **ravish** like enchanting harmony' (*LLL* 1.1.166–7).

eunuch (A) The history of the castrated male in social, political and artistic contexts is very ancient and diverse. Eunuchs were employed in roles as varied as harem attendants, diplomats and holders of high office in Ancient Greece and Rome to highly sought-after **sing**ers in early modern **music** theatre, ecclesiastical **choir**s and opera. Jacopo Peri (1561–1633), one of the major figures in early opera, for example, during his employment at the Medici court in Florence accompanied the group of singers known as the *concerto de' castrati*. There is no evidence,

eunuch

however, that eunuchs ever figured in the English musical provision of the period.

There are no eunuchs having acting/singing parts in Shakespeare's plays, nor were the actors who sang his songs in the plays castrati, but either boy players with a broken but harmonious **voice**, or an older male for whom Shakespeare wrote some of the songs.

(B) Musical references to eunuchs are sometimes comical or derogatory in the Shakespeare canon. One of the items on the comical list of entries for the wedding entertainment in *A Midsummer Night's Dream* is 'The battle with the Centaurs, to be sung / By an Athenian eunuch to the **harp**' (5.1.44–5). This entertainment is discarded in favour of the mechanicals' amateur production of 'Pyramus and Thisbe'.

Coriolanus, hating the humble behaviour urged on him by his mother, uses the eunuch image to express its degradation:

> . . . My **throat** of war be turn'd,
> Which **quier**'d with my **drum**, into a **pipe**
> Small as an eunuch, or the virgin voice
> That babies lull asleep! . . .
> (*Cor* 3.2.112–15)

A bawdy play on 'pipe' is barely disguised here. To Coriolanus, showing humility towards the plebeians amounts to losing his virility. The image of the eunuch, deprived of all of his male traits, is further developed into that of the high-pitched female voice.

A similar pun is observed in Orsino's remark to Viola (disguised as Cesario): 'Thy small pipe / Is as the maiden's **organ**, **shrill** and sound' (*TN* 1.4.32–3), which can be interpreted as referring back to Viola's intention at the beginning of the play to serve Orsino by assuming a false identity, as she explains to the Captain:

> . . . I'll serve this duke;
> Thou shalt present me as an eunuch to him,
> It may be worth thy pains; for I can sing
> And speak to him in many sorts of music
> That will allow me very worth his service.
> (1.2.55–9)

eunuch

The best way of justifying the high-pitched tone of her voice and her ambiguous sexual identity is by passing herself off as a castrato singer. Orsino falls into her trap, and in 1.4.32–3 he 'comments on her body and voice in appropriately musical terms, playing . . . [on her] state of suspension between the conditions of prepubescent male (as actor), fully grown female (as dramatis persona), and castrato singer (her disguise role)' (Elam, p. 35).

In the passage around the song 'Hark, hark the **lark**' in *Cymbeline*, where Cloten prefaces the **musician**s' performance with crude double-entendres, he dismisses its possible failure as a serenade as useless as 'the voice of unpav'd eunuch to boot' (2.3.30). 'Unpav'd' (i.e. without stones) alludes to the absence of testicles in a eunuch (Partridge, pp. 272–3).

(C) Brown, 'How Opera Began' (1970), focuses on Peri and early opera. Though very important in the history of Western music, early opera did not have the far-reaching impact in England it had on the continent.

Elam, 'The Fertile Eunuch' (1996), deals with the theme of castration running throughout *Twelfth Night*, with some attention paid to the musical and vocal spheres.

Partridge, *Shakespeare's Bawdy* (1968).

Rosselli, 'The Castrati as a Professional Group and a Social Phenomenon' (1988).

Sternfeld, *Music in Shakespearean Tragedy* (1967), chs 1–6, on Shakespeare's adult singers.

extemporally see **extempore**.

extempore (A) **Sing**ing a **part** extempore was synonymous with **descant** (or discant) in Elizabethan **music**. Morley attempts to reaffirm this:

> The name of Descant is usurped of the musitions in divers significations . . . they take it for **sing**ing a **part** extempore upon a playne-song, in which sence we commonly use it: so that when a man talketh of a Descanter, it must be understood of one that can extempore sing a part upon a playne song.
>
> (*Introduction*, 1597, p. 70)

extempore

Descant involved singing an improvised **part**, generally in the **treble**, against a slower moving part, usually the tenor, **perform**ing the **plainsong**. The sense of improvisation is found in other definitions, for example John Florio: '*Improvisare*, to sing or speake extempore' (*Worlde of Words*, 1598).

(B) In the Shakespeare canon, this term is usually employed to describe an improvised speech or performance, but in *Venus and Adonis* it is used in its musical nuance. **Lament**ing the grief that her unrequited love for Adonis brings her, Venus 'sings extemporally a **woeful ditty**' (836), which is **echo**ed by the caves and makes the song **tedious** (841). This spontaneous melancholy song contrasts with the frightening **noise**s of the boar-hunt that will cost Adonis his life.

See also **division**, **imitate**, **point**.

F

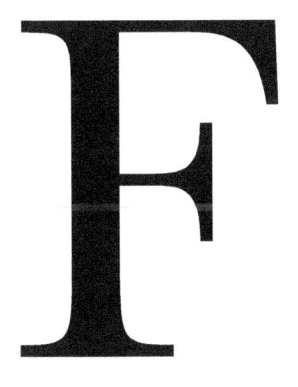

fa (A) The fourth **note** of the Renaissance hexachord. See **ut**.

fading (A) In a general sense 'fading' means the softening or dying away of **sound** at an ending or **cadence** in **music**. More specifically, it is the name of a lively **dance**, mentioned by Beaumont and Fletcher (1611): 'I will have him dance Fading: Fading is a fine **jig**' (*The Knight of the Burning Pestle*, 3.5.9), or it is the refrain 'with a fading' of a bawdy popular **song**.

(B) Shakespeare employs both the cadential and popular song meanings. Portia's wish to help Bassanio choose the right casket is clear when she orders that music be **play**ed to accompany his choice, something she denies her two previous suitors. She says:

> Let music sound while he doth make his choice;
> Then if he lose he makes a **swan**-like end,
> Fading in music. That the comparison
> May stand more proper, my eye shall be the stream
> And wat'ry death-bed for him. He may win,
> And what is music then? Then music is
> Even as the **flourish** when true subjects bow
> To a new-crowned monarch . . .
>
> (*MV* 3.2.43–50)

fading

The outcome of Bassanio's choice will influence the way Portia perceives music: the idea of music dying away springs to Portia's mind when she considers the possibility that the man she loves chooses the wrong casket. On the other hand, music will sound joyful if Bassanio chooses the lead casket.

A bawdy allusion is intended by the servant in *The Winter's Tale* when he describes the nature of Autolycus' **ballad**s (see '**burden**' for a commentary of this passage). These include:

> ... the prettiest **love-songs** for maids, so without
> bawdry, which is strange; with such delicate **burthen**s
> of **dildo**s and fadings, 'jump her and thump her' ...
> (4.4. 193–5)

Phrases such as 'delicate burdens', 'dildos and fadings' and 'jump her and thump her' are found in refrains of the period, referring to the sexually suggestive nature of 'dildo':

> Dainty darling, kind and free,
> Fairest maid I ever see,
> Dear, vouchsafe to look on me;
> Listen when I **sing** to thee
> What I will do
> With a dildo
> Sing do with a dildo.
> (anon. in Jones, 1601, no. 15).

(C) Naylor, *Shakespeare and Music* (1931).
Salzman, 'Dildos and Fadings' (1933).

faint (A) In a musical context, 'faint' refers to **soft**, possibly distant **sound**s and could invoke the effect of **echo** which **sing**ing in a large space would produce.

(B) The only time when this adjective is used by Shakespeare in its musical nuance is found at the beginning of *A Midsummer Night's Dream*. Theseus confronts Hermia with what would happen to her should she decide to disobey her father Egeus and not marry the suitor he has chosen for her. She will either be sentenced to death or be forced to enter a nunnery, where she will have

> . . . to be in shady cloister mew'd,
> To live a barren sister all [her] life,
> **Chaunt**ing faint **hymn**s to the cold fruitless moon.
> (1.1.71–3)

The faint singing in honour of the virgin goddess Diana (the moon) evokes the idea of a life of renunciation which awaits a girl devoting her life to chastity.

fall see **cadence**.

false (relation) (A) The theoretical term 'false' is used to describe the movement of two or more **part**s in counterpoint. It occurs when one part rising has a natural or **sharp** and the other part falling has a **flat** or natural. In Elizabethan theory it was known by various different terms, as Campion notes: 'Relation or reference, or respect not harmonicall is *Mi* against *Fa* in a crosse forme, and it is foure **Note**s, when one being considered crosse with the other doth produce in the **Music**ke a strange **discord**' (*A New Way*, c. 1614, E1v).

False relations can occur either simultaneously or successively between parts. They are dependent on melodic chromatic **alteration** and in their **harsh** discordant **sound** (simultaneous) or strange melodic juxtaposition (successive) make a striking effect. **Madrigal** composers in particular used them for special emotional moments. They are called false because the relationship between the two parts creates ungrammatical **harmony** according to Renaissance rules.

(B) 'False' can be synonymous with 'out of **tune**' and expresses the idea of discord deriving from **jar**ring sounds. This meaning is clear from an exchange between Julia (disguised as a page) and the Host, commenting on a **song** performed by a **consort** of **musician**s in honour of Silvia:

> JULIA: He **play**s false, father.

false (relation)

> HOST: How, out of tune on the **string**s?
> JULIA: Not so; but yet so false that he grieves my very heart-strings.
> ...
> HOST: I perceive you delight not in **music**.
> JULIA: Not a whit, when it jars so.
> (*TGV* 4.2. 59–62; 66–7)

Julia discloses her feelings of jealousy towards Silvia, who is wooed by Thurio and Proteus (the latter is the man Julia loves) by employing musical imagery which reflects her negative emotional state.

When Rosalind (disguised as Ganymede) reproaches Silvius for loving the scornful Phebe, she resorts to a metaphor which conjures up images of disharmony: 'Wilt thou love such a woman? What, to make thee / an **instrument**, and play false **strain**s upon thee? (*AYLI* 4.3.66–7). The relationship between the two is so unbalanced that Phebe can use Silvius as an instrument and 'tune' him as she pleases. It is interesting that both Julia in *The Two Gentlemen of Verona* and Rosalind in *As You Like It* use the adjective 'false' metaphorically after assuming a false identity.

In a sleepy state, Lucius says that 'the strings ... are false' (*JC* 4.3.291) when referring to his instrument (probably a **lute**) on which he played a tune for Brutus. Also in this case the allusion is to an instrument not properly tuned.

Rejecting Venus' advances, Adonis claims that his heart is not open to love: 'For know my heart stands armed in mine **ear**, / And will not let a false sound enter there' (*Ven* 779–80). The 'false sound' which creates 'deceiving harmony' (781) hints at Adonis' conviction that Venus is mistaking lust for love, as becomes clear in a later stanza: 'Call it not love, for Love to heaven is fled / Since sweating Lust on earth usurp'd his name' (793–4).

(C) Haar, 'False Relations and Chromaticism in Sixteenth-Century Music' (1977), deals with issues in music theory mainly relating to continental examples.

fancy (A) Although the term 'fancy' or 'fantasia' designated a specific kind of musical piece in sixteenth and seventeenth-century English **music**, namely a freely invented **instrument**al piece featuring

fancy

differing kinds of compositional techniques but usually beginning with imitative counterpoint, the one occurrence of the term in a musical context in Shakespeare does not seem to refer to the specific kind but rather to the nature of the music itself, according to a definition which Pepusch gave in the early eighteenth century when explaining 'fantasia': 'a Kind of **Air**, wherein the Composer is not tied up to such strict Rules, as in most other Airs, but has all the Freedom and Liberty allowed him for his Fancy or Invention, that can reasonably be desir'd' (*A Short Explication of Such Foreign Words, As are made Use of in Musick Books*, 1724, p. 30).

(B) Justice Shallow's reputation as a frequenter of brothels is highlighted by Falstaff, who observes that he

>   ... Sung those **tune**s to the
> overscutch'd huswives that he heard the **carmen
> whistle**, and sware they were his fancies or his good-nights.
> (*2H4* 3.2.316–18)

The musical terms 'tunes' and 'carmen whistle' (the latter has indecent connotations) introduce further musical conceits evoked by the words 'fancies' and 'good-nights', whilst developing the image of Shallow as a lustful man who fulfils his sexual fantasies at night-time.

fiddle (A) It is usually assumed that 'fiddle' is a colloquial synonym, often with disparaging overtones, for the violin. But in Elizabethan times that was not necessarily so. In some cases the word refers specifically to the violin as opposed generally to any bowed **string**ed **instrument** such as the **treble viol** or **rebec**. Elsewhere, 'fiddle' is used much more loosely and may not even indicate a bowed instrument. Hortensio is called a fiddler though he tries to pass himself off as a **lute**nist (see below). Another disguised character, Barabas in Marlowe's *The Jew of Malta*, is similarly addressed as a 'fiddler', even though he enters with a lute (Manifold, p. 81). The fiddler was a less worthy player, albeit professional, of a stringed instrument. Owen Feltham (*Resolves* c.1620) says that 'it is a kind of disparagement to a man to be a common fiddler. It argues his neglect of better employment, and that he hath spent much time on a thing unnecessarie' (cited by Holman,

fiddle

p. 140). The proverbial locution 'to give one a fiddler's fee', used in negative contexts, for instance in a play of c.1592, *Soliman and Perseda*, (quoted in Tilley, p. 291), shows that fiddle players were not paid high fees for their services.

The term 'fiddle' generally implied an element of crudity, of lack of refinement in contrast to lutes, viols or violins. The constituent parts of the fiddle together with an abundance of Elizabethan musical terms are found in the bawdy poem relating the fiddle to 'a woman fair' set by Robert Jones in his *The Muses Gardin for Delights* (1610):

> As I lay lately in a dream,
> Methought I saw a wondrous thing.
> A woman fair transformed was
> Into a fiddle without a string.
> A metamorphosis so rare
> As almost made me wake for fear.
> O this is rare,
> Yea, very rare,
> A wondrous thing,
> So fair a fiddle diddle diddle
> Should want a string.

The third stanza mentions the tuning **peg** and the bridge and alludes to the fiddle accompanying dancing:

> They'll send her first to some that can
> Put in the peg, and peg her then.
> If that her bridge be broken, so
> As that the fiddle cannot go,
> They'll soon devise some other way
> To make her **sound** the **roundelay**.
> O this is rare, [etc].

Other stanzas include references to the terms: **'consort'**, **'key'**, **'strain'**, **'high'**, **'crack'**, **'diapason'**, 'sound', **'discord'**, 'prick', **'mood'**, 'sing three to one', **note**s in the **gamut** scale' and the 'long' **time**-value.

'Fiddle' could also refer to any bowed stringed instrument in Elizabethan times. It inherited this meaning from Medieval precepts. The word is translated in England in the fifteenth century, as Mary Remnant observes (Appendix A), from the Latin 'viella', 'vidula', 'vitula' as 'fydyll' or 'fyyele'. It could not have had a specific association since the violin and viol were introduced in to England in the early sixteenth century.

The fiddle as violin was primarily employed to accompany dancing either in the highest courtly circles – where dancing was an after-dinner obsession – or at the lowliest get-together in the local tavern. Among the instruments found on the *Mary Rose* were two 'fiddles', according to Remnant's definition having 'a clear distinction between the body and the neck of the instrument, even if they are carved from one piece of wood' and 'a flat or nearly flat back' (p. 61). Mary Anne Alburger links the *Mary Rose* fiddles with fifteenth-century 'fydill in fist' instruments generally associated with traditional rather than art **music**. Moreover, she cites iconographic evidence relating these fiddles to mid-sixteenth-century social contexts in which they were **play**ed together with **pipe**s and **tabor**s. A tabor and three-holed pipe were also found on the *Mary Rose* confirming the suggestion that the fiddles were most likely used to accompany on-board entertainment, especially dancing.

The connection between the fiddle and less refined dancing is taken up in popular **rhyme**s of the time. In Thomas Preston's play, *A lament*able tragedy . . . *conteyning the life of Cambises King of Percia* (printed in 1569), the fiddle is clearly a bowed stringed instrument used to accompany the **dance**: 'They be at hand Sir with stick and fiddle; / They can play a new daunce called Hey didle didle'. In Alexander Montgomerie's *The Cherry and the Slae* (1597) the fiddle and dance are intimately bound up:

> But since you think't an easy thing
> To mount above the moon,
> Of your own fiddle take a spring
> And dance when ye have done.

These verses are almost certainly related to the famous 'Hey diddle diddle / The cat and the fiddle', one of the most popular of all English rhymes. References to cat, fiddle and fiddle-stick are found in a number of English rhymes, most often in connection with dancing. And the link with the tavern can be deduced from the popular name of many inns. It is known, for example, that there was an inn called the 'Catte and Fidle' at Old Chaunge, London by 1587.

fiddle

(B) In the Shakespeare canon, all references to fiddles and fiddlers appear in metaphors with a negative connotation. One case in point is Hortensio's explanation of how the ill-tempered Katherina broke a lute on his head: 'While she did call me rascal fiddler / And **twangling Jack**, with twenty such vild terms' (*Shr* 2.1.157–8). In a later scene, Lucentio condemns Hortensio's wooing of Bianca when he exclaims: 'Fiddler, forbear, you grow too forward, sir' (3.1.1). This and the other negative epithets addressed to Hortensio, for instance 'twangling Jack' show that his disguise is not as successful as he wishes it to be – nobody seems to believe that he is a lutenist.

In *Henry VIII*, Lovell talks in a derogatory manner about a group of English aristocrats who, after spending some time in France, have acquired French mannerisms to the point of losing their English identity. Among the many habits they have learned in France, they: 'Have got a speeding trick to lay down ladies. / A French song and a fiddle has no fellow' (1.3.40–1). The bawdy innuendo implied here ('fiddle' was used as a euphemism for 'penis') effectively adds to the anti-French tone of the scene. Another insulting use of the term is found in the ensuing line: 'The devil fiddle 'em' (42).

Prince Hal observes that the devil is leading the dance when he senses commotion afoot: 'The devil rides upon a fiddle-stick' (*1H4* 2.4.487). The association of the devil with the fiddle in this proverbial expression testifies to the negative nuance applied to this term in early modern England.

In *Romeo and Juliet*, fiddle-stick indicates Mercutio's rapier: 'Here's my fiddle-stick, here's that shall make you dance' (3.1.48). This develops a previous musical pun on '**consort**', which in this context can be interpreted as meaning either 'keep company with' or '**perform** with a consort of **minstrel**s'. The passage sounds like an insult when we consider that it is addressed to a gentleman (Evans, pp. 136–7).

(C) Alburger, 'The "Fydill in Fist" ' (2000).
   Brown, 'The Trecento Fiddle and Its Bridges' (1989).
   Evans, *Romeo and Juliet* (2003).
   Holman, *Four and Twenty Fiddlers* (1993).
   Humphreys, *King Henry IV, Part I* (1960), p. 83.
   Levenson, *Romeo and Juliet* (2000), p. 252.
   Long, *Shakespeare's Use of Music* (1977).

Manifold, *The Music in English Drama* (1956), pp. 24ff. and p. 76, underlines the quality of shabby professionalism associated with fiddlers and the difficulty in trying to recover a definitive meaning for the words 'fiddle' and 'fiddler'.

Remnant, *English Bowed Instruments* (1986).

Tilley, *Proverbs in England* (1966).

Williams, *A Dictionary of Sexual Language* (1994), explains the sexual connotations of the word 'fiddle' and notes that 'fiddle-stick' can mean 'penis' (vol. 1, p. 479), and that 'fiddler' can mean 'sexual partner' (vol. 1, p. 480).

fiddler see **fiddle**.

fiddle-stick see **fiddle**.

fife (A) The Renaissance fife was a small cylindrical transverse **flute** made out of a single piece of wood and having six finger holes. With its narrow bore, it would have made a **shrill** and comparatively **loud sound**. The fife and side-**drum** was a **march**ing and signalling combination for footsoldiers, as opposed to **kettledrum**s and **trumpet**s for cavalry. As such it originated in Swiss and German armies but quickly spread throughout Europe. Regulations for British infantry, surviving from 1557 (quoted in Farmer, variously) indicate that military fifers must 'teach the companye the soundes of the marche, allarum, approache, assaulte, battaile, **retreat**e, skirmishe, or any other challenge that of necessitie should be knowen'. William Byrd's 'The flute and the droome' from his famous miscellany for keyboard, *The Battell* (MLNB, 1591) is a good example of **music** for fife and drum. It is also clear from contemporary sources (e.g. Arbeau, *Orchesography*, 1589), that fifes were used to accompany **dance**s, generally outdoor and not socially exclusive.

(B) There are very few stage directions for fifes in the plays written for professional adult companies in the period 1580–1642; only one play, Robert Wilson's *The Cobbler's Prophecy* (1594), makes use of the fife in a non-military context (Dessen and Thomson, p. 91).

fife

There are two stage directions in Shakespeare's plays referring to this **instrument**. One reads: '*Enter Alcibiades, with Drum and Fife, in warlike manner, and Phrynia and Timandra*' (*Tim* 4.3.48.SD) (see 'drum' for a detailed discussion). The other occurs in a situation which clearly aims to parody military values: '*Enter the Prince marching, and Falstaff meets him* **play***ing upon his truncheon like a fife*' (*1H4* 3.3.87). The fact that the fife is not actually played here is significant. The comical effect of the truncheon being used instead of the musical instrument underlines Falstaff's role as an incompetent and cowardly soldier.

Fifes are mentioned on four occasions in speeches. For instance, Shylock refers to a **masque** which will be accompanied by 'the drum . . . and the wry-neck'd fife' (*MV* 2.5.30). It is likely here that 'drum and fife' refer to the people playing the instruments, as can be deduced by a passage from Barnaby Riche's *Irish Hubbub* (1616): 'A fife is a wry-neckt **musician**, for he always looks away from his instrument' (taken from Brown, p. 51).

In *Othello*, we realize that Iago's insinuations about Desdemona's infidelity are having an effect on Othello when, in a fit of jealousy, the latter renounces the most important values in his life:

> Farewell the neighing steed and the shrill trump,
> The spirit-stirring drum, th' **ear**-piercing fife,
> The royal banner, and all quality,
> Pride, pomp, and circumstance of glorious war!
> (3.3.351–4)

This rejection shows that Iago's 'attack on the private man is resulting in the destruction of the public one' (King, p. 155).

In *Coriolanus*, the Romans celebrate Coriolanus's decision to spare the city as follows: '*Trumpets,* **hoboys**, *drums* **beat***, all together*' (5.4.48.SD). This stage instruction is followed by the second messenger's speech: 'Why, hark you! The trumpets, **sackbut**s, psalteries, and fifes / **Tabor**s and **cymbal**s . . .' (5.4.49–50). If all the instruments mentioned in the speech were intended to be played on the stage, this is one of the most remarkable sound effects in the Shakespeare canon. A reference to a fife is also found in *Much Ado About Nothing*, 2.3.14 (see 'drum').

(C) Brown, *The Merchant of Venice* (1955).
Dessen and Thomson, *A Dictionary of Stage Directions* (1999).

Farmer, *The Rise and Development of Military Music* (1912).
King, '"Then Murder's Out of Tune": The Music and Structure of *Othello*' (1986).

fingering (A) The fingers of both hands are used to **play** most **instrument**s, the exceptions being **brass** (e.g. **trumpet**s, **horn**s) and percussion (e.g. **drum**s, **cymbal**s, **bell**s) where the hand rather than specific individual fingers are needed. To finger an instrument, therefore, is to play an instrument.

In Elizabethan times, all the fingers (although thumb and little finger rarely) were employed in playing keyboard instruments (harpsichord, **virginal, organ**, clavichord). In **perform**ing scalic or figurative passages, so much a feature of virtuosic English virginal **music**, the technique of running long fingers over short (right hand descending, left hand ascending) and short over long (right hand ascending, left hand descending) was highly developed.

Wind instruments (**flute**s, **recorder**s, **hoboy**s, **cornett**s) usually had six holes (known as **stop**s or **ventage**s) which were covered and uncovered (**govern**ed) by the three middle fingers on the right hand and the three middle fingers on the left, separately or in combinations according to what **note** was **sound**ed. The speed at which the fingers moved corresponded to the speed at which the music was being played.

On plucked **string**ed instruments (e.g. **lute, cittern**) the individual fingers of both hands operate in playing. Usually the right-hand fingers pluck the strings whilst the left-hand fingers stop or **fret** the strings on the fingerboard at the appropriate places. On bowed stringed instruments (e.g. violin, **viol**) it is generally the fingers of the left hand which are active in stopping the strings, whereas the right hand fingers clasp the bow and act as a hand rather than as individual fingers.

On any keyboard, wind or stringed instrument, the movement of the fingers is the most obvious visual sign that the instrument is being played and the most specific connection between the player and the instrument. Fingering is the most important element of technique, or level of ability, attained in playing an instrument.

(B) The technique of fingering a keyboard instrument is explained in detail in *Sonnet* 128. The poet observes his lady's '**sweet** fingers ... upon that blessed wood' (2–3), i.e. the virginal's keys, moving with

fingering

'gentle gait' (11), and wishes that, while the instrument can enjoy the **touch** of her fingers, he will soon be able to enjoy the touch of her lips: 'Since saucy **jack**s so happy are in this, / Give them thy fingers, me thy lips to kiss' (13–14).

The musical connotation of 'fingering' sometimes allows Shakespeare to create a pun on the bawdy nuance of the word, which was used as a euphemism either for masturbation or for sexual intercourse (Williams, p. 485). When Hortensio (who is passing himself off as a music teacher) recounts his misadventure with Katherina, he explains that she broke the lute on his head after he 'bow'd her hand to teach her fingering' (*Shr* 2.1.150). The double entendre is even more evident in a later scene. Hortensio is now trying to introduce Bianca to lute-playing and warns her:

> Madam, before you touch the instrument,
> To learn the order of my fingering,
> I must begin with rudiments of art . . .
> (*Shr* 3.1.64–6)

Hortensio is vying with Lucentio for Bianca's attention, and the scene is dominated by sexual tension, evident for instance in Lucentio's advice to Hortensio that he should 'spit in the hole, and **tune** again' (3.1.40) – a metaphor for male orgasm as well as a reference to the tuning technique for the lute.

In *Cymbeline*, before performing the **song** 'Hark, hark, the **lark** at heaven's gate **sing**s' to Imogen, a group of **musician**s are exhorted by Cloten as follows: 'Come on, tune. If you can penetrate her with your / fingering, so; we'll try with **tongue** too' (2.3.14–15). This advice to the musicians, with apparent reference to playing techniques (fingering and tonguing), discloses Cloten's intense sexual desire for Imogen.

Yet another bawdy innuendo can be discerned in Pericles' words while solving the riddle which the King of Antioch proposes to his daughter's suitors. He addresses a cryptic musical metaphor to the Princess:

> You are a fair viol, and your sense the strings;
> Who, finger'd to make man his lawful music,
> Would draw heaven down, and all the gods to hearken;

> But being play'd upon before your time,
> Hell only **dance**th at so **harsh** a **chime**.
> (*Per* 1.1.81–5)

These words convey Pericles's knowledge that the Princess is being sexually abused by her father. In all three passages involving bawdy innuendos, the woman is viewed as a passive instrument in the hands of her would-be lover.

See also **division**.

(C) de Fer, *Epitome musical* (1556), for wind instrument fingering.

Dowland, *Varietie of Lute-Lessons* (1610), for lute fingering.

Ferguson, *Keyboard Interpretation* (1987), pp. 67–73, for Elizabethan keyboard instruments.

Le Huray, *Fingering of Virginal Music* (1981), on the same topic as Ferguson.

Riley, *The Teaching of Bowed Instruments from 1511 to 1756* (1986), for stringed instruments.

Robinson, *The Schoole of Musicke* (1603), for lute fingering.

Williams, *A Dictionary of Sexual Language* (1994).

flat (A) Used as a noun, a 'flat' is the sign (♭) placed before a **note** which lowers it half a tone (semitone). In Elizabethan notation, if a flat occurred in a **key**-signature it related to the third and sixth of the scale, indicating a 'lesser' third or 'lesser' sixth. In the key of G this would relate to the notes B and E.

To '**sing**' or '**play**' flat is to **perform** just below the standard or exact pitch of a note. It is the opposite to **sharp**. When two or more sing or play together, if one performer is flat then the resultant **sound** is unpleasant and **discord**ant.

Notes altered using sharps and flats became known as 'chromatic' notes. Such notes would change the character of a piece. This is alluded to in:

> Come, **woeful Orpheus**, with thy charming lyre,
> And **tune** my **voice** unto thy skilful **wire**;
> Some strange chromatic notes do you devise,
> That best with **mournful accent**s sympathise;

flat

>Of sourest sharps and uncouth flats make choice,
>And I'll thereto compassionate my voice.
>
>(Byrd, 1611, no. 19)

(B) Only once is 'flat' used in its musical meaning by Shakespeare. This happens when Lucetta expresses her doubts about Julia's ability to sing the poem that Proteus has written in her honour. Julia chooses to sing to the tune of 'Light o' love' (*TGV* 1.2.80), but her waiting-woman is very critical of her singing abilities. First, she objects that the tune is 'too sharp' (1.2.88), and then she upbraids Julia for the opposite fault:

>Nay, now you are too flat,
>And mar the **concord** with too **harsh** a **descant**:
>There wanteth but a **mean** to fill your song.
>
>(1.2.90–2)

The dialogue between the two women works on two levels: from a performative viewpoint, the puns on musical terms throughout the scene provide an ideal background to the actual singing. On a metaphorical level, Lucetta's remarks on Julia's singing abilities work as advice to Julia: the young woman needs a male voice to make her descant more harmonious and, by extension, to make her life complete.

See also **harmony**.

flourish (A) Of all the sixteenth-century calls and signals, the flourish is the most improvisatory and musically least structured. This, by default, was its identifiable characteristic although it was often interchanged with **sennet**s and **tucket**s in early modern theatrical performance. In theatre contexts, the flourish was invariably for **trumpet**s or **cornett**s sometimes accompanied by **drum**s. Some examples of flourishes for **recorder**s and **hautboy**s are also observed.

In general, any **instrument** or instruments could **play** a flourish as a short (improvised) warm-up to a longer notated piece. This is the sense given by Thomas in his definition of 'Proludo' in his *Dictionarium Linguae Latinae et Anglicanae* (1587): 'To flourish as **musician**s ... doe before they play in earnest'. See also the definition for 'Proludium' ('a flourish, a voluntarie, a preamble') in the same work by Thomas.

flourish

Unsurprisingly, notated **music** examples of flourishes are very scarce. The Praeludium and Voluntary are not uncommon, especially in keyboard music manuscripts of the period and may suggest something of the improvisatory nature of the flourish. The extent or **degree** of elaboration would depend on the context and the skill of the player. Often, however, just a few **note**s would suffice.

(B) The importance of this **sound** effect in theatrical performance is testified by its frequent occurrence in the plays written for adult professional companies between 1580 and 1642: Dessen and Thomson have identified over 500 examples of stage directions for flourishes in the 500 or so plays analysed in their *Dictionary of Stage Directions*. The term is often found in manuscript play books and in early-printed plays annotated for performance. Flourishes, together with other fanfares such as sennets and tuckets, were effective aural signals to evoke ceremonial and official events in the theatre of Shakespeare and his contemporaries. They were also sometimes used in military contexts, as the direction '*A flourish, as to an assault*' (*The Maid of Honour* 2.3.OSD) suggests (Dessen and Thomson, p. 94). Flourishes and sennets accompanied the entries and exits of royal characters and heads of state, whereas tuckets usually signalled the entrance of persons of lesser degree, heralds and messengers. Flourishes were also used for proclamations.

Instructions for flourishes for combinations of instruments appear in as many as 21 Shakespeare plays. For instance, the drum is used in conjunction with a **wind** instrument in *Coriolanus* 5.5.8.SD ('*A flourish with drums and trumpets*') and in *Antony and Cleopatra* 2.7.133.SD ('*Sound a flourish, with drums*').

As well as in explicit stage directions, this type of fanfare is called for in some speeches, for instance in *Richard III*: 'A flourish, trumpets!' (4.4.149); and in *Titus Andronicus*: 'Why do the Emperor's trumpets flourish thus?' (4.2.49).

Manifold has proposed that flourishes were essentially theatrical signals but that they did not belong to the 'camp or court'. However, this does not seem to be the case when we consider a passage from *The Merchant of Venice*, occurring when Bassanio is trying to guess which casket contains Portia's picture. Hoping for his success, Portia comments:

Let **music** sound while he doth make his choice;

flourish

> Then if he lose he makes a **swan**-like end,
> **Fading** in music. That the comparison
> May stand more proper, my eye shall be the stream
> And wat'ry death-bed for him. He may win,
> And what is music then? Then music is
> Even as the flourish when true subjects bow
> To a new-crowned monarch . . .
>
> (3.2.43–50)

This speech is interspersed with musical metaphors, and links the sounding of a flourish to one of the most **solemn** and meaningful rites in early modern society, i.e. the coronation ceremony. In *Henry VIII*, an elaborate stage direction describes the 'order of the Coronation' for Anne Boleyn. The ceremony starts with '*A lively flourish of trumpets*' (4.1.36.SD) and ends with '*a great flourish of trumpets*' (4.1.36.SD).

Since some stage directions in plays of the age require that the flourish be 'long', Manifold infers that this specification would have been necessary to signal the exception to the rule, and that flourishes were normally two-note calls. However, some stage directions require 'short' flourishes, for instance: '*This short flourish of* **cornett**s*, and shouts within*' (*TNK* 2.5.OSD). A look at Dessen and Thomson's *Dictionary of Stage Directions* reveals that 'flourish' is accompanied by a variety of adjectives, including 'lively', 'untunable' and 'full', for instance '*A full flourish of cornetts*' (*Sophonisba* 3.2.84.SD). It is possible that 'full' here has the same meaning as 'great': the latter, as Shirley suggests, may either refer to the number of instruments employed or to the length of the sound effect. Dessen and Thomson have found examples of flourishes being played 'within' and 'afar off' in non-Shakespearean drama (see also Introduction). The different adjectives and adverbs accompanying stage instructions for flourishes seem to reveal that dramatists and book-keepers alike were keen to signal this sound effect as accurately as possible. Hence, it can reasonably be inferred that flourishes did not follow a strict two-note pattern as Manifold proposes.

'Narrator' figures not directly involved in the development of the plot such as the **Chorus** in Folio *Henry V*, are sometimes introduced by a flourish. It is striking that the entrance of the Prologue to the amateur production of the story of 'Pyramus and Thisbe' put on by the mechanicals in the final scene of Folio *A Midsummer Night's Dream* is preceded by the right-hand marginal indication '*Flor.*[*ish*] *Trum.*[*pets*]'. Such an effect underlines the fictional nature of the play-within-the-play in a comedy which indulges in multilayered metatheatrical games with the audience.

Previous commentators have noted that fanfares can acquire an ironic nuance and that they work as reminders of the contrast between appearance and reality, for instance when weak rulers' entries are underlined by such sound effects. A good example of this is found in the opening scene of *2 Henry VI*. The false sense of security brought about by the marriage between Henry and Margaret of Anjou is conveyed by the use of flourishes. The first entry of the King and his retinue is preceded by the stage direction: '*Flourish of trumpets: then hoboys*' (1.1.OSD). After Margaret has been introduced to the Court, the lords kneel and exclaim:

> Long live Queen Margaret, England's happiness.   *Flourish.*
> (1.1.37)

The tragic irony of this passage, whose theatrical rendition entails symbolic stage action (kneeling) and sound effects (flourish) becomes clear as the story of the Wars of the Roses unfolds.

That the sounding of fanfares can be a superficial display of power is confirmed in a speech by the Princess of France in *Love's Labour's Lost*. Boyet, one of her followers, praises her beauty using flattering terms. The Princess replies:

> Good Lord Boyet, my beauty, though but mean,
> Needs not the painted flourish of your praise:
> Beauty is bought by judgement of the eye,
> Not utt'red by base sale of chapmen's **tongue**s.
> (2.1.13–16)

'Flourish' is usually taken to mean 'embellishment' in this context. However, this noun seems to have a musical connotation, which is even more significant when we consider that in the previous speech Boyet refers to the military signal '**parley**' when he exhorts the Princess to try and persuade the King of Navarre to give back to her father a share of Aquitaine. The passage quoted above exemplifies the linguistic complexity characterising this play. For instance, line 16 uses other words which can be interpreted as building on the musical metaphors by

flourish

punning on the term 'base' in its musical nuance ('**bass**' was also spelt 'base' in early modern English).

(C) Dessen and Thomson, *A Dictionary of Stage Directions* (1999).
Manifold, *The Music in English Drama* (1956).
Shirley, *Shakespeare's Use of Off-Stage Sounds* (1963).

flute (A) The meaning of this term is ambiguous. Today it refers invariably to the transverse flute. But in the early modern period until the end of the eighteenth century, 'flute' could be generic, encompassing **pipe**s, **fife, recorder**s and transverse flute. Or it could be used specifically to indicate a certain kind of flute. It is often difficult to know when the term is being used generically or specifically, unless 'flute' is qualified contextually, for example by contrasting flutes with recorders, or adjectively by words such as transverse (*traverso*) or German (*flûte d'Allemagne*), or by having some idea of what **consort** is implied. The transverse flute, for example, was a member of the peculiarly English mixed consort, mentioned by the anonymous chronicler of *The Honourable Entertainment . . . at Elvetham* (1591) as 'an exquisite consort' of '**Lute**, Bandora, **Base-Viol**l, **Cittern**e, **Treble**-violl, and Flute'. **Music** for this combination of **instrument**s was arranged by Morley in his *Consort Lessons* (1599, 2/1611) and Rosseter, *Lessons for Consort* (1609), and used to accompany the four-**part song**s in William Leighton's *Teares or Lamentacions* (1614).

During the sixteenth century, the transverse flute enjoyed widespread popularity among aristocratic and merchant class circles, including of course both men and women. Furthermore, it was very popular as a consort instrument. Court inventories of establishments across the continent and England indicate that a comparatively large number of instruments was kept. Henry VIII lists 74 flutes in 1547; the imperial court at Stuttgart (1589) records 220 transverse flutes as well as 48 recorders, 113 **cornett**s and 39 viols. These instruments would be intended for professional **play**ers and gentleman amateurs at court.

Like all **wind** consort instruments, flutes were made in different sizes. Martin Agricola illustrates four (discantus, altus, tenor, bassus) in the 1545 revised edition of his *Musica instrumentalis deudsch*. Transverse flutes played an octave higher than their notated pitch. Unlike shawm or recorder consorts, there was no real deep **bass** or large bass instrument. In a mixed consort, therefore, the tenor flute could take the equivalent of the **descant** or altus part.

It is interesting to note that whilst most Renaissance woodwind instruments had basically similar **fingering** systems, the flute was unique, especially in its upper registers. This would suggest that although, say, a recorder player could also play an **hoboy**, he or she would probably not be so adept on a transverse flute. In other words, the transverse flute was an individual instrument and would not easily be doubled or substituted by another instrument by a versatile player. Moreover, it would seem that the transverse flute had a special **soft/sensuous sound**, played 'with trembling **breath**' (Agricola, 1529) or a kind of pervading vibrato not used with other instruments. Comparisons made (by Arbeau, 1589; Praetorius, 2/1619) with German and Swiss military flutes (fifes) make it clear that the transverse flute was a refined indoor instrument.

(B) Flutes are called for in very few stage directions (never in Shakespeare), mainly in relation to funerals (Dessen and Thomson, p. 95). Because of the ambiguity in the usage of the word 'flute' explained above, it is likely that this was synonymous with 'recorder' in some of these directions, for instance in Marston's *Antonio and Mellida* (1599) when a coffin enters accompanied by '**still** flutes' (5.2.208). It has also been argued that 'flute' means 'fife' in a stage direction in *Gorboduc* (1561) describing a battle (quoted in Manifold, p. 70):

> *First the **drum**s and flutes began to sound, during which there came forth upon the stage a company of arquebusiers, and of armed men, all in order of battle. These, after their pieces discharged, and that the armed men had three times **march**ed about the stage, departed, and then drums and flutes did cease.*
>
> (5.1)

In Shakespeare, there are only two references to the flute. The enticing power of flute music transpires from Enobarbus' description of how Cleopatra conquered Antony's love when she was sailing down the River Cydnus. The oars of Cleopatra's barge

>   ... were **silver**,
> Which to the **tune** of flutes kept stroke, and made

flute

> The water which they **beat** to follow faster,
> As amorous of their strokes.
>
> *(Ant* 2.2.194–7)

Words such as 'tune', 'stroke' and 'beat' reinforce the musical connotation of these lines. It is likely that the reference is to the transverse flute: the sensuous sound produced by this instrument makes it particularly suited to the occasion described by Enobarbus, in which Cleopatra's sensuality is brought to the foreground.

In the same play, at the end of the scene of the banquet aboard Pompey's galley, Menas orders that a **flourish** be sounded in honour of the triumvirs:

> These drums, these **trumpet**s, flutes! what!
> Let Neptune **hear** we bid a **loud** farewell
> To these great fellows. Sound and be hang'd, sound out!
> *Sound a flourish, with drums.*
> (2.7.131–3)

Unfortunately the explicit stage direction does not give any details about the type of flute that was expected to be played. However, it is unlikely that a transverse flute would have been used for a fanfare.

(C) Baines, *Woodwind Instruments and their History* (1977), ch. 10 'The Sixteenth Century and the Consorts'; and *The Oxford Companion to Musical Instruments* (1992).

Dessen and Thomson, *A Dictionary of Stage Directions* (1999), p. 95.

Hadden, 'The Transverse Flute in the Middle Ages and Renaissance: Sources, Instruments, Technique' (forthcoming).

Manifold, *The Music in English Drama* (1956).

Puglisi, 'A Survey of Renaissance Flutes' (1988).

Solum, *The Early Flute* (1992), with a chapter on the Renaissance flute by Anne Smith.

frame (A) As a verb in a musical context 'frame' has the same meaning as '**make**', 'invent' or '**compose**'. Campion says in his preface 'To the Reader' in his *Two Bookes of Ayres* (c.1613): 'These **Ayre**s were for the most part framed at first for one voyce with the **Lute**, or **Violl**'. In

frame

his neo-Horatian ayre, 'Come let us **sound** with **melody**' (*A Booke of Ayres*, 1601) Campion has 'Author of **number**, that hath all the world in / Harmonie framed'.

(B) Proteus advises Thurio to 'frame some feeling line' (*TGV* 3.2.75), i.e. compose a poem, in honour of Silvia if he wants to conquer her. In the ensuing lines (77–80) he alludes to the harmonising power of **Orpheus**' lute, thus creating a link between poetry and **music**.

Glendower boasts his connections with the English court in order to discourage Hotspur from criticising his Welsh origin:

> I can speak English, lord, as well as you,
> For I was train'd up in the English court,
> Where being but young I framed to the **harp**
> Many an English **ditty** lovely well.
> (*1H4* 3.1.119–22)

Here the reference could be either to the words of a **song** or 'ayre', or the composition of a poem with a specific musical setting in mind, as the term 'ditty' can signify either.

fret (A) A small gut, wooden, bone or wire strip placed across the fingerboard of certain **string**ed **instrument**s, the position of which **govern**s the pitch of a **note** on any given string. There were two types of fret, namely fixed and tied. The fixed were usually wire or bone, set in to the fingerboard and characteristically found on the **cittern**. The tied were made of gut and held fast with a special knot which could be loosened to move the fret. This type was common on Elizabethan **lute**s and **viol**s. Such instruments were called 'fretted' and placing the finger on the fret was called 'stopping'. Consequently, frets were also called **stop**s. William Barley notes that the

> . . . frets are those strings that are tied about the necke of the Lute, and are ordinarilie eight in number represented and marked with these letters, b.c.d.e.f.g.h.i and they are called stops, in regard that where these letters are found, following the order of the tabliture, and the spaces betwixt the freets must bee stopped with the fingers of the left hand.
> (*New Booke of Tabliture*, 1596)

fret

(B) Frets are mentioned in conjunction with heart strings by Lucrece after she has been raped. Invoking **Philomela** (another victim of rape), she claims that she intends to fix a sharp knife against her heart

> . . . to affright mine eye,
> Who if it wink shall thereon fall and die.
> These means, as frets upon an instrument,
> Shall **tune** our heart-strings to true **languishment**.
> (*Luc* 1138–41)

Like Philomela, Lucrece wishes to vent her despair through **sing**ing but realizes that this will not be enough: the idea of committing suicide is beginning to take shape in her mind. A similar instance is also found in *Henry VIII*, 3.2.104 (see '**chord**' for a detailed comment).

'Fret' is also used in *Hamlet*, 3.2.371 (see '**instrument**' for a detailed discussion). In a more light-hearted context, Hortensio enters with '*his head broke*' (*Shr* 2.1.141.SD) and explains to Baptista that Katherina was responsible for the accident. He was trying to teach her to **play** the lute, but instead of 'break[ing] her to the lute' (147), she 'broke the lute to [him]' (148). He complains:

> I did but tell her she mistook her frets,
> And bow'd her hand to teach her **fingering**;
> When, with a most impatient devilish spirit,
> 'Frets, call you these?' quoth she, 'I'll fume with them.'
> And with that word she strook me on the head.
> (*Shr* 2.1.149–53)

The comical quality of the situation is increased by the pun on 'fingering' which, as well as referring to a playing technique, can have a sexual connotation (Partridge, p. 135).

(C) Grijp, 'Fret Patterns of the Cittern' (1981).
Partridge, *Shakespeare's Bawdy* (1968).

G

galliard (A) Originating in late-fifteenth-century Italy, the galliard was a fairly vigorous courtly **dance** in triple **time**. A variant of the *cinque pas*, Arbeau (*Orchesography*, 1589) described its choreography as a basic pattern of four *grues* (a hop and kick step on alternate feet) and one *saut majeur* (a high leap). It was common, together with **measure**s and **coranto**s, in the revels of English courtly **masque**s. The Agent of Savoy describes one such instance at the *Somerset Masque* (1613): 'The other lords from the masque gave their hands to the bride and the other ladies, and passing up and down they danced only a galliard which lasted a half-quarter of an hour' (transl. Orrell, p. 304).

In late sixteenth- and early seventeenth-century England, a large number of galliards were **compose**d as independent keyboard and **lute** pieces. In many collections, notably MLNB and FWVB, galliards were paired with the **pavan**, contrasted in tempo (slow) and rhythm (duple time). Despite what Morley says in describing their metrical attributes, very few of these galliards were close variants of their associated pavan:

> After every pavan we usually **set** a galliard (that is, a kind of **music**ke made out of the other) causing it go by a measure, which the learned cal *trochaicam rationem*, consisting of a long and short stroke successivelie . . . This is a lighter and more stirring kinde of dauncing then the pavane.
>
> (*Introduction*, 1597, p. 181)

galliard

(B) The liveliness of the dance is encapsulated in the adjective '**nimble**' used by the French ambassador when he defies Henry V's claim on some French dukedoms. On behalf of the Dauphin, he tells Henry: 'there's nought in France / That can be with a nimble galliard won' (*H5* 1.2.251–2). These cautionary words imply that Henry's expectations are unrealistic, and that an English military campaign in France would be anything but easily won.

The galliard is also mentioned by Sir Toby Belch when he asks Sir Andrew Aguecheek:

> Why dost thou not go to church in a galliard, and come home in a coranto? My very walk should be a **jig**.
> I would not so much as make water but in a **sink-a-pace**.
>
> (*TN* 1.3.128–30)

Sir Toby is trying to understand how skilled Olivia's suitor is at dancing, since this was one of the fundamental qualities of a courtier. But what transpires from Sir Toby's words is also his own inclination to indulge in revelling.

See also **caper**.

(C) Neighbour, *The Consort and Keyboard Music of William Byrd* (1978), includes a chapter on the sources and structures of Byrd's pavans and galliards.

Orrell, 'The Agent of Savoy at The Somerset Masque' (1977).

Sorrel, 'Shakespeare and the Dance' (1957).

gamouth see **gamut**.

gamut (A) 'Gamma **ut**' was the name for the first and lowest **note** of the solmization system of letter notation used from the eleventh century to the end of the sixteenth. Just as the Greek alpha and beta, which were the first two letters, came to mean the entire series of letters of a language, the 'alphabet', so gamut came to represent all six letters of the hexachord which made up the Renaissance scale. Most Renaissance teaching manuals and treatises on **music** began with the naming of notes, the so-called scale of music. '... first of all it is needful for him that will learn to **sing** truly, to understand his *Scale*, or (as they commonly call it) the *Gamma-ut* (anon, *Pathway to Musicke*, 1596, A2). William Bathe emphasized the essential pedagogical role of the gamut and referred to the stave on which the scale was notated:

> The Scale of Musick, which is called Gam-ut, conteineth 10 rules, and as many spaces; and is set downe in letters and sillables, in which you must beegin at the lowest word, Gam-ut, and so go upwards to the end still ascending, and learne it perfectly without booke, to say it forwards and backewards.
>
> (*Briefe Introduction to the skill of Song*, c.1592, A4v)

In the late sixteenth century, owing to the extension of the vocal range and the use of more sophisticated **harmony**, the gamut as the basis of music was becoming seriously outmoded. In theory, it prevented the use of notes outside the basic gamut and hindered modulation or moving from one **key** into a related key within the same piece. To obviate these problems, theorists devised a system whereby one note could be identified by two or more syllables of the gamut, such as F **fa** ut or G **sol** ut, etc. Campion refers to this when he says,

> ... the olde *Gam-ut*, in which there is but one **Cliffe**, and one Note, and yet in the same Cliffe he wil sing *re & sol*. It is most true that the first invention of the *gam-ut* was a good invention, but then the distance of Musicke was cancelled within the number of twenty Notes ... the liberty of the latter age hath given Musicke more space both above and below, **alter**ing thereby the former naming of the Notes: the curious observing whereof hath bred much unnecessary difficultie to the learner
>
> (*A New Way*, c.1614, B4r)

During the early seventeenth century, the diatonic scale began to replace the outmoded gamut.

(B) One passage in *The Taming of the Shrew* mentions 'gamut' four times, but in no other play or poem does Shakespeare use this term. The scene in which the passage occurs is characterized by a comical atmosphere: Hortensio and Lucentio, disguised respectively as the music master Litio and the tutor Cambio, are vying for Bianca's attention and are *gamut*

beginning to expose their real identity. Hortensio resorts to a convoluted explanation of the gamut to try to impress Bianca and reveal to her who he really is:

> HORTENSIO: Madam, before you **touch** the **instrument**,
> To learn the order of my **fingering**,
> I must begin with rudiments of art,
> To teach you gamouth in a briefer sort,
> More **pleasant**, pithy, and effectual,
> Than hath been taught by any of my trade;
> And there it is in writing, fairly drawn.
> BIANCA: Why, I am past my gamouth long ago.
> HORTENSIO: Yet read the gamouth of Hortensio.
> BIANCA: [*Reads*] '*Gamouth* I am, the **ground** of all **accord**:
> A *re*, to plead Hortensio's passion;
> B ***mi***, Bianca, take him for thy lord,
> C *fa ut*, that loves with all affection.
> D *sol re*, one cliff, two notes have I,
> E ***la*** *mi*, show pity, or I die.'
> Call you this gamouth? **tut**, I like it not.
>
> (3.1.64–79)

From a theoretical viewpoint, Hortensio's gamut is in the **bass** F fa ut clef. Following the Renaissance system, the **clef** indicates the pitch of the note – in this case D. The name of the note is determined by the hexachord to which it relates – 'sol' to the hexachord starting on G and 're' to the hexachord starting on C.

When this passage is considered from a wider perspective, several interesting points emerge. 'Instrument' refers to the **lute** which Hortensio carries as part of his disguise, but this and other musical terms give rise to a number of bawdy innuendos (e.g. 'instrument' for 'genitalia', and 'fingering' for 'masturbating'). The list of the musical notes in the gamut is interesting in itself for its play on the phonetic level: 'B *mi*' suggests 'be mine', and 'E *la mi*' suggests 'alas! ah me'. (Fabry, p. 183). A similar play on words takes place in the **musician**s' scene in *Romeo and Juliet* (4.5). Bianca's curt reply intimates that she does not like Hortensio's courtship style, and that she is not impressed by his scholarly exposition of music theory.

(C) Fabry, 'Shakespeare's Witty Musician' (1982).
Herrisone, *Music Theory in Seventeenth-Century England* (2000).
Wilson (ed.), *A New Way* (2003), p. 43.

gigge see **jig**.

govern (A) The term 'govern' means to **play** an **instrument** in the sense that the fingers control what is being played. On a **wind** instrument such as a **recorder** or **hoboy**, the fingers and one thumb cover and uncover the holes, **ventage**s or **stop**s according to which **note** is played. The term is used not so much in a musical sense as in a technical meaning of handling an implement. It is rarely used in a musical context. When Morley talks about a '**song** being governed with **flat**s' (*Introduction*, 1597, p. 156) he means that the **key** of the song is determined by flats.

(B) In the Shakespeare canon, 'govern' is used on two occasions with a musical connotation. In *Hamlet*, the Prince tries to teach Guildenstern (who is trying to establish whether Hamlet is mad and then report back to Claudius) how to play the recorder. He exhorts him to:

> . . . Govern these ventages
> with your fingers and thumbs, give it **breath** with
> your mouth, and it will discourse most eloquent **music**.
> Look you, these are the stops.
>
> (3.2.357–60)

The use of a recorder as a stage property works as an effective visual metaphor, allowing Hamlet to convey the message to his 'friend' that he does not want to be an instrument in his hands. A few lines later, he abruptly tells Guildenstern: 'Call me what instrument you will . . . / you cannot play upon me' (370; 372).

In *Much Ado About Nothing*, 'govern' creates a paradoxical effect. Claudio observes that Benedick has changed drastically since falling in love with Beatrice. His jesting spirit has 'crept into a **lute**-string, and [is] now govern'd by stops' (3.2.60). Rather than Benedick governing an instrument, it is the instrument associated with melancholic **mood** that governs him.

govern

grace (A) There were two main categories of ornament in early modern **music**, namely 'graces' and **division**s. Graces were the formal or strict embellishments found almost exclusively in **instrument**al **music**. Divisions were the usually improvised, highly ornate scalic passages favoured by professional **sing**ers and instrumentalists for enlivening conjunct, slower moving melodic lines.

Graces abound in Elizabethan **lute** and **virginal** music. They are indicated by two, possibly three, basic signs. In the lute repertoire an upright cross and a diagonal cross are used. In keyboard music one or two oblique slashes through the tail of a **note** (or immediately above or below notes without tails) are usual. Their exact interpretation is far from clear. The earliest published list of graces with a commentary on their performance appeared in John Playford's *A Breefe Introduction to the Skill of Musick* (1654). Thomas Robinson describes three graces, the 'rellish', the 'fall' and the 'fall with rellish' in his *The Schoole of Musicke* (1603) but does not give their signs or method of performance. A short table of graces with their interpretation, compiled by Edward Bevin probably in the 1630s, is to be found in BL Add. MS 31403. It contains four main signs of which only the first (single slash) relates back to Elizabethan music. An earlier manuscript, BL Egerton MS 2971 contains a table of 'Caracters for ye graces of ye **viol**l' pasted on the final flyleaf. It identifies two main groups of graces, four 'graces with ye hande' and three 'graces with ye bowe'. The principal two graces, the shake and the 'fall' or appoggiatura, emerge as the basis for all the others. Moreover, the interpretation of the graces seems to relate viol and lute performance style and technique, at least as far as ornamentation is concerned.

Graces were an essential characteristic of Elizabethan instrumental music and served both a rhetorical and an articulatory function. They helped express the most important notes of a musical line and, especially in **dance** music, reinforced the structural rhythms of the piece.

(B) 'Grace' and '**tut**' (a type of grace) are mentioned in close proximity by York when he dismisses Bolingbroke's humble gesture of kneeling, comparing it to a pointless musical embellishment: 'Tut, tut! / Grace me no grace, nor uncle me no uncle' (*R2* 2.3.87). 'Grace' is also used in the concluding speech of the play by Bolingbroke, now King Henry IV, when he announces to his courtiers his intention to undertake a pilgrimage to the Holy Land. He wants to obtain divine forgiveness for the murder of Richard:

> I'll make a voyage to the Holy Land,
> To wash this blood off from my guilty hand.
> **March** sadly after, grace my mournings here,
> In weeping after this untimely bier.
>
> (5.6.49–52)

The court's weeping for Richard's death ornaments the King's own grief as graces embellish a **melody** (Robbins, p. 237). Similarly, in the despair following Lucrece's rape, only '**sigh**s and groans and tears may grace the fashion / Of her disgrace' (*Luc* 1319–20).

In a more light-hearted context, Claudio is convinced that the time is right for a **song** since the evening is 'still . . . as hush'd on purpose to grace **harmony**' (*Ado* 2.3.38). On this occasion, human music (*musica humana*) can achieve the harmony that is normally accorded only to the music of the spheres (*musica mundana*) through the employment of ornaments achieved in practical music (*musica instrumentalis*).

(C) Beer, 'Ornaments in Old Keyboard Music' (1952), argues that ornaments explained in later seventeenth-century sources can be applied to Elizabethan music.

Clutton, 'The Virginalists' Ornaments' (1956), adds to the discussion.

Dart, 'Ornament Signs in Jacobean Music for Lute and Viol' (1961), refers to BL Add. MS 31403 and discusses BL Eg. MS 2971 in some detail.

Hunter, 'The Application of Grace Signs in the Sources of English Keyboard Music' (1989), is a detailed account of ornaments.

Poulton, 'Graces of Play in Renaissance Lute Music' (1975), is a brief survey.

Robbins, 'Shakespeare's Sweet Music' (1968).

Shepherd, 'The Interpretation of Signs for Graces in English Lute Music' (1996), is an engaging article on differing approaches to graces and relates lute graces to keyboard signs.

Wulstan, *Tudor Music* (1985), ch. 6, discusses 'Graces in play', especially in keyboard music.

grace

Greensleeves (A) Probably the best-known popular **song tune** of Elizabethan times, it survives in two basic versions on which numerous variants were made. The compound duple rhythm version is found in Dublin, Trinity College MS 408/2 (c.1605); the simple duple rhythm version in Folger Library MS V.b.280 (c.1590).

(B) This **ballad** is mentioned in the dialogue of *The Merry Wives of Windsor* on two separate occasions. When Mrs Ford and Mrs Page realize that Falstaff has written the same love letter to both of them, the former ironically observes that his words 'do no more adhere and keep place together than the / hundred **Psalm**s to the tune of "Greensleeves"' (2.1.62–3). Just as the tune of a popular **love song** is not suitable for a song dedicated to God, so Falstaff's promises of constancy **sound** inappropriate.

Falstaff himself refers to the song when, hoping to be able to satisfy his desire for the two women, he delivers a speech interspersed with references to aphrodisiacs. Among other things, he wishes that the sky would 'rain potatoes' (5.5.19), 'snow eringoes' (i.e. candied roots of sweet holly, 20) – both thought to enhance sexual desire – and '**thunder** to the tune of "Green-sleeves"' (19). These lines reveal Sir John's unsophisticated perception of love.

(C) Duffin, *Shakespeare's Songbook* (2004), pp. 177–9, notates the music for this ballad.

Ward, 'And who but Ladie Greensleeues?' (1990), provides a full account of the ballad.

ground (A) In its most straightforward meaning, 'ground' is the **bass part** or **voice** of a piece of **music** in which *cantus, medius* (**mean** or alto) and tenor parts also occur. More often, the term has a more complicated technical meaning of structural significance. The English ground was a simple **tune** or group of **note**s, generally slow moving, used as the basis (*cantus firmus*) for embellishment or **descant** treatment in another voice or part. When there was repetition of the tune, the ground acted as a sort of ostinato. Often the ground was sited in the bass and sectional variations would be developed upon it as in William Byrd's 'Hughe Ashtons Grownde' (MLNB, 35), in which twelve variations are built upon a regularly recurring bass pattern. Where schematic repetition is not involved, 'ground' is the name given simply to the bass part, the foundation on which the music is built. Often, grounds were connected with **dance**s. An early notated keyboard ground of this kind is Hugh Aston's *Hornepype* (BL Roy.App. 58, c.1540). Others assumed a role not dissimilar from a **drone** and were associated with pastoral contexts: 'To teach our flocks their wonted bounds, / Our **bagpipe**s **play** the shepherds' grounds'. (Weelkes, 1598, no. 23).

(B) The connection between ground and descant is evident in Buckingham's recommendation to Richard that he should pretend he wants to refuse the title of King which is about to be offered to him:

> The Mayor is here at hand. Intend some fear,
> Be not you spoke with but mighty suit;
> And look you get a prayer-book in your hand,
> And stand between two churchmen, good my lord –
> For on that ground I'll make a holy descant –
> And be not easily won to our requests:
> Play the maid's part, still answer nay, and take it.
> (*R3* 3.7.45–51)

The musical nuances of these lines allow Buckingham to expose his plan in an oblique manner: he intends 'to structure a descant on the "ground" (bass) of the theme represented by Richard's pious appearance' (Hammond, p. 248). The variation at line 51 of the proverb 'maids say nay and take it' (Tilley, p. 405) further exploits the musical context of this speech: 'playing the maid's part' could hint at a **song** for two voices, one of which is female.

Trying to dissuade Chiron and Demetrius from quarrelling for Lavinia's love, Aaron warns them: 'Young lords, beware! and should the Empress know / This **discord**'s ground, the music would not please' (*Tit* 2.1.69–70). The reason or 'ground' for the two brothers' quarrel and the disharmony it causes, like a bass **sing**ing a descant unskillfully, would not please Tamora. Musical imagery is used to express the idea of discord elsewhere in the Shakespeare canon. Aaron's suggestion of how the conflict between the two brothers should be overcome goes against the expectation that they should aspire to **harmony**, since he encourages them to rape the object of their desire, a brutal act which will cause further conflict and chaos.

ground

Guiderius and Arviragus decide to sing a **dirge** for the (apparently) dead Imogen, who they believe to be Fidele. The latter exhorts his brother as follows: 'And let us ... though now our voices / Have got the mannish **crack,** sing him to th' ground' (*Cym* 4.2.235–6). The obvious meaning of the expression 'sing to the ground' is 'sing in his honour while he is being buried'. However, the reference to the boys' voices having just broken gives this expression another nuance, i.e. that they can now sing the bass part properly.

See also **burden, dump, gamut**.

(C) Hammond, *Richard III* (2002).
Tilley, *A Dictionary of Proverbs in England* (1966).

H

harmony (A) Whereas today harmony in **music** means almost exclusively the way **voice**s or **part**s relate vertically according to rules and conventions developed from the seventeenth century onwards, in the sixteenth century it had a less technical meaning. At one level it could simply refer to the pleasantness or '**sweet**-sounding' quality of music. In this sense, it signified the melodiousness of a **tune** or the **concord** of several parts: 'the **accord** of diverse **sound**s or **note**s' (Thomas, 'Harmonia'). Not only do the parts sound 'sweet' because of the use of consonances (i.e. thirds, sixths, eighths), they also bind together in 'sweete agreement' (Minsheu, 'Harmonia').

On a philosophical level, the term was used to refer to the 'harmony of the heavens', the music of the spheres. It implied a heavenly concord, effected by music. In this context and others where agreement or concord of several parts making up a whole is implied, harmony became synonymous with 'music'. This concept transpires in Lorenzo's famous speech in *The Merchant of Venice*, 5.1.54–68 (see 'music' for a detailed comment on this passage).

(B) In Shakespeare, visions and apparitions, which often involve the sounding of music on the stage to 'frame' them within the main plot, are intimately connected with the concept of harmony. This is because, more than any other devices, they allow an insight into the supernatural. An illuminating example is observed in *The Tempest*. Just before

harmony

the apparition of the banquet to Alonso, Antonio and their followers, we have a stage direction followed by an interesting exchange:

> **Solemn** and **strange** *music, and Prospero on the top, invisible.*
> ALONSO: What harmony is this? My good friends, hark!
> GONZALO: Marvellous sweet music!
>
> (3.3.17–18)

Music and **dance** accompanying the apparition of the banquet (3.3.19.SD) strongly contrast with the **harsh** sound provided by the **thunder** and lightning effect (3.3.53.SD) and by the entry of Ariel '*like a harpy*' (3.3.53.SD). This scene is permeated with dramatic irony: the creation of practical music on the stage is interpreted by the characters on the main acting area as harmonious music of the spheres. However, the audience is aware that this is a deceptive perception since they can see Prospero on the stage gallery **perform**ing his magic power. In Elizabethan and Jacobean venues, the stage gallery was often occupied by **musician**s: hence, in a seventeenth-century production of the play, the proximity between Prospero and the musicians performing the 'solemn and strange' music would have conveyed multilayered meanings.

In a later scene, Prospero puts on a spectacular **masque** to celebrate the engagement between Ferdinand and Miranda. Among other devices, the masque involves the descent of Juno from the top of the stage. The goddess **sing**s a fertility song and Ferdinand comments that the vision in front of his eyes is 'harmonious charmingly' (4.1.119). The combination of these two words has a very special effect:

> A '**charm**' is both a magic spell and a song, and Ferdinand's praise for the masque suggests that it, like the music which first led him to Prospero and Miranda, has a power beyond the mere delighting of the senses, reflecting instead a divine, cosmic harmony.
>
> (Lindley, p. 187)

Nowhere else in the Shakespeare canon does the integration between practical and world music acquire such a fundamental role in the development of the plot: comments on the delight derived from harmony contribute to the philosophical debate of the relationship between the divine and the human.

As in *The Tempest*, solemn music is **play**ed to underline a vision in

Henry VIII; this time, however, the vision precedes the death of Katherine of Aragon, hence the music is '*sad and solemn*' (4.2.81.SD) rather than '*solemn and strange*' (*Tmp* 3.3.17.SD). The disgraced Queen urges her gentleman usher:

> Cause the musicians play me that sad note
> I nam'd my **knell**, whilst I sit meditating
> On that celestial harmony I go to.
> *Sad and solemn music.*
> (4.2.78–80)

Approaching death, Katherine – and with her the audience – is able to get closer to the harmony of the music of the spheres (*musica mundana*), which is not accessible to human beings in their mortal state.

Strictly connected with the supernatural quality of harmony are its healing powers, as Lysimachus' speech makes clear. He hopes that Marina will be able to cure Pericles' suffering thanks to her 'sweet harmony' (*Per* 5.1.45). When later in the same scene Marina sings to Pericles, this triggers the recognition of the girl as Pericles' long-lost daughter.

Marcus' **lament** over the rape and mutilation of Lavinia is full of terms pointing to the harmonious nature of music, which is now irreparably lost:

> Fair **Philomela**, why, she but lost her **tongue** . . .
> O, had the monster seen those lily hands
> Tremble like aspen leaves upon a **lute**,
> And make the silken **string**s delight to kiss them,
> He would not have **touch**'d them for his life!
> Or had he heard the heavenly harmony
> Which that sweet tongue hath made,
> He would have dropp'd his knife . . .
> (*Tit* 2.4.38; 44–50)

In his invective against the man responsible for Lavinia's miserable state, her uncle compares her to Philomela, who was transformed into a **nightingale** after being raped; the loss of her hands and tongue imply that Lavinia will no longer be able to pursue activities befitting a woman of her social status, namely playing the lute and singing. The use of the word 'heavenly' to describe the harmony produced by

harmony

Lavinia emphasizes the quasi-sacrilegious nature of the violence inflicted on her. The reference to the lute shows that in Marcus' eyes, 'Lavinia has become the **instrument**, now untuned' (Bate, p. 189).

In other contexts, pleasantness and melodiousness intrinsic in the concept of harmony enhance the meaning of political allusions. For instance, the King in *2 Henry VI* reflects on the quarrel between Gloucester and the Bishop of Winchester in musical terms: 'When such strings **jar**, what hope of harmony?' (2.1.55). When political agreement (harmony) is missing, chaos (**discord**) will ensue.

In the sequel to this history play, the King thanks the Lieutenant for treating him kindly during his spell in the Tower:

> . . . I'll well requite thy kindness,
> For that it made my imprisonment a pleasure;
> Ay, such a pleasure as incaged **bird**s
> Conceive, when, after many moody thoughts,
> At last by notes of household harmony
> They quite forget their loss of liberty.
> (*3H6* 4.6.10–15)

Implicit in this exposition is the idea that harmony experienced in a captive state cannot match that experienced in freedom. What the bird can **hear** are simple 'notes' as opposed to the **melodious** full singing (the latter a recurrent image in Elizabethan and Jacobean literature) of other birds.

(C) Bate, *Titus Adronicus* (1995).
   Lindley, *The Tempest* (2002).
   Minsheu, *A dictionarie in Spanish and English* (1599).
   Thomas, *Dictionarium Linguae Latinae et Anglicanae* (1587).

harp (A) With its distinctive triangular shape and ancient symbolic associations, the harp, more than any other **instrument**, has been the subject of iconographic representation throughout the ages. Despite uncertainties over terminology and confusion with other plucked **string**ed instruments (e.g. lyra, cithara), and notwithstanding the diversity of types of instrument found in different regions (e.g. Ireland, Wales), it can be said that in the Middle Ages the harp was a comparatively

harp

small instrument with up to 19 strings. In the Renaissance it expanded and the Italian double-stringed instrument (*arpa doppia*) became favoured in art **music**. The harp was employed variously in both folk and art music contexts as a solo instrument, often accompanying **voice**, or in ensembles. It is found depicted in Christian iconography (especially King David **play**ing or tuning a harp), royal occasions, banquets, processions and domestic or rustic scenes. Men are shown playing the harp either as soloist or in large ensembles in the more public occasions, whilst women generally played in small groups, in more private, domestic settings. Men and women playing different instruments together (e.g. **lute** and harp) are not uncommon in Renaissance pictures.

(B) Stage directions for harps are rare in Renaissance drama (Dessen and Thomson's *Dictionary of Stage Directions* gives only five examples) and are never observed in the plays by Shakespeare. However, there are some interesting references to the harp in the dramatic dialogue. When hearing from King Richard II that he has been sentenced to banishment for life, Mowbray uses an elaborate musical metaphor to express his despair:

> My native English, now I must forgo,
> And now my **tongue**'s use is to me no more
> Than an unstringed **viol** or a harp,
> Or like a cunning instrument cas'd up,
> Or being open, put into his hands
> That knows no **touch** to **tune** the **harmony**.
> (*R2* 1.3.160–5)

In exile, he will no longer speak English and will lose his competence, like an inexperienced **musician** incapable of tuning and playing a stringed instrument which has been enclosed in its **case** for a long time.

In *1 Henry IV*, Glendower defends himself against Hotspur's derogatory remark about his Welsh origins by underlining his connection with the English court where, he says, 'being but young I **frame**d to the harp / Many an English **ditty** lovely well' (3.1.121–2).

There is a reference to the mythological harp played by Amphion to raise the walls of Thebes after Gonzalo mistakenly identifies Carthage with Tunis:

201

harp

>ANTONIO: His word is more than the miraculous harp.
>SEBASTIAN: He hath rais'd the wall, and houses too.
>ANTONIO: What impossible matter will he make easy next?
>(*Tmp* 2.1.88–90)

When choosing the entertainment for the newly wed couples, Theseus discards the first option on offer, 'The battle with the Centaurs, to be sung / By an Athenian **eunuch** to the harp' (*MND* 5.1.44–5).

The blind were commonly associated with harping, as is clear for instance from these lines in Lyly's *Sapho and Phao* (c.1582): 'Harping alwaies upon love, till you be as blind as a harpar' (4.3.34, taken from Tilley, p. 291). An entry in the 1580 *Nottingham Rec.* IV. 194 ('Gevyn to the blynde harpar xij*d*', taken from *OED*) further supports this point, as does a common drinking pledge of the sixteenth and seventeenth centuries: 'Have among you, blind harpers' (Tilley, p. 291). Berowne's words towards the end of *Love's Labour's Lost* are in line with this commonplace association. Recognizing that his courting techniques are too pretentious, he promises that he will never again 'woo in **rhyme**, like a blind harper's **song**' (5.2.405).

(C) *A Checklist of European Harps* (1979).
Dessen and Thomson, *A Dictionary of Stage Directions* (1999), pp. 110–11.
Rensch, *The Harp* (1969).
Riesthuis, *The Historical Harp* (1998).
Tilley, *A Dictionary of Proverbs in England* (1966).

harsh see **discord**.

hautboy see **hoboy**.

hay (A) Of the large number of varying kinds of **branle** described by Arbeau, the hay branle is '**dance**d in duple **time** like the **coranto**. The dancers begin, one at a time in succession, by dancing the **melody** in the manner of the coranto and at the end they interweave and make the hay' (*Orchesography*, 1589, p. 169). It is an old rustic dance and was accompanied by rustic **instrument**s such as **pipe**, **tabor** or **bagpipe**.

Its name may be derived from the French 'la haye', meaning 'artificial hedge' (ibid.). In *A Countercuff given to Martin Junior* (1589), Nashe links the term with other lyric terms: 'You shall shortlie have a Glosse and a Commentarie upon your Epilogue, with certaine Hayes, **Jig**ges, Rimes, **Roundelay**s, and **Madrigal**s'.

(B) Dull mentions the instrument he will use to accompany this dance when he explains to Holofernes and Moth what he intends to do during the pageant of the Nine Worthies: '. . . I will **play** / On the tabor to the Worthies, and let them dance the hay' (*LLL* 5.1.153–4). The pastoral atmosphere that this entertainment for the Princess of France and her ladies-in-waiting is meant to achieve is spoilt in the ensuing scene by the incompetence of the people playing the Worthies, and by the announcement of the death of the King of France, which brings the play to an abrupt end.

hear (A) Robert Burton describes hearing as 'a most excellent outward sense, by which we learn and get knowledge. His object is **sound**, or that which is heard' (Dell and Jordan-Smith, p. 138). In an age of widespread illiteracy like the Elizabethan and Jacobean periods, hearing **music** was the most common form of music reception. Music propagandists such as Morley and Drayton would have us believe that **perform**ing music was both commonplace and highly accomplished. Granted, in courtly, ecclesiastical, aristocratic and mercantile circles, music-making was popular and expertly done. A large number of **madrigal** books and books of **ayre**s were published during the 1590s and the first two decades of the seventeenth century, all cleaving royal or aristocratic patronage and often bought by foreign merchants or English merchants going abroad. Several music treatises and **instrument**al tutors were published, presumably for a ready market of (young) beginners, as their authors sometimes claimed. A large amount of keyboard and instrumental music circulated in manuscripts. But Morley's suggestion that after-dinner **sing**ing was a common custom (*Introduction*, 1597, p. 1), or that spontaneous instrumental and vocal performance was pervasive as suggested by Drayton:

> The English that repyn'd to be delay'd so long

hear

> All quicklie at the hint as with one free **consent**,
> Strooke up at once and sung each to the Instrument
> (*Poly-Olbion*, 1613, 'Fourth Song')

is not borne out by fact.

Hearing music is integral and relative to the Elizabethan soundscape. Folkerth contends that 'the soundscape is not entirely an objective phenomenon, but rather the intersection between the sounds we hear and how we react to and derive meaning from them' (p. 34).

(B) Shakespeare exploits this concept. Hearing music or imagining hearing music can have the desired effect upon both *dramatis personae* and audience. The conventionalities of music – for example, quick, major-**key** for happiness, slow, minor-key for sadness – would pertain whether or not music actually sounded on the stage. It would be sufficient to say that music was of such and such a kind to engender merriment, happiness, sorrow, concern or other emotions connected with the power of music. Even for the Elizabethan reader, imagining hearing music would have achieved the same effect.

Before being murdered in the dungeon at Pomfret Castle, Richard soliloquizes about the meaning of life, comparing it to the musical concept of **time** in relation to **proportion** (or lack of it). At the beginning of his soliloquy Richard asks himself: 'Music do I hear?' (*R2* 5.5.41). Marginal stage directions in different editions of this history play – for instance Q1 (1597) has '*the music plays*' (I4r), and Folio has '*music*' – reveal that music was expected to be played in performance. The audience would have been able to hear the music with Richard, and thus be totally receptive both to the practical and theoretical implications of the speech.

The Host tries to change Julia's melancholic **mood** by having her hear music: 'Come, we'll have you merry: I'll bring you / where you shall hear music' (*TGV* 4.2.31–2). But even though music should have a positive influence on people's moods, in *The Merchant of Venice* Jessica observes: 'I am never merry when I hear **sweet** music' (5.1.69). This is because Jessica realizes that, no matter if the music played by human beings sounds harmonious ('sweet'), it will never be as perfect as the music of the spheres, which cannot be heard by mortals.

In his attempt to affect Benedick's feelings towards Beatrice, Don Pedro asks his followers: 'Come, shall we hear this music?' (*Ado* 2.3.37).

hear

This exhortation is followed by the **song** '**Sigh** no more, ladies', which marks the beginning of Benedick's excursions with love.

The harmonious music of the mermaid has an extraordinary power which cannot be achieved by human music, as Oberon explains:

> . . . once I sat upon a promontory,
> And heard a mermaid on a dolphin's back
> Uttering such **dulcet** and harmonious **breath**
> That the rude sea grew civil at her song,
> And certain stars shot madly from their spheres,
> To hear the sea-maid's music.
> (*MND* 2.1.149–54)

Given the supernatural quality of the mermaid's **voice**, it is not surprising that it can influence the course of natural phenomena.

The opening line of *Sonnet* 8 is addressed to the poet's young friend: 'Music to hear, why hear'st thou music sadly?' Through the use of musical metaphors (evoking theoretical concepts such as '**concord**', '**well-tuned** sounds' and '**bear a part**'), the poet tries to persuade him to get married and have children. On the other hand *Sonnet* 128, also with a musical theme but this time dedicated to the Dark Lady, begins with the line: 'How oft when thou, my music, music play'st'. It indulges in sexual imagery evoked by musical terms such as '**jack**' and '**fingering**'. The two sonnets explore two different aspects, and perceptions, of music: whilst *Sonnet* 8 focuses on how we understand the theoretical implications of music by hearing it, *Sonnet* 128 is about practical music (*musica instrumentalis*) and its effect on our sensual nature.

See also **voice**.

(C) Dell and Jordan-Smith (eds), *The Anatomy of Melancholy* (1938).
Folkerth, *The Sound of Shakespeare* (2002), especially chs 2 and 3.
Smith, B. R., *The Acoustic World of Early Modern England* (1999), pp.101–6, discusses 'listening' and relates it to 'seeing' in early modern times.

hey (ho) (A) Found frequently in the **burden**s or refrains of **song**s 'hey' is most often linked with 'ho' and/or '**nonny** no'. The hey may refer to 'heave' (heave-ho) of working songs found in nautical and other contexts. The characteristic lengthening in utterance is an onomatopoeic

hey (ho)

representation of its emotional significance, generally heaviness, sadness and resignation.

(B) The Shakespeare canon has several songs which use this refrain. It usually expresses a melancholy **mood**, as in 'Sigh no more, ladies, sigh no more' (*Ado* 2.3.62–74), whose main theme is men's unfaithfulness; or in *Twelfth Night*'s concluding song 'When that I was and a little tiny boy' (5.1.389–408), which bestows a vein of sadness to the end of this comedy. This song is one of the few used by Shakespeare which is not traceable in any contemporary sources. Its refrain ('With hey, ho, the **wind** and the rain, / For the rain it raineth every day') is also found in *King Lear*, when the Fool bitterly observes that

> He that has and a little tine wit –
> With hey, ho, the wind and the rain –
> Must make content with his fortunes fit,
> Though the rain it raineth every day.
> (3.2.74–7)

Shakespeare 'seems to have written it, perhaps for use in the comedy, and found it useful to quote it in the later tragedy' (Duffin, p. 449). Certainly, the Fool's reference to the rain enhances the sense of dark despair in this scene dominated by a raging storm which underlines Lear's descent into madness.

The most poignant use is found in one of Ophelia's 'mad' songs, ominously anticipating her death:

> They bore him barefac'd on the bier,
> Hey non nonny, nonny, hey nonny,
> And in his grave rain'd many a tear.
> (*Ham* 4.5.165–7)

In quite a different context, the onomatopoeic combination of 'hey, ho', 'hey nonino', and 'hey ding a ding' in the song 'It was a lover and his lass' (*AYLI* 5.3.16–33) captures the childlike joy that love brings to young people in the springtime. It provides an interesting contrast to **'Blow**, blow, thou winter wind' (2.7.174–90) celebrating the winter (Noble, p. 76) earlier in the same play.

hey (ho)

(C) Duffin, *Shakespeare's Songbook* (2004).
Noble, *Shakespeare's Use of Song* (1923).

high (A) As a musically descriptive term, 'high' refers to relative pitch. All **sound**ing **music** has pitch, that is the relative highness or lowness of the **note**(s) being **play**ed or sung. **Instrument**s and **voice**s **perform** at differing pitches depending on their size and nature. A high-pitched voice, the **treble**, is the property of a pre-pubescent boy or a woman. A **low**-pitched voice is a deep man's **bass**. Similarly, instruments in Elizabethan England were referred to as treble, bass, **mean**, tenor, etc. according to their pitch or register. Pitch is indicated in notated music either by the place on the stave a note-value occupies or by a letter or number written in a **lute** or **organ** tablature. The pitch of a note on the stave is determined by the choice of **clef**. Each voice had its own clef best suited to representing its pitch, today referred to variously as 'treble clef', 'alto clef', 'tenor clef' and 'bass clef'. It was important therefore to choose the correct clef, as Morley attests: 'Now must you diligentlie marke that in which of all these **compass**es you make your musicke, you must not suffer any **part** to goe without the compasse of his rules [i.e. stave], except one note at the most above or below ... It is true that the high and lowe **key**es come both to one pitch, or rather compasse, but you must understand that those **song**s which are made for the high key be made for more life, the other in the low key with more gravetie and staidnesse' (*Introduction*, 1597, p. 166). He then goes on to mention tuning and transposition, that is the **alter**ing of pitch: 'take an instrument, as a *Lute Orpharion, Pandora*, or such like, being in the naturall pitch, and **set** it a note or two lower it wil go much heavier and **dull**er' (ibid.). The pitches instruments and voices performed at in Elizabethan England is uncertain and the subject of considerable debate among present-day commentators and practitioners. Surviving instruments, such as the Oxford **cornett**s and **organ**s, indicate that differing pitches were used. Voices could adapt within their register or 'compass' to whatever pitch was needed to fit accompanying instruments. And whereas certain instruments, especially **string**ed instruments, could be **tune**d a semitone or tone higher or lower to match other instruments less flexible in their tuning (**flute**s, **pipe**s, etc.) in a mixed **consort**, large variables in pitch could not be accommodated. In order to cope with the pitch of the flute it is thought

high

that the pitch of the stringed instruments in Morley's *Consort Lessons* (1609) is higher than normal; in other words, as Morley specifies, the lute to be used is the 'treble'. Likewise, the violin or **viol** would be a treble.

'High' was used synonymously with '**loud**' in opposition to 'low' and '**soft**' music when it signified the music of **wind** instruments in contrast to stringed instruments and invoked the quarrel between Marsyas and **Apollo**.

(B) When Bolingbroke accuses Mowbray of murdering Gloucester, he resorts to acoustic conceits. He says that Gloucester's blood 'cries / Even from the **tongue**less caverns of the earth' (*R2* 1.1.104–5). To this King Richard replies: 'How high a pitch this resolution soars!' (109) and invites Mowbray to defend himself against these accusations. The latter's words build on the acoustic theme: 'O, let my sovereign turn away his face, / And bid his **ear**s a little while be deaf' (111–12). It is often argued that the reference to the high pitch evokes the flight of a hawk to its highest point, and that it serves as a reminder of Bolingbroke's falcon badge (Gurr, p. 62). However, a pun on the musical meaning of 'pitch' was also probably intended.

(C) Gurr, *Richard II* (1984).
Sternfeld, *Music in Shakespearean Tragedy* (1967), pp. 210–14, on 'loud' versus 'soft' music.

hit (it) (A) According to Chappell (vol. 1, p. 239) 'hit' refers to the name of a **dance tune**. He says it is 'mentioned as a dance in the play of *Wily Beguiled*, written in the reign of Elizabeth' (the play was published in 1606 and is ascribed by some scholars to George Peele). Chappell also notes that in 1579 'a ballat intytuled *There is better game, if you could hit it* was licensed to Hughe Jaxon' (ibid.).

(B) In *Love's Labour's Lost* Rosalind and Boyet **sing** the tune 'Can'st thou not hit it' in 4.1.125–8. Duffin (pp. 88–9) claims that it is a **song** for a game and notes that a '**lute** setting for the tune survives in Dublin, Trinity College MS 408/2 (c.1605) under the title *Hit*' and that 'the same tune survives in a setting for keyboard in Paris Conservatoire MS Rés. 1186 (1630–40) as *Can you not hitt it my good man*' (ibid., p. 89). The tune Duffin transcribes is essentially the same as Chappell.

hit (it)

An alternative hypothesis is put forward by Robbins (pp. 257–8). He thinks that the 1579 **ballad** involves a pun on hitting a target, or a deer, and is applied by extension to the concept of 'hitting' a **note**:

> ROSALIND: Thou canst not hit it, hit it, hit it,
> Thou canst not hit it, my good man.
> BOYET: And I cannot, cannot, cannot,
> And I cannot, another can.
> (*LLL* 4.1.125–8)

(C) Chappell, *Popular Music of the Olden Time* (1855–9).
Duffin, *Shakespeare's Songbook* (2004).
Robbins, 'Shakespeare's Sweet Music' (1968).

hoboy (A) It would be a mistake to equate the sixteenth-century English hoboy (hautbois, howeboie) with the modern oboe or even to suggest it was a direct precursor. The history of the 'hautboy', the precursor of the oboe, begins in the mid seventeenth century in France. The Elizabethan hoboy was a member of the shawm family, wooden **instrument**s of different sizes with finger holes, **sound**ed by a single or a double reed. A characteristic shape included a flared **trumpet**-like **bell**. **Consort**s of reed instruments were known generically as shawms (derived from the Latin 'calamus', meaning a reed or reed**pipe**; Ger. *Schalmei*; Fr. *chalemie*), and, according to Praetorius (1619), ranged from the very **low** (and very large) *Gross Doppel Quint-Pommer* to the **high** *Klein Schalmey*. In France, the higher pitched shawms were called hautbois. In England, both the terms 'shawm' and 'hoboy' appeared together in the same context, as in the following description of a spectacle presented to Queen Elizabeth at Kenilworth in July 1575 'This pageaunt was clozd up with a delectable **harmony** of Hautboiz, Schalmz, Cornets, and such oother loud muzik' (Robert Laneham, *A Letter*, ?1575. Cf also George Gascoigne, *The Princelye Pleasures*, 1576, lost; repr in *The Whole Woorks*, 1587). Galpin (*Old English Instruments of Music*, 4/1965) deduced that the latter was a higher-pitched instrument than the former. This quote also reveals another characteristic of the hoboy, that it was associated with '**loud**' (outdoor) **music**.

(B) As with **cornett**s, all stage directions for hoboys in the Shakespeare

hoboy

canon are found in the Folio edition of some tragedies and histories, for instance *Henry VIII, Macbeth, 2 Henry VI, Coriolanus, Hamlet* and *Titus Andronicus*. Of these, three (*Hamlet, 2 Henry VI* and *Titus Andronicus*) also survive in quarto editions antedating Folio. The three quartos of *2 Henry VI* do not prescribe any sound effect when the King and his followers make their first appearance on stage. On the other hand, Folio is very accurate with sound cues:

> **Flourish** *of* **trumpets***: then hoboys. Enter King, Duke Humphrey, Salisbury, Warwick, and Beauford, on the one side; the Queen, Suffolk, York, Somerset, and Buckingham, on the other.*
>
> (1.1.OSD)

In Folio *Titus Andronicus*, the banquet scene in which Tamora eats her own children's flesh is introduced as follows: '*Hoboyes. A table brought in. Enter Titus like a cook, placing the meat on the table, and Lavinia with a veil over her face*' (5.3.25.SD). The equivalent stage instruction in Q1 (1594), Q2 (1600) and Q3 (1611) requires the sounding of trumpets instead. A similar situation is observed with *Hamlet*: whereas Folio prescribes that hoboys be **play**ed before the dumb show acted by the itinerant actors (3.2.135), Q1 (1603) gives no musical cue, and Q2 (1604/5) mentions trumpets. Bate has recently argued that hoboys were preferred here perhaps because this is not an imperial entrance, which was usually underlined by the sounding of trumpets.

Henry VIII makes use of hoboys for different purposes: to herald the entry of Wolsey (1.4.34.SD), to underline the entry of tables for the banquet at Wolsey's palace (1.4.OSD) and during the coronation ceremony for Anne Boleyn (this is one of the most detailed stage directions in the Shakespeare canon, listing the order of the coronation in great detail). It also accompanies the **masque** during the banquet at Wolsey's palace: '*Hoboys. Enter King and others as Maskers, habited like shepherds* [. . .]' (1.4.63.SD).

The main function of the hoboys in the stage directions observed so far is ceremonial. This includes the sounding of the instrument during official courtly events such as processions, banquets and masques; hoboys also accompany dumb shows. Although Manifold rejects the theory that this instrument might evoke supernatural atmospheres, this has been favoured more recently, and is supported by a stage direction found in the early Elizabethan play *Gorboduc* (written c.1561 by Thomas

Norton and Thomas Sackville and published in quarto in 1565). Each of the five acts of this tragedy is preceded by a dumb show described by detailed stage directions, which, in the wording of the text, explain 'the order of the Dumb Show ... and the significance thereof'. Different instruments are called for in each dumb show (violins, cornetts, **flute**s and **drum**s), whose main role is to summarize in an allegorical way the events unfolding in the ensuing act. Significantly, the dumb show in which the goddesses of vengeance appear on stage 'as though from hell' is the only one to require hoboys:

> *First, the music of hautboys began to play, during which there came forth from under the stage, as though from hell, three Furies, Alecto, Megaera, and Tisiphone, clad in black garments sprinkled with blood and flames . . .*
> (*Gorboduc*, Dumb Show before Act 4, 1–4)

A clear connection between the underworld and the sound of this instrument is found in Shakespeare's *Antony and Cleopatra*: '*Music of the hoboy is under the stage*' (4.3.12.SD). This signals that Hercules 'whom Antony lov'd, now leaves him' (4.3.16) and that Antony's fate is sealed. The decision to have a hoboy played from under the stage in this scene might in part have been dictated by considerations of acoustics. As Manifold explains: 'if any instrument has to play under the stage, it had best be the hautboy, whose tone will penetrate almost any obstacle' (p. 61).

Falstaff refers to Justice Shallow's slim build with a series of metaphors, including a musical one: 'the **case** of a **treble** hoboy was a mansion for him' (*2H4* 3.2.326). The treble hoboy required a thin case. It has also been suggested (Melchiori, p. 131) that 'treble' applies to the high-pitched tone of Shallow's **voice**.

(C) Baines, *Woodwind Instruments and their History* (1977), ch. 10 'The Sixteenth Century and the Consorts'.
Bate, *Titus Andronicus* (1995).
Dessen and Thomson, *A Dictionary of Stage Directions* (1999), pp. 115–16.
Duffin, 'Backward Bells and Barrel Bells' (1997 and 1998).
Manifold, *The Music in English Drama* (1956).
Melchiori, *2 Henry IV* (1989).
Praetorius, *Syntagmatis musici tomus secundus* (1619).

hoboy

holding (A) As a musical term 'holding' means a refrain, **burden** or undersong.

(B) The only usage of this musical term in Shakespeare is observed in the scene of the drunken celebration on board Pompey's galley in *Antony and Cleopatra*. Enobarbus exhorts his companions:

> All take hands.
> Make battery to our **ear**s with **loud music**;
> The while I'll place you, then the boy shall **sing**.
> The holding every man shall bear as loud
> As his strong sides can volley.
> (2.7.108–12)

The boy will sing the main **part** while the men will sing the undersong as powerfully as possible. The excesses characterising this feast are encapsulated in the first line of the drinking **song** that follows, 'Come, thou monarch of the vine', dedicated to Bacchus. According to Ross Duffin, it is possible that the song was a 'three-part **round**: one part begins and the others "hold" their own parts ... especially suitable for the three rivals Caesar, Pompey, and Antony' (p. 110). This suggestion is interesting but not entirely convincing. It could be argued that there needs to be a contrast between the solo boy's **voice** and the adult male voices of the others, which the contrast in timbre will effect despite the 'loud' music.

(C) Duffin, *Shakespeare's Songbook* (2004).

hollow (A) In a musical or acoustic context, 'hollow' is usually associated with **sound** or the cavity that produces sound (e.g. the **bird**'s **breast** or person's mouth). As a metaphor it can be interpreted as the emptiness of sound, meaning insincerity, falseness and even **discord**. The place that is hollow lacks **music** in contrast to the place that is full of music. Marston employs it 'in a passage whose musical reference contrasts the music of normal and harmonious life with that of an exile' (Robbins, p. 260). He juxtaposes the hollow cell with the lively court:

hollow

> My cell, 'tis, lady, where instead of **masque**s,
> Music, tilts, tourneys, and such courtlike shows,
> The hollow murmurs of the checkless **wind**s
> Shall groan again, whilst the unquiet sea
> Shakes the whole rock with foamy battery.
> *(The Malcontent* 4.5.12–16)

(B) Shakespeare stresses the quality of emptiness associated with this term in *2 Henry VI*, when the King reacts violently to Suffolk's attempt at comforting him for the death of Gloucester:

> What, doth my Lord of Suffolk comfort me?
> Came he right now to **sing** a **raven**'s **note**,
> Whose dismal **tune** bereft my vital pow'rs;
> And thinks he that the chirping of a **wren**,
> By crying comfort from a hollow breast,
> Can chase away the first-conceived sound?
> (3.2.39–44)

Mentioning the part of a bird's body which produces its **voice** acquires a metaphorical nuance: the King is accusing Suffolk of offering words of circumstance without really meaning them. The choice of 'hollow' (43) allows Shakespeare to pun on 'deceitful' (Knowles, p. 259).

At the eve of the Battle of Shrewsbury, the Prince of Wales reads ominous signs in the **wind**, which he likens to a **trumpet** (an apt comparison in a martial situation). He defines its whistling 'hollow' (*1H4* 5.1.5), thus emphasizing its connection with the discord accompanying war.

References to the hollow parts of the human body associated with the perception and production of sound are sometimes used to conjure up a sense of loss and despair. For instance, the bird which sings at dawn when Romeo and Juliet must be separated is described by Juliet as having 'pierc'd the fearful hollow of [Romeo's] **ear**' (*Rom* 3.5.3). In *Titus Andronicus*, Marcus' horror when he realizes that Lavinia's **tongue** has been cut out is vented through a musical metaphor:

> O, that delightful engine of her thoughts,
> That blabb'd them with such pleasing eloquence,
> Is torn from forth that pretty hollow cage,

hollow

>Where like a **sweet** melodious bird it sung
>Sweet varied notes, **enchant**ing every ear!
>(3.1.82–6)

Like a bird singing in its cage, Lavinia's **tongue** was capable of enchanting those who surrounded her, and its mutilation causes loss of **harmony**.

(C) Knowles, *King Henry VI, Part II* (1999).
   Robbins, 'Shakespeare's Sweet Music' (1968).

horn (A) Like the Renaissance **trumpet**, the horn was not an **instrument** of Western art **music** until much later, or, as Adam Carse put it, the horn did not leave the hunting field and enter 'the sphere of cultured music' until the early eighteenth century (p. 210). The term refers to a large variety of wind instruments whose diverse forms prior to the eighteenth century cannot be confined or classified. These range from primitive single-**note** types made from shells or animal tusks and horns to straight-tube post-horns, bugles and multinote, metal, coiled, curved or hooped horns. There is some evidence that a closely coiled horn (*jegerhorn*) existed in the early sixteenth century, as is attested by Virdung (1511), but further evidence and surviving examples are very rare. The hunting horn (*trompe*), a crescent-shaped instrument with a single coil in the tubing, was found throughout Europe. It is illustrated in Jacques du Fouilloux's treatise, *La vénerie* (c.1561). The spiral horn (*cor à plusieurs tours*) was also known in the sixteenth century. But there is no evidence to support the argument that there was a consistent differentiation between the *trompe* and the *cor*.

Notated horn signalling codes for the hunt date back to fourteenth-century French manuscripts. In the later sixteenth century, some of these codes and their variants were printed on the continent. English codes, according to Eric Halfpenny (1954), were partly derived from them. He cites a manuscript entitled *Directyones to Wynde the Horne* (Somerset Record Office, printed in *Royal Commission on Historical Manuscripts*, 9th Report, 1884, pt 2, p. 495), thought to date from the beginning of the seventeenth century, which contains sixteen calls for the Chase, written in code. In Turbeville's *Noble Art of Venerie* (London, 1575), there are 17 horn calls given in a music notation (on a single

horn

pitch d¹), which seem to represent the English norm. Turbeville identifies the individual phrases of the horn calls as **Wind**es, e.g. 'The Recheat, with three windes'. Compositions, notably for keyboard, based on horn calls were included among the Elizabethan repertory, the most famous being John Bull's 'The King's Hunt' (FWVB II, no. 135).

Ravenscroft includes a hunting **song** in his collection of **catch**es called *Pammelia*:

> **Blow** thy horn, thou jolly hunter,
> Thy hounds for to revive-a,
> Show thyself a good huntsman
> Whilst that thou art alive-a . . .
> (1609, no. 57)

(B) Most stage directions for horns in the Shakespeare canon are connected with hunting, but there are some exceptions. In Folio *3 Henry VI* this instrument is **sound**ed by a messenger from behind the *frons scenae* just before he enters: '*Post blowing a horn within*' (3.3.161.SD). In *1 Henry VI*, Talbot '**wind**s *his horn*. **Drums strike** *up; a* **peal** *of* **ordinance**' (2.3.60.SD). This sequence of sound effects is intended to summon Talbot's soldiers, who save him from the Countess of Auvergne's attempt to imprison him.

In *The Two Noble Kinsmen* (3.1.95.SD, 3.1.108.SD, 3.5.90.SD, 3.5.158.SD, 3.6.106.SD and 3.6.131.SD), *Titus Andronicus* (2.2.OSD, 2.2.10.SD, 2.4.10.SD) and *The Taming of the Shrew* (Ind.i.15.SD) musical cues for horns accompany hunting parties. In Folio *King Lear*, Lear's entry from hunting (1.4.7.SD) is announced by horns. The use of this instrument here parallels the descent in social status suffered by the old King, whose first entry (before he relinquished his powers) was greeted by a ceremonial **sennet** (Shirley, p. 74).

The arrival of Theseus and his train in Q1 (1600) *A Midsummer Night's Dream* is preceded by '*Wind horn*' (4.1.102.SD). The hunting atmosphere is evoked through Theseus' exhortation to one of his followers to

> . . . Find out the forester,

horn

> For now our observation is perform'd,
> And since we have the vaward of the day,
> My love shall **hear** the music of my hounds.
>
> (4.1.103–6)

The horns and the 'music of the hounds' have an effect quite unlike the harmonious music **play**ed throughout the first part of the scene, when the spell on Titania is removed and she is reconciled to Oberon. Later in the same scene, Theseus orders that the sleeping Lysander, Demetrius, Helena and Hermia be awaken as follows:

> Go, bid the huntsmen wake them with their horns.
> *Shout within. Wind horns. They all start up.*
>
> (4.1.138)

While the Queen of the Fairies was brought back to reality through the use of gentle music, the four young mortals are awoken by a **harsh**er sound, which causes them to 'start up'.

The idea that the sound of the horn is unsophisticated is confirmed by a metaphor in *Henry V*, when the Dauphin proudly describes his horse on the eve of the Battle of Agincourt:

> When I bestride him, I soar, I am a hawk; he
> trots the air; the earth sings when he **touch**es it; the
> basest horn of his hoof is more musical than the **pipe** of
> Hermes.
>
> (3.7.15–18)

Even though 'horn' technically refers to the hoof, the pun on the sound produced by the instrument 'horn' is evident from the use of terms such as '**base**', 'musical' and 'pipe'.

During a hunt in the woods, Tamora proposes to Aaron that he becomes her lover:

> And curtain'd with a counsel-keeping cave,
> We may, each wreathed in the other's arms
> (Our pastimes done), possess a golden slumber,
> Whiles hounds and horns and **sweet melodious bird**s

216

> Be unto us as is a nurse's song
> Of **lullaby** to bring her babe asleep.
> (*Tit* 2.3.24–9)

To the lustful and unwomanly Queen of the Goths, the sound of the horn and the barking of hounds are as love conducive as the **melody** of birds singing.

In the opening scene of *King John*, Philip the Bastard ends his soliloquy when he notices Lady Faulconbridge:

> But who comes in such haste in riding-robes?
> What woman-post is this? Hath she no husband
> That will take pains to blow a horn before her?
> (1.1.217–19)

'Horn' is associated with riding and with the arrival of messengers; even more important, the musical pun alludes to her unfaithfulness with King Richard I (which had made her pregnant with Philip).

The horn is harbinger of bad news for Venus, when she is waiting for the outcome of Adonis's boar-hunt:

> She hearkens for his hounds and for his horn;
> Anon she hears them **chaunt** it lustily,
> And all in haste she coasteth to the cry.
> (*Ven* 868–70)

She starts to lose hope when she hears the 'timorous yelping' of the hounds (881) and later discovers that some of them have been badly hurt by the boar; her worst fear is realized when she finds the dead body of Adonis (1030).

(C) Carse, *Musical Wind Instruments* (1939).
Halfpenny, 'Tantivy: An Exposition of the "Ancient Hunting Notes"' (1954).
Heater, 'Early Hunting Horn Calls and their Transmission' (1995).
Morley-Pegge, *The French Horn* (1973), ch. 2, discusses the evolution of the horn.
Shirley, *Shakespeare's Use of Off-Stage Sounds* (1963).
Virdung, *Musica getutscht* (1511).

horn

hornpipe (A) The hornpipe was a popular **dance**, possibly related to the **jig**, which could be danced and sung: 'And lovely Graces, with wanton satyrs come and **play**, / Dancing and **sing**ing, a hornpipe or a **roundelay**' (Watson, 1590, no. 6).

Baskervill notes that 'like the jig, the hornpipe seems to have been used by groups of men and women somewhat in the manner of country dance' (p. 360) and concludes that 'there are many other allusions to the hornpipe as a dance for a number of participants, especially as a round dance' (ibid.).

(B) The only time this dance is mentioned by Shakespeare is in a rustic context. Before the sheep-shearing feast, the Clown observes that the shearers – 'three-man song-men all' (*WT* 4.3.42) – are 'most of them **mean**s and **base**s' (43). The only exception is represented by 'one Puritan amongst them, and he sings **psalm**s to horn-pipes' (44). The Puritan is the only singer in the three-**part** song to have a **high**-pitched **voice**, but because of his religious convictions he despises singing for frivolous purposes and dancing, and therefore he sings psalms to hornpipe music, or, perhaps, fits religious words to secular **tune**s.

(C) Baskervill, *The Elizabethan Jig* (1929).

hubbub see **whoobub**.

hum (A) As a non-verbal **sound**, 'hum' is often associated with the buzzing of bees and other insects. In the Shakespeare canon, it is used as a synonym for '**drone**' or '**burden**'. It can also mean the wordless sounding of a **tune** quietly uttered although Shakespeare does not use it in this sense.

(B) Lucrece likens humming to the **sing**ing of a burden when she compares her situation to that of **Philomela** who, after being raped by Tereus, was transformed into a **nightingale**:

> Come, Philomele, that sing'st of ravishment,
> Make thy sad grove in my dishevell'd hair;

>As the dank earth weeps at thy **languishment**,
>So I at each sad **strain** will strain a tear,
>And with deep groans the **diapason** bear;
>For **burthen**-wise I'll hum on Tarquin still,
>While thou on Tereus **descant**s better **skill**.
>   (*Luc* 1128–34)

In this stanza aural conceits merge with imagery of sexual violation ('groans', 'bear', 'burthen'). 'Humming', with its connotation of persistent **noise** and constant refrain ('burthen'), mirrors Lucrece's obsession with the violence which was inflicted on her and will drive her to commit suicide.

When Caliban, Stephano and Trinculo in a drunken state plot to murder Prospero, Ariel confounds them by **play**ing **music** while invisible. This frightens Stephano and Trinculo. Caliban tries to reassure them:

>Be not afeard, the isle is full of noises,
>Sounds, and **sweet air**s, that give delight and hurt not.
>Sometimes a thousand **twang**ling **instrument**s
>Will hum about mine **ear**s . . .
>   (*Tmp* 3.2.135–8)

The magical atmosphere of the island is reflected in its music and sounds. The sound of the 'twangling' (i.e. plucked) **string**ed instruments is continuous, as 'hum' with its related meaning of 'burden' suggests (Lindley, p. 169).

Anxious to persuade King Henry to move war against France, the Archbishop of Canterbury explains to him that he has loyal subjects ready to fight on his side. He compares the hierarchy in the kingdom to that of a colony of bees. Among the duties carried out in a well-ordered society are those of

>The singing masons building roofs of gold,
>The civil citizens kneading up the honey,
>The poor mechanic porters crowding in
>Their heavy burthens at his narrow gate,
>The sad-ey'd justice, with his surly hum,

hum

> Delivering o'er to executors pale
> The lazy yawning drone . . .
> (*H5* 1.2.198–204)

Musical imagery permeates this speech and the placing of 'hum' between the polysemic terms 'burthens' and 'drone' reinforces its musical associations with these two words.

(C) Lindley, *The Tempest* (2002).

human music (*musica humana*) see **music**.

hymn (A) The origins of the term lie in Ancient Greek pagan **song**s (e.g. Delphic hymn) and early Christian liturgical songs. In both, the essential meaning was a song of **praise**. Whilst the hymn was usually found in religious contexts in the early modern period, as a song of praise to God, it also kept its secular associations and could be used in a more general, non-Christian, way as an occasional or ceremonial song.

In Christian worship, there was often little distinction between a **psalm** and a hymn. In the late sixteenth century, English Protestants brought back with them from Europe metrical psalm **tune**s which quickly became incorporated into English practice. In 1562, John Day published Sternhold and Hopkins' metrical psalter which in its various editions remained in use as the principal book authorized for use in the Church of England for well over 100 years (and in fact continued in its 'New Version' until the nineteenth century when it was replaced by the first specifically designated 'hymn' books). The earliest English hymns, therefore, are to be found in this 1562 metrical psalter. They are musically simple and rhythmically straightforward.

If hymns intended for church use during the Elizabethan period were contained in the metrical psalter, then there was a body of sacred songs which existed outside the Church, probably intended for domestic use like the **madrigal** and **ayre**. Such collections include Hunnis' *Handful of Honisuckles* (1583) and Amner's *Sacred Hymnes* (1615).

(B) Hymns are associated with solemn contexts in the Shakespeare canon, for instance when Claudio pays homage to the tomb of the *hymn*

supposedly dead Hero. He reads the epitaph for Hero and then orders: 'Now, **music, sound**, and sing your **solemn** hymn' (*Ado* 5.3.11). The text that follows deals with the theme of sorrow accompanying death, but is not that of a psalm. In *King John*, the reference to the dying **swan** 'who **chaunt**s a **doleful** hymn to his own death' (5.7.22) is another example of the association between death and the singing of hymns.

Theseus warns Hermia that, unless she follows her father's wish and pledges to marry Demetrius, she must either die or enter a convent. If she chooses the latter, she will have:

> . . . to be in shady cloister mew'd,
> To live a barren sister all your life,
> Chaunting **faint** hymns to the cold fruitless moon.
> (*MND* 1.1.71–3)

The apparently Christian meaning of 'hymn' in this context acquires a more pagan nuance when the reference to the goddess of chastity Diana (the moon) at line 73 is considered: 'the anachronistic Christian image of a cloistered nun coalesces with that of a pagan priestess hymning Diana . . . , more appropriate to the Athens of Theseus' (Foakes, p. 50). This association is also found in *The Merchant of Venice*, when Lorenzo exhorts a group of **musician**s to 'wake Diana with a hymn' (5.1.66): this scene is set at night-time, hence Diana stands for the moon.

After Capulet discovers Juliet's apparent death on the day of her wedding to Paris, he wants to **change** the 'solemn hymns' which had been intended to be sung for the wedding ceremony into 'sullen **dirge**s' (*Rom* 4.5.88). Unlike the examples examined so far, in this context hymns are associated with a joyous ceremonial occasion.

See also **anthem**.

(C) Foakes, *A Midsummer Night's Dream* (1984).
Temperley, *The Hymn Tune Index* (1998), includes extensive commentary.
Watson, *The English Hymn* (1997).

I

imitate (A) As a technical term, 'imitate' has a specific meaning in **music** written in **part**s. It refers to the copying of one part by another in counterpoint and in Elizabethan times was called 'fuge'. Morley says, 'we call that a Fuge, when one part beginneth, and the other **sing**eth the same, for some number of **note**s (which the first did sing)' (*Introduction*, 1597, p. 77). In a more general sense it is found in connection with working or composing music from a model, as Morley reminds us when his 'pupil' asks: 'I wil by the grace of God diligentlie observe these rules, therefore I pray you give us some more examples which we may imitate, for how can a workeman worke, who hath had no patterne to instruct him' (ibid., p. 167).

(B) In her inconsolable despair Lucrece compares herself to **Philomela**, who vented her distress at Tereus' rape by singing after being transformed into a **nightingale**. Lucrece exhorts Philomela to 'sing of ravishment' (1128) and then begins to contemplate suicide:

> And whiles against a thorn thou **bear**'st thy part
> To keep thy **sharp** woes waking, wretched I,
> To imitate thee well, against my heart
> Will fix a sharp knife to affright mine eye,
> Who if it wink shall thereon fall and die.

imitate

> These **mean**s, as **fret**s upon an **instrument**,
> Shall **tune** our heart-**string**s to true **languishment**.
> (*Luc* 1135–41)

There is an abundance of musical puns in this and the preceding stanza, most notably the allusion to singing in parts, which gives 'imitate' the added sense of a musical **echo**.

See also **compose, point, report**.

incantation (A) In a general sense, 'incantation' refers to spontaneous or inspirational **sing**ing often associated with forms of religious ritual going back to pre-history. More specifically it refers to sung or **chant**ed sets of words – a **charm** or spell – used to engender a magical effect. The oldness of the spell was thought to give it extra power.

(B) This term is used only once by Shakespeare, when Joan of Arc conjures up some fiends before being captured by the English. She observes that her 'ancient incantations are too weak' (*1H6* 5.3.27). This part of the scene is dominated by Joan's waning magic powers: as a female practitioner of the occult, she is not given the ability to control her powers to the same extent as her male counterparts in other plays by Shakespeare (Austern, pp. 196–7). There may be a musical nuance in Joan's reference to 'incantations' because of the intimate link between the supernatural (be it good or bad) and **music**. If the adjective 'ancient' is taken to mean 'of ancient origin' rather than 'often-used', this reinforces Joan's connection with the world of witchcraft (Burns, p. 261).

(C) Austern, ' "Art to Enchant" ' (1990), on the function of music in magical and supernatural dramatic contexts.

Burns, *King Henry VI, Part I* (2000).

Gouk, *Music, Science and Natural Magic in Seventeenth-Century England* (1999).

Walker, *Spiritual and Demonic Magic from Ficino to Campanella* (1958), on music and magic.

instrument (A) In a musical context, the generic term 'instrument'

instrument

signifies the object used to make **music** in contrast to the human **voice** which **sing**s. It is appropriate, therefore, to refer to instrumental music as opposed to vocal music. The two come together when instruments are used to accompany singing.

The sixteenth century had for long been regarded by musicologists as essentially a period of vocal music with instrumental music a subsidiary genre, taking second place a long way behind vocal polyphony and solo song. The importance of instruments in the early modern period, however, should not be underestimated. It is a mistake to regard them as vocal substitutes. Whilst there is a substantial repertoire of sixteenth-century music suitable for either voices or instruments, many kinds of instrumental music clearly showed an independence and idiomatic approach quite distinct from vocal music.

Although the physical shape and **sound** of every instrument of the Renaissance was separately identifiable, most instruments were grouped into families or **consort**s (e.g. **viol**s, violins, **recorder**s, shawms, etc.). Reference, therefore, to a recorder or a viol, for example, could mean either a specific type of recorder or viol, or simply any member of the recorder or viol family. Moreover, certain instruments were known by several names (e.g. recorder, **flute, pipe**, etc); alternatively, one name (e.g. **fiddle**) could indicate a number of different instruments. Hence, alluding to 'instrument' could imply either a specific type or an unidentified type.

In addition to iconographic evidence, many instruments of the period actually survive in differing states of preservation. It is possible, therefore, to know what these instruments looked like (taking care to identify later additions or alterations) and how they might have **sound**ed. Towards the end of the twentieth century, a huge revival in interest in early musical instruments resulted in many being copied in modern reproductions and **play**ing techniques restored and refined.

It is often not possible to know precisely which instruments were employed in instrumental cues in plays and **masque**s but certain conventions governing usage and consort combinations allow us to make informed decisions. '**Still** music', for example, may indicate **soft** instrumental music. A viol consort would be more appropriate than a shawm band. '**Loud** music' signifies noisy **wind** instruments.

(B) There is only one stage direction in the Shakespeare canon requiring unspecified 'instruments': '*Here is heard a sudden **twang** of instruments, and* *the rose falls from the tree*' (*TNK* 5.1.168.SD). 'Twang' suggests that (plucked) **string**ed instruments would have been employed in contrast to the '*still music of records*' (136.SD) earlier in this scene full of supernatural omens and involving a number of spectacular effects.

In the dialogue, 'twangling instruments' are mentioned by Caliban among the noises which fill the island (*Tmp* 3.2.137). Elsewhere, Rosalind chides Silvius, who is in love with Phebe: 'Wilt thou love such a woman? What, to make thee / an instrument, and play **false strain**s upon thee? (*AYLI* 4.3.67–8). Rosalind is implying that Silvius is letting Phebe exert too much power over him (at line 70 she calls him a 'tame snake'): that this is an undesirable situation is clear when he is told that false strains are being played on him. This choice of words conveys the idea that tension and power games are intrinsic in love relationships, and that these result in one party being weaker than the other.

A similar tension emerges in *Hamlet*, when the protagonist expresses his distrust for Rosencrantz and Guildenstern:

> Why, look you now, how unworthy a thing
> you make of me! You would play upon me, you would
> seem to know my **stop**s, you would pluck out the
> heart of my mystery, you would **sound** me from my
> lowest **note** to the top of my **compass**; and there is
> much music, excellent voice, in this little **organ**, yet
> cannot you make it **speak**. 'Sblood, do you think I am
> easier to be play'd on than a pipe? Call me what
> instrument you will, though you **fret** me, yet you
> cannot play upon me.
>
> (3.2.363–72)

The 'little organ' (367) is a recorder which Hamlet is holding in his hands, unsuccessfully trying to make Guildenstern play it. 'Fret' (371) has a similar effect here to 'strain' in *As You Like It*. Its musical nuance overlaps with other meanings of the word, including 'irritate', 'consume' and 'devour'. Harold Jenkins has noted that 'Hamlet switches from wind to stringed instrument for the sake of the pun on "fret"' (p. 309). But he seems to disregard the fact that this word appears in a context where Hamlet mentions different playing techniques (playing on the stops, plucking and fretting) to express his discomfort at the idea of being manipulated. The Prince's speech concludes with a clear provocation:

instrument

'Call me what / instrument you will, though you / fret me, you cannot play upon me' (370–2). In other words, no matter how his two 'friends' and the Danish court label the Prince, he will not let them control him.

The Taming of the Shrew is the Shakespeare play with the largest number of references to 'instrument'. Hortensio's disguise as a **lute** teacher (a trick which allows him to approach and woo Bianca) provokes a series of bawdy innuendos, as in the lively exchanges between Hortensio, Lucentio (himself disguised as a schoolmaster) and Bianca in 3.1. The girl exhorts Hortensio to play his 'instrument' (25) while she listens to Lucentio's lecture.

> BIANCA: His lecture will be done ere you have tun'd.
> HORTENSIO: You'll leave his lecture when I am in **tune**?
> LUCENTIO: That will be never, tune your instrument.
> ...
> HORTENSIO: Madam, my instrument's in tune.
> BIANCA: Let's **hear**. O fie, the **treble jar**s.
> LUCENTIO: Spit in the hole, man, and tune again.
> (3.1.23–25; 38–40)

Commentators have been inclined to think that these references are strictly musical – when it was difficult to tune the lute, spitting in the treble **peg**-hole (e.g. Morris, p. 220) would facilitate this process. However, the sexual undertones of these passages are equally strong: the desire of both men to have intercourse with Bianca transpires from their references to the penis (the 'instrument' waiting to be tuned). The expression 'spit in the hole' is equally interesting as it refers to male orgasm during intercourse. 'Spit' refers to seminal emission (Williams, vol. 2, p. 1288), and 'hole' is a shape-metaphor for female genitalia (Partridge, pp. 155, 243). Later, Hortensio explains to Bianca that he must teach her the musical scale: 'before you **touch** the instrument / to learn the order of my **fingering**' (3.1.64–5). Once again, the bawdy tone of these lines is clear: the technique of fingering a wind instrument is here superimposed to the erotic image of masturbation.

In a more serious context, Northumberland reports Gaunt's death to King Richard: 'His **tongue** is now a stringless instrument, / Words, life, and all, old Lancaster hath spent' (*R2* 2.1.149–50). The idea of death is conveyed through the image of an instrument deprived of its strings and therefore incapable of producing any sound.

(C) Baines, *The Oxford Companion to Musical Instruments* (1992).
Jenkins, *Hamlet* (1982).
Morris, *The Taming of the Shrew* (1981).
Partridge, *Shakespeare's Bawdy* (1968).
Williams, *A Dictionary of Sexual Language* (1994).

J

jack (A) The jack is the small piece of wood into which a quill or leather plectrum is inserted so that when raised it plucks a metal **string** on a harpsichord, spinet or **virginal** to make it **sound**. A release mechanism allows the jack to fall back into place without sounding the string once the player lifts his/her finger from the key. On the virginal, the jacks are clearly visible. They generally run in a diagonal line from front left to right back.

(B) In *The Taming of the Shrew*, Hortensio (disguised as a **music** teacher) enters with '*his head broke*' (2.1.141.SD) after trying unsuccessfully to teach Katherina to **play** the **lute**. Questioned by Baptista, he explains how the girl abused him after breaking the **instrument** on his head:

> ... she did call me rascal **fiddler**
> And **twang**ling Jack, with twenty such vild terms,
> As had she studied to misuse me so.
> (2.1.157–9)

'Jack' can be interpreted as a derogative form of address, or even as a euphemism for 'penis' (Williams, vol. 1, p. 480). However, 'twangling' gives a musical flavour to the term: 'twangle' can mean 'to play upon [a stringed instrument] in a petty or trifling manner' (*OED*): the disparaging way in which Katherina treats Hortensio may reveal that she intuitively realizes he is not the music expert he purports to be.

jack

In *Sonnet* 128, 'How oft when thou, my music, music play'st', Shakespeare explains that the 'wood' (the **key**s of an instrument, probably the **virginal**) is 'blessed' (2) by the **touch** of his mistress's fingers. He envies 'those jacks that **nimble** leap / To kiss the tender inward' (5–6) of her hand: 'nimble', an appropriate adjective for a female player, suggests that she is particularly skilled, which results in the jacks moving in a swift and agile way. Some editors believe that the image evoked at line 5 is incorrect, since it is the keys rather than the jacks which touch the lady's fingers. However, this is not necessarily the case when we consider another metaphor in the same sonnet. Shakespeare claims that his lips would **change**

> . . . their state
> And situation with those dancing chips,
> O'er whom thy fingers walk with gentle gait.
> (9–11)

Clearly, 'chips' means 'keys': hence, the image of the jacks touching the palm of the hand 'works by extension of the metaphor' (Robbins, p. 271). The sonnet concludes with the poet's wish: 'Since saucy jacks so happy are in this, / Give them thy fingers, me thy lips to kiss' (13–14). 'Jacks' provides the opportunity for a pun on 'men' and virile attributes, and hints at the woman's promiscuity, a concept analysed from a more pessimistic stance in other sonnets, e.g. *Sonnets* 129, 133 and 134.

(C) Robbins, 'Shakespeare's Sweet Music' (1968).
Williams, *A Dictionary of Sexual Language* (1994).

jangle (A) To jangle is 'to make a **noise**, as **Bell**s when rung in no set **Tune**' (Bailey, 1730). This was the most common musical meaning in Elizabethan times, that is the **discord**ant **sound** made by bells rung in an arbitrary and uncontrolled pattern. The clashes made by the reverberations of the bells would result in a cacophonous polyphony.

(B) Of the four usages of this word in the Shakespeare canon, two have a musical connotation. During an exchange which provides comic relief from Pericles' shipwreck, three fishermen discuss greediness – with a possible topical hint at 'the tradition of Tudor polemic against

jangle

enclosures' (Hoeniger, p. 44). They compare 'rich misers' (*Per* 2.1.29) to whales who swallow smaller fish. Similarly, these men swallow 'the whole parish, church, steeple, bells, and all' (34). To this comment another fisherman replies that, had he been swallowed, he would 'have kept such a jangling of the bells' (41) which would have caused the miser to vomit the whole parish. The biblical image of Jonah being swallowed and then vomited by a whale influences this passage, but the musical reference gives it an originality of its own.

After being insulted by Hamlet, who tells her to go to a nunnery (which in Shakespeare's day could also mean 'brothel'), a distressed Ophelia reflects on his mental state:

> What a noble mind is here o'erthrown!
> . . .
> [I] now see that noble and most sovereign reason
> Like **sweet** bells jangled out of **time**, and **harsh** . . .
> (*Ham* 3.1.150, 7–8)

The musical metaphor of bells **ring**ing harshly because they are not keeping a rhythmical pattern ironically foreshadows Ophelia's 'mad' songs in 4.5. Both practical **music** on the stage and music as a metaphor are intimately linked to the mental state of the main characters of this play.

(C) Bailey, *Dictionarium Britannicum* (1730).
Hoeniger, *Pericles* (2001).

jar (A) The word 'jar' was a descriptive term in Elizabethan **music** referring to the unpleasant **sound** made when **instrument**s were **play**ed out of **tune** or when the **string**s on an instrument (e.g. **viol, lute**) were not tuned. This sense persisted into the eighteenth century, confirmed by John Kersey's definition: 'Jarr . . . in *Musick* to disagree, or go out of Tune' (*Universal English Dictionary*, 6th edn, 1706). The unpleasantness could be further compounded if instruments were played out of **time** as well so that their several **part**s were not in **harmony**.

(B) Hortensio, disguised as a lute teacher, approaches Bianca and vies with Lucentio for her attention. He tells her that he is ready to teach her how to play the lute: 'Madam, my instrument's in tune' (*Shr* 3.1.38). However, Bianca is less than impressed and replies that the instrument is not tuned properly since 'the **treble** jars' (39). The use of a musical instrument as a stage property allows Shakespeare to underline visually the musical imagery pervading this scene. Hortensio's reference to his instrument being 'in tune' suggests his desire to be in harmony with Bianca but also has a sexual connotation, further developed in Lucentio's suggestion that Hortensio should 'spit in the hole' (40) to tune the lute properly (see 'instrument' for a detailed discussion). By remarking that the lute jars, Bianca is telling Hortensio that she is not in tune with him and rejects his suit.

Later in the play, the word 'jar' is used more conventionally. Lucentio addresses Hortensio with a reconciliatory speech in the final scene:

> At last, though long, our jarring **note**s agree,
> And time it is, when raging war is done,
> To smile at scapes and perils overblown.
> (5.2.1–3)

A sense of restored harmony is conveyed in this description of the two rivals in love **sing**ing in **concord** ('notes' is synonymous with '**songs**' in this context).

The image of jarring strings conveys the idea of political unrest in *2 Henry VI*, where the King comments on the quarrel between Gloucester and the Bishop of Winchester: 'When such strings jar, what hope of harmony?' (2.1.55). Similarly, in *1 Henry VI* Exeter remarks that 'this jarring **discord** of nobility / . . . doth presage some ill event' (4.1.188, 91). Musical metaphors of discord as opposed to harmony are often used in political contexts.

Before the touching reconciliation between Cordelia and Lear, the former prays that her father will recover from insanity:

> O you kind gods!
> Cure this great breach in his abused nature,
> Th' untun'd and jarring senses, O, wind up
> Of this child-changed father!
> (*Lr* 4.7.13–16)

Lear's mental state is compared to a stringed instrument which needs to

jar

be tuned by 'winding up' or turning its **peg**. This speech is followed by the sounding of soothing music to accompany Lear's recovery: the contrast between the harmony of practical music on the stage and musical discord evoked by Cordelia's words could not be more powerful.

Helen discloses her anxiety about Bertram's possible amorous adventures during his visit at the French court when she observes: 'his jarring [will have] concord, and his discord **dulcet**' (*AWW* 1.1.172). This interesting oxymoron is created by pairing opposite musical concepts: 'jar' with 'concord', and 'discord' with 'dulcet'. Another paradoxical effect is achieved in *As You Like It* when Duke Senior declares ironically: 'If he [Jaques], compact of jars, grow musical, / We shall have shortly discord in the spheres' (2.7.5–6). Since the music of the spheres was considered to be the most harmonious type of music, it would be impossible for it to be discordant. Hence, the Duke implies that Jaques will never be able to 'grow musical' and in tune.

See also **noise**.

jay see **bird**.

jig (A) There are two main types of Elizabethan jig, sometimes distinguished today by different spellings, namely 'jig' and 'jigg'. The first is a **dance** and the second a short comedy or 'farce' acted at the end of a play. Morley includes jig as one of the 'many other kindes of daunces' after his brief descriptions of **pavan**s, **galliard**s, **almain**s, **branle**s, etc. (*Introduction*, 1597, p. 181). As a term used for a type of dance, it does not seem to have had a specific meaning. It probably involved leaping and a lively tempo and was sometimes associated specifically with the north of Britain. Florio described the Scottish jig as 'full of leapings' (*A Worlde of Words*, 1598). **Music** for jigs found in stylized keyboard miscellanies of the period confirm the lack of uniformity of character. Byrd's 'A Gigge' (FWVB II, p. 237) is a lively **piece** in compound rhythm employing a simple **tune** of popular origin. In contrast, Richard Farnaby's 'Noboddys gigge' (FWVB II, p. 162) is a much more sedate piece in simple binary rhythm (known as 'Scots **measure**') whose tune derives from the farce-jigg *Pickleherring* (see Baskervill, pp. 281–4; 515–18). Two examples by John Bull ('A Gigge' FWVB II,

p. 258 and 'Dr Bulls myselfe' FWVB II, p. 257) are rhythmically more sophisticated and lack the spontaneity and appeal of Byrd's jig. Though similar to the **coranto**, the jig seems to have been a particularly English dance and is not mentioned, for example, by Arbeau in *Orchesography* (1589) or Praetorius in *Terpsichore* (1612). It is, however, found as a type in contemporary Dutch collections such as Starter's *Friesche Lust-hof* (1621) and Adriaen Valerius' *Neder-Landtsche Gedenck-Clanck* (1626).

The stage jigg is defined by Dart/Tilmouth as 'a short burlesque comedy for two to five characters, sung in verse to one or more well-known tunes, interspersed with much lively dancing and **perform**ed by a team of professional comedians' (Grove Online, 'Jigg'). The famous Elizabethan clown, Richard Tarleton, is thought to have been one of the first major exponents of the form on the London stage during the 1570s and 80s. He was succeeded by William Kemp who also exported the vogue for the jigg to the continent, notably after he had taken the Earl of Leicester's players to Copenhagen in 1586 and later to Saxony. During the 1590s, a jigg customarily concluded a play on the London stage, or it might have been performed as a comic relief during an interlude in a tragedy or history. In the early 1600s, the jigg tended towards either the bawdy and rowdy and became identified with the more seedy north London public theatres such as the Red Bull, the Curtain and especially the Fortune; or the more refined romantic type presented by the players of the Bankside houses, the 'round' Globe and the Swan.

(B) The liveliness of the jig (dance) is sometimes evoked in the Shakespeare canon, for instance in *Much Ado About Nothing* (2.1.74–5) (see '**cinque pas**'), and in *Twelfth Night* (1.3.129) (see '**galliard**'). On both occasions, the jig is compared and contrasted to other types of dance popular in Shakespeare's day. In *The Passionate Pilgrim*, the poet **lament**s the loss of his love, as a result of which all his 'merry jigs are quite forgot' (17.5). A sombre **mood** has replaced the sense of cheer that love used to bring him.

In *Love's Labour's Lost* reference is made to the jig as a tune rather than a dance when Armado is told by his servant Moth that he should 'jig off a tune' (2.1.11) in order to conquer Jaquenetta's love. In a later scene, the expression 'tune a jig' (4.3.166) is used.

The term 'jig' can acquire pejorative connotations. When a poet tries to act as a peacemaker between Brutus and Cassius, Brutus insults the

jig

poet by calling him a 'jigging fool' (*JC* 4.3.137), meaning that he is only capable of composing bad verses but has no understanding of the politics of war. Hamlet calls himself a 'jig-maker' (*Ham* 3.2.125) when he is about to have the play by the itinerant actors performed in front of the Danish court. He implies that he is a great provider of entertainment, but since the 'Mousetrap' is intended to prove that the King has murdered his brother, the entertainment that Hamlet is about to provide is anything but light-hearted. Earlier in the same play, Hamlet says of Polonius that 'he's for a jig or a tale of bawdry' (2.2.500), thus reminding the audience of the jig's association with the obscene.

(C) Baskervill, *The Elizabethan Jig* (1929), is a thorough account of the stage jigg.

Berger, 'Against the Sink-a-Pace' (1982), argues that the references to dances in *Much Ado About Nothing* try to justify the patriarchal values upheld in that play.

Gurr, *The Shakespearean Stage* (1992), pp. 173–6.

Sternfeld, *Music in Shakespearean Tragedy* (1967), talks briefly about the various dance kinds in Shakespeare.

van den Borren, *The Sources of Keyboard Music in England* (1913), pp. 300–3, includes a short but useful account of the jig.

Wilson, 'Elgar, Naylor and "The Cobbler's Jig": An Enquiry Reopened' (1993), discusses an interesting example of the English jig in Dutch sources.

jigg see **jig**.

K

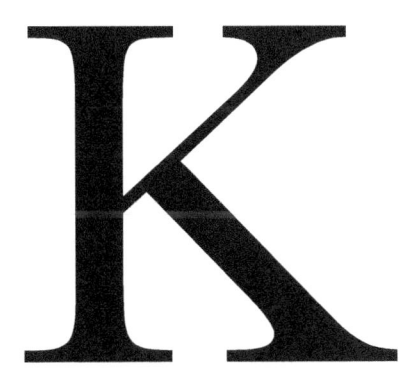

keep time see **time**.

kettledrum see **drum**.

key (A) The key is fundamental to the practice and understanding of Western tonal **music** from the early modern period to the present day. It governs melodic contour and harmonic vocabulary. In his *A New Way of Making Fowre Parts in Counterpoint* (c.1614), Campion was in no doubt about its importance:

> Of all things that belong to the making up of a Musition, the most necessary and usefull for him is the true knowledge of the Key or **Mood**e, or Tone, for all signifie the same thing, with the closes belonging unto it, for there is no **tune** that can have any **grace** or **sweet**nesse, unlesse it be bounded within a proper key, without running into strange keyes which have no affinity with the **air**e of the **song**.
>
> (*A New Way*, c.1614, D4r)

Before the sixteenth century, the relationships of pitches in music was controlled by the system of modes, of which there were eight. During the late sixteenth and early seventeenth century, the theory of keys

key

gradually replaced **mode**s. To begin with only six or seven keys were commonly notated. It was not until the early eighteenth century that the complete twenty-four were used in a systematic and interconnected way through the so-called 'Circle of Fifths'.

Key depends on certain defining elements, namely the behaviour of the **bass**, the **cadence**s or closes used, the start and finish pitches of a **piece** and the **sharp**s and **flat**s employed. Elizabethan theorists were aware of these principles to varying degrees. Dowland stressed the importance of the start pitch and possibly the **harmony**: 'A *Key* is the opening of a Song, because like as a *Key* opens a dore, so doth it the Song' (*Micrologus*, 1609, p. 8). Morley was very anxious, like Campion, that a piece should begin and end in the same key and that modulation (to a strange key) was forbidden:

> A great fault, for every key hath a peculiar **ayre** proper unto it selfe, so that if you goe into another then that wherein you begun, you **change** the aire of the song, which is as much as to **wrest** a thing out of his nature, making the asse leape upon his maister and the Spaniell beare the loade . . . . if you begin your song in *D **sol re***, you may end in *a re* and come againe to *D sol re*, etc.'
>
> (*Introduction*, 1597, p. 147)

The start and finish key area became known as the tonic and was determined by the predominant pitch of the **melody** and the bass. The particular use of accidentals (sharps and flats) not only helped identify keys, it distinguished between major and minor keys, each with their own characteristics of mood. Morley warned against writing in the wrong key and the use of unusual accidentals: 'The musick is in deed true, but you have set it in such a key as no man would have done . . . wheras by the contrary if your song were prickt [i.e. notated] in another key any young scholler might easilie and perfectlie **sing** it' (ibid., p. 156).

The choice of key could also indicate the types of **voice**s intended depending on the arrangement of **clef**s. Morley stated that there were two combinations: 'All songs made by the **Musician**s, who make songs by discretion, are either in the **high** key or in the **low**e key' (*Introduction*, 1597, p. 165). The different vocal ranges were thereby accommodated. A high-key voice was therefore one in its upper range or **compass**; a low-key voice occupied its low register.

(B) The instances of 'key' as musical metaphors in Shakespeare are all of a theoretical nature, for example in *The Two Noble Kinsmen*, when one of the three queens whose husbands have been killed by Creon appeals to Hippolyta and asks her to convince Theseus to fight against Creon. Although the Queen of the Amazons is renowned for her military achievements, she should **speak** to Theseus 'in a woman's key' (1.1.94) and even cry to be more persuasive. Here, emphasis is laid on the relationship between key and pitch (women's key is high-pitched); moreover, Hippolyta must be careful not to change the key, i.e. the tone of her plea to Theseus, and not to let her combative side emerge.

Interestingly, the relationship between Theseus and Hippolyta is explored using a similar metaphor in an earlier play, *A Midsummer Night's Dream*. Four days before their wedding, the Duke of Athens tells Hippolyta:

> Hippolyta, I woo'd thee with my sword,
> And won thy love doing thee injuries;
> But I will wed thee in another key,
> With pomp, with triumph, and with revelling.
> (1.1.16–19)

In this case a change of key – from the martial to the nuptial – is vital in order to reach lasting balance between them.

The concept of harmony derived by singing in the same key is found in another metaphor in *A Midsummer Night's Dream*. Helena remembers with nostalgia the days when she and Hermia were good friends and both sang 'in one key' (3.2.206) as if their voices 'had been incorporate' (208). In *Much Ado About Nothing*, the same idea is put forward once again. Benedick expresses puzzlement at Claudio's appreciative comments about Hero and asks him: 'Come, in what key shall a man take you to go in the song?' (1.1.185). Benedick is wondering if Claudio is serious or whether he is joking, and wishes he could be in tune with him.

In the concluding scene of *The Comedy of Errors*, Egeon asks Antipholus of Ephesus (whom he mistakenly believes to be Antipholus of Syracuse) whether he recognizes his face. When the long-lost twin son replies in the negative, Egeon asks him if he can at least recognize his voice. At his son's second negative answer, he **lament**s:

key

> Not know my voice! O time's extremity,
> Hast thou so **crack**'d and splitted my poor **tongue**
> In seven short years, that here my only son
> Knows not my feeble key of untun'd cares?
>
> (5.1.308–11)

If the fundamental pitches of the key are uncertain, then the music will go 'out of key' and sound **discord**ant. Egeon is implying that grief and care have caused his voice to become feeble and discordant.

See also **gamut**.

(C) Wilson (ed.), *A New Way* (2003), p. 59.

knell (A) The knell is the **sound**ing of a **bell** rung slowly and **solemn**ly to announce that someone has died. It followed the tolling of the passing-bell which signified that someone was dying or being executed: 'executions were accompanied by the **ballad** "Fortune my foe" whose **mournful tune** was intoned to the baleful **burden** of the passing-bell' (Wulstan, p. 49). The knell was rung intermittently, in pairs of **note**s, sometimes as a burden to a six-note **peal** (presumably muffled) as is attested by several keyboard pieces (e.g. 'The buriing of the dead' interpolated from *Elizabeth Rogers* **Virginal** *Book* BL Add MS 10337 into Byrd's 'The Battell'; the 'knell' in 'A Batell & no Battell' attributed to Bull, MB 19, p. 117) and Weelkes' three-**voice** setting of 'In black mourn I' (*The Passionate Pilgrim*, 1599) where the knell sounds in the lowest voice on 'rings **doleful** knell' whilst the upper two **part**s **sing** the six-note descending figure of the 'winding bell':

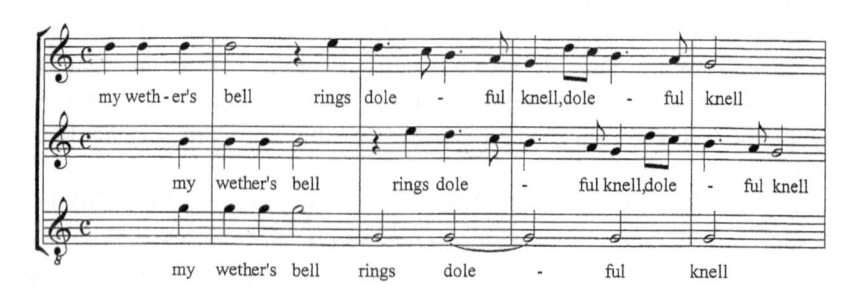

'Knell' is also used figuratively as a portent of death or sometimes a doleful cry can stand as a metaphor for the knell or death bell.

(B) The dying Katherine of Aragon urges her usher to

> Cause the **musician**s **play** me that sad note
> I nam'd my knell, whilst I sit meditating
> On the celestial **harmony** I go to.
> (*H8* 4.2.78–80)

There follows the stage direction '*Sad and **solemn music***' (80.SD). The practical music (*musica instrumentalis*) played on the stage helps Katherine in her transition between life and death. Only after her death can she hope to enjoy the perfect harmony created by the music of the spheres (*musica mundana*), since this is denied to human beings in their mortal state.

At the end of his famous monologue preceding the murder of Duncan, Macbeth **hears** the bell **ring** (*Mac* 2.1.61.SD) – his wife's signal that the time is right to commit regicide – and observes:

> I go, and it is done; the bell invites me.
> **Hear** it not, Duncan, for it is a knell,
> That summons thee to heaven or to hell.
> (62–4)

This powerful musical metaphor portending death acquires even more significance since it has a concrete aural counterpart in **perform**ance.

Another interesting metaphorical use of the term is found in *Henry VIII*, when two gentlemen talk about Buckingham's reaction when he heard his sentence of death:

> When he was brought again to th'bar, to hear
> His knell rung out, his judgement, he was stirr'd
> With such an agony he sweat extremely,
> And something spoke in choler, ill, and hasty.
> (2.1.31–4)

Reading out the death sentence sounds like the ringing of a death bell to the fated Duke.

239

knell

Leontes, convinced that his wife Hermione is pregnant with Polixenes' child, reflects that he will be pursued by the disgrace of cuckoldry till his dying day: 'contempt and **clamor** / Will be my knell' (*WT* 1.2.189–90). In his fit of unfounded jealousy, Leontes juxtaposes the two contrasting concepts of knell and clamour.

Lucrece's sense of inconsolable sadness is touchingly described in musical terms:

> For sorrow, like a heavy hanging bell,
> Once set on ringing, with his own weight goes;
> Then little strength rings out the doleful knell.
> (*Luc* 1493–5)

The hopelessness possessing her soul has drawn her into a spiral of despair which she can only overcome by committing suicide – the 'doleful knell' aptly anticipating her fate.

Ariel's **song** 'Full fathom five' (*Tmp* 1.2.397–405), which leads Ferdinand to believe that his father has drowned in the shipwreck, makes reference to 'sea-nymphs [who] hourly ring his knell' (403). Another song, 'Tell me where is fancy bred', which accompanies Bassanio's choice of casket (*MV* 3.2.63–72) contains the line 'Let us all ring fancy's knell' (70). Duffin notes that these two songs have a similar versification, and that the term 'knell' as well as the refrain 'ding dong bell' appears in both, and conjecturally sets 'Tell me where is fancy bred' (for which no tune survives) to the music of 'Full fathom five' (p. 381).

(C) Duffin, *Shakespeare's Songbook* (2004).
Wulstan, *Tudor Music* (1985)

knock see **strike**.

knoll'd see **bell; knell**.

L

la The sixth **note** of the Renaissance hexachord. See **ut**.

lament see **dirge**.

languishment (A) In a musical sense, 'languishment' is associated with weeping, sadness and melancholy and derives from the French (*languissant*) and Italian (*lamentatione*) as imported into late sixteenth and seventeenth-century English **music**. It is characterized by slow minor **mode music**.

(B) After Lucrece has been raped, she invokes **Philomela** (who was transformed into a **nightingale** after suffering the same fate as Lucrece):

> Come, Philomele, that **sing**'st of ravishment,
> Make thy sad grove in my dishevell'd hair;
> As the dank earth weeps at thy languishment,
> So I at each sad **strain** will strain a tear.
> (*Luc* 1128–31)

The sophisticated musical metaphor is sustained when Lucrece expresses her intention to fix a **sharp** knife against her heart:

languishment

> ... to affright mine eye,
> Who if it wink shall thereon fall and die.
> These means, as **fret**s upon an **instrument**,
> Shall **tune** our heart-**string**s to true languishment.
> (1138–41)

The use of 'languishment' in two consecutive stanzas helps to evoke Lucrece's feeling of sadness and despair, which ultimately leads her to commit suicide.

See also **motion**.

lark see **bird**.

lauda see **laudes**.

laudes (A) The Medieval 'Laudes' were religious poems derived from biblical, liturgical and popular devotional texts and **set** to secular **song tune**s. They originated in thirteenth-century north Italian monastic foundations, particularly Franciscan. The poetic forms of the sacred texts were modelled on secular *ballata* types. The tunes of the monophonic *Lauda* ranged from **chant** to popular song types. In the later fifteenth and sixteenth century, the Venetian polyphonic *Lauda* became widespread although it did not supplant the solo song version. *Lauda* **sing**ing was adopted in a variety of everyday devotional contexts, ranging from private contemplation to public gatherings. Savonarola, for example, encouraged the singing of *lauda* throughout the churches and religious communities of Florence. A poignant case of private devotion is reported in Grove Online:

> The great Florentine *lauda* poet Feo Belcari (1410–84) was informed of the death of his sister in a Florentine convent with a letter describing how in her final moments she 'entered into a devout state and began singing the *lauda* that begins *Partiti core et vane all'amore*, then upon her request her close companions gathered and sang a *lauda* that eased her passage from this life.
>
> ('lauda': Grove Online)

(B) Shakespeare uses 'laudes' in *Hamlet* (Q2, 1604/5); Folio has 'tunes' instead. In the former, when Gertrude gives her touching description of Ophelia's death by drowning, she explains that Ophelia '**chaunt**ed **snatch**es of old laudes / As one incapable of her own distress' (M1v). Jenkins (1982) and Edwards (1985) think that this word is synonymous with 'songs of **praise**'; the latter argues that crazy **hymn**-singing might have marked Ophelia's death (p. 212). However, if Shakespeare used 'laudes' in the nuance of the term described above, it would reinforce the connection with the popular quality of the songs sung by Ophelia during her madness.

(C) Barr, *The Monophonic Lauda and the Lay Religious Confraternities of Tuscany and Umbria in the Late Middle Ages* (1988), scrutinizes the background and differing aspects of the Lauda.
    Edwards, *Hamlet* (1985).
    Jenkins, *Hamlet* (1982).
    Macey, 'The Lauda and the Cult of Savonarola' (1992); and *Bonfire Songs* (1998).
    Wilson, Barbara, 'Madrigal, Lauda and Local Culture in Trecento Florence' (1997).

lay (A) The lay was a simple **song**, possibly of French origin and in certain contexts indicating a **dance** song, substituting for **roundelay**. When not a dance song, it has a sad **lament**ing character, as in:

> Fair Daphne, gentle shepherdess, sat weeping
> Good Thyrsis' loss. The swains their flocks left keeping,
> Attending all on Daphne's **mournful** lays,
> Whose ditties were her griefs and Thyrsis' praise.
>   (East, 1618, no. 14)

As a dance song, opposite emotions of mirth and merriment prevail, as in:

> Up, merry mates! To Neptune's praise
> Your **voice**s high advance.
> The wat'ry nymphs shall dance;

lay

> And Aeolus shall **whistle** to your lays.
> (Dowland, 1612, no. 19)

(B) 'Lay' can also be 'a short lyric or poem intended to be sung' (*OED* 4.1). Shakespeare uses this meaning in *Sonnet* 100 when exhorting his inspiring Muse to '**Sing** to the **ear** that doth thy lays esteem, / And gives thy pen both skill and argument' (7–8). The same nuance is found in *Sonnet* 102, in which the poet develops the theme of loss of inspiration. He remembers with melancholia the time when the love between him and his friend 'was new, and then but in the spring / When I was wont to greet it with my lays' (5–6).

Marina's grace and elegance are captured in Gower's description that she 'sings like one immortal, and she dances / As goddess-like to her admired lays' (*Per* 5. Ind.3–4). While the allusion in this case is unmistakably to a dance song, in *Hamlet* a different meaning is observed. Gertrude recounts the drowning of Ophelia in poetical terms. The girl sang in the water

> ... But long it could not be
> Till that her garments, heavy with their drink,
> Pull'd the poor wretch from her **melodious** lay
> To muddy death.
> (5.1.180–3)

The melodious quality of her song conjures up an image of serenity soon to be disrupted by her 'muddy' death.

'Lay' sometimes indicates **bird**song, for instance when Suffolk explains to Queen Margaret that the Duchess of Gloucester will become a victim of his scheming. He likens his cunning plotting to 'a **choir** of such enticing birds / That she will light to listen to the lays' (*2H6* 1.3.89–90). *The Phoenix and Turtle* opens with an invocation to 'the bird of **loud**est lay' (1) to summon the birds for the funeral procession of the phoenix and the dove. In *Sonnet* 98, the poet laments that 'the lays of birds' (5) in spring bring him no pleasure since his young friend is not with him.

lesson (A) The sixteenth-century term 'lesson' is used to denote a pedagogical **piece** written for keyboard or **lute** or mixed **consort**

generally for domestic consumption. The first known appearance of the word is on the title page of the second English edition (London, 1574) of Adrian Le Roy's *Instruction pour apprendre la tablature du luth* (1567): 'with a briefe instruction how to **play** on the lute by tablature, to conduct and dispose thy hand upon the lute, with certaine easie lessons for that purpose'. Collections of lessons for various **instrument**s were published in England in the late sixteenth and early seventeenth centuries, including Barley's *A New Booke of **Cittern**e Lessons* (1593) [lost], Morley's *First Booke of Consort Lessons* (1599) for mixed consort, Rosseter's *Lessons for Consort* (1609), Robinson's *New Citharen Lessons* (1609) and Robert Dowland's *Varietie of Lute Lessons* (1610).

(B) In their attempt to impress Bianca, Lucentio (disguised as a tutor) and Hortensio (disguised as a lute teacher) try to outdo one another by means of witty exchanges. However, the girl does not appreciate this and puts them in their place:

> Why, gentlemen, you do me double wrong
> To strive for that which resteth in my choice.
> I am no breeching scholar in the schools,
> I'll not be tied to hours, nor 'pointed times,
> But learn my lessons as I please myself...
> (*Shr* 3.1.16–20)

The meaning of 'lessons' applies both to the **music** that Hortensio wants to teach, and to Latin, of which Lucentio is supposedly an expert. But more interesting is Hortensio's use of the word when he is about to teach Bianca the **gamut** and tries to get rid of his rival in love. He addresses Lucentio as follows: 'You may go walk, and give me leave a while; / My lessons **make** no music in three **part**s' (59–60). On the surface, Hortensio is saying that he does not intend to teach music for three instruments or **voice**s (parts), but the more oblique message is that he will not accept rivalry in his courtship of Bianca.

(C) Harwood, 'Rosseter's *Lessons for Consort* of 1609' (1965), is a study of Rosseter and the domestic function of consort lessons.

long (A) The long was one of the eight **note**-values of white mensural

long

notation in the Medieval and Renaissance periods. So in its strict usage it had a specific **time** value which was twice the **breve** and four times the duration of the semibreve. By the sixteenth century, it had come to be a comparatively slow or long-lasting note. In a more general musical sense 'long' is used to indicate a duration opposite to short but of no determinate time-value.

(B) The final scene of *The Taming of the Shrew* is dominated by a sense of reconciliation, as pointed out by Lucentio's opening speech: 'At last, though long, our **jar**ring notes agree, / And time it is, when raging war is done' (5.2.1–2). While expressing the idea that this **harmony** was long overdue, the use of 'long' enhances the musical metaphor. There is also a connection between duration and the resolution of **discord** in that, according to the Renaissance rules of counterpoint, discord could only be resolved by following strict durational principles.

The beginning of Lucrece's painful account of her rape is described in the following terms:

> And now this pale **swan** in her wat'ry nest
> Begins the sad **dirge** of her certain ending:
> 'Few words', quoth she, 'shall fit the trespass best,
> Where no excuse can give the fault amending.
> In me moe woes than words are now depending,
> And my **lament**s would be drawn out too long
> To tell them all with one poor tired **tongue**.
> (*Luc* 1611–17)

Likening Lucrece to a swan is pertinent in a context of imminent death: she has resolved to commit suicide after revealing to her husband who the rapist is. The length of her lament, or dirge, could also allude to the length of the notes.

In *Love's Labour's Lost*, 3.1 is dominated by a musical theme. Moth **sing**s 'Concolinel' when Armado – in love with Jaquenetta – exhorts him to 'make passionate' (3.1.1) his sense of **hear**ing. Moth then advises Armado on how to conquer a woman's love. Among other things, he should 'keep not too long in one **tune**, but / a snip and away' (21–2). Since the common phrase in early modern English would have been 'a **snatch** and away', it is possible that 'long' had a musical connotation, intended to create a contrast with the brevity characterising a snatch.

long

See also **bird, minim, pricksong**.

(C) Apel, *The Notation of Polyphonic Music* (1953).

loud (A) The descriptive term 'loud' denotes the comparative volume or intensity of a musical **sound**. In Elizabethan times it also referred to 'outdoor' or noisy **instrument**s such as **trumpets, drum**s, **cornett**s, **hoboy**s, shawms and **pipe**s. In certain contexts it could imply coarseness. The **brazen noise** of loud **music** contrasted with the quiet stillness of **soft** music, **play**ed by **string**ed instruments. 'The achievements of heroes of battle [in ancient Rome] were celebrated with music loud and wild', whereas 'the soft, dignified music of strings was the means of paying homage to the Deities and of inducing wisdom in the magistrates' (Sternfeld, p. 209). This opposition between loud and soft music permeates Shakespeare's drama and its symbolic role is important to the understanding of Shakespeare's theatrical intent.

(B) There are three stage directions in the Shakespeare canon prescribing loud sounds. Two are in a battle context: '*A loud **alarum***' (*3H6* 2.6.OSD), and '*Loud alarum*' (*JC* 5.2.2.SD). The third introduces a festive scene in *Timon of Athens*: '*Hoboys playing loud music. A great banquet served in . . .*' (1.2.OSD). The intensity of the music is meant to emphasize the **solemn**ity of Timon's lavish banquet in honour of his courtiers.

Speeches hinting at the use of loud music and sounds are very often found in martial scenes, as for instance in Aeneas' command to the Trojan trumpeter: 'Trumpet, **blow** loud, / Send thy **brass** voice through all these lazy tents' (*Tro* 1.3.256–7). The Greek general Agamemnon later incites Ajax with similar energy: 'With starting courage, / Give with thy trumpet a loud **note** to Troy' (4.5.2–3). He then exhorts his soldiers: '**Beat** loud the **taborin**s, let the trumpets blow' (275).

In *King John*, The Bastard's speech before his army's clash with that of the Dauphin evokes the potent sounds of drums in battle:

> Indeed your drums, being beaten, will cry out;
> And so shall you, being beaten. Do but start
> An **echo** with the **clamor** of thy drum,

loud

> And even at hand a drum is ready brac'd
> That shall reverberate all as loud as thine.
> Sound but another, and another shall
> (As loud as thine) **rattle** the welkin's **ear**,
> And mock the deep-mouth'd **thunder** . . .
> (5.2.166–73)

The loud sound of martial instruments is mentioned metaphorically by Blanche when, on her wedding day, she begs her husband (the Dauphin) not to move war against her uncle. To the Dauphin's exhortation 'Father, to arms!', she passionately replies:

> Upon thy wedding day?
> Against the blood that thou hast married?
> What, shall our feast be kept with slaughtered men?
> Shall braying trumpets and loud churlish drums,
> Clamors of hell, be **measure**s to our pomp?
> (*Jn* 3.1.300–4)

The musical nuance of 'measures', a word which in its common usage suggests moderation, acquires a particular significance in a metaphor conveying the idea of conflict and loud sounding of battle instruments.

Loud sounds are mentioned in a light-hearted metaphor in *The Taming of the Shrew*. Petruchio confirms his intention to woo Katherine notwithstanding her reputation as a spiteful woman. He claims that, since he has heard 'loud 'larums, neighing steeds, and trumpets' **clang**' (1.2.206) in battle, he can certainly put up with the sounds made by a 'woman's **tongue**' (207).

More rarely, loudness is mentioned by Shakespeare in relation to vocal and instrumental music. When courting Olivia on behalf of Orsino, Viola (disguised as Cesario) explains to the countess that Orsino wishes to woo her and 'write loyal **canton**s of contemned love, / And sing them loud even in the dead of night' (*TN* 1.5.270–1).

In *King Lear* (Q1, 1608), a doctor – a secondary character found only in this version of the play – helps the King recover from his insanity. He asks to bring Lear to the presence of Cordelia, and commands: 'Louder the music there' (4.7.24). The introduction of music with its healing powers provides a serene background to the reconciliation between the old king and his youngest daughter later in the scene.

loud

During the drunken feast on board Pompey's galley, Enobarbus instructs his fellow revellers to sing the song 'Come, thou monarch of the vine' and **dance** to it. He says: 'All take hands. / Make battery to our **ear**s with the loud music' (*Ant* 2.7.108–9). The singing would have probably been accompanied by the beating of drums, as the phrase 'make battery' suggests. Loudness is apt in a context where chaos and drunkenness dominate.

See also **consort, harmony, jar, measure, shrill, tune**.

(C) Duffin, 'Backward Bells and Barrel Bells' (1997 and 1998).
Sternfeld, *Music in Shakespearean Tragedy* (1967).

love song (A) A particular kind, 'love song' is a major category of **song** in Elizabethan times. Whilst not defined by particular musical features, the texts of the songs are characterized by amorous themes generally of a light nature. Campion, for example, devoted the second half of his *Two Bookes of Ayres* (c.1613) to 'Light Conceits of Lovers'. The first part had been devoted to 'Divine and Moral Songs'.

(B) The habit of indulging in love songs as part of the courtship ritual is almost invariably ridiculed in the Shakespeare canon, for instance by Jaques when he begs Orlando (in love with Rosalind): 'I pray you mar no more trees with writing / love-songs in their barks' (*AYLI* 3.2.259–60). Among the skills possessed by the lover Valentine, he '**relish**[es] a love-song like a **robin**-redbreast' (*TGV* 2.1.20). Romeo's love for Rosaline is described in an ironic way as having been 'stabb'd with a white wench's black eye, run through / the **ear** with a love-song' (*Rom* 2.4.14–15).

A similarly jocular tone is intended by the servant when he says that Autolycus 'has the prettiest love-songs for maids, so without / bawdry, which is strange' (*WT* 4.4.193–4). He then goes on to explain that these songs have 'delicate **burthen**s of **dildo**s and **fading**s' (195): the sexual innuendos created by terms such as '**burden**' and 'dildo' of course belie the servant's statement at line 193.

The only exception to the ironic use of 'love song' is observed in *Twelfth Night*. When offered the choice of what type of song he would like to **hear**, Sir Toby enthusiastically says: 'A love-song, a love-song' (2.3.37). Feste then intones 'O mistress mine' (39–52). Whilst the first

love song

stanza celebrates the positive outcome of courtship thus confirming the light-hearted nature of love songs, the second stanza insists on the mutability of love (Wells, pp. 220–1) and proposes a less optimistic view of this feeling.

See also **bird**.

(C) Wells, *Elizabethan Mythologies* (1994), pp. 208–24, focuses on the role of music in *Twelfth Night*.

See also bibliography under '**song**'.

low (A) Whilst indicating relative musical pitch, 'low' also conventionally connects with '**soft**' **music** in Renaissance topoi to mean the gentle music of **string**ed **instrument**s in opposition to the **high** and **loud** musics of **wind** instruments.

(B) *Julius Caesar* has three stage directions in martial contexts prescribing that **sound**s must be 'low', in contrast to stage directions for 'loud' martial sounds found elsewhere in the play: these indications for practical music aim to give the impression that the sounds in question are heard from a distance. The first of the stage directions, '*Low* **march** *within*' (4.2.24.SD), precedes the entry of Cassius and his army (4.2.29.SD): 'within' tells us that the march would have been **play**ed in the tiring-house rather than on the stage (see also Introduction). Later in the play, '*low* **alarums**' (5.3.96.SD; 5.5.23.SD) are heard during the Battle of Philippi. Nowhere else in the Shakespeare canon do we find specific indications for 'low' sounds.

'Low' is used in connection with **voice** on some occasions. For instance, in the song 'O mistress mine' the lady is exhorted to wait for her true love 'that can sing both high and low' (*TN* 2.3.41). When Cleopatra tries to dissemble her jealousy after discovering that Antony has married Octavia, she comments that he will not be in love with her for long, since Octavia is 'low-voic'd' (*Ant* 3.3.13) rather than '**shrill**-tongu'd' (12). The implication is that a low-pitched voice is not desirable in a woman. On the other hand, when King Lear is holding Cordelia's dead body he remembers her voice which 'was ever soft, / Gentle, and low, an excellent thing in woman' (*Lr* 5.3.273–4). In this case however 'low' may refer to Cordelia's calm manner of speaking rather than to her vocal pitch.

There is also a reference to the pitch range (**compass**) of a **recorder** when Hamlet confronts Guildenstern: 'you would sound me from my / lowest **note** to the top of my compass' (*Ham* 3.2.366–7). Hamlet is aware that Guildenstern is spying on him on behalf of Claudius, and uses this musical metaphor to vent his frustration at the knowledge that he is being manipulated.

See also **soft**.

lullaby (A) In Elizabethan times lullaby was a folk or popular **song** used by the mother or nurse to lull a child to sleep. It would therefore be a quiet gentle song with a rocking-motion rhythm. One of the most famous lullabies of the sixteenth century known today is the so-called Coventry Carol, 'Lully, lulla, thow littell tyne child'. It comes from the Shearmen and Tailor's late Medieval play, *The Nativity and Slaughter of the Innocents* and is sung by the mothers of the Innocents after the shepherds' song. The musical setting, according to Rastall (p. 69), is probably contemporary with the play's revision of 1534. Lullabies have both generic and specific connections with other kinds of songs, including laments, serenades, **charm**s and narrative verses. One of the most exquisite Elizabethan lullabies is Byrd's setting, with its associations with Christmastide and the slaughter of the innocents:

> Lulla, lullaby.
> My **sweet** little baby, what meanest thou to cry?
> Be still, my blessed babe, though cause thou hast to mourn,
> Whose blood most innocent to shed the cruel king hath sworn.
>   (Byrd, 1588, no. 32)

(B) The fairies of *A Midsummer Night's Dream* **sing** and **dance** around Titania at her request to make her fall asleep. The chorus of the song 'You spotted snakes with double **tongue**' exhorts **Philomela** (the **nightingale**) to

> Sing in our **sweet** lullaby,
> Lulla, lulla, lullaby, lulla, lulla, lullaby.
> Never harm,
> Nor spell, nor charm,

lullaby

>Come our lovely lady nigh.
>So good night, with lullaby.
>(2.2.14–19)

It is ironic that, as soon as the fairies leave after singing this lullaby meant to protect Titania from magic spells and danger, the Queen of the Fairies falls victim to Oberon's spell and falls in love with the ass-headed Bottom.

When Tamora uses the word 'lullaby', it has an ominous ring to it. After urging Aaron to become her lover, she explains that their love-making would be followed by

>... a golden slumber,
>Whiles hounds and **horn**s and sweet melodious **bird**s
>Be unto us as is a nurse's song
>Of lullaby to bring her babe asleep.
>(*Tit* 2.3.26–9)

The evocation of an idyllic atmosphere and childlike innocence is followed by the brutal reality of the murder of Bassianus and the rape of Lavina, instigated by Tamora and Aaron.

When Antigonus is about to abandon baby Perdita, he expresses his aversion to following Leontes' order:

>... Weep I cannot,
>But my heart bleeds; and most accurs'd am I
>To be by oath enjoin'd to this. Farewell!
>The day frowns more and more; thou'rt like to have
>A lullaby too rough ...
>(*WT* 3.3.51–5)

The merciless weather will be the only lullaby for the baby in her state of abandonment.

(C) Rastall, *The Heaven Singing* (1996), examines the Coventry plays and songs in early English religious drama.

lute (A) The lute is the ubiquitous plucked **string**ed **instrument** of the Renaissance when it was used either in a solo capacity, or in

lute

consorts and larger ensembles, or to accompany **song** (see '**ayre**'). It is one of the most often depicted instruments with its characteristic pear shape, steeply angled **peg**box or head and bulbous vaulted back. It is also distinguished by its **fret**ted neck on which are strung, generally, six courses of strings, and by the ornamental rose soundhole carved on the flat belly which some commentators (e.g. Wells, 1981) find numerically symbolic. In both its practical use and symbolic role, the lute is one of if not the most important instrument of the early modern period. Its origins lay in the ancient Arab world where it was known as the 'Ud', and it remained popular throughout Europe until the late seventeenth century, surviving into the eighteenth as an archaic instrument. It saw a significant revival as a period instrument in the second half of the twentieth century. No 'authentic' Elizabethan theatrical production involving music would be complete without the lute.

More so than the **viol**, the other quintessential Elizabethan instrument, the lute is to be found in both domestic amateur and public professional environments – the viol is usually associated more exclusively with the latter. As its popularity in England grew in the mid sixteenth century, instruction books on how to **play** the lute were published. The earliest (now lost) were *The Sceyence of Lutynge*, printed by John Alde in 1565, and *An Exortation to all Kynde of Men How they shulde Learn to play of the Lute*, printed by Robert Ballard in 1567. Then followed several books in English (which have survived) taken from a French original by Le Roy. These included **music** examples and were *A Briefe and easye Instrution* [sic] (1568), 'englished by J. Alford Londenor' and William Barley's *A New Booke of Tabliture* (1596). Thomas Robinson's *The Schoole of Musicke* (1603) is a teaching manual for lute written in a dialogue (compare Morley's *Introduction*, 1597), 'between a Knight, having children to be taught, and Timotheus, who should teach them'. Concluding the series of English Renaissance lute instruction books is Robert Dowland's *Varietie of Lute-Lessons* (1610), based on Besard's *Thesaurus harmonicus* (1603) and incorporating observations on lute playing by John Dowland, Robert's father.

John Dowland was the most accomplished English lutenist and composer of the time. He is named in *The Passionate Pilgrim* 8, as the **musician**, Spenser as the poet:

> If music and **sweet** poetry agree,
> As they must needs (the sister and the brother),

lute

> Then must the love be great 'twixt thee and me,
> Because thou lov'st the one, and I the other.
> Dowland to thee is dear, whose heavenly **touch**
> Upon the lute doth **ravish** human sense;
> Spenser to me, whose deep conceit is such
> As passing all conceit, needs no defense.
>
> (1–8)

Dowland's virtuoso talent was not rewarded in England with a court appointment, at least not for many years. He was, however, recognized in continental Europe as one of the leading players. Other luminaries in England who played at court and in the theatres included John Johnson, Robert Johnson, Francis Cutting, Philip Rosseter, Francis Pilkington, Daniel Bacheler, Robert Jones and Alfonso Ferrabosco (father and son).

The lute was important not only as a solo instrument for which a large body of **dance** music and other pieces survives but also as the omnipresent accompanying instrument in the ayre. In addition, it was a crucial member of the especially English mixed consort in which it acted as a **harmony** instrument, filling in the parts the **cittern** and bandora didn't play as accompaniment to the **melody** instruments (**flute** and viols). In the context of the English courtly **masque**, large numbers of lutes of differing sizes were employed. In Campion's *Lord Hayes Masque* (1607) there are a number of '**bass**e and **mean**e' lutes in the orchestra. Ben Jonson's *Oberon* (1611) recalls that '20 lutes for the Prince's dance' were used.

(B) Like the viol, the lute depended on the **Apollo**nian associations of string music for its symbolic meaning. The lute is '**soft**', 'sweet', 'gentle' and 'dignified', fit for lofty sentiments and passions. It suggests artistry and refinement in comparison, say, to the cittern and bandora, and represents Apollonian control and restraint, the music of love and **concord**,of harmony, the music of the spheres, as in Berowne's meditation on love:

> Love's feeling is more soft and sensible,
>   . . . as sweet and musical,
> As bright Apollo's lute, strung with his hair.

> And when Love speaks, the voice of all the gods
> Make heaven drowsy with the harmony.
> (*LLL* 4.3.334; 339–42)

It is not clear from where Shakespeare derived the image of Apollo stringing his lute with his hair (see 'Apollo' for a detailed comment), but the idea conjured up by this image is that Apollo and his instrument are inseparable.

The power to calm troubled situations is embodied in Orphic music, particularly **Orpheus** singing and playing the lute. His lyric verse is his poetic voice; his lute symbolizes his affective music. In *The Two Gentlemen of Verona*, the two-sided nature of Orpheus' art, music and poetry, shows that they share in their attempt to bring order and control to worldly things. This is evident from Proteus' words of advice to Thurio:

> For Orpheus' lute was strung with poets' **sinews**,
> Whose golden touch could soften steel and stones,
> Make tigers tame, and huge leviathans
> Forsake unsounded deeps, to dance on sands.
> (3.2.77–80)

Only by being in control of both music and poetry will Thurio be able to conquer Silvia.

A similar concept is found in *Henry VIII*, when one of Queen Katherine's attendants sings a lute song:

> Orpheus with his lute made trees,
> And the mountain tops that freeze,
> Bow themselves when he did sing.
> . . . In sweet music is such art,
> Killing care and grief of heart
> Fall asleep, or **hear**ing, die.
> (3.1.3–5; 12–14)

These words about cosmic balance reflect the Queen's frustrated desire for harmony in her marriage (she will be ordered to accept Henry's request for divorce later in the same scene). Katherine's exhortation to her attendant before the song 'Take thy lute, **wench**, my soul grows sad with troubles' (3.1.1) indicates that a lute was actually

lute

played on the stage. This line points to the association between stringed instruments, particularly lutes, and melancholy, especially of those in love.

Similarly, Claudio refers to the sad lute in describing (with a tinge of irony) Benedick's melancholy, brought on by thwarted love. As a result, his 'jesting spirit . . . is now / crept into a lute-string, and now **govern**'d by **stops**' (*Ado* 3.2.59–60).

The calming effect of Orpheus' music is famously portrayed in the passage towards the end of the *The Merchant of Venice* (5.1.54–88), reflecting on the 'sweet power of music': although obviously intended, Orpheus' lute is not specifically mentioned.

When Hal compares Falstaff, among other similes, to a 'lover's lute' (*1H4* 1.2.75), his reference to melancholic symbolism is ambivalent depending on a knowledge of opposites and parody. The lute is a symbol of virtue and calm, happiness and fidelity in love. Its ambivalence lies in its juxtaposition between idealized love and the carnal lusts of the flesh. The lute's 'significance as a symbol of vice',

> depends essentially on the idea of parody. Characteristic of evil is its propensity for mocking and perverting the true forms of virtue – something at which Falstaff is notably adept. Thus, although the iconography of the lover's lute to which Hal compares the melancholy Falstaff may be arcane, its meaning in this context is clear enough. This is plainly no symbol of virtue. For undoubtedly the **sound** that Falstaff is used to hearing in the Eastcheap tavern is . . . the lascivious pleasing of a lute.
> (Wells, 1994, p. 53)

The same imagery is employed in marking *Richard III*, in his opening soliloquy, as inclining to vice rather than virtue:

> And now, in stead of mounting barbed steeds,
> To fright the souls of fearful adversaries,
> He **caper**s nimbly in a lady's chamber
> To the lascivious pleasing of a lute.
> (*R3* 1.1.10–13)

The lute as a symbol of love and peace, domesticity and calm as opposed to war and destruction is implicit not only in this passage but

lute

elsewhere in Shakespeare. With some irony, the 'unbroken' state of Katherina is depicted in the contrasted images of war and peace:

>HORTENSIO: I think she'll sooner prove a soldier,
>Iron may hold with her, but never lutes.
>BAPTISTA: Why then thou canst not break her to the lute?
>HORTENSIO: Why no, for she hath broke the lute to me.
>   (*Shr* 2.1.145–8)

That Katherina will not learn to play the lute but rather breaks it over the head of Hortensio further reveals her lack of refined etiquette and that she is no easy lover. Graceful and educated maids, fit for wooing, must demonstrate various domestic skills, including playing and singing to the lute, as a reference in *Pericles* indicates:

>. . . or when to th'lute
>She sung, and made the night-**bird** mute,
>That still **record**s with moan.
>   (4 Cho. 25–7)

The vivid incongruity of the lute in war is used to telling effect in *1 Henry VI* as Talbot addresses the dying Salisbury:

>He beckons with his hand and smiles on me,
>As who should say, 'When I am dead and gone,
>Remember to avenge me on the French.'
>Plantagenet, I will, and like thee, Nero,
>Play on the lute, beholding the towns burn.
>   (1.4.92–6)

This image recalls Grafton, *Chronicle* 1.61: 'He commanded the City of Rome to be set on fyre, and himself in the meane season, with all semblant of joy, sitting in an high Tower . . . played upon the **harp**e, and sang the destruction of Troy' (taken from Cairncross, p. 30). The outmoded harp, common at the early Tudor court, has been replaced in Shakespeare by the more familiar Elizabethan lute.

The night before the Battle of Philippi, Brutus commands his boy Lucius to play 'a sleepy tune' upon his instrument. Commentators agree that the stage direction '*Music and a Song*' (*JC* 4.3.266.SD) indicates

lute

that Lucius' music is a lute song or ayre, since he must sing and play at the same time. The reference to the lute with its pleasant domestic associations heightens the atmosphere of artificial calm before the storm of battle, and draws upon the Orphic tradition of the calming properties of the lute song as in *Henry VIII*.

In the scene portraying Ophelia's madness, *Hamlet* (Q1, 1603) employs the stage direction: '*Enter Ofelia playing on a lute, and her haire down singing*' (G4v). A wig creating the effect of dishevelled hair would have visually signified the girl's state of insanity; the boy actor was also expected to accompany himself on a lute while singing the bawdy songs. Neither of the two later versions of the tragedy, Q2 (1604/5) and Folio, indicates that a lute must be used.

(C) Batchelor, 'Daniel Bacheler: The Right Perfect Musician' (1988).
Cairncross, *King Henry VI, Part I* (1962).
Coelho (ed.), *Performance on Lute, Guitar and Vihuela* (1997), has an extensive discussion on lute playing.
Forrester, 'An Elizabethan Allegory and Some Hypotheses' (1994).
Gill, 'The Elizabethan Lute' (1959).
Harwood, 'Thomas Robinson's "General Rules" ' (1978).
Holman, *Dowland: Lachrimae* (1999).
Hulse, 'Francis and Thomas Cutting: Father and Son?' (1986).
Lumsden, 'The Sources of English Lute Music' (1955), analyses repertoire.
Lundberg, 'Sixteenth- and Seventeenth-Century Lute-Making' (1974), focuses on lute construction.
Newton, 'English Lute Music of the Golden Age' (1938–9).
Poulton, *John Dowland* (1982).
Scott, 'Elizabeth I as Lutenist' (1976).
Smith, *A History of the Lute from Antiquity to the Renaissance* (2001), is a general history of the instrument.
Spring, *The Lute in Britain* (2001), provides the most comprehensive account of the English Renaissance lute.
Ward, *Music for Elizabethan Lutes* (1992).
Wells, 'Number Symbolism in the Renaissance Lute Rose' (1981); and *Elizabethan Mythologies* (1994).

lute-string see **lute**.

madrigal (A) The madrigal was one of the most popular vocal forms in sixteenth-century Europe, which mainly used vernacular lyric poetry set most often to three to six **voice**s. Beginning in northern Italy (notably Florence) in the late fifteenth century, it was exported northwards throughout Europe until it reached England in the late sixteenth century. As a generic term, it encompassed many kinds of musical and poetical forms. In general, its identity was defined by its use of secular texts and equal-voiced polyphony. In its specific usage, 'madrigal' was employed to distinguish between it and the **canzonet** and villanelle.

Though an offshoot of the Italian, the English madrigal enjoyed a separate existence from the 1580s to c.1630. The English madrigal appeared at a time when there was a vogue for Italian culture, especially poetry. Italian madrigals had been circulating in manuscripts for a decade before the first printed collection, Nicholas Yonge's anthology of various kinds of Italian madrigals set with new English words, the *Musica transalpina* (1588). This publication signalled the start of two decades of intense activity. The Italian madrigal composer best known in England, and one of the most prolific, was Luca Marenzio (1553–99). The most influential and best-known English madrigal composers were George Kirbye (d.1634), Thomas Morley (1557–1602), Thomas Weelkes (?1576–1623), John Ward (1571–1638) and John Wilbye (1574–1638).

The English madrigal was essentially a 'light' kind. It usually set

madrigal

anonymous poetry of no great literary merit or consequence, although the poetry it used was especially apt for musical setting. Its content was often amorous and a wide variety of stanzaic forms were employed. References to local English *personae* (e.g. Jack and Jill) and quasi-pastoral scenes characterize the textual imagery.

The madrigal offered the composer ample opportunity to demonstrate writing **music** in **part**s (counterpoint) and setting words in clever and representational ways (word painting). Variety was the essence of the madrigal. Morley, one of England's outstanding exponents, says:

> As for the musick it is next unto the Motet, the most artificiall and to men of understanding most delightfull. If therefore you will **compose** in this kind you must possesse your selfe with an amorus humor (for in no composition shal you prove admirable except you put on, and possesse your selfe wholy with that vaine wherein you compose) so that you must in your musicke be wavering like the **wind**, sometime wanton, somtime drooping, sometime grave and staide, otherwhile effeminat, you may maintaine **point**s and revert them, use triplaes and shew the verie uttermost of your varietie, and the more varietie you shew the better shal you please.
>
> (*Introduction*, 1597, p. 180)

This intense variety in the melodic and rhythmical elements of the music and the fact that the polyphony tended to mask the words for the hearer meant that the madrigal was less suited to plays and dramatic contexts than the **ayre**. It was, therefore, rarely found in courtly entertainments, **masques** or the professional theatre. The English madrigal was principally intended for domestic consumption. Morley gives an example of where and when the madrigal was used: 'supper being ended, and Musicke bookes, according to the custome being brought to the table: the mistresse of the house presented mee with a part, earnestly requesting mee to **sing**' (*Introduction*, 1597, p. 1).

Madrigals were printed in sets of part-books, the number of books equalling the number of voices employed in the collection. Each singer would sing from his or her book. The fact that the madrigal was printed in Elizabethan England places it alongside the ayre as a Protestant form in contrast to keyboard music which was cultivated by Catholic composers and circulated in manuscript copy (the most famous collection being the FWVB, c.1619).

madrigal

(B) There is only one occurrence of 'madrigal' in the Shakespeare canon. In *The Merry Wives of Windsor*, Evans sings to overcome his fear of the imminent duel (which in the end doesn't take place) with Caius. He sings the **tune** derived from Marlowe's poem, *The Passionate Shepherd to His Love*, which begins with the line 'To shallow rivers, to whose falls' but after the line '**Melodious bird**s sing madrigals' (3.1.18) he intones the opening line of a metrical version of **Psalm** 137 ('By the rivers of Babylon, there we sat down, yea, we wept, when we remembered Zion'). It is probably the sadness characterizing both the madrigals mentioned in Marlowe's lyric and Psalm 137 which prompts this connection in Evans's mind (Oliver, p. 70).

(C) Kerman, *The Elizabethan Madrigal* (1962), considers the effect of the Italian madrigal in England.
 Oliver, *The Merry Wives of Windsor* (1971).
 Pike, *Pills to Purge Melancholy* (2004).
 Roche, *The Madrigal* (1990), contains a chapter on the English form; this study is one of the most succinct and accessible of the many commentaries on the madrigal.

make (A) In discussing who invented or **compose**d the different elements of the early seventeenth-century English courtly **masque**, Walls draws attention to the term 'make' which appears in some of the printed *Descriptions* or texts of masques (for example, Campion's *Somerset Masque*, 1613). He says the 'term seems now to have a rather naïve (or perhaps *faux naïf*) ring to it, but in the early seventeenth century it was synonymous with "compose" ' (p. 35). He goes on to point out that 'maker' was also used to denote a poet, the term derived from the Greek word *Poiein*, as Ben Jonson (in *Timber or Discoveries*) and Sir Philip Sidney (in *The Defence of Poesy*) attest. Walls concludes that the 'verb "make" obviously bore the same connotations as "create" does now' (ibid.). When used in a musical context, 'make' implies not only the **perform**ance but also the creation of music. It combines both a theoretical and practical application as for example in:

> Hoarse **sound**s the **voice** that praiseth not her name,
> For no **ground** else could make the **music** such,
> Nor other hand could give so **sweet** a **touch**.
> (Daniel, 1606, no. 4)

make

(B) Of the over 1,500 usages of 'make' in the Shakespeare canon, some have a distinctly musical flavour, as for instance in the Induction to *The Taming of the Shrew* when the lord exhorts his followers to 'make a **dulcet** and a heavenly sound' (Ind.i.51) in order to awake the drunken Christopher Sly. This pleasant music will trick Sly into believing that he is the lord of the house. Later in the same play, Hortensio is disguised as a **lute** teacher and is competing with Lucentio for Bianca's attention. He addresses his rival as follows: 'You may go walk, and give me leave a while; / My **lesson**s make no music in three **part**s' (3.1.59–60), in other words, not resulting in music being 'made' for three persons to **sing** or **play** together.

A darker meaning of 'make' is observed when Pericles tells King Antiochus' daughter:

> You are a fair **viol**, and your sense the **string**s;
> Who, finger'd to make man his lawful music,
> Would draw heaven down, and all the gods to hearken;
> But being play'd upon before your time,
> Hell only **dance**th at so **harsh** a **chime**.
>   (*Per* 1.1.81–5)

Pericles is hinting at the incestuous nature of the relationship between Antiochus and his daughter ('viol' and 'finger' have sexual connotations). This relationship is unnatural and can only create unpleasant and harsh sounds, instead of proper harmonious music.

In a convoluted speech interspersed with musical conceits, Moth advises Armado on how to woo Jaquenetta successfully. For instance, he should learn different dances and singing techniques. It is these and other skills that 'make them men of **note** / ... men that most are affected [inclined] to these' (*LLL* 3.1.24–5). The straightforward meaning of these lines (men will be noticed by the women they love if they are skilled at dancing and singing) plays on the musical meaning of 'note', and possibly hints at the ability to 'make music'.

Iago cynically comments that he will 'set down the **peg**s that make this music' (*Oth* 2.1.200), i.e. disrupt the **harmony** between Desdemona and Othello by spreading the rumour that Cassio and Desdemona are in love (see 'peg' for a commentary of this passage).

(C) Walls, *Music in the English Courtly Masque* (1996).

march (A) Whilst march does not necessarily require **music**, when it does the **instrument**s involved provide primarily a repetitive rhythmical accompaniment. Consequently, a percussive instrument (e.g. **drum, bell, cymbal**) is the most important, sometimes only, instrument needed. More elaborate marches would involve outdoor instruments such as **trumpet**s, **pipe**s, **hoboy**s and **cornett**s.

The march was usually associated with military signal music. All marches share a basic duple-**time** (walking) pulse but were differentiated by their speeds (tempi) and rhythms. Sir John Hawkins, for example, wrote that 'the old English march [of Elizabethan times] of the foot was formerly in high estimation . . . its characteristic is dignity and gravity, in which respect it differs greatly from the French, which, as it is given by Mersennus is brisk and alert' (p. 229).

Marches of various nationalities and function were clearly identifiable as Byrd shows in his famous 'The Battel' (MLNB, 1591) miscellany for keyboard. It includes 'The March of the footemen', 'The March of the horsemen', 'The Irish March' and 'The **Bagpipe** and the Drum'. Conventionally, the drum accompanied the footmen, the trumpet the cavalry. The combination of bagpipe and drum indicates a military march. Francis Markham in his *Five Decades of Epistles of Warre* (1622) refers to marches of different nations: 'a *March* according to the nature and custom of the country (for divers countries have divers Marches)' (Decade I, Epistle 5 'Of Drummes and Phiphes').

Marches were used for specific occasions such as funeral processions (dead marches) or victory parades, again characterized by tempo and rhythm. When instruments in addition to drums **play**ed, the **mood** of the march could be enhanced further by the **key**: minor for **solemn**, major for joy. Marches performed in the theatre would be simple and concise, whereas some military marches could be extensive and elaborate.

(B) In Shakespeare, stage directions for marches and marching are mainly found in historical plays and tragedies. **Sound** effects could either be achieved on stage, or from behind the *frons scenae* – the latter is clearly indicated, for instance, by '*March afar*' (*AWW* 3.5.37.SD), and '*A march afar off*' (*3H6* 1.2.68.SD). Instructions such as '*A march*' (*3H6* 2.1.OSD; 2.1.94.SD; 2.2.80.SD) seem to have purposely been left generic: they could be modified to suit different

263

march

performances in which musical instruments may or may not have been available (see also Introduction). If the latter was the case, then the actors' movements would have sufficed to evoke the atmosphere of a march.

Sometimes it is clear that the march is meant to be accompanied by instruments. For instance, Alcibiades enters '*with Drum and **Fife**, in warlike manner*' (*Tim* 4.3.48.SD). The use of both instruments in this case is quite unusual, since the drum is more commonly employed for marches, as in *1 Henry VI* for the French march '*with drum and soldiers*' (1.2.OSD) before Orléans. The syntax of this stage direction seems to reveal that 'drum' refers to the person carrying and **beat**ing the instrument on the stage, rather than to an offstage sound effect. This play differentiates between the English and the French march (stage directions at, respectively, 3.3.30 and 3.3.32).

The rhythm of the march changed not only according to nationality, but also to the occasion (Edelman, p. 212). One such occasion would be a funeral, as in *Coriolanus*, which concludes with the following stage direction: '*Exeunt, bearing the body of Martius. A dead march sounded*' (5.6.154.SD). Another funeral for an important character (Henry V), this time in *1 Henry VI*, is punctuated by a march: '*Dead march. Enter the funeral of King Henry the Fifth [. . .]*' (1.1.OSD). A dead march was characterized by a muffled drum (Manifold, pp. 30–1). This sound would have been particularly poignant at the end of *King Lear*, when the dead bodies of the old King and Cordelia would have been carried off stage '*with a dead march*' (5.3.327.SD).

The dialogue sometimes contains clear hints that a march is to be accompanied by instruments. We find such clear indication in Montgomery's order to his troops in York: 'Drummer, **strike** up, and let us march away' (*3H6* 4.7.50), followed by the stage direction '*The Drum begins to march*' (4.7.50.SD).

After the Battle of Towton, Warwick orders his followers: 'And now to London with triumphant march' (*3H6* 2.6.87). In *Henry V*, a march is referred to as 'merry' (1.2.195), whereas in *Richard III* Richard talks about 'dreadful marches' (1.1.8), and in *Antony and Cleopatra* Antony exhorts Cleopatra to '**make** a jolly march' (4.8.30) through Alexandria to celebrate his victory over Caesar. All of these adjectives seem to point to musical accompaniment.

(C) Edelman, *Shakespeare's Military Language: A Dictionary* (2000), pp. 210–13, explains in detail the different meanings acquired by the noun and verb 'march' and the meaning of sound effects used to evoke martial atmospheres.

Hawkins, *A General History of the Science and Practice of Music* (1776).
Manifold, *The Music in English Drama* (1956).
Shirley, *Shakespeare's Use of Off-Stage Sounds* (1963), pp. 67–71.

mask see **masque**.

masque (A) **Music, dance** and visual spectacle were the essence of the Jacobean masque although Ben Jonson would also have us believe (in his famous 'Expostulation with Inigo Jones', 1622) that the words, the 'poetry', were more important: he believed the poetry was the 'soul' of the masque, the rest its 'body'. The form of the masque in the early seventeenth century represented a coalescence of elements of Henrician Interludes and Elizabethan Entertainments. Whilst every masque was unique and no predetermined fixed form for the genre emerged, certain main events in the course of the entertainments helped provide structure and generic identity. The most important event was the entry of the noblemen and/or ladies, the masquers, in costume or disguises. In most Jacobean masques there were three main masquers' entries or dances punctuated by **song**s. Immediately preceding the first entry was the 'discovery' or presentation of the theme of the masque usually embracing an abbreviated mythological scene or emblem combined with contemporary allusion referring to the occasion of the masque, such as a marriage or national event. The second entry marked the emblem of the masque. After the third entry and song the masque proper dissolved into what was time-wise the most substantial element, namely 'the revels' or social dancing when the masquers joined with members of the invited audience in less formalized dances. The masque often concluded with a song of farewell and final dance. From around 1609, courtly masques frequently began with an antimasque whose content, theme and presentation contrasted with the main masque and was performed by professional dancers-cum-actors. With the presence of an antimasque, the entry of the noble masquers, signifying the resolution or dispersal of the 'antic' prelude, was even more marked.

masque

Masques were artistically diffuse, involving many differing elements and therefore a number of different creators including writer (author), composer (there could be several), dance master(s), costume maker and set designer or 'architect' (usually Inigo Jones). No one person 'made' all the words, music, dances and *mis-en-scène*, although Campion was responsible for both the words and songs in his first masque, *The Lord Hayes* (1607).

Masque music usually comprised solo **lute ayre**s, dialogue songs, ensemble vocal and **instrument**al music and a variety of other kinds as appropriate (including **madrigal**s and motets). In some masques, the orchestra was large (in *Hayes* more than 40 **play**ers are needed) and included a mixture of lutes, **string**ed instruments, **hoboy**s, **recorder**s, **cornett**s and **trumpet**s. It was, however, rare for all the instrumentalists to play together; generally they played in distinct **consort**s at different points in the masque.

Masques were very lavish, extravagant productions, seeming the more luxurious because most were performed on one night only. None was done more than twice. The costs were outrageous, generally borne by the royal court or the Inns of Court. Exceptionally, individuals were known to pay: Sir Francis Bacon met the £2,000 it cost to mount the *Masque of Flowers* (1614); Sir William Knollys paid for the Entertainment (masque) for Queen Anne at Cawsome (Caversham) House (April 1613). Most of the court masques were presented at the Banqueting House, Whitehall and contemporary accounts suggest they lasted at least three hours. Most of the time was given to the dances of the revels. 'Masques normally began somewhere between eight and ten o'clock at night' (Walls, p. 329) and there are reports that some continued through the night (e.g. *Tethys Festival* and *Tempe Restored*).

(B) That the masque was considered to be an occasion for courtly display of wealth and pomp is evident in Norfolk's narration of the one that took place in France during Henry VIII's visit (*H8* 1.1.13–26). This masque, staged during the first night of revelries, was surpassed by the celebrations of the following night:

> . . . Now this masque
> Was cried incomparable; and th'ensuing night
> Made it a fool and beggar.
>
> (26–8)

masque

This episode is found in Holinshed's and Hall's chronicles, but the speech may allude to the celebrations for the wedding of Princess Elizabeth in 1613 (Foakes, p. 9).

A masque is one of the options for entertainment in *A Midsummer Night's Dream* after the weddings between Theseus and Hippolyta and the two young couples, as Theseus' question to his Master of the Revels indicates:

> Come now; what masques, what dances shall we have,
> To wear away this long age of three hours
> Between our after-supper and bed-time?
>
> (5.1.32–4)

A wedding between members of the aristocracy was only one of several official occasions for which masques were commissioned. It is also worth noting that the usual duration of a courtly masque is noted in this passage.

Shylock warns his daughter against this excessive type of entertainment when he realizes that Lorenzo and his friends are in celebratory **mood**:

> What, are there masques? Hear you me, Jessica:
> Lock up my doors, and when you **hear** the **drum**
> And the vile **squealing** of the wry-neck'd **fife**,
> Clamber not you up to the casements then,
> Nor thrust your head into the public street
> To gaze on Christian fools with varnish'd faces;
> But stop my house's **ear**s, I mean my casements;
> Let not the **sound** of shallow fopp'ry enter
> My sober house . . .
>
> (*MV* 2.5.28–36)

The musical component of the masque is stressed throughout the speech. Shylock makes reference to the practice sometimes adopted by masquers to start the celebration on the streets before proceeding into the palace where the masque was staged. The accompaniment of drums and fifes was also common. The image of the 'wry-neck'd fife' ('fife' here refers to the **musician** rather than the instrument) squealing in a vile manner anticipates Shylock's open expression of disapproval

267

masque

of masques. He fears that, by listening to the musicians and watching the masquers, Jessica may be contaminated by superficial Christian foolery as opposed to Jewish sobriety.

A pejorative meaning of this term is found also in *Julius Caesar*, when during the Battle of Philippi Antony is described (anachronistically) as 'a masker and a reveller' (5.1.62) by his enemy Cassius. In *Twelfth Night*, Sir Andrew Aguecheek reveals his fondness for revelry when he says that he delights 'in masques and revels' (1.3.113).

In the concluding scene of *Love's Labour's Lost*, the entry of the King of Navarre and his lords before the staging of the pageant of the Nine Worthies is preceded by the sounding of a trumpet (5.2.156.SD) and by Boyet's exhortation to the Princess and her ladies: 'The trumpet sounds, be mask'd; the maskers come' (5.2.157). Then, we have the stage direction: '*Enter Blackmoors with music, the Boy with a speech, and the rest of the Lords disguised*' (5.2.158.SD). The sound of the trumpet seems to serve the purpose of announcing royalty, whereas the musicians in the King's train would have provided the musical background to the ensuing masque (158–309). Black Africans (blackamoors) were employed, for instance, in Ben Jonson's *Masque of Blackness* of 1605.

In *King John*, the Bastard defines his imminent battle against the Dauphin as a 'harness'd masque' (5.2.132). This is an unusual metaphorical allusion, which likens the movements of the soldiers in armour to those of masquers, and the military sounds to those of the music accompanying a masque.

(C) Bevington and Holbrook (eds), *The Politics of the Stuart Court Masque* (1998), includes essays on dance and music, as well as an authoritative overview of the current state of scholarship by Martin Butler.

Chan, *Music in the Theatre of Ben Jonson* (1980).

Foakes, *Henry VIII* (1964).

Lindley, *The Court Masque* (1984), is an introduction to differing aspects of the masque; and *Thomas Campion* (1986), pp. 174–234, includes a study of Campion's masques.

Orgel, *The Jonsonian Masque* (1981), analyses production and literary subjects; *The Illusion of Power* (1975), a seminal discussion of the politics of the genre.

Sabol, *Four Hundred Songs and Dances from the Stuart Masque* (1978), provides a selection of the music of the songs and dances and also contains a very helpful introduction to the subject of the masque.

masque

Walls, *Music in the English Courtly Masque* (1996), is the fullest and best account of the role of music in the English masque, together with a discussion of the identity of the genre and a useful bibliography.

Welsford, *The Court Masque* (1927), was, and to a certain extent still is, the standard authority on the masque.

Wilson, 'Some Musico-poetic Aspects of Campion's Masques' (1990), examines Campion's masques.

mean (A) On the **lute** the mean is the second **string** or 'small mean'. In vocal **music**, it is the middle **part** between top and bottom (**treble** and **bass**). Today we would call it either an alto or a tenor **voice** depending on its range or *tessitura*. Charles Butler defined it reasonably precisely: 'The Mean is so called, becaus it is a midling or mean **high** part, betweene the Countertenor, (the highest part of a man) and the Treble, (the highest part of a boy or woman:) and therefore may bee sung by a mean voice' (p. 42). In Elizabethan music in four or more parts, the mean usually came next below the treble. In the eighteenth century, 'mean' became obsolete and was replaced by 'alto' or 'tenor'.

(B) Of the over 500 usages of 'mean' and 'means' in the Shakespeare canon, very few have a musical connotation and are connected to vocal music. One such usage is observed when Berowne speaks about Boyet in a derogatory manner and observes that 'he can **sing** / A mean most meanly' (*LLL* 5.2.327–8). The pun on 'mean' as a synonym for 'unpleasant' and 'inferior' is intended here: clearly, Boyet is anything but a good singer.

Lucetta warns Julia, who is trying to sing the song written in her honour by Proteus, that: '[You] mar the **concord** with too **harsh** a **descant**: / There wanteth but a mean to fill your song' (*TGV* 1.2.91–2). The improvisation of a two-voice polyphony ('descant') is incomplete without the contribution of the tenor. Similarly, Julia's life will not be fulfilled until she accepts Proteus' love.

Another use of this word to indicate a middle vocal part is found in *The Winter's Tale*, where the Clown tells us that his sister has made:

269

mean

> ... Four and twenty nosegays for the shearers (three-man song-men all, and very good ones), but they are most of them means and **base**s ...
> (4.3.41–3)

The Clown is pointing to the lack of an upper part in this three-man song. The subtitle of Ravenscroft's second collection of **catch**es, **roundelays** and imitative part songs, his *Deuteromelia* (1609), was: *The Second part of Musicks melodie, or melodius Musicke. Of Pleasant Roundelaies; K.H. mirth, or Freemens Songs. And such delightfull Catches.* Most of these songs are for three (male) voices. 'Freemens Songs' is probably a corruption of 'three mens songs' and K.H. stands for 'King Henry'. The songs Ravenscroft published relate to those part-songs of Henry VIII's court found in the so-called 'King Henry VIII Manuscript' (BL MS Add. 31922, printed in MB 18).

See also **ayre**.

(C) Butler, *Principles of Musik* (1636).

measure (A) Usually associated with **dance**, the measure is the speed at which a piece of **music** goes. This is sometimes referred to as the beat and to measure is to beat **time**. Ravenscroft defined measure as 'a Quantity of the length and shortnes of Time, either by Naturall **sound**s pronounced by the **Voice**, or by Artificiall, upon **Instruments**' (*Briefe Discourse*, 1614, p. 1). This could imply either a fast or a slow tempo. Rules governing tempo were not so clearly stated in the sixteenth and seventeenth centuries as they were in later periods when tempo words (e.g. Allegro, Moderato, Lento) and (in the nineteenth century onwards) metronome marks were included in the score. The best indicators were the **mood** of a piece: fast for happy, slow for sad, and any relationship a piece had to a dance. Specific types of dances were allied to certain tempi. A more theoretical way of determining tempo was based on the kinds of notation or rhythmic **mode** used.

Because of their essential rhythmical quality, dances were referred to as measures, in some cases quite specifically as in the passing-measures **pavan** (derived from the Italian '*passamezzo*'). The steps of the dance were the measures and were related to the tempo of the accompanying music.

measure

(B) Shakespeare invariably uses this word as a synonym for 'dance'. For instance, the final scene of *Love's Labour's Lost* plays on two different meanings of 'measure': the act of determining quantity, on the one hand, and the dance on the other. The King of Navarre and his three lords are disguised as Muscovites and are wooing the Princess of France and her three ladies-in waiting. However, the women are aware of their disguise and decide to exchange masks, thus confounding their suitors. The following passage is built on the King's false assumption that he is addressing the Princess instead of Rosaline:

> KING: Say to her that we have measur'd many miles,
> To tread a measure with her on this grass.
> BOYET: They say that they have measur'd many a mile
> To tread a measure with you on this grass.
> ROSALINE: It is not so. Ask them how many inches
> Is in one mile: if they have measured many,
> The measure then of one is eas'ly told.
> (5.2.184–90)

Rosaline's knowledge that the suitors come from a country closer than Russia transpires here. The King then asks her: 'in our measure ... vouchsafe one **change**' (209) but she declines. 'Change' refers to the phases of the moon – a topic of conversation brought up by Rosaline at line 203 – but also to the **round**s of a dance (David, p. 144). The King is surprised at her rejection (he still believes that he is talking to the Princess of France):

> KING: Why take we hands then?
> ROSALINE: Only to part friends.
> Curtsy, **sweet** hearts – and so the measure ends.
> KING: More measure of this measure ...
> (219–22)

He renews his invitation (222) to no avail. The puns on 'measure' and 'change' in these passages work particularly well in productions which choose to **play** music in the background following Rosaline's words 'Play, music, then!' (211). This type of musical cue is widely used in Elizabethan and Jacobean plays, and in this specific case would have worked as an instruction to the **musician**s who accompany the King

271

measure

of Navarre and his followers (they are part of the French entourage as the stage direction at 5.2.157 instructs).

The expression 'tread a measure' found in *Love's Labour's Lost*, 5.2.187 evokes a 'grave or stately dance' (*OED* 15a). This meaning is also implied by Touchstone when he claims that he has 'trod a measure' (*AYLI* 5.4.44) to convince Duke Senior that he is a courtier; and by Venus when, after Adonis' death, she prophesies that love will always be accompanied by sorrow and contradiction, such as 'teaching decrepit age to tread the measures' (*Ven* 1148). The implication here is that the art of dancing can only be mastered by the young.

Beatrice's advice to Hero concerning marriage provides a theoretical exposition of this and other kinds of dance:

> ... For hear me,
> Hero: wooing, wedding, and repenting, is as a
> Scotch **jig**, a measure, and a cinquepace; the first
> suit is hot and hasty, like a Scotch jig, and full
> as fantastical; the wedding, mannerly-modest, as
> a measure, full of state and ancientry; and then
> comes repentance, and with his bad legs falls into
> the cinquepace faster and faster, till he sink into
> his grave.
>
> (*Ado* 2.1.72–80)

The measure is by far the most stately and moderate of the three dances, whereas the jig and the cinquepace are more lively and less formal (see '**cinque pas**' for a detailed analysis of this passage).

The stately nature of the dance is also emphasized in Gaunt's attempt to comfort Bolingbroke after the latter has been banished by the King. Gaunt advises his son to make a virtue of necessity and to use his imagination in order to make his exile more bearable:

> Suppose the **sing**ing **bird**s musicians,
> The grass wheron thou tread'st the presence strow'd,
> The flowers fair ladies, and thy steps no more
> Than a delightful measure or a dance.
>
> (*R2* 1.3.288–91)

'Tread' manages to connect seamlessly two different ideas: walking on grass (289) and dancing a measure (291). Gaunt conjures up an image of courtly entertainment, and the pleasure derived from listening to music and dancing. No wonder that Bolingbroke's response to this speech is not as positive as his father had hoped.

(C) Berger, 'Against the Sink-a-Pace' (1982), argues that the references to dances in *Much Ado About Nothing* try to justify the patriarchal values upheld in that play.

David, *Love's Labour's Lost* (1951).

Mullally, 'More about the Measures' (1994); and '*Measure* as a Choreographic Term in the Stuart Masque' (1998).

Ward, 'The English Measure' (1986).

melodious see **melody**.

melody (A) For the Elizabethans 'melody' conjured up the idea of a **sweet tune** apt for **sing**ing. Thus 'melodious **bird**s' would be sweet singing birds. A melody would necessarily comprise rhythm (in due **proportion**s), pitches and words or, as Dowland reports, 'Plato defines melody to consist of **harmony, number** & words; harmony naked of it selfe: words the ornament of harmony, number the common friend & uniter of them both' (*The First Booke of Songes*, 1597, Dedicatory epistle). **Instrument**s, the neo-Platonic argument goes, are not so good at expressing melody as the singing **voice**. Thus the ideal is the human voice (the melody) accompanied by instruments as in the **lute** song or **ayre**. The term 'ayre' used to signify lute song derives from this notion of a vocal melody accompanied by lute in contrast to say the **madrigal** where several voices **imitate** each other's melodies in polyphony.

When a melody serves as a theme or motive it could also be called the 'ayre'. Campion argues that the **bass** can have the melody or theme: 'But I will plainely convince by demonstration that contrary to some opinions, the Base containes in it both the Aire and true iudgement of the **Key**' (*A New Way*, c.1614, B6v).

(B) The singing of birds is often mentioned in conjunction with melody, as in *The Merry Wives of Windsor*, 3.1.18 (see 'madrigal' for a detailed

melody

discussion). The same applies to the opening scene of *The Two Noble Kinsmen* where a boy sings about 'bird melodious, or bird fair' (1.1.17), and in *The Rape of Lucrece* when the 'sweet melody' (1108) of birds makes Lucrece even more resolved to commit suicide instead of giving her some consolation.

Strange as it may appear, *Titus Andronicus* – one of the most violent plays in the Shakespeare canon – has the largest number of references to 'melody' and 'melodious' (five). For instance, the lascivious Tamora tries to entice Aaron into becoming her lover when they meet in the forest:

> My lovely Aaron, wherefore look'st thou sad,
> When every thing doth make a gleeful boast?
> The birds **chaunt** melody in every bush . . .
> (2.3.9–11)

She then describes what would happen after their love-making:

> We may, each wreathed in the other's arms
> (Our pastimes done), possess a golden slumber,
> Whiles hounds and **horn**s and sweet melodious birds
> Be unto us as is a nurse's song
> Of **lullaby** to bring her babe asleep.
> (2.1.25–9)

The pastoral descriptions of the forest in these two passages have a more sinister quality than it may appear at first. Tamora is the major instigator of the despicable events which take place later in the scene, most notably the murder of Bassianus, and the rape and mutilation of Lavinia. Evocation of childhood innocence through musical metaphors is cruelly ironic, since Tamora is responsible for Lavinia's brutal loss of sexual innocence. It is also interesting that Marcus uses yet another image of musical melody to vent his horror when he realizes that Lavinia's **tongue** has been cut. He observes that her tongue 'like a sweet melodious bird . . . sung / Sweet varied **note**s, **enchant**ing every **ear**' (3.1.85–6).

The musical nuance of 'air' (ayre) and its relationship with 'melody' is evident in Titus' speech commenting on the death of a fly:

melody

> ... How if that fly had a father and mother?
> How would he hang his slender gilded wings
> And buzz **lament**ing doings in the air!
> Poor harmless fly,
> That, with his pretty buzzing melody,
> Came here to make us merry! ...
> (3.2.60–5)

Even at the height of his madness, which leads him to compare the buzzing of a fly with a melody, Titus does not go as far as calling it 'sweet', a term more appropriate for the melodious singing of birds. He chooses the adjective 'pretty' instead.

Venus articulates with a musical oxymoron her attraction to Adonis' voice, which is like 'melodious **discord**, heavenly tune **harsh sound**ing' (*Ven* 431). On the other hand, no such paradoxical effect is to be found in King Henry IV's reflection on his lack of sleep:

> Why rather, sleep, liest thou in smoky cribs,
> Upon uneasy pallets stretching thee,
> And hush'd with buzzing night-flies to thy slumber,
> Than in the perfum'd chambers of the great,
> Under the canopies of costly state,
> And lull'd with sound of sweetest melody?
> (*2H4* 3.1.9–14)

While passion transpires in Venus' unusual combination of musical terms, Henry's soliloquy has quite a different impact. The contrast between the melodious nature of courtly **music** and the noise of buzzing night-flies in the houses of his subjects aims to reinforce the importance of the King's hierarchical position in society.

See also **hum**.

(C) Wilson (ed.), *A New Way* (2003), p. 46.

metre (A) Related to **measure**, 'metre' is used in connection with the rhythm and scansion of a literary poem. When the metre of a poem is replicated in **music** then that music is said to be in such a metre, for example '**ballad**' metre. The potential interrelationships in art **song** between musical rhythm and poetic metre were explored by **lute**-song

metre

composers, in particular, Campion, Dowland and John Daniel. Equally, English poets experimented in making verses to fit pre-existent music. Notable parodical exercises were some of Sir Philip Sidney's *Certain Sonnets* (c.1577–82) and Thomas Watson's *Italian Madrigalls Englished* (1590). It was common practice to fit ballads to popular songs and adapt **tune**s to ballads.

(B) In response to Glendower's boasting that he has had close connections with the English court and is skilled in poetry and music, Hotspur replies that he 'had rather be a kitten and cry mew / Than one of these same metre **ballet-monger**s' (*1H4* 3.1.127–8). This is a derogatory comment about the repetitiveness of ballad metres and the 'low repute of street ballads' (Humphreys, p. 93) which were commonly sold by pedlars. By implication, Hotspur is criticizing poetry as a whole.

In *Sonnet* 17, the poet exhorts his young friend to have children, who will prove to posterity that the beauty of the young man described by the poet was real. Otherwise the poet's verses will

> Be scorn'd, like old men of less truth than **tongue**,
> And your true rights be term'd a poet's rage,
> And stretched metre of an antique song.
>
> (10–12)

The poet is afraid that he will be accused of following his own inspiration and giving a false portrayal of the young man. As a result, his poem ('song') will be judged to be strained ('stretched') and old-fashioned ('antique'). Line 12 acquires a wider meaning when set against the vocabulary characterising *Sonnet* 17 as a whole. The polysemic quality of terms such as '**part**s' (4), '**grace**s' (6) 'heavenly' (8) and '**touch**es' (8) – often employed in music treatises of the Renaissance – aims to create musical nuances.

(C) Duffin, *Shakespeare's Songbook* (2004), examines Shakespeare's use of ballads, and popular songs.

Duncan-Jones, *Shakespeare's Sonnets* (1997), p. 16.

Humphreys, *King Henry IV, Part I* (1960).

Maynard, *Elizabethan Lyric Poetry and Its Music* (1986), discusses aspects

metre

of joining rhythm and metre in English Renaissance popular and art songs.

Weil, *The First Part of Henry IV* (1997).

mi The third **note** of the Renaissance hexachord. See **ut**.

minikin (A) The thin **high**-pitched catgut **string**s on a violin or other similar stringed **instrument** are called the 'minikin'.

(B) Before the mock trial of Lear's ungrateful daughters, Edgar, who is faking madness, **sing**s:

> Sleepest or wakest thou, jolly shepherd?
> Thy sheep be in the corn,
> And for one blast of thy minikin mouth,
> Thy sheep shall take no harm.
> (*Lr* 3.6.41–4)

Commentators often observe that these lines refer to the shepherd's summoning of sheep in order to prevent them from accessing the cornfield, where they can get bloated and die (Foakes, p. 289). The 'blast' of the 'minikin mouth' may be the shepherd's **shrill** cry to call his flock, since the minikin is used for the **treble** strings and by extension, means 'a high-pitched **voice**' (*OED* A.I.2). Robbins has an alternative explanation: '"minikin mouth" probably refers to the mouthpiece of the pibcorn, or **hornpipe**, a **hollow** instrument with finger holes and **horn** at each end' (p. 310).

In *Romeo and Juliet* (Q1, 1597) there is also reference to 'minikin'. One of the **musician**s dismissed after the wedding celebrations between Paris and Juliet have been cancelled (4.5) is called 'Matthew Minikin'. This name changes to 'Simon **Catling**' in all later versions of the play, i.e. Q2 (1599), Q3 (1609), Q4 (c. 1622) and Folio. (See 'catling' for a detailed comment).

See also **pipe**.

(C) Foakes, *King Lear* (1997).

Robbins, 'Shakespeare's Sweet Music' (1968).

minim

minim (A) The minim is a **note** or 'character of **time**'. It is a time-value equal to half a semibreve (which was a white note without a tail, or as Dowland states, 'a Figure, which is round in forme of an egge, or (as *Franchinus* sayeth) Triangular' (*Micrologus*, 1609, p. 39) or two **crotchet**s. It was one of the eight notes of white mensural notation (see '**breve**'). Dowland described its written form as 'a Figure like a *Sembreefe*, having a tayle, ascending or descending' (ibid.). During the sixteenth century, the minim became the basic unit of **measure** or time, only to be replaced by the crotchet in the seventeenth century.

(B) There is only one reference to 'minim' in the Shakespeare canon, in Mercutio's exposition of Tybalt's duelling skills:

> ... He fights as you sing a **prick-song**, keeps time, distance, and **proportion**; he **rest**s his minim rests, one, two, and the third in your bosom ...
>
> (*Rom* 2.4.20–3)

Like a piece of **music**, the art of duelling has to rely on precisely observed rhythm and tempo to be successful. Tybalt 'will make two feints, with the briefest possible pause between each, and then on the third beat, he will strike' (Evans, p. 106). The unit pulse is the minim. Therefore, when he pauses, he 'rests' for the duration of a minim, known also in music as 'minim rest'.

(C) Apel, *The Notation of Polyphonic Music* (1953).
Evans, *Romeo and Juliet* (2003).

minstrel (A) A minstrel was a professional entertainer and/or **musician**, most often a **fiddler** or a **sing**er, who was paid for his or her services, that is his/her minstrelsy. The origin of the term is uncertain but Roger North (1728) claimed it derived from a monastery church or minster:

> There will be small show of skill in **music**k in England except what belonged to the cathedrall churches, and monasterys (when such were) and for that reason the consortiers wherever they went, (from

ministers, as the word was) were called minstrells, and then the whole faculty of musick [was called] the minstrelsie.

(Chan and Kassler, ff. 128–128v)

If there was a specific connection with the Church, it lapsed as the Middle Ages progressed so that minstrels could be found in a variety of secular contexts. Minstrels were expected to provide musical and sometimes poetical entertainment on demand. Consequently, their repertoire was either improvised or **perform**ed from memory. Groups of minstrels could be called upon to entertain at more formal occasions such as banquets and weddings.

Although minstrels enjoyed a comparatively high standing as entertainers in the Middle Ages, their reputation declined significantly during the sixteenth century, as the Acts of Parliament and Royal Proclamations controlling the activities and apparel of minstrels and players attest. At the beginning of the century, minstrels attracted some esteem as the 'Act agaynst wearing of costly Apparrell' (1 Hen. VIII. C.14, 1510) confirms: 'Provided ... that this acte be not prejudiciall nor hurtfull to eny Woman or to eny ambassatures Hencemen Harroldes of armes Mynstrelles Players in enterludes ...'. By the 1570s, minstrels had been reduced to the status of vagabonds and beggars, unless exceptionally they received the patronage of nobility. It is interesting to note that the decline in minstrelsy coincided with the rise in printed music and poetry. It may be that the improvised entertainment of the Medieval performer was supplanted by the more formalized art of the Renaissance specialist.

(B) Shakespeare makes interesting use of the word 'minstrel'. A comical exchange takes place between Peter (the servant of Juliet's nurse) and the musicians who have been asked to **play** at the wedding of Juliet and Paris, and who have been dismissed after Juliet's (apparent) death. The musicians, more interested in their remuneration than in music, are addressed by Peter who says that, instead of money, he will give them 'the minstrel' (*Rom* 4.5.115). This derogatory comment, implying that a minstrel is not a real artist, shows that Shakespeare and his fellow playwrights and actors were well aware of the 1572 'Acte for the punishment of Vacabondes and for the Relleif of the Poore & Impotent', which put minstrels and actors who did not enjoy the patronage of a member of the aristocracy in the same league as vagabonds, rogues and sturdy beggars.

minstrel

Earlier in the same play, Mercutio too has a negative connotation of the term in mind when he defies his enemy Tybalt, after the latter accuses him of '**consort**ing' with Romeo. This word allows Mercutio to build on the pun:

> Consort! what, dost thou make us minstrels?
> And thou make minstrels of us, look to **hear** nothing
> but **discord**s. Here's my **fiddle-stick**, here's that shall
> make you **dance**. 'Zounds, consort!
>
> (3.1.46–9)

Apart from the obvious meaning of 'consort' ('keep company with'), the musical nuance ('perform with a consort of minstrels') is evident. The rapier that the young man is carrying is compared to a fiddle-stick. Mercutio obviously feels degraded by being compared to a humble minstrel.

In *Love's Labour's Lost*, Berowne remarks that the King should not **compose** love poetry: 'Tush, none but minstrels like of sonneting!' (4.3.156). This remark underlines the connection between lyric poetry and minstrels, and once again is used pejoratively. The King himself refers to the minstrel's profession in anything but flattering terms. He explains why and in what capacity he wants to employ Armado:

> ... Our court you know is haunted
> With a refined traveller of Spain,
> A man in all the world's new fashion planted,
> That hath a mint of phrases in his brain;
> One who the music of his own vain **tongue**
> Doth **ravish** like **enchant**ing **harmony**;
> ...
> How you delight, my lords, I know not, I,
> But I protest I love to hear him lie,
> And I will use him for my minstrelsy.
>
> (1.1.162–7; 174–6)

Armado is a caricatural, pedantic self-conceited character. He comes from Spain, the greatest enemy of England, a country 'lost in the world's debate' (1.1.173), i.e. warfare. That the King wants to use him as a minstrel proves that this profession was not as highly reputed in Shakespeare's time as it was in the Middle Ages.

At the height of her despair, Lucrece considers the possible consequences of the violence she has suffered. She fears that her rape will become a popular theme for stories and songs:

> The nurse to still her child will tell my story,
> And fright her crying babe with Tarquin's name;
> The orator to deck his oratory
> Will couple my reproach to Tarquin's shame;
> Feast-finding minstrels, tuning my defame,
> Will tie the hearers to attend each line,
> How Tarquin wronged me, I Collatine.
> (*Luc* 813–19)

Here, the minstrel is described as an itinerant figure who offers his services at feasts and does not enjoy courtly patronage.

(C) Anderson, Pettitt and Schröder, *The Entertainer in Medieval and Traditional Culture* (1997), provides an account of the heyday of minstrelsy.
 Chan and Kassler, *Roger North's 'The Musicall Grammarian'* (1990).
 Chappell, 'English Minstrelsy from 1270 to 1480', in *Popular Music of the Olden Time* (1855–9), vol. 1, pp. 28–47.
 Rastall, *Minstrels Playing* (2001).

minstrelsy see **minstrel**.

mode (A) In the twelfth and thirteenth centuries, rhythmic notation was determined basically by the rhythmic modes. Six modes contained stereotyped patterns based on groupings of **long**s (*longa*) and shorts (*brevis*). Until the advent of the **time**-signature, the precise rhythm had to be deduced from the groupings of **note**s and **rest**s, and context. As note-values in Western **music** slowed down from the thirteenth century to the seventeenth, so the system of modal rhythmic notation was subdivided into smaller time-values according to 'Time' (**breve** into semibreve) and 'Prolation' (semibreve into **minim**). Although the modal system had become largely obsolete by the end of the sixteenth century, it was still discussed by theorists. Morley, for example, has a detailed section on Mode (*Introduction*, 1597, pp. 12–36).

mode

'Mode' was also used in Renaissance theory to mean **'key'** or 'tone'. Campion, for instance, misleadingly conflates the terms: 'Of all things that belong to the making up of a Musition, the most necessary and usefull for him is the true knowledge of the Key or Moode, or Tone' (*A New Way*, c.1614, D4r). Morley, similarly, wrongly equated the Medieval term 'mode' with key and tone: 'The perfect knowledge of these **air**es ["keys"] (which the antiquity termed *Modi*) was in such estimation amongst the learned, as therein they placed the perfection of **music**ke' (*Introduction*, 1597, p. 147). Mode, or tonal character, was part of key but a key was not the same as a mode.

(B) There are no unequivocal uses of 'mood' or 'mode' in a musical sense in Shakespeare. Some editors gloss 'mood' in *2 Henry IV* as alluding to a musical meaning when the dying King talks to his son about the dangers implicit in becoming a monarch. King Henry admits to the unpopularity of his rule, and concludes:

>   . . . And now my death
> **Change**s the mood, for what in me was purchas'd
> Falls upon thee in a more fairer sort;
> So thou the garland wear'st successively.
>   (4.5.198–201)

The polysemic quality of 'mood' is played on to achieve an interesting effect: 'mood' can mean 'state of mind', equivalent to 'musical key' or 'tone', but also 'pace of life', recalling the temporal meaning of 'mood' in music.

See also **degree, proportion**.

(C) Apel, *The Notation of Polyphonic Music* (1953), pp. 220–58 explains the rhythmic modes.

Owens, 'Concepts of Pitch' (1998), pp. 220–4.

Rastall, *The Notation of Western Music* (1998).

Robbins, 'Shakespeare's Sweet Music' (1968).

Wilson (ed.), *A New Way* (2003) pp. 75–6, analyses 'mood' as 'key' or 'tone'.

mood see **mode**.

morris dance

morris dance (A) The morris dance, a ceremonial display **dance**, possibly of Moorish origins (hence its name), was imported into Europe through Spain in Medieval times. It came to England in the fourteenth century and during the fifteenth century seems to have developed unique characteristics still in evidence in the twentieth century, as Baskervill notes:

> So far as Elizabethan allusions to the morris go, they indicate that this dance also has remained much the same. Six seems to have been the usual number of dancers in the sixteenth century as at the present time. Laneham describes the morris dance performed before Elizabeth at Kenilworth in 1575 as 'a lively morisdauns, according too the auncient manner, six daunserz, Mawdmarion, and the fool'.
>
> (p. 352)

Hand gestures (*chironomia*) were an essential feature and were emphasized by scarves fastened to the sleeves and by morris 'napkins' held in the hands of the dancers (see woodcut depiction in Kemp's *Nine Daies Wonder*). Similarly, feet movements were characterized by the dancers wearing little **bell**s on their leggings, a feature derived from the Medieval continental form of the dance.

The English 'morris', though related, was different from the *morisque* described by Arbeau (*Orchesography*, 1589, p. 177). In England it became connected with rustic gatherings and occasions for interpersonal relationships, especially in the springtime at 'semi-social dancing around the May pole' (Baskervill, p. 363): 'Our country swains in the morris dance / Thus woo and win their brides' (Weelkes, 1597, no. 11).

Another lyric suggests an appropriate rustic **instrument**al accompaniment:

> Hark, hark I **hear** some dancing
> And a **nimble** morris prancing.
> The **bagpipe** and the morris bells
> That they are not far hence us tells.
> Come let us all go thither,
> And dance like friends together.
> (Weelkes, 1600, no. 8)

Although it was a very popular dance only one **music** example is found

morris dance

in Elizabethan sources. The anonymous 'The King's Morisco' (FWVB ii. 373) is a short **piece** of five episodes in duple rhythm and a sixth in triple **metre**.

(B) This term is used twice in its musical sense by Shakespeare. In *All's Well That Ends Well*, the Clown boasts to the Countess of Rossillion that he suits perfectly a courtly environment, as he has an 'answer that fits all questions' (2.2.15). To illustrate his point, he declares that his answer is as fit '. . . as a pancake for / Shrove Tuesday, a morris for May-day, as the nail to / his hole, the cuckhold to his horn . . .' (23–5). This is only part of the list of commonplaces uttered by the Clown, and reveals that morris dancing on May Day was a widely known and popular custom in Shakespeare's time.

The Dauphin advises his father that the French should show defiance towards the English, with

> . . . no show of fear,
> No, with no more than if we **hear**d that England
> Were busied with a Whitsun morris-dance.
> (*H5* 2.4.23–5)

The Dauphin treats the English with contempt and arrogance. In his mind, a morris dance on Whit Sunday (the seventh Sunday after Easter) was such a common event that it did not deserve any special notice.

(C) Baskervill, *The Elizabethan Jig* (1929), pp. 352–3, describes the steps of the morris.

Lowe, 'Early Records of the Morris in England' (1957), is a useful description of the early English morris.

Ward, 'The Morris Tune' (1986), includes a list of early modern pieces labelled 'morris' and various 'morris' tunes from sixteenth and seventeenth-century sources.

motion (A) In differing contexts 'motion' had several meanings in Elizabethan **music**. It could refer to musical speed or tempo, as Morley describes it:

If the subject be light, you must cause your musicke go in motions,

motion

which carrie with them a celeritie or quicknesse of **time**, as **minim**es, **crotchet**s and quavers: if it be **lament**able, the **note** must goe in slow and heavie motions, as semibreves, **breve**s and such like.

(*Introduction*, 1597, p. 178)

Immediately preceding this observation, Morley also defines 'motion' as what we call modulation, that is the logical movement of the music from one **key** into another. Morley specifically refers to modulation from major into minor and minor into major; major expressing 'masculine virility' and minor signifying 'effeminate and languishing' emotions (ibid., p. 177).

The music made by the movement of the celestial bodies was called the 'motion of the spheres' and as an element of speculative music was a common topos in Elizabethan literature. Campion, for example, has: 'To his **sweet lute, Apollo** sung the motion of the spheres / The wondrous order of the stars, whose course divides the years (*Fourth Booke*, no. 8, c.1617).

(B) This metaphysical concept is found in Lorenzo's speech to Jessica on the starry sky at night:

> There's not the smallest orb which thou behold'st,
> But in his motion like an **angel sing**s,
> Still quiring to the young-ey'd cherubins,
> Such **harmony** is in immortal souls,
> But whilst this muddy vesture of decay
> Doth grossly close it in, we cannot **hear** it.
> (*MV* 5.1.60–5)

The motion of the stars has a supernatural quality resembling the singing of angels: the divine nature of the harmony produced by the movements of the spheres means that it cannot be heard by mortals.

The conceits of divine power and motion are paired also in *Sonnet* 128, albeit in a more oblique way. The poet describes his mistress when she skilfully **play**s the **virginal**s. He envies the **jack**s set in motion by her hands. The lines 'Upon that blessed wood whose motion **sound**s / With thy sweet fingers' (2–3) recall the movement of the keys which operate the jacks of the virginal. The **instrument** is 'blessed' both *motion*

because it is **touch**ed by the lady the poet loves, and because it produces harmonious music with its divine associations.

There are two instances in the Shakespeare canon when 'motion' in a musical context alludes to dancing rather than music. The King of Navarre, disguised as a Muscovite, thinks that he is talking to the Princess of France (in fact he is addressing Rosaline, who has exchanged masks with the Princess after they have been warned of the King and his followers' disguise). He invites her to **dance**: 'The music plays, vouchsafe some motion to it' (*LLL* 5.2.216). She rejects his offer with a witty reply: they should take hands only to 'curtsy' (221) and end the **measure** (221) ('measure' here as elsewhere in Shakespeare is used as a synonym for 'dance').

The second instance is found in *All's Well That Ends Well*, when Lafeu talks to the King of France about the wonders that the medicine about to be presented to him by Helen can work:

> . . . I have seen a medicine
> That's able to breathe life into a stone,
> Quicken a rock, and make you dance **canary**
> With spritely fire and motion. . .
>
> (2.1.72–5)

The reference to the dance canary, characterized by lively movements, is particularly apt to express the idea of recovery from an illness.

See also **languishment**.

mournful (A) In **music**, 'mournful' is an emotional expression of extreme sadness and despair and is usually associated with death or dying. It may describe either the mode of **sing**ing or **play**ing:

> Grief, press my soul, that I may never find relief,
> Since wearied life is still prolonged by uttered grief.
> . . . And as my singing is a mournful **swan**-like crying,
> So let my living be a senseless life, a dying.
>
> (Handford, 1609, no. 5);

or the music itself:

> Out from the vale of deep despair
> With mournful **tune**s I fill the air,
> To satisfy my restless ghost.
> (Ward, 1613, no. 21)

(B) Lucius' concluding speech in *Titus Andronicus* states that, whereas Lavinia and Titus will be accorded **solemn** funeral rites, Tamora is not worthy of such an honour. Hence, 'No funeral rite, nor man in mourning weed / No mournful **bell** shall **ring** her burial' (5.3.196–7). The sounding of the funeral bell as formal ritual is not appropriate for the death of the cruel Tamora.

The **nightingale**'s singing is described as 'mournful **hymn**s [which] hush the night' (*Son* 102, 10). The use of this adjective is apposite in a sonnet where this **bird** is identified with **Philomela**, who was transformed into a nightingale after being raped by Tereus, and as a result was able to vent her anguish through her **song**.

See also **dirge, doleful, woeful**.

music (A) The use of the term 'music' involves several different meanings current in Elizabethan England. It can refer to notated music, or to music as **perform**ed by **sing**ers or **instrument**alists (practical music), or to the **sound** (actual or imagined) of music, or to neo-Platonic theories about the symbolic role of music (speculative music) or, in the early seventeenth century, to the representational function of the 'new music'. 'Music' can also refer to a group of **musician**s, on or off the stage.

Elizabethan writers seem reluctant to commit themselves to a definition of music. Morley (*Introduction*, 1597) says 'amongst so many who have written of musicke, I knew not whom to follow in the definition' (Annotations to part 1). He then proceeds to offer several interpretations:

> The most aunicent of which is by *Plato* set out in his *Theages* thus. Musicke (saith he) *is a knowledge . . . whereby we may rule a company of singers* [i.e. **choir**] . . . But in his *Banquet* he giveth this definition. *Musick*, saith he, *is a science of love matters occupied in harmonie and rythmos.*

These two aspects of music are found stated elsewhere, for example,

music

in the anonymous *Pathway to Musicke* (1596): 'Musicke is a science, which teacheth how to **sing** skilfullie; that is, to deliver a **song sweet**ly, **tune**ably, and cunningly' (A ii). Morley then goes on to invoke the two major divisions proposed by Boethius (c.475–525), the early Medieval philosopher and mathematician who transmitted Ancient Greek theory:

> *Boetius* distinguisheth and theoricall or speculative musicke he defineth ... As for the division, Musicke is either *speculative* or *practicall*. *Speculative is that kinde of musicke* which by Mathematical helpes, seeketh out the causes, properties, and natures of soundes by themselues, and compared with others proceeding no further, but content with the onlie contemplation of the Art. *Practical* is that which teacheth al that may be knowne in songs, eyther for the understanding of other mens, or making of ones owne.
>
> (Annotations to part 1)

This division of music into, on the one hand, the aesthetic properties of music and, on the other, the rudiments or theoretical rationale of making music were commonplace in Elizabethan definitions. In his translation of Ornithoparcus' *Micrologus* (1609), Dowland is happy to reiterate the Boethian subdivisions of speculative music: '*Boëtius* ... doth shew ... that Musicke is three-fold. The *Worlds Musicke: Humane Musicke*: and *Instrumentall Musicke*' (p.[i]). These will be discussed below in section (3). For the sake of convenience, music is divided here into three main categories: (1) practical music, (2) affective music and (3) speculative music. In turn (1) and (3) are further subdivided. There is also an additional section (4) on representational music, the 'new music' of the seventeenth century.

(1) *Practical music*

(a) *Vocal music*. Vocal music, particularly sacred polyphony – music historians have argued – was the predominant kind of music in the Renaissance and all other forms grew out of it. Certainly, all the major composers primarily wrote vocal music, although not always sacred polyphony. The main categories of English vocal music are: (i) secular songs, **ayre**s, **consort** songs, **ballad**s, **madrigal**s, **catch**es, **round**s, **canzonet**s; and (ii) sacred **anthem**s, motets, masses, songs ('*cantiones* *sacrae*'), **hymn**s, **psalm**s. These categories are determined by the kinds of texts used, and how and where the pieces are to be performed. They are not mutually exclusive. Sacred hymns, for example, could be regarded as 'songs', suitable for a domestic context, whereas some consort songs and ayres have religious texts apt for church use. Both main categories include forms that can be performed either by solo **voice**(s) and accompaniment or by several voices together in vocal polyphony. Some (e.g. ayres, consort songs, verse anthems) generally include instruments (**lute**s, **viol**s), others (e.g. madrigals, motets) are sung unaccompanied.

Access to vocal music in Elizabethan England was not difficult. Most, including Latin motets and masses, was printed and published in collections (especially after 1575). A great deal also circulated in manuscript copy, some of which has survived to this day. Performance venues varied, according to type of music, from domestic to courtly, private to public. Cathedrals, colleges and a surprising number of parish churches supported choirs and uniquely English choral music was **compose**d for their consumption. Choirboys from the royal chapels, Westminster Abbey and St Paul's Cathedral sang (and acted) in the theatres as well. Madrigals and ayres would be sung at home by both male and female **perform**ers – Morley claims it was a common after-dinner activity:

> Supper being ended, and Musicke bookes, according to the custome being brought to the table: the mistresse of the house presented mee with a **part**, earnestly requesting mee to sing.
>
> (*Introduction*, 1597, p. 1)

There is plenty of evidence that singing was popular and beneficial (see 'song'). Among the illiterate, popular songs and ballads were well known.

(b) *Instrumental music*. Whilst many forms derive from vocal music, much Renaissance instrumental music is independent and highly idiomatic. That which is independent can be classified according to the instrument for which it was written. Consequently, we get lute, **cittern**, viol, keyboard and **wind** music as well as music for mixed consorts. The large majority of pieces is intended for ensembles of instruments of differing pitches. Only the keyboard repertoire, and to a lesser extent the lute repertoire, is supplied for the solo instrument.

music

Instrumental teaching manuals and treatises reveal that **play**ing instruments was to be encouraged among amateurs, both male and female, as much as it was the preserve of the highly skilled professionals. It was the mark of a lady or a gentleman to be able to play upon a lute, viol or **virginal**. More common folk would aspire to play **pipe**s, **fiddle**s or plucked **string**ed instruments such as the cittern. Instrumental music, be it notated or improvised, was common in Elizabethan society at all levels. Unlike vocal music, not much of it was printed. The great collections of English keyboard music, for example, the so-called Fitzwilliam Virginal Book and William Byrd's *My Ladye Nevells Booke*, survived in manuscript. Instrumental music for plays and courtly **masques** was not published, with one or two isolated exceptions. Some printed (pedagogical) collections of consort music were issued, but these were comparatively few.

When music is mentioned in the Shakespeare canon in a non-specific way, instrumental music is generally implied.

(2) *Affective music*
Shakespeare refers to the **concord**ant or harmonious sound of music. In contrast to Medieval music, Renaissance music was built upon consonances, what were thought to be pleasing or 'sweet sounding' intervals such as thirds, and sixths. Fifths and octaves (**diapason**s) were also consonant. Grating fourths and seconds, characteristic of Medieval sonority, were to be used sparingly and within the controlled context of smoothly flowing polyphony. By the end of the sixteenth century, the tonality (major or minor) and the tempo of a piece of music could determine whether the **mood** was sprightly and cheerful or grave and **solemn**. The cult of melancholy, especially in the music of John Dowland and Thomas Weelkes, was a significant movement and particularly effective in certain vocal and instrumental pieces (e.g. Dowland's *Lachrimae*, 1604).

The impact and significance of **hear**d music in the Elizabethan and Jacobean theatre have often been overlooked by literary scholars and musicologists, intent on analysing a dramatic text but reluctant to assess the effect of an audible song. This is possibly because 'musicology fastidiously declares issues of musical signification to be off-limits to those engaged in serious scholarship' (McClary, p. 4). Whilst we cannot be certain what actual music was performed in first productions, we must be careful to remember, from our critical vantage point, that

music

Shakespeare's performative music (songs and instrumental cues) was intended to be heard and that its signification was aural. As Jacquelyn Fox-Good stipulates:

> Shakespeare's songs ... are expressions of an embodied voice, different in kind from words on a page, and also from words merely spoken in performance. It is through sound that music (in most periods, but certainly ... in the English Renaissance) involves and also provokes, *moves* the body, leads to (and through) what Roland Barthes has subtly described as "the grain of the voice". This is especially true for vocal music.
> (p. 220)

Ophelia's singing, for example, must be heard as song because in singing she is

> constituting her own story, using her own voice for her own grief, and for rage and protest. More generally, she helps us to see how and why music could serve, even to the point of conventionality, the function that it did, not only in *Hamlet* but in much of Shakespeare's drama
> (ibid., p. 222).

(3) *Speculative music*
The symbolic associations of music and its powers to affect human emotions were derived from the neo-Platonic philosophies contained in the writings of the sixth-century A.D. Roman philosopher and mathematician, Boethius. Although his five books on the philosophy of music, the *De Institutione Musica* (printed in 1491–2), were not particularly well known in England, Elizabethans referred to Boethius as the main source of ideas about music. Students at the universities (Oxford and Cambridge) spent two terms studying music, '*in musica Boetium*', as an adjunct to the study of mathematics. Francis Meres is in no doubt about Boethius' importance: '*Boëtius* is esteemed a Prince and captaine in Musicke' (*Palladis Tamia*, 1598, p. 288). Dowland regards him as the most influential of the Medieval theorists, 'to whom among the Latine writers of Musicke, the praise is to be given' (*Micrologus*, 1609, [i]).

For Boethius, a musician is not so much a performer as a thinker about both music and the 'science' of making music. He divides music into *musica mundana*, *musica humana* and *musica instrumentalis*.

music

(a) *Musica mundana.* The first level, the 'music of the world', was concerned with the cosmic order of the heavens, the stars and planets in allegorical '**harmony**' or music. This was termed the 'music of the spheres' and was 'caused by the motion of the Starres, and violence of the Spheres' (Dowland, *Micrologus*, 1609, p. 1). How music is involved in the motion of the spheres is explained by Dowland in the previous sentences:

> When God ... had devised to make this world moveable, it was necessary, that he should governe it by some active and mooving power, for no bodies but those which have a soul, can move themselves ... Now that **motion** ... is not without sound: for it must needs be that a sound be made of the very wheeling of the Orbes ... The like sayd Boëtius, how can this quick-moving frame of the world whirle about with a dumb and silent motion? From this turning of the heaven, there cannot be removed a certaine order of Harmonie. And nature will ... that extremities must need sound deepe on the one side, & **sharp** on the other.
>
> (ibid.)

These sounds are the music of the spheres, of 'heavenly' or 'celestial' music as it is often called.

(b) *Musica humana.* The second definition given by Boethius, 'human music', has to do with the 'harmony' or music within man's being, the relation of his soul to his body, a state of well-being, of equilibrium both within himself and in relation to the world about him. Boethius refers to it as 'temperament', 'that which unites the incorporeal activity of the reason with the body ... as it were a tempering of **high** and **low** sounds into a single consonance'. This includes the notion of concord, of 'sweet music'. Dowland encapsulates this in his (translated) definition of *Humane Musick*:

> The Concordance of divers elements in one compound, by which the spirituall nature is ioyned with the body, and the reasonable part is coupled in concord with the unreasonable, which proceedes from the uniting of the body and the soule ... we loath and abhorre **discord**s, and are delighted when we **hear**e harmonicall concords, because we know there is in our selves the like concord.
>
> (*Micrologus*, p. 1)

music

Here is a clumsy explanation of the Elizabethan aesthetic of the pleasing nature of music, its 'concord of sweet sounds'. If music, or by extension the music of man, is unpleasant or 'out of tune' as the Boethian concept has it, then it (music) or man is discordant both within himself and in comparison with his world. If, on the other hand, that music is 'in tune' then there is concord. Dowland presumes authority in citing Boethius: '*Concordance* (as saith *Boëtius*) is the due mingling of two or more voices' (*Micrologus*, p. 78), '. . . A *Discord* (as saith *Boëtius*) is the hard and rough thwarting of two sounds, not mingled with themselves' (ibid., p. 79). Why concords should have sounded pleasing in early modern Western culture, and discords unpleasing is not certain. Renaissance counterpoint was based on concords, whose treatment is unequivocally stated, as the great theorist, Zarlino, affirms in his *Istitutioni armoniche*, Venice, 1558, Lib. III. This theory was transmitted to England by Morley (*Introduction*, 1597). Discords may interrupt concords in a strictly controlled manner. That is, they must be prepared and resolved. Discord may act as a foil to concord, but according to the Renaissance aesthetic of music, concord must prevail. Concord and discord served as metaphors for order and chaos, sanity and madness, joy and sorrow, peace and war, good and evil, reason and irrationality, love and hatred, and other emotional opposites.

The concept of *musica humana* cannot be separated from the curative powers ascribed to music: 'this concept was derived ultimately from the Greek theory of *ethos*, which ascribed to each of the various **mode**s a distinctive character capable of producing specific and unique emotional effects' (Dunn, p. 392).

(c) *Musica instrumentalis*. The third Boethian definition, revolves round the elements of making and writing music: the musician not only **make**s music, he thinks about what he is doing in relation to the world about him. He also questions how he is creating music and needs to be conversant with the technicalities of music. For Boethius this was the mathematical rationale behind the intervals of music and the Pythagorean relationships between differing pitches, for example the octave was 2:1, the fifth 3:2, etc. This could be shown, for example, in the different lengths of strings (on the kythara) and the sound they made. The technical aspects of music – how music is made – make up the essence of *musica instrumentalis*. For the Elizabethan, these were the theoretical and performative terms used by players, singers and composers.

music

Just as today, 'musician' is an all-embracing term encompassing performers (instrumentalists and singers: amateur or professional, male or female, classical or popular, live or recorded), composers and arrangers, teachers and writers, so it was in Elizabethan times, referring to practitioners, composers and theorists alike. The term, generally when in the plural, was most commonly applied to instrumental performers constituting an ensemble or consort. In Tudor London, established groups were formally recognized and given the responsibility of professional music making. In 1604, for example, the Worshipful Company of Musicians of London received its first charter, granted by King James. The term 'musician' replaced the Medieval '**minstrel**'. Minstrels had also formed themselves into Guilds or Fraternities, as the charter granted by Edward IV to his 'beloved minstrels' in 1469 testifies. The terms 'minstrel', 'musician' and 'wait' remained interchangeable until the early seventeenth century. Henry Walker (known to have had connections with Shakespeare at Blackfriars) was described as both 'citizen and minstrel of London' and, in his Will (proved 30 August 1616), as a 'Musition of London'.

In his treatise on counterpoint (c.1614), Campion refers to 'musitions' as both theorists and composers rather than as performers (in doing so he most often uses the singular 'musition'). In his preface to his treatise, for example, he says that 'there can be no greater hindrance to him that desires to become a Musition, then the want of the true understanding of the Scale' (*A New Way*, c.1614, B3v). Campion's musician here must first learn and understand the theory of music. Other writers clearly intend singers or instrumentalists, as Hollybrand defines the term: 'a musician or player on instruments'. Dowland, however, warns against simply assuming 'musician' means a performer and reminds his reader that the musician is also a philosopher: 'he is truely to be called a *Musitian*, who hath the faculty of speculation and reason, not he that hath onely practicke fashion of singing ... He is called a Musitian, which taketh upon him the knowledge of Singing by weighing it with reason, not with the servile exercise of practise, but the commanding power of speculation, and wanteth neither speculation nor practise' (*Micrologus*, 1609, p. 4).

(4) *Representational music*
During the last decade of the sixteenth century and the first of the seventeenth changes occurred in music in both compositional practice

and performative style. Composition moved from what twentieth-century musicologists called the Renaissance style to the Baroque. The auditory signification of music changed from the notional power it had to reflect the feelings and senses of its recipients, through perfectly regulated harmony, to its ability to characterize the emotions of a subject, mood or person by rhythm, tempo and tonality, instantaneously reflecting the emotional content of the text it was representing. In other words, its function changed from symbolic association to dramatic representation. Nowhere are these two attributes – new compositional style and emotion and meaning – more clearly felt than in Monteverdi's 'seconda pratica', the new music emanating from northern Italy and embodied initially in the new madrigals and then most extensively in the innovatory genre, opera. Whilst the vogue for opera did not sweep into England, the effect of the new music, transmitted per the works of Giulio Caccini, was felt among cultured and artistic circles. That this was true for Shakespeare is manifest in his use of music in the late plays, notably *The Tempest*. Whilst neo-Platonic theories of the symbolic power of music persist in *The Tempest*, the aural effect of music and its emotional impact are more prominent and significant. This play 'determinedly sets out to question' (Lindley, p. 19) the Renaissance concept and role of music as expounded, for example, by Lorenzo in *The Merchant of Venice* (5.1), so that by 'stressing the essentially rhetorical nature of music and dramatising the way in which it is used to manipulate and control, Shakespeare questions the traditional view of its God-derived power' (ibid.). Shakespeare's new music is the music of humans interacting, with their shared emotions, concerns and ambitions.

(B) The idea of music in all its guises pervades Shakespeare's poetry and plays, from the early comedies and histories to the late romances, ranging from elaborate musical metaphors in the dialogue to practical stage instructions. The term 'music' occurs in every play except for *3 Henry VI* and *King John*.

Practical instrumental and/or vocal music are indicated in stage directions and dialogue to mark the solemnity of specific occasions. For instance, ceremonial music is played during the procession at the coronation of Anne Boleyn (*H8* 4.1.36.SD). Wedding scenes sometimes require music in *The Taming of the Shrew* (3.2.183.SD), and *Romeo and Juliet* (4.4.21.SD): the latter is an aborted celebration. Music is also used

music

in light-hearted contexts, most notably when one of Bianca's suitors, Hortensio, disguises himself as a music teacher to make approaches to her (*Shr* 2.1.56 and 82; 3.1.7, 10 and 60). Such disguise causes a series of comical misunderstandings and lively repartee between Hortensio and other *dramatis personae*.

When characters fall in love, music and songs are often heard. Among the most widely known and quoted lines suggesting the practice of playing music in love contexts are those spoken by Orsino at the very beginning of *Twelfth Night*:

> If music be the food of love, play on,
> Give me excess of it; that surfeiting,
> The appetite may sicken, and so die.
> (1.1.1–3)

These words well encapsulate the Duke of Illyria's propensity towards lovesickness.

Music and a song help Bassanio choose the lead casket: Portia bestows this privilege only on him (the previous two suitors, Morocco and Arragon, make their choice without any music in the background). Portia's hope that music will have a positive influence on Bassanio's choice is evident from her words:

> Let music sound while he doth make his choice;
> Then if he lose he makes a **swan**-like end,
> **Fading** in music. That the comparison
> May stand more proper, my eye shall be the stream
> And wat'ry death-bed for him. He may win,
> And what is music then? Then music is
> Even as the **flourish** when true subjects bow
> To a new-crowned monarch . . .
> (*MV* 3.2.43–50)

The song 'Tell me where is fancy bred' (63–72) soon after this speech accompanies Bassanio while he '*comments on the caskets to himself*' (3.2.62.SD).

Romeo's encounter with Juliet at Capulet's feast happens when '*Music plays, and they* **dance**' (*Rom* 1.5.25.SD) immediately after Capulet's exhortation 'Come, musicians, play!' (25). In a similar situation in *Henry*

music

VIII, the King expresses his admiration for Anne Boleyn when they dance to music during a feast: '*Music. Dance.*' (1.4.76.SD).

Benedick realizes that he loves Beatrice when he hears music accompanying the song '**Sigh** no more, ladies, sigh no more' (*Ado* 2.3.34, 36.SD, 37, 41, 45 and 85). Thurio serenades Silvia accompanied by musicians (*TGV* 4.2.15.SD, followed by seven references to music in the dialogue, at lines 17, 31, 35, 55, 66, 68 and 86) who sing 'Who is Silvia?' (39–53). Another courtship situation is introduced by references to music in the dialogue (*Cym* 2.3.11 and 12) and the entry of musicians (2.3.13.SD) who accompany Cloten's song 'Hark, hark, the **lark** at heaven's gate sings' (20–6). A parody of courtship is observed when Falstaff flirts with Doll:

> *Enter Music.*
> PAGE: The music is come, sir.
> FALSTAFF: Let them play. Play, sirs. Sit on my knee, Doll.
> (*2H4* 2.4.225–6)

Sick and dying characters sometimes call for soothing music, for instance Henry IV. Knowing that his death is approaching, he says:

> Let there be no **noise** made, my gentle friends,
> Unless some **dull** and favorable hand
> Will whisper music to my weary spirit.
> (*2H4* 4.5.1–3)

To this Warwick replies with an order to 'Call for the music in the other room' (4.5.4): the 'other room' is probably the stage gallery where musicians would have been positioned (Melchiori, p. 157).

Oncoming death is announced by music also in *Richard II*. In a moving soliloquy just before being murdered in the dungeon at Pomfret Castle, the King ponders:

> (*The music plays*). Music do I hear?
> Ha, ha, keep **time**! How sour sweet music is
> When time is broke, and no **proportion** kept!
> So is it in the music of men's lives.
> And here have I the daintiness of ear
> To check time broke in a disordered string;

297

music

> But for the concord of my state and time
> Had not an ear to hear my true time broke.
> I wasted time, and now doth time waste me;
> For now hath time made me his numb'ring clock.
> (5.5.41–50)

Richard's helplessness and despair are expressed through musical terms and metaphors; the references to the sense of hearing are metatheatrical reminders of the music played in the background during the speech. The Boethian concept of *musica humana* emerges from these lines: order, proportion and concord in life – in its private and public aspect – are irreparably lost when death is approaching. In this wretched state, Richard concludes that music has no healing power for him:

> This music mads me, let it sound no more,
> For though it have holp mad men to their wits,
> In me it seems it will make wise men mad.
> (61–3)

On the other hand, the healing power of music is emphasized in *King Lear* in the scene where Lear recovers from madness. Before Cordelia approaches her father, the doctor, who has cured the old King, exclaims: '**Loud**er the music there' (4.7.24). This cue is found in Q1 (1608)) but is absent from Folio – in the latter the character of the doctor is omitted.

Another play which insists on the idea of 'music as a healing agent' (Hart, p. 316) is *Pericles*. Gower, who acts as a **chorus** figure throughout, establishes this at the very beginning of this romance:

> To sing a song that old was sung,
> From ashes ancient Gower is come,
> Assuming man's infirmities,
> To glad your ear and please your eyes.
> It hath been sung at festivals,
> On ember-eves and holy-ales;
> And lords and ladies in their lives
> Have read it for restoratives.
> (1.Cho. 1–8)

In the same play, the Ephesian lord Cerimon calls for '**rough**' (3.2.88) music in the scene where the apparently dead Thaisa is revived: this moment is linked to the Phrygian religious ceremonies centring on the cult of Diana of Ephesus. Such ceremonies employed **jar**ring music, 'notorious for its "savagery" ' (Hart, p. 320). Hence, Cerimon's use of 'rough' to describe the music in this scene is appropriate, and most editors' emendation of 'rough' to 'still' is not necessary.

An obvious parallel can be drawn between the reviving of Thaisa and another 'resuscitation' scene, this time in *The Winter's Tale*: Hermione, apparently dead, is restored to life by Paulina. This enables the final touching reconciliation between Leontes and his wife, whom he had unjustly accused of adultery. To the surprise of all the characters on stage, what appears to be the statue of Hermione starts to walk to the sound of music after Paulina's exhortation:

> Music! awake her! **strike**!
> 'Tis time; descend; be stone no more; approach;
> Strike all that look upon with marvel . . .
> (5.3.98–100)

As Dunn has observed 'the use of music here could be considered . . . as a typical use of *musica instrumentalis* to underscore a dramatic climax. But it is, of course, as an example of music's restorative powers that it gains its chief importance' (p. 399).

Music and magic are two other inseparable elements in Shakespeare's plays: 'even by its very nature, music was not unlike magic, for both were considered at their simplest and most basic to be arts of **number** and proportion with an affinity for the secret, contemplative aspects of things' (Austern, p. 194). It is therefore not surprising that *The Tempest*, whose main character is a skilled magician, has the largest number of references to music in the Shakespeare canon. Through Prospero, who uses music and magic to manipulate other characters, 'Shakespeare questions the traditional view of its God-derived power' (Lindley, p. 19). Lindley quotes as an example of Prospero's controlling powers the seemingly well intentioned order that 'heavenly music' be played (5.1.52) to help Alonso, Antonio, Sebastian and their followers regain their sanity. However, a closer look at Prospero's speech discloses a darker purpose, since he informs Ariel that the aim of such music is 'to work mine end upon their senses' (5.1.53).

Vocal songs and instrumental music help the audience understand

music

the nature of the different characters, and in some instances where its 'discordant, anarchic dimension' (Iselin, p. 137) emerges, it can be interpreted as a challenge to the very authority represented by Prospero. For instance, Stephano, Trinculo and Caliban are unable to sing in harmony in 3.2. They are plotting the murder of Prospero but the invisible Ariel manages to distract them by playing on his **tabor** and pipe:

> STEPHANO: ... Come on, Trinculo, let us sing. *Sings.*
> 'Flout 'em and scout 'em,
> And scout 'em and flout 'em!
> Thought is free.'
> CALIBAN: That's not the tune.
> *Ariel plays the tune on a tabor and pipe.*
> STEPHANO: What is this same?
> TRINCULO: This is the tune of our catch, play'd by the picture of Nobody.
>
> (3.2.120–7)

Here, 'coupled with the practical function [of music] is an apparent hint at speculative music's theory of temperament ... As there is chaos in their [Stephano's, Trinculo's, and Caliban's] individual lives, there will be confusion and failure in their joint conspiracy to murder Prospero' (Dunn, p. 401). But even though the conspirators' plot is doomed to fail, their drunken song expresses the desire for freedom and equality (Iselin, p. 145), thus questioning the essence of Prospero's power on the island and its inhabitants.

Another interesting occurrence of music in *The Tempest* is '*Solemn and strange music*' (3.3.17.SD), played during the banquet scene, in which Ariel accuses Alonso, Antonio and Sebastian of being 'men of sin' (53). After the stage direction and before Ariel's apparition as a harpy, we have:

> ALONSO: What harmony is this? My good friends, hark!
> GONZALO: Marvellous sweet music!
>
> (3.3.18–19)

Both characters are probably talking about affective music (see section 2 above) since they use words associated with it ('harmony' and 'sweet').

The adjective 'solemn' (3.3.17.SD) points in the same direction: this is observed in several contemporary masques and plays to evoke either ceremonial or melancholy atmospheres (Lindley, p. 138). From a theatrical stance, there is 'contrast in mood between the "shapes" who dance in gracefully with the banquet and Ariel who flaps in darkly and causes it to vanish' (Shirley, pp. 110–11).

Music takes place in a magic context also in *A Midsummer Night's Dream*, 4.1, when Titania awakes from the spell which was cast upon her (81, 83, 83.SD and 85). Oberon and Titania dance while leaving the stage (89): the harmony that their reconciliation brings is emphasized both aurally and visually in this scene.

In *Macbeth* a dark supernatural atmosphere involving the presence of the three witches and Hecate is evoked by two stage directions (3.5.33.SD and 4.1.43.SD): both call for music followed by a song. The direction in 3.5 prescribes: '*Music, and a song. Sing within*: ' "Come away, come away, etc." ' (3.5.33.SD). Act 3, scene 5 is one of the most debated scenes in the whole Shakespeare canon: Middleton is generally considered to be its author on the grounds that another play by this dramatist, *The Witch*, contains a reference to the same song (see for instance Braunmuller, p. 256, who supports this theory; and Muir, pp. xxxii–xxxiv, who maintains that another anonymous writer was responsible for 3.5). Authorship questions aside, it can be surmised that it is probably the macabre and sinister tone of *Macbeth* which ultimately dictated the choice of making minimal use of music. And when music is called for it has the paradoxical effect – sometimes observed in early modern drama – of representing the occult on the stage (Austern, p. 206).

The framing role of devices such as inductions, masques and visions is often highlighted by music, for instance in *Love's Labour's Lost* when Ferdinand and his lords enter disguised as Russians, along with '*Blackmoors with music*' (5.2.157.SD): in this case, 'music' is probably synonymous with 'musicians', who were expected to play on stage. Another example is found in the second Induction of *The Taming of the Shrew* (35.SD) when Sly is being tricked into believing that he is a lord.

Pericles, like the other romances (*Cymbeline*, *The Winter's Tale* and *The Tempest*), resorts to music on several occasions: 'in addition to its basic function of adding a philosophical framework for the plot, music also serves as a dramatic device to intensify the climax of the action' (Dunn,

music

p. 396). This is evident towards the end of the play, after Pericles recovers from insanity and discovers that his daughter Marina is still alive. The ensuing dialogue is revealing:

> PERICLES: . . . But what music?
> HELICANUS: My Lord, I hear none.
> PERICLES: None?
> The music of the spheres! List, my Marina.
> LYSIMACHUS: It is not good to cross him, give him way.
> PERICLES: Rarest sounds! Do ye not hear?
> LYSIMACHUS: Music, my lord? I hear.
> PERICLES: Most heavenly music!
> It nips me unto list'ning, and thick slumber
> Hangs upon mine eyes. Let me **rest**.
>
> (5.1.226–35)

What emerges from these lines is the Boethian idea of *musica mundana* and its divine quality, which appropriately introduces Pericles' vision of the goddess Diana. 'Rest' at line 235 just before Pericles falls asleep is an excellent linguistic choice which elaborates on the musical theme of the speech.

It is not clear whether music would have actually been played at this moment in original performances of the play. From a strictly theoretical viewpoint, world music cannot be perceived by the human ear, but in performance it is likely that such music would have been made audible. The choice of whether to play music would have been dictated by acting conditions and availability of musicians. The absence of musical cues in this part of the scene does not mean that music 'sounded' only in Pericles' imagination, since his words could have been intended to work as implicit stage directions. If music was indeed played during a performance, 'rest' would have been an effective cue to the musicians to stop playing. Scholars such as Sternfeld (p. 245) and McIntosh believe that music would have been played, but the latter makes the point that '*musica mundana* is audible only to Pericles and the audience' (p. 106). In performance, the other onstage characters would have maintained the fiction that they could not hear the music. This type of anti-realistic stage action, which allowed the audience to become aware of situations unknown to a number of characters, was often employed on the Shakespearean stage, for example when two characters are instructed to exchange aside comments to the exclusion of others, or when a character is 'invisible' to everyone except one person (as is the case with Ariel in *The Tempest*, who can only be seen by Prospero).

The music of the spheres is also mentioned in *Twelfth Night*, 3.1.110. An interesting intersection of the concepts of sweet music and music of the spheres is found in the final scene of *The Merchant of Venice*, when Lorenzo addresses Jessica as follows:

> How sweet the moonlight sleeps upon this bank!
> Here will we sit, and let the sounds of music
> Creep in our ears. **Soft** stillness and the night
> Become the **touch**es of sweet harmony.
> Sit, Jessica. Look how the floor of heaven
> Is thick inlaid with patens of bright gold.
> There's not the smallest orb thou behold'st
> But in his motion like an **angel** sings
> Still quiring to the young-ey'd cherubins;
> Such harmony is in immortal souls,
> But whilst this muddy vesture of decay
> Doth grossly close it in, we cannot hear it.
>   (5.1.54–65)

Lorenzo is keen to emphasize that the music of the spheres cannot be heard by mere mortals. However, he goes on to exhort some musicians to play a hymn and 'with sweetest touches pierce your mistress' ear' (67). The closest humans can get to the perfection of *musica mundana*, the music of the spheres – visually reflected in the harmony and brightness of the stars – is through the audible 'sweet' sounds created by musicians.

One of the most fascinating instances of visions is in *Cymbeline*. The captive Posthumus Leonatus has just fallen asleep:

> *Solemn music. Enter (as in an apparition) Sicilius Leonatus, father to Posthumus, an old man, attired like a warrior; leading in his hand an ancient matron, his wife and mother to Posthumus, with music before them. Then, after other music, follows the two young Leonati, brothers to Posthumus, with wounds as they died in the wars. They circle Posthumus round as he lies sleeping.*
>   (5.4.29.SD)

music

'Solemn music' was probably intended to conjure up a melancholy mood, since the people appearing to Posthumus are dead. They call Jupiter, who descends onto the stage in a highly spectacular fashion '*in **thunder** and lightning, sitting upon an eagle*' (5.4.92.SD) and throwing a thunderbolt. A similar instruction for music is found in *Henry VIII*, when the sick Katherine falls asleep and has a vision. On this occasion, we have '*sad and solemn music*' (4.2.80.SD) immediately before the elaborate stage direction for the vision, which concludes with the indication '*the music continues*' (4.2.82.SD). In both *Cymbeline* and *Henry VIII*, the supernatural is intimately connected with music, as it is in *Pericles* 5.1.226–35 (see above).

'*Solemn music*' (*Cymbeline* 4.2.186.SD) also accompanies the entry of Arviragus carrying the body of the apparently dead Imogen. That in this case 'solemn' is meant to evoke sombreness is evident from Guiderius' remarks 'solemn things / Should answer solemn accidents' (191–2) and 'O melancholy / Who ever yet could sound thy bottom?' (203–4). The musical nuance of the second quotation works as a linguistic reminder of the instrumental music in performance.

Musica instrumentalis as theorized by Boethius is sometimes alluded to in relation to broken music and is closely associated with 'music in parts'. Hence, 'broken' also evokes the idea of something which is not complete in itself, as for instance when King Henry asks Katherine, who can only speak a little English, to marry him:

> . . . Come, your answer in broken music;
> for thy voice is music and thy English broken; therefore,
> queen of all, Katherine, break thy mind to me in
> broken English – wilt thou have me?
>
> (*H5* 5.2.243–6)

The concluding scene of this history play provides a (temporary) harmonious solution to the war between England and France thanks to the marriage between Henry and the daughter of the French King. In a play dominated by battles and military sound effects, the focus on music at this point is all the more appropriate.

Pandarus' song 'Love, love, nothing but love' (*Tro* 3.1.115–24) is introduced with puns on music 'in parts' (18) and his comment 'Here is good broken music' (49), to which Paris replies:

> You have broke it, cousin; and by my life
> you shall make it whole again – you shall piece it out
> with a piece of your performance.
>
> (50–2)

The concord of sweet music 'in parts' and music-induced melancholy are employed in *Sonnet* 8, which calls upon musical imagery. The young man is sad and Shakespeare wonders:

> Music to hear, why hear'st thou music sadly?
> Sweets with sweets war not, joy delights in joy.
> Why lov'st thou that which thou receiv'st not gladly,
> Or else receiv'st with pleasure thine annoy?
>
> (1–4)

He is urged to contemplate marital union:

> If the true concord of **well-tuned** sounds,
> By unions married, do offend thine ear,
> They do but sweetly chide thee, who confounds
> In singleness the parts that thou shouldst bear.
>
> (5–8)

Pleasing music in parts – for several voices or instruments – is 'sweet', concordant or well-tuned just as husband and wife are in marital bliss or harmony.

A similar juxtaposed repetition of 'music' occurs in *Sonnet* 128 'How oft when thou, my music, music play'st / Upon that blessed wood . . .' (1–2). Here the lover imagines his mistress ('my music' – this is one of the sonnets dedicated to the Dark Lady) making music, presumably by playing the virginals (see also '**jack**'). The lines 'With thy sweet fingers, when thou gently sway'st / The wiry concord that mine ear confounds' (3–4) indicate that the philosophy of speculative music is involved ('sweet', 'concord' and 'confounds'), juxtaposed, as it were, with the more practical aspects of the mechanism of the virginals being played ('Blessed wood', i.e. the keys, the 'wiry' strings and 'those jacks' which pluck the strings to make them sound).

(C) Atlas, *Anthology of Renaissance Music: Music in Western Europe, 1400–1600* (1998), provides an overview of music in the Renaissance.

music

Austern, ' "Art to Enchant" ' (1990), studies the relationship between magic and music in English Renaissance drama.

Braunmuller, *Macbeth* (1997).

Duffin, *Shakespeare's Songbook* (2004), has an introduction by Stephen Orgel with some compelling observations on music in English Renaissance drama.

Dunn, 'The Function of Music in Shakespeare's Romances' (1969), surveys Renaissance musical ideology as reflected in Shakespeare's later plays.

Fox-Good, 'Ophelia's Mad Songs' (1995), gives a feminist intepretation of the function of music in *Hamlet*.

Gooch and Thatcher (eds), *A Shakespeare Music Catalogue* (1991), lists music cues and incidental music in the plays, and discusses the role of music in the Introduction.

Hart, 'Cerimon's "Rough Music" ' (2000), is an insightful analysis of the healing and sacred power of music in connection with the Phrygian cult of the goddess Diana.

Iselin, ' "My Music for Nothing" ' (1995), scrutinizes the role of vocal and instrumental music in *The Tempest*, and its potentially subversive power.

Kisby, *Music and Musicians in Renaissance Cities and Towns* (2001).

Lindley, *The Tempest* (2002).

Long (ed.), *Music in English Renaissance Drama* (1968), is a seminal study.

Lowinsky, *Music in the Culture of the Renaissance and Other Essays*, ed. Bonnie Blackburn (1989), focuses on the relationships between music and other arts.

McClary, *Feminine Endings: Music, Gender, and Sexuality* (1991).

McIntosh, 'Musical Design in *Pericles*' (1973), explores the role of music in this romance in relation to Boethius' concepts of *musica instrumentalis, humana* and *mundana*.

Manifold, *The Music in English Drama, from Shakespeare to Purcell* (1956), is a 'classic' study of the importance of the aural sphere in Renaissance drama.

Melchiori, *The Second Part of Henry IV* (1989).

Muir, *Macbeth* (1984).

Owens, *Composers at Work* (1996), includes aspects of music historiography and attempts to identify Renaissance musical style.

Palisca, *Studies in the History of Italian Music and Music Theory* (1994), includes discussion of *seconda pratica* and the 'defense' of modern music.

Seng, *The Vocal Songs in the Plays of Shakespeare* (1967), locates the songs in the plays in their dramatic contexts.

Shirley, *Shakespeare's Use of Off-Stage Sounds* (1963), analyses the importance of music and sound effects in the Shakespeare canon.

Sternfeld, *Music in Shakespearean Tragedy* (1967), is a seminal study of the role of music in Shakespeare.

Tomlinson, *Monteverdi and the End of the Renaissance* (1987), focuses on music in late Renaissance thought.

Wilson (ed.), *A New Way* (2003), p. 43.

Wulstan, *Tudor Music* (1985), is a lively account of music in England between 1485 and 1625.

Most modern editions of Shakespeare's plays give limited accounts of the different nuances of 'music' both in stage directions and dialogue, and provide variable references to philosophical and music treatises influential in the Renaissance period.

musician see **music**.

N

nightingale see **bird**.

nimble (A) Meaning 'dexterous' and 'quick' and connected with leaping, 'nimble' is rarely found in musical contexts. When it does occur its significance is clear. For instance, in:

> Pretty wantons, **sweet**ly **sing**
> In honour of the smiling Spring.
> Look how the light-winged chirping **choir**
> With nimble skips the Spring admire.
> (Peerson, 1620, no. 17)

the **bird**s make quick and effective melodic leaps as they sing.

(B) There are three musical usages of this term in Shakespeare. The birds' singing is described as 'nimble', i.e. joyful and virtuosic when Lucrece addresses them as follows: '**Relish** your nimble **note**s to pleasing **ear**s, / Distress likes **dump**s when **time** is kept with tears' (*Luc* 1126–7). Lucrece is beginning to contemplate suicide to overcome the shame caused by the violence she has suffered, hence the birds' harmonious and **pleasant** warbling does not suit her distressed **mood**.

In *Sonnet* 128, the poet admires the Dark Lady while she is **play**ing the **virginal**:

nimble

> How oft when thou, my **music**, music play'st
> Upon that blessed wood whose motion **sound**s
> With thy sweet fingers . . .
> Do I envy those **jack**s that nimble leap
> To kiss the tender inward of thy hand.
> (1–3; 5–6)

'Nimble' indicates the woman's **skill** as a virginal player, which causes the jacks of the **instrument** to move up and down ('leap') in a swift and effortless manner (see also 'jack' for a commentary of this passage).

Trying to dissuade Henry V from moving war against France, the French ambassador warns him that 'there's nought in France / That can be with a nimble **galliard** won' (*H5* 1.2.251–2). 'Nimble' evokes the liveliness of this vigorous triple-time **dance**, which also involves a leaping step (*saut majeur*).

noise (A) The indefinite term 'noise' is most often used to describe **loud**, unmusical **sound**s, the meaning in common usage today. But in Elizabethan times it could also have several musical meanings. It could refer to pleasant **music** as in Spenser's 'heavenly noise', the sound of **angel**s **sing**ing (*The Faerie Queene* 1.12), or the '**melodious** noiz', according to Robert Laneham (*A Letter*, London 1575, p. 43), made by the **consort** of **instrument**s at the entertainment at Kenilworth in July 1575. Or it could signify an ensemble of instruments or **voice**s as in:

> In midst of woods or pleasant grove
> Where all **sweet bird**s do sing . . .
> The **charm** was good, the noise full sweet.
> Each bird did **play** his **part**.
> (Mundy, 1594, no. 27)

In George Gascoigne and Francis Kinwelmershe's play, *Jocasta* (1566), Holman notes (p. 132) that the dumb-show was accompanied by 'a **doleful**l and straunge noyse of **viol**les, Cythren, Bandurion, and such like' (i.e. a mixed consort). The band of instruments which **perform**s at the conclusion of Act 2 of Martson's *The Dutch Courtesan* (1603–4) is referred to as 'M. Creakes noyse'.

noise

(B) Some stage directions for noises in Shakespeare's plays indicate that this effect must take place 'within', i.e. behind the *frons scenae*, and are meant to convey the idea of turmoil or of crowds celebrating an important occasion – an effective aural device which conjured up specific atmospheres aurally rather than visually (see also Introduction). For instance, the entry of Katherine of Aragon is preceded by the stage direction: '*A noise within, crying*: "Room for the Queen!" ' (*H8* 1.2.8.SD). Later in the same play, 5.3 opens with the indication: '*Noise and tumult within*', followed by the entry of a porter and his man trying to restrain the crowd who want to attend the christening of Princess Elizabeth. Other examples of noises 'within' are found in *The Tempest* (1.1.60.SD), *Coriolanus* (3.1.259.SD), *Hamlet* (4.5.96.SD; 4.5.110.SD; 4.5.153.SD), *The Two Noble Kinsmen* (5.4.39.SD), *Antony and Cleopatra* (5.2.232.SD) and *2 Henry VI* (3.2.121.SD).

Indications for noise of hunters occur in *The Tempest* (4.1.254.SD) and *The Two Noble Kinsmen* (3.1.OSD); a hunting situation is evoked also by stage directions prescribing noise of **horn**s in *The Merry Wives of Windsor* (5.5.29.SD) and *Titus Andronicus* (2.2.OSD). The '*noise of a seafight*' is heard in *Antony and Cleopatra* (3.10.OSD). *The Tempest* opens with the indication for '*a tempestuous noise of* **thunder** *and lightning*' (1.1.OSD), which immediately sets the mood for the scene of the shipwreck. The same effect is found also in 2.2.OSD.

In Shakespeare's poetry and dramatic dialogue, this term is often used in its negative connotation, for instance when the howling of dogs is described by Venus as an 'ill resounding noise' (*Ven* 919), an ominous prelude to the discovery of the dead body of Adonis; or when Hamlet criticizes the groundlings' taste by observing that they can only appreciate 'dumb-shows and noise' (*Ham* 3.2.12).

Another significant instance is found in King Henry IV's order to his courtiers:

> Let there be no noise made, my gentle friends,
> Unless some **dull** and favorable hand
> Will whisper **music** to my weary spirit.
>   (*2H4* 4.5.1–3)

The dying King wants to avoid the disturbance caused by noise, and wishes to **hear** soothing sleep-inducing ('dull') music instead.

However, the term does not always have a pejorative connotation. For

noise

instance, martial sounds are sometimes referred to as 'noise'. Bolingbroke discloses to his troops the tactic he has chosen to approach Flint Castle: 'Let's **march** without the noise of threat'ning **drum**' (*R2* 3.3.51). The 'noise of drums' is also mentioned in *Coriolanus* (2.3.54), as is the sounding of a **parley** (referred to as 'noise' once again) in *2 Henry VI* (4.8.3). In a non-martial context, Caliban uses the term in a positive sense when he tries to reassure Stephano and Trinculo: 'Be not afeard, the isle is full of noises, / Sounds, and sweet **air**s, that give delight and hurt not' (*Tmp* 3.2.135–6).

In *As You Like It*, 'noise' acquires yet another nuance when Jaques asks one of the lords to sing in order to celebrate the killing of a deer: 'Sing it [the **song**]. 'Tis no matter how it be in **tune**, / so it make noise enough' (4.2.8–9). Line 9 refers to the choral singing which would have been required by the **burden** of the song 'What shall he have that kill'd the deer' (10–18). Jaques' words disclose that his main concern, rather than the quality of the singing, is that as many hunters as possible join in the celebratory song.

'Noise' can also be 'the correct noun of assemblage of **trumpet**s, and for **fiddle**s and **flute**s as well' (Manifold, p. 42). This alternative meaning is observed when the noise of hunting horns is alluded to by Titus Andronicus. He exhorts his followers to '**ring** a hunter's **peal** / That all the court may **echo** with the noise' (*Tit* 2.2.5–6). These lines precede the stage direction instructing to '***wind*** *horns in a peal*' (2.2.10.SD) and are ironically suggestive when set against Lavinia's **silence** in 2.4. after her tongue has been cut out.

See also **clamour, clangor, din**.

(C) Dessen and Thomson, *A Dictionary of Stage Directions* (1999), pp. 150–1.
Holman, *Four and Twenty Fiddlers* (1993).
Manifold, *The Music in English Drama* (1956).

nonino, nonny-(no) see **hey**.

note (A) The essential musical term 'note' can have various interrelated meanings. In notated music, it is the mark or sign used in notation to indicate the pitch and duration of a musical **sound**. In the

note

sixteenth century, individual marks came to represent separate notes, but the older practice of joining several notes together in one mark, known as a ligature, was still occasionally used. Put simply, a 'note' 'is that by which the **high**ness, or **low**ness of a **Song** is expressed' (Dowland, *Micrologus*, 1609, p. 6). But 'note' can also mean the sound of the written symbol. Or it can be employed to stand for a **tune** or song such as the 'note' of a **bird**. In his preface to his treatise on counterpoint, Campion attempts as a point of clarification to draw his reader's attention to the various usages of 'note':

> Likewise the word Note is sometimes used proprely, as when in respect of the forme of it, we name it a round or square Note; in regard of the place we say, a Note in rule or a Note in space; so for the **time**, we call a **Brief**e or Sembriefe a **long** Note, a **Crotchet**, or Quaver a short note. Sometime the word Note is otherwise to be understood, as when it is, *signum pro signato*, the signe for the thing signified: so we say a **Sharp**e, or **flat** Note, meaning by the word Note, the sound it signifies; also we terme a Note high, or low, in respect of the sound. The word Note simply produced, hath yet another signification, as when we say this is a **sweet** Note, or the Note I like, but not the words, wee then meane by this word Note, the whole tune, putting the **part** for the whole: But this word Note with addition, is yet far otherwise to be understood, as when we say a whole Note, or a halfe Note; wee meane a perfect or imperfect Second, which are not Notes, but the severall distances betweene two Notes, the one being double as much as the other; and although this kinde of calling them a whole and a halfe Note, came in first by abusion, yet custome hath made that speech now passable.
>
> (*A New Way*, c.1614, B3r–B3v)

(B) Shakespeare often uses 'note' in its meaning of 'song'. The final scene of *The Taming of the Shrew* opens with a reconciliatory speech by Lucentio:

> At last, though long, our **jar**ring notes agree,
> And time it is, when raging war is done,
> To smile at scapes and perils overblown.
> (5.2.1–3)

note

The musical metaphor excellently fits a play where **music** is central to the development of the plot – Hortensio's disguise as a music teacher causes a number of comical incidents.

In another comedy, Antipholus of Syracuse, trying to resist his attraction to Luciana, exhorts her not to entice him with her 'note' (*Err* 3.2.45). 'Note' acquires an ironic slant in Hamlet's reproach to Guildenstern and Rosencrantz when he understands that his 'friends' are trying to establish whether he has gone insane and report back to Claudius:

> Why, look you now, how unworthy a thing
> you make of me! You would **play** upon me, you would
> seem to know my **stop**s, you would pluck out the
> heart of my mystery, you would sound me from my
> lowest note to the top of my **compass** . . .
>
> (*Ham* 3.2.363–7)

Through this elaborate metaphor, the Prince is conveying the idea that he knows that Guildenstern and Rosencrantz want to grasp the whole range ('from the lowest note to the top of my compass') of his most intimate thoughts and feelings. At the end of the speech, he makes clear to them that he will not let this happen by resorting to musical vocabulary once again: 'Call me what **instrument** you will . . . you / cannot play upon me' (370–1).

'Note' is mentioned in relation to birds on several occasions. For instance, Bottom **sing**s to overcome his fear when the other mechanicals flee from him:

> The **woosel cock** so black of hue,
> With orange-tawny bill,
> The **throstle** with his note so **true**,
> The **wren** with little quill . . .
> The finch, the sparrow, and the **lark**,
> The **plain-song cuckoo** grey,
> Whose note full many a man doth mark
>
> (*MND* 3.1.125–8;130–2)

This is a metatheatrical moment: the ass-headed Bottom sings about the singing of birds and is admired by Titania, who exclaims: 'I pray

note

thee, gentle mortal, sing again. / Mine **ear** is much enamored of thy note' (3.1.137–8). She goes on to praise Bottom's physical appearance. Since Titania is under a spell, it is clear that she is deceived about both the singing and the appearance of Bottom. It can be inferred that Bottom's singing was intended to be anything but pleasant. The fact that his song is about the **melodious** singing of birds contributes to the scene's comical slant.

In *As You Like It*, Amiens too sings about songs in connection with birds at the beginning of 2.5:

> Under the greenwood tree
> Who loves to lie with me,
> And turn his merry note
> Unto the sweet bird's **throat**.
> (1–4)

Human beings should attune their song to that of a bird to achieve perfection and make it as pleasant as possible.

The 'note' of birds can acquire sad connotations, as when Marcus realizes that Lavinia has been deprived of her **tongue**:

> O, that delightful engine of her thoughts,
> That blabb'd them with such pleasing eloquence,
> Is torn from forth that pretty **hollow** cage,
> Where like a sweet melodious bird it sung
> Sweet varied notes, **enchant**ing every ear!
> (*Tit* 3.1.82–6)

The image of the bird singing melodiously is reinforced by the comparison between Lavinia's mouth and a bird's cage. This euphemistic musical description embodies a marked contrast to the visual impact of the mutilated Lavinia on the stage and manages to convey in a powerful way the horror of the violence inflicted on the young woman.

At the nadir of her despair another victim of rape, Lucrece, warns the birds not to try to raise her spirits with their singing: '**Relish** your **nimble** notes to pleasing ears, / Distress likes **dump**s when time is kept with tears' (*Luc* 1126–7).

The sadness of separation is encapsulated in Romeo's speech when, under sentence of banishment, he has to leave Juliet after spending the night with her. Juliet protests that the bird heard by her lover is the **nightingale**, not the lark. Romeo wishes the same thing:

> I'll say yon grey is not the morning's eye,
> 'Tis but the pale reflex of Cynthia's brow;
> Nor that is not the lark whose notes do **beat**
> The vaulty heaven so high above our heads.
> (*Rom* 3.5.19–22)

However, he knows that it is dawn and that he must leave. The ensuing exchange between the young lovers elaborates on the musical imagery by employing terms such as '**discord**', '**division**' and 'sharps' among others.

In *The Taming of the Shrew* we find the use of 'note' in a context of musical notation. Disguised as a music teacher, Hortensio is trying to impress Bianca with his version of the **gamut**:

> '**Gamouth** am I, the **ground** of all **accord**:
> *A re*, to plead Hortensio's passion;
> *B mi*, Bianca, take him for thy lord,
> *C fa ut*, that loves with all affection.
> *D sol re*, one **cliff**, two notes have I,
> *E la mi*, show pity, or I die.'
> (3.1.73–8)

The meaning of 'one cliff (i.e. **clef**), two notes have I' is not entirely clear. It relates to a controversy in contemporary progressive music theory where one note can have two names (*sol* or *re*) depending on the position of the *ut* on the stave. Campion addresses the problem as follows:

> In like manner there can be no greater hindrance to him that desires to become a Musition, then the want of the true understanding of the Scale, which proceeds from the errour of the common Teacher, who can doe nothing without the olde Gam-ut, in which there is but one Cliffe, and one Note, and yet in the same Cliffe he wil sing re & sol.
> (*A New Way*, c.1614, B3v–B4r)

note

It is possible that 'clef' is Hortensio's love and the 'two notes' his real and assumed personalities (Morris, p. 222).

In martial contexts, the sounding of **alarum**s is sometimes referred to as the 'note', probably to emphasize that this military signal is characterized by a specific range of notes. This happens when the Constable of France, eager to fight at Agincourt and confident that the French will win, orders triumphantly:

> ... Then let the **trumpet**s sound,
> The **tucket sonance** and the note to mount;
> For our approach shall so much dare the field,
> That England shall couch down in fear, and yield.
> (*H5* 4.2.34–7)

That the 'note to mount' alludes to a precise range of notes is evident because it is mentioned in connection with the 'tucket sonance', which refers to another set of trumpet notes. In another martial situation, this time in *Troilus and Cressida*, the Greek commander Ajax is incited by his general Agamemnon to give 'a **loud** note to Troy' with the trumpet (4.5.3).

See also **chord, degree**.

(C) Folkerth, *The Sound of Shakespeare* (2002), pp. 91–8, notes the vital function carried out by the aural dimension when transformations occur in *A Midsummer Night's Dream*.
Morris, *The Taming of the Shrew* (1981).
Wilson (ed), *A New Way* (2003), p. 43.

number (A) In Elizabethan poetic theory and practice, 'number' could mean either rhyming **accent**ual lyric poetry or neo-classical quantitative verse. In the former, 'number' referred to the numerosity of the syllables in a line. In the latter, it meant the equivalent of the foot in classical scansion. The polemic raged until the early seventeenth century with Sidney and Campion, among others advocating English **metre** adopting classical theories of prosody, vigorously opposed by Gabriel Harvey, Samuel Daniel and other 'native' poets arguing for the promotion of accentual rhyme. As an oblique reference to **music**, 'number' meaning 'rhyme' indicates lyric poetry which is either meant for music or is characteristically musical.

number

(B) Shakespeare's use of 'number' in relation to musical poetry accords to its signification of rhyme, for instance in *Sonnet* 17 when he wishes that he could describe appropriately his friend's many positive qualities: 'If I could write the beauty of your eyes, / And in fresh numbers number all your **grace**s . . .' (5–6). In *Love's Labour's Lost*, Holofernes asks Nathaniel to read 'a staff, a stanza, a verse' (4.2.104) ('staff' could mean either 'stanza' or 'musical stave') of a **canzonet**, whose content alludes to the neo-platonic doctrine of human versus divine music (114–18). The musical overtones of this exchange are amplified in Holofernes' response to the canzonet, which he wants to supervise:

> You find not the apostrophas, and so miss
> the **accent**. Let me supervise the canzonet.
> Here are only numbers ratified, but for
> the elegancy, facility, and golden **cadence** of poesy,
> > *caret*.
> > (4.2.119–23)

Even though the sonnet is read rather than sung, when the pedant remarks that the canzonet lacks in metrical correctness ('numbers ratified'), it is possible that he is trying to show off his musical knowledge. He makes a similar attempt earlier in the scene when he **hum**s the **note**s of the **gamut** (100), albeit in the wrong order.

(C) Attridge, *Well-weighed Syllables* (1974), deals with quantitative versus accentual poetry.

Lindley, *Lyric* (1985), has a lively discussion of the lyric's relationship with music, and a possible definition of the genre.

Wilson, 'Number and Music in Campion's Measured Verse' (forthcoming), focuses on the Elizabethan meaning of 'number' and its relationship with music.

O

ordinance see **ordnance**.

ordnance (A) Strictly speaking, 'ordnance' is not a musical term but one connected with warfare and military activity. A piece of ordnance was an artillery weapon such as a cannon or musket and was referred to as either a 'small' or 'great piece' equivalent to today's light or heavy artillery. In the Elizabethan playhouse, however, stage directions for ordnance functioned in a similar way to stage directions for straightforward **sound** effects, and involved the evocation of the sound of cannon or gunpowder artillery (Edelman, p. 241).

(B) There are two stage directions for ordnance in military contexts (*1H6* 2.3.60.SD and *2H6* 4.1.OSD); Hamlet's **solemn** funeral is also marked by this sound effect: '*Exeunt march*ing; *after the which, a* **peal** *of ordinance are* [sic] *shot off*' (Folio *Ham* 5.2.403.SD).

Salisbury is killed by 'a piece of ord'nance' (*1H6* 1.4.15) in Orléans; Exeter threatens the Dauphin with war by telling him that Henry V's 'ordinance' (*H5* 2.4.126) will be the English reply to the barrel of tennis balls that the Dauphin had sent to mock the English claims to the French crown.

Claudius orders: 'Let all the battlements their ord'nance fire' (*Ham* 5.2.270) to signal the beginning of the fencing contest between Hamlet and Laertes. Petruchio feels confident that he will be able to put up with

ordnance

Katherina's spiteful personality, since he is used to **hear**ing sounds more frightening than 'a woman's **tongue**' (*Shr* 1.2.207), among which is that of the 'great ordnance in the field' (203).

(C) Edelman, *Shakespeare's Military Language: A Dictionary* (2000).

organ (A) Despite its antiquity, the fundamental principle of the organ has remained unchanged since the Ancient Greek and Roman **instrument**, the *hydraulis*. Essentially, the organ is a **wind** instrument in which a metal or wooden **pipe** is **sound**ed when a key is depressed on a keyboard. When the key is **play**ed, air generated by bellows is **blow**n through the pipe. (In the *hydraulis*, the air pressure was controlled by water level. This system had been displaced by the second century AD.) Until the late nineteenth century, the bellows were operated by hand. Organs varied in size according to the number and dimensions of pipes they had.

Unlike its ancient forebears, the organ in Western culture from at least the eighth century was the provenance of monastic churches and ecclesiastical locations, though mainly for ceremonial rather than liturgical use. As the organ developed through the Middle Ages and Renaissance, several kinds emerged. There were the larger fixed organs, especially developed by builders in the Netherlands and Germany, who exerted a strong influence throughout continental Europe. In addition, smaller, fixed organs, sometimes called chamber organs, and small movable organs ('portative') also existed. In Henry VIII's inventory (1547) there was 'a payre of portatives' in a privy chamber, whereas in the chapel were the larger fixed 'organes'. ('Payre' does not necessarily mean two, cf. pair of scissors, pair of trousers, pair of **virginal**s). The Regal was a small 'reed' organ without pipes.

In Tudor England, organs were to be found in cathedrals, chapels and in a surprising number of parish churches. Smaller chamber organs are known to have existed in royal and stately homes. But the overwhelming occurrence of the organ is in sacred rather than secular contexts. During the later sixteenth century, especially after 1570, the playing and building of organs, particularly in parish churches, suffered a serious decline as a direct consequence of Protestant antipathy to **music** in church services except for the accompanied **sing**ing of **psalm**s. That decline was to some extent halted soon after Elizabeth's

organ

death in 1603, although organs were not reintroduced until the eighteenth and especially nineteenth centuries.

After his return to England following extensive continental travels (including Turkey), the pre-eminent English organ builder, Thomas Dallam, completed several major projects and helped restore English organ building considerably after years of misfortune. In 1605–6 he installed a new organ in King's College Chapel, Cambridge, which comprised Great and Chaire cases (see below). Back in London, Dallam worked on the organ in Westminster Abbey (1606–7) and from about 1607 took over the care of the organs in the royal chapels. In 1608–9 he built a new organ for Norwich Cathedral. In 1609–10 he extensively reworked the organs in St George's Chapel, Windsor. Robert Cecil, Earl of Salisbury, employed Dallam for the installation of the new organ at Hatfield House in 1611, 'setting up and perfecting the great wind instrument' for which he was handsomely paid £53. The organ Dallam installed in Worcester Cathedral in 1613 is one of the very few pre-Restoration organs for which we have details. It comprised eight **stop**s in the Great case and five in the Chaire. After Worcester, Dallam worked on organs for Eton College Chapel (1613–14), the chapel of the Palace of Holyrood House, Edinburgh (1616), Wells Cathedral (1620), All Saints, Wakefield (1620), Durham Cathedral (1621–2) and Bristol Cathedral (1629).

If Dallam was the most significant organ builder of the Jacobean revival, the leading builders and **tune**rs of the earlier Tudor period were the Howe family. John Howe the older worked on organs at York Minster (1485), St Mary at Hill, London (1500), Eton College (1505–6) and St Stephen Walbrook, London (1507). His son, John Howe the younger, is known to have lived 'at the sign of the Organe Pype' in the parish of St Stephen, Walbrook. His son, Thomas, attempted to keep the family business going but was eventually defeated by the worsening Elizabethan suppression of organ building.

Although comparatively modest in size, larger Tudor organs could boast a number of 'stops' (ranks of pipes or 'registers') housed in one or two (organ) cases, referred to as the 'Great' organ and the 'Chaire' organ, the latter situated behind the player. The stops of differing pitches and timbres were called 'fflutes', 'pryncipalls' or '**diapason**s'. The player would use one or more stops by pulling out the draw-stop located near the keyboard, thus allowing the air to resonate the pipe as appropriate. In some instances, terminology peculiar to English usage, indicates that 'stops' were so called because they shut off the rank of pipes. In France, in contrast, 'stops' were called '*tirants*' (pull [stops]).

(B) In *All's Well That Ends Well,* Helen tries to convince the King of France to take a remedy prepared by her recently departed father (a physician). Although the seriously ill King is reluctant to follow her advice at first, he finally changes his mind: 'Methinks in thee some blessed spirit doth **speak** / His powerful sound within an organ weak' (2.1.175–6). 'Organ' can have other meanings: the most obvious is the organ of speech. 'Weak' and the other adjectives appearing at line 176 ('powerful' and 'sound') are excellently chosen in a scene where the King's state of health is the main preoccupation. 'Sound' used in proximity to 'organ' gives a musical nuance to the line: the King, trusting in the remedy's miraculous healing power, is probably hinting at the organ as a sacred instrument. His mention of the 'blessed spirit' (175) reinforces this reading.

There are two references to organ in *Hamlet*. The first occurs when the Prince soliloquizes about his intention to observe Claudius's reaction when the itinerant actors put on a play which portrays the murder of a king by the hands of a usurper:

> . . . I have **hear**d
> That guilty creatures sitting at a play
> Have by the very cunning of the scene
> Been strook so to the soul, that presently
> They have proclaim'd their malefactions:
> For murther, though it have no **tongue**, will speak
> With most miraculous organ.
> (2.2.588–94)

As in *All's Well That Ends Well*, there seems to be a correlation between two different meanings of 'organ': as part(s) of the body enabling speech and as a sacred instrument. Later in the play, Hamlet compares a **recorder** (a wind instrument) to a 'little organ' (i.e. windpipe) with 'much music' and an 'excellent **voice**' (3.2.368).

Orsino exhorts the disguised Viola (who is passing herself off as Cesario) to woo Olivia by proxy. He argues that Cesario's 'small pipe' (his voice) 'is as the maiden's organ, **shrill** and sound, / And all is semblative a woman's **part**' (*TN* 1.4.33–4). With the word 'part'

organ

Shakespeare creates a metaphor which is at the same time theatrical and musical. He aims to draw attention to the gender of the young male actor, who is playing the role of a girl disguised as a boy, and to the quality of his **high**-pitched, unbroken voice – hence the adjectives 'shrill' and 'sound'. The use of 'organ' in relation to 'pipe' provides the foundation for the musical pun.

Alonso hears the accusations directed against him, Sebastian and Antonio after the banquet disappears in front of his and his followers' eyes. Ariel's magic trick has the effect of causing a sense of deep guilt in Alonso, who is convinced that

> ... the **thunder**,
> That deep and dreadful organ-pipe, pronounc'd
> The name of Prosper; it did **base** my trespass.
> Therefore my son i' th'ooze is bedded...
> (*Tmp* 3.3.97–100)

Here as in *All's Well That Ends Well*, the organ is associated with the religious sphere. The locution 'base my trespass' is a reminder of the Lord's Prayer. Clearly, 'base' is used in its musical meaning and is also 'a pun on the baseness of Alonso's actions' (Lindley, p. 178).

When King John is delirious after being poisoned by a monk, he sings and asks to be brought into an orchard. Prince Henry consents to his request and **lament**s his father's imminent death:

> ... 'Tis strange that death should sing.
> I am the cygnet to this pale **faint swan**
> Who **chaunt**s a **doleful hymn** to his own death,
> And from the organ-pipe of frailty sings
> His soul and body to their lasting **rest**.
> (*Jn* 5.7.20–4)

The image of the swan that dies singing (used elsewhere in Shakespeare) seamlessly blends with the image of the organ pipe as the organ of speech and as the musical instrument. The effect is heightened when Henry refers to the 'doleful hymn' (22) and the soul and body which will come to 'their lasting rest' (24), with their powerful religious overtones.

(C) Bicknell, *The History of the English Organ* (1996).

Elam, 'The Fertile Eunuch' (1996), deals with the implications that Orsino's reference to Viola's voice has on the theme of castration in *Twelfth Night*.

Lindley, *The Tempest* (2002).

Owen, 'Towards a Definition of the English Renaissance Organ' (1986).

Temperley, *The Music of the English Parish Church* (1979), vol. 1, p. 40.

Vaughan, *The Tempest* (1999), p. 241.

Wilson, Michael, *The Chamber Organ in Britain* (2001).

organ pipe see **organ**.

organ stop see **organ**.

Orpheus (A) The Orpheus myth derives from many sources going back to classical antiquity. The fullest accounts, well known in Elizabethan England, either in their original Latin or in translation or in vernacular paraphrase, come from Virgil *Georgics* IV and Ovid *Metamorphoses*, Books X and XI. (Ovid is a particularly important source for Shakespeare.) The tale of Orpheus, as Sternfeld reminds us:

> ... concerns a **Thracian sing**er of magic and 'divine' power. This divinity usually derives from **Apollo**, the Greek god of **music**, and in many versions of the story Orpheus is the son of Apollo and the Muse Calliope. In other versions the connection with Apollo is more mysterious, but it is only rarely that Orpheus is not at least his protégé. The divine power of Orpheus' **song** is able to move rocks and beasts as well as humans. Even more miraculously, it overcomes the power of Hades.
>
> (1986, p. 20)

According to most stories, it is Orpheus' divine singing that allows him to regain Euridice from Hades. It is not Orpheus' special musical and poetical attributes that make him stand out in Renaissance allegory, it is the 'symbolism of the *figura* of Orpheus that distinguishes him from other musical figures of antiquity (such as Arion and Amphion)'

Orpheus

(Sternfeld, 1988, p. 180). The figure of Orpheus represents far more than the popular 'fabula', the magical power of his music and his unending love of Euridice. 'Orpheus becomes a sage, a courageous seeker after divine wisdom, a conqueror of death, a religious prophet . . . , an *allegory* for Apollo, Dionysus, Osiris, or Christ' (ibid., p. 179).

The story of Orpheus provided the basis for much music and drama at the beginning of the seventeenth century, notably in Italy for opera, as for example in Peri's *Euridice* (Florence, 1600) and Monteverdi's *Orfeo* (Mantua, 1607). It has continued to do so right up to the present day, including works by Gluck, Offenbach, Stravinsky and Birtwistle, to name but a few. Elements of the Orpheus myth, particularly to do with the soothing power of music, found their way into English drama and literature of the early modern period, for example in Campion's *Lords Masque* (1613) and Davenant's *The Temple of Love* (1635).

(B) The soothing power of Orphic **lute** music is evoked in Proteus' advice to Thurio:

> For Orpheus' lute was **strung** with poets' **sinew**s,
> Whose golden **touch** could soften steel and stones,
> Make tigers tame, and huge leviathans
> Forsake unsounded deeps to **dance** on sands.
> (*TGV* 3.2.77–80)

Music and poetry are inseparable and exert a harmonizing power over the hardest stones and the wildest creatures: Thurio will need to master both arts if he wants to conquer Silvia's love.

In *Henry VIII*, a similar image of the power of Orpheus' lute over nature is evoked in a song:

> Orpheus with his lute made trees,
> And the mountain tops that freeze,
> Bow themselves when he did sing.
> (3.1.3–5)

After the song, Queen Katherine is ordered by Wolsey and Campeius to accept Henry's request of divorce, which she desperately (and unsuccessfully) tries to oppose. The song about cosmic balance reflects her desire for **harmony** in her marriage. The singer accompanies herself on a lute, as is clear from the Queen's request at the beginning of the scene: 'Take thy lute, **wench**, my soul grows sad with troubles. / Sing, and disperse 'em if thou canst' (3.1.1–2). The lute as a stage property is an effective visual reminder of the themes developed in the song.

In the final scene of *The Merchant of Venice*, Jessica complains that she is 'never merry' when she **hear**s '**sweet** music' (5.1.69). Lorenzo reminds her that a herd of wild colts can be tamed by music:

> . . . Therefore the poet
> Did feign that Orpheus drew trees, stones, and floods;
> Since nought so stockish, hard, and full of rage,
> But music for the **time** doth change his nature.
> (5.1.79–82)

According to most commentators, the poet in question is Ovid, who narrated the story of Orpheus in *Metamorphoses*. Once again, the harmonising and calming power of Orphic music is emphasized.

The myth of Orpheus and Eurydice is alluded to just before Tarquin commits rape. Lucrece pleads to be spared and her words have the effect of delaying the violence: 'His unhallowed haste her words delays, / And moody Pluto winks while Orpheus **play**s' (*Luc* 553). Like Orpheus' music in the underworld, which charmed Pluto's **ear**s, Lucrece's pleas have a temporary, if ultimately futile, effect on Tarquin.

(C) Sternfeld, 'The Orpheus myth' (1986); and 'Orpheus, Ovid and Opera' (1988).

Wilson, 'Shakespeare's "Fair Viols, Sweet Lutes, and Rude Pipes" as Symbolic Musics' (1998).

owl see **bird**.

P

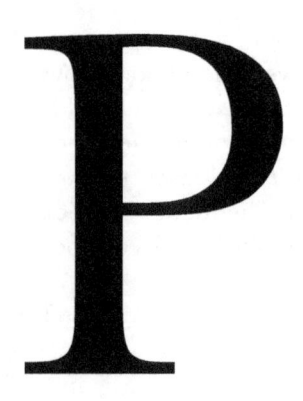

Pabylon see **Babylon**.

parley (A) The military term derives from the French *'parler'* (to speak). To **beat** or **sound** a parley is to give a signal, generally in a battle situation, that one side wants to hold a meeting with the other. A **drum** would be beaten or **trumpet** sounded to indicate that one side wished to hold talks, for example in a siege when the besieged sought to discuss terms of surrender. There is also evidence that a parley might be sounded by the besiegers in order to ask leave to bury their dead.

(B) There are several explicit indications that trumpets must be used for parleys in the Shakespeare canon, for instance when at Shrewsbury *'the trumpet sounds a parley'* (*1H4* 4.3.29.SD) is followed by the entry of Sir Walter Blunt who listens to Hotspur's grievances against the King. A similar stage direction is found in *1 Henry VI*: *'Trumpets sound a parley'* (3.3.35.SD).

During the siege of Corioles, Martius orders one of his followers: 'Come, **blow** thy blast' (*Cor* 1.4.12), another unmistakable reference to the use of trumpets. This cue is followed by the explicit stage direction: *'They sound a parley. Enter two Senators with others on the walls of Corioles'* (1.4.12.SD).

The use of trumpets can also be inferred from the lines spoken by Bolingbroke before Flint Castle:

parley

> Go to the rude ribs of that ancient castle;
> Through **brazen** trumpet send the **breath** of parley
> Into his ruin'd **ear**s . . .
>
> (*R2* 3.3.32–4)

A sound effect follows: '*The trumpets sound. Richard appeareth on the wall*' (3.3.61.SD). This type of staging was standard in plays by Shakespeare and his contemporaries for scenes which display two enemy factions holding a parley. Usually, after the sounding of trumpets or the beating of drums, one or more representatives of one party are instructed to appear on an elevated area (the stage gallery in a public playhouse) standing for a besieged castle or town, while the other party occupies the main stage. The symbolism evoked by the sound effect and the use of the acting space on two levels were effective devices in a theatre which did not rely on scenery and other realistic devices (see also Introduction). A similar staging was implied in *Henry V* during the besieging of Harfleur, when Gower's line 'the town sounds a parley' (3.2.136) is preceded by the sound cue '*A parley*' (3.2.135.SD).

In *Macbeth*, a horrified Macduff reacts with decisiveness after discovering the murder of Duncan:

> Awake, awake!
> **Ring** the **alarum-bell**! Murther and treason!
> . . .
> Ring the bell.   *Bell rings.*
>
> (2.3.73–4; 80)

As Lady Macbeth enters, she exclaims: What's the business, / That such a hideous trumpet calls to parley / The sleepers of the house? (81–3). At first, it seems strange that she calls the bell a 'hideous trumpet': however, it is possible here that she is subconsciously expressing her sense of guilt, which makes her feel that she is being summoned by enemies. Furthermore, her words assume a quasi-biblical tone conjuring up as they do the image of the Last Judgement. The sleepers of the house 'rising in their night-shirts and flocking on to the stage by every entrance . . . present a visual resemblance to the spirits rising from their graves on the Last Day' (Jones, p. 17).

Sometimes, parleys are mentioned in metaphors, for instance when Iago cunningly uses a military image to appeal to the soldier Cassio

parley

while trying to awaken in him lustful feelings for Desdemona: 'What an eye she has! Methinks it sounds a / parley to provocation' (*Oth* 2.3.22–3). He elaborates on this a few lines later: 'When she speaks, is it not an alarum to love?' (26).

Tarquin's cowardly assault on Lucrece while she is asleep in her bed is described in terms of a siege and subsequent attack on a town. For instance, when Tarquin puts his hand on her **breast**, Shakespeare likens his hand to a battering ram hitting an ivory wall. When the woman is awoken, he does not show much pity towards her: 'First like a trumpet doth his **tongue** begin / To sound a parley to his heartless foe' (*Luc* 470–1). A frightened Lucrece asks him 'under what color he commits this ill' (476). The word 'color', besides meaning 'pretext', also has a military connotation (a flag or standard of a regiment) and builds on the martial imagery preceding the act of rape.

(C) Dessen and Thomson, *A Dictionary of Stage Directions* (1999), pp. 157–8.

Jones, *The Plays of T. S. Eliot* (1960).

Muir, *Macbeth* (1984).

parrot see **bird**.

part see **bear a part**.

passamezzo see **pavan**.

passy measures see **pavan**.

pavan (A) The Renaissance 'pavan' was a slow stately **dance** of Italian origin (*pavana* means 'of Padua'). Arbeau was the first to record its **measure**s:

The pavan is easy to dance as it is merely two *simples* [single steps] and one *double* [double step] forward and two *simples* and one *double*

pavan

backward. It is **play**ed in duple **time** [*mesure binaire*], you will take note that in dancing it the two *simples* and the *double* forward are begun with the left foot, and the two *simples* and one *double* backward are begun with the right foot.

(*Orchesography*, 1589, p. 57)

Whilst declining in popularity by the time Arbeau described it (as he notes), the pavan maintained its attractiveness in English courtly circles in the later sixteenth and early seventeenth centuries. **Music** for pavans survives in a variety of sources for **lute**, keyboard and **consort**. Morley regarded the pavan in high esteem, next only behind the fantasy in 'gravity and goodness': 'A kind of staide musicke, ordained for grave dauncing, and most commonlie made of three **strain**es, wherof everie straine is plaid or sung twice' (*Introduction*, 1597, p. 181).

There are a large number of examples of pavans in English manuscript and printed sources. In these, the pavan is often the first of several dances. Quicker dances, such as the **galliard** in triple metre, followed the slower pavan. Sometimes the quicker dances were melodically or harmonically related to the pavan. Keyboard arrangements of consort pavans from the early Tudor court survive, such as *King Harry the VIIIth Pavyn* (BL. Royal App. 58, ed. in MB 67, no. 41). The simple homophonic style found in contemporary continental and Elizabethan settings of the 1580s was displaced by the more complicated, technically sophisticated **piece**s of later Elizabethan composers such as William Byrd, whose ten pavans in MLNB demonstrate a high degree of originality and skill. The gravity of the form is sometimes emphasized as in the titles 'pavana dolorosa' (e.g. Peter Philips FWVB i. p. 321), 'pavana lachrymae' (e.g. Dowland *Lachrymae*, 1604) and John Bull's 'Melancholy Pavan' (MB 19, p. 13).

In addition to pavans bearing titles designating **mood**, pavans also included titular prefixes denoting musical characteristics. The passamezzo or passing measures pavan was very popular in Europe from the 1540s and was developed in England during the last two decades of the sixteenth century and into the seventeenth. It was characterized by a specific repeating **bass**, the *passamezzo antico*, equivalent to modern-day minor tonality. The 'quadran' pavan used the *passamezzo moderno*, a bass in major tonality, and slightly different from the *antico* bass. Passamezzo pavans were often followed by a galliard or saltarello using the same bass or harmonic pattern.

pavan

(B) *Twelfth Night* is the only Shakespeare play where reference to this dance by name occurs, when Sir Toby makes an ironic comment about Dick Surgeon's drunkenness: 'Then he's a rogue, and a passy measures pavin' (5.1.200). ('Panin' found in Folio is a misprint for 'pavin'. Commentators as early as Malone – in his Shakespeare edition of 1790 – have noted that the middle letter has been inverted.) Sir Toby is associated with the lively **caper** (1.3.141) and is frustrated by the slowness of the Surgeon who is likened to the staid dance. The passamezzo music is bass heavy: this is appropriate for the heavy exaggerated steps that accompany drunkenness.

(C) Caldwell, *English Keyboard Music before the Nineteenth Century* (1973), includes discussion of a wide variety of English pavans.

Neighbour, *The Consort and Keyboard Music of William Byrd* (1978), provides a discussion of Byrd's pavans.

Sternfeld, *Music in Shakespearean Tragedy* (1967), pp. 250–2, offers a definition of pavan and scrutinizes its occurrences as 'measure'.

pavin see **pavan**.

peal (A) A peal indicates the **loud sound** of **instrument**s, for instance **bell**s, and can also mean 'a discharge of guns or cannon so as to produce a loud sound' (*OED* 5).

(B) In the theatre of Shakespeare's day, references to 'peal' often included musical instruments with military significance, and were associated with **ordnance**. It was a peal of chambers (short cannon), indicated by the stage direction '*Chambers discharg'd*' (*H8* 1.4.48.SD) which is thought to have caused the Globe theatre to burn down during a production of *Henry VIII* in 1613.

When Titus invites his followers to join the hunt, he wants them to '**ring** a hunter's peal, / That all the court may **echo** with the **noise**' (*Tit* 2.2.5–6). A stage direction some lines later tells us exactly which instruments were intended to be used: '***Wind horn**s in a peal*' (2.2.10.SD). (Other stage directions in the Shakespeare canon prescribing a peal are discussed under 'ordnance').

Moth uses the expression 'Peace, the peal begins' (*LLL* 5.1.44) with an ironic intention when he likens the pedantic exchanges between Holofernes, Armado and himself to a peal of bells. The phrase 'ring a peal' was used to describe a torrent of words (David, p. 123).

(C) David, *Love's Labour's Lost* (1951).
Dessen and Thomson, *A Dictionary of Stage Directions* (1999), p. 160.

peg (A) The peg is the small wooden tuning key at the top end of the fingerboard of a **string**ed **instrument** (e.g. **viol, lute, cittern**, etc.) which when turned raises or lowers the pitch of an individual string. The viol, for example, has six pegs, one for each string. They are arranged on each side of the 'head' or pegbox, which is often ornately carved.

(B) According to the stage direction in Q1 *Othello* (1622) (this stage direction is omitted in Folio), when Othello arrives in Cyprus and embraces Desdemona, '*they kiss*' (2.1.198.SD), effectively articulating: 'And this, and this, the greatest **discord** be / That e'er our hearts shall make' (2.1.197–8). In this harmonious meeting, Shakespeare's musical imagery is omnipresent. Iago observes that the lovers are **well tuned**, but determines to destroy that **harmony** or **music** by **alter**ing (**flat**tening is implied) the pitch of the strings, thus putting them out of tune and causing discord: 'O you are well-tun'd now! / But I'll **set** down the pegs that **make** this music' (199–200). The implications are that marital bliss will be undone or untuned by the workings of human evil. As Lawrence Ross points out:

> the official 'Homilie of the State of Matrimonie' ... warned Elizabethan married folk to be careful of falling into just such false security as Othello: ... 'For the divell will assay to attempt all things to interrupt and hinder your hearts and godly purpose, if yee will giue him entry ... [with] divers griefes and displeasures'.
>
> (p. 113)

This use of pegs as musical imagery invoking 'discord' is found in *Othello* and nowhere else in early modern drama. It is surprising that this neat and effective metaphor was not employed more frequently.

(C) Dodd, ' "But I'll set down the pegs that make this music" ' (1967).

peg

King, ' "Then Murder's Out of Tune": The Music and Structure of *Othello*' (1986), analyses the musical imagery pervading *Othello* and its relationship with the theme of loss of harmony.

Ross, 'Shakespeare's "Dull Clown" and Symbolic Music' (1966).

Sternfeld, *Music in Shakespearean Tragedy* (1967).

percussion see **thunder**.

perform (A) Although common in musical parlance today, the term was rare in Elizabethan times meaning the **play**ing or **sing**ing of **music** either in private or in public. More often used was '**sound**' [a **note, instrument**, etc.] or words specifying the manner of performance, such as 'sing', '**dance**', '**chant**', '**warble**', 'play', etc. Occasionally the word is found with its executorial musical meaning, as when Gibbons writes in the dedicatory epistle to Sir Christopher Hatton: 'Songs of this Nature are usually esteemed as they are well or ill performed' (*First Set of Madrigals*, 1612).

(B) The term appears only once in a musical context in the Shakespeare canon, and then in connection with dance, in a passage in *Macbeth* usually ascribed to Thomas Middleton. The scene shows the apparitions conjured up by the Witches and Hecate in reply to Macbeth's queries. Just before the Witches disappear, the First Witch exhorts her sisters as follows:

> I'll **charm** the **air** to give a sound,
> While you perform your antic **round**;
> That this great king may kindly say
> Our duties did his welcome pay.
> *Music. The Witches dance and vanish.*
>   (4.1.129–32)

The 'antic round' in this case is a dance rather than a song, and discloses the sinister power of the world of the occult through the use of practical music on the stage.

See also **rehearse**.

(C) Austern, ' "Art to Enchant" ' (1990), considers the relationship between the occult and practical music in Renaissance theatre.

Wulstan, *Tudor Music* (1985), focuses on performing different types of English Renaissance music.

Philomela (Philomel, Philomele) see **bird**.

Phoebus see **Apollo**.

pie see **bird**.

piece (A) Although not used in its eighteenth and nineteenth-century way to mean an entire small-scale composition or movement of a musical opus, 'piece' is found in Elizabethan times used to describe a **song** or part of a musical work. It was also conventionally used in 'a piece of **ordnance**' to signify a cannon or other artillery weapon.

(B) A marginal stage direction in Q2 *Hamlet* (1604/5) prescribes: '**Drum, trumpet**s*, and shot.* **Florish***, a peece goes off*' (N4v). This indicates that a cannon was expected to be shot off-stage to signal the beginning of the fencing contest between Hamlet and Laertes. There are also some instances of 'piece' in the dialogue which refer to the aural sphere. For instance, the Master Gunner of Orléans informs his boy that he has placed 'a piece of ord'nance' (*1H6* 1.4.15) which will kill Salisbury.

In *Twelfth Night*, Orsino wants to **hear** 'that piece of song / That old and antique song' (2.4.2–3) which he and Viola (disguised as Cesario) heard the previous night and which momentarily soothed Orsino's passion for Olivia. This request confirms the Duke's proneness to self-indulging melancholia, and his tendency to make 'a spectacle of his passion' (Wells, p. 215), while also hinting at Viola's feelings for him. This is the first use of 'piece' in a musical sense in the English language.

In *Troilus and Cressida*, Paris tells Pandarus that he wants to hear a 'piece of your **perform**ance' (3.1.52). This cue occurs in a context permeated with musical allusions, and hints at Pandarus' performance of the song 'Love, love, nothing but love' (115–24) later in the scene.

See also **music**.

piece

(C) Dessen and Thomson, *A Dictionary of Stage Directions* (1999), p. 163.
Wells, *Elizabethan Mythologies* (1994).

pipe (A) Either on its own or connected with a descriptive term, 'pipe' is a simple generic term to denote a wide range of differing kinds of **wind instrument**, including **recorder**, flute, **fife**, flageolot, shawm, **tabor** and pipe, **bagpipe**, hornpipe, panpipe, organ pipe and **whistle**. Sometimes 'pipe' is used in connection with the **sing**ing **voice**.

Pipes were made from many kinds of materials and were generally a single tube in which several finger holes were cut in order for the player to produce different **note**s or pitches. From earliest times they were fashioned out of natural materials such as wood, reed-cane and straw, and were employed in rustic contexts, often to 'serve primitive magic and ritual' (Baines, p. 171). In classical antiquity, the divergent double pipe with its reedy nasal **sound** replaced the old single fluty whistle, becoming the *aulos* of the Greeks and the *tibia* of the Romans. Both the sound and shape of these classical pipes were known to the Elizabethans. The sixteenth century saw the culmination of the diverse Medieval types of pipes. After Shakespeare's time, they were either to be known by specific names or become largely obsolete, banished to the confines of rustic obscurity.

(B) One interesting use of 'pipe' occurs when the Greek commander Ajax orders that a **trumpet** be sounded before Troy: 'Thou, trumpet, there's my purse. / Now crack thy lungs, and split thy **brazen** pipe' (*Tro* 4.5.7–8). Ajax is addressing a trumpeter: hence 'brazen pipe' is a metonymic transposition for the trumpeter's **throat** (*Riverside Shakespeare*, p. 513).

In *Othello*, the Clown dismisses a group of **musician**s as follows: 'Then put up your pipes in your bag, for I'll / away. Go, vanish into air, away!' (3.1.19–20). The dialogue preceding these lines draws on an allusion to the classical myth of Marsyas' disastrous contest with **Apollo**, in which the pipe – the classical *aulos* – is compared unfavourably with the refined **lute** – the *kythara* or lyre of Plato and others. There is also a possible sexual innuendo in these lines, since they seem to expand on a word-play on 'tail' (7–8), a reference to the penis.

The rustic, often peasant origins of the simple traditional pipe are

pipe

commonly adduced in literature. This pipe, the 'shepherd's pipe', is made from materials such as corn stalks, river reeds or grass and is the 'pipe of green corn' of Chaucer, the 'oaten pype' in Spenser's 'January' (*Shepherds Calendar*, 1597), and Watson's 'My Muse shall pipe but on an oaten quill' in *Eclogue upon the Death of Walsingham* (1590). A similar usage is found, for instance, in a line of the concluding **song** of *Love's Labour's Lost*: 'When shepherds pipe on oaten straws' (5.2.903). Titania reminds Oberon of when he 'in the shape of Corin sat all day / **Play**ing on pipes of corn' (*MND* 2.1.66–7). In *The Passionate Pilgrim* we have: 'My shepherd's pipe can sound no deal' (17.17) when the poet **lament**s the sense of loss caused by his mistress's inconstancy. References to rustic straw pipes are a pastoral commonplace with precedents in classical antiquity going back to Theocritus.

Elsewhere, this imagery is used with an ironic twist as in the villainous Richard's 'weak piping **time** of peace' (*R3* 1.1.24) which is characterized not by martial music but by the rustic pipe, also invoking on a more sophisticated level the pipe's polarity to the **string**ed instrument, the 'lascivious pleasing of a lute' (13).

On the eve of the Battle of Agincourt, an impatient Dauphin comments in the following terms about his horse:

> . . . the earth sings when he **touch**es it; the
> basest **horn** of his hoof is more musical than the pipe of
> Hermes.
> (*H5* 3.7.16–18)

The 'pipe of Hermes' recalls classical mythology (Ovid, *Metamorphoses* I, 677) where Hermes lures the monster Argus to sleep by playing his pipe (Walter, p. 84). The harmonizing or civilizing power of Hermes exercised through poetry and music was often employed in Elizabethan mythological imagery. The subduing of the monster by music is emblematic of social order and universal law embodied in the monarch, an idea particularly current in Elizabethan philosophy (Brooks-Davies, 1983).

On the other hand, the notion of the lowly pipe is exploited when Guildenstern has his recorder **lesson**. Hamlet exhorts him to: '**Govern** these **ventage**s / with your fingers and thumbs, / Give it **breath** . . . and it will discourse most eloquent music' (*Ham* 3.2.357–60). Later, Hamlet suggests that Guildenstern should not try to 'play upon' him (i.e. to control him) given that he is incapable of mastering a simple

pipe

instrument like the pipe. The ability to 'govern' or play a pipe as analogous to controlling the mind and emotions is found in Hamlet's observation:

> . . .and blest are those
> Whose blood and judgement are so well co-meddled,
> That they are not a pipe for Fortune's finger
> To sound what **stop** she please.
>
> (3.2.68–71)

In the Induction to *2 Henry IV* the prologue-like figure of Rumour warns us that the mind can be distracted by dishonourable thoughts and deeds:

> . . . Rumor is a pipe,
> **Blow**n by surmises, jealousies, conjectures,
> And of so easy and so plain a stop
> That the blunt monster with uncounted heads,
> The still-discordant wav'ring multitude,
> Can play upon it . . .
>
> (15–20)

The high-pitched voice of a woman is compared to the sound of a pipe when Orsino remarks of Viola's voice: 'Thy small pipe / Is as the maiden's organ, **shrill** and sound' (*TN* 1.4.32–3). The implications of these lines cannot be overstated: the 'small pipe' is 'at once the **treble** voice and undeveloped member of the boy actor, which is simultaneously . . . female vocality and genitality together' (Elam, p. 35). Similar implications are found in *Coriolanus*:

> Away, my disposition, and possess me
> Some harlot's spirit! My throat of war be turn'd,
> Which **quier**'d with my drum, into a pipe
> Small as an **eunuch**, or the virgin voice
> That babies lull asleep! . . .
>
> (3.2.111–15)

Coriolanus delivers this speech after being persuaded by Volumnia to appease the plebeians' anger. To his combative and soldierly nature, the

pipe

fact that he will not be allowed to express his contempt for the plebeians amounts to prostitution and loss of virility.

The imagery of a **high**- versus **low**-pitched voice is enlarged upon in Jaques' famous speech on the seven ages of man. When a man reaches his sixth age:

> . . . his big manly voice,
> Turning again toward childish treble, pipes
> And whistles in his sound . . .
> (*AYLI* 2.7.161–3)

Mention of **Philomela**'s pipe (8) in *Sonnet* 102 aptly recalls the shrill high-pitched voice of a treble or soprano, confirming that Shakespeare's song**bird** was female.

See also **organ**.

(C) Baines, *Woodwind Instruments and their History* (1977).
Brooks-Davies, *The Mercurian Monarch* (1983).
Elam, 'The Fertile Eunuch: *Twelfth Night*, early modern Intercourse, and the Fruits of Castration' (1996).
Partridge, *Shakespeare's Bawdy* (1968), p. 434.
Schlesinger, *The Greek Aulos* (1939).
Smith, 'The Contest of Apollo and Marsyas: Ideas about Music in the Middle Ages' (1979).
Walter, *Henry V* (1954).

plainsong (A) Morley's approach to teaching counterpoint is based on the Renaissance principle of composing one or more **part**s against a 'plainsong tenor'. Although some of the **tune**s used may bear resemblance to Medieval ecclesiastical **chant**s, Morley uses the term to mean a basic or simple tune, as in: 'now here be diverse other examples of plainsong, which you may **sing** by your selfe' (*Introduction*, 1597, p. 8). The term when used in a religious context is derived from the late Medieval *cantus planus*, an alternative name for monophonic (Gregorian) chant, and is more appositely called 'plainchant'. When employed in a polyphonic composition, be it religious or secular, the plainsong invariably acts as a tenor or **ground** on which other parts build more florid **music** (**descant**).

plainsong

(B) The **song** 'The **woosel cock** so black of hue' (*MND* 3.1.125–33) intoned by the ass-headed Bottom lists different **bird**s and the qualities which make them unique. Among them is 'the plain-song **cuckoo** grey' (131): this use of the term hints at the basic repetitive nature of this bird's song. The same meaning of simple tune is implied in *Henry VIII* when Lovell contrasts his 'plain-song' (1.3.45) with the 'French song' (41): whereas the former embodies English honesty and integrity, the latter is artificially elaborate and reflects the deviousness and potential for seduction implicit in French music.

Nym's comment parodying Henry V's famous speech 'Once more unto the breach, dear friends' (*H5* 3.1.1–34) during the attack on Harfleur uses 'plain song' in an interesting way:

> . . . The knocks are too hot; and for mine own part, I have not a case of lives. The humo[u]r of it is too hot, that is the very plain-song of it.
>
> (3.2.3–6)

His fear of being killed in battle is articulated through sensorial conceits including aural metaphors. In his frightened state, 'plain song' equals 'simple truth' but also hints at the role he is undertaking during the battle, which is associated with the part in a song.

(C) Apel, *Gregorian Chant* (1958), is the standard work on chant.

Hiley, *Western Plainchant: A Handbook* (1993), is a detailed survey and contains a bibliography.

Iselin, ' "My Music for Nothing" ' (1995), explores the potentially subversive power of music in Shakespeare.

play (A) To play refers specifically to **perform**ing on an **instrument** as opposed to **sing**ing a song as in:

> Then I forthwith took my **pipe** . . .
> And upon a heavenly **ground** . . .
> Played this **roundelay**.
> (Dowland, 1603, no. 12)

Another example is: 'Like as the **lute** delights, or else dislikes, / As is his art that plays upon the same' (Daniel, 1606, no. 4. Poem by Samuel Daniel, sonnet 57 in *Delia*).

Consequently, when **music** is referred to as playing, that reference is almost invariably to instrumental music. Playing upon an instrument caused music to **sound** although not always audibly to mere humans (as when the concept of *musica mundana* or music of the spheres is evoked):

> Hark! **hear** you not a heavenly **harmony**?
> Is't Jove, think you, that plays upon the spheres?
> Heavens! Is not this a heavenly **melody**,
> Where Jove himself a **part** in music **bear**s?
> (Bateson, 1604, no. 22)

(B) Stage directions in the Shakespeare canon instructing that music be played sometimes specify which instrument is required, as in *The Tempest*: '*Ariel plays the **tune** on a **tabor** and pipe*' (3.2.124.SD). In Q1 *Hamlet* (1603), we have: '*Enter Ophelia playing on a lute, and her haire down singing*' (G4v). The lute accompanies her irreverent bawdy songs and the dishevelled hair is an indicator of her state of insanity. The **solemn**ity of the banquet hosted by Timon is signalled by: '**Hoboy**s *playing **loud** music. A great banquet serv'd in . . .*' (*Tim* 1.2.OSD). The central entertainment of the banquet consists of a **masque** '*of Ladies, as Amazons, with lutes in their hands, dancing and playing*' (1.2.130.SD).

More often however there are generic indications for music (sometimes referring to the **musician**s themselves), without any specification about the nature of the instruments to be played. This happens for instance in another banquet scene: '*Music plays. Enter two or three servants with a banket*' (*Ant* 2.7.OSD). Or in *The Merchant of Venice* where we have: '*Play Music*' (5.1.68.SD). The imperative tone of this stage direction may indicate that this was an addition by a theatrical annotator addressing the musicians during rehearsals. Vague as these stage directions for music may appear to a modern reader, they were nonetheless very useful in a theatre where the number of musicians available at any given performance was, like many other resources, variable.

Sometimes lines in the dramatic dialogue work as cues for music, called for to underline the **mood**s of different occasions ranging from happiness in love at wedding celebrations to sadness in death at

play

funerals. For instance, Duke Senior commands: 'Play, music' (5.4.178) towards the end of *As You Like It*, when order and harmony are finally restored and celebrated. Similarly, at the end of *Much Ado About Nothing*, Benedick uses the same cue (5.4.121) to celebrate the triumph of positive feelings. Quite a different effect is achieved in *Henry VIII* when Katherine of Aragon orders: 'Cause the musicians play me that sad **note** / I nam'd my **knell**' (4.2.78–9). The disgraced Queen knows that she is dying and wants to find some comfort in the soothing power of music during her transition between the mortal world and the 'celestial harmony' (80) she is hoping to achieve.

Another interesting example occurs at the opening of *Twelfth Night*, which immediately establishes Orsino's proneness to melancholy. His first words are:

> If music be the food of love, play on,
> Give me excess of it; that surfeiting,
> The appetite may sicken, and so die.
> (1.1.1–3)

It is not clear in which area of the stage the music was intended to be played during this scene. It is possible that a **consort** of musicians would have started playing on the main stage before the entrance of Orsino, or perhaps that they would have occupied the stage gallery if a public playhouse was used. Alternatively, playing could have taken place in the tiring-house rather than in full view of the audience (see Introduction for a discussion of the areas where aural effects were normally achieved in Elizabethan playhouses). Music – both instrumental and vocal – is heard on several occasions in this play, and underlines the theme of love as it is perceived by different characters. Orsino has a tendency to make 'a spectacle of his passion' (Wells, p. 215), a trait confirmed in 2.4, when he wants Feste to sing for him an 'old and antique song' (3) which has the power to 'relieve my passion much' (4). When Curio leaves to look for Feste, Orsino orders the musicians 'to play the tune the while' (14), once again indulging in his feelings for Olivia in a public way.

An unusual use of the verb 'play' is observed when, at the eve of the Battle of Shrewsbury, the Prince of Wales interprets ominously the signals given out by the weather:

> The southern **wind**

play

> Doth play the **trumpet** to his purposes,
> And by his **hollow** whistling in the leaves
> Foretells a tempest and a blust'ring day.
>
> (*1H4* 5.1.3–6)

In this prosopopoeia the whistling wind is described as playing a trumpet, an instrument with strong martial associations (trumpets were commonly used, for instance, to sound **alarum**s).

The act of playing an instrument acquires metaphorical nuances when Hamlet tries to persuade Guildenstern to learn how to play the **recorder**. The latter protests that he cannot play the instrument, and Hamlet confronts him:

> . . . You would play upon me, you would seem to know my **stop**s, you would pluck out the heart of my mystery, you would sound me from my lowest note to the top of my **compass**; and there is much music, excellent **voice**, in this little **organ**, yet cannot you make it **speak**. 'Sblood, do you think I am easier to be play'd on than a pipe? Call me what instrument you will, though you **fret** me, yet you cannot play upon me.
>
> (3.2.364–72)

Thanks to the use of polysemic terms such as 'stops', 'note', 'compass', 'voice', 'organ' and 'instrument', the speech works on two different levels: on a superficial level, it is about the practical art of mastering an instrument, but at the same time it is about the political art of manipulating, or 'playing on', people's minds. Hamlet's ultimate message to his 'friend' (who in fact wants to establish on behalf of Claudius whether the Prince is faking his madness) is that he will not tolerate anyone exerting control over him.

See also **false, ply, strain**.

(C) Dessen and Thomson, *A Dictionary of Stage Directions* (1999), pp. 165–6.

Wells, *Elizabethan Mythologies* (1994), studies the correlation between love and music in *Twelfth Night*.

pleasant

pleasant (A) In rare musical contexts, 'pleasant' is used in connection with **sing**ing, as in: '**Sound**ing on high in Daphne's praise / Pleasant songs and **roundelay**s' (Youll, 1608, no. 16).

(B) In *Sonnet* 102, we are told that the summer is 'less pleasant now' (9) that the **nightingale** does not sing. This image is based on the belief that this **bird** only sang at the beginning of the summer and stopped this activity by the end of July (Duncan-Jones, p. 102). It evokes the pleasantness of the bird's melodious singing as reflected in the summer climate.

In *The Winter's Tale* the Clown declares his passion for **ballad**s, which he describes by means of paradox: 'I love a ballad but even too well, if it be **doleful** matter / merrily set down, or a very pleasant thing indeed and sung **lament**ably' (4.4.188–9). Here, the topic of the ballad ('**mournful**' as opposed to 'light-hearted') is contrasted with the **mode** of delivery of this popular form of song (quick and lively as opposed to slow and sad).

(C) Duncan-Jones, *Shakespeare's Sonnets* (1997).

ply (A) Not often found in a musical sense, 'ply' is used generally in literary and artistic contexts to mean the enthusiastic application of an act, as in Spenser's 'During which time her gentle wit she plyes / To teach them truth' (*The Faerie Queene*, 1.6.19).

(B) When Polonius instructs Reynaldo to spy on Laertes (who has just left for Paris), he concludes his recommendations by saying: 'And let him ply his **music**' (*Ham* 2.1.69). This sentence could be interpreted in two ways: Polonius is either asking Reynaldo to let Laertes carry on with whatever he wants to do, or he wishes that Laertes would become skilful in music since 'music was one of the essential accomplishments of the gentleman' (Jenkins, p. 233).

(C) Jenkins, *Hamlet* (1982).

point (A) A point is a small group of **note**s with a separately identifiable melodic and rhythmic contour (a motivic cell) which can be used as

point

the theme or motive in imitative counterpoint. As Butler puts it, 'A Point is a certain number and order of observable Notes in any one **Part**e, iterated in the same or in divers Partes' (*Principles of Musik*, 1636, p. 71). 'Point', 'fuge' and 'imitation' are synonymous for Morley: 'We call that a Fuge, when one part beginneth, and the other **sing**eth the same, for some **number** of notes (which the first did sing)' (*Introduction*, 1597, p. 76). Today the term is obsolete but in Elizabethan **music** theory and practice it was common. Points were used as much in **instrument**al music as they were in vocal. The **madrigal** was particularly fond of exploiting points whereas the fantasia, according to Morley, was the principal kind of instrumental music in which 'a **musician** taketh a point at his pleasure, and **wrest**eth and turneth it as he list, making either much or little of it according as shall seeme best in his own conceit' (ibid., p. 181).

(B) Though 'point' is used many times by Shakespeare, principally in non-musical contexts, it occasionally has a musical connotation, as for example when Westmorland asks the Archbishop of York why the latter has decided to turn his '**tongue** divine / To a **loud trumpet** and a point of war' (*2H4* 4.1.51–2). The phrase 'point of war', now obsolete, means 'a short phrase **sound**ed on an instrument as a signal' (*OED*, 9a), a martial signal.

When Pericles is finally reunited with his daughter Marina, he exclaims:

> O heavens bless my girl! But hark, what music?
> Tell Helicanus, my Marina, tell him
> O'er, point by point, for yet he seems to dote,
> How sure you are my daughter. But what music?
> (*Per* 5.1.223–6)

To the amazement of other onstage characters, he claims that what he is **hear**ing is the music of the spheres (*musica mundana*), but since this was not supposed to be audible to mortals, it is difficult to establish if music was intended to be **play**ed during a **perform**ance (see 'music' for a review of different positions on this matter). What is important to note here is that the reference to 'point' happens in a scene where music carries out a fundamental role in plot development. Earlier in the same scene Marina sings for Pericles, and soon after this passage the goddess

343

point

Diana appears to him, although any musical signification of Diana is not exploited here.

(C) Kerman, 'Byrd, Tallis, and the Art of Imitation' (1967).

practical music (*musica instrumentalis*) see **music**.

praise (A) '**Sing**ing someone's praise', either literally or metaphorically, was common in Elizabethan literature. Heroic ladies, or the objects of amorous desire, were often the subjects of vocal praising as in:

> Come, shepherd swains . . .
> Sing not a **note** of mirth, but **sigh** with me . . .
> For she is dead, who while she lived was such
> As in her praises none could sing too much.
>   (East, 1618, no. 16)

Elsewhere, Campion's amorous suitor regales his unresponsive 'rosy cheeked' lady: 'Yet will I never cease her praise to sing, / Though she gives no regard' (*Second Booke*, c.1613, no. 20).

In many cases the object of praise is holy or divine as versified by John Hopkins in his metrical version of **Psalm** 47:

> Sing praises to our God, sing praise,
> Sing praises to our King,
> For God is king of all the earth,
> All thankful praises sing.
>   (Mundy, 1594, no. 7)

(B) A religious connotation of praise is intended when Charles exalts Joan's vital role in the recapture of Orléans:

> 'Tis Joan, not we, by whom the day is won;
> For which I will divide my crown with her,
> And all the **priest**s and friars in my realm
> Shall in procession sing her endless praise.
>   (*1H6* 1.6.17–20)

praise

The fact that religious men rather than laymen will be singing her praise indicates the saint-like status that she enjoys. This is even clearer when Charles concludes his speech by claiming that Joan will become the new patron saint of France after she dies: 'No longer on Saint Denis will we cry, / But Joan de Pucelle shall be France's saint' (28–9).

Sonnet 5 of *The Passionate Pilgrim*, whose text is also found in *Love's Labour's Lost* (4.2.105–18), follows the more conventional line of praise to a lady whose love is craved by the poet. The poem concludes with the couplet: 'Celestial as thou art, O, pardon love this wrong, / That sings heaven's praise with such an earthly **tongue**' (13–14). In the poet's eyes, the object of his love has divine qualities, hence praising her acquires a quasi-religious overtone.

See also **Te Deum, psalm, hymn**.

pricksong (A) A fairly common term in Elizabethan times, 'pricksong' indicates notated as opposed to unwritten, improvised **music**. Specifically it means music written on staff notation as opposed to tablature, as the title of Tobias Hume's *The First Part of* **Ayre**s (1605) makes clear: 'some in Tabliture, and some in Pricke-Song'. In an age of widespread illiteracy, written **song**s would be, almost exclusively, **compose**d art music in contrast to the many kinds of improvised folk **ballad**s and popular songs. In the preface 'To the Reader' of his *Second Booke of Ayres* (1601), Robert Jones reminds his readers that the 'prickesong **Note**s' he is using are 'Semibreefe, Minnum, Chrochet, Quaver', in other words the note-values of modern notated music.

Some confusion has arisen over the use of the word 'pricke' in Elizabethan sources. A prick note is a dotted note, that is one that is lengthened by a half. Morley calls this the 'pricke of augmentation' and says that 'the pricke [signifieth] the halfe of the note going before to be holden out' (*Introduction*, 1597, p. 12). This is the meaning of 'you maie hold the first note with a pricke' in Coprario's *Rules How to Compose* (Wilson (ed.), p. 91/c.1610, fol. 11v). It is easy to see how the confusion has arisen. A little later, Coprario talks about 'if they rise in quavers you maie nott use them with a pricke in a song' (Wilson (ed.), p. 92/c. 1610, fol. 13v).

(B) The only use of this term in Shakespeare is found in a speech by Mercutio, who says of Tybalt that *pricksong*

> ... He fights
> as you **sing** a prick-song, keeps **time**, distance, and
> **proportion**; he **rest**s his **minim** rests, one, two, and the
> third in your bosom ...
>
> (*Rom* 2.4.20–3)

Musical metaphors are employed to describe opponents engaged in a fencing context (see 'minim' for a detailed analysis). The use of 'prick-song' with its implications of accuracy, predictability and control of notation stresses the idea of precision characterizing the art of duelling.

(C) Gibbons, *Romeo and Juliet* (1980), p. 142.

Krummel, *English Music Printing* (1975), focuses on English printed music.

Rastall, *The Notation of Western Music* (1998), is a good introduction to music notation.

Wilson (ed.), *A New Way* (2003).

priest (A) Shakespeare confines **sing**ing priests to the Histories. Those priests would be Roman Catholic and monastic. Their singing, therefore, would be monodic **chant**ing.

(B) The Dauphin praises Joan of Arc's recapture of Orléans and promises that 'all the priests and friars in my realm / Shall in procession sing her endless **praise**' (*1H6* 1.6.19–20). The Catholic context of this play makes this allusion all the more appropriate. The same conclusion can be drawn in relation to Henry V's famous soliloquy before the Battle of Agincourt. Praying for a victory against all odds, he reminds God that he has had two chantries built for Richard II, where 'the sad and **solemn** priests / Sing **still** for Richard's soul' (*H5* 4.1.300–1).

The **swan**, often associated with death, is compared to a singing priest in *The Phoenix and Turtle*:

> Let the priest in surplice white,
> That **defunctive music** can,
> Be the death-divining swan,
> Lest the **requiem** lack his right.
>
> (13–16)

The mournful associations of this **bird** make it apt to officiate at the funeral of the phoenix and the turtle dove.

See also **chantry, plainsong**.

(C) Apel, *Gregorian Chant* (1958), discusses the traditional music of the Roman Catholic Church and its plainchant.

proportion (A) A difficult term from **music** theory, 'proportion' is the relationship between sections of a **piece** of music in differing rhythms and tempi. The most common proportional **change** in Renaissance music concerned moving from duple **metre** into a faster triple metre. 'Proportion', therefore, was the speed of the new tempo in relation to the former either in diminution or in augmentation. Morley defines it as:

> either of equalitie or unequalitie. *Proportion of equalitie*, is the comparing of two aequall quantities together ... *Proportion of inequalitie*, is when two things of unequall quantitie are compared together, and is either of the more or lesse inaequalitie. *Proportion of the more inequalitie* is, when a greater number is set over and compared to a lesser, and *in Musicke doeth alwaies signifie diminution. Proportion of the lesse inequalitie* is, where a lesser number is set over, and compared to a greater, as 2/3, *and in Musicke doeth alwaies signifye augmentation.* ... in all proportions the upper number signifieth the semibriefe, and the lower number the stroke, so that as the upper number is to the lower, so is the semibriefe to the stroke.
>
> (*Introduction*, 1597, pp. 27–8)

Rhythm and tempo became clearer with the introduction of the metrical bar-line and the **time** signature. The upper **note** signified the number of **beat**s or strokes in a bar, whose quantity or unit pulse was indicated by the lower number, thus a bar in **minim**s would have a lower number 2, in **crotchet**s it would have a lower number 4, in quavers a lower number 8, etc. A piece in 2/4 would be in duple time whereas a piece in 3/4 or 3/8 would be in triple time.

The theory of proportion originated in Medieval mensural notation and was a complex issue due to the three main metrical categories, namely **Mode**, Prolation and Time. The mathematical basis for the

proportion

system of proportions goes back to the early sixth century and Boethius. The mathematical ratios were used to diminish or increase the value of notes within a section. The whole system depended on the principle of a fixed unit of time, namely the *tactus* or rhythmical beat. Consequently, if the beat is lost proportion cannot be kept.

The idea that proportion contained quantity or '**numbers**' and depended on a regular beat or **accent** did not escape Campion's attention in his treatise on quantitative verse in neo-classical English poetry, his *Observations in the Art of English Poesie* (1602), in which musical parallels and interrelationships are cited to reinforce his argument: 'The world is made by Simmetry and proportion, and is in that respect compared to Musick, and Musick to Poetry ... What musick can there be where there is no proportion observed? (Vivian (ed.), p. 35).

Campion knew that musical rhythm was governed by the relationship of the shorter notes to the longer and that in classical verse a similar relationship was thought to exist between long and short syllables. That durational principle **govern**ed the scansion or metre of a line of poetry. Such a system, Campion asserts, could be applied beneficially to English poetry in place of accentual **rhyme**d doggerel. This theory was effectively dismissed by Daniel Samuel in his *A Defence of Ryme*, published the following year.

(B) A wording similar to the concluding line of Campion's passage quoted above is found in *Richard II*, which was published in 1597, five years before Campion's *Observations*. Richard soliloquizes about the futility of human life before being murdered:

> (*The music **play**s*). Music do I **hear**?
> Ha, ha, keep time! How sour **sweet** music is
> When time is broke, and no proportion kept!
> So is it in the music of men's lives.
> (5.5.41–4)

As in music, loss of **harmony** in life has extremely negative consequences. In Richard's case, it ultimately causes his death.

The concept of proportion is also found in a metaphor which likens fencing to music. Mercutio says of Tybalt:

proportion

> ... O, he's the
> courageous captain of compliments. He fights
> as you **sing** a **prick-song**, keeps time, distance, and
> proportion; he **rest**s his minim rests, one, two, and the
> third in your bosom ...
>
> (*Rom* 2.4.19–23)

Rhythm and tempo have to be scrupulously observed for duelling to be successful. Proportion has to be kept by following the time-value represented by the minim. (See 'minim' for a detailed discussion of this passage).

See also **degree, mood**.

(C) Apel, *The Notation of Polyphonic Music* (1953), pp. 145–95, considers the use and notation of proportions in music.

Attridge, *Well-weighed Syllables* (1974), is an excellent account of the so-called quantitative movement in English poetry.

Campion, *Observations in the Art of English Poesy*, ed. Vivian (1966).

de Ford, 'Tempo Relationships between Duple and Triple Time in the Sixteenth Century' (1995).

psalm (A) The texts of the psalms come from the Hebrew Scriptures of the Bible known as the Old Testament. Often referred to as the Psalms of David, the Book of Psalms or Psalter was translated into Greek (the Septuagint) in the early Middle Ages and thence into Latin (the Vulgate). It contained 150 items or sacred poems. Early English translations, such as Coverdale's (1535), were based on the Vulgate.

Musical settings of psalms had been used in religious worship from earliest times and plainchant psalms were common in Roman Catholic worship in the Middle Ages. During the last years of Henry VIII's reign and those of Edward VI (1547–53) the effects of the Protestant Reformation were felt increasingly in England. This meant that much of the musical practice of Roman Catholicism was swept away. Instead of **chant**ing psalms, vernacular translations in metrical **rhyme** were introduced. One of the first publications was Myles Coverdale's *Goostly psalmes and spirituall* **song**es *drawn out of the holy Scripture* (c.1539). It contained thirteen metrical psalms as well as metrical versions of

psalm

canticles, the Lord's Prayer, the Creed and German and Latin **hymn**s. Another early collection of metrical psalms was Robert Crowley's *Psalter of David newely translated into Englysh **metre*** (1549). It was the first complete English metrical psalter and contained **tune**s harmonized in **part**s similar to the Lutheran collections of *geistliche Lieder*. It was not, however, successful. Thomas Sternhold's small selection of metrical psalms, issued in 1549, did gain favour, especially at court. During Mary's reign (1553–8) the Latin rite was restored and metrical psalms were cultivated on the continent. Sternhold and Hopkins' famous psalter was published in Geneva in 1556. Elizabeth's accession to the throne in 1558 saw the return of the English rite and the Queen's Injunctions of 1559 allowed the resumption of metrical psalm **sing**ing. The first English edition of the Sternhold and Hopkins psalter was published by John Day in 1560. The first complete edition was published in 1562.

The singing of metrical psalms became increasingly widespread in cathedrals and churches throughout England coinciding with the publication each year of a new edition of 'Sternhold and Hopkins'. The impact on religious worship of the return of Puritan refugees, notably Dutch, was significant, especially in the 1560s. In 1559, Jan Utenhove, the great Dutch psalmist, came back to London from exile in Emden, where he had been forced to flee during the Marian years. His early psalm paraphrases had been published in London by Steven Mijerdman during the Edwardian era and were intended for the exiled Dutch Protestant Church in London. On his return, subsequent psalters by Utenhove were published by John Day in London. The complete edition, *De psalmen Davidis, in Nederlandsicher sangsryme* was published in 1566, the year after Utenhove's death.

The tunes of the metrical psalms were basically simple, syllabic, easily sung lines. They were published either as single-line (monophonic) tunes or harmonized in four parts in homorhythmic chordal fashion. In contrast to the more florid settings of polyphonic cathedral **music**, they reflected the simplicity and austerity of the Puritan creed. During Elizabeth's reign a large number of books of metrical psalms were published. Their aim was accessibility to a large cross section of the population. Thomas Este published his *The Whole Booke of Psalmes* in 1592 so that 'the unskilfull with small practice may attaine to sing that part, which is fittest for their **voice**'. William Barley's *The Whole Booke of Psalmes* (1599) repeated the accessibility blurb and was printed in a

psalm

cheap pocket-sized version. Richard Alison's *The Psalmes of David in Metre* (1599) are musically very straightforward.

(B) Interestingly, Shakespeare mentions 'psalm' in light-hearted contexts, for instance when Mistress Ford remarks that Falstaff's words 'do no more adhere and keep place together than the / hundred Psalms to the tune of "**Green-sleeves**" ' (*Wiv* 2.1.62–3). This comment appears in Folio (there is no such reference in the two quarto versions antedating Folio) and has evoked a debate in the scholarly community, since editors have interpreted, and sometimes emended, 'hundred' in different ways. It is common knowledge that there are 150 psalms – no Elizabethan psalters printed a selection of 100 psalms. This has led Wells and Taylor to emend the phrase to 'the hundred and fifty psalms' (p. 490). This makes no sense because each psalm had its own tune and it would be meaningless to compare the psalms as a totality with one tune. Other scholars simply emend 'hundred' to 'hundredth'. In the eighteenth century, Rowe adopted this reading as did Quiller Couch and Dover Wilson in their 1921 Cambridge edition of *The Merry Wives of Windsor*. Oliver, on the other hand, keeps 'hundred' on the grounds that Rowe's interpretation in part spoils Mistress Ford's joke since there is 'even less likelihood of all hundred (or so) psalms being sung or fitted to the lively tune of "Greensleeves" ' (p. 40). But Oliver's emendation ignores the fact that there are 150 psalms.

From a musical point of view the obvious solution is to emend 'hundred' to 'hundredth'. Mistress Ford's remark has an ironic intention: having just realized that Falstaff is trying to seduce both her and Mistress Page, Mistress Ford implies that his promises of constancy to each of the two women sound as inappropriate as the singing of the 'Old Hundredth' psalm tune to the tune of the popular **love song**, 'Greensleeves'. The 'Old Hundredth' is a dour slowish tune in four-square rhythm with a **solemn** descending four-**note** pattern at its beginning whereas 'Greensleeves' is a sprightly compound duple-**metre** tune with an ascending **melody** at its opening. In other words, the tunes could hardly be more dissimilar. The moralistic opposition between psalms and **ballad**s is neatly expressed on the title page of William Daman's *The Psalmes of David in English meter* (1579), where psalms are 'to the use of the godly Christians for recreating themselves, in stede of fond and unseemely Ballades'.

In *1 Henry IV*, 2.4.133 'psalm' is used by Falstaff (see '**weaver**' for a

psalm

detailed comment) and alludes to the reputation of weavers as psalm singers. In *The Winter's Tale*, the rustic atmosphere of the sheep-shearing feast is created by the three-part song intoned by the shearers. According to the Clown, most of their voices belong to the middle and low range ('**mean**s and **base**s', 4.3.43), except for that of a Puritan who has a **high**-pitched voice but refuses to sing and **dance** for the sake of entertainment. Instead, he 'sings psalms to **horn-pipe**s' (44).

(C) Frost, *English & Scottish Psalm & Hymn Tunes* (1953), contains bibliographical details of Elizabethan publications and the music of the psalm tunes.

Kümin, 'Masses, Morris and Metrical Psalms: Music in the English Parish, c.1400–1600' (2001).

Le Huray, *Music and the Reformation in England* (1978), ch. 11, concentrates on the metrical psalm in England.

Leaver, *'Goostly Psalmes and Spirituell Songes'* (1991).

Oliver, *The Merry Wives of Windsor* (1971).

Wells and Taylor, *William Shakespeare: The Complete Works* (1986).

psaltery (A) The psaltery was a simple plucked **string**ed **instrument** of the zither family in which the wire strings were laid out horizontally in a flat wooden box. The box could take many different shapes. The most common was the triangular form, but there were wing shapes, irregular triangular shapes and also quadrangular forms. A distinctive kind, known as the *istrumento di porco*, was essentially triangular with concave cheeks, the so-called 'pig's head' shape. The psaltery was popular throughout Europe in the Middle Ages but was supplanted by the harpsichord during the sixteenth century.

(B) In *Coriolanus*, a messenger notes that Rome is pervaded by a festive mood when its citizens are informed that Coriolanus has decided to spare the city, thanks to his mother's intercession:

> . . . Why, hark you!
> The **trumpet**s, **sackbut**s, psalteries, and **fife**s,
> **Tabor**s and **cymbal**s, and the shouting Romans,
> Make the sun **dance**. Hark you!
>
> (5.4.48–51)

psaltery

This is the only instance in the Shakespeare canon where psalteries are mentioned. The messenger's remark was intended to bring the audience's attention to the **music** and **sound**s which were expected to be achieved from behind the tiring-house walls, as the stage direction '*A shout within*' (5.4.51.SD) suggests. The liveliness characterising this scene is short-lived, as the play ends with the indication that a dead **march** (with its sombre connotations) be sounded while Coriolanus' dead body is brought off stage.

It is interesting to note that, even if it appears in a pagan context, this passage **echo**es Psalm 150:

Praise ye the Lord . . .
   Praise him with the sound of the trumpet: praise him with the psaltery and **harp**.
   Praise him with the timbrel and dance: praise him with stringed instruments and **organ**s.
   Praise him upon the **loud** cymbals: praise him upon the **high** sounding cymbals.

(verses 1; 3–5)

Q

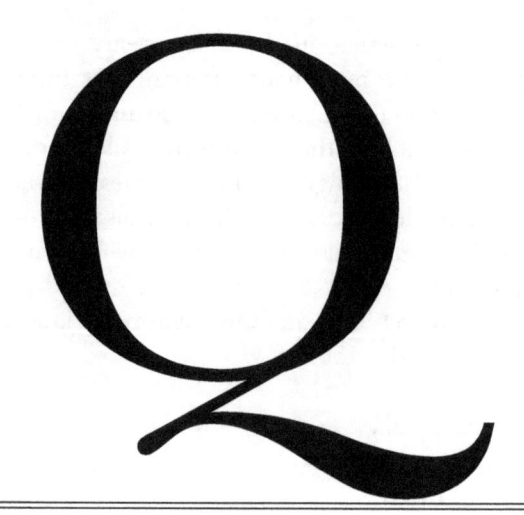

quier see **choir**.

quire see **choir**.

R

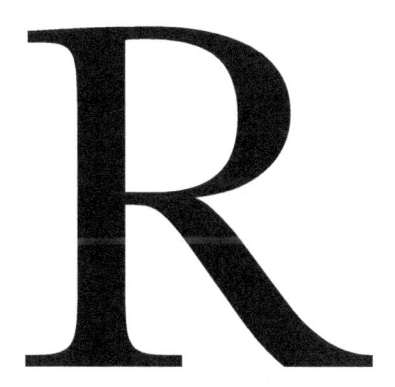

rattle (A) There are a number of different kinds of rattle classified under two main types, namely the ratchet or cog rattle and the shaken rattle. The ratchet is a wooden **instrument** with a blade constructed so that the free end 'rattles' against the teeth of a wooden cogwheel. A **noise** is made by swinging the rattle around. According to Baines, ratchet rattles were used by night watchmen and outcasts in Medieval times. Shaken rattles make a less brittle **sound**. They use seeds, shells or teeth to make the noise. One common type was the dried pig's bladder with small pebbles, dried seeds or peas inside which, when shaken on a stick by the 'Fool', was a common sight at May Day festivities and Eastertide religious ceremonies. The rattle is often one of the first instruments a child comes in contact with and as a simple, noise-making instrument dates back to prehistoric times. The essential defining characteristic of the rattle is the noise it makes in contrast, for example, to the 'jingle' or 'ding' of **bell**s, which in some contexts (e.g. metal pellet bells) could be counted as rattles.

(B) In *The Merry Wives of Windsor*, Mrs Page explains her plan to ridicule Falstaff: some children dressed as fairies and elves, with 'rattles in their hands' (4.4.52), will ambush him after **sing**ing a 'diffused song' (55). Like the instruction to *'burthern dispersedly'* (*Tmp* 1.2.381.SD) the stage direction 'diffused', with reference to the song 'Come unto these yellow sands' in *The Tempest*, means 'divided among [the children] as a kind of **part**-song' (Oliver, p. 120).

rattle

Sounds are described as 'rattling' on four occasions, for instance when Antony orders his followers to celebrate his victory against Caesar by mixing powerful martial sounds with more light-hearted ones: 'With **brazen din** blast you the city's **ear**, / Make mingle with our rattling **taborine**s' (*Ant* 4.8.36–7). In *King John*, the Bastard defies the Dauphin to battle. His speech is centred on the image of the martial **drum**s being struck, and plays on two different meanings of '**beat**' ('strike an instrument' and 'defeat'). The sound of the drum is then compared to the rattling **thunder**:

> Indeed your drums, being beaten, will cry out;
> And so shall you, being beaten. Do but start
> An **echo** with the **clamor** of thy drum,
> And even at hand a drum is ready brac'd
> That shall reverberate all as **loud** as thine.
> Sound but another, and another shall
> (As loud as thine) rattle the welkin's ear,
> And mock the deep-mouth'd thunder . . .
>
> (5.2.166–73)

The noise of thunder is also described as 'rattling' by Prospero. He lists the magic powers he is about to renounce, among which is his ability to give lightning 'to the dread rattling thunder' (*Tmp* 5.1.44). In *Antony and Cleopatra*, before Cleopatra commits suicide, she remembers Antony:

> . . . His **voice** was propertied
> As all the **tune**d spheres, and that to friends;
> But when he meant to quail and shake the orb,
> He was as rattling thunder . . .
>
> (5.2.83–6)

The contrast between the loud noise of thunder and the **harmony** of heavenly **music** (the music of the spheres, also known as *musica mundana*) appropriately evokes opposite sides of Antony's personality.

(C) Baines, *The Oxford Companion to Musical Instruments* (1992).
Oliver, *The Merry Wives of Windsor* (1971).

raven see **bird**.

ravish (A) When associated with **music**, 'ravish' can have both philosophical and sensual meanings. With the first it refers to the power that music has to affect the emotions, to transport the soul (to heaven) or to overwhelm with passion. Campion describes the ecstatic power of music to ravish in:

> Follow your Saint, follow with **accent**s **sweet**;
> Haste you, sad **note**s, fall at her flying feet.
> There wrapped in cloud of sorrow, pity move,
> And tell the ravisher of my soul I perish for her love.
> But if she scorns my never-ceasing pain.
> Then burst with **sigh**ing in her sight, and ne'er return again.
>
> All that I sung still to her **praise** did tend.
> Still she was first, still she my **song**s did end.
> Yet she my love and music both doth fly,
> The music that her **echo** is, and beauty's sympathy.
> Then let my notes pursue her scornful flight;
> It shall suffice that they were breathed, and died for her delight.
> (1601, no. 10)

On a sensual level, music had the power to ravish the senses, to give delight and intense pleasure as Barnfield claims in his reference to Dowland's **lute play**ing. His 'heavenly **touch** / Upon the lute doth ravish human sense' (*PP* Sonnet 8, 5–6).

(B) Mortimer comments on the beauty of Glendower's daughter and on the **charm** of the language she speaks using a musical metaphor:

> . . thy **tongue**
> Makes Welsh as sweet as ditties highly penn'd,
> Sung by a fair queen in a summer's bow'r,
> With ravishing **division**, to her lute.
> (*1H4* 3.1.205–8)

The embellishment that the practice of division entailed has a powerful

ravish

effect on him. Mortimer's theoretical exposition is followed by practical music on the stage when the woman '*sings a Welsh song*' (3.1.244.SD).

The smug personality of Armado is highlighted by the King of Navarre:

> ... Our court you know is haunted
> With a refined traveller of Spain,
> A man in all the world's new fashion planted,
> That hath a mint of phrases in his brain;
> One who the music of his own vain tongue
> Doth ravish like **enchant**ing **harmony**.
> (*LLL* 1.1.162–7)

Armado can only delight himself with the 'music of his own vain tongue', but fails to achieve the same effect on those who surround him. That the King's opinion of the Spaniard is anything but high is confirmed by his intention to make him his **minstrel** (a term which had acquired pejorative connotations in Shakespeare's day).

re The name 're' is the second **note** of the Renaissance hexachord. See **ut**.

Recheat see **horn**.

rebec (A) The rebec was common in Western art and folk **music** of the Middle Ages and Renaissance. It was a smallish bowed **instrument** with between one and five gut **string**s, classed as a bowed **lute** or **fiddle**. Made from a single piece of wood, it had a vaulted back and tapered from its body to the neck. Its **play**ing position varied according to geographical custom. In England and in Northern Europe it was played up at the shoulder or on the chest, like a fiddle. In Southern Europe and North Africa it was held in a down position in the lap, more like a **viol da gamba**.

The rebec is more easily identifiable with Medieval music, especially from the fourteenth century onwards, than it is with the later Renaissance. In the seventeenth century it was superseded by the Kit, a kind of narrow violin, and already known in the sixteenth century as the reference to '**Harp**es, lutes, kyttes, basens and drommes' in *The Cristen State of Matrimony* (1543) suggests.

In art music, the rebec is sometimes specified in sixteenth-century instrumental and vocal **consort** music. Like the fiddle, it was also used to accompany art **song**s and **dance**s. Rebecs are listed in court inventories. They were **part** of the incidental music, contrasted with the **loud** ceremonial music, played at major court banquets, as the Venetian secretary, Sagudino, recounts of an Henrician feast (July, 1517): 'In the centre of the hall there was a stage on which were some boys, some of whom sang, and others played the lute, rebeck and harpsichord' (Sanuto). The rebec was often one of the instruments depicted being played by professional Medieval and Renaissance **minstrel**s, as the well known carving on the Minstrels' Pillar at St Mary's Church, Beverley (E. Yorks) (post 1520) indicates. In folk or rustic music, the iconographical and literary evidence shows that rebecs were played at village revels together with **wind** instruments such as **pipe, horn** or **bagpipe**.

(B) 'Rebec' is used only once in the Shakespeare canon. In *Romeo and Juliet*, one of the **musicians** dismissed after the discovery of the apparently dead body of Juliet on her wedding day to Paris is called Hugh Rebeck (4.5.133). This part of the scene has several musical puns which seem to reveal that Hugh Rebeck and his fellow musicians are not particularly sophisticated (see also '**catling**', '**silver**' and '**soundpost**').

(C) Brown, 'The Trecento Fiddle and Its Bridges' (1989).
Downie, 'The Rebec: An Orthographic and Iconographic Study' (1981).
Holman, *Four and Twenty Fiddlers* (1993), esp. ch. 3 'Mynstrelles with Straunge Soundes'.
Sanuto, *I diarii* (1889).

record (A) As a verb, 'record' is most frequently found in connection with **bird**s **sing**ing, as in: 'Now birds record new **harmony**, / And trees do **whistle melody**' (from Thomas Watson, 'With fragrant flowers we strew the way', *Entertainment . . . at Elvetham*, 1591); or: 'Each chirping bird records a piping **voice**' (Weelkes, 1597, no. 1).

Essentially the word means 'to sing' but a sense of recall and repetition in the act of singing is further implied. It can also be applied to

record

humans, as in: '**Sound** out, my voice, with **pleasant tune**s recording / The new delight that love to me inspireth' (Kirbye, 1597, no.9)

(B) Gower, who acts as **Chorus** in *Pericles*, introduces the fourth act by explaining that Marina '. . . hath gain'd / Of education all the **grace**' (Pro., 8–9). He narrates of when

> . . . to th' **lute**
> She sung, and made the night-bird mute
> That still records with moan . . .
> (25–7)

The **nightingale**'s **woeful song** was surpassed in excellence by Marina's lute **play**ing: as a result, the bird had to stop singing. Reference to the nightingale's song is also found in *The Two Gentlemen of Verona*, when Valentine is yearning for Silvia in the forest. He observes:

> Here can I sit alone, unseen of any,
> And to the nightingale's complaining **note**s
> Tune my distresses and record my woes.
> (5.4.4–6)

The proneness of the lover to indulge in his feeling of melancholy and unfulfilment is encapsulated in Valentine's use of 'record', which evokes the idea of repetition.

recorder (A) The English name for this very popular Renaissance **pipe** derives from the supposition that it was the easiest and best **instrument** for 'recording' a **tune**, recording in the sense of remembering or reiterating. A **minstrel** could be a 'recorder', a rememberer or reminderer, and thus the pipe he **play**ed upon became his recorder. The earliest occurrence of the term in England was reported in the late fourteenth century and first appears in English literature in the early fifteenth century in Lydgate's poem, *The Fall of Princes* (c.1438): 'Pan, god off Kynde, with his pipes sevene / Off recorderis fond first the melodies'. On the continent the instrument was known as a kind of **flute**, e.g. *fleute a neufte trous, flauto diritto* or *Blockflöte*.

Renaissance recorders (the best collection is housed in the

Kunsthistorisches Museum, Vienna) differ from their successors, the multi-jointed Baroque recorders, in that they were turned from one piece of wood. They characteristically had six tuned (finger) holes, whereas the Baroque recorder had seven. They made a reasonably full, without being **loud**, warm **sound**, ideally suited to **consort performing**, and said (e.g. by Girolamo Cardano, *De Musica*, c.1546) to relate most closely to vocal sonority. This would partly explain why so much of the recorder consort repertory was originally vocal polyphony.

The standard recorder consort in the early sixteenth century was **bass**, two tenors and a **treble**. By the later part of the century this had increased to five (e.g. Norwich 1584–5 five-player consort described as 'being a whole **noise**'), and more generally six instruments. The consorts attached to the royal courts comprised six players. The recorder may also have substituted occasionally for the (transverse) flute in mixed consorts, as the Matthew Holmes consort books (Cambridge University Library Dd. 5. 21) of c.1595 attest.

The surviving repertory of these recorder consorts (e.g. Cambridge Fitzwilliam MS 734) suggests that their main **music** was arrangements of **dance**s, motets and **madrigal**s in four, five, and six **part**s. Jeronimo Bassano's fantasias (c.1580) for recorder consort demonstrate a more elaborate style of original recorder music which may have been played in professional circles.

The recorder was popular with amateur players as a well as professional **musician**s. Among the aristocracy, it was preferred by ladies; gentlemen may have thought it unseemly when compared with the **lute** and **viol**, not least because it was played from the mouth. Castiglione warns that it should only be played in private surroundings, especially when ladies are present.

In Renaissance iconography, the recorder lost its Medieval heavenly symbolism (**angel**s playing in pairs around the Blessed Virgin Mary) and became associated with sexual pleasures and relationships. The recorder was often employed to depict 'Vanitas', the sensuous pleasures of worldly being. In the Elizabethan theatre, recorders are often part of supernatural or heavenly symbolism, and are sometimes associated with death. One curious extension of this, noted by Lasocki, is their presence at mock funerals (when the deceased later recovers) in Jacobean theatre, for example in Marston's *Sophonisba* (1606) and Middleton's *A Chaste Maid in Cheapside* (1613).

recorder

(B) In the Shakespeare canon, '***Still*** *music of records*' is required in *The Two Noble Kinsmen* (5.1.136.SD). This stage direction underlines Emilia's plea at the altar of Diana that, between her two suitors Palamon and Arcite, the one who loves her more should conquer her. The **soft** sound of the recorders during the first part of her speech is in contrast to the **harsh**er '*sudden **twang** of instruments*' (5.1.168.SD) heard just before a rose falls from a rose tree – a sign that the goddess has been listening to Emilia's prayer.

Commenting on the Prologue to 'Pyramus and Thisbe', performed by the mechanicals at her wedding, Hippolyta compares Quince's efforts as an actor to those of a child learning to play the recorder: 'Indeed he hath play'd on this prologue like / a child on a recorder – a sound, but not in government' (*MND* 5.1.122–3). An unskilled musician would not be able to **govern** – i.e. play with a certain degree of skill – the instrument. Similarly, Quince's clumsy attempts at acting disclose that he is an amateur.

After the staging of the 'mousetrap' by the itinerant actors in *Hamlet*, most courtiers leave the stage with the upset Claudius. Hamlet, who remains behind with Horatio, asks for music: 'Come, some music! Come, the recorders!' (3.2.291). The players enter with recorders (3.2.344.SD) while Rosencrantz and Guildenstern are urging the Prince to justify his behaviour to his mother. Hamlet asks Guildenstern to play on one of the recorders. When the latter protests that he has 'not the **skill**' (3.2.362), Hamlet exclaims:

> Why, look you now, how unworthy a thing
> you make of me! You would play upon me, you would
> seem to know my **stop**s, you would pluck out the
> heart of my mystery, you would sound me from my
> lowest **note** to the top of my **compass**; and there is
> much music, excellent **voice**, in this little **organ**, yet
> cannot you make it **speak**. 'Sblood, do you think I am
> easier to be play'd on than a pipe? Call me what
> instrument you will, though you **fret** me, yet you
> cannot play upon me.
>
> (3.2.363–72)

Through this musical metaphor Hamlet discloses his total distrust for his school friends and his knowledge that they are in league with Claudius.

The verbal imagery of this speech is reinforced in **perform**ance by the presence of the recorder as a visual signifier.

(C) Baines, *Woodwind Instruments and their History* (1977), ch. 10 'The Sixteenth Century and the Consorts'.
    Castiglione, *The Book of the Courtier* (1528).
    Dessen and Thomson, *A Dictionary of Stage Directions* (1999), pp. 177–8.
    Griscom and Lasocki, *The Recorder: A Guide to Writings about the Instrument for Players and Researchers* (1994).
    Hunt, *The Recorder and Its Music* (1977).
    Lasocki, 'Professional Recorder Players in England, 1540–1740' (1983); and 'The Recorder in the Elizabethan, Jacobean and Caroline Theater' (1984).
    Thomson, John (ed.), *The Cambridge Companion to the Recorder* (1995).

reed see **voice**.

rehearsal see **rehearse**.

rehearse (A) Specifically in **music** and drama, 'rehearse' means 'to practise' or 'run through' beforehand, usually several times, in an informal or private environment in preparation for a more formal uninterrupted public **perform**ance. It can also mean 'recite or speak aloud' (*OED*, 1a).

(B) In *A Midsummer Night's Dream*, Shakespeare uses 'rehearse' and 'rehearsal' with the former meaning in relation to the mechanicals' preparation of their production of 'Pyramus and Thisbe'. Titania may also have this meaning in mind when she exhorts her followers to bless the house of the newly weds:

> First, rehearse your **song** by **rote**,
> To each word a warbling **note**.
> Hand in hand, with fairy **grace**,
> Will we sing, and bless this place.
> (5.1.397–400)

rehearse

In an age when professional singers could perform complicated music at sight without much rehearsal, those who had to take time in rehearsing, presumably would not be as **skill**ed.

relish (A) An ornament common in **lute** and keyboard **music** and sometimes applied to vocal music. It was a simple or complicated trill depending on whether a single or double relish was indicated. It was regarded as an attractive **grace** and in its application enhanced the appeal of the music, as Samuel Daniel reminds us: 'If any pleasing relish here I use / Then judge the world her beauty gives the same' (*Delia*, no. 57).

Birds, we discover from contemporary literature, are particularly adept at **sing**ing relishes: 'Come, blessed bird, and with thy sugared relish / Help our declining **choir** now to embellish' (Morley, 1601, no. 24).

(B) When Speed lists the **skill**s that Valentine has acquired as a lover, he observeves that he has learnt 'to relish a **love-song**, like a **robin**-redbreast' (*TGV* 2.1.20). Another reference to the graceful singing of birds is found in a more serious context, after Lucrece has been raped and is beginning to meditate suicide. In her despair, she warns the birds as follows: 'Relish your **nimble note**s to pleasing **ear**s, / Distress likes **dump**s when **time** is kept with tears' (*Luc* 1126–7).

(C) Grove Online, 'Ornament'.
Mace, *Musick's Monument* (1676), contains an explication of the relish for the lute.

report (A) In **music** 'report' can have various shades of meaning from the repetition of a **note** or musical phrase by another (e.g. **bird**s **sing**ing to each other), a response in **sound** (e.g. to an **echo**), to simply an undefined musical **noise** stimulated by some occurrence. Samuel Daniel, for example, invokes the sense of response in his sonnet 'Like as the **lute** delights':

> Her **touch** doth cause the **warble** of the sound,
> Which here I yield in lamentable wise,

> A wailing **descant** on the **sweet**est **ground**,
> Whose due reports gives honour to her eyes.
> (*Delia*, no. 57)

It can be more specifically related to echo as in: 'Ay me, Echo, sweetly sing, / Nymphs and swains reporting' (East, 1610, no. 1).

(B) When Queen Margaret, the Duchess of York and Queen Elizabeth curse Richard, his reaction is decisive:

> A **flourish, trumpet**s! **strike alarum, drum**s!
> . . .
> Either be patient and treat me fair,
> Or with the **clamor**ous report of war
> Thus will I drown your exclamations.
> (*R3* 4.4.149; 152–4)

He hopes that the reverberating military sounds can overpower the women's **voice**s which are revealing unwelcome truths. However, the three women are not intimidated by these powerful aural signals.

In *Richard II*, the dying John of Gaunt voices his opinion about the pitiful condition of the realm. He believes that the King will listen to him as 'the **tongue**s of dying men / Enforce attention like deep **harmony**' (2.1.5–6). These lines initiate a series of musical and sound conceits, culminating in Gaunt's hope that his 'death's sad tale may yet undeaf his [the King's] **ear**' (16). His brother York dashes his hopes by developing the musical imagery:

> No, it is **stop**p'd with other flattering sounds,
> As **praise**s, of whose taste the wise are fond,
> Lascivious **metre**s, to whose venom sound
> The open ear of youth doth always listen;
> Report of fashions in proud Italy,
> Whose manners still our tardy, apish nation
> Limps after in **base** imitation.
> (17–23)

Whilst 'report' here applies to news of fashion, the musical context intensifies its meaning to include 'imitation'. There are subtle plays

report

both on the phonetic and semantic level of these carefully chosen words. For instance, the verb 'stop' reminds us of the **stop**s of an **instrument** such as a **recorder** or an **organ**, and the adjective 'base' calls to mind the musical term **bass**. Hence, 'report' also acquires a musical meaning. There may be an oblique reference to the influence of Italian music in England, in particular to the **madrigal**, which had spread throughout Europe during the sixteenth century and had been imported into England in the 1580s. It may be significant that Shakespeare, out of sympathy with the vogue for the madrigal, refers to the term only once in his plays (see 'madrigal').

(C) Kerman, *The Elizabethan Madrigal* (1962).

Roche, *The Madrigal* (1990), ch. 8, examines the effect of the Italian madrigal in England.

requiem (A) A requiem was a special mass sung at funerals, commemorations of the dead or at certain other **solemn** occasions, public or private. The name derives from the Introit: 'Requiem aeternam dona eis, Domine' ('Grant them eternal rest, O Lord'). Each section of the Requiem mass has its own plainchant **melody**. Those in use in the sixteenth century were evocative and of poignant beauty.

(B) In *Hamlet*, the importance of the requiem as a Christian rite of passage between death and afterlife is clear from the doctor's recommendation that the burial ceremony for Ophelia is not formal:

> We should profane the service of the dead
> To **sing** sage requiem and such rest to her
> As to peace-parted souls.
> (5.1.236–8)

Ophelia's burial is conducted with 'maimed rites' because of the ambivalence of her death. Though the gravedigger reports that Christian burial has been allowed, the doctor is clearly still anxious about the legitimacy of the ceremony.

The only other instance in which this word is used by Shakespeare is in *The Phoenix and Turtle*, when the **swan** is exhorted to celebrate the funeral of the phoenix and the turtle dove:

requiem

> Let the **priest** in surplice white,
> That **defunctive music** can,
> Be the death-divining swan,
> Lest the requiem lack his right.
> (13–16)

The swan was commonly associated with death, and is therefore the most appropriate **bird** to officiate at such a sad occasion.
　See also **dirge**.

(C) Luce, 'The Requiem Mass from its Plainsong Beginnings to 1600' (1958).

rest (A) Morley defines 'rests' as 'signified the whole length of the **note**s in **silence**' (*Introduction*, 1597, p. 12). They can vary in length according to the context and structural demands of the **music**. In **song**, words often determine where rests occur. In **instrument**al music, form and texture tend to control silences. In notated music, they are indicated by signs with specific durational meanings.

(B) This term is used in its musical nuance in *Romeo and Juliet* when Mercutio alludes to the mensural quality of the pause in his explanation of Tybalt's fencing skills: '[he] keeps **time**, distance, and / **proportion**, he rests his **minim** rests' (2.4.21–2). (See 'minim' for a detailed commentary.) In *Hamlet* 'rest' is used twice in the space of two lines when the Prince is dying (5.2.358; 360), with a pun on the lack of **sound** engendered in a 'rest'. (See 'silence' for a detailed commentary.)

retrait see **retreat**.

retreat (A) The retreat is a military signal usually **sound**ed by **trumpet**s during or at the end of an engagement. In his famous multi-movement work *The Battell* for keyboard, William Byrd has 'The retreat' (MLNB no. 4) as the last movement. It is a simple **piece** with a slow four-**note** descending 'trumpet' figure repeated over a static **bass** followed by quicker scalic figuration, presumably representing the retreat itself:

retreat

[musical notation]

etc.

According to Gervase Markham, the retreat ('Goe to your Colours' as he calls it) is one of the trumpet 'soundings' (I2v) with which the soldier must be familiar. It 'is a Retrayt for the Horseman, and brings him off being ingaged, for as oft as he heares it, he must retire and goe backe to his Colour' (I3r).

(B) There are several stage directions for 'retreat' in Shakespeare's drama, mainly in his history plays and tragedies. During a performance in the Elizabethan playhouse, this and other military sound effects would have worked as an aural metonymy for events that could not be represented on the stage on a full scale. An excellent example is the following stage direction:

> **Alarum**. *Enter Richard and Richmond; they fight; Richard is slain. Then, retreat being sounded, enter Richmond, Derby, bearing the crown, with other lords, etc.*
>
> (*R3* 5.5.OSD)

The alarum followed by the retreat would have been enough to convey the unfolding of the Battle of Bosworth field to an early modern audience. A similar synecdochic quality is found in *King John*, where the end of the Battle of Angiers is conveyed through '*Alarums, excursions, retreat*' (3.3.OSD).

As with other sound and **music** effects, stage directions can specify that the retreat be sounded from within the tiring-house (see Introduction for an analysis of the areas used for music and sound effects). This happens for instance in *King Lear*, when we witness the battle between Cordelia's and her sisters' armies through the perspective of the blind

Gloucester: '*Alarum and retreat within*' (5.2.4.SD). The stage direction is followed by Edgar's narration of Lear and Cordelia's defeat and imprisonment.

After the indication '*A retreat is sounded*' (*1H4* 5.4.158.SD), a wounded Prince Harry observes triumphantly that 'the trumpet sounds retreat, the day is our[s]' (159). Quite a different **mood** is evoked by Bedford to his fellow English soldiers in Orléans: 'Here sound retreat, and cease our hot pursuit' (*1H6* 2.2.3), followed by the stage direction '*Retreat*' (2.2.3.SD).

See also **flourish, parley, sennet, tucket**.

(C) Dessen and Thomson, *A Dictionary of Stage Directions* (1999), pp. 179–80.

Markham, *The Souldiers Accidence* (1625).

rhyme see **ditty**.

ring see **bell**.

robin see **bird**.

rote (A) In his *An Introduction to the Skill of Musick* (1674), John Playford mentions learning 'to **play** [music] by rote or **ear** without Book' (II, p. 110). Learning **music** by rote implies the mechanical repetition of a **piece** for the sake of memorizing it rather than understanding it. Playford may also be suggesting that learning by rote is best suited to the musically illiterate. In an age when professional **sing**ers could **perform** complicated polyphonic or ensemble music at sight without much **rehearsal**, those who had to take time learning the **note**s by repetition, presumably would not be as **skill**ed.

Contemporary lyric poems confirm that learning by rote was best suited to the simple minded:

> Upon a hill the bonny boy,
> **Sweet** Thyrsis, sweetly played . . .
> His **pipe** and he could not agree,

rote

> For Milla was his note.
> This silly pipe could never get
> This lovely name by rote.
> (Weelkes, 1608, no. 5)

(B) 'Rote' is used by Shakespeare in a musical sense in *A Midsummer Night's Dream*, when Titania instructs the fairies on how to bless the house of the newly-weds:

> First, **rehearse** your song by rote,
> To each word a warbling note.
> Hand in hand, with fairy **grace**,
> Will we **sing**, and bless this place.
> (5.1.397–400)

As is often the case, music and **dance** are connected in early modern drama. Since the fairies are not professional singers and since they are performing as an ensemble, they have to rehearse their song by rote.

(C) Playford, *An Introduction to the Skill of Musick* (1674).

rough see **music**.

round (A) The round is a kind of **song** for three or more **voice**s in which a single vocal line or **melody** is repeated at regular metrical intervals to form a polyphonic unity (i.e. a song in **parts**). Unlike the **catch**, the melody is a continuous unbroken line. The melody is usually repeated several times and the **piece** comes to an end when all the voices have completed the melody.

Curiously, Morley does not include 'round' in his *Introduction* (1597), although he defines 'canon' at some length and refers briefly to 'catch'. The English term 'round' comes from the early sixteenth century. According to Stevens, the first use of the word is found in BL Add. MS 31922: 'Now let vs syng this round all thre / sent george graunt hym the victory' (fol. 103). In this early Henrician court songbook, thought to date from the second decade of the sixteenth century, there are twelve genuine English rounds, some with **instrument**al **ground-bass** accompaniment.

Rounds can be reasonably sophisticated, composed songs, without reaching the intellectual heights and complexity of the puzzle canon, a genre cultivated by court composers from Henry VIII onwards. Several fine rounds from the late sixteenth and early seventeenth centuries, variously ascribed to William Byrd, survive in late seventeenth and eighteenth-century printed collections. Ravenscroft's *Pammelia* (1609) is the earliest printed English source of rounds, as well as other kinds of fashionable songs. His *Melismata: Musicall Phansies, Fitting the Court, Citie and Countrey Humours* (1611) includes nine 'Citie' and 'Countrey' rounds.

In Elizabethan times certain song types were conventionally linked with dancing even though surviving songs themselves do not often indicate a connection with **dance**. We know from contemporary commentary (e.g. Webbe, *A Discourse of English Poetrie,* 1586) that songs were **perform**ed for dancing, either as '**sing**ing daunce, or dauncing song'. Moreover, it was not uncommon practice to set ditties to dances as the examples in the miscellany *A Handfull of Pleasant Delites* (1584) and Dowland's books of songs attest. As Baskervill points out, 'this conventional union explains the large number of terms that were used interchangeably for song and for dance. **Carol**, "round" or "roundel", and "**ballet**" or "**ballad**" came out of the Middle Ages, and they remained in use for both song and dance in spite of the change in meaning that "ballad" underwent in the sixteenth century' (p. 10).

As a singing dance, the round or roundelay was frequently employed in Elizabethan literature in a pastoral or quasi-pastoral context, notably by Spenser. It became synonymous with the 'shepherd's **jig**' (see Baskervill, p. 14). In Greene's *Menaphon* (1589), for example, the shepherd Doron asks that a roundelay (or jig) be **sound**ed whilst he sings.

(B) In *A Midsummer Night's Dream*, the world of the fairies is associated with round dances. At the end of her quarrel with Oberon, Titania makes him a peace offer when she asks him to join her and her fairy attendants and to 'patiently dance in our round' (2.1.140); however, he rejects her offer and swears that he will take vengeance upon her. Titania's entry at the beginning of the following scene is accompanied by her exhortation to her train: 'Come, now a roundel and a fairy song' (2.2.1). The wording of this cue and the text of the song (9–24) reveal that the fairies did not accompany the dance to a round; rather, the song *round*

has the form chosen most often by Shakespeare for his own songs, that of refrain-song. [. . .] The form suggests that each stanza would be sung by a solo voice, with the refrain sung by all the fairies [. . .] The lyric is not a rondel in form; Titania's request for 'a roundel and a fairy song' suggests that the fairies danced a round before their song, or that they accompanied the refrain with dancing.

(Maynard, p. 178)

Later, Puck promises that he will mislead the mechanicals who are fleeing from Bottom: 'I'll follow you, I'll lead you about a round' (3.1.106). 'A round' can be interpreted either as meaning 'in a ring-dance' (Brooks, p. 5) or 'a way which turns in a circle' (Foakes, p. 83). Puck's line reinforces the connection between the supernatural world of the fairies and the dancing of rounds.

A similar connection, this time with the sinister world of witchcraft, is found in *Macbeth* in a passage generally ascribed to Thomas Middleton After conjuring up apparitions for Macbeth, the Witches and Hecate decide to disappear in a spectacular way. The First Witch exclaims:

> I'll **charm** the **air** to give a sound,
> While you perform your antic round;
> That this great king may kindly say
> Our duties did his welcome pay.
> *Music. The Witches dance and vanish.*
>
> (4.1.129–32)

From the stage direction in this passage, it is clear that there is no singing in this context. The 'antic round' may be the same dance as in 1.3.32–7. It would probably have been regarded as 'a macabre version of a Jacobean courtly entertainment' (Braunmuller, p. 197) by Shakespeare's contemporaries.

(C) Baskervill, *The Elizabethan Jig and Related Song Drama* (1929).
Braunmuller, *Macbeth* (1997).
Brooks, *A Midsummer Night's Dream* (1983).
Foakes, *A Midsummer Night's Dream* (1984).
Maynard, *Elizabethan Lyric Poetry and its Music* (1986), considers the relationship between music and different literary genres (among them poetry, plays and masques) during the Elizabethan age.

Stevens, 'Rounds and Canons from an Early Tudor Song-Book' (1951) discusses puzzle canons and rounds and offers definitions; and Stevens (ed.), *Music at the Court of Henry VIII* (1969) is a critical edition of BL Add. MS 31922.

Vlasto, 'An Elizabethan Anthology of Rounds' (1954).

roundel see **dance, round**.

roundelay see **dance, lay, round**.

rude (A) In his **ayre** ('To his **sweet lute**', c.1617, no. 8) depicting the contest between **Apollo** and Pan, Campion contrasts the 'sweet lute' of Apollo with the 'rude **pipe**' of Pan, juxtaposing the sophisticated **string**ed **instrument** of the god of **music** with the vulgar **wind** instrument of the rustic Pan.

(B) Whilst Shakespeare does not identify his pipes as 'rude' he does use the term in other musical contexts to mean 'un**skill**ed', 'unlearned', '**harsh**'. For instance, when Troilus refers to 'rude **sound**s' (*Tro* 1.1.89) he intends unmusical **discord**ant **noise**; in this musical metaphor he also opposes 'rude' and 'civil', meaning 'impolite' versus 'cultured'.

Oberon contrasts the delicate and harmonious sounds uttered by a mermaid and the 'rude sea' (*MND* 2.1.152) which 'grew civil at her **song**' (152). 'Rude' aptly describes the wild force of the sea, which expresses itself through harsh noise as well as other manifestations (see '**dulcet**' for more comments on this passage). Another natural phenomenon, the wind, is described as having a 'rude **breath**' (*AYLI* 2.7.179), a reference to its overwhelming noise.

In *King John*, the Bastard describes Peter, who has predicted the end of King John's reign, as having sung his prophecy 'in rude harsh-sounding **rhyme**s' (4.2.150). In this case the allusion may be not only to Peter's lack of skill in delivering his verses, but also to the seditious content of his prediction (as a result of which he is sentenced to death by the King).

See also **concord, discord**.

S

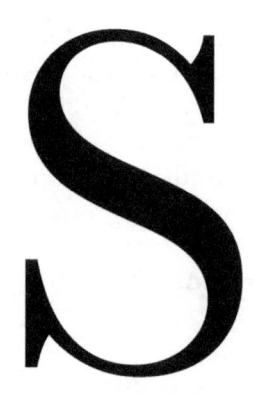

sackbut (A) Sackbut is the early English name, in use from the late fifteenth century, for the Italian '*trombone*'. In France and the Low Countries it was called the *sacquboute* (e.g. Tinctoris c.1487) – the earliest reference from the Burgundian court in 1468 is to the '*trompette saiqueboute*'. In Germany it was the '*posaune*'. The name 'trombone' displaced 'sackbut' in the eighteenth century although the distinctive feature of this **brass instrument**, the forward projecting slide, continued.

The sackbut customarily **play**ed the lower **part**(s) in the shawm or **cornett** ensembles of the Renaissance. When Henry VIII received the Emperor Charles V in London in 1522, according to Edward Hall, 'they passed to the conduite in Cornehill ... and over the arches wer two towers, the one full of Trompettes and the other full of Shalmes and shagbuttes whiche played continually' (p. 638). The cornett and sackbut ensemble was used in cathedrals to accompany the **choir**, and the instrument was part of the standard equipment of the town band or 'waits'. Secular **music** for sackbuts and cornetts was printed in England during the seventeenth century, e.g. in John Adson's *Courtly Masquing Ayres* (1621) and Matthew Locke, *Music for His Majesty's Sagbutts and Cornets* (1661).

(B) In his 1598 inventory of the stage props belonging to the Admiral's Men (see Introduction for more details), Henslowe lists a sackbut among other instruments. Though seldom mentioned in stage directions of Renaissance plays (Dessen and Thomson cite only two instances in their

Dictionary of Stage Directions) it must frequently have been used in the actual music of the theatre.

Coriolanus is the only Shakespeare play where a reference to the sackbut is made. This occurs when the Romans are preparing to welcome Volumnia's entry in triumph into the city. The celebration entails playing several instruments at a time, including **trumpet**s, suckbuts, **psalteries, fife**s, **tabor**s and **cymbal**s (5.4.49–50), as is clear from a messenger's speech. The jubilant **mood** is brought about by Volumnia's success in persuading her son Coriolanus to spare Rome. The lively atmosphere evoked by the **sound**ing of these instruments works as a foil to the sombre dead **march** sounded at the end of the play – only two scenes later (5.6.154.SD) – when the dead body of Coriolanus is taken offstage according to the military tradition.

(C) Dessen and Thomson, *A Dictionary of Stage Directions* (1999), p. 186.

Duffin, 'The *trompette des menestrels* in the 15th-century *alta capella*' (1989).

Hall, *The Union of the Two Noble and Illustre Families of Lancaster and York* (facsimile reprint, 1965).

Myers, 'Slide Trumpet Madness: Fact or Fiction?' (1989).

Polk, 'The Trombone, the Slide Trumpet and the Ensemble Tradition of the Early Renaissance' (1989).

sautry see **psaltery**.

scornful (A) The adjective 'scornful' is found in musical contexts with its normal meaning of unworthy or contemptuous. **Music**, especially in **song**, can heighten the sense of contempt as Campion sharply defines in his:

> All that I sung still to her **praise** did tend.
> Still she was first, still she my songs did end.
> Yet she my love and music both doth fly,
> The music that her **echo** is, and beauty's sympathy.
> Then let my **note**s pursue her scornful flight;
> It shall suffice that they were breathed, and died for her delight.
> (1601, no. 10)

scornful

(B) In the final scene of *The Merry Wives of Windsor*, Falstaff's plan to seduce Mistress Page and Mistress Ford is frustrated when some boys dressed as fairies (whom Falstaff mistakes for real fairies) are instructed to **dance** around him and 'sing a scornful **rhyme**' (5.5.91). The text of the song that follows ('Fie on sinful fantasy') ridicules Falstaff's lustful feelings for the two women.

screech owl see **bird**.

sennet (A) The most exclusive, least used signal in military and courtly contexts was the sennet. The term is probably derived from the Italian Military **Music** *Sarasinetta* (this term, current from the fifteenth century, disappears from Italian Military Music sources around 1620). Whilst some critics argue that *sarasinetta* is an earlier version of *serenade*, others contend that '*sara*' (or '*sero*') may be a contraction of '*sereno*' or '*serenissimo*', an honorary title bestowed on nobles of high rank such as the Venetian Doge, and that '*sinetta*' (or '*seneda*') equates to '*sonata*' (or '*seneda*'). If the latter is the more correct interpretation, then *sarasinetta* could mean a **piece sound**ed for the highest nobility. Such interpretation is strengthened by the title of a piece of music **compose**d by Cesare Bendinelli, *Fanfare Sarasinetta*, for the coronation ceremony of the Doge Marino Grimani in 1595.

The *sarasinetta* was musically distinct from other **trumpet** signals (see '**tucket**'). Only a very few *sarasinette* survive, but these tell us that longer 4/2 bars were employed and that slightly higher trumpet harmonics (4–10) prevailed, as in Bendinelli (1614), f. 8 'Sarasinetta' no. 2:

A short (improvised) passage normally opens the final section. This is distinguished from the rest of the sennet by its step-wise notation in contrast to the arpeggiated contour of the rest. Clearly the sennet was a more sophisticated signal than other solo-line trumpet calls.

sennet

The lowest person of rank a sennet would accompany was a prince or victorious military general. Otherwise, only kings and emperors were announced by a sennet. Of the extant *sarasinette*, most are found in Magnus Thomsen's *Trumpet Book*, c.1596 (Copenhagen, Kongelige Bibliotek, GL.kgl, Saml. 1875a) – Thomsen was a German trumpeter employed by the Danish court; and only a few (including the one for the Doge Marino Grimani) in Cesare Bendinelli (*Tutta l'arte della trombetta*, 1614).

In Tudor England, the sennet was reserved for personages of the highest rank. In *The Souldiers Exercise* (1639), Gervase Markham refers to 'other Soundings . . . a Call for Summons, a Senet for State . . . [which] have reference to the greatest Officers, and those have no need of my Instruction'. The 'Call for Summons' is probably the toccata (see **tucket**') and the 'Senet for State' is the *sarasinetta*.

(B) In the theatre of the Elizabethan and Jacobean ages, trumpets would have been used for sennets and would have underlined ceremonial entrances and, sometimes, exits. Even though there is no mention of sennets in the dialogue of Shakespeare's plays, stage directions for this type of fanfare are found in a number of his historical plays and tragedies: except for one, they all appear in Folio. Two directions for 'sennets' in Folio *3 Henry VI* (1.1.205.SD) and in Folio *Richard III* (4.2.OSD) are more generically indicated as 'trumpets' in their counterpart quarto editions. These peculiarities acquire further significance when we consider what happens in the extant play texts of the early modern professional theatre. From the exhaustive review of indications for sennets found in *A Dictionary of Stage Directions*, it can be surmised that the tendency to signal this type of fanfare was more prominent in the seventeenth century than in the late sixteenth century. The development of this specialized musical code seems to go hand in hand with the employment of professional **musician**s in the theatre (for instance the **consort** at the Blackfriars).

Failure to note that Shakespeare's stage directions for sennets appear almost exclusively in Folio (which was published in 1623) have led commentators to offer misleading statements. Downey, for example, argues that 'there are fifteen references to the sennet in Shakespeare's plays . . . More than half the references occur in plays written between 1584–92. Could this have been caused by the arrival of the *Italian Military Music* at that time?' (p. 92). In fact, the use of the specific term 'sennet' in the early seventeenth century rather than the late sixteenth is

sennet

testament to Shakespeare and his company's awareness of the latest trends emanating from Italy.

The only instance of the word 'sennet' in an early edition of a Shakespeare play other than Folio is found in Q1 *King Lear* (printed in 1608), B1v: '*Sound a Sennet. Enter one bearing a coronet* [. . .]'. The sounding of a sennet is also prescribed in Folio *King Lear*, where we have: '*Sennet. Enter King Lear* [. . .]'. This first entry by Lear and his retinue is thematically very important. As Frances Shirley has argued:

> It [the sennet] is sounded for the old King's only entrance as the ruler of England. After he has divided his country between Goneril and Regan, he leaves with only a **flourish**. Later in the play, hunting **horn**s announce his approach. The change in fanfare goes hand-in-hand with the diminishing respect accorded to the old man by his two daughters.
>
> (p. 74)

The fact that the change in Lear's status is aurally emphasized by different types of **wind instrument** sounds shows how familiar these must have been to early-modern playgoers.

Shirley has also noted that sennets sometimes work as ironic reminders of a weak monarch's inability to rule despite his outward display of power, for instance in the *Henry VI* plays. Similarly, when we see Macbeth enter '*as King*' (*Mac* 3.1.10.SD) for the first time after his coronation in Scone, we cannot help but feel that the sennet accompanying him and his wife is meant to emphasize that he is dressed 'in borrowed robes', especially because Duncan's previous entries are underlined by less formal fanfares ('flourish' at the beginning and end of 1.4, and '**hoboy**s' at the beginning of 1.6).

The dramatically ironic insertion of sennets also applies to the indication of this sound effect (5.2.374.SD) in Folio *Henry V* (the only version with the prologue, **chorus**es and epilogue). These sennets accompany the exit of Henry, his followers and the French court when Henry is the undisputed victor and has just obtained the hand of Katherine. This seemingly triumphant **mood**, expressed by Henry's final line ('And may our oaths well kept and prosp'rous be!', 5.2.374) is soon dispelled by the Chorus's concluding speech, which ominously reminds the audience of the troubled times awaiting England when Henry VI will succeed to the throne.

One of the most spectacular uses of the sennet is observed in *Henry VIII*. The opening stage direction of 2.4 begins with the indication: '*Trumpets, sennet, and* **cornet**s'. These are followed by the entry of a large number of characters assembling in a hall in Blackfriars for the divorce proceedings between Henry and Katherine of Aragon. These sound effects – as well as the processional entry of the characters with stage props symbolising constituted power – are intended to emphasize the official tone of this scene, in which the disgraced Queen courageously pleads her case. The use of ceremonial sound effects strongly contrasts with the personal sphere evoked in the following scene: here, a **lute** accompanies a melancholy **song** and introduces Katherine's sad reflections in the intimate setting of her apartments.

(C) Bendinelli, *Tutta l'arte della trombetta* (MS, 1614).
Dessen and Thomson, *A Dictionary of Stage Directions* (1999).
Downey, 'The Trumpet and its Role in Music of the Renaissance and Early Baroque' (1983).
Grove Online, 'Signal (1) Military Signals'.
Markham, *The Souldiers Exercise* (1639).
Shirley, *Shakespeare's Use of Off-Stage Sounds* (1963).

set (A) When we talk about setting something to **music** today we imply a formal act, of writing it down, of composing. Thus the act of setting words to music results in a **song**. For the Elizabethans, 'set' did not have the same restricted meaning, though it could still mean setting words to music as in Daniel's 'Can **doleful note**s to **measure**d **accent**s set' (1606, no. 13). When discussing his 'Rules to be observed in **ditty**ing' (i.e. setting words to music), Morley uses 'dispose', 'apply', '**make**', 'express', 'cause', '**frame**'. He only uses 'set' to mean 'place', as in 'to shewe you in a worde the use of the **rest**s in the dittie, you may set a **crotchet** or **minim**e rest above a comma or colon' (*Introduction*, 1597, p. 179). On the other hand, the compound 'set down' (in an appropriate context) did mean 'put something into writing'.

(B) The Clown in *A Winter's Tale* refers to the composition of **ballad**s in paradoxical terms. He claims that he loves a ballad 'if it be doleful matter merrily set down, / or a very **pleasant** thing indeed and sung **lament**ably' (4.4.189–90). No wonder that somebody as ignorant

set

about ballads as the Clown does not recognize Autolycus (who has robbed him) in his disguise as a pedlar and ballad seller.

In *Othello* (2.1.200), 'set down' is also used in a musical context, but in this case the verb is synonymous with 'un**tune**' (see '**peg**' for a commentary of the relevant passage).

sharp (A) The comparative term 'sharp' can have several interrelated meanings in a musical context. It can refer to the **high**-pitched incisive **sound** of a **voice** or **instrument** such as a **fife** or **whistle**. Most often it indicates the half-tone raised pitch of a **note** in contrast to the lowered half-tone pitch signified by the **flat**. In other words, a note can be either natural, sharp or flat, as Morley states: 'no note of it selfe [is] either flatt or sharpe, but compared with another, is sometime flatt and sometime sharpe: so that there is no note in the whole Scale which is not both sharpe and flatt' (*Introduction*, 1597, p. 7). A flat **key** in Elizabethan times would be equivalent to the minor key; a sharp key equates to the diatonic major.

Occasionally in early modern contexts, 'sharp' can mean a note that is out of **tune** by being sounded higher than it should. This would seem unpleasant to the **ear**, especially if the sharp note clashed with one or more that were in tune. Word-play on 'sharp' as a piercing sound and a sharp implement is found in the elegy on Sir John Shelton, who was 'slain with fatal sword'. 'Sharp' is juxtaposed with 'flat', as in **music**:

> Let every sharp in sharp tune figure
> The too sharp death he hath endured;
> Let every flat show flat the rigour
> Of Fortune's spite to all inured.
> (Carlton, 1601, no. 12)

(B) 'Sharp' acquires a musical connotation on three occasions in the Shakespeare canon, in relation to the concept of notes out of tune. In *The Two Gentlemen of Verona*, Julia tries to sing Proteus' love letter, written in **rhyme**, 'to the tune of "light o' Love" ' (1.2.80) but her waiting-woman Lucetta is far from being impressed and says she does not like it because ' 'tis too sharp' (89), i.e. sung **high**er than it should be. When Julia sings it **low**er, Lucetta protests once again: 'Nay, now you are too flat' (91). She suggests that Julia needs a tenor voice to make her singing *sharp*

more harmonious. The elaborate musical references in this scene are aimed to reinforce Lucetta's support of Proteus' suit.

In *Romeo and Juliet*, Juliet vents her grief after dawn has broken and the banished Romeo must leave her. She exhorts him to go as hastily as possible and then observes:

> It is the **lark** that sings so out of tune,
> **Strain**ing **harsh discord**s and unpleasing sharps.
> Some say the lark makes **sweet division**;
> This doth not so, for she divideth us.
> (3.5.27–30)

This powerful speech subverts the conventional **praise** of the lark's pleasant singing: to Juliet, the **bird** sings out of tune because it causes separation (division) between her and Romeo.

Anticipating his encounter with Cressida, Troilus cannot conceal his excitement. He asks himself what impact the emotion of the meeting will have on him:

> . . . Death, I fear me,
> Sounding destruction, or some joy too fine,
> Too subtile, potent, tun'd too sharp in sweetness
> For the capacity of my ruder powers.
> (*Tro* 3.2.22–5)

Troilus fears that his encounter with Cressida will reveal his unrefined nature ('ruder powers'). The musical metaphor elucidates 'a paradox of taste: to raise sweetness to an extreme pitch would be to lose the sense of sweetness altogether' (Palmer, p. 193). The reference to 'sweetness' is particularly apposite. 'Sweetness' concerns intervals of thirds and sixths: these intervals are crucially affected by sharps (and flats). If the intervals were too sharp, their pleasantness would be seriously impaired.

(C) Palmer, *Troilus and Cressida* (1982).

shrill (A) The term 'shrill' describes a **high**-pitched piercing **sound** or an **instrument** or **voice** producing such a sound. High **trumpet**s *shrill*

are often referred to as 'shrill': 'In fields abroad, where trumpets shrill do sound' (Byrd, 1588, no. 22).

Pipes such as (**descant**) **recorder**s, **whistle**s and **fife**s are also frequently shrill as are certain **bird**s: 'O come, come, come abroad, / And **hear** the shrill birds **sing**' (Peerson, 1620, no. 1). In one example, the image of the pipe ('recorder') sounding and bird singing ('**record**') is compounded: 'Then **tune** to us, **sweet** bird, thy shrill recorder' (Thomas Morley (ed.), *The Triumphes of Oriana*, 1610, no. 24).

(B) In *Titus Andronicus*, Tamora's account of the hunt places emphasis on the sounds and **noise**s accompanying it:

> . . . the babbling **echo** mocks the hounds,
> Replying shrilly to the **well-tun'd horn**s,
> As if a double hunt were heard at once.
> (2.3.17–19)

The sound of a different **wind** instrument, this time the trumpet, is defined as 'shrill' by Othello (*Oth* 3.3.351). In *Henry V* the shipmaster's 'shrill whistle . . . doth order give' (*H5* Pro.3.9) during the Channel crossing of the English fleet on its way to France.

After Gloucester's failed suicide attempt, his son Edgar (who wants him to believe that he has been spared by divine intervention) tries to convince him that he has just fallen from the edge of a cliff:

> From the dread summit of this chalky bourn
> Look up a-height, the shrill-gorg'd **lark** so far
> Cannot be seen or heard. Do but look up.
> (*Lr* 4.6.57–9)

Edgar's apparent cruelty in asking his father to look up when he knows that he is blind, is justified by the fact that he has assumed a false identity and pretends to have just met him by chance. To the blind Gloucester, it is the description of the voice of the lark which creates the illusion that he is now at the bottom of the cliff.

Another bird, the cockerel, is qualified as having a 'shrill-sounding **throat** [voice]' (*Ham* 1.1.151), heralding the morning like a trumpeter. The voice of the Soothsayer is 'shriller than all the **music**' (*JC* 1.2.16) of the **flourish**es being **play**ed in honour of Caesar: it warns him of the danger he faces on the Ides of March. According to Cleopatra, Antony cannot remain in love with Octavia for a long time since she is 'low-voic'd' (*Ant* 3.3.13) rather than 'shrill-**tongu'**d' (12), the latter a desirable quality for a female voice.

side-drum see **drum**.

sigh (A) The sigh was a distinctive rhetorical gesture in Renaissance vocal **music**. It was used as an expressive element in sad, sorrowful and melancholic **madrigal**s and **ayre**s. In the Italian madrigal it is most often found in combination with words for weeping, tears, sadness and piety characterized by evocative dissonant **harmony** and articulated by short off-**beat silence**s (quasi exhalations), as in Willaert's madrigal 'I vidi in terra' (*Musica Nova*, 1559, no. 17) at the words '*lagrimar . . . et sospirando dir parole*'. This musical rhetoric was imported into England in the late sixteenth century, as Morley notes (recalling Italian practice):

> When you would expresse sighes, you may use the **crotchet** or **minim**e **rest** at the most, but a longer then a minime rest you may not use, because it will rather seeme a breth taking then a sigh, an example wherof you may see in a very good **song** of *Stephano venturi* to five **voice**s upon this dittie *quell'aura che spirando a paura [sic] mia?*' for coming to the word *sospiri* (that is sighes) he giveth it such a natural grace by breaking a minime into a crotchet rest and a crotchet.
>
> (*Introduction*, 1597, p. 178)

The device was employed by madrigal and **lute**-song composers to great effect. John Dowland's famous melancholic ayre 'Flow my tears' incorporates a typical setting at the words:

> Never may my woes be relieved,
> Since pity is fled,
> And tears, and sighs, and groans my weary days
> Of all joys have deprived.
>
> (1600, no. 2)

sigh

Another good example is 'I sit, I sigh, I weep, I faint, I die' from his ayre, 'Come again **sweet** love' (1597, no. 17). The idea of expressing sadness through music, signified by the topos of the sigh, is nicely put in Dowland's:

> Sorrow was there made fair,
> And Passion wise, tears a delightful thing;
> **Silence** beyond all speech a wisdom rare.
> She made her sighs to **sing**,
> And all things with so sweet a sadness move
> As made my heart at once both grieve and love.
>
> (1600, no. 1)

(B) Of the many uses of 'sigh' in the Shakespeare canon, only a few have a musical connotation. After singing 'Concolinel' on Armado's request, Moth advises him on how he should woo Jaquenetta:

> ... **jig** off
> a **tune** at the **tongue**'s end, **canary** to it with your
> feet, humor it with turning up your eyelids, sigh
> a **note** and sing a note, sometime through the **throat**,
> as if you swallow'd love with singing love,
> sometime through the nose, as if you snuff'd up
> love by smelling love ...
>
> (*LLL* 3.1.11–17)

The allusions to **dance**s (jig and canary) and music are intended to highlight the overstated manners that accompany the process of falling in love. The **mood** swings experienced by the wooer are well expressed by the contrasting ways of sighing and singing 'a note'.

Edmund places emphasis on the dissonant nature of sighing when he devises his evil plan against Edgar. When the latter is entering, Edmund concludes his soliloquy by saying:

> Pat! he comes like the catastrophe in the old comedy.
> My cue is villainous melancholy, with a sigh like
> Tom o' Bedlam. – O, these eclipses do portend these
> **division**s! *Fa, sol, la, mi.*
>
> (*Lr* 1.2.134–7)

sigh

Edmund is expected to **hum** the notes in a **discord**ant way: 'sigh' points to the divisions he is about to cause, both in a political and in a musical sense.

In the song 'Sigh no more ladies' (*Ado* 2.3.62–74), 'sigh', found at the beginning of the first stanza, makes an effective contrast with 'sing' at the beginning of the second stanza. Even though 'sigh' in this context is synonymous with 'lament', the musical overtones of these two words would hardly have escaped a Renaissance audience.

See also **doleful**.

silence (A) Both as a concept and an aural experience, 'silence' signifies the absence of **sound**, nowhere more eloquently expressed than in Daniel's:

> Eyes, look no more, for what hath all the earth that's worth the sight?
> **Ear**s, **hear** no more, for what can breathe the **voice** of true
> delight? . . .
> Silence, lock up my words and scorn these idle sounds of air.
> (1606, no. 16)

In mensural **music** notation, silence was indicated by **rest**s, each one having a specific duration according to the type of sign (vertical stroke in Renaissance music). Silence was often emotively connected with death and dying. Gibbons' famous '**Silver swan**', for example, sang one more time before dying and remaining silent forever:

> The silver swan, who living had no **note**,
> When death approached unlocked her silent **throat** . . .
> Thus sang her first and last, and sung no more.
> (1612, no. 1)

(B) Although this term appears over 80 times in the Shakespeare canon, there is only one occasion when it seems to acquire a specific musical nuance. Hamlet may well be punning on 'rest' and 'silence' as he dies, as transpires from the following exchange:

> HAMLET: O, I die, Horatio,
> The potent poison quite o'er-crows my spirit.

silence

> I cannot live to hear the news from England,
> But I do prophesy th' election lights
> On Fortinbras, he has my dying voice.
> So tell him, with th' occurrents more and less
> Which have solicited – the rest is silence.
> HORATIO: Now cracks a noble heart. Good night, **sweet** prince,
> And flights of **angel**s sing thee to thy rest!
>
> (*Ham* 5.2.352–60)

Hamlet's 'dying voice' conjures up the aural imagery developed in the allusion to 'silence' and 'rest'; in its turn, the latter is linked to the image of the **sing**ing angels. This scene is pervaded by aural signals on and off the stage, which make the musical allusion to 'silence' all the more significant: **trumpet**s and **drum**s announcing the entry of the fated royal party (5.2.224.SD), the sounding of these **instrument**s during the fencing context between Hamlet and Laertes (5.2.278.SD; 5.2.283.SD), the **ordnance** (5.2.283.SD) and, just before Hamlet dies, the sounding of a **march** (5.2.348.SD).

silver (A) In extolling the virtues of **music** and its heavenly powers, Sir John Davies wrote: 'If music did not merit endless **praise** / Would heavn'ly spheres delight in silver **sound**' ('Hymn in Praise of Music', *Poetical Rhapsody*, 1602, ed. Rollins, vol. 1, p. 201). Alluding to the vibrant clear sound of silver with its gentle tone and resonant qualities, many poets employed the metaphor in various connections. Campion knowingly combines '**sweet**, silver, sound' in his **masque song**, '**Time**, that leads the fatal **round**': '. . . and Venus sweetly **sing**s, / With heavenly **note**s **tune**d to sound of silver **string**s' (*Lord Hayes Masque*, 1607, no. 5). In comparing Amphion's lyre and **Orpheus' lute**, Arion's **harp** 'distilling silv'ring sound' is found in Weelkes': 'What have the gods their **consort** sent from heaven / To **charm** my senses with heaven's **harmony**?' (*Madrigals*, part 2, 1600, nos 3–4). 'Silver tuned strings' are contrasted with '**shrill, ear**-piercing **noise**s', as Sternfeld notes (p. 241), in the induction to the anonymous *Mucedorus*.

(B) This term is used on two different occasions in *Romeo and Juliet*. The first occurrence is in the balcony scene, when Romeo and Juliet declare their mutual love, and Romeo exclaims: 'How silver-sweet sound lovers' *silver*

tongues by night / Like **soft**est music to attending ears!' (2.2.165–6). The **voice**s ('tongues') of lovers are so full of gentle sounds that they acquire the quality of music. Whilst 'silver' is used here in a conventional way, it is employed to achieve a surprising effect later, when the **musician**s who were supposed to **play** at the wedding between Juliet and Paris are dismissed (this happens after the apparently dead body of Juliet is discovered). Asked by Peter to explain the meaning of the phrase 'music with her silver sound' (4.5.129), the first musician replies that it means that 'silver hath a sweet sound' (131), and the second musician adds that 'musicians sound for silver' (135). Clearly, these musicians are more interested in the money they can make out of playing rather than in the aesthetic qualities of music.

Pericles is able to recognize his daughter Marina (who until that moment he believes to be dead) when he observes that she is 'as silver-voic'd' (*Per* 5.1.110) as his wife Thaisa. Since this comment occurs after Marina has sung for Pericles, its musical connotations are unmistakable. They refer to the heavenly quality of her singing, which is noted by Gower earlier in the play: 'She sings like one immortal' (5.Ind.3).

(C) Sternfeld, *Music in Shakespearean Tragedy* (1967), pp. 101–5, discusses 'silver strings', 'silver sound', 'silver voice' and 'silver-sounding tales'.

sinew see **catling, string**.

sing see **song**.

sink-a-pace see **cinque pas**.

skill (A) Morley equates skill in **music** (in particular **sing**ing) with being learned in other arts in contrast to being ignorant (*Introduction*, 1597, p. 1). Most writers on music in the late sixteenth century used the word 'skill' to mean an ability to sing or **play** well upon an **instrument**. William Bathe called his second treatise, *A Brief Introduction to the Skill of Song* (c.1592). Other writers employ the term to indicate a high level of accomplishment in composition. Campion, for example,

skill

introduces the term at the beginning of his treatise 'Of Counterpoint' when referring to composers of multi-**voice** polyphonic works: 'The **part**s of Musicke are in all but foure, howsoever some skilfull Musitions have composed songs of twenty, thirty, and forty parts' (*A New Way*, c.1614, B6r).

(B) When Guildenstern protests that he cannot play the recorder which Hamlet is showing him, he has this musical meaning of 'skill' in mind: 'But these (*stops*) cannot I command to any utt'rance / of **harmony**. I have not the skill' (*Ham* 3.2.361–2). (See also 'stop' and '**govern**' for a comment of this and the ensuing passages).

Thurio decides to employ 'some gentlemen well skill'd in music' (*TGV* 3.2.91) in order to serenade Silvia, i.e. a **consort** of professional **musician**s as is later demonstrated by the stage direction instructing Thurio to enter with '*musicians*' (4.2.15.SD) who play and sing the song 'Who is Silvia?' (39–53).

Lucrece compares herself to **Philomela** (who was transformed into a **nightingale** after Tereus raped her) and, in a sexually suggestive stanza remarks: 'For **burthen**-wise I'll **hum** on Tarquin still, / While thou on Tereus **descant**s better skill' (*Luc* 1133–4). Lucrece is probably alluding to the nightingale's greater ability to sing than her own.

(C) Wilson (ed.), *A New Way* (2003), p. 46.

snatch (A) The term 'snatch' means a small section of a **tune** or **song**. Its frequent association with **catch** suggests a section of a male three-**voice**d comic song. Otherwise, it does not refer to any specific song type.

(B) Shakespeare uses this word only once with a musical connotation. In Q2 *Hamlet* (1604/5) Ophelia '**chaunt**ed snatches of old **laudes**' (M1v – Folio *Ham* has 'tunes' instead of 'laudes') while drowning. Her distressed state explains why she could only remember sections, rather than the whole text, of the songs she was intoning. (See also 'laudes' for a commentary of this passage.)

soft (A) Contemporary usage of the term in the Elizabethan theatre and courtly **masque** suggest that it meant 'gentle' rather than necessarily 'quiet' **music**. Peter Walls argues, for example, that 'the adjective in "a soft musique of twelve **Lutes** and twelve voyces" – *Tethys Festival* [1610], l. 303 – is probably intended to indicate something about the sophistication and quality rather than the volume' (p. 152). Used as an opposite to '**loud**', it meant **string**ed as opposed to **wind instrument**s.

(B) Two stage directions in *The Tempest* call for 'soft music' when supernatural events are displayed. The 'shapes' appearing in the banquet scene enter *'to soft music'* (3.3.82.SD), as does Iris (4.1.59.SD) during the masque which Prospero has put on to celebrate the betrothal of Ferdinand and Miranda. Both scenes have an abrupt ending. The banquet scene shows Ariel in the shape of a harpy making Alonso, Sebastian and Antonio face their sins; the masque is interrupted hastily by Prospero when he remembers the 'foul conspiracy of the beast Caliban' (140), i.e. his plot to assassinate him with the help of Stephano and Trinculo. Contrary to what would be expected, soft music here acquires a sinister quality, and confirms the ambivalent role of music in this play. Ultimately, it reminds us that human happiness is ephemeral.

(C) Walls, *Music in the English Courtly Masque* (1996).

sol The fifth **note** of the Renaissance hexachord. See **ut**.

solemn see **music**.

Solomon (A) The **ballad** entitled 'King Solomon' uses the same **tune** as 'There dwelt a man in **Babylon**' (Duffin, p. 247).

(B) In a speech using terms relating to **dance** and **music**, Armado confesses his love for Jaquenetta to his page Moth:

> I do affect the very **ground** (which is **base**)
> where her shoe (which is baser) guided by her foot

Solomon

> (which is basest) doth tread.
> ... Yet was Sampson so tempted,
> and he had an excellent strength; yet was Salomon so
> seduced, and he had a very good wit.
>
> (*LLL* 1.2.167–9; 173–5)

Armado's conceited personality and proneness to exaggeration lead him to compare himself to biblical figures. Furthermore, the 'reference to the tune draws attention to the irony of using a fabled biblical king for a frivolous love **song**' (Duffin, p. 247).

Later in the play, when Berowne finally admits his feelings for Rosaline, he also alludes to the ballad when he mentions 'profound Salomon [who] tune[s] a **jig**' (4.3.166). It is interesting that in the previous line there is a reference to Hercules, whose name also appears in the ballad 'King Solomon'.

(C) Duffin, *Shakespeare's Songbook* (2004).

sonance (A) Used as both a noun and a verb, 'sonance' is synonymous with '**sound**'.

(B) There is only one use of this term in the Shakespeare canon. Before the Battle of Agincourt, the Constable exhorts the French thus:

> ... Then let the **trumpet**s sound
> The **tucket** sonance and the **note** to mount;
> For our approach shall so much dare the field,
> That England shall couch down in fear, and yield.
>
> (*H5* 4.2.34–7)

Trumpet signals in martial contexts were intended for the cavalry (see Markham), and the tucket is no exception What transpires here is the Constable's confidence that the French numeric superiority will guarantee them victory. He (mistakenly) hopes that the sound of the military signal and the **noise** of the approaching French cavalry will be enough to scare the English.

(C) Markham, *The Souldiers Accidence* (1625).

song (A) As an all-embracing term, 'song' refers to **music** that is produced by the **voice** (vocal music). The act of making that music is called singing. Songs generally employ a verbal text, but this is not always the case as in **bird**song. The term can have either general or specific meanings. In Elizabethan times, 'song' was used for a wide variety of vocal music, including **ayre**s or **lute** songs, **part** songs, **madrigal**s, **consort** songs, sacred songs (*cantiones sacrae*), **ballad**s, **catch**es, etc. These genres were for either solo voice or for several voices. Today we tend to think of song as a solo voice medium. Occasionally, 'song' could mean the text of a poem that would be suitable for singing (e.g. Byrd, 1589). Or it could refer to the subject of the song, e.g. song of mourning, song of night, song of sixpence, song of love, etc. Different professions were attributed with special kinds of song, e.g. reapers, ploughmen, balladmongers, etc. Birds were known by their song, the **lark**, the **nightingale**, the **thrush**, the **jay**, to name but a few. 'Song' was also used to distinguish vocal music from **instrument**al, although certain **piece**s of instrumental music, especially those with literary titles, could be termed 'songs' – equivalent to the nineteenth-century 'songs without words'. Another usage, obliquely related to music, is found in the modern phrase 'going for a song' meaning that something is very cheap, not worth much. This is the significance in 'I know a man that had this tricke of melancholy hold a goodly Mannor for a song' (*AWW* 3.2.9).

That songs and singing were popular in Elizabethan England is attested by the large number of songs that were printed. For the most part, this was to satisfy a newish market, that of the domestic recreational or amateur singer. Such notated songs, either in manuscript or printed songbook were sometimes called '**prick**e **song**' as opposed to improvised or **extempore** singing (**division**), usually done by accomplished or professional **musician**s. Songs could be **perform**ed in a variety of different ways including solo unaccompanied, solo accompanied, in vocal polyphony or in a mixture of voices and instruments. The solo singer could accompany him/herself, on the lute or other plucked **string**ed instrument, or could be accompanied by a separate consort. In many Renaissance songbooks the precise accompaniment is not stipulated.

Virtually all the English music treatises between 1560 and 1630 deal with singing, both as a guide to learning the rudiments of music and as an approach to composition. Morley's great treatise, his *A Plaine and*

song

Easie Introduction to Practicall Musicke (1597) is divided into three sections. 'The first teacheth to sing with all things necessary for the knowledge of pricktsong.' 'The second treateth of **descant**e and to sing two parts in one upon a **plainsong** or **ground**, with other things necessary for a descanter.' 'The third and last part entreateth of composition of three. Foure, five or more parts with many profitable rules to that effect.' In the prefatory material to his *Psalmes, Sonets, & Songs* (1588), Byrd emphasizes the importance of singing for the betterment of man:

> Reasons briefely set downe by th'auctor, to perswade every one to learne to sing.
>
> First, it is a knowledge easely taught, and quickly learned, where there is a good Master, and an apt Scoller.
>
> 2 The exercise of singing is delightfull to Nature, & good to preserve the health of Man.
>
> 3 It doth strengthen all parts of the brest, & doth open the **pipe**s.
>
> 4 It is a singuler good remedie for a stutting & stammering in the speech.
>
> 5 It is the best meanes to procure a perfect pronunciation, & to make a good Orator.
>
> 6 It is the onely way to know where Nature hath bestowed the benefit of a good voyce: which guift is so rare, as there is not one among a thousand, that hath it: and in many, that excellent guift is lost, because they want Art to expresse Nature.
>
> 7 There is not any Musicke or Instruments whatsoever, comparable to that which is made of the voyces of Men, where the voices are good, and the same well sorted and ordered.
>
> 8 The better the voyce is, the meeter it is to honour and serve God therewith: and the voyce of man is chiefly to be imployed to that ende.

(B) References to song, singing and those who sing pervade Shakespeare's works. In the plays, stage directions for songs and singing can be of a general nature; sometimes they are followed by the text of the song or by details about its theme. In a number of cases when songs are accompanied by music, the instruments needed are also specified; singing can happen in conjunction with dancing or can be expected to take place in a specific area of the stage (Dessen and Thomson, pp. 200–1; 207–8). The dialogue often refers to songs and singing when explicit stage directions are found, but there are also examples of allusions to songs confined to the dramatic dialogue.

Among the most interesting explicit instructions for actors to sing, is the one found in Q1 *Hamlet* (1603): '*Enter Ophelia **play**ing on a lute, and her hair down singing*' (G4v). A wig creating the effect of dishevelled hair would have visually signified the girl's state of insanity; the boy actor was also expected to accompany himself on a lute while singing the bawdy songs (see below for a detailed commentary).

At the beginning of 2.2 of *A Midsummer Night's Dream*, Titania orders the fairies: 'Sing me now asleep; / Then to your offices, and let me rest' (7–8). There follows the direction '*Fairies sing*', which was probably accompanied by a **dance** as the opening line by Titania suggests: 'Come, now a **roundel** and a fairy song' (2.2.1). The lyrics 'Never harm, nor spell, nor **charm**, / Come our lovely lady nigh' (16–17) acquire an ironic connotation: as soon as the fairies depart, Oberon casts the spell on Titania which will make her fall in love with the ass-headed Bottom.

The magical atmosphere imbuing *A Midsummer Night's Dream* is reflected in its ample use of music and song: in a subtle metatheatrical game with the audience, it sometimes serves a comical purpose. For example, just after the magic spell is cast on Bottom, the other mechanicals abandon him and, to overcome his fear, he starts singing 'The **woosel cock**'. The text of this song was probably **set** to the **tune** of 'Whoop, do me no harm, good man', whose title is mentioned in *The Winter's Tale*, 4.4.198 (Duffin, p. 478). Titania, awakened by Bottom's song, comments:

> I pray thee, gentle mortal, sing again.
> Mine **ear** is much enamored of thy **note**;
> So is mine eye enthralled to thy shape.
> (3.1.137–9)

Clearly, Titania's ears must be as deceived as her eyes: it is likely that the actor playing Bottom would have sung in a way which was anything but enthralling. Bottom's song would have created a contrast to the harmonious song sung by the fairies in the previous scene, 'You spotted snakes' (2.2.9–19). Interestingly, the latter has no surviving **melody** but 'fits remarkably well to the same tune as "Robin Goodfellow", a song alluded to elsewhere in this play' (Duffin, p. 480).

song

The harmony at the end of this comedy is underlined by the fairies' blessing on the house and on the newly wed couples:

> OBERON: Through the house give glimmering light
> By the dead and drowsy fire,
> Every elf and fairy sprite
> Hop as light as bird from brier,
> And this **ditty**, after me,
> Sing, and dance it trippingly.
> TITANIA: First, **rehearse** your song by **rote**,
> To each word a warbling note.
> Hand in hand, with fairy **grace**,
> Will we sing, and bless this place.
>
> (5.1.391–400)

There follows another **rhyme**d speech, which in Folio is indented and italicized, and is introduced by the italicized heading '*The Song*'. In contrast, both Q1 (1600) and Q2 (1619) assign that speech to Oberon and do not differentiate it from the rest of the dialogue. Scholars are divided on the question of whether the Folio or quarto version is the more correct: for instance, Noble (pp. 55–7) believes that Folio is the correct version, whereas Foakes maintains that the song suggested in the passage quoted above is missing (p. 133). From the wording of the speeches, it transpires that the singing was accompanied by a dance, probably a **round**, as is suggested by two earlier references (2.1.86 and 2.2.1 discussed above). Titania's instruction to rehearse the song (5.1.397) seems to parallel the concern expressed by the mechanicals while rehearsing 'Pyramus and Thisbe'. (See '**warble**' for a commentary of this passage.)

Sometimes there are references to song structure, for instance when Celia tells Rosalind: 'I would sing my song without a **burthen**; / Thou bring'st me out of tune' (*AYLI* 3.2.247–8). It is likely that Celia is referring to **burden** in its meaning as 'undersong', which would be sung throughout the stanza, rather than at the end of it like a refrain. The musical metaphor employed by Celia reveals that she is frustrated because Rosalind is asking pressing queries about the identity of the man who is dedicating love poems to her, and she feels that she is no longer in tune with her cousin (see 'burden' for a more detailed analysis of this passage). This metaphor is appropriate in a play where vocal singing acquires a prominent role, for instance with 'Under the greenwood tree' (2.5.1–8; 38–45), 'Blow, blow, thou winter wind' (2.7.174–90), 'What shall he have that kill'd the deer?' (4.2.10–18), 'It was a lover and his lass' (5.3.16–33) and 'Wedding is great Juno's crown' (5.4.141–6).

In *Measure for Measure*, 'Take, O, take those lips away' (4.1.1–6) is sung by a boy while he enters with Mariana at the beginning of 4.1. The text alludes to Mariana's state as an abandoned lover: this is the only time that a song is found in this stern play. When Duke Vincentio (disguised as a friar) arrives, Mariana orders the boy to interrupt his singing and to go away. She then apologizes to Vincentio:

> I cry you mercy, sir, and well could wish
> You had not found me here so musical.
> Let me excuse me, and believe me so,
> My mirth it much displeas'd, but pleas'd my woe.
> (10–13)

To which Vincentio replies: ' 'Tis good; though music oft hath such a charm / To make bad good, and good provoke to harm' (14–15). The song and the ensuing debate on the dangers implicit in pleasurable activities serve 'the vital function of placing the episode within the main thematic preoccupations of the play' (Lindley, 1990, p. 80). They exemplify the dilemma that faces most of the characters in this play, who on the surface display aversion towards pleasure and yet often – if involuntarily – reveal their attraction to it.

Sometimes songs and singing are mentioned in connection with other musical terms, or can be preceded (or followed) by sound effects on the stage. Exemplary in both regards is the concluding scene of *Hamlet*. Upon realising that Hamlet has died, Horatio exclaims:

> Now cracks a noble heart. Good night, sweet prince,
> And flights of **angel**s sing thee to thy **rest**!
> Why does the **drum** come hither?
> (*Ham* 5.2.359–61)

The religious image of the angels singing while escorting Hamlet to heaven points to the **harmony** and peace that await Hamlet in the afterlife. There is also a pun on the word 'rest' with its musical

song

connotation which echoes the last line delivered by Hamlet: 'The rest is **silence**' (5.2.358). It is possible that Horatio has Ophelia in mind when he refers to the singing angels, since she is remembered for her singing during her madness and also, according to Gertrude's account, while she is dying: 'she **chaunt**ed **snatch**es of old **laud**s / As one incapable of her own distress' (4.7.177–8). The **beat**ing of a military drum immediately after references to silence and harmonious singing, brings the audience back to the reality of the imminent succession of Fortinbras to the throne of Denmark. The funeral ceremony accorded to the Prince is in line with the military tradition: Fortinbras commands that 'the soldiers' music and the rite of war / **Speak** loudly for him' (5.2.399–400) and concludes the play with the order to the soldiers to shoot. The staging of the funeral with its military sounds could not be further removed from the image of the angels singing Hamlet harmoniously to his rest.

Hamlet comments on the skull just dug up that it 'had a **tongue** in it, and could sing once' (*Ham* 5.1.75). His jocular remark contrasts with the doctor's stern comment later in the scene that Ophelia cannot be buried with proper funeral rites, given that the cause of her death is 'doubtful' (5.1.227). The doctor says:

> We should profane the service of the dead
> To sing a **requiem** and such rest to her
> As to peace-parted souls.
> (5.1.236–8)

His word-play on 'rest', a musical pun used more than once in this play, is noteworthy in this sombre context.

In *Twelfth Night*, instrumental and vocal music on the stage provide the opportunity for meditation on the meaning of true love, for instance when Orsino discusses this topic with Viola (disguised as Cesario) after ordering that a song be played (2.4.1–41). Completely unaware of Viola's gender and of the fact that she is in love with him, his remarks are full of ironic echoes and confirm his proneness to self-indulging melancholia. The feeling of melancholia and pain accompanying love are epitomized by Feste's song 'Come away, come away, death', sung at the end of this conversation (2.4.51–66); ultimately, this song and 'O mistress mine' (2.3.39–52) 'embody the paradoxical truth about romantic love that is the play's subject' (Wells, p. 223). Viola is closely

song

associated with the musical sphere: at the beginning of the play, the girl announces her intention to disguise herself as a **eunuch** and enter the service of the Duke. She claims that she 'can sing / And speak to him in many sorts of music' (1.2.57–8), i.e. that she is versed both in vocal and instrumental music (see 'eunuch' for a detailed analysis). She refers to her musical ability throughout the play, for instance when she courts Olivia by proxy, and explains that she can 'write loyal **canton**s of contemned love, / And sing them loud even in the dead of night' (1.5.270–1).

Songs can serve another important function, since they sometimes 'give women a voice, literally as well as figuratively – a voice by and large denied to them by the literary high culture of Renaissance England' (Smith, p. 26). It is undeniable that in the Shakespeare canon, songs allow women to express themselves more freely within a society which expects decorum and decency from them. With their explicit sexual content, the tunes sung by Ophelia in her madness (*Ham* 4.5) fall into this category, as does Desdemona's 'Willow song' (an addition found only in Folio *Othello*, 4.3) with its popular tone. This type of spontaneous song was frowned upon by Puritans in early modern England. There are several Elizabethan and Jacobean examples of attacks on music, which often associate this form of art with the female, 'longed for but also feared' (Fox-Good, p. 233). The songs delivered by these women have a role of 'provoking music' (Lindley, 1990, p. 88), which not only reveals a character's feelings and anxieties but also preoccupations about society as portrayed in a specific play. In a similar way, music could acquire an uncontrolled disorderly quality as for instance in Caliban's drunken songs (ibid., p. 20), and 'may thus be viewed as . . . a potential form of debate' (Iselin, p. 136). However, most of the other songs in *The Tempest* seem to support the traditional neo-platonic theory. A good example is provided by Ariel's songs to Ferdinand – 'Come unto these yellow sands' (1.2.375–87) and 'Full fadom five' (1.2.397–405). These are inseparable from Prospero's artistic vision, and encapsulate the encounter between the civilized and the natural world (Chan, p. 324). The setting of 'Full fadom five' by Robert Johnson (who was associated with Shakespeare's playing company) 'points both to a narrative significance in the words and to the poetry as a formal whole, in this way emphasizing its conceptual significance – as a microcosm of the meaning of the island' (ibid., p. 325).

See also **breast**, **throat**.

song

(C) Chan, *Music in the Theatre of Ben Jonson* (1980), ch. 7, concentrates on *The Winter's Tale* and *The Tempest* and gives a detailed account of the influence of the masque on Jacobean drama and of the relationship between art and playgoers.

Dessen and Thomson, *A Dictionary of Stage Directions* (1999), pp. 200–1; 207–8.

Duffin, *Shakespeare's Songbook* (2004), brings together lyrics and notation of the songs connected with the Shakespeare canon.

Foakes, *A Midsummer Night's Dream* (1984).

Fox-Good 'Ophelia's Mad Songs' (1995), offers a thorough analysis, from a feminist perspective, of the contents and musical form (e.g. harmonic structure and metre) of the songs in *Hamlet*, arguing that the 'mad' songs allow Ophelia to free herself from the code of passivity imposed on women in early modern society.

Iselin, ' "My Music for Nothing" ' (1995), focuses on the traditional and subversive role of vocal and instrumental music in *The Tempest*.

Lindley, 'Shakespeare's Provoking Music' (1990), argues that songs in Shakespearean drama go beyond the purely conventional, and that they carry out a vital thematic function within the play; *The Tempest* (2002).

Noble, *Shakespeare's Use of Song* (1923), is a seminal study on the topic.

Owens, 'Concepts of Pitch in English Music Theory' (1998), 183–246.

Seng, *The Vocal Songs in the Plays of Shakespeare* (1967), explores the dramatic role of each song he cites.

Smith, *The Acoustic World of Early Modern England* (1999).

Wells, *Elizabethan Mythologies* (1994), has a chapter dedicated to the role of songs in *Twelfth Night*.

Wilson (ed.), *A New Way* (2003), pp. 14–26, provides a list and brief survey of English music treatises.

See also 'music' section C.

sound (A) To the largely illiterate Elizabethan audience, the sound of **music** would have more significance and impact than any other form of musical transmission. This is one of the most important underlying precepts in Shakespeare's use of music. And yet he rarely acknowledges it in his use of 'sound'. In the great majority of cases, when sound is employed in a musical context it is as a verb in connection with 'all the lofty **instrument**s of war' (*1H4* 5.2). Sound, for the most part, was to be actually **hear**d rather than imagined. The bellman sounded his **bell** to signify the time of day. The **trumpet** signal was a clearly recognizable martial or ceremonial sound. When Shakespeare does not specify trumpets or military signals and has what seems the more general 'music sounds' he calls for **soft** instrumental music to **play**.

When sound is heard imaginatively, the neo-platonic ethos of heavenly music is invoked. The **motion** of the spheres results in sound which becomes music, and that music has the power to influence celestial and earthly existences. Thus musical sounds can have the power to effect ideas, actions and relationships. (For a fuller discussion of the music of the spheres, see 'music'.)

In other contexts, 'to sound means not only to produce sound, but also to measure the depth of something, to establish its boundaries, to define it spatially' (Folkerth, p. 25). In this sense there is a relationship to music in that musical sound has a quantitative element or intensity. Folkerth argues that

> in early modern culture, sound is considered a privileged mode of access to the deeply subjective thoughts, emotions, and intentions of others. We find this association between sound and the deeply subjective self articulated throughout Shakespeare's works. In them, the practice of 'sounding out' others is frequently represented not only as an important method of surveillance, but also as a way of representing characters' emotional proximity to each other.
>
> (p. 33)

In one Shakespeare passage (*Ham* 3.2.363–72) this interpretation is couched within a musical framework (see below).

Audiences today are much more aware of the sound musical instruments might have made in Elizabethan theatres, thanks to the work of musicologists, period instrument makers and players. The Globe theatre permanent exhibition in London, for example, includes a section on music. Not only does it have examples of instruments from the Elizabethan period, it also offers the visitor sound-bites so that they can hear those instruments. In the Globe production (2002) of *Twelfth Night*, the authenticity of the production extended to using period instruments and contemporary music so that it had an aural dimension unusual in the modern theatre.

sound

(B) A number of explicit stage directions in the Shakespeare canon prescribe that military and ceremonial instruments and/or signals have to be sounded. These include indications for battles such as '*sound **alarum***' (*Tro* 1.1.88.SD). '*Sounds a **parley***' (*Tim* 5.4.2.SD) follows Alcibiades' order to parley with the senators of Athens: 'Sound to this coward and lascivious town / Our terrible approach' (1–2). Similarly, in *1 Henry VI*, Joan of Arc's command to 'summon a parley' (3.3.35) is followed by '*trumpets sound a parley*' (3.3.35.SD), and is preceded by '***drum*** *sounds afar off*' (3.3.28.SD) to signify the English army's marching towards Paris. '*A **retreat*** *is sounded*' in *Coriolanus* (1.9.OSD) and *1 Henry IV* (5.4.158.SD). '*A dead **march***' is '*sounded*' (*Cor* 5.6.154.SD) while the dead body of Coriolanus is carried offstage in solemn fashion at the end of the play. Indications of the type '*sound **flourish***' (*Ant* 2.7.133.SD), '*a **tucket*** *sounds*' (Folio *MV* 5.1.121.SD) and '*sound a **sennet***' (Q1 *King Lear*, B1v) accompany the entry of characters of rank (see respective entries for relevant examples).

Exhortations such as 'Sound, trumpet' (*Lr* 5.3.109), 'Sound, trumpets, and set forward, combatants' (*R2* 1.3.117), 'Sound retreat, and cease our hot pursuit' (*1H6* 2.2.3) and 'Sound drums and trumpets' (*3H6* 5.7.45) are frequent in the dramatic dialogue and were intended to work as cues to **musician**s to play their instruments in martial and combat scenes.

There are also instances in Shakespeare where 'sound' is used in connection with music on a more philosophical level rather than with sound effects. In the first scene of the Induction to *The Taming of the Shrew*, some characters plot to trick Sly into believing that he is a lord; when he wakes from his drunken state, musicians will be playing for him making 'a **dulcet** and a heavenly sound' (Ind.i.51). The **harmony** of music is required to create a conducive atmosphere also in *The Merchant of Venice* when Bassanio is trying to choose the right casket and Portia (who hopes for a positive outcome) orders: 'Let music sound while he doth make his choice' (3.2.43). The '**true concord** of **well tuned** sounds' (*Son* 8.5) is invoked by the poet when he exhorts his friend to get married in a sonnet pervaded by musical conceits.

A repentant Claudio reads out the epitaph he has written for the (apparently) dead Hero and then, to enhance the **solemn**ity of the ceremony in her honour, he orders: 'Now, music, sound, and sing your **solemn hymn**' (*Ado* 5.3.11). This is followed by the **song** 'Pardon, goddess of the night' (12–21).

sound

In an unusual metaphor, Orsino juxtaposes sound and smell when he remarks that the music being played in the background, which he considers to be the 'food of love' (*TN* 1.1.1):

> . . . came o'er my **ear** like the **sweet** sound
> That **breath**es upon a bank of violets,
> Stealing and giving odor . . .
>
> (5–7)

The practice of 'sounding out' people as explained by Folkerth (see above) is nicely illustrated when Hamlet attempts to teach his 'friend' Guildenstern (who has been sent by Claudius to establish whether Hamlet is faking his madness) to learn to play the **recorder**. Hamlet reproaches Guildenstern: 'you would sound me from my / **low**est **note** to the top of my **compass** . . . / yet cannot you make it [the recorder] **speak**' (*Ham* 3.2.366–7; 369). The use of a musical instrument as a stage property during this (supposed) **lesson** in practical music gives the speech a far deeper metaphorical significance: it allows Hamlet to reveal his knowledge that Guildenstern wants to extract information from him.

See also **knell, voice**.

(C) Elam, 'Collective Affinities' (2002), reviews the 2002 *Twelfth Night* production at the Globe and its use of 'authentic' Renaissance music.

Folkerth, *The Sound of Shakespeare* (2002).

McGee, *Medieval and Renaissance Music: A Performers' Guide* (1985), contains a survey of style and historical performance practice in Renaissance music.

Pattison, *Music and Poetry of the English Renaissance* (1948), opens with a chapter on 'Music in Sixteenth-Century Society'.

Smith, *The Acoustic World of Early Modern England* (1999), ch. 3, explores the 'soundscapes of early modern England' in both town, court and country.

Woodfill, *Musicians in English Society from Elizabeth to Charles I* (1953), devotes a large part of his book to the role of music and musicians.

Wulstan, *Tudor Music* (1985), ch. 3, discusses the sound-role of music in the everyday world of Elizabethan citizens.

sound-post (A) The small cylindrical piece of pine wood fitted

sound-post

within the body of a violin or related instrument between the front and the back and closely beneath the bridge is called a 'sound-post'. It has two functions. One is structural, providing strength to the body of the **instrument**. The other is acoustical, transmitting vibrations from the front to the back evenly throughout the body. The exact position of the sound-post and the type and quality of wood used are crucial to the tone of the instrument. It is not surprising therefore that the sound-post has been described as the 'soul' of the instrument, as its Italian name 'anima' and French 'âme' suggest.

(B) This technical term is found only once in Shakespeare's works, in *Romeo and Juliet*. One of the three **musician**s dismissed after the (apparent) death of Juliet on her wedding day to Paris is called 'James Soundpost' (4.5.136). His companions also have **music**al names, connected with the violin: Hugh **Rebec**k and Simon **Catling**. The light-hearted tone of this part of the scene contrasts with the **mournful** tone of the first part. Hugh Rebeck's statement that music has a '**silver sound** because musicians sound for silver' (4.5.134) leaves us with the impression that these musicians are more interested in the money that can be made from **play**ing at feasts than in the artistic value of music.

speak (A) When referring to an **instrument** speak means 'to **sound**'. It is most often used in connection with **wind** instruments and is still used today in particular with reference to **organ pipe**s.

(B) In Shakespeare, martial and ceremonial instruments sometimes 'speak' almost as if they were verbalizing through their sounds the wishes of the person who commands them to be **play**ed. This is evident when Macduff, who has a strong desire for revenge after Macbeth has had his family slaughtered, orders the assault on Macbeth's castle: 'Make all our **trumpet**s speak, give them all **breath** / Those **clamor**ous harbingers of blood and death' (*Mac* 5.6.9–10). Edmund too expresses his wish to engage in a fight with his half-brother Edgar when he orders 'Trumpets, speak!' (*Lr* 5.3.151), the signal that the fight can begin. Claudius can barely disguise his eagerness to see the fencing contest between Hamlet and Horatio when he gives directions on how it must be announced: 'Let the **kettle[drum]** to the trumpet speak / The trumpet to the cannoneer without' (*Ham* 5.2.275–6). The **solemn** funeral of Coriolanus is accompanied by a dead **march** as Aufidius commands the drummer: '**Beat** thou the drum, that it speak mournfully' (*Cor* 5.6.149).

In *Othello* the Clown asks some **musician**s after they have played: 'have your instruments been in / Naples, that they speak i' th' nose thus?' (3.1.3–4), a reference to the sound of the **bagpipe**s but also to syphilis – commonly known as the Neapolitan disease in Shakespeare's time (Partridge, p. 197).

'Speak' acquires a technical meaning when Don Pedro asks a reluctant Balthasar to sing '**Sigh** no more, ladies'. In the ensuing dialogue, they exchange puns on the meaning of '**crotchet**' and '**note**':

> BALTHASAR: Note this before my notes:
> There's not a note of mine that's worth the noting.
> DON PEDRO: Why, these are very crotchets that he speaks –
> Note notes, forsooth, and nothing.
>
> (*Ado* 2.3.54–7)

'Crotchet' can mean either 'quarter-note' or 'whim'. 'Note' is another polysemic term. It means 'take notice of', 'brief comment' and has, of course, a musical nuance. Hence 'speaking crotchets' obliquely refers to 'playing notes'.

(C) Partridge, *Shakespeare's Bawdy* (1968).
See also 'sound' section C.

spheres (music of the) see **music**.

squealing (A) The term 'squealing' denotes a **loud** unpleasant **high**-pitched **sound** sometimes associated with **bagpipe**s, children and swine.

(B) The unpleasantness of this sound is mentioned by Shylock when he warns Jessica against the excesses of **masque**s:

> What, are there masques? Hear you me, Jessica:
> Lock up my doors, and when you **hear** the **drum**
> And the vile squealing of the wry-neck'd **fife** . . .

squealing

> ... Stop my house's **ear**s, I mean my casements;
> Let not the sound of shallow fopp'ry enter
> My sober house ...
>
> (*MV* 2.5.28–30; 34–6)

The 'fife' in this case is the **musician** rather than the **instrument**: the juxtaposition of two unpleasant images shows how much Shylock disapproves of masques, which he associates with Christianity as opposed to Jewishness. The first image is that of the wry neck of the fifer – Barnaby Riche tells us that 'a fife is a wry-neckt musician, for he always looks away from his instrument' (taken from Brown, p. 51). The second unpleasant image conjured up by Shylock is that of the **shrill** loud sound of the instrument.

See also **speak**.

(C) Brown, *The Merchant of Venice* (1955).

still (A) In Elizabethan times, 'still' refers either to continuous **music**, when the word follows the noun (e.g. '**recorder**s still'), or to quiet or **soft** music, when the adjective precedes the noun (e.g. 'still music'). Conventionally the latter would apply to **string**ed **instrument**s such as the **viol** and **lute**. **Wind** instruments were most often thought to be **loud**. Consequently, if wind instruments are to **play** softly they are designated 'still' as in Marston's stage direction '*The still **flute**s sound softly*' (*Antonio's Revenge*, 1602, 4.3).

(B) In several early modern stage directions, phrases such as 'music still' or '**alarum**s still' are indications for music and sound effects to continue (Dessen and Thomson, p. 216). This is explicit in '*Alarum continues still afar off*' (*Cor* 1.5.3.SD) heard during the Battle of Corioles. Another interesting usage in the Shakespeare canon is found in the scenes portraying Lear's descent into madness (2.4, 3.1, 3.2 and 3.4), where sound effects for a storm mirror the state of confusion in the King's mind. The stage direction '*storm still*', which appears at the beginning of 3.1, 3.2 and 3.4. provides continuity in the sound effects.

'Still' is sometimes synonymous with 'soft', for instance in *As You Like It* where '*Still music*' (5.4.108.SD) underlines the **solemn**ity of the multiple wedding celebration at the end of the play. It accompanies

still

Hymen's speeches about the sanctity of marriage, and precedes the **song** 'Wedding is great Juno's crown' (141–6). In *The Two Noble Kinsmen*, Emilia prays at the altar of Diana that, between Palamon and Arcite, the one who loves her more should conquer her. During the first part of her speech '*Still music of record[er]s*' (5.1.136.SD) is **hear**d. Playing these instruments softly is appropriate in a scene focusing on religious devotion.

(C) Dessen and Thomson, *A Dictionary of Stage Directions* (1999).

Sternfeld, *Music in Shakespearean Tragedy* (1967), pp. 242–3 discusses 'still' only as quiet music and accepts the dubious editorial substitution of 'still' for 'rough' in *Pericles* 3.2, 'The rough and woeful music' (88) (see 'music').

stop (A) A 'stop' is the finger hole on a **wind instrument** such as the **recorder** or **hoboy** which, when covered or stopped, **alter**s the pitch of the **note** being **sound**ed. There are generally six stops on a woodwind instrument. A stop on a **string**ed instrument is called the **fret**. When stops are called **ventages** (e.g. *Ham* 3.2.357), a wind instrument is indicated. Stops on a harpsichord or **virginal** are small handoperated devices located near the keyboard. They control a row of **jack**s so that they can be brought into **play** if desired. An early reference to keyboard stops occurs in the Privy Purse Expenses of Henry VIII: 'ii payer of Virginalls in one coffer with iii stoppes' (Rimbault, *History of the Pianoforte*, 1860, p. 33). **Organ**s also have several stops which the player can use to change registers.

(B) *Hamlet* has three references to stops in one scene. At the beginning of 3.2, the Prince comments that 'blest are those' (68) 'that . . . are not a **pipe** for Fortune's finger / To sound what stop she please' (70–1). The meaning implied here, that men should not let themselves be influenced by external events, is elaborated on later in the scene, when Rosencrantz and Guildenstern are trying to find out on behalf of the King whether Hamlet is faking his madness. Hamlet encourages Guildenstern to play a **recorder** and demonstrates how to use its stops or ventages: '**Govern** these ventages . . . / Look you, these are the stops' (3.2.357; 360). The latter objects that he cannot play that instrument, which leads Hamlet to rebuke him:

stop

> Why, look you now, how unworthy a thing
> you make of me! You would play upon me, you would
> seem to know my stops, you would pluck out the
> heart of my mystery, you would sound me from my
> lowest note to the top of my **compass**; and there is
> much **music**, excellent **voice**, in this little organ, yet
> cannot you make it **speak**. 'Sblood, do you think I am
> easier to be play'd on than a pipe? Call me what
> instrument you will, though you fret me, yet you
> cannot play upon me.
>
> (3.2.363–72)

This elaborate musical metaphor indicates that Hamlet is aware of his friends' real intentions, and that he does not intend to be manipulated.

The Prologue's address to the audience in *2 Henry IV* opens with a musical allusion: 'Open your **ear**s, for which of you will stop / The vent of **hear**ing when **loud** Rumor speaks?' (Ind. 1–2). He sustains this metaphor when he compares himself to a pipe:

> . . . Rumor is a pipe
> **Blow**n by surmises, jealousies, conjectures,
> And of so easy and so plain a stop
> That the blunt monster with uncounted heads,
> The still-**discord**ant wav'ring multitude,
> Can play upon it . . .
>
> (Ind. 15–20)

Like Hamlet in his speech to Guildenstern, Rumor implies that controlling the stops of a wind instrument is quite a straightforward technique.

The only allusion to stops in relation to stringed instruments is found when Claudio ironically comments that Benedick's jesting spirit has 'crept into a **lute**-string, and [is] **govern**'d by stops' (*Ado* 3.2.60) since he has fallen in love with Beatrice. The lute was associated with melancholy caused by love, and the frets (or stops) of the lute symbolize Benedick's surrender to this feeling.

See also **peg, tune, viol**.

strain (A) A strain is the phrase, line or section of a **piece** of **music**.

406

strain

As a temporal unit, it can have structural significance, as Campion suggests: 'In Musick we do not say a straine of so many **note**s, but so many sem'briefes' (*Observations*, 1602, ed. Vivian, p. 35). He goes on to qualify the use of 'strain', for example, in an **ayre** where the lines of a **song** may need extra **beat**s in order to be in **proportion**: 'For we find in Musick that oftentimes the straines of a song cannot be reduct to true **number** without some **rest**s prefixt in the beginning and middle, as also at the **close** if need requires' (ibid., pp. 39–40).

Morley affirms the sectional meaning when he defines the **canzonet** as: 'Little shorte songs (wherin little arte can be shewed being made in straines, the beginning of which is some **point** lightlie touched, and everie straine repeated except the middle)' (*Introduction*, 1597, p. 180).

The meaning of 'strain' in relation to individual notes and context is nicely articulated in the opening of the elegy on the death of Sir John Shelton:

> **Sound** saddest notes with rueful moaning;
> **Tune** every strain with tears and weeping;
> Conclude each close with **sigh**s and groaning.
> (Carlton, 1601, no. 11)

When not used in a specific sense, the term can simply mean a 'tune' or 'melodic line': 'Sing we, **dance** we on the green, / And fill these valleys with our **melodious** strains' (Pilkington, 1613, no. 16).

As a verb, it is used specifically to mean 'tightening **string**s' on a musical **instrument** such as **lute, harp** or **viol**; or it can mean 'to **play** upon an instrument' or 'to employ the **voice** to sing'.

(B) Orsino refers to a specific phrase or section of a piece of music when, in his melancholy mood caused by his unrequited love for Olivia, he orders his **musician**s to play it again: 'That strain again, it had a dying **fall**' (*TN* 1.1.4). The 'fall' or '**cadence**' of this section probably entailed a diminution of pitch and **loud**ness, such as in Dowland's famous ayre 'Flow my Tears', published in 1600, which has been used in various modern productions (e.g. at the new Globe in Southwark in 2002).

In Juliet's comment that the **lark** 'sings out of tune, / Straining **harsh discord**s and unpleasing **sharp**s' (*Rom* 3.5.27–8) the conventional **praise** of this **bird**'s harmonious singing is subverted. 'Straining' here means 'using the voice'.

strain

On the eve of the Battle of Philippi, Brutus feels anxious and lonely and asks his servant Lucius, who is falling asleep:

> Bear with me, good boy, I am much forgetful.
> Canst thou hold up thy heavy eyes awhile,
> And **touch** thy instrument a strain or two?
>
> (*JC* 4.3.255–7)

The instrument was probably a lute, since Lucius later refers to its 'strings' (291). It is likely that Brutus was requesting a light-hearted tune which would help him overcome his fears and doubts.

In a passage loaded with musical conceits, Lucrece invokes **Philomela** (transformed into a **nightingale** after being raped by Tereus) in the following terms:

> Make thy sad grove in my dishevell'd hair;
> As the dank earth weeps at thy **languishment**,
> So I at each sad strain will strain a tear,
> And with deep groans the **diapason bear**:
> For **burthen**-wise I'll **hum** on Tarquin still,
> While thou on Tereus **descan**ts better **skill**.
>
> (*Luc* 1129–34)

These lines express the same ideas as Carlton's elegy quoted above. The **high** descant is underlined by the voice, which works as a kind of **ground**. The image of sexual violation is hinted at by terms such as 'groans' and '**burden**'.

There may be a musical nuance also in the concluding couplet of *Sonnet* 90, in which the poet, fearing that his friend intends to leave him, exhorts him to do it now 'while the world is bent my deeds to cross' (2). He concludes that 'other strains of woe, which now seem woe[ful], / Compar'd with loss of thee will not seem so' (13–14). 'Strain' used in a context of love-induced pain evokes musical nuances, since this feeling of sadness was often expressed through music.

(C) Partridge, *Shakespeare's Bawdy* (1968), pp. 92–3; 149.

strike (A) To strike is to initiate the **sound** of an **instrument** by making physical contact, through the hands or by means of an

strike

implement (a stick or hammer). In Elizabethan musical treatises it most often refers to **play**ing the **lute**: 'now for your right hand, called the striking hand leane upon the bellie of the Lute' (Thomas Robinson, *Schoole of Musicke*, 1603, Bv). This word is also found, especially in literature, in the context of sounding **drum**s or **bell**s or combinations of instruments that make up a signal (e.g. **alarum**).

(B) The order to strike up drums is found in martial contexts in several historical plays and tragedies, among them *2 Henry IV* (4.2.120), *Richard III* (4.4.149 and 179), *Timon of Athens* (4.3.169; 5.4.85), *King Lear* (5.3.81) and *3 Henry VI* (2.1.204; 4.7.50; 5.3.24). In *King John* the Dauphin declares his readiness to engage in battle with the English with a powerful musical metaphor: 'Strike up the drums, and let the **tongue** of war / Plead for our interest and our being here' (5.2.164–5). The Bastard uses '**beat**' as a synonym for 'strike' in his defiant reply, punning on the military and musical nuances of the word: 'Indeed your drums, being beaten, will cry out; / And so shall you, being beaten' (166–7). A similar effect is achieved in *1 Henry VI* when Talbot remembers that the dying Salisbury was a valiant soldier: 'Whilst any **trump** did sound, or drum struck up, / His sword did ne'er leave striking in the field' (1.4.80–1). The striking of the drum in battle and the action of striking the enemy with a sword are juxtaposed.

Troilus' command to 'strike a free **march**' to Troy (*Tro* 5.10.30) has puzzled scholars. 'Free' possibly means that the marching order is not intended to be formal (Bevington, p. 352); this would 'take the Trojans briskly back to the city' (Palmer, p. 301). The rhythm of the march would have been established by the beating of drums.

The use of 'strike' in its musical connotation is sometimes observed in non-military situations. The joyous atmosphere at the end of *Much Ado About Nothing* is accentuated by Benedick's exhortation: 'Strike up, **pipe**rs' (5.4.128). 'Piper' in Shakespeare's day could be synonymous either with '**bagpipe**r' or with the more generic term '**musician**'.

When Paulina is about to 'revive' what the other characters believe to be the statue of Hermione, she **solemn**ly commands: '**Music**! awake her! strike!' (*WT* 5.3.98). In a more light-hearted scene earlier in the play, the Clown also gives the order to 'strike up' (4.4.161 and 165) and 'a **dance** of Shepherds and Shepherdesses' (4.1.165.SD) follows. As in *Much Ado About Nothing*, the rustic dance would have required the instrumental accompaniment of pipes.

strike

The most conspicuous allusion to striking the lute is found in *Sonnet* 8, built on elaborate musical imagery. Encouraging his young friend (who is addressed as 'music to **hear**' in the opening line of the sonnet) towards marriage, the poet observes:

> Mark how one **string, sweet** husband to another,
> Strikes each in each by mutual ordering;
> Resembling sire, and child, and happy mother,
> Who all in one, one pleasing **note** do **sing**.
> (9–12)

The **harmony** derived from marital union resembles that of the music produced by a stringed instrument. For instance, lutes were strung with pairs of strings for each course, except the **bass**. Those pairs had to be in **tune** ('harmony') otherwise the lute would sound out of tune and its music would be **discord**ant. 'Strikes each in each' is also suggestive of sexual union (Duncan-Jones, p. 127).

See also **trumpet**.

(C) Bevington, *Troilus and Cressida* (1998).
Duncan-Jones, *Shakespeare's Sonnets* (1997).
Palmer, *Troilus and Cressida* (1982).

string (A) Stringed **instrument**s such as the **lute, viol**, violin (**fiddle**) and **harp** are so-called because of the sets of strings stretched across their bodies which when bowed or plucked vibrate to make a **sound** through the soundboard. Until superseded by steel, strings were made from animal gut, normally sheep gut (erroneously called 'catgut'). During the sixteenth century, Italy was famous for the manufacture of strings, particularly Rome, where gut from very young sheep was extracted and made, after a lengthy process, into strings of various sizes and densities. In his 'Other Necessary Obseruations belonging to the Lute' ('For Chusing of Lute-strings') in *Varietie of Lute-lessons* (1610), John Dowland notes that the best 'small' (i.e. thin or **high**er pitched) strings 'come from *Rome* and other parts of *Italy*' (D1v) and that the best 'great' or **low**er strings 'come out of Germany' (D1v). He advises potential buyers that the 'best time for the Marchant is to provide his strings at Michaelmas, for then the string-makers bring their best strings which were made in the Summer to *Franckford*, and *Lypzig* Martes. Contranly at Easter they bring their Winter strings, which are not so good' (D1v).

Strings in keyboard instruments were generally made of metal wire. They varied in thickness and length from the deep **bass** (long and fat) to the high **treble** (short and thin).

(B) *Richard II* has three references to strings. After Mowbray has been banished from England for life, he observes:

> My native English, now I must forgo,
> And now my **tongue**'s use is to me no more
> Than an unstringed viol or a harp.
> (1.3.160–2)

The impossibility of speaking his language in a foreign country makes him feel like an instrument which cannot produce any sound because it has been deprived of its strings. In another scene, Northumberland informs King Richard of Gaunt's death. He compares the latter's tongue to an instrument which cannot produce sounds because it has no strings: 'His tongue is now a stringless instrument, / Words, life, and all, old Lancaster hath spent' (*R2* 2.1.149–50). Later, a metaphor referring to stringed instruments **play**ing out of **time** is used by Richard in his disconsolate soliloquy at Pomfret Castle:

> (*The **music** plays.*) Music do I **hear**?
> Ha, ha, keep time! How sour **sweet** music is
> When time is broke, and no **proportion** kept!
> So is it in the music of men's lives.
> And here have I the daintiness of **ear**
> To check time broke in a disordered string.
> (5.5.41–6)

The musical metaphor of loss of **harmony** and proportion exemplifies the chaos in Richard's public and private life, which ultimately leads to his death.

Broken time and **discord**ant strings are recurrent images in the Shakespeare canon. Lucius (Brutus' servant) describes the strings of the instrument – probably a lute – which he has just played as '**false**' (*JC* 4.3.291). During his speech on the importance of hierarchical harmony

string

in the army and in society at large, Ulysses resorts to musical language throughout and concludes: 'Take but **degree** away, un**tune** that string, / And hark what discord follows' (*Tro* 1.3.109–10). This idea is similar to that put forward by Richard in the passage quoted above: when degree is ignored, chaos and disharmony will ensue. In yet another expression of fear of political unrest, King Henry VI wonders: 'when such strings [Gloucester and the Bishop of Winchester] **jar**, what hope of harmony?' (*2H6* 2.1.55).

A pun on musical strings and heart strings is found when Julia observes that Proteus (who is courting Silvia by having music played in her honour) 'plays false' (*TGV* 4.2.59). Surprised by this comment, the Host asks her: 'How, out of tune on the strings?' (60). She replies: 'Not so; but yet so false that he grieves my / very heart-strings' (61–2). This comment betrays Julia's jealousy when she is trying to pass herself off as a page, but the Host does not understand the pun and continues the conversation exclusively on a musical level.

The lute is described as being 'strung with poets' sinews' (*TGV* 3.2.77), and 'strung with [**Apollo**'s] hair' (*LLL* 4.3.340) (see '**Orpheus**', 'Apollo' and 'lute' for a detailed comment). A sexual connotation is implied when the daughter of Antiochus is compared to a viol whose strings need to be fingered 'to **make** man his lawful music' (*Per* 1.1.82, see 'viol').

(C) Abbott and Segerman, 'Strings in the 16th and 17th centuries' (1974); 'Gut Strings' (1976), which deals with the problems of using gut strings on period instruments.

strung see **string**.

swan see **bird**.

sweet (A) 'Sweet' is used frequently in Elizabethan times specifically in connection with **music** to mean 'pleasing' and implying **concord** and **harmony**, as in:

> Music divine, proceeding from above,
> Whose sacred subject oftentimes is love,

> In this appears her heavenly harmony,
> Where **tune**ful concords sweetly do agree.
>   (Tomkins, 1622, no. 24)

Those that make harmonious music make it sweetly: 'The merry **nightingale** she sweetly sits and **sing**s' (Ravenscroft, *Pammelia*, 1609, no. 20); or: 'Pretty wantons, sweetly sing / In honour of the smiling Spring' (Peerson, 1620, no. 17).

(B) Whilst Simonides praises the 'delightful pleasing harmony' (*Per* 2.5.28) of sweet music, Jessica in *The Merchant of Venice* explains to Lorenzo that it does not have its intended effect on her: 'I am never merry when I **hear** sweet music' (5.1.69). (See 'music' for a discussion of the context of this line.) Another reference to the beneficial power of sweet music is found in the **song** '**Orpheus** with his **lute**' (*H8* 3.1.3–14) sung to soothe Katherine of Aragon's sad **mood**. The second stanza mentions Orpheus' 'sweet music' (12), which is capable of 'killing care and grief of heart' (13).

There are two instances when the phrase 'sweet music' achieves a paradoxical effect. Close to death, Richard II bitterly observes: 'How sour sweet music is / When **time** is broke, and no **proportion** kept!' (*R2* 5.5.42–3). This musical metaphor begins a soliloquy in which the distressed King ponders on the lack of harmony in his public and private life. In another history play, Richard III praises Tyrrel, who has just agreed to murder the young princes in the Tower, in the following terms: 'Thou sing'st sweet music' (*R3* 4.2.78). To the ruthless Richard, the most unnatural of acts is as pleasant and harmonious as 'sweet music'.

T

tabor (A) The tabor is a small **drum** (pronounced 'tabber' in folk **song** circles) most often with a gut snare **strung** across one or both ends. It is suspended from the wrist of one hand (usually left) and **beat**en by a small stick held in the other hand, or sometimes by the fingers. The shape of the tabor varies from a shallow to a deep drum, the latter having come into existence in the fifteenth century (e.g. the Provençal '*tambourin*'). The tabor is commonly **play**ed in association with a **pipe** by the same person, although the larger tabors, slung from the shoulder, are more often played by a single person without a pipe.

In combination with the pipe, the tabor is usually played by the right hand and the pipe by the left. This arrangement emphasizes the importance of the drum which beats **time** for the **dance**rs. As if to confirm this, the player is called a taborer, not a piper (see for instance *The Tempest* 3.2.151; and *The Two Noble Kinsmen* 3.5.OSD and 3.5.23). A well-known reference occurs in William Kemp's *Nine Daies Wonder* (1600), in which the famous Shakespearean comic actor records how he **morris dance**d to Norwich accompanied by his 'taborer' Thomas Slye, as depicted on the title page. Kemp's fame as a dancer after the tabor, both in England and on the continent, is alluded to in:

> Since Robin Hood, Maid Marian,
> And Little John are gone-a,
> The hobby horse was quite forgot,
> When Kemp did dance alone-a,

> He did labour
> After the tabor.
> For to dance
> Then into France.
> (Weelkes, 1608, no. 20)

The tabor was invariably associated with dancing, or with activities where a repetitive rhythmic accompaniment would be appropriate, such as juggling. With a pipe it was a very effective one-man band and was especially popular in England. Tabor and pipe playing crossed social boundaries and was not confined to any one type of event. It ranged from accompanying courtly dances to rural and sea-faring gatherings. Three types of tabor pipe, for example, were discovered on the *Mary Rose*. As a rustic **instrument**al combination it was particularly connected with morris dancing in England, as has already been noted in connection with William Kemp.

(B) Although there are several textual references to the tabor in the Shakespearean canon, there is only one stage direction mentioning the **instrument**: '*Ariel plays the* **tune** *on a tabor and pipe*' (*Tmp* 3.2.124.SD). The scene where this stage direction occurs strongly relies on the aural dimension thanks to its use of song and **music**; there are also musical allusions in the dramatic dialogue. While leaving the stage at the end of the scene, Stephano says to his drunken friends: 'I would I could see this taborer' (3.2.150), a cue meant to reinforce the theatrical illusion that Ariel is invisible to the onstage characters. The supernatural power of Ariel's music is evident when the spirit recounts how he was able to **charm** Caliban, Trinculo and Stephano and to lead them into a 'filthy-mantled pool' beyond Prospero's cell (an act which averts the murder plot against Prospero):

> . . . Then I beat my tabor,
> At which like unback'd colts they prick'd their **ear**s,
> Advanc'd their eyelids, lifted up their noses
> As they smelt music.
> (4.1.175–8)

Some of the references in the dialogue of Shakespeare's plays may have worked as implicit stage directions to play this instrument, as for

tabor

instance in *Coriolanus*, when a messenger informs Menenius and Sicinius that:

> The **trumpet**s, **sackbut**s, **psalteries**, and **fife**s,
> Tabors and **cymbal**s, and the shouting Romans,
> Make the sun dance. Hark you!
>
> (5.4.49–51)

The celebratory mood is caused by the triumphant entry of Volumnia into Rome. Earlier in the same play, the pastoral associations of the drum are indicated in Cominius' welcoming words to Caius Martius, victorious from his assault on the Volscian city of Corioles:

> The shepherd knows not **thunder** from a tabor
> More than I know the **sound** of Martius' **tongue**
> From every meaner man.
>
> (1.6.24–6)

In *Much Ado About Nothing*, Benedick disparagingly comments on the transformation undergone by the soldier Claudio when he has decided to woo Hero:

> . . . I have known when there was no music with him but the drum and the fife, and now had he rather **hear** the tabor and the pipe . . .
>
> (2.3.12–15)

The symbolic contrast of the pipe and tabor's peaceful associations with the trumpet/fife and drum's war-like theme emerges from Benedick's words. This notion is recalled by John Aubrey: 'Before the late civill warres, the tabor and pipe were commonly used, especially Sundays and Holy-dayes . . . Now it is almost all lost; the drumme and trumpet have putt all that peaceable music to **silence**' (Clark, vol. 2, p. 319). Ironically, it will not be long until Benedick makes the same choice as Claudio: before the end of the scene, he falls in love with Beatrice.

The pan-social presence of the tabor to accompany dancing is evident when Dull explains how he intends to contribute to the pageant of the Nine Worthies: 'I'll make one in a dance, or so; or I will play / On

tabor

the tabor to the Worthies, and let them dance the **hay**' (*LLL* 5.1.153–4). The habit of dancing to tabor and pipe to emphasize rustic associations is mentioned in *The Winter's Tale*, 4.4.182–3. In *Twelfth Night*, Viola's remark to Feste shows that he probably carried a tabor as part of his costume: 'Dost thou / live by the tabor?' (3.1.1–2).

See also **taborine**.

(C) Baines, *Woodwind Instruments* (1977).
Clark (ed.), *Briefe Lives* (1898).
Galpin, *Old English Instruments of Music* (1910; R/1965).
Palmer, 'Musical Instruments from the Mary Rose' (1983).

taborer see **tabor**.

taborine (A) It is not clear exactly what 'taborines' are. According to *OED*, a 'taborine' is a kind of **drum**, less wide and longer than a **tabor**, and struck with a stick. *OED* adds that the taborine accompanies the **flute** [sic]. This definition seems to do little more than place the taborine in the tabor and **pipe** category. It does not appear to take into account the various sizes of tabors that are known to exist, or their differing regional characteristics.

Another meaning, derived from the French '*tambourins*', may refer to the **tune**s and **dance**s of the pipe and tabor repertoire. Or 'taborine' may indicate a larger military drum not used to accompany recreational dancing, and therefore unconnected with 'pipe and tabor'.

(B) It is likely that the two references to 'taborine' in the Shakespeare canon are the English form for the French '*tambourine*' and Italian '*tamburello*' or '*tamburino*', an **instrument** of ancient origin. This is 'a shallow, single-headed frame drum with a wooden frame in which metal disks or jingles are set' (*The New Harvard Dictionary of Music*, p. 834), which can be **play**ed with a stick or shaken.

On both occasions, Shakespeare introduces the taborine in the company of **trumpet**s, for instance when Agamemnon exhorts his men to welcome Hector: '**Beat loud** the taborines, let the trumpets **blow**' (*Tro* 4.5.274). In *Antony and Cleopatra*, after defeating Caesar, Antony wishes to celebrate his victory through the streets of Alexandria in great style:

taborine

> ... Trumpeters,
> With **brazen din** blast you the city's **ear**,
> Make mingle with our rattling taborines,
> That heaven and earth may **strike** their **sound**s together,
> Applauding our approach.
>
> (4.8.35–9)

Here, it is possible that Shakespeare had the 'tambourine' in mind: the adjective 'rattling' is suggestive of the sound made by metal disks or jingles, and well befits the festive atmosphere of the occasion.

(C) Galpin, *Old English Instruments of Music* (1965).
The New Harvard Dictionary of Music (1986).

Te Deum (A) The ancient Christian **hymn** of **praise** *Te Deum Laudamus* ('We praise thee, O God') was adopted by the Anglican Church for Morning Prayer. The *Book of Common Prayer* of 1549 (revised in 1552), on which the Anglican liturgy was based, kept the Latin titles of **psalm**s and hymns: hence, those who did not speak Latin would have easily recognized them. Outside the liturgical sphere, *Te Deum* is known to have been sung on the battlefield to celebrate victory.

The numerous collections of canticles with settings in English in the period following the Reformation show how popular choral worship was: according to *Grove*, 'between 1565 and 1644 (when choral services were discontinued) more than sixty full services were composed, together with a further 20 collections of canticles from Matins to Evensongs, some twenty-five for Matins (mainly consisting of the *Te Deum* only)' (p. 153).

(B) In *Henry V*, at the end of the Battle of Agincourt, Henry exhorts his men with the following words: 'Do we all holy rites: / Let there be sung *Non Nobis* and *Te Deum*' (4.8.122–3). It is not by chance that Henry mentions both *Non Nobis* (Psalm 115 in the *Book of Common Prayer*, beginning with the words 'Not unto us, O Lord, not unto us, but unto thy name give the glory') and *Te Deum* at this point. As Steven Marx has noted, 'the miraculous military victory commemorated in the *Non Nobis* is the core event of salvation in the Bible, the model of all of God's interventions in human history' (p. 85). *Non Nobis* followed by the hymn of praise to God is very appropriate at the end of a battle which the English won against all odds, and which cost them comparatively few lives. Holinshed's account, closely followed by Shakespeare, tells us that only 29 Englishmen died against 10,000 Frenchmen. Even though modern historians have calculated that there were probably around 600 casualties on the English side, the outcome of the Battle of Agincourt was nonetheless an outstanding achievement for Henry V: understandably, this was interpreted as a sign of divine intervention by Shakespeare's contemporaries.

Reference to the canticle *Te Deum* is also found in *Henry VIII*, when a gentleman narrates that, at the end of the Anne Boleyn's coronation ceremony at Westminster Abbey, the best **musician**s of the kingdom 'together sung *Te Deum*' (4.1.92).

(C) *Grove*, 'Anthem' (2001).
Marx, 'Holy War in Henry V' (1995).
Noble, *Shakespeare's Biblical Knowledge* (1935).

tedious (A) Used in opposition to 'brief', 'tedious' implies that a poem, tale or **song** was long, slow and possibly irritating.

(B) Shakespeare uses this term only once in a musical context, when he refers to Venus' **ditty lament**ing her unrequited love for Adonis. The caves **echo** her song, which as a result 'was tedious, and outwore the night' (*Ven* 841). There are many other references to **noise**s and **music** in this part of the poem, ranging from the singing of the **lark** at dawn to the yelping of the hounds accompanying Adonis during the ill-fated boar hunt.

Thracian (A) Thrace was a region in the north of Greece in classical antiquity. The adjective is sometimes associated with classical poets and **musician**s, especially **Orpheus**.

(B) In the concluding scene of *A Midsummer Night's Dream*, Theseus is given a list of possible entertainments for the newly wed couples. Among these is 'The riot of the tipsy Bacchanals, / Tearing the Thracian **sing**er in their rage' (5.1.48–9). However, he decides to discard this and

Thracian

other options in favour of the mechanicals' play. The 'Thracian singer' is Orpheus, renowned for the soothing and harmonizing power of his **music**, who was torn to pieces by the 'drunken rout' of Maenads (Dionysus' followers).

After realising that Lavinia has been raped and mutilated, her uncle Marcus launches an invective against the person (whose identity he does not yet know) responsible for brutalizing her:

> ... Had he **hear**d the heavenly **harmony**
> Which that **sweet tongue** hath made,
> He would have dropp'd his knife and fell asleep,
> As Cerberus at the Thracian poet's feet.
> (*Tit* 2.4.48–51)

When trying to recover his dead wife Eurydice, Orpheus was able to placate the three-headed guardian dog of the underworld thanks to his harmonious music. Marcus believes that Lavinia's sweet **voice** would have had a similar effect on her rapist if only he had listened to it.

(C) The translation of Ovid's *Metamorphoses* by Arthur Golding (1567) recounts the episode of the killing of Orpheus in Book XI.

three see **lesson**, **mean**.

throat (A) **Voice** production, be it speaking or **sing**ing, is generated in the larynx – a part of the throat containing the vocal cords. Thus 'throat', in a musical context, refers to singing. As a metaphor for the singing voice, and by extension song, it is found most often in association with **bird**s singing:

> **Sweet**, when thou sing'st I leave my careful nest ...
> The chattering day-birds can no counsel keep.
> Thou tell'st thy sorrows in a **soft** sweet **note**,
> But I proclaim them with the **loud**est throat.
> (Jones, 1607, nos. 14–15)

In a number of poems, 'throat' is juxtaposed with '**breast**' to heighten the sense that the throat is the voice-box which articulates the emotions

throat

of the breast, often in sad **lament**ing contexts. One of the most famous examples is Orlando Gibbons' 'The **Silver Swan**' madrigal (*recte* **consort** song):

> The silver swan, who living had no note,
> When death approached unlocked her silent throat;
> Leaning her breast against the reedy shore,
> Thus sung her first and last, and sung no more.
> (1612, no. 1)

Another example is Sir Philip Sidney's:

> The **nightingale**, so soon as April bringeth . . .
> Her throat in **tune**s expresseth
> What grief her breast oppresseth.
> (*Certain Sonnets*, no. 4 set by Bateson, 1604, no. 3)

(B) In Shakespeare, 'throat' sometimes alludes to the production of voice, **music** and **sound**. For instance, after agreeing to appease the plebeians, Coriolanus feels that he is prostituting himself:

> Away, my disposition, and possess me
> Some harlot's spirit! My throat of war be turn'd,
> Which **quier**'d with my **drum**, into a **pipe**
> Small as an **eunuch**, or the virgin voice
> That babies lull asleep! . . .
> (*Cor* 3.2.111–15)

In the act of faking respect for the plebeians, his voice will acquire a **high** pitch like that of a eunuch or of a virgin. As a result it will lose its virile tone, which used to be in **harmony** with the sounding of the drum during his military campaigns. The bawdy allusion to the 'small pipe' enhances the idea of emasculation pervading this speech.

Othello describes shooting cannons as 'mortal engines, whose **rude** throats / Th' immortal Jove's dread **clamor**s counterfeit' (*Oth* 3.3.355–6) when comparing their **noise** to that of **thunder** ('Jove's clamors'). The deep sound mentioned here differs from the high-pitched sound of the cockerel, described by Horatio in *Hamlet*. This bird 'is the trumpet to the morn [with a] / **shrill**-sounding throat' (1.1.150–1).

throat

Moth explains to Armado, who has just exhorted him to sing 'Concolinel', how a **love song** is best sung:

> . . . **sigh** a note and sing a note, sometime through the throat
> as if you swallow'd love with singing love,
> sometime through the nose, as if you snuff'd up
> love by smelling love . . .
>
> (*LLL* 3.1.14–17)

The allusion here is to different singing techniques, differentiating between breathing in (a sigh note) and breathing out (singing through the throat). Even in this jocular context, Shakespeare reveals a knowledge of singing technique, namely the difference between head voice and chest voice.

See also **tongue**.

(C) Elam, 'The Fertile Eunuch' (1996), explores among other subjects the relationship between castration and musical metaphors in Shakespeare.

Partridge, *Shakespeare's Bawdy* (1968).

throstle see **bird**.

thrush see **bird**.

thunder (A) Not strictly speaking a musical term, 'thunder' is associated with a **loud** percussive **noise**. The use of thunder in the early modern theatre is a metaphor for a storm and, by extension, **discord** through supernatural intervention.

(B) Stage directions for thunder, often followed by lightning, demonstrate how important this special effect was in the theatre of Shakespeare's time whenever supernatural, ominous or awe-inspiring atmospheres were introduced to the audience. The **sound** effect was produced by rolling a cannon-ball down a wooden trough, the so-called 'thunder run', or by **drum**s or cannon-fire.

Not surprisingly, two plays dominated by magic, *Macbeth* and *The Tempest*, have several stage directions for thunder. Both plays open with thunder and lightning – in *Macbeth* this special effect introduces the witches, and in *The Tempest* it evokes the storm which causes the shipwreck of Alonso's ship. A *'noise of thunder'* (*Tmp* 2.2.OSD) accompanies Caliban's entry in the scene where he meets the drunken Stephano and his companion Trinculo for the first time. Even though the thunder in this comical situation may seem to have a different purpose from that of the thunder heard in the shipwreck scene, it serves an important thematic function. It ultimately reminds us that every action on the island is being manipulated by Prospero, who creates more thunder effects during the banquet scene (3.3.52.SD; 3.3.82.SD).

'*Thunder*' precedes entries of the witches in *Macbeth* not only in the opening scene, but also in 1.3 (OSD), 3.5 (OSD) and 4.1 (OSD). Two other indications for thunder in the Shakespeare canon are intended to create an atmosphere of witchcraft. The first is in *1 Henry VI* (5.3.4) when Joan of Arc conjures up 'fiends' (5.3.7.SD) in a desperate attempt to elicit their supernatural help in her fight against the English. The second is in *2 Henry VI*, when Eleanor evokes a spirit that foretells the fate of Henry and other noblemen. The ceremony is described in detail in a prescriptive stage direction:

> *Here do the ceremonies belonging, and make the circle; Bolingbrook or Southwell reads,* 'Conjuro te, etc.'. *It thunders and lightens terribly; then the Spirit riseth.*
>
> (1.4.23.SD)

The adverb 'terribly' suggests that the thunder and lightning effect was expected to be as powerful and impressive as possible. The subsequent departure of the spirit – probably through the trapdoor to suggest its connection with the underworld – is also accompanied by '*thunder and lightning*' (1.4.40.SD).

The idea of political unrest is expressed through thunder and lightning in *Julius Caesar* when the conspirators meet (1.3.OSD). The indication '*Thunder* **still**' (1.3.100.SD) reveals that this sound effect would have probably been heard in the background throughout the scene.

The most spectacular scene involving thunder is found in *Cymbeline*, where Jupiter '*descends in thunder and lightning, sitting upon an eagle: he throws a thunderbolt*' (5.4.92.SD). Jupiter would have been lowered onto the main

thunder

stage – or alternatively left mid-air at the stage gallery level – from the cover over the stage or 'heavens' to signify his divine nature. He would then have been hoisted up to the same area as the stage direction '*Ascends*' (5.4.113) suggests. This special effect would have been made all the more remarkable by the use of a stage property symbolizing a thunderbolt along with the sound effect.

Of the dozens of references to the noise of thunder in the dialogue of Shakespeare's plays, some are specifically connected to the musical sphere. For instance, Hippolyta describes the barking of the hounds during a hunt in unconventional terms: 'I never heard / so musical a discord, such **sweet** thunder' (*MND* 4.1.117–18). The adjectives 'musical' and 'sweet' preceding two terms which suggest lack of **harmony** ('discord' and 'thunder') achieve an interesting paradoxical effect.

After Ariel's denunciation of Alonso, Sebastian and Antonio as 'three men of sin' (*Tmp* 3.3.53), Alonso is deeply shocked and guilt-ridden. He claims that

> . . . the thunder,
> That deep and dreadful **organ-pipe**, pronounc'd
> The name of Prosper; it did **base** my trespass.
> (97–9)

The forces of nature play an important role in this scene, where thunder is heard before Ariel's apparition as a harpy (3.3.52.SD) and his subsequent accusations. The actual sound effect acquires a metaphorical meaning in Alonso's speech. The phrase 'base my trespass' puns on the musical sense of '**bass**' while reminding us of the Lord's Prayer (Lindley, p. 178). (See also 'bass' for a detailed commentary.)

The threatening **sound** of the military **drum** is likened to that of thunder when Coriolanus is feared dead in battle. Titus Lartius praises Coriolanus' military valour:

> . . . with thy grim looks and
> The thunder-like percussion of thy sounds,
> Thou mad'st thine enemies shake, as if the world
> Were feverous and did tremble.
> (*Cor* 1.4.58–61)

Emphasis is placed on the awe-inspiring effect of thunder.

In *Henry VIII* there is a reference to 'the youths that thunder at a playhouse' (5.3.60). This metatheatrical comment implies that the noisy behaviour of some members of the audience felt threatening and unpredictable from the actors' viewpoint.

An intriguing musical allusion can be found when Cominius realizes that Coriolanus is still alive:

> The shepherd knows not thunder from a **tabor**
> More than I know the sound of Martius' **tongue**
> From every meaner man.
>
> (*Cor* 1.6.24–6)

Cominius implies that Coriolanus' **voice** is deep and inspires respect in the same way as a drum with its deep sound has a more powerful effect on the **ear** than the tabor with its lighter sound. This speech works as an oblique reminder that the sound effect of thunder was achieved by the **beat**ing of drums in the Elizabethan and Jacobean theatre.

See also **wind**.

(C) Astington, 'Descent Machinery in the Playhouses' (1985), provides a review of staging techniques adopted in the early modern theatre for ascents and descents.

Dessen and Thomson, *A Dictionary of Stage Directions* (1999), p. 230.

Lindley, *The Tempest* (2002).

Thomson, 'The Meaning of Thunder and Lightning: Stage Directions and Audience Expectations' (1999).

timbrell see **cymbal**.

time (A) Timing of a **note**, according to Morley, is 'a certayne space or length, wherein a note may be holden in **sing**ing' (*Introduction*, 1597, p. 9). Time in **music**, therefore, is the appropriate placing of a note in its context according to its length and the tempo of the music. If correct time is adhered to by the **perform**ers then the music is harmonious and ordered. If time is inaccurate, broken or lost, then the music becomes **discord**ant and chaotic. Strict time or tempo is particularly *time*

vital in polyphonic music or when music accompanies dancing, as Campion suggests:

> Kind are her answers
> But her performance keeps no day;
> Breaks time, as **dance**rs
> From their own music when they stray.
> (*Third Booke*, c.1617, no. 7)

'Time' in Medieval and Renaissance music specifically referred to the **proportion**s of the notes in relation to **mood** and Prolation. Mood is based on the rhythmic pulse of a **long**; Time is dependent on **breve**s and Prolation on **minim**s. Since the end of the sixteenth century, tempo (or **degree** as it was often called) has slowed and the unit pulse has become the **crotchet**, and still is to this day.

(B) In the Shakespeare canon there are specific references to 'breaking time' and 'keeping time'. After singing 'It was a lover and his lass' (*AYLI* 5.3.16–33), the two Pages are upbraided by Touchstone, who observes that 'the note was very un**tune**able [untuneful]' (35). To this, one of the Pages replies by defending his and his friend's singing ability: 'You are deceiv'd, sir, we kept time, we / lost not our time' (37–8). Touchstone's ensuing line, 'I count it but time / lost to **hear** such a foolish song' (39–40), plays wittily on the concept of time in its meanings of 'duration, period' and of 'musical tempo', as well as on the content of the song, in which the phrase 'spring time' is repeated four times. His comment also reveals that music was regarded as a marker of time in early modern England (Smith, p. 80).

Malvolio upbraids the drunken party who are keeping Olivia's household awake in the middle of the night with their **catch**-singing. He ends his list of reproaches by asking them: 'Is there no respect of place, persons, nor time in you? (*TN* 2.3.90–1). To which Sir Toby replies: 'We did keep time, sir, in our catches' (93). In his drunken state, he confuses 'time' in the sense meant by Malvolio (hour of the night) with its musical counterpart (inability to keep time, which leads to discord).

When the ghost of the King of Denmark appears to Hamlet in the Queen's closet, Gertrude cannot see it and tells her son that the apparition 'is the very coinage of your brain' (*Ham* 3.4.136), but Hamlet insists that what he has seen is real and that he is not mad:

> My pulse as yours doth temperately keep time,
> And **make**s as healthful music. It is not madness
> That I have utter'd . . .
>
> (140–2)

The conceit of the pulse **beat**ing in a regular **mode** and therefore keeping time encapsulates the connection between music and health (both of the body and of the mind) often evoked in Renaissance drama, in which recovery from illness is sometimes underlined by music.

Before being murdered in the dungeon at Pomfret Castle, Richard delivers a powerful soliloquy:

> (*The music **play**s*). Music do I hear?
> Ha, ha, keep time! How sour **sweet** music is
> When time is broke, and no proportion kept!
> So is it in the music of men's lives.
> And here have I the daintiness of **ear**
> To check time broke in a disordered **string**;
> But for the **concord** of my state and time
> Had not an ear to hear my true time broke.
> I wasted time, and now doth time waste me;
> For now hath time made me his numb'ring clock.
>
> (*R2* 5.5.41–50)

This is a highly elaborate musical metaphor, in which the time when a man's life ends is analysed in relation to the political sphere: the breaking of time leads to loss of order and proportion, and can only result in death.

(C) Smith, *The Acoustic World of Early Modern England* (1999).

tirra-lyra (A) According to the first edition of *Grove Dictionary of Music* (1889, vol. 4, Appendix, p. 805), the term is derived from the ancient Provençal '**burden**' or 'refrain', 'ture-lure'. Two early modern dictionaries, John Florio's *A worlde of wordes, or most copious, and exact dictionarie in Italian and English* (1598) and Randle Cotgrave's *A dictionarie of the French and English tongues* (1611), mention this term. The former states that 'tirelirare' is 'to **sing** or chirp as a **lark**e', while the latter tells us that 'tirelirer' means 'to **warble**, or sing like a larke', and that

tirra-lyra

'tirelire', also spelt 'tirelyre', is 'the warble, or song of a lark'. The English form was used in literature as a suggestive cry of the lark, particularly the skylark, whose **note** is **shrill** and joyous.

(B) The sense of gaiety created by the lark's note is conveyed in Autolycus' song 'When daffodils begin to peer', which celebrates the coming of spring. One of its earliest signs is the singing of '**sweet bird**s' (*WT* 4.3.6). Among these is 'The lark, that tirra-lyra **chaunt**s, / With heigh, with heigh, the **thrush** and the **jay**! (9–10).

(C) Duffin, *Shakespeare's Songbook* (2004), p. 438.

toll (A) **Bell**s can either be rung or tolled. The latter is effected by a single pull on the rope attached to the mechanism that **sound**s the bell, or by a single stroke to one side of the bell, as for example when a clock **chimes**. The difference between **ring**ing and tolling is heard in the volume and speed of the chime. Tolling is quieter and slower. The most obvious example of this difference is in the transition from the 'passing-bell' (tolled) to the death **knell** (rung). John Donne probably alludes to this transition when he writes: 'The bell rings out, the pulse thereof is changed; the tolling was a **faint** and intermitting pulse, upon one side; this stronger, and argues a better life. His soule is gone out' (Wulstan, p. 50). Wulstan reminds us that the 'change of timbre between the passing-bell and death knell is also noted by Thomas Dekker in his *Lanthorne & Candlelight* (1608, xxii)' (ibid.). In his 'Goe nightly cares' (*A Pilgrimes Solace*, 1612, no. 9), as Wulstan also notes, John Dowland represents the three-**note** toll of the passing-bell and the ring of the knell. In the slower middle section of the **song**, the bell tolls at 'O give me time to draw my weary **breath**. Or let me die'. When a bell chimes the hours of the day, especially a church bell, it is described as tolling.

(B) The tolling of clocks is referred to in *Henry V* when the **Chorus** describes the atmosphere in the two opposing camps before the Battle of Agincourt. The aural dimension pervades this speech: for instance, the audience is informed that the steeds pierce 'the night's dull **ear**' (4.Chor. 11), and that the 'armorers ... / give dreadful note of preparation' (12–14). When 'the clocks do toll / And the third hour of drowsy morning name' (15–16), it causes the 'condemned English' (22) to ponder on the danger awaiting them, whilst the French, confident in their military superiority, play at dice. To the English, who fear a defeat in battle, the tolling of the hour evokes the tolling of the bell for the dead.

In *2 Henry IV*, Northumberland observes that the person who announces the death of a friend has a

> . . . losing office, and his **tongue**
> **Sound**s ever after as a sullen bell,
> Rememb'red tolling a departing friend.
> (1.1.101–3)

A prolonged tolling of the bell was sometimes commissioned for the dead (Duncan-Jones, p. 252): these lines, like those mentioning the 'sullen bell' in *Sonnet* 71 (2), may well allude to this custom.

(C) Duncan-Jones, *Shakespeare's Sonnets* (1997).
  Wulstan, *Tudor Music* (1985).

tongs and bones (A) The use of 'tongs' in **music** is rare, whereas 'bones' is common, especially in a rustic context. Pairs of wooden sticks (tongs) and pairs of dried animal bones would be clattered together to make primitive rhythmical music.

(B) That tongs and bones were not highly thought of is clear from a passage in *A Midsummer Night's Dream*. Titania, in love with the ass-headed Bottom, expresses her wish to '**hear** some music' (4.1.28), to which he promptly replies: 'I have a reasonable good **ear** in music. Let's / have the tongs and the bones' (4.1.29–30). Similar to his understanding of acting, Bottom's grasp of music is basic: 'his musical preferences do not even extend to **instrument**s capable of **melody**' (Folkerth, p. 97). Putting these words in his mouth testifies to the unrefined connotations that these instruments evoked in Shakespeare and his contemporaries. The stage direction following this speech found in Folio confirms this view: '*Music tongs, rural music*'. Onstage music was intended to be as simple as possible.

(C) Folkerth, *The Sound of Shakespeare* (2002).

tongue

tongue (A) As a metaphor for **voice**, in a musical context 'tongue' can either mean 'to **sing**', as in:

> We'll **tune** our voices to the **lute**
> And **instrument**s of **sweet**est **sound**;
> No tongue shall in thy **praise** be mute,
> That doth thy foes and ours confound.
> (Alison, 1606, no. 24)

or 'to give voice to an instrument', especially a **wind** instrument such as a **trumpet**, where the tongue articulates the sound. In other words, 'to tongue' is to make an instrument sound.

(B) Romeo's happiness and anticipation at the thought of marrying Juliet transpires from the speech which he addresses to her:

> Ah, Juliet, if the measure of thy joy
> Be heap'd like mine, and that thy skill be more
> To blazon it, then sweeten with thy **breath**
> This neighbor **air**, and let rich **music**'s tongue
> Unfold the imagin'd happiness that both
> Receive in either by this dear encounter.
> (*Rom* 2.6.24–9)

The topos of the sweetness of a mistress's breath blends with the musical meaning of words such as 'measure', 'air' (pronounced in the same way as '**ayre**') and 'breath'; it culminates in the exposition of Juliet's harmonious voice, which is like music to Romeo.

Desperate at the death of her beloved, Venus wonders: 'Whose tongue is music now?' (*Ven* 1077). Ferdinand finds the '**harmony** of [women's] tongues' (*Tmp* 3.1.41) enticing. Helena, envying Hermia's beauty and grace, remarks: 'My tongue should **catch** your tongue's sweet **melody**' (*MND* 1.1.189). In all these instances, emphasis is placed on the harmony brought about by the voice of people who are loved or admired.

'Tongue' is employed in some powerful martial metaphors. The sound of the **drum**s **beat**en for a **parley** is a 'tongue of war' (*Jn* 5.2.164) according to the Dauphin. In another military context, Westmoreland worries that the Archbishop of York's 'tongue divine'

tongue

(*2H4* 4.1.51) will be turned into 'a loud trumpet and a **point** of war' (52) in times of civil unrest. The moments preceding the rape of Lucrece are described in similar terms: 'First like a trumpet doth his [Tarquin's] tongue begin / To sound a parley to his heartless foe' (*Luc* 470–1). Lucrece's body is compared to a besieged city which must surrender to the enemy's brutality, announced by a parley. Before murdering Duncan, Macbeth fears that the King's virtues 'will plead like **angel**s, trumpet-tongu'd, against / The deep damnation of his taking-off' (*Mac* 1.7.19–20). The tragic consequences that regicide will bring about are foreshadowed in the biblical image of the angels sounding the trumpets on Judgement Day.

In *A Midsummer Night's Dream*, when 'the iron tongue of midnight hath told twelve' (5.1.363), i.e. the midnight **bell** has struck twelve, the celebrations for the newly wed couples draw to an end. The metallic sound of the bell is described with a similar prosopopoeia in *King John*: 'the midnight bell / . . . with his iron tongue and **brazen** mouth' (3.3.37–8). On the other hand, Don Pedro's description of Benedick's outspoken personality is described by comparing it to inanimate objects:

> . . . He hath a heart as sound as a bell, and his tongue is the clapper, for what his heart thinks, his tongue **speak**s . . .
> (*Ado* 3.2.12–14)

Pitch and tone are sometimes commented on, as when Julius Caesar observes that he can hear 'a tongue shriller than all the music' (*JC* 1.2.16) of the **flourish**es in his honour. This voice belongs to the Soothsayer, who warns Caesar to beware the Ides of March. One of the six knights in *The Two Noble Kinsmen* is described in adulatory terms by Pirithous who, among other qualities such as the knight's youth and beauty, notes that: 'When he speaks, his tongue / Sounds like a trumpet' (4.2.112–13).

After resolving to commit suicide, Lucrece calls her maid:

> This plot of death when sadly she had laid,
> And wip'd the brinish pearl from her bright eyes,
> With untun'd tongue she hoarsely calls her maid.
> (*Luc* 1212–14)

431

tongue

Lucrece's hoarse and disharmonic voice reflects her state of despair, and contrasts with the '**soft** slow tongue, true mark of modesty' (1220), with which the maid (unaware of the events of the previous night) greets her.

See also **breast, throat**.

touch (A) **String**ed **instrument**s such as the **lute** and **harp** were **play**ed by the fingers plucking or 'touching' the strings. 'Touch', therefore, means to play an instrument and the touch is the particular **sound** an instrument makes when it is played. It is invariably an individual characteristic and even today we talk, for example, about a pianist's 'touch', meaning the special sound generated by a particular player. In his beautiful musical imagery-rich sonnet, *Delia*, no. 57, Samuel Daniel encapsulates the special senses associated with touch:

> Like as the lute delights, or else dislikes,
> As is his art that plays upon the same . . .
> For no **ground** else could **make** the **music** such,
> Nor other hand could give so **sweet** a touch.
> (Daniel, 1607, no. 4)

(B) A direct reference to the lute being 'touched' is found in Sonnet 8 of *The Passionate Pilgrim*, where Dowland is said to have a 'heavenly touch / Upon the lute [which] doth **ravish** human sense' (5–6). When Brutus orders his servant Lucius to 'touch thy instrument a **strain** or two' (*JC* 4.3.257) in order to help him forget his anguish before the Battle of Philippi, he is referring to a stringed instrument (probably a lute). This is later confirmed by Lucius' allusion to the instrument's strings (291).

After being sentenced to banishment for life, Mowbray cannot disguise his despair:

> My native English, now I must forgo,
> And now my **tongue**'s use is to me no more
> Than an unstringed **viol** or a harp,
> Or like a cunning instrument cas'd up,
> Or being open, put into his hands
> That knows no touch to **tune** the **harmony**.
> (*R2* 1.3.160–5)

touch

Like an inexperienced player incapable of tuning and playing a stringed instrument which has been enclosed in its case for a long time, Mowbray's linguistic competence will decline while he is in exile.

The beneficial power of music on human beings and animals alike is stressed by Lorenzo in his speech to Jessica. He hopes that the **musician**s he has employed will be able to 'pierce [Portia's] **ear** / And draw her home with music' (*MV* 5.1.67–8) thanks to their 'sweetest touches' (67), i.e. their **skill** in playing their stringed instruments. Even though music played by mortals is not as perfect as the music of the spheres, it can still have a notable soothing effect (79), as is demonstrated by what happens to wild colts:

> If they but **hear** perchance a **trumpet** sound,
> Or any **air** of music touch their ears,
> You shall perceive them make a mutual stand,
> Their savage eyes turn'd to a modest gaze,
> By the sweet power of music . . .
> (75–9)

The sexual overtones of this term – 'touch' could mean 'a sexual caress, a copulation' (Partridge, p. 264) – is played on in a comical scene in *The Taming of the Shrew* where Hortensio is disguised as a lute teacher. A bawdy innuendo is implied when he exhorts Bianca in the following terms:

> Madam, before you touch the instrument,
> To learn the order of my **fingering**,
> I must begin with rudiments of art.
> (3.1.64–6)

'Instrument' and 'fingering' enhance the sexual connotation of 'touch'. No wonder that Hortensio's clumsy attempt to woo Bianca makes a bad impression on her, and is doomed to failure.

(C) Partridge, *Shakespeare's Bawdy* (1968).
    Poulton, *John Dowland* (1982).

toy

toy (A) In a general poetic and musical context 'toy' is used to mean a 'light conceit' or 'idle **fancy**' often of an amorous nature. Baskervill (p. 88) notes that it was 'a favourite term among the cultured to designate any slight or unworthy composition, but it was also employed in a somewhat more specific way for frivolous dramatic devices, very much as Marlowe, Shakespeare and Jonson use "**jig**"'. In a specific musical context it can refer to a **tune**, often a **ballad** tune usually with **dance** associations, as in Thomas Ford's *Musicke of Sundrie Kindes. The Second* [Book] (1607), 'Pavens, Galiards, **Almain**es, Toies, Iigges, Thumpes and such like', or: '**Sing** after, fellows, as you hear me, / A toy that seldom is seen-a' (Ravenscroft, *Pammelia*, 1609, no. 74); or it can mean a 'light' piece of no great import such as 'A Toye' by Giles Farnaby (FWVB II. 421), a simple short piece in two main sections.

(B) 'Toy' is used twice with its musical connotation by Shakespeare. In *The Two Gentlemen of Verona*, Lucetta refers to Proteus' courtship of Julia in musical terms. He has sent Julia a letter in **rhyme**, which can be sung 'to a tune' (1.2.77). The dialogue between the two women in this scene is characterized by musical puns with bawdy nuances, as the following passage reveals:

> LUCETTA: Give me a **note**, your ladyship can **set**.
> JULIA: As little by such toys as may be possible:
> Best **sing** it to the tune of 'Light o' love'.
> LUCETTA: It is too heavy for so light a tune.
> JULIA: Heavy? Belike it hath some **burden** then?
> (1.2.78–82)

While on the surface Lucetta and Julia are talking about technical musical terms, allusions to sexual intercourse are evident. Terms such as 'heavy' and 'burden' are suggestive in this respect. 'Toy' refers to the widely popular ballad 'Light o' love' (also mentioned in *Much Ado About Nothing* 3.4.45–6 and *The Two Noble Kinsmen* 5.2.54), but has also an erotic connotation, as it can mean 'a toying, a love-trick; an amorous (especially if sexual) caress; . . . penis' (Partridge, pp. 264–5).

When Mistress Quickly intones the refrain 'And down, down, adown-a' (*Wiv* 1.4.43), the foolish French physician Caius asks her in his stilted English: 'Vat is you sing? I do not like des toys' (44). This term implies criticism of the song, which is dismissed as unrefined by this pompous character.

(C) Baskervill, *The Elizabethan Jig* (1929).
    Partridge, *Shakespeare's Bawdy* (1968)

treble (A) The treble is the **high**est pitch or **note** in **music**. It may also refer to the highest **sing**ing or **instrument**al part in a group of **perform**ers. Campion affirms that the '**part**s of Musicke are in all but foure ... The **Base** which is the lowest part and foundation of the whole song: the *Tenor*, placed next above the *Base*: next above the *Tenor* the **Mean**e or *Counter-Tenor*, and in the highest place the *Treble*' (*A New Way*, c.1614, B6r). Usually boys, sometimes girls, sang the treble whilst men (or older boys) sang the mean (or alto), tenor and **bass** parts. Instruments were grouped in families or **consort**s so that the highest was called the treble (e.g. treble violin, treble **hoboy**, treble **viol**). On the **lute**, the highest pitched **string** was known as the treble. And the **clef** indicating the highest pitches in notation was called the treble.

(B) There are three instances when Shakespeare uses this word with its musical connotation. In *2 Henry IV* Falstaff comments ironically on Justice Shallow's slim build: 'the **case** of a treble hoboy was a mansion for him' (3.2.326). As if to emphasize the slimness of the 'case', Shakespeare refers to the 'treble hoboy'. It is also possible that Falstaff is alluding to Shallow's high-pitched **voice** (Melchiori, p. 131).

Jaques' famous speech on the seven ages of man resorts to musical and sound imagery throughout. This imagery is sustained in the description of the sixth age:

>   ... his big manly voice,
> Turning again toward childish treble, **pipe**s
> And **whistle**s in his sound ...
>   (*AYLI* 2.7.161–3)

The high-pitched treble with its unmanly connotations is here compared unfavourably with the virile qualities of the bass voice.

treble

Bianca refers to the lute string known as 'treble' when she reproaches Hortensio for failing to **tune** his lute. 'O fie, the treble **jar**s' (*Shr* 3.1.39), she responds to his comment that his 'instrument's in tune' (38). Hortensio is disguised as a music teacher, but is increasingly disclosing his real identity by showing that he is not the music expert he claims to be.

See also **melody**.

(C) Melchiori, *2 Henry IV* (1989).

Triton (A) A sea-deity of Greek mythology, Triton is often depicted as a man whose legs have become a fish tail, holding a trident and **blow**ing a shell **trumpet** or **horn**. Musical tritons appeared in court **masque**s, such as Jonson's *Masque of Blackness* (1605) and Daniel's *Tethys Festival* (1610), where they had 'trumpets of writhen shells in their hands' (Lindley, p. 57, l. 126).

(B) Accused by Sicinius of having an opinion of the citizens which 'shall remain a poison' (*Cor* 3.1.88), Coriolanus defiantly replies:

> Shall remain?
> Hear you this Triton of the minnows?
> (3.1.88–9)

Playing on 'shall' and 'shell', Coriolanus evokes the image of Neptune's trumpeter blowing the conch. He is implicitly demeaning the role of Sicinius as a tribune of the people by comparing him to a minor sea deity. The musical metaphor is continued later when Coriolanus talks about 'horn and **noise**' (95) when further describing Triton.

(C) Lindley, *The Court Masque* (1984).
 Wells, *Elizabethan Mythologies* (1994).

troll (A) When referring to **sing**ing, 'troll' means 'passing a **part**' from one **voice** to another as in a **round** or **catch** or in a **psalm** when verses are sung alternatively by different halves of the **choir**. Elizabethan sources which mention the trolling of psalms suggest that this antiphonal practice was distracting to worshippers. The practice, however, can still be found today in English cathedrals and churches, especially during choral evensong. 'Troll' can also mean 'to sing in a **loud** and jovial fashion'. The sense of passing parts around and singing merrily is captured by Thomas Ravenscroft:

> **Hey** down a down,
> Behold and see,
> What song is this,
> Or how may this be?
> Three parts in one,
> Sing all after me,
> With hey down a down,
> Troll the berry,
> Drink and be merry.
> (*Pammelia*, 1609, no. 13)

(B) This musical term is found only once in the Shakespeare canon. In a drunken state, Caliban exhorts Stephano and Trinculo to 'troll the catch' (*Tmp* 3.2.117) that Stephano has taught him. However, Ariel's intervention frustrates their efforts: the spirit, invisible to the three would-be conspirators, confounds them by **play**ing the catch on a **tabor** and **pipe**.

(C) Fellowes, *English Cathedral Music* (1969), pp. 14–19, analyses antiphonal singing of psalms.

true (A) The descriptive term 'true' is used in **music** to mean a **note** or **sound** that is fully resonant and in **tune**. Its opposite, were it to exist, would be a faulty note and not a **false** note, which has a different theoretical meaning (see '**false relation**').

(B) In *Sonnet* 8, the young man is encouraged to overcome his reservations about getting married. The poet reminds him of the serenity which derives from 'the true **concord** of **well-tuned** sounds' (5), i.e. from the harmony between husband, wife and their children. The link between tune and 'true' sounds could not be more evident.

true

In Bottom's **song** 'The **woosel cock** so black of hue' (*MND* 3.1.125–33), there is a reference to the melodious singing characterising the song **thrush** or mavis: 'the **throstle** with his note so true' (127).

true time see **time**.

trump see **trumpet**.

trumpet (A) The trumpet was not an **instrument** of Western art **music** until the seventeenth century. Before then, various kinds of trumpets were associated with military and civic occasions, generally outdoors, when one or several instruments together would **play** fanfares or signals. As the sixteenth century progressed, the type of instrument became more standardized so that when Monteverdi wrote for trumpets in his opera, *Orfeo* (1607), they had evolved into a more refined **high**er-pitched instrument. At the beginning of the century, S. Virdung illustrated the three main Renaissance trumpets in his *Musica getutscht* (Basle, 1511). The narrow folded zigzag or S-shaped *Thurnerhorn* ('Tower-man trumpet') was the most old-fashioned and was used almost exclusively by town **musician**s, notably the tower watchmen. The *Clareta* or claret trumpet was the smallest of the three, more suited to **sound**ing the higher harmonics and quite possibly able to incorporate a slide, thereby giving it more versatility. The *Felt trumet* was a larger, more robust instrument often referred to as the 'Italian trumpet'. By the early seventeenth century, according to Praetorius (*Syntagma*, 1619), the *Felt Trumet* and *Clareta* were effectively the same and the *Thurnerhorn* virtually obsolete. What distinguished trumpets, or rather trumpeters, at the beginning of the seventeenth century was the range and *tessitura* in which they specialized.

The highest order of trumpeters was the courtly-military, enjoying royal or noble patronage. Renaissance sovereigns and high noblemen sought to reflect their status in the quality and size of their courtly corps of trumpeters. The next order were the military signallers and the lower orders comprised municipal servants commanded to play at civic occasions or keep watch in designated rooms in municipal or church towers. The Tower-man, or *Thurmer*, would sound alarms or mark the passing hours. The corps of military trumpeters and (kettle) **drum**mers increasingly began to distinguish between the more accomplished players who had been professionally taught and mere field signallers, so that by the seventeenth century the identification was complete. Moreover, the trumpet-**kettledrum** band was divided into sections comprising players responsible for playing **note**s at differing pitches and subsequently of increasing technical virtuosity in the higher registers. The five **part**s from bottom up were the *basso, vulgano, alto e basso, principale* and *clarion*. Notated music for military and courtly 'privileged' trumpeters survives (e.g. Italian sonatas and toccatas), together with archival material (for example, a correspondence between the royal Danish court at Copenhagen and the electoral Saxon court at Dresden concerned with court trumpeters and their music), undermining therefore the theory that Renaissance trumpeters were musically illiterate and could not learn or transmit their music in manuscript or print. In non-military contexts, distinctions persisted between the superior Town Bands and the lowly Tower-men, although by the end of the sixteenth century it was not uncommon to discover Tower-men perfectly capable of artistic playing as opposed to mere **blow**ing.

Trumpets were employed in the theatre of Shakespeare's time for various purposes, sometimes in conjunction with **drum**s; it appears that **cornett**s were preferred to the **loud**er trumpets in indoor theatres. In military contexts, **alarum**s, **retreat**s and **parley**s often required the sounding of trumpets. As is clear from Gervase Markham's *The Souldiers Accidence* (1625), trumpets were associated with the cavalry whereas drums were associated with the infantry. The sounding of trumpets also accompanied the entrance of characters of rank. Indications for a **flourish** or a **sennet** are usually of a generic nature, but there are instances when it is specified whether trumpets or cornetts must be used; on the other hand, a **tucket** was normally sounded by a trumpet.

The sketch of the Swan theatre drawn by the Dutch scholar Johannes de Witt when he was visiting London in 1596 shows a trumpeter in the hut above the stage cover or 'heavens'. Shakespearean scholars generally agree that trumpets were sounded three times to announce the beginning of a **perform**ance. Stage directions and dialogue from contemporary play texts clearly point to this practice, for instance Robert Greene's *Alphonsus King of Aragon* (1599) and Ben Jonson's *Every Man Out of His Humour* (1600).

trumpet

Another invaluable piece of evidence is given by Philip Henslowe's inventories of stage properties, costumes and play books belonging to the Admiral's Men. In these inventories, drawn up in 1598, the Rose impresario recorded three trumpets along with a drum, a **treble viol**, a **bass** viol, a bandore, a **cittern** and a **sackbut**. Whereas only one specimen of each of the other instruments was listed by Henslowe, as many as three trumpets are mentioned. This points to the popularity of this instrument in Renaissance staging practices.

Some manuscript and printed play books annotated for performance place instructions for mid-scene sound effects such as 'Sound Trumpet(s)' in the margins of the pages: this device would have been useful for those in charge of achieving sound effects during a performance, since it visually isolates this category of effects from other indications for mid-scene stage business. It is also important to note that the practice of using the noun 'trumpet' to denote the musician as well as the instrument was widely adopted in theatrical jargon.

(B) The paucity of cues for 'trumpeters' in the Shakespeare canon proves this point: there are only two occasions when trumpeters are exhorted to act, specifically in *1 Henry VI*: 'Go to the gates of Burdeaux, trumpeter, / Summon their general unto the wall' (4.2.1–2); and in *Antony and Cleopatra*: 'Trumpeters, / with **brazen din** blast you the city's **ear**' (4.8.34–5).

The use of trumpets in battle scenes is signalled in both explicit stage directions and in cues for stage business in the dialogue, mainly in historical plays and tragedies. Sometimes, early modern play texts specify that the sounding of trumpets has to take place 'within' or 'afar off' (i.e. from behind the tiring-house wall). (See also Introduction.) An example in Shakespeare's plays is found in Folio *King Lear*: '*Trumpet answers within*' (5.3.116.SD). The absence of this and of several other detailed stage directions in Q1 *King Lear* (1608) is one of the reasons which has led critics to argue that Folio is the more theatrical of the two versions.

Bolingbroke's order to the Earl of Northumberland to sound a parley before Flint Castle points to the physical intensity of the sounding of trumpets onstage: 'Go to the rude ribs of that ancient castle; / Through brazen trumpet send the **breath** of parley' (*R2* 3.3.32–3). Later in the same scene, a stage direction (61) explicitly signals that trumpets are to be sounded and that Richard enters on the walls to parley with his enemies. That trumpets were also used to signify retreats can be surmised, for instance, from a passage in *1 Henry IV*. The stage direction '*A **retrait** is sounded*' (5.4.158.SD) is followed by Prince Henry's words to Lancaster: 'The trumpet sounds retrait, the day is our [sic]' (5.4.159).

The opening scene of *King John* works as an ominous prelude to the tragic events with which this history play is concerned. It shows King John in the middle of a discussion with Chatillon, the ambassador from France, at the end of which he dismisses Arthur's claims to the English throne. Answering Chatillon's threat that a war may ensue with France, he exclaims:

> Be thou as lightning in the eyes of France;
> For ere thou canst **report**, I will be there;
> The **thunder** of my cannon shall be heard.
> So hence! Be thou the trumpet of our wrath,
> And sullen presage of your own decay.
> (1.1.24–8)

This aural metaphor, involving the anachronistic reference to gunpowder and mentioning a martial instrument, prepares the audience for the sieges and battles displayed later on the stage, during which the actual sounding of trumpets is often required.

Trumpets announce ceremonial entries (and sometimes departures) of characters of rank. One of the most effective uses of the trumpets for such purpose is found in Q1 *Titus Andronicus* (1594). Just before Titus Andronicus serves Tamora a pie containing the flesh of her own sons, a stage direction reads: '*Trumpets sounding, a table brought in. Enter Titus like a cook, placing the dishes, and Lavinia with a veil over her face*' (K2r). The **shrill** sound of the trumpet clashes with Lavinia's dumbness. In Folio *Titus Andronicus*, **hoboy**s are played instead.

Jorgensen has argued that 'Kings and ranking military officers had their specially identifying trumpet music' (p. 23). For instance, the sounding of a trumpet which announces Othello's arrival in Cyprus is immediately recognized by Iago when he exclaims: 'The Moor! I know his trumpet' (*Oth* 2.1.178). This remark, accompanying the sound effect, puts an end to Iago's aside comment. The aside allows the audience to become aware of Iago's intention to exploit the friendly relationship between Cassio and Desdemona for his villainous purposes. Thus, the

trumpet

evocation of the public sphere created by the trumpet at this point contrasts with the references to the private and sexual spheres in Iago's previous comments. Characters of rank are recognized by a specific trumpet sound also in *All's Well That Ends Well* (3.5.9), *Titus Andronicus* (5.3.16), *Troilus and Cressida* (4.4.140) and *King Lear* (2.1.79).

Images of emotions, intentions or secrets being disclosed are sometimes established by using a musical metaphor involving a trumpet. When Antiochus realizes that his incestuous relationship with his daughter has been discovered by Pericles, he reveals in a soliloquy that he wants to have Pericles murdered:

> He must not live to trumpet forth my infamy,
> Nor tell the world Antiochus doth sin
> In such a loathed manner.
>
> (*Per* 1.1.145–7)

In *The Winter's Tale*, Paulina tries to help the disgraced Hermione after the latter has given birth to Perdita. She decides to take the baby to Leontes and to plead for Hermione's cause:

> If I prove honey-mouth'd, let my **tongue** blister;
> And never to my red-look'd anger be
> The trumpet any more . . .
>
> (2.2.31–3)

These words barely disguise Paulina's passionate and outspoken nature.
See also **clang**.

(C) Altenburg, *Untersuchungen zur Geschichte der Trompete* (1973).
Baines, *Brass Instruments* (1976).
Bate, *The Trumpet and Trombone* (1978).
Bendinelli, *Tutta l'arte della trombetta* (1614).
Blackburn, 'Music and Festivals at the Court of Leo X: A Venetian View' (1992).
Carter, *Music in Late Renaissance and Early Baroque Italy* (1992).
Dessen and Thomson, *A Dictionary of Stage Directions* (1999), pp. 237–8.
Downey, 'A Renaissance Correspondence Concerning Trumpet Music' (1981); 'The Trumpet and its Role in Music of the Renaissance and Early Baroque' (1983); 'The Renaissance Slide Trumpet: Fact or

trumpet

Fiction?' (1984); and 'The Danish Trumpet Ensemble at the Court of King Christian III' (1991).

Duffin, 'The *trompette des menestrels* in the 15th-century *alta capella*' (1989).

Fantini, *Modo per imparare a sonare di tromba* (1638).

Farmer, *The Rise and Development of Military Music* (1912); and *Military Music* (1950).

Foakes, *Henslowe's Diary* (2002), p. 318.

Grove, 'Trumpet'.

Gurr, *The Shakespearean Stage* (1992), pp. 131–2.

Jorgensen, *Shakespeare's Military World* (1956).

Kobbe, 'The Trumpet in Camp and Battle' (1898).

Markham, *The Souldiers Accidence* (1625).

Myers, 'Slide Trumpet Madness: Fact or Fiction?' (1989).

Polk, 'The Trombone, the Slide Trumpet and the Ensemble Tradition of the Early Renaissance' (1989).

Shirley, *Shakespeare's Use of Off-Stage Sounds* (1963), pp. 41–50.

Tarr, *Die Trompete / La trompette* (1977).

trumpeter see **trumpet**.

tucket (A) The most important function of Cavalry Signal **Music** (as Downey calls it, p. 69) was to transmit military commands in the field. The **trumpet** was the **instrument** used and the 'Cavalry **March**' or Tucket was one such signal. The other four Cavalry Signals were 'Boots and Saddles', 'Mount-up', 'To the Standard' and 'The Watch'. Each command had a separately identifiable signal motif, recognizable primarily by its rhythm. That rhythm was based on the word-rhythm of the command, as Bendinelli's mnemonics suggest, e.g. 'boutes selles' ('Boots and Saddles') and 'ranante' ('Cavalry March'):

These four Cavalry Signals could be preceded and followed by another signal called variously, according to nationality, Toccata, Ingangk, Toc[c]ada, Tucket or Entrée. This Downey terms the Signal Toccata in *tucket*

order not to confuse it with the Cavalry March or Tucket. The Signal Toccata was used only when there was ample time to **sound** the Cavalry Signal. Sometimes the Cavalry March would replace the Signal Toccata. This seems to be especially the case in English signalling.

The etymology of the Cavalry March signal, the Tucquet or Tucket is derived from the Italian '*toccata*'.

Downey refers to trumpet signals not used in the field and having an ornamental function as 'Occasional Military **Music**' (p. 69). The toccata or tucket was sounded to announce the arrival of a royal person or high-ranking military person. The 'occasional' toccatas are related to the Signal Toccatas but are more extensive and complicated in musical form.

(B) The indication 'tucket' is not as frequently signalled in the drama of the period as the more generic **flourish**. Dessen and Thomson, whose *Dictionary of Stage Directions* counts on a database of c.22,000 entries taken from plays belonging to adult professional companies between 1580 and 1642, note that 'of the roughly twenty signals for a tucket many are in the Shakespeare canon' (p. 239). Like other trumpet sounds, tuckets were connected with the military world. They were also used to announce the arrival of a messenger. Furthermore, as Manifold suggests, 'persons of importance had their *own* tuckets, by which they could be recognized at a distance' (p. 28). Recognition of characters by a tucket is clear, for instance, from Folio *King Lear*, where we have: '*Tucket within*' (2.1.77.SD and 2.4.181). In both cases, exchanges between onstage characters make it clear that the tuckets in question are for, respectively, the Duke of Cornwall and Goneril. No sound effect is indicated in the quarto editions of 1608 and 1619.

The indication '*A tucket afar off*' (*AWW* 3.5.OSD), like 'within', means that an area behind the tiring-house wall would have probably been used to give the impression that the sound was coming from far away (see Introduction for more details on the areas of purpose-built playhouses from which sound effects would have been achieved). Tuckets are also required in *Timon of Athens* (1.2.114.SD), Folio *Troilus and Cressida* (1.3.212.SD) and *Richard II* (1.3.25.SD).

In Folio *The Merchant of Venice* 'A tucket sounds' precedes the arrival of Bassanio (5.1.121.SD). In the ensuing line, Lorenzo addresses Portia: 'Your husband is at hand, I hear his trumpet' (5.1.122). The sounding of a trumpet before the denouement (Portia and Nerissa reveal that they were disguised respectively as a lawyer and her clerk) has the effect of bringing the audience back to reality after the sounding of music during the first part of the scene, dominated by the exchanges between the lovers Lorenzo and Jessica. Lorenzo's line would have worked as a cue: the explicit stage instruction for a tucket is in fact found only in Folio, characterized by a larger number of musical cues than Q1 (1600) and Q2 (1619).

The entries of the French herald Montjoy before the Battle of Agincourt are signalled as follows in Folio *Henry V* (as with *The Merchant of Venice*, in this history play the stage directions for music are absent from Q1, 1600): '*Tucket. Enter Montjoy*' (3.6.113; 4.3.78). However, when Montjoy concedes the French defeat at the end of the battle, his entry (4.7.65) is not preceded by any sound effect. This apparent inconsistency in the way of announcing the entry of the herald may serve an important thematic purpose: the absence of a fanfare here reflects a more subdued attitude by the French after their unexpected – and disastrous – defeat. The words spoken by Gloucester at line 67 ('His eyes are humbler than they us'd to be') further support this interpretation. Thus, it is difficult to agree with Shirley's view that 'we should hear it [Montjoy's tucket] again . . . We would know it by this time and have an instant to wonder if the Frenchman still dares to ask for ransom' (p. 82).

The only instance of the use of this word in the Shakespeare dialogue is found once again in *Henry V*, when the Constable incites the French before the Battle of Agincourt:

> . . . Then let the trumpets sound
> The tucket **sonance** and the **note** to mount;
> For our approach shall so much dare the field,
> That England shall couch down in fear, and yield.
> (4.2.34–7)

This is an accurate description of the military usage of the tucket: as Gervase Markham (1625) reminds us, like other trumpet sounds, it is a signal for the cavalry.

tucket

(C) Bendinelli, *Tutta l'arte della trombetta* (1614).
Byrne, 'The English March and Early Drum Notation' (1997).
Dessen and Thomson, *A Dictionary of Stage Directions* (1999).
Downey, 'The Trumpet and its Role in Music of the Renaissance and Early Baroque' (1983).
Edelman, *Shakespeare's Military Language: A Dictionary* (2000), pp. 368–9.
Farmer, *The Rise and Development of Military Music* (1912).
Manifold, *The Music in English Drama* (1956).
Markham, *The Souldiers Accidence* (1625).
Shirley, *Shakespeare's Use of Off-Stage Sounds* (1963).
Tarr, 'Cesare Bendinelli' (1977).

tune (A) As a noun the 'tune' is the distinctive series of **note**s or **melody** that characterizes a **song** or instrumental **piece**. The tune usually appears at the beginning in the uppermost or **treble part**, as in **ayre**s or **ballad**s, or in the principal 'singing' part, as in consort songs. In contrapuntal pieces such as **madrigal**s and motets, all the parts have the tune at one point or another. Sometimes tunes were known specifically by their titles, such as '**Greensleeves**' (mentioned, for instance, in *The Merry Wives of Windsor* 2.1.63 and 5.5.19), 'Fortune my foe', 'Walsingham', etc.

As a verb, 'tune' can have several meanings. Connected with melody, 'to tune it' can mean 'to sing'. Or this verb can refer to the process by which **instrument**s are made to **sound** harmonious, for example by raising or lowering the pitch of their different **string**s, usually by very small adjustments of the tuning **peg**s, as on the **lute, viol**, violin or harpsichord (or **virginal**). **Wind** instruments, notably **trumpet**s and **sackbut**s, can be tuned by varying the length of their tubes. **Drum**s are tuned by increasing the tension of the membrane or skin. The sense of adjusting the pitch to bring the strings of an instrument into **harmony** can be extended to the **voice**, as in Campion's poem, 'Tune thy **Music**ke to thy hart / Sing thy ioy with thankes' (*Two Bookes of Ayres*, The First, c.1613, no. 8) where '**Concord** pleaseth more, the lesse 'tis **strain**ed'. 'To sing' or 'to **play** out of tune' is to violate the pleasing harmonious sounds normally produced when **perform**ing in tune.

(B) In his narration of Antonio's betrayal, Prospero explains to Miranda that her uncle took advantage of his powerful position in the Dukedom of Milan:

> ... Having both the **key**
> Of officer and office, set all hearts i' th' state
> To what tune pleas'd his **ear** ...
> (*Tmp* 1.2.83–5)

Antonio thus managed to usurp Prospero's rightful title. 'Key' is a signifier of his high status in the dukedom and also introduces the musical metaphor to describe his manipulative abilities. Furthermore, 'Antonio's metaphorical power to control or direct his subjects is literalised in Prospero's employment of music as a means of dictating action throughout the play' (Lindley, p. 102).

'Tune' is sometimes synonymous with 'song'. In a drunken state, Stephano sings 'I shall no more to sea' (2.2.42) and declares that it is 'a very scurvy tune' (44). He then intones another song, which he calls a 'scurvy tune too' (55). 'Scurvy', which in this context means 'worthless', 'contemptible' reflects traits of Stephano's personality and may also hint at his inability to sing in a pleasing manner. 'Tune' is mentioned in another scene involving the presence of Stephano, Trinculo and Caliban, this time to refer to the musical accompaniment of a song. The three characters are drunk and cannot sing in harmony because Ariel (invisible to them) confounds them:

STEPHANO: Come on, Trinculo, let us sing.   *Sings.*
'Flout 'em and scout 'em ...
CALIBAN: That's not the tune.
   Ariel plays the tune on a **tabor** *and* **pipe**.
STEPHANO: What is this same?
TRINCULO: This is the tune of our **catch**, play'd by the picture of Nobody.
(3.2.120–1; 124–7)

Like the singing in the previous scene, this must have been anything but pleasing to the ear.

The Two Gentlemen of Verona has a lively exchange between Julia and Lucetta which entails singing to the tune of 'Light o' Love' (1.2.77–92). (See '**burden**' and 'toy' for a detailed discussion). This early comedy

447

tune

has several uses of the term: the most technical occur in 4.2, when **musician**s arrive to sing beneath Silvia's window. Thurio exhorts them: 'Now, gentlemen, / Let's tune, and to it lustily a while' (24–5). Realising that Julia looks sad while listening to the song, the Host wonders whether it is because she thinks that one of the musicians plays 'out of tune on the strings' (60). On both occasions, the allusion is to the process of making the different instruments sound in harmony. It is difficult to tell which stringed instrument the Host thinks may be out of tune, since mixed **consort**s had several stringed instruments (among them lute, bandora and different types of viol).

'Tune' is also used in the sense of 'tuning an instrument' in *The Taming of the Shrew* when Hortensio, disguised as a music teacher in 3.1, unsuccessfully tries to impress Bianca with his lute playing. His clumsy attempt to display supposed musical expertise fails: he is incapable of tuning the instrument, as is clear from the exchanges at lines 24–48 (see 'instrument' for a detailed discussion).

Speeches in political contexts sometimes resort to musical metaphors, as in *Richard II*. Shocked by the harshness of the sentence imposed on him (he has been banished for life) Mowbray addresses the King with powerful and moving words. He compares his **tongue**, which in exile will no longer speak English, to a 'cunning instrument cas'd up' (1.3.163) which, even if opened, will fall into the hands of somebody 'that knows no **touch** to tune the harmony' (165). In another history play, Henry VI angrily apostrophizes Suffolk, who has just announced to him the death of Gloucester. He accuses him of singing 'a **raven**'s note / Whose dismal tune bereft my vital pow'rs' (*2H6* 3.2.40–1). A raven's tune can only be 'dismal', i.e. **discord**ant and thus unpleasant to the ear.

The nature of tunes sung or played is sometimes alluded to. For instance, Autolycus claims that among the ballads he is selling, there is 'one to a very **doleful** tune' (*WT* 4.4.262). Before being visited by the ghost of Caesar on the eve of the Battle of Philippi, Brutus observes that one of his servants is playing and singing 'a sleepy tune' (*JC* 4.3.267). Falstaff threatens Prince Hal that he will have ballads written to mock him which will be 'sung to filthy tunes' (*1H4* 2.2.45).

Adonis rejects Venus' attempts to seduce him with a musical metaphor which highlights Venus' sensual and alluring nature:

> If love have lent you twenty thousand tongues,
> And every tongue more moving than your own,

>   Bewitching like the wanton mermaids' songs,
>   Yet from mine ear the tempting tune is **blow**n.
>   (*Ven* 775–8)

In *Much Ado About Nothing*, after Beatrice's 'conversion' to love, Hero jokingly remarks to her: 'Do you speak in the sick tune?' (3.4.42). Beatrice replies: 'I am out of all other tune, methinks' (43). In this light-hearted conversation, the two women imply that being in love causes pain and anguish similar to that experienced by a sick person.

'Tuning' in its meaning of 'being in harmony' achieves a paradoxical effect when mentioned in relation to murder in *Othello*. Othello has just killed Desdemona and still believes that Cassio was her lover. Hearing that Cassio has only been wounded but not killed by Roderigo, he concludes that harmony cannot be achieved since one of the 'adulterous' lovers is still alive (King, p. 158). He exclaims: 'Then murther's out of tune, / And **sweet** revenge grows **harsh**' (5.2.114–15). On the other hand, in *Cymbeline* Guiderius resorts to the opposite image: the devastating effect of death results in lack of harmony. He announces that the (apparent) death of Fidele prevents him from singing a **dirge** in his honour 'for notes of sorrow out of tune are worse / Than **priest**s and fanes that lie' (5.2.241–2).

Harmony can be achieved even in harsh conditions, as Nestor explains. He observes that, during a storm, the courageous creature

>   As rous'd with rage, with rage doth sympathize,
>   And with an **accent** tun'd in self-same key
>   Retires to chiding fortune.
>   (*Tro* 1.3.52–4)

Regrettably, lack of discipline in the Greek army makes it impossible for the soldiers to adapt themselves to difficult conditions and to reach an acceptable degree of harmony.

See also **bird, discord**.

(C) King, '"Then Murder's Out of Tune": The Music and Structure of *Othello*' (1986).

Lindley, *The Tempest* (2002).

tut

tut (A) 'Tut' is a **lute** and lyra-**viol** articulation embellishment or '**grace**', certainly known about and used in the later seventeenth century and most probably integral in lute **play**ing style in the late sixteenth century. The earliest description we have of 'tut' is one by Thomas Mace:

> The *Tut*, is a *Grace*, always **perform**ed with the *Right Hand*, and is a *sudden taking away the* **Sound** *of any* **Note**, and in such a manner, as it will seem to cry *Tut*; and is very *Pritty*, and *Easily done*, Thus. When you would perform *This Grace*, it is but to **strike** your *Letter,* [i.e. note indicated by a letter on the tablature] (which you intend shall be so *Grac'd*), with one of your *Fingers*, and immediately *clap on your next striking Finger, upon the* **String** *which you struck*; in which doing, you suddenly *take away the Sound of the Letter*, which is that, we call the *Tut*; and if you do it clearly, it will seem to **speak** the word *Tut*, so plainly, as if it were a *Living Creature, Speakable*.
>
> (p. 109)

The earliest published explication of English graces is the table printed in John Playford's *A Breefe Introduction to the Skill of Musick* (1654). It was reproduced in Christopher Simpson's *The Division Violist* (1659), where a debt to 'the ever famous Charles Colman Doctor of **Music**k' is acknowledged. It does not contain 'tut', unsurprisingly, since Simpson's treatise is not intended for lutenists or lyra-viol players.

That the interpretation of later seventeenth-century graces could be applicable to late sixteenth and early seventeenth-century ones is confirmed as it were by comparing ornament signs in both sixteenth and seventeenth-century sources. Whilst the latter had increased their number and changed their system, similarities in usage between the two are discernable. The 'shake' and the 'fall' were the basic graces on which more elaborate ones were embellished. English **musician**s of the later seventeenth century had been brought up in early seventeenth-century performance practices and unspecific examples of continuity of practice are recognizable in printed sources, notably Charles Butler's *Principles of Musik*, printed in 1636 but relating to late sixteenth-century practice, and Campion's *A New Way*, first printed c.1614 but reprinted by Playford in several editions of his famous *Introduction to the Skill of Musick* from 1654 onwards, with short annotations by Christopher Simpson.

Mace's 'tut' is equivalent to the French *'étouffement'* which is found in earlier seventeenth-century French lute **music**. Because French lutenists and their music were known in Elizabethan London, and English lutenists travelled in France (Dowland, for example, was in Paris as early as 1580), it is likely that the French style and technique were familiar to the English.

(B) If 'tut' was known to the Elizabethans, then the comical scene involving Hortensio (disguised as a music teacher) trying to impart a lute **lesson** to Bianca may well contain a pun on the term. After Hortensio has explained his **gamut** to her, she replies: 'Call you this gamouth? Tut, I like it not' (*Shr* 3.1.79). Not only is the musical context unmistakable, it is also couched within a lute lesson. Just as the lute grace is a rhetorical gesture, '**stop**ping the sound', so Bianca's remark to Hortensio is a 'put down'.

In *Richard II*, York says to the kneeling Bolingbroke. 'Tut, tut, / Grace me no grace, nor uncle me no uncle' (2.3.85–6). The adjacency of 'tut' and 'grace' is striking and surely not coincidental. In both cases analysed here, Shakespeare's use of 'tut' coincides with the sense and usage of the musical ornament or grace.

(C) Craig-McFeely, 'English Lute Manuscripts and Scribes 1530–1630' (1993), makes no reference to 'tut'.

Dart, 'Ornament Signs in Jacobean Music for Lute and Viol' (1961), provides a discussion of signs in an early seventeenth-century BL MS (Egerton 2971).

Mace, *Musick's Monument* (1676).

twang (A) 'Twang' can have various applications but is usually the **sound** made when a **string** on an **instrument** such as a **harp, lute** or violin is plucked quite hard. Its usage suggests that it intends a not altogether **pleasant** sound, resulting in resonant **high**-pitched **noise**s. Thus, to twang an instrument is to pluck its strings forcibly. (It is worth noting that the term 'pluck' is not used in a musical meaning in Shakespeare, even when it occurs in a musical context such as in *Hamlet* 3.2.362–6.)

'Twang' also implies an uneducated way of **play**ing a stringed instrument. When used in connection with vocal sounds or speech it refers to **accent** or dialect.

twang

(B) One stage direction in Shakespeare indicates a '*sudden twang of instruments*' (*TNK* 5.1.168.SD) before a rose falls from a rose tree at the altar of Diana. This sound effect is interpreted as a 'gracious' (173) sign by Emilia, who knows that the goddess is listening to her prayers.

'Twang' relates to vocal sounds in *Twelfth Night*. After challenging Cesario to a duel, Sir Andrew is urged to put on 'a swaggering accent **sharp**ly twang'd off' (3.4.180) while swearing in order to show an air of valour and superiority. It is interesting that the high-pitched ('sharp') quality of twanging is underlined in a vocal rather than instrumental context.

When Caliban and his drunken companions Stephano and Trinculo plot to assassinate Prospero, Ariel plays **music** while invisible and confounds them. Caliban reassures his fellow conspirators:

> Be not afeard, the isle is full of noises,
> Sounds, and **sweet air**s, that give delight and hurt not.
> Sometimes a thousand twangling instruments
> Will **hum** about mine **ears** . . .
>
> (*Tmp* 3.2.135–8)

The pejorative connotation implicit in 'twangling' intimates the potentially dangerous and subversive power that music can exert over the human mind, a theme which is present throughout *The Tempest*.

When Katherina insults Hortensio (disguised as a music teacher) by labelling him a 'rascal **fiddler** / And twangling **Jack**' (*Shr* 2.1.157–8) she highlights his incompetence as a player. These lines engage the audience in a subtle metatheatrical game, since they reveal that Hortensio's disguise is not as effective as he was hoping.

twangling see **twang**.

U

ut (A) The name 'ut' is the first syllable or **note** of the Renaissance hexachord. The others are: re (the second), mi (the third), fa (the fourth), sol (the fifth), la (the sixth). The system was thought to have been devised in the eleventh century in Italy by Guido d'Arezzo, who observed that the verse of a **hymn**, written in the eighth century by Paulus Diaconus for the feast day of St John the Baptist, began each phrase with a note of the hexachord in ascending order:

> *Ut* queant laxis *Re*sonare fibris
> *Mi*ra gestorum *Fa*muli tuorum
> *Sol*ve polluti *La*bii reatum, Sancte Ioannes.
>   (*Liber Usualis*, 1952, p. 1504)

He adopted the syllables sung to these notes as the basis for his solmization system, which was used virtually unchanged for five centuries and more. The syllables were usually associated with the six notes, C,D,E,F,G,A or G,A,B,C,D,E.

Although it continued to be employed as the starting point for teaching beginners **music**, the hexachord began to be replaced at the end of the sixteenth century by the diatonic major/minor octave scale. The main problem some practical and theoretical **musician**s (e.g. Burmeister, Campion) identified in the hexachord system was that one note could have two different names in the same **piece**. This meant, in addition to a certain confusion, that it was not possible to

ut

change key ('modulate') in a piece as the new musical language of the burgeoning baroque style began to demand. The major/minor scale system developed and persisted into the twentieth century when it was challenged and to some extent replaced by atonality. It still, however, forms the basis of practical and theoretical music teaching today.

(B) Since all or some of the hexachord notes are mentioned in conjunction in Shakespeare's plays, they are treated here under 'ut' for the sake of convenience.

The whole hexachord is delivered by Hortensio, disguised as a **lute** teacher, in *The Taming of the Shrew*, 3.1.74–9 (see '**gamut**' for a detailed commentary). In *Love's Labour's Lost*, Holofernes, aptly described as 'the Pedant' in the stage direction at the beginning of 4.2, is asked by Jaquenetta (who is illiterate) to read the love letter she has received from Armado. Holofernes is willing to display his knowledge of various subjects, and replies in a cryptic style. After quoting a passage from an Italian eclogue, he goes on to show off his understanding of music. He **hum**s the hexachord: '*Ut, re, sol, la, mi, fa*' (4.2.100). The fact that he gets the scale wrong shows that he is not as learned as he makes himself out to be.

In *King Lear*, Edmund hums some of these notes in a **discord**ant manner while Edgar enters:

> Pat! he comes, like the catastrophe in the old comedy.
> My cue is villainous melancholy, with a **sigh** like
> Tom o' Bedlam. – O, these eclipses do portend these
> **division**s! *fa, sol, la, mi.*
>
> (1.2.134–7)

This is the moment when Edgar succumbs to the plot that Edmund has devised against him. 'Divisions' can be understood to mean 'discords' but can also have a musical nuance, which introduces the discord of the following notes intoned by Edmund. The atmosphere of 'villainous melancholy' is thus successfully achieved.

In *Romeo and Juliet*, a comical exchange occurs between Peter and the musicians who have just been dismissed after the apparent death of Juliet on the day of her wedding to Paris. Peter asks them to **play** a **tune** for him, which they refuse to do. The first musician derogatorily calls him a 'serving-creature' (4.5.116), and there ensues a musical exchange between the two men:

> PETER: Then will I lay the serving-creature's dagger on your pate. I will carry no **crotchet**s, I'll *re* you, I'll *fa* you. Do you note me?
> FIRST MUSICIAN: And you *re* us and *fa* us, you note us.
> (117–20)

Peter has the Italian meaning of 're' (the note D) and 'fa' (F) in mind: these words also mean, respectively, 'king' and 'to do, to make' (the latter can have sexual connotations). Peter is saying that he refuses to accept any whimsical **fancy** (one of the non-musical meanings of 'crotchet') on the part of the musician. He will crown (i.e. hit on the head) the musician with his dagger, and will do him in (i.e. assault him). The pun is elaborated upon even further 'when the first musician acknowledges that to be re'd and fa'd is to be noted, . . . [thus shifting] Peter's use of "note" (understand) to "know" in the carnal sense' (Fabry, p. 183).

(C) Fabry, 'Shakespeare's Witty Musician' (1982), comments on the passage from *Romeo and Juliet* quoted above, and compares it to *The Taming of the Shrew* 3.1.74–9.

Owens, 'Concepts of Pitch in English Music Theory, c.1560–1640' (1998), is the best discussion of the hexachord system in Renaissance England.

V

vent see **ventage**.

ventage see **stop**.

vestal (A) A vestal was one of the four (later six) virgin priestesses commanded to tend the altar fire in the Temple of Vesta in ancient Rome. By association the term was used to describe a chaste and pure woman.

(B) Of the nine occurrences of this term in Shakespeare, only one makes reference to the musical sphere. In *Pericles*, two frequenters of the brothel in Mytilene realize the errors of their ways, and resolve that from then on they will be virtuous. One of them suggests: 'Shall's go **hear** the vestals **sing**?' (4.5.7). The beneficial influence of **music** on the two penitent sinners is all the more significant because it is associated with the sacred status of the virgin priestesses.

vial see **viol**.

viol (A) Although the viol was introduced into the English court in the early sixteenth century, there is no evidence to suggest the **instrument** became popular as a gentleman's instrument until after 1580. The revels accounts of 1515 are the first to include the viol as belonging to an ensemble **play**ing **dance music**. The great royal inventories of the 1540s show that the King owned a good many instruments including a number of viols both 'great and smale'. It is possible that the court violinists also played the viols in **consort**s either for courtly entertainment or dancing. We know that from about the middle of the century, learning to play the viol became part of the education of a number of **choir**boys at the Chapel Royal, St Paul's and Westminster. These child viol players took part in ceremonial and theatre **perform**ances, playing incidental music and accompanying **song**s. As they reached adulthood and found employment, their influence as violists spread (Woodfield, 1984). Evidence indicates that towards the end of the century, an increasing number of Elizabethan stately homes owned a set or 'chest' of viols, suggesting that the instrument was becoming popular among the nobility outside the immediate confines of the royal court.

Like the **lute**, the viol is one of the most important instruments of the Renaissance, with its distinctive appearance and **sound**. Highly skilled makers, such as John Rose (father and son), helped to give the English viol its classic shape (Woodfield, 1984). It is a bowed **string**ed instrument, not dissimilar from a violin, but with a wide **fret**ted neck with five or six strings. Like the cello, it is played in a downwards vertical position, held between the knees or lower leg, hence its name, 'viol da gamba' (i.e. 'leg viol'). The characteristic convex bow is held with the palm of the hand facing upwards (the opposite to the violin bow).

The viol was particularly suited to consort music and was made in different sizes, ranging from **high treble** to **low bass**. The middle-range instruments, standard treble, tenor and bass, were the most common in viol consorts. The sound of the viol is comparatively quiet but its tone is distinctive in its reedy nasal quality. It is ideally suited to slowish smooth-flowing music, and less appropriate for quick **accent**ed **piece**s (such as faster dance forms). In England, the viol was most often found in consorts of between three and five instruments rather than as a solo instrument. In the early seventeenth century, the polyphonic fantasia emerged as the preferred genre for viol consort, notably at the hands of the court composer, Alfonso Ferrabosco the younger. Next in popularity was consort music for the slow stately dance, the **pavan**. This idiomatic viol music developed, out of which grew the art of *viol*

playing **division**. The viol became an indispensable member of the mixed consort, an ensemble special to English music – treble and bass viols, **flute, cittern**, lute and bandora. The viol's special role in playing divisions or ornaments sometimes led to this type of consort being called a '**broken**' consort, i.e. 'break division'.

The timbre of the viol made it particularly good at accompanying **sing**ing. Almost all the lute songs or **ayre**s published between 1597 and 1622 contained a part for bass viol. **Madrigal**s were often designated as 'Apt for Viols and Voyces'. And the consort song, popular in the children's companies plays, was specifically intended for solo **voice**(s) and a consort of viols.

(B) Social refinement, quietude and the healing power of string music are emblematic of the viol. In *2 Henry IV*, the King's request from his sickbed for quiet or '**still**' music implies soothing string music:

> Let there be no **noise** made, my gentle friends,
> Unless some dull and favorable hand
> Will whisper music to my weary spirit.
>
> (4.5.1–3)

Lear's 'un**tun**'d and **jar**ring senses' (*Lr* 4.7.15) are probably cured by string (viol) music (Sternfeld, p. 242). In *Pericles*, Cerimon revives Thaisa to the accompaniment of music:

> The **rough** and **woeful** music that we have,
> Cause it to sound, beseech you.
> The vial once more. How thou stir'st, thou block!
> The music there! I pray you give her **air**.
> Gentlemen, this queen will live. Nature awakes,
> A warmth breathes out of her . . .
>
> (3.2.88–93)

In this musically unambiguous context, the reference to 'vial', paradoxically, is probably not to the stringed instrument. It is more likely a reference to the small jar or bottle containing smelling salts used to revive those in a fainting condition. As has been pointed out above, the occurrence of the solo viol is rare. A solo lute would have been preferred. However, Shakespeare rarely misses a chance for word-play, and the use of the word 'vial' here may also obliquely hint at the music with its magical healing powers, just as in the next line 'give her air' may involve a pun on the 'air' we breath and the song form (see 'ayre').

The likening of the viol to the human body, especially the female figure, is present in sixteenth-century literature in varying degrees of explicitness. This sexual imagery is employed by Shakespeare when Pericles unravels the secret of the incestuous relationship between King Antiochus and his daughter, and expresses his opinion about the Princess:

> You are a fair viol, and your sense the strings;
> Who, finger'd to make man his lawful music,
> Would draw heaven down, and all the gods to hearken;
> But being play'd upon before your **time**,
> Hell only danceth at so **harsh** a **chime**.
>
> (1.1.81–5)

Any present-day viol maker will tell how badly an unseasoned immature viol sounds: this fact is used tellingly here. The sexual overtones of this speech cannot be ignored: the oblique reference to the female body established by 'viol' continues with **fingering** which, as well as referring to a playing technique, also means 'masturbate' (Partridge, p. 135).

Sir Andrew Aguecheek's supposed ability to play the 'viol de gamboys' and speak 'three or four languages / word for word without book' (*TN* 1.3.26–7) are the marks of an educated gentleman. Why Shakespeare uses the masculine form of 'gamba' here is not clear. This could be an oblique reference to the famous viol player and composer Tobias Hume, who was fat and also had a penchant for (young) boys. It is, after all, Sir Toby Belch who damns Sir Andrew with such faint praise. But there is no hard evidence to support this intriguing theory. Moreover, the viol is not unusually called the 'viol de gambo' in Elizabethan sources. Ungerer maintains that bawdy is implicit in this 'sexualised musical metaphor' (p. 87). This is unlikely because jokes about viol da gambas in early modern poetry and drama invariably refer to female players.

See also **case**.

(C) Ashbee and Holman, *John Jenkins and his Time: Studies in English Consort Music* (1996).

viol

Ashbee, Holman, Lasocki and Kisby, *A Biographical Dictionary of English Court Musicians, 1485–1714* (1998).
Dolmetsch, *The Viola da Gamba* (1968).
Pallis, 'The Instrumentation of English Viol Consort Music' (1969).
Partridge, *Shakespeare's Bawdy* (1968).
Remnant, *English Bowed Instruments from Anglo-Saxon to Tudor Times* (1986).
Sternfeld, *Music in Shakespearean Tragedy* (1967).
Ungerer, 'The Viol da Gamba as a Sexual Metaphor in Elizabethan Music and Literature' (1984).
Woodfield, *The Early History of the Viol* (1984); and *English Musicians in the Age of Exploration* (1995).

viol da gamba, viol de gamboys see **viol**.

virginal (A) The virginal or virginals was a small harpsichord with one set of **string**s and **jack**s. The application of the term 'virginal' was often not precise, being used in England for all types of harpsichords until the mid seventeenth century. Praetorius (1619) concluded that 'In England, all such **instrument**s, whether large or small, are termed *Virginall*. In France, *Espinettes*. In the Netherlands, *Clavicymbel* and also *Virginall*. In Germany, *Instrument* (in the narrow sense of the word)' (ch. 38). When it was used specifically, it referred to a small harpsichord in which the strings ran at right angles to the keys and the **case** had basically a rectangular shape.

The origin of 'virginal' as a name for the instrument, first found in late fifteenth-century Europe, is uncertain. Although Elizabeth I is known to have been an accomplished **play**er, there is no evidence to associate the derivation of the term with 'the virgin queen'. Its name, however, may have something to do with the instrument's particular association with female players as, for example, the title page of *Parthenia or The Maydenhead of the first musicke that euer was printed for the Virginalls* (c.1612–13) attests.

All the English virginals that survive are rectangular. Their cases are distinctive. Generally of oak, the outsides of the lids are plain whereas the insides are highly decorated, often with landscape scenes including stylized figures. The virginal came to England in the early sixteenth century, probably from the Netherlands. It became a popular keyboard

virginal

instrument in both household domestic and courtly circles, and by the early seventeenth century a large repertoire existed for it. This has survived almost exclusively in manuscript sources, the most famous being William Byrd's *My Ladye Nevells Booke* (1591) and the huge compendium compiled during the first two decades of the seventeenth century, the so-called *Fitzwilliam Virginal Book*. This **music** could also have been played on a variety of contemporaneous keyboard instruments and was not necessarily restricted to the virginal. On the other hand, all of it can be **perform**ed very successfully on the virginal, thereby emphasizing the versatility of the instrument, rather like the domestic upright piano of today which has its own special qualities, but which can be used to play the entire piano repertoire.

(B) Palomon and Arcite, while remembering the women they had loved in the past mention the Lord Steward's daughter who once had an encounter with Arcite in an arbour. Palomon asks: 'What did she there, coz? play o' th' virginals?' (*TNK* 3.3.34). We learn that the girl played the instrument for a while and then something else happened which made her 'groan' (3.3.35). In early modern English 'groaning' referred to 'a woman's cry or groan of pain at losing her virginity' (Partridge, p. 149). The image of the girl playing the virginals (an instrument with an allusive name) and the reference to groaning enhance the bawdy tone of the speeches. The comic exchanges between the two cousins provide some degree of relief between two darker scenes, occupied by the soliloquies of the Gaoler's daughter, who is going insane.

Leontes' irrational jealousy is unleashed by the affectionate exchanges between Hermione and Polixenes. Among other things, he observes that his wife is 'virginalling' upon Polixenes' palm (*WT* 1.2.125). This intransitive verb is now obsolete and means 'to tap with the fingers as on a virginal' (*OED* 2). In this context too the term acquires a sexual nuance – words such as 'bawcock' (121), 'nose' (121) and 'neat' (i.e. horned, 123) are uttered just before the reference to virginalling.

See also **organ, jack**.

(C) Apel, *The History of Keyboard Music to 1700* (1972).
Caldwell, *English Keyboard Music before the Nineteenth Century* (1973).
Ferguson, *Keyboard Interpretation from the 14th to the 19th century* (1987).
Partridge, *Shakespeare's Bawdy* (1968).

voice (A) The sixteenth century was quintessentially the age of vocal **music**, music for solo voice or polyphonic **sing**ing ('music in **part**s'). It was also a time when **instrument**al music, either as an alternative to or independent of vocal music, was forging ahead. Consequently, 'voice' was often used to distinguish singing from **play**ing instrumental music. Many Elizabethan **madrigal** publications were titled 'apt for **Viol**s and Voyces'; a number of **lute ayre** books were designated to be sung either by several voices or by 'one Voyce to an Instrument'. Singing with an instrument was often referred to as 'tuning the voice to . . .', as in: 'We'll **tune** our voices to the lute / And instruments of **sweet**est **sound**' (Alison, 1606, no. 24).

Sometimes, musical characteristics were distinguished from speaking tones by the use of the term 'voice': 'Thy voice is as an **echo** clear, which music doth beget; / Thy speech is as an oracle which none can counterfeit' (Thomas Campion, *Third Booke*, c.1617, no. 13). 'Voice' could therefore also mean song.

By the late sixteenth century there were four standard categories of singing voice, dependent on *tessitura* or pitch. They were generally called in descending order, **treble**, countertenor (alto) or **mean**, tenor and **bass**. In England, the treble was usually higher than the continental equivalent (the *cantus*) and the mean higher than the countertenor or alto. Most English music treatises give descriptions of the voices, although there is not always much consistency. Campion (*A New Way*, c.1614) says there are essentially four voices, namely Bass, Tenor, Countertenor or Meane and Treble. Charles Butler, in his retrospective *Principles of Musik* (1636) defines five voices, namely the 'deep' bass, the **'plainsong'** tenor, the countertenor 'because it answereth the tenor', the mean so-called 'because it is a middling or mean **high** part between the countertenor and the treble' and the treble 'sung with a high clear sweet voice'. In professional cathedral **choir**s, boys sang treble and mean parts. In domestic circles women would sing the high parts of madrigals and ayres. At court and in the theatre, boys from the cathedral and chapel choirs, notably St Pauls and the Chapel Royal, would sing when required.

(B) There are some general references to the quality of singing voices in Shakespeare. For instance, Balthasar tries to avoid singing '**Sigh** no more ladies' by warning Don Pedro who has asked him to sing: 'O good my lord, tax not so bad a voice / To slander music any more than once'

voice

(*Ado* 2.3.44–5). After **hear**ing the song, Benedick agrees with Balthasar's view of his singing ability:

> And he had been a dog that should have
> howl'd thus, they would have hang'd him, and
> I pray God his bad voice bode no mischief.
> (79–81)

Amiens expresses his reluctance to sing the second stanza of 'Under the greenwood tree' in similar terms when he tells Jaques: 'My voice is ragged, I cannot please you' (*AYLI* 2.5.15).

However, more interesting are the metatheatrical allusions to the ambiguous state of boy actors' voices when they take on female roles. These allusions are based on the Renaissance belief that the change of voice of males at puberty was caused by the enlargement of the wind-pipe (which in its turn reflected the enlargement of the body as a whole) which caused 'larger' (**loud**er) sound (Smith, p. 227). Hence, when Portia announces that she will disguise herself as a doctor of law, she is aware that her voice will have to sound different: 'And [I'll] speak between the **change** of man and boy / With a reed voice . . .' (*MV* 3.4.66–7).

Orsino comments that Cesario (Viola in disguise) has a 'small pipe' which 'is as the maiden's **organ, shrill** and sound / And all is semblative a woman's part' (*TN* 1.4.33–4). The sexual and aural dimension evoked by terms such as 'pipe', 'organ' and 'part', as well as the theatrical role ('part') played by the boy actor, are juxtaposed in a very effective way and evoke the difficulties with which young actors had to contend when taking on female roles.

In the final scene of *Henry V*, the King proposes to Katherine in the following terms:

> . . . Come, your answer in **broken** music;
> for thy voice is music and thy English broken; therefore,
> queen of all, Katherine, **break** thy mind to me in
> broken English – wilt thou have me?
> (5.2.243–6)

On a superficial level, Henry is jokingly referring to Katherine's stilted English, but on a more subtle level this speech works as a metatheatrical

voice

reminder of the fact that the voice of the boy actor playing Katherine would soon break.

An explicit comment on the different quality of male and female voices is found in Scroop's remark that 'boys, with women's voices, / Strive to **speak** big' (*R2* 3.2.113–14). These boys have not yet reached puberty, and have to make a conscious effort to try and emulate the 'bigger' voice of a post-pubescent male. On the other hand, in *Cymbeline* Arviragus observes that his and Guiderius' voices have 'got the mannish **crack**' (4.2.236), i.e. that they have finally broken.

(C) Arkwright, 'Elizabethan Choirboys Plays and their Music' (1913–14).

Elam, 'The Fertile Eunuch' (1996).

Jeffreys, *The Life and Works of Philip Rosseter* (1990), ch. 2, has a short account of the boy actors/singers in the Blackfriars Theatre.

Monson, *Voices and Viols in England* (1982).

Smith, *The Acoustic World of Early Modern England* (1999).

Wilson (ed.), *A New Way* (2003).

Wulstan, *Tudor Music* (1985), ch. 8, discusses vocal pitch and ranges, vocal quality and characteristics of the individual voices.

W

warble (A) Used as both noun and adjective, 'warble' is an intensely descriptive musical term with various shades of meaning. Generally, it refers to melodic **sing**ing in a quivering, throaty, fluctuating manner. It is often applied to **bird**s singing, or to singing like a bird, specifically in a **soft** and delicate way (prettily or **sweet**ly), as in: 'Shaded with olive trees sat Celestina singing, / Than the warbling birds more sweet **harmony ring**ing' (Greaves, 1604, no. 1). It can also be merely a less than complimentary substitute for 'sing'.

(B) Of the five usages of this term in Shakespeare, four are synonymous with 'sing', as in Jaques's exhortation 'come, warble, come' (*AYLI* 2.5.37), followed by the text of the second stanza of 'Under the greenwood tree' and by the indication that the characters have to sing it '*all together*' (2.5.37.SD). The same meaning is implied in Armado's request to his page Moth that he must 'warble [and] make passionate my sense of **hear**ing' (*LLL* 3.1.1); a song at the beginning of this scene pertinently conveys Armado's feelings of love for Jaquenetta.

At the end of *A Midsummer Night's Dream* Titania instructs the fairies on how to **rehearse** their song to bless the house:

> First, rehearse your song by **rote**,
> To each word a warbling **note**.

warble

> Hand in hand, with fairy **grace**,
> Will we sing, and bless this place.
> (5.1.397–400)

The singing was expected to be **pleasant** and **melodious**, in line with the ending of the comedy, which is blessed by marital harmony. The pleasantness of the singing is confirmed by the phrase 'fairy grace' (399). In the same play Helena laments that her friendship with Hermia is no longer as strong as it used to be:

> We, Hermia, like two artificial gods,
> Have with our needles created both one flower,
> Both on one sampler, sitting on one cushion,
> Both warbling of one song, both in one **key**.
> As if our hands, our sides, **voice**s, and minds
> Had been incorporate . . .
> (*MND* 3.2.203–8)

Once again, it is the harmonious quality implicit in warbling which is emphasized: the present lack of harmony between the two young women fills Helena's heart with nostalgia for the old days.

'Warble' alludes to the melodious singing of a bird when Lucrece is compared to **Philomela** (who was transformed into a **nightingale** after being raped). Whilst 'Philomele had ended / The **well-tun'd** warble of her nightly sorrow' (*Luc* 1079–80), Lucrece wishes that dawn would never come, since this will only deepen her sense of pain and shame for her rape. She then weeps and sobs (1087–8), two actions quite different from the bird's composed and balanced expression of grief through its warbling.

(C) Folkerth, *The Sound of Shakespeare* (2002), pp. 91–8, explores the acoustic imagery used throughout *A Midsummer Night's Dream* to express physical and emotional proximity.

wassail (A) A wassail is a drinking **song** or **carol**, often associated with Christmastide. It is used in connection with drinking alcohol in excess and therefore has ironic, even jocular, overtones.

wassail

(B) When Hamlet tells Horatio and Marcellus that the newly-crowned king 'doth wake to-night and takes his rouse, / Keeps wassail . . .' (*Ham* 1.4.8–9), he refers to a 'drinking-hail', which would have been accompanied by celebratory **sing**ing. The evocation of the warm and festive **mood** within the castle makes a striking contrast to the cold atmosphere surrounding the three men on the guard-platform.

Berowne is very sceptical about Boyet's singing abilities and accuses him of being a 'wit's pedlar [who] retails his wares / At wakes and wassails, meetings, markets, fairs' (*LLL* 5.2.317–8). Catering for occasions such as carousals and fairs, which imply unsophisticated **music**, is only appropriate for somebody who sings 'A **mean** most meanly' (328).

weaver (A) In Renaissance England, weavers were mainly Calvinist refugees from the Netherlands (Milward, p. 153). They were keen **psalm-sing**ers, a fact which is alluded to twice in the Shakespeare canon.

(B) In *1 Henry IV*, while drinking sack Falstaff observes: 'I would I were a weaver, I could **sing** psalms' (2.4.133). That Falstaff is aspiring to the piousness of Dutch weavers may be indicated in an earlier line, where he promises that he will 'sew nether-stocks' (116) (Bevington, p. 185). The use of 'psalms' is found in Q1 (1598), whereas Folio changes 'psalms' to 'all manners of songs', which shows that the 1606 Act of Parliament to Restrain the Abuses of Players was followed scrupulously when this edition was prepared (Kastan, p. 214).

Intent on revelling in the middle of the night, Sir Toby asks his companions: 'Shall we rouse the night-**owl** in a **catch** that will draw / three souls out of one weaver?' (*TN* 2.3.58–9). Catches were songs for three or more **part**s, hence the implication is that the power of **music** on the soul is three times as effective in the case of this three-part catch which Sir Toby intends to sing with Sir Andrew and Feste (Warren and Wells, p. 126). Since catches often had a bawdy content, it appears that Sir Toby's words reveal his hope that the weavers may be touched by a type of music quite unlike the religious singing they are used to.

(C) Bevington, *1 Henry IV* (1987).
Kastan, *1 Henry IV* (2002).
Mahood, *Twelfth Night* (1968).

weaver

Milward, *Shakespeare's Religious Background* (1973), refers to the Dutch origin of weavers in sixteenth-century England.

Warren and Wells, *Twelfth Night* (1994).

well-tuned (A) 'Well-tuned' can mean either literally an **instrument** that has been carefully and expertly tuned or **voice**s or instruments that are in perfect agreement or **harmony**. For a discussion of the former see '**tune**'; the latter may also invoke a philosophical meaning as in Campion's 'Let well-tuned words amaze / With harmony divine' (*Third Booke*, c.1617, no. 12) which recalls the neo-Platonic philosophies about the relationship between the human world and the celestial world embodied in the word 'harmony'. A similar concept is found in Kirbye's :

>That Muse, which sung the beauty of thy face
>In **sweet** well-tuned **song**s
>And harmony that pleased.
>   (*Madrigalls*, 1597, no. 16)

(B) Shakespeare seems to have had the first meaning in mind when he has Tamora describe aurally a hunt in progress:

>. . . the babbling **echo** mocks the hounds,
>Replying **shrill**y to the well-tun'd **horn**s,
>As if a double hunt were heard at once.
>   (*Tit* 2.3.17–19)

The horns are in agreement with each other thus providing important aural signals for the hunters; the echo of the hounds' barking contributes to the harmony of the **sound**s characterizing this hunt.

Iago's aside remark that Desdemona and Othello are 'well tun'd now' (*Oth* 2.1.199) reflects the love and **concord** reigning between wife and husband, which Iago intends to disrupt. A similar image of marital harmony is introduced in *Sonnet* 8 when the poet exhorts his friend to contemplate marriage, which produces 'concord of well-tuned sounds' (5). In another poetical work, the **nightingale**'s 'well-tun'd **warble**' (*Luc* 1080) suggests the harmonious quality of this **bird**'s song.

See also **accord, concent**.

(C) Ratcliffe, *Campion: On Song* (1981), is a challenging deconstructionalist reading of 'Now winter nights'.

wench (A) Musical wenches are rare in Elizabethan literature. A reference to a **lute-play**ing young maid servant occurs in Coverdale's translation of the Bible (1535), as noted in *OED*: 'Take thy lute (saie men to her) and go about the citie, thou art yet an unknowne wensche' (Isaiah 23.16).

(B) There is one reference to 'wench' in Shakespeare when Queen Katherine commands her servant to play a lute **song** to help assuage her despair at the realization that her marriage with Henry is over: 'Take thy lute, wench, my soul grows sad with troubles. / **Sing**, and disperse 'em if thou canst. Leave working' (*H8* 3.1.1–2).

whistle (A) As a physical object, a whistle is a small **pipe** made usually out of metal, wood or clay and can take a variety of forms. The **bird** whistle, generally made of clay, could **imitate** the **sound**s of various species, notably **nightingale**, quail, turtle-dove and **cuckoo**. The metal boatswain's pipe was a slightly elongated duct whistle which sounded different signals depending on how the hand was cupped over its end. Three were discovered in the wreck of the *Mary Rose*.

The **shrill noise** of the whistle can be made without an **instrument**. By pursing the lips and **blow**ing fairly hard, a shrill piercing sound can be emitted. As with the instrument, a limited number of **note**s can be made. A distinctive pattern of notes may be identified with a particular kind of whistle.

(B) Jaques' description of the sixth age of man includes the observation that the

> . . . big manly **voice**,
> Turning again toward childish **treble**, pipes
> And whistles in his sound . . .
> (*AYLI* 2.7.161–3)

It is the shrill quality and small size of a whistle which prompts this conceit.

whistle

Whistling is sometimes connected to specific professions. For instance, Falstaff refers to the **carman's** [cart driver's] **whistle** with its bawdy connotation when hinting at Justice Shallow's habit of visiting prostitutes (*2H4* 3.2.316–18).

The mariners' whistle is mentioned twice in *Pericles*. During a powerful storm which is jeopardizing Pericles' journey to Tyre, the Prince comments on the dangerousness of the elements: 'The seaman's whistle / Is as a whisper in the **ear**s of death' (3.1.8–9). Later, Marina remembers that, on the day when she was born:

> Never was waves nor wind more violent,
> ... The boatswain whistles, and
> The master calls, and **treble**s their [the mariners'] confusion.
> (4.1.59; 63–4)

'Trebles' enhances the musical connotation of this speech, since it can be interpreted as meaning 'to increase threefold' (*OED* 1), but also as 'to emit a shrill sound'(*OED* 3). Whistling was an efficient way of carrying out orders, and was also 'a badge of office' (Lindley, p. 92) for both Master and Boatswain. Yet another scene set at sea during a storm confirms this. The boatswain exhorts the mariners to 'tend to th' master's whistle' (*Tmp* 1.1.6) in this perilous situation. At the beginning of *Henry V*, Act 3, the **Chorus** narrates Henry and his army's crossing of the Channel on their way to Harfleur, and asks the audience to imagine that they are hearing 'the shrill whistle which doth order give / To sounds confus'd' (3.Chor.9–10).

In *A Midsummer Night's Dream*, the 'whistling **wind**' (2.1.86) provides the ideal background for the fairies' **dance**. On the other hand, the same phenomenon is perceived as ominous at the eve of the Battle of Shrewsbury. In the words of the Prince of Wales:

> The southern wind
> Doth **play** the **trumpet** to his purposes,
> And by his **hollow** whistling in the leaves
> Foretells a tempest and a blust'ring day.
> (*1H4* 5.1.3–6)

In this martial situation, likening the wind to a herald is most apt.

(C) Lindley, *The Tempest* (2002).
Palmer, 'Musical Instruments from the *Mary Rose*' (1983).

whoobub (A) Although not specifically a musical term, 'whoobub' is sometimes found in early modern literature associated with the **noise** of **shrill bagpipe**s (e.g. Spenser, *The Faerie Queene* 3.10.43). In general it refers to noisy cacophony, shouting or ranting.

(B) This term is used twice by Shakespeare. In *The Winter's Tale*, Autolycus comments that, had the Old Shepherd not interfered 'with a whoobub against his daughter and the King's son' (4.4.616), he could have carried on undisturbed stealing purses during the sheep-shearing feast. The Shepherd's strong reaction is caused by his discovery that Florizel, who is wooing his reputed daughter Perdita, is the son of the King of Bohemia. This courtship is unacceptable given the (supposed) gap in social status between Perdita and Florizel. Autolycus' speech has several musical terms suggesting pleasantness such as '**ballad**' (598), '**song**' (606, 613) and '**tune**' (607), which make 'whoobub' stand out for its negative connotation.

The Gaoler's daughter in *The Two Noble Kinsmen* is looking forward to her meeting in the woods with Palamon, whom she has just freed from prison. Realising that his escape will soon be noticed, she observes that 'within this hour the whoobub / Will be all o'er the prison' (2.6.35–6). 'Whoobub' expresses the idea of unrest and confusion associated with the noise made by a crowd, in this case Palamon's fellow inmates.

wind (A) When applied to musical **instrument**s, 'wind' refers to instruments which are **blow**n as opposed to **string**ed instruments which are plucked or bowed, and **drum**s which are hit or **beat**en. Allusions to the **sound** of the wind '**sing**ing' or 'whistling' or, more ominously, 'howling' can have musical overtones. When whistling, the wind blows an imaginary **pipe**.

'Wind' as a verb means 'blow a wind instrument' and is used in connection with **horn**s during hunting scenes (examples are discussed in detail under 'horn').

(B) Wind instruments are mentioned in *Othello* 3.1. This scene opens with the entry of Cassio and **musician**s – the latter have been

wind

employed to **play** outside the lodgings of newly wed Othello and Desdemona. Cassio's choice of **music** does not seem to be appropriate for the occasion (King, p. 155), as the Clown's comic repartee with one of the musicians indicates:

> CLOWN: Why, masters, have your instruments been in Naples, that they **speak** i'th'nose thus?
> MUSICIAN: How, sir, how?
> CLOWN: Are these, I pray you, wind instruments?
> MUSICIAN: Ay, marry, are they, sir.
> CLOWN: O, thereby hangs a tail.
> MUSICIAN: Whereby hangs a tale, sir?
> CLOWN: Marry, sir, by many a wind instrument that I know . . .
>
> (3.1.3–11)

The musical context provides the Clown with an opportunity for indecent puns. The instruments speaking 'in the nose' are probably **bagpipe**s (these are described by Shylock as singing 'i' th' nose', *MV* 4.1.49). However, there is a clear allusion to syphilis, which in early modern England was called the 'Neapolitan disease' or 'malady of France' (Partridge, pp. 186 and 197), and which affects the nose among other parts of the body. The reference to wind instruments (10) also implies a joke on flatulence.

In a more serious context, Emilia observes that the outcome of the fight between Arcite and Palomon 'is proclaim'd / By the wind instruments' (*TNK* 5.3.93–4). A stage direction appearing a few lines before this comment tells us exactly which instruments were expected to be played to announce Arcite's victory: '**Cornet**s. *Cry within*, "Arcite, Arcite!"' (5.3.88.SD). The combat was rendered aurally from behind the *frons scenae* rather than visually on the main stage, a device commonly adopted in the theatre of Shakespeare's time (see Introduction for details on the areas of Elizabethan venues used for sound effects).

More frequent in the Shakespeare canon are general allusions to the sound caused by the wind, as when Trinculo observes that 'another storm [is] brewing, I **hear** it / sing it i' th' wind' (*Tmp* 2.2.19–20). A similar expression is found in: 'a man may hear this show'r sing in the wind' (*Wiv* 3.2.37). In both cases the implication is that the rising wind announces the arrival of rain.

wind

Sometimes the sound of the wind preceding a storm is compared to that of specific wind instruments. The Prince of Wales tells his followers that the southern wind 'doth play the **trumpet**' (*1H4* 5.1.4) and 'foretells a tempest and a blust'ring day' (6). This speech, delivered before the Battle of Shrewsbury, has ominous overtones: the evocation of the wind blowing the trumpet anticipates the sounding of a military trumpet (5.1.8.SD) on the stage.

On the other hand, the blowing of the wind is likened to the sounding of a pipe when Titania explains how the elements are influenced by the lack of harmony between her and Oberon:

> . . . the winds, piping to us in vain,
> As in revenge, have suck'd up from the sea
> Contagious fogs . . .
> (*MND* 2.1.88–90)

The winds piped in vain because Oberon spoilt the ringlets that Titania and her followers wanted to **dance**. Line 88 recalls Luke 7.31: 'We have piped unto you and ye have not danced' (Brooks, p. 32). However, the rural atmosphere characterizing this passage gives the speech a secular tone.

See also **ayre, breath, thunder**.

(C) Brooks, *A Midsummer Night's Dream* (1983).
    King, '"Then Murder's Out of Tune": The Music and Structure of *Othello*' (1986).
    Partridge, *Shakespeare's Bawdy* (1968).

wire see **fret, string**.

woeful (A) Rarely found in musical contexts, when it is, 'woeful' intends sorrow, affliction and distress expressed in slow sad **music**.

(B) In his famous speech about the seven ages of man, Jaques describes the lover as '**sigh**ing like furnace, with a woeful **ballad** / Made to his mistress' eyebrow' (*AYLI* 2.7.148–9). Jaques' intention is ironic: he reveals a lover's proneness to exaggeration in praising his mistress by

473

woeful

'combining the catalogue of physical beauties and the sonnets on trivial subjects' (Latham, p. 56). In *Venus and Adonis*, the **ditty** (in this case synonymous with '**song**') sung **extempore** by Venus is described as 'woeful' (836) since it expresses her grief at Adonis' rejection of her advances.

In *Pericles*, a play in which the healing power of music is a recurrent theme, Cerimon orders that music be **play**ed when he revives Thaisa: 'The **rough** and woeful music that we have, / Cause it to sound, beseech you' (3.2.88–9). The music for this 'resuscitation' rite belongs to the Phrygian religious ceremonies centring on the cult of Diana of Ephesus, which employed **jar**ring ('rough') music, 'notorious for its "savagery"' (Hart, p. 320).

See also **doleful**.

(C) Hart, 'Cerimon's "Rough Music"' (2000), provides an insightful analysis of the healing and sacred power of music in connection with the Phrygian cult of Diana.

Latham, *As You Like It* (1975).

woosel cock see **bird**.

world music (*musica mundana*) see **music**.

wren see **bird**.

wrest (A) To wrest is to turn or to screw the tuning **peg**s on a **string**ed **instrument** so as to tighten or slacken the strings, thereby altering the pitch of the string according to the tuning. Morley uses the term in the sense of 'turning' or 'manipulating' a musical motif or **point** in imitative counterpoint:

> The fantasie . . . is, when a **musician** taketh a point at his pleasure, and wresteth and turneth it as he list, making either much or little of it according as shall seeme best in his own conceit.
>
> (*Introduction*, 1597, p. 181)

(B) This term occurs uniquely in *Troilus and Cressida*. Ulysses blames the weakness of the Greek army on Achilles, who spends his time in his tent with Patroclus 'mocking [the] designs' (1.3.146) of his peers and superiors. He warns his general Agamemnon about one of Achilles' most despicable pastimes:

> . . . Sometime, great Agamemnon,
> Thy topless deputation he puts on,
> And like a strutting **play**er, whose conceit
> Lies in his hamstring, and doth think it rich
> To **hear** the wooden dialogue and **sound**
> 'Twixt his stretch'd footing and the scaffolage,
> Such to-be-pitied and o'er-wrested seeming
> He acts thy greatness in; and when he speaks,
> 'Tis like a **chime** a-mending, with terms unsquar'd.
> (1.3.151–9)

The pretentiousness of Achilles' actions is condemned. He is compared to a foolish over-ambitious actor who is ultimately incapable of achieving his goal. The metaphor on acting blends seamlessly with the two later musical metaphors thanks to the use of 'wooden' and 'sound' (155). The image of the actor delivering speeches on the wooden stage anticipates those of the overwrested tuning peg and of the un**tune**d **bell** whose sound is not harmonious.

Bibliography

Modern-spelling Editions of Shakespeare's Works
Bate, Jonathan, *Titus Andronicus*, London: Routledge, 1995.
Bevington, David, *1 Henry IV*, Oxford: Clarendon Press, 1987.
——, *Troilus and Cressida*, Walton-on-Thames: Nelson, 1998.
Braunmuller, A. R., *Macbeth*, Cambridge: Cambridge University Press, 1997.
Brockbank, Philip, *Coriolanus*, London: Methuen, 1976.
Brooks, Harold F., *A Midsummer Night's Dream*, London: Methuen, 1983.
Brown, John Russell, *The Merchant of Venice*, London: Methuen, 1955.
Burns, Edward, *King Henry VI, Part I*, London: Thomson Learning, 2000.

Cairncross, Andrew S., *King Henry VI, Part I*, London: Methuen, 1962.

Daniell, David, *Julius Caesar*, Walton-on-Thames: Nelson, 1998.
David, Richard, *Love's Labour's Lost*, London: Methuen, 1951.
Dorsch, T. S., *The Comedy of Errors*, Cambridge: Cambridge University Press, 1988.
Duncan-Jones, Katherine, *Shakespeare's Sonnets*, London: Arden Shakespeare, 1997.

Edwards, Philip, *Hamlet*, Cambridge: Cambridge University Press, 1985.
Evans, Blakemore, *Romeo and Juliet*, updated edn, Cambridge: Cambridge University Press, 2003.

Foakes, R. A., *The Comedy of Errors*, London: Methuen, 1962.
——, *Henry VIII*, London: Methuen, 1964.
——, *A Midsummer Night's Dream*, Cambridge: Cambridge University Press, 1984.
——, *King Lear*, Walton-on-Thames: Nelson, 1997.

Gibbons, Brian, *Romeo and Juliet*, London: Methuen, 1980.
Greenblatt, Stephen, Walter Cohen, Jean E. Howard, and Katharine Eisaman Maus, *The Norton Shakespeare*, New York and London: Norton, 1997.
Gurr, Andrew, *Richard II*, Cambridge: Cambridge University Press, 1984.

Hammond, Antony, *King Richard III*, London: Arden Shakespeare, 2002.

Bibliography

Hattaway, Michael, *The First Part of King Henry VI*, Cambridge: Cambridge University Press, 1990.
Hibbard, George Richard, *Love's Labour's Lost*, Oxford: Clarendon Press, 1990.
Hoeniger, F. D., *Pericles*, London: Arden Shakespeare, 2001.
Honigmann, E. A. J., *Othello*, London: Nelson, 1996.
Hughes, Alan, *Titus Andronicus*, Cambridge: Cambridge University Press, 1994.
Humphreys, A. R., *King Henry IV, Part 1*, London: Methuen, 1960.

Jenkins, Harold, *Hamlet*, London: Methuen, 1982.

Kastan, David Scott, *1 Henry IV*, London: Arden Shakespeare, 2002.
Kermode, Frank, *The Tempest*, London: Methuen, 1954.
Knowles, Ronald, *King Henry VI, Part II*, London: Thomson Learning, 1999.

Latham, Agnes, *As You Like It*, London: Methuen, 1975.
Levenson, Jill, *Romeo and Juliet*, Oxford: Oxford University Press, 2000.
Lindley, David, *The Tempest*, Cambridge: Cambridge University Press, 2002.
Lothian, J. M., and T. W. Craik, *Twelfth Night*, London: Methuen, 1975.

Mahood, M. M., *Twelfth Night*, Harmondsworth: Penguin, 1968.
Mares, Francis, *Much Ado About Nothing*, Cambridge: Cambridge University Press, 1988.
Melchiori, Giorgio, *The Second Part of Henry IV*, Cambridge: Cambridge University Press, 1989.
Morris, Brian, *The Taming of the Shrew*, London: Methuen, 1981.
Muir, Kenneth, *Macbeth*, London: Methuen, 1984.

Nosworthy, J. M., *Cymbeline*, London: Methuen, 1955.

Oliver, H. J., *The Merry Wives of Windsor*, London: Methuen, 1971.

Pafford, J. H. P., *The Winter's Tale*, London: Methuen, 1963.
Palmer, Kenneth, *Troilus and Cressida*, London: Methuen, 1982.

Sanders, Norman, *The First Part of King Henry the Sixth*, London: Penguin, 1981.

Vaughan, Virginia Mason, and Alden T. Vaughan, *The Tempest*, Walton-on-Thames: Nelson, 1999.

Walter, J. H., *Henry V*, London: Methuen, 1954.
Warren, Roger, and Stanley Wells, *Twelfth Night*, Oxford: Clarendon Press, 1994.

Weil, Herbert, and Judith Weil, *The First Part of King Henry IV*, Cambridge: Cambridge University Press, 1997.
Weis, Rene, *King Lear: A Parallel Text Edition*, London: Longman, 1993.
Wells, Stanley, and Gary Taylor, *William Shakespeare: The Complete Works*, Oxford: Clarendon Press, 1986.
Woudhuysen, H. R., *Love's Labour's Lost*, Walton-on-Thames: Nelson, 1998.

Articles, books, dissertations and Online resources

Abbott, Djilda, and Ephraim Segermann, 'Strings in the 16th and 17th centuries', *GSJ*, 27 (1974): 48–73.
——, 'The Cittern in England before 1700', *LSJ*, 17 (1975): 24–48.
——, 'Gut Strings', *EM*, 4 (1976): 430–7.
Adson, John, *Courtly Masquing Ayres* (London, 1621), ed. Peter Walls, 3 vols, *English Instrumental Music of the Late Renaissance*, London: London Pro Musica Edition, 1975–6.
Alburger, Mary Anne, 'The "Fydill in Fist": Bowed String Instruments from the Mary Rose', *GSJ*, 53 (2000): 12–24.
Aldrich, Richard, 'Shakespeare and Music', in *Musical Discourse from the 'New York Times'*, Essay Index Reprint Series, Freeport, NY: Books for Library Press, 1967, pp. 126–47.
Alexander, Gavin, 'The Elizabethan Lyric as Contrafactum: Robert Sidney's "French Tune" Identified', *ML*, 84/3 (August 2003): 378–402.
Allen, David G., and Robert A. White (eds), *Subjects on the World's Stage: Essays on British Literature of the Middle Ages and the Renaissance*, Newark, NJ: University of Delaware Press, 1995.
Altenburg, Detlef, *Untersuchungen zur Geschichte der Trompete im Zeitalter der Clarinblaskunst, 1550–1800*, Regensburg: G. Bosse, 1973.
Amner, John, *Sacred Hymns of 3, 4, 5 and 6 parts for Voices and Vyols*, London, 1615.
Anderson, Fleming, Thomas Pettitt, and Reinhold Schröder (eds), *The Entertainer in Medieval and Traditional Culture: A Symposium*, Odense: Odense University Press, 1997.
Anderson, Warren D., *Ethos and Education in Greek Music: The Evidence of Poetry and Philosophy*, Cambridge, MA: Harvard University Press, 1966.
——, *Music and Musicians in Ancient Greece*, Ithaca and London: Cornell University Press, 1994.
Andrews, Hilda (ed.), *My Lady Nevells Booke of Virginal Music*, London: Curwen, 1926 (reprinted New York: Dover Publications, 1969).
Apel, Willi, *The Notation of Polyphonic Music, 900–1600*, Cambridge, MA.: The Medieval Academy of America, 1953.
——, *Gregorian Chant*, Bloomington: Indiana University Press, 1958.
——, *The History of Keyboard Music to 1700*, tr. Hans Tischler, Bloomington: Indiana University Press, 1972.

Bibliography

Arbeau, Thoinot, *Orchesography*, 1589, tr. Mary Stewart Evans, ed. Julia Sutton, New York: Dover Publications, 1967.
Arkwright, G. E. P., 'Elizabethan Choirboys Plays and their Music', *Proceedings of the Musical Association*, 40 (1913–14): 117–38.
Ashbee, Andrew, *Records of English Court Music*, 6 vols, 1–4, Snodland: Ashbee Publications, 1986–91; 5–6, Aldershot: Scolar, 1991–2.
Ashbee, Andrew, and Peter Holman (eds), *John Jenkins and his Time: Studies in English Consort Music*, Oxford: Clarendon Press, 1996.
Ashbee, Andrew, Peter Holman, David Lasocki, and Fiona Kisby, *A Biographical Dictionary of English Court Musicians, 1485–1714*, 2 vols, Aldershot: Ashgate, 1998.
Astington, John, 'Descent Machinery in the Playhouses', *MaRDiE*, 2 (1985): 119–33.
——, 'Malvolio and the Eunuchs: Texts and Revels in *Twelfth Night*', *ShS*, 46 (1993): 23–34.
Atlas, Allan W. (ed.), *Anthology of Renaissance Music: Music in Western Europe, 1400–1600*, New York: Norton, 1998.
Attridge, Derek, *Well-weighed Syllables: Elizabethan Verse in Classical Metres*, London: Cambridge University Press, 1974.
——, *The Rhythms of English Poetry*, London: Longman, 1982.
Austern, Linda Phyllis, ' "Art to Enchant": Musical Magic and its Practitioners in English Renaissance Drama', *JRMA*, 115 (1990): 191–206.
——, *Music in English Children's Drama of the Later Renaissance*, Philadelphia and Reading: Gordon and Breach, 1992.

Bailey, Nathan, *Dictionarium Britannicum*, London, 1730.
Baines, Anthony, *Bagpipes*, Oxford: Oxford University Press, 1960.
——, *Brass Instruments*, London: Faber, 1976.
——, *Woodwind Instruments and their History*, 3rd edn, London: Faber, 1977.
——, *The Oxford Companion to Musical Instruments*, Oxford: Oxford University Press, 1992.
Barr, Cyrilla, *The Monophonic Lauda and the Lay Religious Confraternities of Tuscany and Umbria in the Late Middle Ages*, Kalamazoo: Medieval Institute Publications, Western Michigan University, 1988.
Baskervill, Charles Read, *The Elizabethan Jig and Related Song Drama*, Chicago: University of Chicago Press, 1929.
Basler Jahrbuch für historiche Musikpraxis, 5 (1981): 11–262 (issue devoted to the cornett incl. E. H. Tarr, 'Ein Katalog erhaltener Zinken').
Batchelor, Anne, 'Daniel Bacheler: The Right Perfect Musician', *LSJ*, 28 (1988): 3–12.
Bate, Philip, *The Trumpet and Trombone: An Outline of their History, Development, and Construction*, 2nd edn, London: Benn, 1978.

Beck, Sidney (ed.), *The First Book of Consort Lessons: Collected by Thomas Morley*, New York: C. F. Peters Corporation, 1959.

Beckerman, Bernard, *Shakespeare at the Globe, 1599–1609*, New York: Macmillan, 1962.

——, 'Theatrical Plots and Elizabethan Stage Practice', in *Shakespeare and Dramatic Tradition: Essays in Honor of S. F. Johnson*, eds W. R. Elton and William B. Long, Newark: University of Delaware Press, 1989, pp. 109–24.

Beer, R., 'Ornaments in Old Keyboard Music', *Music Review*, 13 (1952): 3–13.

Bendinelli, Cesare, *Tutta l'arte della trombetta* (MS 1614), in Documenta musicologica, 2nd series, no. 5, Kassel: Bärenreiter, 1975.

Bentley, G. E., *The Jacobean and Caroline Stage*, 7 vols, Oxford: Clarendon Press, 1940–68.

——, *The Profession of Dramatist in Shakespeare's Time, 1590–1642*, Princeton: Princeton University Press, 1971.

Berger, Harry J. R., 'Against the Sink-a-Pace: Sexual and Family Politics in *Much Ado About Nothing*', *ShQ*, 33/3 (Autumn 1982): 302–13.

Berger, Thomas L., William C. Bradford, and Sidney L. Sondergard, *An Index of Characters in Early Modern English Drama. Printed Plays, 1500–1660*, Cambridge: Cambridge University Press, 1998.

Bergeron, David M. (ed.), *Pageantry in the Shakespearean Theater*, Athens, GA: University of Georgia Press, 1985.

Berry, Herbert (ed.), *The First Public Playhouse: The Theatre in Shoreditch, 1576–1598*, Montreal: McGill-Queen's University Press, 1979.

Bevington, David, *From 'Mankind' to Marlowe: Growth of Structure in the Popular Drama of Tudor England*, Cambridge, MA: Harvard University Press, 1962.

——, and Peter Holbrook (eds), *The Politics of the Stuart Court Masque*, Cambridge: Cambridge University Press, 1998.

Bicknell, Stephen, *The History of the English Organ*, Cambridge: Cambridge University Press, 1996.

Binnall, P. B. G., 'A Man of Might', *Folk-Lore*, 51/52 (1941–2): 72.

Blackburn, Bonnie J., 'Music and Festivals at the Court of Leo X: A Venetian View', *Early Music History*, 11 (1992): 1–37.

Blayney, Peter W. M., 'The Publication of Playbooks', in *A New History of Early English Drama*, eds J. D. Cox and D. S. Kastan, New York: Columbia University Press, 1997, pp. 383–422.

Block, E. A. 'Chaucer's Millers and their Bagpipes', *Speculum*, 29 (1954): 293–43.

Bodleian Library Broadside Ballads Online (www.bodley.ox.ac.uk/ballads).

Bonta, Stephen, 'Further Thoughts on the History of Strings', *Catgut Acoustical Society Newsletter*, 26 (1976): 21–6.

Bowles, E. A, '*Haut* and *Bas*: the grouping of musical instruments in the Middle Ages', *Musica Disciplina*, 8 (1954): 115–40.

Bibliography

Bowles, E. A, 'Iconography as a Tool for Examining the Loud Consort in the Fifteenth Century', *Journal of the American Musical Instrument Society*, 3 (1977): 100–13.

Bowsher, Julian, *The Rose Theatre: An Archaeological Discovery*, London: Museum of London, 1998.

Bowsher, Julian and Simon Blatherwick, 'The Structure of the Rose', in *New Issues*, ed. F. J. Hildy, New York: Peter Lang, 1990, pp. 55–78.

Boyd, Morrison Comegys, *Elizabethan Music and Musical Criticism*, Philadelphia: University of Pennsylvania Press, 1940.

Boyden, David, *The History of Violin Playing from Its Origins to 1761 and Its Relationship to the Violin and Violin Music*, London: Oxford University Press, 1965.

Bradley, David, *From Text to Performance in the Elizabethan Theatre: Preparing the Play for the Stage*, Cambridge: Cambridge University Press, 1992.

Brett, Philip (ed.), *Consort Songs, 1570–1625*, MB 22, 2nd rev. edn, London: Stainer and Bell, 1974.

Brissenden, Alan, *Shakespeare and the Dance*, London: Macmillan, 1981.

Bronson, Bertrand Harris, *The Traditional Tunes of the Child Ballads*, 3 vols, Princeton: Princeton University Press, 1959–72.

——, *The Singing Tradition of Child's 'Popular Ballads'*, Princeton: Princeton University Press, 1976.

Brooks-Davies, Douglas, *The Mercurian Monarch: Magical Politics from Spenser to Pope*, Manchester: Manchester University Press, 1983.

Brophy, James, 'Shakespeare's "Saucy Jacks" ', *English Language Notes*, 1 (September 1963): 11–13.

Brown, Alan, *Elizabethan Keyboard Music*, MB 55, London: Stainer and Bell, 1989.

Brown, Howard M., 'How Opera Began: an Introduction to Jacopo Peri's *Euridice* (1600)', in *The Late Italian Renaissance 1525–1630*, ed. Eric Cochrane, London: Macmillan, 1970, pp. 401–43.

——, *Embellishing Sixteenth-century Music*, London: Oxford University Press, 1976.

——, 'The Trecento Fiddle and Its Bridges', *EM*, 17/3 (1989): 311–29.

Bücker, Josephine, 'Der Einfluss der Musik auf den englischen Wortschatz im 16. und 17. Jahrhundert', PhD dissertation, Universität Köln, 1926. Printed Düsseldorf: L. Schwann, 1926.

Bukofzer, Manfred, *Studies in Medieval and Renaissance Music*, New York: Norton, 1950.

Butler, Charles, *Principles of Musik*, London, 1636.

Buxton, John, *Elizabethan Taste*, London: Macmillan, 1963.

Byrne, Maurice, 'The English March and Early Drum Notation', *GSJ*, 50 (1997): 43–80.

Caldwell, John, *English Keyboard Music before the Nineteenth Century*, Oxford: Blackwell, 1973.
——, *The Oxford History of English Music*, vol. 1, Oxford: Clarendon Press, 1991.
Caldwell, John, Edward Olleson, and Susan Wollenberg (eds), *The Well Enchanting Skill: Essays in Honour of Frederick W. Sternfeld*, Oxford: Clarendon Press, 1990.
Calore, Michela, 'Elizabethan Stage Conventions and Their Textual Verbalization in the Drama of the 1580s and 1590s', PhD dissertation, Reading University, 2001.
——, 'Elizabethan Plots: A Shared Code of Theatrical and Fictional Language', *Theatre Survey*, 44/2 (November 2003): 249–61.
——, 'Battle Scenes in the Queen's Men's Repertoire', *Notes & Queries*, 50/4 (December 2003), 394–9.
Campion, Thomas, *A New Way of Making Fowre Parts in Counterpoint*, London: Thomas Snodham, c.1614.
——, *Observations in the Art of English Poesy*, 1602, ed. Percival Vivian, *Campion's Works*, Oxford: Clarendon Press, 1966.
Carolan, N., 'Shakepeare's Uilleann pipes', *Ceol*, 5/1 (1981): 4.
Carpenter, Naan Cooke, 'Shakespeare and Music: Unexplored Areas', in *Shakespeare and the Arts*, eds Stephen Orgel and Sean Keilen, New York and London: Garland, 1999, pp. 123–35.
Carse, Adam, *Musical Wind Instruments: A History of the Wind Instruments used in European Orchestras and Wind-Bands from the Later Middle Ages up to the Present Time*, London: Macmillan, 1939.
Carson, Neil, *A Companion to Henslowe's Diary*, Cambridge: Cambridge University Press, 1988.
Carter, Tim, *Music in Late Renaissance and Early Baroque Italy*, London: Batsford, 1992.
Castiglione, Baldassare *The Book of the Courtier*, 'Done into English by Sir Thomas Hoby, anno 1561', Venice, 1528.
Cauthen, Irby B., Jr (ed.), *Gorboduc or Ferrex and Porrex, by Thomas Sackville and Thomas Norton*, Regents Renaissance Drama Series, London: Edward Arnold, 1970.
Chambers, E. K., *The Elizabethan Stage*, 4 vols, Oxford: Clarendon Press, 1923.
Chan, Mary, *Music in the Theatre of Ben Jonson*, Oxford: Oxford University Press, 1980.
Chan, Mary, and Jamie Kassler (eds), *Roger North's 'The Musicall Grammarian' 1728*, Cambridge: Cambridge University Press, 1990.
Chappell, William, *Popular Music of the Olden Time*, 2 vols, London: Cramer, Beale, and Chappell, 1855–9 (reprinted New York: Dover Publications, 1965).

Bibliography

Chappell, William, and Joseph W. Ebsworth (eds), *The Roxburghe Ballads*, 9 vols, London: Ballad Society, 1869–99.

Charlton, Andrew, *Music in the Plays of Shakespeare: A Practicum*, New York and London: Garland, 1991.

A Checklist of European Harps, New York: publication of the Metropolitan Museum of Art, 1979.

Chickering, Howell, 'Hearing Ariel's Songs', *Journal of Medieval and Renaissance Studies*, 24 (1994): 131–72; reprinted in *Shakespeare and the Arts*, eds Stephen Orgel and Sean Keilen, New York and London: Garland, 1999, pp. 65–106.

Child, Francis J., *The English and Scottish Popular Ballads*, 5 vols, Cambridge, MA: Harvard University Press, 1882–98.

Clark, Andrew (ed.), *Briefe Lives, Chiefly of Contemporaries, set down by John Aubrey, between the years 1669 and 1696*, Oxford: Clarendon Press, 1898.

Clutton, Cecil, 'The Virginalists' Ornaments', *GSJ*, 9 (1956): 99–100.

Cochrane, Eric (ed.), *The Late Italian Renaissance 1525–1630*, London: Macmillan, 1970.

Coelho, Victor Anand (ed.), *Performance on Lute, Guitar and Vihuela: Historical Practice and Modern Interpretation*, Cambridge: Cambridge University Press, 1997.

——, *The Cambridge Companion to the Guitar*, Cambridge: Cambridge University Press, 2003.

Colaco, Jill, 'The Window Scenes in Romeo and Juliet and Folk Songs of the Night's Visit', *Studies in Philology*, 83 (1986): 138–57.

Collins, Stephen L., *From Divine Cosmos to Sovereign State: An Intellectual History of Consciousness and the Idea of Order in Renaissance England*, Oxford: Oxford University Press, 1989.

Collver, Michael, and Bruce Dickey, *A Catalog of Music for the Cornett*, Bloomington: Indiana University Press, 1996.

Cooper, Thomas, *Thesaurus linguae romanae & britannicae*, London, 1565.

Cox, John D., and David Scott Kastan (eds), *A New History of Early English Drama*, New York: Columbia University Press, 1997.

Craig-McFeely, Julia, 'English Lute Manuscripts and Scribes 1530–1630', PhD dissertation, Oxford University, 1993. www.craigmcfeely.force9.co.uk/thesis.html

Cressy, David, *Bonfires and Bells: National Memory and the Protestant Calendar in Elizabethan and Stuart England*, Berkeley: University of California Press, 1989.

Crookes, David Z. (ed. and tr.), *Michael Praetorius: Syntagma Musicum II. De Organographia Parts I and II*, Oxford: Clarendon Press, 1986.

Cunningham, James P., *Dancing at the Inns of Court*, London: Jordan, 1965.

Cutts, John P., 'Jacobean Masque and Stage Music', *ML*, 35 (1954): 185–200.

——, 'Music and the Supernatural in *The Tempest*: A Study in Interpretation', *ML*, 39 (October 1958): 347–58.

Cutts, John P. (ed.), *La Musique de scène de la troupe de Shakespeare*, Paris: Editions du Centre National de la Recherche Scientifique, 1971.
Cyr, Mary, 'A 17th-century Source of Ornamentation for Voice and Viol: British Museum MS Egerton 2971', *Royal Musical Association Research Chronicle*, 9 (1971): 53–72.

Daniel, Samuel, *Delia, with the complaint of Rosamand*, London, 1592.
Dart, Thurston, 'The Cittern and its English Music', *GSJ*, 1 (1948): 46–63.
——, 'The Repertory of the Royal Wind Music', *GSJ*, 11 (1958): 93–106.
——, 'Ornament Signs in Jacobean Music for Lute and Viol', *GSJ*, 14 (1961): 30–3.
Day, John, *Certaine Notes*, London, 1565.
de Fer, Jambe, *Epitome musical*, Lyons, 1556.
de Ford, R., 'Tempo Relationships between Duple and Triple Time in the Sixteenth Century', *Early Music History*, 14 (1995): 1–51.
Dell, Floyd, and Paul Jordan-Smith (eds), *The Anatomy of Melancholy*, New York: Tudor Pub. Co., 1938.
Dessen, Alan C., *Elizabethan Stage Conventions and Modern Interpreters*, Cambridge: Cambridge University Press, 1984.
——, *Recovering Shakespeare's Theatrical Vocabulary*, Cambridge: Cambridge University Press, 1995.
Dessen, Alan C., and Leslie Thomson, *A Dictionary of Stage Directions in English Drama, 1580–1642*, Cambridge: Cambridge University Press, 1999.
de Somogyi, Nick, *Shakespeare's Theatre of War*, Aldershot: Ashgate, 1998.
Dobbins, Frank (ed.), *The Oxford Book of French Chansons*, Oxford: Oxford University Press, 1987.
Dodd, Wayne, ' "But I'll set down the pegs that make this music" ', *Neuphilologische Mitteilungen*, 68/3 (1967): 321–6.
Dolmetsch, Mabel, *Dances of England and France, 1450–1600*, London: Routledge and Kegan Paul, 1949.
——, *Dances of Spain and Italy, 1400–1600*, London: Routledge, 1954.
Dolmetsch, Nathalie, *The Viola da Gamba; its Origins and History, its Technique and Musical Resources*, 2nd edn, London: Hinrichsen Edition, 1968.
Doughtie, Edward, 'Words for Music: Simplicity and Complexity in the Elizabethan Air', *Rice University Studies*, 51 (1965): 1–12.
Doughtie, Edward (ed.), *Lyrics from English Airs, 1597–1622*, Cambridge, MA.: Harvard University Press, 1970.
Doughtie, Edward, *English Renaissance Song*, Boston, MA: Twayne, 1986.
Dowland, John (tr.), *Micrologus*, London, 1609.
Dowland, Robert, *Varietie of Lute-Lessons*, London, 1610.
Downey, Peter, 'A Renaissance Correspondence Concerning Trumpet Music', *EM*, 9/3 (July 1981): 325–9.

——, 'The Trumpet and its Role in Music of the Renaissance and Early Baroque', PhD dissertation, Queen's University, Belfast, 1983.

——, 'The Renaissance Slide Trumpet: Fact or Fiction?', *EM*, 12/1 (February 1984): 26–33.

——, 'The Danish Trumpet Ensemble at the Court of King Christian III: Some Notes on its Instruments and its Music', *Årbog for musikforskning*, 19 (1991): 7–17.

Downie, M. A., 'The Rebec: An Orthographic and Iconographic Study', PhD dissertation, University of West Virginia, Morgantown, 1981.

Duckles, Vincent, 'Florid Embellishment in English Song of the Late 16th and Early 17th Centuries', *Annales Musicologiques*, 5 (1957): 329–45.

——, 'The Music for the Lyrics in Early Seventeenth-Century English Drama: A Bibliography of Primary Sources', in *Music in English Renaissance Drama*, ed. John H. Long, Lexington, KY: University of Kentucky Press, 1968, pp. 117–60.

Duffin, Ross W., 'The *trompette des menestrels* in the 15th-century *alta capella*', *EM*, 17/3 (1989): 397–402.

——, 'Backward Bells and Barrel Bells: Some Notes on the Early History of Loud Instruments', *Historic Brass Society Journal*, 9 (1997): 111–29; 10 (1998): 174–5.

——, *Shakespeare's Songbook*, New York: Norton, 2004.

Dunn, Catherine M., 'The Function of Music in Shakespeare's Romances', *ShQ*, 20/4 (1969): 391–405.

Early English Books Online (www.lib.umi.com/eebo).

Edelman, Charles, *Brawl Ridiculous: Swordfighting in Shakespeare's Plays*, Manchester: Manchester University Press, 1992.

——, *Shakespeare's Military Language: A Dictionary*, London: The Athlone Press, 2000.

Edwards, Warwick 'The Performance of Ensemble Music in Elizabethan England', *PRMA*, 97 (1970–1): 113–23.

——, 'The Instrumental Music of "Henry VIII's Manuscript" ', *The Consort*, 34 (1978): 274–82.

Egan, Gabriel, 'The Situation of the "Lords Rooms": A Revaluation', *RES*, 48 (1997): 297–309.

Elam, Keir, *The Semiotics of Theatre and Drama*, London: Methuen, 1980.

——, 'The Fertile Eunuch: *Twelfth Night*, early modern Intercourse, and the Fruits of Castration', *ShQ*, 47/1 (1996): 1–36.

——, 'Collective Affinities', *Around the Globe*, 22 (Autumn 2002), 7–9.

Fabry, Frank, 'Shakespeare's Witty Musician', *ShQ*, 33/2 (1982): 182–3.

Fantini, G., *Modo per imparare a sonare di tromba*, Frankfurt, 1638 (English translation, ed. E. H. Tarr, 1975).
Farmer, Henry G., *The Rise and Development of Military Music*, London: William Reeves, 1912.
——, *Military Music*, London: Parrish, 1950.
Fellowes, Edmund H. (ed.), *The English School of Lutenist Songwriters*. First series, 16 vols, London: Stainer and Bell, 1920–32; second series, 8 vols, London: Stainer and Bell, 1925–6. Rev. as *The English Lute Songs*, ed. Thurston Dart et al., London: Stainer and Bell, 1959–.
——, *English Cathedral Music*, 5th edn, rev. Jack Westrup, London: Methuen, 1969.
Fenlon, Iain (ed.), *Man and Music: The Renaissance*, London: Macmillan, 1989.
Ferguson, Howard, *Keyboard Interpretation from the 14th to the 19th Century*, Oxford: Oxford University Press, 1987.
Finney, Gretchen, *Musical Backgrounds for English Literature: 1580–1650*, New Brunswick, NJ: Rutgers University Press, 1961.
Foakes, R. A., *Illustrations of the English Stage, 1580–1642*, London: Scolar Press, 1985.
Foakes, R. A. (ed.), *Henslowe's Diary*, 2nd edn, Cambridge: Cambridge University Press, 2002.
Folkerth, Wes, *The Sound of Shakespeare*, London: Routledge, 2002.
Forrester, Peter S., 'Citterns and their Fingerboard', *Lute Society Journal*, 23/1 (1983): 15–20.
——, 'An Elizabethan Allegory and Some Hypotheses', *The Lute*, 34 (1994): 11–14.
Fox-Good, Jacquelyn A., 'Ophelia's Mad Songs: Music, Gender, Power', in *Subjects on the World's Stage*, eds David G. Allen and Robert A. White, Newark: University of Delaware Press, 1995, pp. 217–38.
Friedman, Albert B., *The Ballad Revival*, Chicago and London: University of Chicago Press, 1961.
Frost, Maurice, *English & Scottish Psalm & Hymn Tunes, c.1543–1677*, London: Oxford University Press, 1953.

Galpin, Francis W., *Old English Instruments of Music*, 4th edn, rev. Thurston Dart, London: Methuen, 1965.
Gerould, Gordon H., *The Ballad of Tradition*, Oxford: Clarendon Press, 1932.
Gill, Donald, 'The Elizabethan Lute', *GSJ*, 12 (1959): 60–2.
Godwin, Joscelyn, 'The Renaissance Flute', *The Consort*, 28 (1972): 70–81.
Golding, Arthur (tr.), *The XV Bookes of P. Ovidius Naso, entytuled Metamorphosis*, London, 1567.
Gooch, Bryan, and David Thatcher (eds), *Shakespeare Music Catalogue*, 5 vols, Oxford: Clarendon Press, 1991.

Gouk, Penelope, *Music, Science and Natural Magic in Seventeenth-Century England*, New Haven, CT: Yale University Press, 1999.

Greene, Richard L. (ed.), *The Early English Carols*, 2nd edn, Oxford: Clarendon Press, 1977.

Greer, David, 'The Part-Songs of the English Lutenists', *PRMA*, 94 (1967–8): 97–110.

——, 'Five Variations on "Farewel Dear loue" ', in *The Well Enchanting Skill*, eds John Caldwell et al., Oxford: Clarendon Press, 1990, pp. 213–29.

Greg, W. W., *Dramatic Documents from the Elizabethan Playhouses: Stage Plots, Actors' Parts, Prompt Books*, 2 vols, Oxford: Clarendon Press, 1931.

Grijp, Louis Peter, 'Fret Patterns of the Cittern', *GSJ*, 34 (1981): 62–97.

Griscom, Richard, and David Lasocki, *The Recorder: A Guide to Writings about the Instrument for Players and Researchers*, New York: Garland, 1994.

The Grove Dictionary of Music Online (www.grovemusic.com).

The New Grove Dictionary of Music, 2nd edn, eds Stanley Sadie and John Tyrell, London: Macmillan, 2001.

Gurr, Andrew, *The Shakespearean Stage, 1574–1642*, 3rd edn, Cambridge: Cambridge University Press, 1992.

——, *Playgoing in Shakespeare's London*, 2nd edn, London: Cambridge University Press, 1996.

——, *The Shakespearian Playing Companies*, Oxford: Clarendon Press, 1996.

——, *The Shakespeare Company, 1594–1642*, Cambridge: Cambridge University Press, 2004.

Gurr, Andrew, and Mariko Ichikawa, *Staging in Shakespeare's Theatres*, New York: Oxford University Press, 2000.

Haar, James, 'False Relations and Chromaticism in Sixteenth-Century Music', *JAMS*, 30 (1977): 391–418.

Hadaway, Robert, 'The Cittern', *EM*, 1 (1973): 77–81.

Hadden, Nancy, 'The Transverse Flute in the Middle Ages and Renaissance: Sources, Instruments, Technique', in *The Cambridge Companion to the Flute*, ed. J. M. Thomson, Cambridge: Cambridge University Press, forthcoming.

Halfpenny, Eric, 'Tantivy: An Exposition of the "Ancient Hunting Notes" ', *PRMA*, 80 (1954): 43–58.

Hall, Edward, *The Union of the Two Noble and Illustre Families of Lancaster and York*, facsimile reprint of edn originally published London, 1809, under the superintendence of Sir Henry Ellis and others, New York: AMS, 1965.

Hapgood, Robert, 'Hearing Shakespeare: Sound and Meaning in *Antony and Cleopatra*', *ShS*, 24 (1971): 1–12.

Harbage, Alfred, *Annals of English Drama, 975–1700*, 3rd edn, rev. Sylvia Stoler Wagonheim, London: Routledge, 1989.

Harrán, Don, 'Verse Types in the Early Madrigal', *JAMS*, 22 (1969): 27–53.

Harris, David G. T., 'Musical Education in Tudor Times (1485–1603)', *PRMA*, 65 (1938–9): 109–39.
Hart, Alfred, 'The Number of Lines in Shakespeare's Plays' *RES*, 8 (1932): 19–28.
——, 'The Length of Elizabethan and Jacobean Plays', *RES*, 8 (1932): 139–54.
——, 'The Time Allotted for Representation of Elizabethan and Jacobean Plays', *RES*, 8 (1932): 395–413.
Hart, Elizabeth, 'Cerimon's "Rough Music" ', *ShQ*, 51/3 (Fall 2000): 313–31.
Harting, James, *The Ornithology of Shakespeare*, Old Woking: Gresham Books, 1978; facsimile reprint of 1st edn, London: J. Van Voorst, 1871.
Hartshorne, C., 'The Relation of Bird Song to Music', *The Ibis*, 100 (1958): 421–45.
Harwood, Ian, 'Rosseter's *Lessons for Consort* of 1609', *LSJ*, 7 (1965): 15–23.
——, 'Thomas Robinson's "General Rules" ', *LSJ*, 20 (1978): 18–22.
——, 'A Case of Double Standards? Instrumental Pitch in England c.1600', *EM*, 9 (1981): 470–81.
——, 'Instrumental Pitch in England c.1600', *EM*, 11 (1983): 76–7.
Hattaway, Michael, *Elizabethan Popular Theatre: Plays in Performance*, London: Routledge and Kegan Paul, 1982.
Hawkins, John, *A General History of the Science and Practice of Music* (1776), a new edition, London: Novello, Ewer & Co., 1875.
Head, Matthew, 'Birdsong and the Origins of Music', *JRMA*, 122 (1997): 1–23.
Heater, E. M. 'Early Hunting Horn Calls and their Transmission', *Historic Brass Society Journal*, 7 (1995): 123–41.
Herrisone, Rebecca, *Music Theory in Seventeenth-Century England*, Oxford: Oxford University Press, 2000.
Hildy, Franklin J. (ed.), *New Issues in the Reconstruction of Shakespeare's Theatre*, New York: Peter Lang, 1990.
Hiley, David, *Western Plainchant: A Handbook*, Oxford: Clarendon Press, 1993.
Hindley, Charles (ed.), *Roxburghe Ballads*, 2 vols, London: Reeves and Turner, 1873–4.
Hinman, Charlton (ed.), *The First Folio of Shakespeare*, 2nd edn with a new introduction by Peter Blayney, New York and London: Norton, 1996.
Hodges, Walter, 'Reconstructing the Rose', in *New Issues*, ed. F. J. Hildy, New York: Peter Lang, 1990, pp. 79–94.
——, *Enter the Whole Army: A Pictorial Study of Shakespearean Staging, 1576–1616*, Cambridge: Cambridge University Press, 1999.
Holborne, Anthony, *The Cittharn Schoole*, London, 1597.
Hollander, John, *The Untuning of the Sky: Ideas of Music in English Poetry, 1500–1700*, Princeton: Princeton University Press, 1961.
Holman, Peter, *Four and Twenty Fiddlers: The Violin at the English Court, 1540–1690*, Oxford: Clarendon Press, 1993.

Bibliography

Holman, Peter, *Dowland: Lachrimae (1604)*, Cambridge: Cambridge University Press, 1999.

Honigmann, E. A. J., and Susan Brock, *Playhouse Wills, 1558–1642: An Edition of Wills by Shakespeare and his contemporaries in the London Theatre*, The Revels Plays Companion Library, Manchester: Manchester University Press, 1993.

Horowitz, Maryanne, Anne Cruz, and Wendy Furman (eds), *Renaissance Rereadings, Intertext and Context*, Urbana and Chicago: University of Illinois Press, 1988.

Hosley, Richard, 'Shakespeare's Use of a Gallery over the Stage', *ShS*, 10 (1957): 77–89.

——, 'Was there a Music-Room in Shakespeare's Globe?', *ShS*, 13 (1960): 113–23.

Howard, Skiles, 'Hands, Feet, and Bottoms: Decentering the Cosmic Dance in *A Midsummer Night's Dream*', *ShQ*, 44/3 (Autumn 1993): 325–42.

Howatson, M. C., and Ian Chilvers (eds), *The Concise Oxford Companion to Classical Literature*, Oxford: Oxford University Press, 1996.

Hulse, Lynn, 'Francis and Thomas Cutting: Father and Son?', *LSJ*, 26 (1986): 73–4.

Hunt, Edgar, *The Recorder and Its Music*, revised and enlarged edn, London: Eulenberg Books, 1977.

Hunter, Desmond, 'The Application of Grace Signs in the Sources of English Keyboard Music, c.1530–c.1650', dissertation, National University of Ireland, 1989.

Ingram, William (ed.), *The English Professional Theatre, 1530–1660*, Cambridge: Cambridge University Press, 2000.

Iselin, Pierre, ' "My Music For Nothing": Musical Negotiations in *The Tempest*', *ShS*, 48 (1995): 135–45.

Jeffery, Brian, 'Antony Holborne', *Musica Disciplina*, 22 (1968): 129–205.

Jeffrey, David L. (ed.), *By Things Seen: Reference and Recognition in Medieval Thought*, Ottawa: University of Ottawa Press, 1979.

Jeffreys, John, *The Life and Works of Philip Rosseter*, Aylesbury: Robertson Publications, 1990.

Jellis, Rosemary, *Bird Sounds and Their Meaning*, London: British Broadcasting Corporation, 1977.

Jensen, Richard d'A., 'Birdsong and the Imitation of Birdsong in the Music of the Middle Ages and the Renaissance', *Current Musicology*, 40 (1985): 50–65.

Jones, C. Fenwick, 'Wittenwiler's *Becki* and the Medieval Bagpipe', *JEGP*, 48 (1949): 207–28.

Jones, David E., *The Plays of T. S. Eliot*, London: Routledge and Kegan Paul, 1960.

Jones, Edward, *The Performance of English Song 1610–1670*, New York and London: Garland, 1989.

Jones, Robert, *The Muses Gordin for Delights, Or the fift Booke of Ayres*, London: William Barley, 1610.

Jorgens, Elsie Bickford, 'The Singer's Voice in Elizabethan Drama', in *Renaissance Rereadings, Intertext and Context*, eds Maryanne Horowitz et al., Urbana and Chicago: University of Illinois Press, 1988.

Jorgensen, Paul A., *Shakespeare's Military World*, Los Angeles: University of California Press, 1956.

Kastan, David Scott, and Peter Stallybrass (eds), *Staging the Renaissance: Reinterpretations of Elizabethan and Jacobean Drama*, New York: Routledge, 1991.

Keenan, Siobhan, *Travelling Players in Shakespeare's England*, Basingstoke: Palgrave Macmillan, 2002.

Kenney, Sylvia, ' "English Discant" and Discant in England', *MQ*, 45 (1959): 26–48.

——, 'The Theory of Discant', in *Walter Frye and the 'Contenance Angloise'*, New Haven, CT: Yale University Press, 1964, pp. 91–122.

Kerman, Joseph, *The Elizabethan Madrigal: A Comparative Study*, New York: American Musicological Society, 1962.

——, 'Byrd, Tallis, and the Art of Imitation', *Aspects of Medieval and Renaissance Music: A Birthday Offering to Gustave Reese*, London: Dent, 1967.

King, Rosalind, ' "Then Murder's Out of Tune": The Music and Structure of *Othello*', *ShS*, 39 (1986): 149–58.

Kisby, Fiona (ed.), *Music and Musicians in Renaissance Cities and Towns*, Cambridge: Cambridge University Press, 2001.

Kite-Powell, Jeffrey T. (ed.), *A Practical Guide to Historical Performance: The Renaissance*, New York: Garland, 1989.

Kittredge, George Lyman, *The English and Scottish Popular Ballads*, ed. Francis Child, 5 vols, Boston and New York: Houghton Mifflin, 1882–98.

Klotz, Sebastian, 'Why "Music with her Silver Sound"?', in *Shakespeare Jahrbuch*, 123 (1987), 130–8.

——, 'William Shakespeare und Thomas Morley im Goldenen Zeitalter der Musik: Historische Koordinaten zu ihren Schaffen', *Beiträge zur Musikwissenschaft*, 31 (1989): 24–38.

Knapp, Peggy A., 'The Orphic Vision of *Pericles*', *Texas Studies in Literature and Language*, 15 (Winter 1974): 615–26.

Knight, G. Wilson, *Myth and Miracle. An Essay on the Mystic Symbolism of Shakespeare*, London: Burrow, 1929.

Knutson, Roslyn Lander, *The Repertory of Shakespeare's Company, 1594–1613*, Fayetteville: University of Arkansas Press, 1991.

——, 'The Repertory', in *A New History of Early English Drama*, eds J. D.

Bibliography

Cox and D. S. Kastan, New York: Columbia University Press, 1997, pp. 461–80.

Kobbe, G., 'The Trumpet in Camp and Battle', *Century Magazine*, 61 (1898): 537–43.

Kossick, S. G., 'Musical Imagery in Shakespeare', *Unisa English Studies*, 20 (April 1982): 6–9.

Krummel, Donald William, *English Music Printing, 1553–1700*, London: Bibliographical Society, 1975.

Kümin, Beat, 'Masses, Morris and Metrical Psalms: Music in the English Parish, c.1400–1600', in *Music and Musicians in Renaissance Cities and Towns*, ed. Fiona Kisby, Cambridge: Cambridge University Press, 2001, pp. 70–81.

La Rue, Helen, 'The Problem of the Cymbala', *GSJ*, 35 (1982): 86–99.

Lasocki, David, 'Professional Recorder Players in England, 1540–1740', dissertation, University of Iowa, 1983.

——, 'The Recorder in the Elizabethan, Jacobean and Caroline Theater', *American Recorder*, 25 (1984): 3–10.

Latham, Alison (ed.), *The Oxford Companion to Music*, new edition, Oxford: Clarendon Press, 2002.

The Latine Grammar of P. Ramus Translated into English, London, 1585.

Leaver, Robin, *'Goostly Psalmes and Spirituall Songes': English and Dutch Metrical Psalms from Coverdale to Utenhove, 1535–1566*, Oxford: Clarendon Press, 1991.

Le Huray, Peter, *Music and the Reformation in England, 1549–1660*, 2nd edn, Cambridge: Cambridge University Press, 1978.

Le Huray, Peter (ed.), *Fingering of Virginal Music*, London: Stainer and Bell, 1981.

Lester, Joel, *Between Modes and Keys: German Theory 1592–1802*, Stuyvesant, NY: Pendragon, 1989.

Lewis, C. O., 'Incipient Tonal Thought in 17th-century English Theory', *Studies in Music*, London, ONT: University of Western Ontario, 6 (1981), 24–47.

Lindley, David (ed.), *The Court Masque*, Manchester: Manchester University Press, 1984.

——, *Lyric*, London: Methuen, 1985.

——, *Thomas Campion*, Leiden: Brill, 1986.

——, 'Shakespeare's Provoking Music', in *The Well Enchanting Skill*, eds John Caldwell et al., Oxford: Clarendon Press, 1990, pp. 79–90.

——, *Court Masques: Jacobean and Caroline Entertainments, 1605–1640*, Oxford: Clarendon Press, 1995.

The Liber Usualis with Introduction and Rubrics in English, Tournai: Desclée & Co., 1952.

Long, John H. (ed.), *Music in English Renaissance Drama*, Lexington, KY: University of Kentucky Press, 1968.

——, *Shakespeare's Use of Music: A Study of the Music and its Performance in the Original Production of Seven Comedies*, New York: Da Capo Press, 1977.
Long, William B., ' "A Bed/For Woodstock": a Warning for the Unwary', *MaRDiE*, 2 (1985): 91–118.
——, '*John a Kent and John a Cumber*: An Elizabethan Playbook and its Implications', in *Shakespeare and Dramatic Tradition: Essays in Honor of S. F. Johnson*, eds W. R. Elton and William B. Long, Newark: University of Delaware Press, 1989, pp. 125–43.
——, ' "Precious Few": English Manuscript Playbooks', in *A Companion to Shakespeare*, ed. David Scott Kastan, Oxford: Blackwell, 1999, pp. 414–33.
Lowe, Barbara, 'Early Records of the Morris in England', *Journal of the English Folk Dance and Song Society*, 8/2 (1957): 61–82.
Lowinsky, Edward, *Music in the Culture of the Renaissance and Other Essays*, ed. Bonnie Blackburn, 2 vols, Chicago: University of Chicago Press, 1989.
Luce, H. T. 'The Requiem Mass from its Plainsong Beginnings to 1600', dissertation, Florida State University, 1958.
Lumsden, David, 'The Sources of English Lute Music (1540–1620)', 3 vols, PhD dissertation, University of Cambridge, 1955.
Lundberg, R., 'Sixteenth- and Seventeenth-century Lute-making', *Journal of the Lute Society of America*, 7 (1974): 31–50.

McAlindon, Thomas, *Shakespeare's Tragic Cosmos*, Cambridge: Cambridge University Press, 1991.
McClary, Susan, *Feminine Endings: Music, Gender, and Sexuality*, Minneapolis: University of Minnesota Press, 1991.
McGee, Timothy, *Medieval and Renaissance Music: A Performer's Guide*, Toronto: University of Toronto Press, 1985.
McIntosh, William, 'Musical Design in *Pericles*', *English Language Notes*, 11 (December 1973): 100–6.
McJannet, Linda, *The Voice of Elizabethan Stage Directions: The Evolution of a Theatrical Code*, London: Associated University Presses, 1999.
McMillin, Scott, '*The Book of Sir Thomas More*: A Theatrical View', *MP*, 68 (1970–1): 10–24.
——, *The Elizabethan Theatre and 'The Book of Sir Thomas More'*, Ithaca: Cornell University Press, 1987.
——, 'Building Stories: Greg, Fleay, and the Plot of *2 Seven Deadly Sins*', *MaRDiE*, 4 (1989): 53–62.
McMillin, Scott, and Sally-Beth MacLean, *The Queen's Men and Their Plays*, Cambridge: Cambridge University Press, 1998.
Mace, Thomas, *Musick's Monument, or, a Remembrancer of the best practical Musick*, London, 1676.

Macey, Patrick, 'The Lauda and the Cult of Savonarola', *Renaissance Quarterly*, 45 (1992): 439–83.

——, *Bonfire Songs: Savonarola's Musical Legacy*, Oxford: Oxford University Press, 1998.

Maguire, Laurie, *Shakespearean Suspect Texts: The 'Bad' Quartos and Their Contexts*, Cambridge: Cambridge University Press, 1996.

Maitland, J. A. Fuller, and W. Barclay Squire (eds), *The Fitzwilliam Virginal Book*, 2 vols, Leipzig: Breitkopf and Härtel, 1899 (reprinted New York: Dover Publications, 1963).

Manifold, John S., *The Music in English Drama, from Shakespeare to Purcell*, London: Rockliff, 1956.

Marder, Louis, 'Shakespeare's "Lincolnshire Bagpipe" ', *N&Q*, 195/2 (Sept. 1950): 383–5.

Markham, Francis, *Five Decades of Epistles of Warre*, London, 1622.

Markham, Gervase, *The Souldiers Accidence, or an Introduction into Military Discipline*, London, 1625.

——, *The Souldiers Exercise: in Three Books*, London, 1639.

Marx, Steven, 'Holy War in Henry V', *ShS*, 48 (1995): 85–97.

Masten, Jeffrey, 'Playwrighting: Authorship and Collaboration', in *A New History of Early English Drama*, eds J. D. Cox and D. S. Kastan, New York: Columbia University Press, 1997, pp. 357–82.

Maynard, Winifred, *Elizabethan Lyric Poetry and Its Music*, Oxford: Clarendon Press, 1986.

Mehl, Dieter, *The Elizabethan Dumb Show: The History of a Dramatic Convention*, London: Methuen, 1965.

Meyer-Baer, Kathi, *Music of the Spheres and the Dance of Death: Studies in Musical Iconology*, Princeton: Princeton University Press, 1970.

Meyerheim, Edgar, 'Shakespeare's Use of Musical Terms for Characterization and Imagery', MA thesis, New York University, 1959.

Milward, Peter, *Shakespeare's Religious Background*, London: Sidgwick & Jackson, 1973.

Minsheu, John, *A Dictionarie in Spanish and English, first published into the English tongue by Ric. Percivale Gent.*, London, 1599.

Monson, Craig, *Voices and Viols in England, 1600–1650: The Sources and the Music*, Ann Arbor: UMI Research, 1982.

Montague, Jeremy, and Gwen Montague, *Minstrels and Angels: Carvings of Musicians in Medieval English Churches*, Berkeley, CA: Fallen Leaf, 1998.

Moody, E. Prior, 'Imagery as a Test of Authorship', *ShQ*, 6 (Autumn 1955): 381–6.

Moore, John Robert, 'The Tradition of Angelic Singing in English Drama', *JEGP*, 22 (1923): 89–99.

——, 'Songs of the Public Theaters in the Time of Shakespeare', *JEGP*, 28 (1929): 166–202.
Morehen, John, 'The English Consort and Verse Anthems', *EM*, 6 (1978): 381–5.
Morley, Thomas, *A Plaine and Easie Introduction to Practicall Musicke*, London, 1597.
——, *A Plain and Easy Introduction to Practical Music*, ed. R. Alec Harman, London: Dent, 1952.
Morley-Pegge, Reginald, *The French Horn*, rev. edn, London: Ernest Benn, 1973.
Morris, Ernest, *Bells of All Nations*, London: Robert Hale, 1951.
Mullally, Robert, 'More about the Measures', *EM*, 22 (1994): 414–38.
——, '*Measure* as a Choreographic Term in the Stuart Masque', *Dance Research*, 16 (1998), 67–73.
Myers, Herbert W., 'The *Mary Rose* "Shawm" ', *EM*, 11 (1983): 358–60.
——, 'Slide Trumpet Madness: Fact or Fiction?', *EM*, 17/3 (1989): 383–9.

Naef, Irene, *Die Lieder in Shakespeares Komödien: Gehalt und Funktion*, Berne: A. Francke, 1976.
Naylor, Edward, *Shakespeare and Music*, new edn, London and Toronto: Dent, 1931.
Negri, Cesare, *Le gratie d'amore*, Milan, 1602.
Neighbour, Oliver, *The Consort and Keyboard Music of William Byrd*, London: Faber, 1978.
The New Harvard Dictionary of Music, ed. Don Michael Randel, Cambridge, MA: Belknap Press of Harvard University Press, 1986.
Newton, Richard, 'English Lute Music of the Golden Age', *PRMA*, 65 (1938–9): 63–90.
Noble, Richmond, *Shakespeare's Use of Song: With the Text of the Principal Songs*, Oxford: Oxford University Press, 1923.
——, *Shakespeare's Biblical Knowledge and Use of the Book of Common Prayer*, New York: Macmillan, 1935.
Nosworthy, J. M., 'Music and its Function in the Romances of Shakespeare', *ShS*, 11 (1958), 60–9.

Oakley, Cletus, 'Shylock's "Woollen Bagpipe" ', *TLS* (29 Jan. 1960): 65.
O'Neill, David G., 'The Influence of Music in the Works of John Marston', *ML*, 53 (1972): 122–33; 293–308; 400–10.
Onions, C. T., *A Shakespeare Glossary*, 3rd edn, enlarged and rev. Robert D. Eagleson, New York: Oxford University Press, 1986.
Orgel, Stephen, *The Illusion of Power: Political Theater in the English Renaissance*, Berkeley and London: University of California Press, 1975.
——, *The Jonsonian Masque*, reprinted New York and Guildford: Columbia University Press, 1981.

Bibliography

Orgel, Stephen, *The Authentic Shakespeare, and Other Problems of the Early Modern Stage*, New York and London: Routledge, 2002.

Orgel, Stephen, and Sean Keilen (eds), *Shakespeare and the Arts*, New York and London: Garland, 1999.

Orrell, John, 'The Agent of Savoy at The Somerset Masque', *RES*, 28 (1977): 301–4.

——, *The Human Stage: English Theatre Design, 1567–1640*, Cambridge: Cambridge University Press, 1988.

——, 'Beyond the Rose: Design Problems for the Globe Reconstruction', in *New Issues*, ed. F. J. Hildy, New York: Peter Lang, 1990, pp. 95–118.

Osborne, James M., 'Benedick's Song in *Much Ado*', *The Times* (London: 17 November 1958): 11.

Osborne, James M. (ed.), *The Autobiography of Thomas Wythorne*, Oxford: Clarendon Press, 1961.

Owen, Barbara, 'Towards a Definition of the English Renaissance Organ', *Early Keyboard Studies Newsletter*, 3 (1986): 1.

Owens, Jessie Ann, *Composers at Work: The Craft of Musical Composition, 1450–1600*, New York: Garland, 1996.

——, 'Concepts of Pitch in English Music Theory, c.1560–1640', in *Tonal Structures in Early Music*, ed. Cristle Collins Judd, New York: Garland, 1998, pp. 183–246.

The Oxford English Dictionary Online (www.oed.com).

Page, Christopher C., *Voices and Instruments of the Middle Ages: Instrumental Practice and Songs in France*, London: Dent, 1987.

Palisca, Claude, *Studies in the History of Italian Music and Music Theory*, Oxford: Clarendon Press, 1994.

Pallis, M., 'The Instrumentation of English Viol Consort Music', *Chelys*, 1 (1969): 27–35.

Palmer, Frances, 'Musical Instruments from the *Mary Rose*', *EM*, 11/1 (Jan. 1983): 53–60.

Partridge, Eric, *Shakespeare's Bawdy*, 3rd edn, London and New York: Routledge, 1968.

Pattison, Bruce, *Music and Poetry of the English Renaissance*, London: Methuen, 1948.

Payne, Ian, *The Almain in Britain, c.1549–c.1675: A Dance from Manuscript Sources*, Aldershot: Ashgate, 2003.

Peters, Julie Stone, *Theatre of the Book, 1480–1880: Print, Text, and Performance in Europe*, Oxford: Oxford University Press, 2000.

Pike, Lionel, *Pills to Purge Melancholy: The Evolution of the English Ballet*, Aldershot: Ashgate, 2004.

Playford, John, *An Introduction to the Skill of Musick*, 7th edn, corrected, London, 1674.
Polk, Keith, 'The Trombone, the Slide Trumpet and the Ensemble Tradition of the Early Renaissance', *EM*, 17/3 (1989): 389–97.
Poulton, Diana, 'Graces of Play in Renaissance Lute Music', *EM*, 3 (1975): 107–14.
——, *John Dowland*, rev. edn, London: Faber, 1982.
Praetorius, Michael, *Terpischore*, 1612.
——, *Syntagma musici tomus secundus*, Wolfenbüttel, 1618–19.
Price, David, *Patrons and Musicians of the English Renaissance*, Cambridge: Cambridge University Press, 1981.
Price, Percival, *The Carillon*, Oxford: Oxford University Press, 1933.
——, *Bells and Man*, Oxford: Oxford University Press, 1983.
Prior, Roger, 'Jewish Musicians at the Tudor Court', *MQ*, 69 (1983): 253–65.
Puglisi, Filadelfio, 'A Survey of Renaissance Flutes', *GSJ*, 41 (1988): 67–82.
Pulver, Jeffrey A., *A Dictionary of Old English Music and Musical Instruments*, London: Kegan Paul, Trench, and Trubner, 1923.

Rasmussen, Eric, 'The Revision of Scripts', in *A New History of Early English Drama*, eds J. D. Cox and D. S. Kastan, New York: Columbia University Press, 1997, pp. 441–60.
Rastall, Richard, *The Heaven Singing*, Cambridge: D. S. Brewer, 1996.
——, *The Notation of Western Music: An Introduction*, rev. edn, London: Dent, 1998.
——, *Minstrels Playing*, Woodbridge: D. S. Brewer, 2001.
Ratcliffe, Stephen, *Campion: On Song*, London: Routledge, 1981.
Remnant, Mary, *Musical Instruments of the West*, London: Batsford, 1978.
——, *English Bowed Instruments from Anglo-Saxon to Tudor Times*, Oxford: Clarendon Press, 1986.
Rensch, Roslyn, *The Harp: its History, Technique and Repertoire*, London and New York: Duckworth, 1969.
Riche, Barnaby, *Farewell to Militarie profession*, London, 1581.
Riesthuis, A. (ed.), '*The Historical Harp: Proceedings of the International Harp Symposium, Berlin, 1994*', Berlin, 1998.
Riley, M. W., *The Teaching of Bowed Instruments from 1511 to 1756*, Ann Arbor: UMI Research, 1986.
Ripin, Edwin M. 'A Re-evaluation of Virdung's *Musica getutscht*', *JAMS*, 29 (1976): 189–223.
Robbins, Martin L., 'Shakespeare's Sweet Music: A Glossary of Musical Terms in the Works of Shakespeare (With Additional Examples from the Plays of Lyly, Marston and Jonson)', PhD dissertation, Brandeis University, 1968.
——, 'The Musical Meaning of "Mode" in 2 Henry IV', *English Language Notes*, 8 (1971): 252–7.

Robinson, Thomas, *The Schoole of Musicke*, London, 1603.
——, *New Citharen Lessons*, London, 1609.
Roche, Jerome, *The Madrigal*, 2nd edn, Oxford: Oxford University Press, 1990.
Rollins, Hyder E., 'The Black-letter Broadside Ballad', *PMLA*, 34 (1919): 258–339.
Rollins, Hyder E. (ed.), *Old English Ballads, 1553–1625*, Cambridge: Cambridge University Press, 1920.
—— *A Handefull of Pleasant Delites*, Cambridge, MA: Harvard University Press, 1924.
—— *Pepys Ballads*, 8 vols, Cambridge, MA: Harvard University Press, 1929–32.
Ross, Lawrence, 'Shakespeare's "Dull Clown" and Symbolic Music', *ShQ*, 17 (1966): 107–28.
Rosselli, John, 'The Castrati as a Professional Group and a Social Phenomenon, 1550–1850', *Acta Musicologica*, 60 (1988): 143–79.
Rothery, Guy, *The Heraldry of Shakespeare*, Westminster: Morland Press, 1930.
Routley, Erik, *The English Carol*, London: Herbert Jenkins, 1958.
Rueger, Christoph, *Musical Instruments and Their Decoration: Historical Gems of European Culture*, tr. Peter Underwood, London: David and Charles, 1986.
Rutter, Carol Chillington (ed.), *Documents of the Rose Playhouse*, rev. edn, Manchester: Manchester University Press, 1999.

Sabol, Andrew (ed.), *Four Hundred Songs and Dances from the Stuart Masque*, Providence: Brown University Press, 1978.
Sachs, Curt, *World History of the Dance*, London: Dent, 1937.
——, *The History of Musical Instruments*, London: Dent, 1942.
Salomon, Brownell, 'Visual and Aural Signs in the Performed English Renaissance Play', *RD*, 5 (1972): 143–69.
Salzman, L. F., 'Dildos and Fadings', *Times Literary Supplement* (7 September 1933): 592.
Sanuto, M., *I diarii*, eds F. Stefano, G. Berchet, and N. Berozzi, 24, Venice, 1889, col. 541.
Schlesinger, Kathleen, *The Greek Aulos*, London: Methuen, 1939.
Scholes, Percy, *The Puritans and Music in England and New England*, Oxford: Oxford University Press, 1934; reprinted 1969.
Scott, David, 'Elizabeth I as Lutenist', *LSJ*, 18 (1976): 45.
Seng, Peter J., 'Songs, Time, and the Rejection of Falstaff', *ShS*, 15 (1962), 31–40.
——, *The Vocal Songs in the Plays of Shakespeare. A Critical History*, Cambridge, MA: Harvard University Press, 1967.
Shepherd, Martin, 'The Interpretation of Signs for Graces in English Lute Music', *The Lute*, 36 (1996): 37–84.

Shirley, Frances Ann, *Shakespeare's Use of Off-Stage Sounds*, Lincoln: University of Nebraska Press, 1963.

Simonds, Peggy Muñoz, *Myth, Emblem, and Music in Shakespeare's 'Cymbeline': An Iconographic Reconstruction*, London and Toronto: Associated University Presses, 1992.

Simpson, Christopher, *The Division-Violist*, London, 1659; 2nd edn 1667. Facs edn of 1667 edn, London: Curwen, 1955.

Simpson, Claude M., *The British Broadside Ballad and its Music*, New Brunswick, NJ: Rutgers University Press, 1966.

Smith, Bruce R., 'The Contest of Apollo and Marsyas: Ideas about Music in the Middle Ages', in *By Things Seen: Reference and Recognition in Medieval Thought*, ed. David Jeffrey, Ottawa: University of Ottawa Press, 1979, pp. 81–107.

——, *The Acoustic World of Early Modern England: Attending to the O-Factor*, Chicago: University of Chicago Press, 1999.

Smith, Douglas A., *A History of the Lute from Antiquity to the Renaissance*, Lexington, VA: Lute Society of America, 2001.

Smith, Gregory (ed.), *Elizabethan Critical Essays*, 2 vols, Oxford: Clarendon Press, 1904.

Solum, John, *The Early Flute*, Oxford: Clarendon Press, 1992.

Sorrel, W., 'Shakespeare and the Dance', *ShQ*, 71 (1957): 367–84.

Spiessens, G., 'De Bergamasca', *Musica Antiqua*, 6 (1989): 154–61.

Spink, Ian, *English Song: Dowland to Purcell*, London: Batsford, 1974.

Spring, Matthew, *The Lute in Britain: A History of the Instrument and its Music*, Oxford: Oxford University Press, 2001.

Steele, John, and Francis Cameron (eds), *John Bull: Keyboard Music*, MB 14, 19, with additional material by Thurston Dart, 3rd edn, rev. Alan Brown, London: Stainer and Bell, 2001.

Stern, Tiffany, *Rehearsal from Shakespeare to Sheridan*, Oxford: Clarendon Press, 2000.

Sternfeld, F. W., 'Dramatic and Allegorical Function of Music in Shakespeare's Tragedies: The Symbolism of Trumpets – Pipes versus Strings – Music of the Spheres – Sweet and Harsh Tuning', *Annales musicologiques*, 3 (1955): 265–82.

——, 'Twentieth-Century Studies in Shakespeare's Songs, Sonnets, and Poems', *ShS*, 15 (1962): 1–30.

——, *Music in Shakespearean Tragedy*, rev. edn, London: Routledge and Kegan Paul, 1967.

——, 'Echo et répétition dans la poésie et la musique', in *La Chanson à la Renaissance*, ed. J. M. Vaccaro, Tours: CESR, 1981.

——, 'The Orpheus myth and the libretto of *Orfeo*', in *Claudio Monteverdi Orfeo*, ed. John Whenham, Cambridge: Cambridge University Press, 1986.

Bibliography

Sternfeld, F. W., 'Orpheus, Ovid and Opera', *JRMA*, 113/2 (1988): 172–202.
——, *The Birth of Opera*, Oxford: Clarendon Press, 1993.
Sternfeld, F. W., and Christopher R. Wilson (arr.), 'An Old English Carol', *Oxford Carols*, London: Oxford University Press, 1978.
Sternfeld, F. W., and Christopher R. Wilson, 'Music in Shakespeare's Work', in *William Shakespeare: His World, His Work, His Influence*, 3 vols, ed. John F. Andrews, New York: Charles Scribner's Sons, 1985, vol. 2, pp. 417–24.
Stevens, Denis, *The Mulliner Book*, MB 1, rev. edn, London: Stainer and Bell, 1973.
Stevens, John, 'Rounds and Canons from an Early Tudor Song-Book', *ML*, 32/1 (January 1951): 29–37.
——, 'Shakespeare and the Music of the Elizabethan Stage: An Introductory Essay', in *Shakespeare and Music*, ed. Phyllis Hartnoll, London: Macmillan, 1964, pp. 3–48.
Stevens, John (ed.), *Music at the Court of Henry VIII*, MB 18, 2nd edn, London: Stainer and Bell, 1969.
——, *Music and Poetry in the Early Tudor Court*, rev. edn, Cambridge: Cambridge University Press, 1979.
Strahle, Graham, *An Early Music Dictionary: Musical Terms from British Sources*, Cambridge: Cambridge University Press, 1995.
Styan, J. L., *Shakespeare's Stagecraft*, Cambridge: Cambridge University Press, 1967.

Talbert, Ernest, *The Problem of Order: Elizabethan Political Commonplaces and an Example of Shakespeare's Art*, Chapel Hill: University of Carolina Press, 1962.
Tarr, Edward, *Die Trompete/La trompette*, Bern: Hallwag, 1977.
——, 'Cesare Bendinelli', *Brass Bulletin*, 17 (1977): 31–45; 21 (1978): 13–25.
Teague, Frances N., *Shakespeare's Speaking Properties*, London: Associated University Presses, 1991.
Temperley, Nicholas, *The Music of the English Parish Church*, 2 vols, Cambridge: Cambridge University Press, 1979.
——, *The Hymn Tune Index: A Census of English-Language Hymn Tunes in Printed Sources from 1535 to 1820*, Oxford: Oxford University Press, 1998.
Thomas, Bernard, 'The Renaissance Flute', *EM*, 3 (1975): 2–10.
Thomas, Thomas, *Dictionarium Linguae Latinae et Anglicanae*, London, 1587.
Thomsen, Magnus, *Trumpet Book*, Copenhagen: Kongelige Bibliotek, GL. Kgl. Saml. 1875.
Thomson, John Mansfield (ed.), *The Cambridge Companion to the Recorder*, Cambridge: Cambridge University Press, 1995.
Thomson, Leslie, 'Broken Brackets and 'Mended Texts: Stage Directions in the *Oxford Shakespeare*', *RD*, 19 (1988): 175–93.

——, 'The Meaning of Thunder and Lightning: Stage Directions and Audience Expectations', *Early Theatre*, 2 (1999): 11–24.
Till, David, 'Ornamentation in English Song manuscripts, 1620–1660', BLitt thesis, Oxford, 1975.
Tilley, Morris P., *A Dictionary of Proverbs in England*, 2nd printing, Ann Arbor: University of Michigan Press, 1966.
Toft, Robert, *Tune thy Musicke to thy Hart. The Art of Eloquent Singing in England 1597–1622*, Toronto: University of Toronto Press, 1993.
Tomlinson, Gary, *Monteverdi and the End of the Renaissance*, Oxford: Clarendon Press, 1987.
——, *Music in Renaissance Magic: Toward a Historiography of Others*, Chicago and London: University of Chicago Press, 1993.
Trousdale, Marion, 'A Second Look at Critical Bibliography and the Acting of Plays', *ShQ*, 41 (1990): 87–96.
Tyler, James, 'Checklist for Music for the Cittern', *EM*, 2 (1974): 25–9.

Ungerer, Gustav, 'The Viol da Gamba as a Sexual Metaphor in Elizabethan Music and Literature', *Renaissance and Reformation*, 8/2 (1984), 79–90.

van den Borren, Charles, *The Sources of Keyboard Music in England*, tr. J. E. Matthew, London: Novello, 1913.
Virdung, Sebastian, *Musica getutscht*, Basle, 1511.
Vlasto, Jill, 'An Elizabethan Anthology of Rounds', *MQ*, 40/2 (April 1954): 222–34.

Waldo, Tommy Ruth, *Musical Terms and Rhetoric: The Complexity of Shakespeare's Dramatic Style*, Salzburg Studies in English Literature, Salzburg: Institut für englische Sprache und Literatur, Universität Salzburg, 1974.
Waldo, Tommy Ruth, and T. W. Herbert, 'Musical Terms in *The Taming of the Shrew*: Evidence of Single Authorship', *ShQ*, 10:2 (Spring 1959): 185–99.
Walker, Daniel Pickering, *Spiritual and Demonic Magic from Ficino to Campanella*, London: Warburg Insitute, 1958.
Walls, Peter, *Music in the English Courtly Masque, 1604–1640*, Oxford: Clarendon Press, 1996.
Warburton, Carol, 'Music as Basic Metaphor in Shakespeare's Plays', PhD dissertation, University of Miami, 1981.
Ward, John M., 'The "Dolfull Domps" ', *JAMS*, 4 (1951): 111–21.
——, 'Music for *A Handefull of pleasant delites*', *JAMS*, 10 (1957): 151–80.
——, 'Apropos *The British Broadside Ballad and Its Music*', *JAMS*, 20 (1967): 28–86.
——, 'Curious Tunes for Strange Histories', in *Words and Music: The Scholar's*

Bibliography

View, ed. Laurence Berman, Cambridge, MA: Harvard University Press, 1972, pp. 339–58.

——, 'The Maner of Dauncyng', *EM*, 4 (1976): 127–42.

——, 'A Dowland Miscellany', *Journal of the Lute Society of America*, 10 (1977): 5–105.

——, 'Sprightly & Cheerful Musick: Notes on the Cittern, Gittern and Guitar in 16th- and 17th-century England', *LSJ*, 21 (1979–81).

Ward, John M. (ed.), *The Dublin Virginal Manuscript*, London and New York: Schott, 1983.

——, 'The English Measure', *EM*, 14 (1986): 15–21.

——, 'The Morris Tune', *JAMS*, 39 (1986): 294–331.

——, 'Newly Devis'd Measures for Jacobean Masques', *Acta Musicologica*, 60 (1988): 111–42.

——, 'And who but Ladie Greensleeues?', in *The Well Enchanting Skill*, ed. John Caldwell et al., Oxford: Clarendon Press, 1990, pp. 181–211.

——, *Music for Elizabethan Lutes*, Oxford: Oxford University Press, 1992.

Warlock, Peter, *The English Ayre*, London: Humphrey Milford, 1926.

Warren, Charles W., 'Music at Nonesuch', *MQ*, 54 (1968): 47–57.

Watson, John Richard, *The English Hymn: a Critical and Historical Study*, Oxford: Clarendon Press, 1997.

Watt, Tessa, *Cheap Print and Popular Piety, 1550–1640*, Cambridge: Cambridge University Press, 1991.

Wells, Robin Headlam, 'Number Symbolism in the Renaissance Lute Rose', *EM*, 9 (1981): 32–42.

——, *Elizabethan Mythologies: Studies in Poetry, Drama and Music*, Cambridge: Cambridge University Press, 1994.

Wells, Stanley, and Gary Taylor (eds), *William Shakespeare: A Textual Companion*, Oxford: Clarendon Press, 1987.

Welsford, Enid, *The Court Masque: A Study in the Relationship Between Poetry and the Revels*, Cambridge: Cambridge University Press, 1927.

Werstine, Paul, 'Narratives About Printed Shakespeare Texts: "Foul Papers" and "Bad" Quartos', *ShQ*, 41 (1990): 65–86.

Wey, James J., 'Musical Allusion and Song as Part of the Structure of Meaning of Shakespeare's Plays', PhD dissertation, Catholic University of America, Washington DC, 1957.

Wienpahl, Robert W., *Music at the Inns of Court During the Reigns of Elizabeth, James, and Charles*, Ann Arbor: University Microfilms International for the Department of Music, California State University, Northridge, 1979.

Williams, Clare (tr.), *Thomas Platter's Travels in England, 1599*, London: Jonathan Cape, 1937.

Williams, Gordon, *A Dictionary of Sexual Language and Imagery in Shakespearean and Stuart Literature*, 3 vols, London: The Athlone Press, 1994.

Wilson, Barbara, 'Madrigal, Lauda and Local Culture in Trecento Florence', *Journal of Musicology*, 15 (1997): 137–77.
Wilson, Christopher R., 'Thomas Campion's "Ayres filled with parts" reconsidered', *The Lute*, 23/2 (1983): 3–12.
——, *Words and Notes Coupled Lovingly Together: Thomas Campion, a Critical Study*, New York: Garland, 1989.
——, 'Some Musico-poetic Aspects of Campion's Masques', in *The Well Enchanting Skill*, eds John Caldwell et al., Oxford: Clarendon Press, 1990, pp. 91–105.
——, 'Elgar, Naylor and "The Cobbler's Jig": an Enquiry Reopened', *ML*, 74/1 (February 1993): 39–43.
——, 'Shakespeare's "Fair Viols, Sweet Lutes, and Rude Pipes" as Symbolic Musics', *Lute News*, 4 (December 1998): 7–12.
Wilson, Christopher R. (ed.), *A New Way of Making Fowre Parts in Counterpoint by Thomas Campion*, Aldershot: Ashgate, 2003.
——, 'Number and Music in Campion's Measured Verse', *John Donne Journal of America*, 25 (2006), 267–91.
Wilson, Michael I., *The Chamber Organ in Britain, 1600–1830*, Aldershot: Ashgate, 2001.
Wilson, Wilfrid G., *Change Ringing. The Art and Science of Change Ringing on Church and Hand Bells*, London: Faber and Faber, 1965.
Winternitz, Emanuel, *Musical Instruments and their Symbolism in Western Art*, London: Faber and Faber, 1967.
Woodfield, Ian, *The Early History of the Viol*, Cambridge: Cambridge University Press, 1984.
——, *English Musicians in the Age of Exploration*, Stuyvesant, NY: Pendragon Press, 1995.
Woodfill, Walter L., *Musicians in English Society from Elizabeth to Charles I*, Princeton: Princeton University Press, 1953.
Wright, Peter M., 'Stage Directions for Music and Sound Effects in 2–3 Henry VI: "No Quarrel, but a Slight Contention" ', in *Shakespeare Performed: Essays in Honor of R. A. Foakes*, ed. Grace Ioppolo, London: Associated University Presses, 2000, pp. 72–87.
Wulstan, David, *Tudor Music*, London: Dent, 1985.
Würzbach, Natascha, *The Rise of the English Street Ballad, 1550–1650*, tr. Gayna Walls, Cambridge: Cambridge University Press, 1990.

Yates, Frances A., *A Study of Love's Labour's Lost*, Cambridge: Cambridge University Press, 1936.

Index

SHAKESPEARE'S WORKS

All's Well that Ends Well   air, ballad, canary, compose, coranto, cornett, discord, dulcet, jar, march, morris dance, motion, organ, song, trumpet, tucket
Antony and Cleopatra   alarum, ballad, bell, brazen, burden, din, ear, flourish, flute, hoboy, holding, loud, low, march, noise, play, rattle, shrill, sound, taborine, trumpet
As You Like It   ballad, bird, burden, carol, clamor, ditty, false, hey (ho), instrument, jar, love song, measure, noise, note, pipe, play, rude, song, still, time, treble, voice, warble, whistle, woeful

Comedy of Errors   bell, case, ear, key, note
Coriolanus   accent, ballad, blow, choir, cornett, cymbal, dance, din, drum, eunuch, fife, flourish, hoboy, march, noise, parley, pipe, psaltery, sackbut, sound, speak, still, tabor, throat, thunder, Triton
Cymbeline   air, bird, choir, crack, ear, eunuch, fingering, ground, music, thunder, tune, voice

Hamlet   alarum, angel, bell, bird, breath, chanson, chant, chorus, compass, dirge, drum, ear, fret, govern, hey (ho), hoboy, instrument, jangle, jig, laudes, lay, low, lute, noise, note, ordnance, organ, piece, pipe, play, ply, recorder, requiem, rest, shrill, silence, skill, snatch, song, sound, speak, stop, throat, time, wassail
Henry IV, Part 1   bagpipe, ballad, bass, bird, division, drone, fiddle, fife, frame, harp, hollow, lute, metre, parley, play, psalm, ravish, retreat, sound, trumpet, tune, weaver, whistle, wind
Henry IV, Part 2   alarum, anthem, ballad, beat, bell, blow, brawl, burden, carman's whistle, case, chime, clang, dull, fancy, hoboy, melody, mode, music, noise, pipe, point, stop, strike, toll, tongue, treble, viol, whistle
Henry V   ballad, bass, chantry, chorus, compose, concent, coranto, flourish, galliard, horn, hum, morris dance, music, nimble, note, ordnance, parley, pipe, plainsong, priest, sennet, shrill, Te Deum, toll, tucket, voice, whistle
Henry VI, Part 1   alarum, aloud, cornett, discord, drum, horn, incantation, jar, lute, march, ordnance, parley, piece, praise, priest, retreat, sound, strike, thunder, trumpet
Henry VI, Part 2   alarum, aloud, bell, bird, blow, breast, choir, consort, flourish, harmony, hoboy, hollow, jar, lay, noise, ordnance, string, thunder, tune
Henry VI, Part 3   bell, bird, breast, clang, dance, drum, harmony, horn, loud, march, sennet, sound, strike
Henry VIII   choir, chord, cornett, dance, fiddle, flourish, fret, harmony, hoboy, knell,

505

Index

lute, masque, music, noise, Orpheus, peal, plainsong, play, sennet, sweet, Te Deum, thunder, wench

Julius Caesar   bell, bird, false, jig, loud, low, lute, masque, shrill, strain, string, thunder, touch, tune

King John   beat, bell, bird, blow, brazen, chant, clamor, doleful, echo, horn, hymn, loud, masque, organ, rattle, retreat, rude, strike, tongue, trumpet

King Lear   alarum, aloud, angel, beat, bird, burden, drum, hey (ho), horn, jar, loud, low, march, minikin, music, retreat, sennet, shrill, sigh, sound, speak, still, strike, trumpet, tucket, ut, viol

Love's Labour's Lost   air, Apollo, ballad, bear a note, brawl, cadence, canary, canzonet, cittern, complement, dance, drum, enchant, flourish, harp, hay, hit (it), jig, long, lute, make, masque, mean, measure, minstrel, music, number, peal, pipe, praise, ravish, sigh, Solomon, string, tabor, throat, ut, warble, wassail

Macbeth   air, alarum, angel, bear a part, bell, bird, charm, clamor, concord, dance, division, drum, hoboy, knell, music, parley, perform, round, sennet, speak, thunder, tongue

Measure for Measure   air, aloud, charm, song

Merchant of Venice   air, angel, bagpipe, bear a part, bird, change, choir, concord, cornett, dulcet, dull, ear, fading, fife, flourish, hear, hymn, knell, lute, masque, motion, music, Orpheus, play, sound, squealing, sweet, touch, tucket, voice

Merry Wives of Windsor   Babylon, bird, canary, caper, compass, Greensleeves, madrigal, melody, noise, psalm, rattle, scornful, toy, wind

Midsummer Night's Dream   air, ballad, bergomask, bird, breath, carol, catch, chant, choir, clamor, dance, discord, ditty, ear, echo, eunuch, faint, flourish, harp, hear, horn, hymn, key, lullaby, masque, music, note, pipe, plainsong, recorder, rehearse, rote, round, rude, song, Thracian, thunder, tongs and bones, tongue, true, warble, whistle, wind

Much Ado About Nothing   air, ballad, bell, burden, case, cinque pas, crotchet, dance, ditty, drum, dull, dump, fife, govern, grace, hear, hey (ho), hymn, jig, key, lute, measure, music, play, sigh, sound, speak, stop, strike, tabor, tongue, tune, voice

Othello   alarum, almain, bagpipe, bell, bird, fife, make, parley, peg, pipe, set, shrill, song, speak, throat, trumpet, tune, well-tuned, wind

Passionate Pilgrim   ditty, doleful, jig, lute, pipe, praise, ravish, touch

Pericles   bell, chime, dance, din, fingering, harmony, jangle, lay, lute, make, music, point, record, silver, string, sweet, trumpet, vestal, viol, whistle, woeful

Phoenix and Turtle   anthem, chorus, defunctive, lay, priest, requiem

Rape of Lucrece   alarum, bear a diapason, bird, descant, diapason, dirge, discord, doleful, dump, ear, fret, grace, hum, imitate, knell, languishment, long, melody, minstrel, nimble, note, Orpheus, parley, relish, skill, strain, tongue, warble, well-tuned

Index

Richard II   bird, brazen, breath, case, dance, grace, harp, hear, high, instrument, measure, music, noise, parley, proportion, report, sound, string, sweet, time, touch, trumpet, tucket, tune, tut, voice

Richard III   alarum, caper, clamor, descant, flourish, ground, lute, march, pipe, report, retreat, sennet, strike, sweet

Romeo and Juliet   accent, alarum, beat, bell, bird, case, catling, change, concent, consort, crotchet, dirge, division, doleful, dump, echo, fiddle, hollow, hymn, love song, minikin, minim, minstrel, music, note, pricksong, proportion, rebec, rest, sharp, silver, sound-post, strain, tongue, ut

Sonnets   alter (116), bear a part (8), bell (71), bird (29), burden (102), choir (73), concord (8; 128), dull (102), fingering (128), hear (8; 128), jack (128), lay (98;   100; 102), metre (17), motion (128), mournful (102), music (8; 128), nimble (128), number (17), pipe (102), pleasant (102), sound (8), strain (90), strike (8), toll (71), true (8), well-tuned (8)

Taming of the Shrew   accord, alarum, Apollo, bass, breve, burden, clang, clef, dulcet, echo, fingering, fret, gamut, horn, instrument, jack, jar, lesson, long, loud, lute, make, music, note, ordnance, sound, touch, treble, tune, tut, twang, ut

Tempest   air, bass, beat, burden, catch, charm, dance, ditty, harmony, harp, hum, instrument, knell, music, noise, organ, play, rattle, soft, song, tabor, thunder, tongue, troll, tune, twang, whistle, wind

Timon of Athens   beat, case, drum, ear, fife, loud, march, play, sound, strike, tucket

Titus Andronicus   alarum, bell, bird, chant, ear, echo, enchant, flourish, ground, harmony, hoboy, hollow, horn, lullaby, melody, mournful, noise, note, peal, shrill, Thracian, trumpet, well-tuned

Troilus and Cressida   accent, alarum, Apollo, beat, blow, brazen, catling, chime, clamor, clef, crack, degree, discord, dull, loud, music, note, piece, pipe, rude, sharp, sound, strike, string, taborine, trumpet, tucket, tune, wrest

Twelfth Night   accent, air, Babylon, breast, breath, canton, caper, catch, chant, chantry, cinque pas, coranto, eunuch, galliard, hey (ho), jig, loud, love song, low, masque, music, organ, pavan, piece, pipe, play, song, sound, strain, tabor, time, twang, viol, voice, weaver

Two Gentlemen of Verona   anthem, bird, burden, change, compose, concord, consort, dance, descant, dump, ear, false, flat, frame, hear, love song, lute, mean, music, Orpheus, record, relish, sharp, skill, string, toy, tune

Two Noble Kinsmen   burden, cornett, dirge, echo, flourish, horn, instrument, key, melody, noise, recorder, still, tabor, tongue, twang, virginal, whoobub, wind

Venus and Adonis   alarum, anthem, bird, chant, choir, discord, ditty, echo, extempore, false, horn, measure, melody, noise, tedious, tongue, tune, woeful

Winter's Tale   bagpipe, ballad, bass, bear a part, bird, burden, chant, dance, doleful, fading, hornpipe, knell, love song, lullaby, mean, music, pleasant, psalm, set, strike, tabor, tirra-lyra, trumpet, tune, virginal, whoobub

507

Index

OTHER WORKS

Alphonsus King of Aragon   trumpet
Antonio and Mellida   flute
Antonio's Revenge   still
Apology for Actors   alarum
Bussy D'Ambois   bell
Chaste Maid in Cheapside   recorder
Cobbler's Prophecy   fife
Defence of Poesy   almain
Dutch Courtesan   noise
Every Man Out of His Humor   trumpet
Fall of Princes   recorder
Faerie Queene   noise, ply, whoobub
Fedele and Fortunio   dump
Gorboduc   flute, hoboy
Honest Whore, Part 2   cittern
How a Man May Choose a Good Wife from a Bad   Apollo
The Jew of Malta   division, fiddle
Jocasta   noise
Knight of the Burning Pestle   fading
Lord Hayes Masque   lute, silver
Love's Cure   cittern
Maid of Honour   flourish
Malcontent   brawl, hollow
Match me in London   cittern
Menaphon   round
Mucedorus   silver
Nine Daies Wonder   tabor
Sapho and Phao   harp
Shepheards Calendar   pipe
Somerset Masque   make
Sophonisba   flourish, recorder
Sylva Sylvarum   consort
Teares of the Muses   bear a part
Tethys Festival   soft
Wily Beguiled   hit (it)
Women Beware Women   canary
Wonderful Year   canary